LITERACY ASSESSMENT AND METACOGNITIVE STRATEGIES

Literacy Assessment and Metacognitive Strategies

A Resource to Inform Instruction, PreK–12

Stephanie L. McAndrews

THE GUILFORD PRESS
New York London

A Division of Guilford Publications, Inc.
370 Seventh Avenue, Suite 1200, New York, NY 10001
www.guilford.com

Printed in the United States of America

This book is printed on acid-free paper.

Last digit is print number: 9 8 7 6 5 4 3 2 1

Library of Congress Cataloging-in-Publication Data

Names: McAndrews, Stephanie L., 1964– author.
Title: Literacy assessment and metacognitive strategies : a resource to inform instruction, PreK-12 / Stephanie L. McAndrews.
Description: New York : The Guilford Press, [2020] | Includes bibliographical references and index.
Identifiers: LCCN 2019056122 | ISBN 9781462543700 (paperback) | ISBN 9781462543717 (hardcover)
Subjects: LCSH: Language arts—Ability testing. | Literacy—Evaluation. | Reading—Ability testing. | Teacher–student relationships.
Classification: LCC LB1576 .M143 2020 | DDC 372.6—dc23
LC record available at *https://lccn.loc.gov/2019056122*

First, to my loving husband, Peter,
for his encouragement and enduring patience

Second, to my daughters, Laura and Katherine,
for sharing their love of learning

Finally, to my grandchildren,
Rio and Maya, who were my inspiration
for emphasizing multicultural and multilingual literacy
and are my hope for the future

About the Author

Stephanie L. McAndrews, PhD, is Professor and Director of the Literacy Program at Southern Illinois University Edwardsville (SIUE). At SIUE, she developed the Master of Science in Literacy Education degree, the Post-Master's Literacy Specialist Certificate program, and the Cougar Literacy Clinic. Dr. McAndrews is an experienced classroom teacher, reading specialist, and Reading Recovery teacher, and is certified in Structured English Immersion. She is an active contributor to the Literacy Research Association, the Association of Literacy Educators and Researchers, and the International Literacy Association. She is also a board member of the Illinois Reading Council, for which she has served as president of the Lewis and Clark Reading Council and the College Instructors of Reading Professionals special interest group. She is a former long-time editor of *The Reading Teacher* journal. Widely published, Dr. McAndrews has presented at national and international conferences, worked on assessment initiatives with the Illinois State Board of Education, and consulted with school districts in Illinois, Missouri, and Guatemala. Her primary goal is to enhance the literacy development of PreK–12 students by cultivating literacy leaders who are knowledgeable about literacy processes and can make informed instructional and programmatic decisions.

Preface

Literacy Assessment and Metacognitive Strategies: A Resource to Inform Instruction, PreK–12 was written for literacy specialists, coaches, interventionists, classroom teachers, and other educators who work to support students' language and literacy development in prekindergarten through grade 12. Attaining such a position is generally a result of advanced education and/or literacy/reading specialist certification. Because a person in this position often supports development in listening, speaking, reading, writing, viewing, and visually representing, throughout this book the position is referred to as a "literacy specialist." A position statement from the International Literacy Association (ILA, 2018) recommends that the roles of the literacy specialist include instruction, assessment, and leadership for the classroom, family, school, and community. This expanded role includes collaboration with classroom teachers, special education teachers, speech–language pathologists, other professionals, and family members to enhance each student's literacy development. Therefore, the assessments and strategies included in this book are not just for a literacy specialist to use with students; they can be modeled or used as resources for all people who work with students. After the data from the initial and ongoing assessments are analyzed and evaluated, instruction can be planned that addresses the strengths and needs of each student by using specific strategies to help the student learn more about applying literacy processes when learning.

HOW WAS THIS BOOK DEVELOPED?

This book is based on current research on effective literacy practices; my years of piloting these practices; and my experiences as a classroom teacher, reading specialist, Reading Recovery teacher, literacy consultant, and university literacy professor. These experiences have provided ongoing insight into the complex decision-making process involved in supporting a student's language, reading, and writing development. As a reflective practitioner, I have analyzed, adapted, and created numerous literacy assessments and instructional strategies. The initial assessments and strategies were part of a 6-year longitudinal study of the effectiveness of my instruction and my students' learning while I was a reading specialist and doctoral student at the University of Arizona (McAndrews, 1999). As a literacy professor, I began organizing literacy assessments and strategies into annually adapted course packets. My graduate students in the Literacy Specialist Program and I have researched, piloted, and adapted each of these assessments and strategies. I also used feedback from literacy specialist candidates who used these assessments and strategies with students in classrooms and in the university literacy clinic to expand, adapt, or delete each assessment and strategy according to its usefulness in assessing and enhancing students' literacy learning. That course packet grew into one of the International Reading Association's bestselling books, *Diagnostic Literacy Assessments and Instructional Strategies: A Literacy Specialist's Resource* (McAndrews, 2008). I have significantly expanded, revised, and updated the original text based on current research and pedagogy. This book includes new information on culturally responsive teaching and on teaching English language learners. It also encompasses understanding, assessing, and teaching viewing and visually representing, which are important with the advent of digital technology.

HOW IS THIS BOOK ORGANIZED?

Literacy Assessment and Metacognitive Strategies incorporates assessments and strategies for multiple literacy processes that meet the Standards for the Preparation of Literacy Professionals 2017 (ILA, 2018) and the Common Core State Standards (National Governors Association Center for Best Practices & Council of Chief State School Officers, 2010). I worked with the ILA to be sure that all six literacy modalities (reading, writing, speaking, listening, viewing, and visually representing) were included in the new standards (ILA, 2018).

The first chapter is the introduction to the book, and the second chapter focuses on building relationships. Chapters 3 through 7 each begins with background information about the topics and provides information and resources to assess and teach an essential process in literacy. To guide the reader, important words are boldfaced and defined within the text.

Chapter 1 is an introduction to literacy, assessment, and instruction. It first provides a definition of literacy, introduces the various literacy processes, and describes the social-constructivist and sociocultural theoretical foundation of the text. It describes the purpose and types of assessment: *of* learning, *as* learning, and *for* learning. Next, it describes instructional design, including the gradual-release-of-responsibility model and the whole–part–whole methodology. The assessment and instruction decision-making cycle is discussed, as are the ways educators use it to inform the planning, implementation, and evaluation and feedback for students' learning and improved instruction. Teaching frameworks and general strategy instruction are also described, along with understanding diverse learners and differentiating the content, process, product, and environment.

Chapter 2 focuses on the importance of building relationships with others to help students develop positive attitudes and motivation toward literacy and learning. In keeping with current sociocultural theory, the important role of learning about each student's culture, language, and interests is described. The assessment section includes a variety of student and family interviews, surveys, and communication documents. Strategies are included for learning about each student, and for incorporating the ideas in the teacher's instruction and interactions to enhance the student's attitude and motivation for learning.

Chapters 3 through 7 each address a different literacy process: language development; word analysis; reading fluency; listening, reading, and viewing comprehension; and writing composition and visual representation. These processes are not discrete concepts. Rather, each is related, and they are often dependent on one's knowledge of the others. All of these five chapters include the following sections (or groupings of sections): "Understanding," "Goals," "Assessments," and "Strategies." The "Understanding" section or sections in each chapter provide background information for understanding the specific literacy process covered in that chapter. The "Goals" section or sections specify the goals for student learning for each literacy process. The "Assessments" section or sections describe literacy assessments, almost all of which my graduate students and I have developed. These literacy assessments are used to gather qualitative, not just quantitative, data on each student's literacy strengths and areas for improvement. For most assessments, the purpose, procedure, scoring, and analysis are provided with a full or partial example to demonstrate the assessment and instructional implications more fully. Occasionally, suggestions for adaptations or differentiation are provided. The assessment data can then be used by the literacy specialist or other educator to develop instructional objectives, and by the student to develop personal literacy goals. The final section or sections of each chapter provide specific literacy strategies that educators can model, and that students can use to develop literacy and independent problem-solving abilities and then apply to new experiences to engage in lifelong learning. These strategies are plans to improve one's performance in learning and can be used for self-assessment as well as ongoing assessment of a student's learning. Although my students and I have developed or adapted some of the strategies, the others have come from conferences, professional development resources, published texts, and my interactions with practicing professionals. Every effort has been made to credit the source for each strategy.

The selection of assessments and instructional strategies has been based on my piloting them since 1986 during instruction in literacy clinics, resource rooms, classrooms, and tutoring sessions, as well as on current teachers' and literacy specialists' using them and providing me with feedback. These strategies were found to be beneficial not only for students who had reading and writing difficulties, but also for typically developing students.

It should be noted that the assessments and strategies are organized in each chapter in the order in which most educators would want to administer or teach them. This is not meant to be a prescriptive order; the order for administering the assessments or teaching the strategies depends on particular students' needs. Not all students will get all assessments, but if a student's skills or needs are unclear, the first assessment should be given first. Also, although the assessments are intended to be administered individually, many of them can be adapted for use with small groups or a whole class. In addition, the grade levels listed with each strategy indicate approximate developmental levels. The strategies chosen should be within a student's zone of proximal development; that is, these should be tasks that the student can do successfully with support (see Chapter 1 for a fuller discussion). If the student is able to complete the task successfully with no support, there is no need to devote additional instruction to it. If the student cannot complete the task, even with significant support, then instruction needs to be differentiated by content, process, product, or environment.

Chapter 3 includes understanding, assessments, and strategies for learning the interrelated language systems of phonetics, syntactics, morphemics, semantics, and pragmatics. These assessments and strategies are useful for native English speakers as well as English language learners. While this chapter emphasizes the oral language of speaking, listening, and orally presenting, it is also the foundation for developing written and visual literacy.

Chapter 4 includes understanding, assessments, and strategies for applying phonological awareness, alphabetic principle, emergent text concepts, word identification, spelling, and handwriting to read and write words.

Chapter 5 includes understanding, assessments, and strategies for improving word accuracy (using the grapho-phonemic, morphemic, syntactic, and semantic cueing systems) and prosody (phrasing, expression, intonation, and pace) to convey meaning while reading.

Chapter 6 includes understanding, assessments, and strategies for improving comprehension of written and visual texts. Comprehension of a variety of genres, text structures, and formats is included.

Chapter 7 includes understanding, assessments, and strategies for improving composition of written and visual texts. Whereas Chapter 6 focuses on understanding others' texts, Chapter 7 focuses on creating texts with a variety of genres, text structures, and formats (written, digital, multimedia, and visual and performing arts).

Reproducible copies of assessments, strategy tools, and other resources are available in the Appendix. It is important to note that not all assessments or strategies are appropriate for every student. The decisions should be made on the basis of the literacy specialist's foundational knowledge of literacy theory and development, the learner's background knowledge and interests, and the complexity of the text or literacy task. The goal of this book is to provide the literacy specialist or other educator with a range of assessments and instructional strategies that can be carefully selected to meet the literacy needs of individual students to help them become lifelong learners. A literacy leader can use the resources in this book to support teachers and paraprofessionals in selecting and analyzing appropriate assessments and instructional strategies.

A note on language: I have given careful thought to pronoun use. When discussing people (such as teachers and students) in general, I use "they/them/their" to indicate a gender-neutral pronoun. In addition, the word *teacher* in this text refers to anyone who teaches or assesses students including but not limited to classroom, reading, and special education teachers; literacy specialists; speech–language pathologists; psychologists; tutors; and teacher aides.

ACKNOWLEDGMENTS

This book is a result of my collaboration and learning from many colleagues and teaching professionals, including members of the Literacy Research Association and the Association for Literacy Educators and Researchers. I especially appreciate my Southern Illinois University Edwardsville (SIUE) colleague Shadrack Msengi, with whom I have collaborated on literacy research, presentations, and publications.

I want to thank all the teachers and university students at SIUE who piloted the assessments, taught literacy lessons, collected student samples, and gave helpful feedback. I also want to thank my friends and colleagues from the University of Arizona: John Bradley, Ken Goodman, Yetta Goodman, Patty Anders, Kathy Short, and Carolyn Carter. Their support, wisdom, and love of literacy inspire me to carry on their passion for literacy.

Finally, in memory of Kenneth S. Goodman (1927–2020), I fondly regard him as not only the "grandfather of whole language," but as a fierce advocate for children and the teachers who teach them.

Contents

Purchasers of this book can download and print copies of the reproducible forms and assessments at *www.guilford.com/mcandrews-forms* for personal use or use with students (see copyright page for details).

Chapter 1

Introduction to Literacy, Assessment, and Instruction

UNDERSTANDING LITERACY

The definition of literacy has evolved from an exclusive focus on reading and writing to encompass a more inclusive and expansive perspective that reflects communication in our modern and technological society. **Literacy** is the desire and ability to make and communicate meaning by listening, speaking, reading, writing, viewing, and visually representing ideas, in order to attain goals, to develop knowledge and potential, and to make a contribution to and fully participate in the community and wider society (Msengi & McAndrews, 2016b).

Literacy Modalities

There are six literacy modalities: listening, speaking, reading, writing, viewing, and visually representing. These literacy modalities are related to each other on the basis of two parameters: the medium of communication (oral, written, or visual) and the direction of communication (receptive or expressive) (Msengi & McAndrews, 2017). Communication is a two-way process; it is the responsibility of the person expressing the information as well as the person receiving the information to make sure that the ideas are clearly understood (see Figure 1.1). In one study, when teachers integrated all six literacy modalities with appropriate strategies during teaching and student learning experiences, almost all of the students were better able to understand and effectively communicate the content (Msengi & McAndrews, 2016b). Using multiple modalities also improves student engagement by providing diverse experiences and ways of representing information. The communication can take place via face-to-face interactions, electronic media, or text. While the literacy modalities are interrelated, for clarification they are defined separately here.

The **listening modality** is the active process of receiving and actively trying to comprehend the spoken and sometimes unspoken messages from the speaker's point of view.

FIGURE 1.1. Literacy modalities.

	Oral Language	Written Language	Visual Language
Receptive Comprehension Thinking	Listening	Reading	Viewing
Expressive Composition Sharing Ideas	Speaking	Writing	Visually Representing

Active listening is a process that consists of four stages: sensing and attending; understanding and interpreting; remembering; and responding (Steinberg, 2007). Sensing and attending involve the focused perception of both verbal and visual stimuli. Understanding and interpreting involve assigning meaning to and evaluating the messages received. Remembering is the storing of meaningful information. Finally, responding is demonstrating that the listener was paying attention, tried to understand, and was interested in what the speaker was saying. Responding is a way of acknowledging, clarifying, paraphrasing, summarizing, sympathizing, empathizing, and commenting about the message (Steinberg, 2007).

The **speaking modality** is the vocalized form of communicating meaning based on the syntactic combination of words. In addition, there are paralinguistic properties that can modify meaning, such as the tone and pitch of the voice, body language, gestures, and facial expressions used to communicate meaning. Sign language is a gestural form of communication often used by people who are deaf. Speech, in addition to its use in communication, can be internally used by mental processes to enhance and organize thinking in the form of an interior monologue (Vygotsky, 1978).

The **reading modality** is a complex transaction between the reader and written language, through which the reader attempts to reconstruct the writer's message while connecting the text to their background knowledge (Goodman, 1996). Reading is not just a decoding process of reading the words; it is an active process in which readers use integrated strategies to strive to understand the author's meaning while at the same time building their own meaning.

The **writing modality** is communication primarily through written words. It represents language and emotion with words in a grammatical structure and context, with the added dependency of conventions of print, including spelling, punctuation, capitalization, paragraphs, and layout. It can allow one to communicate a message with clarity to a larger audience than through face-to-face conversations. Unlike speech, the written mode provides an opportunity to revise and correct. It is also a method of preserving records of communication.

The **viewing modality** is the comprehension of ideas and information through our eyes. It incorporates the ability to interpret, use, and appreciate images and visual media. This text focuses on three areas of visual literacy: (1) interpreting illustrations, paintings, and photographic images; (2) reading and analyzing graphical devices such as maps, charts, graphs, diagrams, three-dimensional models, and realia; and (3) interpreting digital, video, and multimedia presentations as well as performance arts.

The **visually representing modality** is the communication of ideas and information through the creation and sharing of two- or three-dimensional, static or moving visual images. The creator needs to consider how the visual elements and principles of design are used together to communicate meaning. Visual media often contain additional information that is not included in, but is supported by, accompanying written or oral text.

Literacy Processes

Literacy, as conceptualized in this text, includes multiple integrated processes such as language development (listening and speaking); word analysis (phonological awareness, the alphabetic principle, word identification, spelling, and emergent text concepts); reading fluency (word accuracy, phrasing, expression, intonation, and pace); reading, listening, and viewing comprehension; and writing composition and visual representation (see Figure 1.2). Although the assessment and development of each of these processes is described in separate chapters, it is important to note that these are not discrete processes, but are interrelated and dependent on the knowledge of the other processes. Language development, both in and out of school, plays an important role in the comprehension and composition of ideas, and therefore language is the first process to be addressed.

Literacy development begins at birth and continues throughout one's lifetime. **Emergent literacy** is a gradual process that takes place over time from birth until a child can read, write, and communicate in what is considered to be a "conventional" sense—a term coined by Marie Clay (1993). **Advanced literacy** or **full literacy** is the ability to apply critical analysis, inference, and synthesis to oral, written, and visual material, and then to communicate with accuracy and coherence, as well as to use information and insights as the basis for informed decisions and creative thought. As adults, while we have strengths in some areas of literacy, we continue to develop our literacy processes and knowledge.

Historically, teachers were taught the importance of incorporating **content area literacy,** which focuses on study skills that can be used to help students learn from disciplinary texts (Shanahan & Shanahan, 2012). While this may be important, it is not sufficient. Students need a much more in-depth understanding of applying literacy in the content areas, now referred to as disciplinary literacy. **Disciplinary literacy** is the "specialized knowledge and abilities possessed by those who create, communicate and use knowledge within each of the disciplines" (Shanahan & Shanahan, 2012, p. 7). Learners need to do much more than just understand the information in textbooks. For example, if they are in a scientific field, they need to learn how to gather information from other experts, collect data, analyze data, and draw conclusions; then they need to communicate their findings

FIGURE 1.2. Literacy processes.

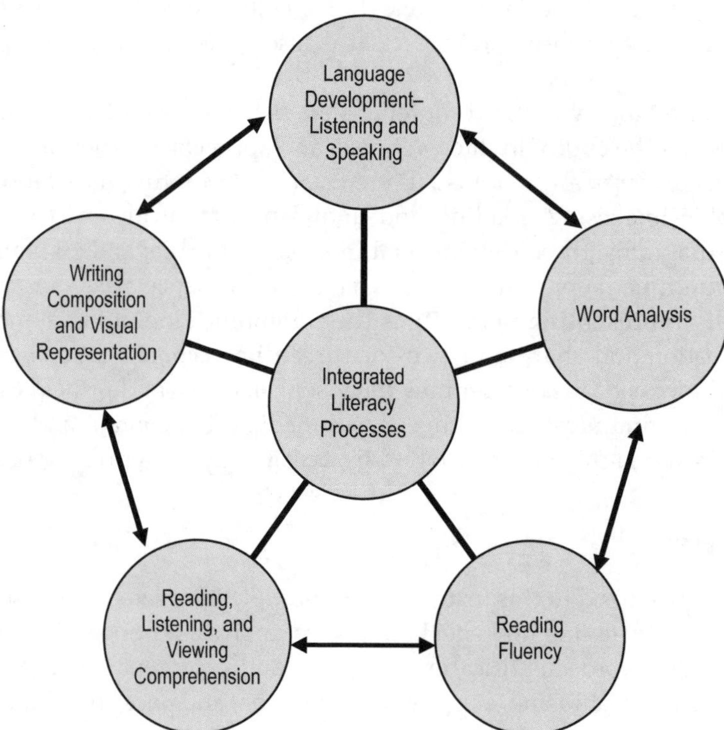

orally, visually, and in written form in order to persuade others to think differently. Therefore, there has been a philosophical shift from teaching content area literacy to teaching disciplinary literacy. Each field has its own type of literacy, such as digital literacy, media literacy, data literacy, mathematical literacy, scientific literacy, critical literacy, civic literacy, and musical literacy, to name a few.

As educators, it is our job to understand our students' current strengths, needs, and interests; to differentiate our instruction; and to develop their enthusiasm for learning during meaningful and authentic literacy experiences. While many of the careers and interests that our students will pursue in the future may not have been developed yet, we can prepare them by giving them opportunities to inquire and apply literacy and problem-solving strategies while collaborating with and learning from others.

Literacy from a Linguistic Perspective

Literacy is based on a foundation of linguistics. **Linguistics** is the study of language and its structure, and involves an analysis and integration of phonetics, morphemics, syntactics, semantics, and pragmatics. **Phonetics** is the study of speech sounds. **Morphemics** or morphology is the study of the formation of words, while **syntactics** or syntax is the study of the formation of sentences. **Semantics** is the study of meaning, and **pragmatics** is the study of language use. In sociolinguistics, which overlaps with pragmatics, there is an emphasis on the effect of society on the way language and literacy are understood and communicated. When these linguistic elements are combined with **orthography**, the writing system of a language, literacy is developed and enhanced. Both teachers and students need to understand explicitly how language and literacy work (Hudson, 2004). A deeper understanding of language is necessary for its intellectual benefits, as it improves the language skills of reading, writing, speaking, and listening (Hudson, 2004). Language and literacy are mostly learned from experience of usage in the interaction with others.

Social-Constructivist and Sociocultural Theories

The learning theories that teachers hold implicitly or explicitly influence their teaching, learning, and assessment practices (Scarino & Liddicoat, 2009). This text is based on the philosophy that teaching and learning are socially constructed, sociocultural, and multimodal literacy-based processes. In **social constructivism**, knowledge is individually constructed and socially mediated through the interaction with others. "Language and culture are frameworks through which humans experience, communicate, and understand reality" (Vygotsky, 1978, p. 39). Instruction should focus not only on how adults and peers create a community of learners that influence individual learning (Vygotsky, 1978), but also on how cultural beliefs and attitudes influence how instruction and learning should take place (Freire, 1970). Teachers should provide collaborative, authentic learning experiences that incorporate and value each student's **funds of knowledge**—the knowledge, skills, and experiences that are acquired through interactions in their community, family life, and culture (Gonzáles, Moll, & Amanti, 2005).

Teachers need to consider both what learners are able to do independently and what they can do with the support of social interaction. According to Vygotsky (1978), an individual's learning potential depends on mediation or the learning supports made available, such as reminders, examples, models, graphics, explanations, questions, elaborations, and specific feedback of strengths and areas for improvement. A sociocultural approach to teaching and learning is one that values and incorporates a learner's prior experiences, social participation, and use of mediating devices (language, tools, and technologies) within the context of authentic experiences (Scarino & Liddicoat, 2009). The final theory is that literacy—especially disciplinary literacy—is a multimodal process integrating not only oral and written literacy, but visual literacy (Msengi & McAndrews, 2016b). In our changing world of technology, we need to attend more to comprehending and representing visual information, and to the cultural importance of the visual and performing arts. A goal of this text is to develop supportive, culturally, and linguistically responsive educators who advocate for all students and facilitate their learning with the resources and strategies they need to be lifelong learners, informed decision makers, and successful citizens in our world.

UNDERSTANDING ASSESSMENT

Assessment is the process of gathering both qualitative and quantitative data about attributes of student learning and teaching through tests, observations, work samples, interviews, self-reflection, and other means. It is important to understand and communicate to others the purposes and types of assessment, possible ways to analyze the assessment data, and the implications for instructional decisions based on these data. Assessment evaluates not only the student's learning, but the teacher's instruction.

Assessment for, as, and of Learning

There are three purposes of assessment: assessment *for* learning, assessment *as* learning, and assessment *of* learning (Cooper, 2006). In addition, there are different types of assessments: norm-referenced, criterion-referenced, curriculum-based, and performance-based.

Assessment for learning, also known as **formative assessment**, is the process of gathering and analyzing data before and during teaching to identify what students know and can demonstrate, and what misconceptions they may have. Assessment for learning provides opportunities for the teacher to share the criteria for learning expectations and to provide specific oral and written feedback based on those learning expectations. This ongoing information is used by teachers to adjust or differentiate their teaching. Students are usually aware of what they are expected to learn and what the criteria for the assessment are. Often these assessments examine the students' processes of learning, not just the products. Assessment during the process of learning shows the students their strengths and needs, as well as their amount of change or development during the completion of a task.

Assessment as learning occurs when students assess themselves and their peers throughout the learning process and create learning goals. Students analyze their performance, or that of their peers, on the basis of specified criteria; they identify their strengths and areas for improvement, and determine how they can enhance their learning (Abromeit, 2001). Students use metacognitive strategies to monitor their own learning, identify what they know and can do, ask questions, and use feedback and self-assessment to help them in the next steps in learning. Ross (1998) suggests that in order to support self-evaluation, educators involve their students in defining the criteria to judge their performance, teach them how to apply the criteria to their own work, give them feedback on their self-evaluations, and help them develop productive goals and action plans. Several of the assessments in this book are specifically designed for peer and self-assessment. When students become involved in the learning process, they gain confidence in understanding what they are expected to learn and to what standard.

Assessment of learning, or **summative assessment**, takes place at the conclusion of instruction or at the end of a learning unit. It provides information and feedback about what was learned. The assessment should match the goals and objectives for student learning. This type of assessment assesses the product of what each student has learned and evaluates the student's learning based on standards. Assessment of the product becomes more meaningful for students when they are not only aware of the steps of the process to complete the task, but also when they are aware of evaluation criteria ahead of time.

Types of Assessment

Norm-referenced assessments are broad measures of achievement; they compare a student's performance to that of a national or representative sample of same-age or same-grade students. The tests are generally administered to groups. The format tends to have more traditional question structures, such as multiple-choice. Norm-referenced reports include a variety of numeric or quantitative data, such as percentile ranks, stanines, grade equivalent scores, raw scores, and scaled scores. A **percentile rank** identifies the percentage of a student's peer group (age or grade level) who took the assessment that the student's score surpassed. A **stanine** is a standard score representing a range of scores within an interval in a nine-point scale, with a mean of five and a standard deviation of two. **Grade and age equivalent scores** are estimates of the performance that an average student at a grade or age level is assumed to demonstrate. However, they can be very misleading because the scores are not stable and the standard changes by grade or age. Students may be one to two grade levels below their actual grade level and still be in the average range. A **raw score** is the number of correct responses on each subtest. A **scaled score** is a conversion of a student's raw score on a test to a common scale that allows a numerical comparison between students.

Norm-referenced achievement tests are often used as institutional assessments to provide the school boards, school administrators, and the general public evidence of the effectiveness of school programs at the curricular and programmatic levels. Examples of norm-referenced assessments (current at the time of this writing) are the *Woodcock–Johnson IV Tests of Cognitive Abilities* (Schrank, McGrew, & Mather, 2014), the *Gates–MacGinitie Reading Tests* (Nelson Assessment, 2017), the *Iowa Assessments* (University of Iowa College of Education, 2019), and the *Stanford Achievement Test* (Pearson, 2010). Results are measured against the stated missions of a school or specific program within them (Gunning, 2004). In the past, the primary means of identification for placement in special education was comparing the results of an intelligence test with a standardized achievement test. Now teachers must demonstrate that a significant amount of intervention was provided prior to testing or placing a child in special education. The data from these norm-referenced tests can complement other forms of assessment; however, they often only provide general information, such as approximate achievement level or expected level of achievement. They often do not measure literacy the way it is taught or used; therefore, this text does not cover the administration of norm-referenced tests.

Both norm-referenced and criterion-referenced tests must be reliable and valid (Gunning, 2004). **Reliability** is a measure of the consistency and dependability of results if students repeat the test. **Validity** is the degree to which test scores appropriately reflect the level of knowledge and skills that a test is designed to measure. Effective tests must also have **content validity**, meaning that they measure skills and strategies in the same way in which they were taught.

Criterion-referenced assessments are measures of student performance against a defined set of learning requirements or expectations. Most criterion-referenced tests measure knowledge, skills, and abilities as defined in learning standards or curricula developed by state educational agencies or school districts. The test results are reported in terms of what a student knows or is able to do as compared to each defined criterion. Therefore, these tests are more useful for making instructional decisions than norm-referenced tests, where the scores are compared to other students. Criterion-referenced tests often use "passing" or "cut" scores to place the students into categories such as basic, proficient, and advanced. Weaknesses of some criterion-referenced tests is that they may have arbitrary cut scores, may not include qualitative data (such as what the student understood) or an analysis of mistakes, and may not assess literacy skills or strategies in an authentic manner. Some tests use brief passages and multiple-choice tests, such as those found in many basal reader tests or technology-based assessments (Gunning, 2004). Another type of criterion-referenced test is an **informal reading inventory**, in which students read complete passages and are evaluated based on an analysis of their word accuracy, cue and strategy use, retelling, and free response to comprehension questions. This analysis can provide placement levels for reading instruction, as well as identify strengths and needs to inform instruction.

Diagnostic assessment, a specific type of criterion-referenced assessment, allows for an in-depth analysis of a student's current knowledge, skills, and strategies in order to gain an understanding of the student's literacy processes. Predominantly qualitative data on students' specific strengths and areas for growth help teachers identify specific objectives to be taught and how to teach them. A teacher can reinforce a student's strengths and background knowledge and use it to help the student make connections to new learning. An analysis of the student's specific miscues or mistakes, and patterns of mistakes, provides windows into the student's thinking, so that the teacher can clarify misconceptions through constructive feedback. An informal reading inventory with an analysis of miscues, oral reading strategies, and comprehension elements is an example of a diagnostic assessment, along with most of the assessments in this book.

Curriculum-based assessment, also called **curriculum-based measurement (CBM)** or **progress monitoring**, is the repeated, direct assessment of targeted skills to monitor student process in areas such as reading, spelling, writing, and math. The assessments are designed to used material from the curriculum to measure student mastery. Benchmarks of progress are defined and assessed on a regular, ongoing (often weekly) basis. Administration of each measure typically takes 1–5 minutes. Quantitative data are usually displayed graphically to allow monitoring of student performance according to benchmarks. Some of these assessments, such as the *Fountas and Pinnell Benchmark Assessment and Scholastic Inventories,* provide opportunities to read from and respond to authentic texts; others, such as AIMSweb (2006), assess isolated skills such as the number of words read or spelled correctly in 1 minute. Although these timed tests of isolated skills are easy to give and easy to report their scores to the public, they generally do not provide any qualitative data for specific analysis of a student's strengths and areas for growth, which would be required to plan appropriate individualized instruction.

Performance-based assessment or **authentic assessment** measures students' ability to apply higher-order thinking skills and knowledge learned in class or from their experiences to perform, create, or produce something with transferable real-world application. Students demonstrate what they know and are able to do, and the quality of their performance is evaluated on the basis of specific criteria. This type of assessment emphasizes the process of how students learn, rather than just the product of what students learned (Gunning, 2004). Running records (Clay, 1993), miscue analysis (Goodman, 1987), oral and written retellings, think-aloud protocols, analysis of written compositions, observations, anecdotal records, checklists, rating scales, and rubrics are used to evaluate students' literacy development. To determine students' interests, attitudes, and beliefs, teachers can use questionnaires and interviews. Self-evaluation, another form of authentic assessment, is of critical importance because students reflect on their own learning, put together portfolios of their own work, and make goals and plans for future learning. These self-evaluations can include the students' using checklists, rubrics, logs, journals, conferences, and literacy development portfolios to evaluate their own learning. This text includes a variety of criterion-referenced and performance-based assessments because they provide not only ongoing quantitative data (such as reading levels), but, more importantly, qualitative data on how each student processes language, reading, writing, and visual information.

Deciding on Appropriate Assessments

No single assessment tool will meet all of the learning goals and suit the learning styles of every student. Multiple assessment tools need to be used to identify students' strengths and areas for growth to make instructional decisions. As an educator seeking to choose the right assessment, you need to ask yourself the right questions:

- Does the assessment align with your teaching goals and philosophy?
- Does it measure what you are currently teaching? Does it align with the current learning objectives, or does it keep testing the same battery of skills even if they were not recently taught?
- Does it measure what it says it measures? For instance, if you want to measure reading comprehension, does the assessment focus on identifying the main idea of the passage, understanding vocabulary in context, making inferences, and identifying the author's purpose, or does it simply assess the ability to select a word to fit in a sentence and call this "reading comprehension"?
- Does it measure what is important? For example, if you want to measure reading and the purpose of reading is comprehension, then comprehension must be assessed. Since students do not need to read and write nonsense words, then this skill should not be assessed.
- Does the assessment provide both quantitative and qualitative data about students' specific strengths and areas for growth?
- Can incorrect responses be analyzed to identify patterns of thinking or misconceptions?
- How will the assessment information be used to inform the next teaching and student learning experiences?
- Does it assess higher-order thinking or just rote memorization?
- Does the assessment match student's skill or developmental levels? Was the student successful with much of the assessment, or was the student at the frustration level and continues to be tested at this level?
- Does the assessment match the students' language and cultural knowledge? Are the students English language learners? Are the assessment items related to concepts that are unfamiliar in their culture or experiences?
- How frequently should the same assessment be given? What new strategies or information has been taught since the last assessment that indicates another administration would be beneficial?
- What impact does the amount of time given for responding to the assessment items have on students' learning and anxiety? Is the emphasis on processing speed or on whether a student can use thinking strategies to respond accurately?

UNDERSTANDING INSTRUCTION

The purpose of **instruction** is to help people learn and to transfer and transform their learning through the use of metacognitive strategies in order to problem-solve and communicate ideas to others. Metacognition allows students to apply, monitor, and regulate strategy use; develop insight into how they learn with their own strengths and weaknesses; and use this insight to improve their learning (Flavell, 1979). **Learning** is a continuous process of gaining knowledge and skills through experience, interaction with others, study, and being taught. Teachers should encourage **student-centered learning** by involving them in decisions during planning, implementation, and assessment. What students learn, how they learn it, and how their learning is assessed are all driven by the students' needs and abilities, as well as their interests. Students should have opportunities to lead and share their learning with others.

Gradual-Release-of-Responsibility Model

The **gradual-release-of-responsibility model**, developed by Pearson and Gallagher (1983), shifts the responsibility of learning from the teacher to the eventual independence of the learner. This is accomplished through instructional scaffolding, based on Vygotsky's concept of the zone of proximal development (to be discussed later). There are four phases in the gradual-release-of-responsibility model: At first the responsibility rests predominantly on the teacher, with focused instruction and guided instruction; it is then gradually shifted to the student, with collaborative learning and independent learning (Fisher & Frey, 2014).

- **Focused instruction:** "I do it." The teacher explains the lesson purpose, introduces the topic in context, models the strategies and skills with a think-aloud, and notices how students respond.
- **Guided instruction:** "We do it." In small instructional groups, the teacher guides students toward using different skills, strategies, and procedures independently, by providing prompts, questions and specific feedback on strengths and areas for growth.
- **Collaborative learning:** "You do it together." Students work in small groups on activities that allow them to deepen their understanding through exploring, problem solving, discussion, and thinking with their peers.
- **Independent learning:** "You do it alone." Students use the skills and knowledge they acquired to demonstrate their learning and pose new questions.

Guidelines for teaching strategies, skills, or tasks within the gradual-release-of-responsibility model (modified from Fisher & Frey, 2014) are as follows:

- Name the strategy, skill, or task.
- State the purpose of the strategy, skill, or task.
- Provide a context and authentic purpose for using it.
- Explain when the strategy or skill is used.
- Use analogies to link prior knowledge to new learning.
- Demonstrate how the skill, strategy, or task is completed, using multiple modes of oral, written, and visual communication.
- Explain and identify each step with criteria for acceptability. Give examples of correct and incorrect responses.
- Alert learners about possible misconceptions or errors to avoid.
- Provide guided instruction with feedback based on the criteria.
- Provide collaborative learning with feedback based on the criteria.
- Provide independent task and assess the use of the new skill in context.
- Promote student self-monitoring.
- Reinforce this strategy in future lessons and literacy experiences.

Whole–Part–Whole Instruction

Students benefit more from instruction when strategies and skills are not taught in isolation, but are framed in the **whole–part–whole** instructional methodology (Knowles,

Holton, & Swanson, 2015; Strickland, 1998). In this methodology, the teacher introduces the "whole" or how the learning is applied in context; students practice the "parts"; and then the students recombine the parts and apply them in a new context or "whole." Here is an example:

Whole: The teacher states that the objective is to read and write words with the *-ea* vowel digraph. The teacher starts by reading an authentic story that contains the preferred vowel digraph. The students next use the think–pair–share approach to arrive at the definition of a vowel digraph, and then highlight the words in the story containing the vowel digraph *-ea*.

Part: Students sort the words by sound: /ē/, *eat*; /ĕ/, *bread*; /ā/, *great*. They read the words. Next, they write and read additional words with the same sounds and spelling patterns.

Whole: Students write their own stories, using at least three words with each of the sounds of the *-ea* vowel digraph. They then highlight the words with the *-ea* vowel digraph, and read their stories aloud to the group.

Elements of Effective Instruction

There are five elements of effective instruction that, when integrated into learning experiences, foster students' engagement with the goal of improving their outcomes and achievement (Great Schools Partnership, 2018).

1. Create a learning environment that supports all students to take risks, ask questions, and make and learn from mistakes. The physical space, routines/procedures, and development of positive relationships constitute a physically, socially, and emotionally safe environment.
2. Identify and share clear outcomes that anchor and guide the choices of instructional activities, materials, practice assignments, and assessment tasks. Outcomes are understood and used by students to set goals, guide learning, and prompt self-reflection.
3. Provide varied content, materials, and methods of instruction, so that students can explore ideas and information in varied ways and access learning through multiple entry points. Teachers select content and materials to engage and meet the needs of all learners.
4. Provide students with opportunities to practice what they are learning, and give timely, specific feedback based on their current performance in relation to the desired outcomes.
5. Coach and teach students to engage in higher-order thinking through instructional activities and practice.

During instruction, teachers need to **actively listen** by paraphrasing, checking perceptions, questioning, and soliciting elaboration; **pause** to allow students to process information; **prompt** students to use literacy and learning strategies; and **probe** students to monitor their learning, internalize strategies, and check for understanding. The design of curriculum, instruction, and assessments should prompt complex thinking, integration of concepts and ideas, and transfer of learned skills to new material or novel situations.

Instructional Design

Instructional design is based on a variety of constructs, such as backward design, diagnostic teaching, zone of proximal development, Bloom's taxonomy of cognitive levels, Camborne's model of literacy development, and lesson frameworks such as those developed by Fountas and Pinnell.

Backward Design

Backward design is the planning of instructional/learning experiences with the final outcome and assessment in mind. Wiggins and McTighe (2005) have identified three stages of backward design:

1. Identify desired results. To establish goals, big ideas, and skills, ask, "What do I want students to understand, know, and be able to do?"
2. Determine acceptable evidence of learning. To gather assessment evidence, ask, "How will I assess their learning during and after the task?"
3. Plan learning experiences and instruction. To plan learning events, ask, "Which learning activities will lead students to the desired results?"

Diagnostic Teaching

In planning instruction, it is also necessary to understand diagnostic teaching. **Diagnostic teaching** is the process of "using assessment and instruction at the same time to identify the instructional modifications that enable readers (and writers) to become independent learners" (Walker, 2011, p. 5). It is important to include formative assessment throughout the learning process, not just summative assessment at the end.

Zone of Proximal Development

To motivate and encourage learning, materials and learning experiences should be within a student's zone of proximal development. The **zone of proximal development**, as defined by Vygotsky (1978, p. 86), is "the distance between the actual developmental level as determined by independent problem-solving and the level of potential development as determined through problem-solving under adult guidance or in collaboration with more capable peers." In other words, instruction should take place at a level at which the student is able to do the task successfully with some scaffolding (see Figure 1.3).

Bloom's Taxonomy

As educators, our primary goal is to develop our students' knowledge and problem-solving abilities by providing experiences that enhance their higher-order thinking. Bloom (1956) developed a method of classification for thinking behaviors that were believed to be important in the processes of learning, known as **Bloom's taxonomy**, with six hierarchical levels of cognitive complexity. From lowest to highest, these six levels are knowledge, comprehension, application, analysis, synthesis, and evaluation. Many educational objectives and strategies have been based on this taxonomy.

FIGURE 1.3. Chart illustrating levels below, within, and above the zone of proximal development.

Below the zone of proximal development ←	Within the zone of proximal development ←	Above the zone of proximal development
Independent level—Easy	Instructional level—Just right	Frustration level—Too hard
Student can read, write, communicate, or complete task on his/her own.	Student can read, write, communicate, or complete task with support.	Student is unable to read, write, communicate, or complete task even with support.

According to Forehand (2005), although teachers have used Bloom's taxonomy since the late 1950s to encourage students to use higher-order thinking, a former student of Bloom's, Lorin Anderson, led a new group of cognitive psychologists, curriculum theorists, and instructional researchers to update the taxonomy. These scholars felt that the original taxonomy did not reflect the depth of knowledge. This revision, which is available in complete and abridged editions (Anderson & Krathwohl, 2001), includes several changes in terminology and structure, which permit its broader use as a tool for planning, instruction, and assessment. The terminology of the six categories has been changed from nouns to verbs; the top two levels have been switched; and the bottom level has been renamed. Forehand describes the structural changes from the original one-dimensional form to the revised two-dimensional form. The knowledge dimension examines the kind of knowledge to be learned, while the cognitive process dimension examines the process used to learn. The knowledge dimension has four levels: factual, conceptual, procedural, and metacognitive. The cognitive process dimension has six levels: remembering, understanding, applying, analyzing, evaluating, and creating. In addition, each of the four knowledge dimension levels is subdivided into either three or four categories; for example, the factual dimension is divided into factual knowledge, knowledge of terminology, and knowledge of specific details and elements. Forehand explains that the subcategories are most helpful to teachers in both writing objectives and aligning standards with the curriculum. They are also helpful in assessing students throughout the learning process. Table 1.1 describes the revised taxonomy's cognitive processes, verbs for objectives, and correlated assessments for learning.

Cambourne's Model of Literacy Development

An effective model of literacy learning, developed by Cambourne (1988), demonstrates how literacy development occurs. Students are engaged in literacy when they have been immersed in it and have had numerous demonstrations of how texts are constructed and used. Teachers should maintain high but achievable expectations; however, the responsibility of learning remains with the students. Students need numerous opportunities to use their developing literacy processes. Teachers should expect and allow approximations, as this is how learning occurs. Finally, students need to receive specific, timely, and constructive feedback. When these elements are in place, learners are likely to continue to engage in literacy activities for their own purposes. In Cambourne's model, there are seven conditions in planning instruction: (1) immersion in the content and context, (2) demonstration of practical and concrete models, (3) clear description of learning expectations, (4) striving for students to take responsibility for their own learning, (5) recognition of approximations

TABLE 1.1. Revised Bloom's Taxonomy

Cognitive process	Verbs for objectives	Assessment
Creating	*assemble, construct, create, design, develop, formulate, compose, invent, generating*	Can the student put elements together to create a new product, idea, or point of view?
Evaluating	*appraise, argue, defend, judge, select, support, critique, evaluate, justify, recommend, conclude*	Can the student make and support judgments based on criteria?
Analyzing	*compare, contrast, differentiate, experiment, predict, categorize, separate, relate, analyze*	Can the student distinguish between different parts and determine how the parts are related to each other and to the overall structure?
Applying	*demonstrate, dramatize, act out, illustrate, interpret, solve, use, infer, show*	Can the student use the information in a new way or context?
Understanding	*classify, describe, explain, discuss, identify, locate, report, select, paraphrase, translate, summarize, arrange, give examples.*	Can the student construct meaning for oral, written, and visual information to explain the ideas or concepts?
Remembering	*define, list, memorize, recall, repeat, state, label, match*	Can the student recall relevant information from long-term memory?

toward learning expectations, (6) opportunities for practice and application of new learning, and (7) providing continuous feedback, support, and celebrations.

Fountas and Pinnell's Continuum of Literacy Learning

Effective instruction comes from careful planning of the entire literacy program. Pinnell and Fountas (2010) have developed a continuum of literacy learning that contributes to students' literacy development and can be used to design and manage the instructional program. This continuum consists of the following seven curriculum components (Pinnell & Fountas, 2010, p. 3):

- **Interactive read-aloud and literature discussion:** Students engage in deep discussion with one another about a text that they have heard read aloud or one they have read independently.
- **Shared and performance reading:** Students read together or take roles in reading a shared text. They reflect the meaning of the text with their voices.
- **Writing about reading:** Students extend their understanding of a text through a variety of writing genres and sometimes with illustrations.
- **Writing:** Students compose and write their own examples of a variety of genres, written for a variety of purposes and audiences.
- **Oral, visual, and technological communication:** Students present their ideas through oral discussion and presentation or through the use of technology.
- **Phonics, spelling, and word study:** Students learn about the relationships of letters to sounds, as well as the structure of words, to help them in reading and spelling.
- **Guided reading:** Students read a teacher-selected text in a small group; the teacher provides explicit teaching and support for reading increasingly challenging text.

UNDERSTANDING THE CYCLE OF DECISION MAKING FOR ASSESSMENT AND INSTRUCTION

Teachers need to make many important decisions about assessment and instruction in order to enhance their students' literacy development and lifelong learning. "Assessment and instruction should be inextricably linked in a recursive, ongoing, and dynamic way" (Vogt & Shearer, 2007, p. 91). Paris and colleagues (1992) have developed phases of decision making for authentic literacy assessments; these include identifying dimensions of literacy, identifying attributes of literacy, collecting evidence of literacy proficiency by various methods, scoring student work samples, and interpreting and using the data. In a different model, Walker (2011) has identified five roles of diagnostic teachers: reflecting, planning, mediating, enabling, and responding. The **cycle of decision making for assessment and instruction** my colleagues and I follow, which is based on multiple models, includes nine integrated phases (see Figure 1.4). Each phase is described in detail on the following pages. These decision-making phases are important so that the instruction can be based on each

FIGURE 1.4. Cycle of decision making for literacy assessment and instruction.

learner's strengths and areas for growth, rather than on a predetermined instructional sequence in a program.

Phase 1. Get to Know Students

In order to plan how to teach students, a teacher needs to know what motivates and interests them, and what background experiences or funds of knowledge they bring to the classroom. Students' learning is also influenced by their peers, family, and community, as well as by their culture, language(s), and level of development. When teachers understand students, they are better able to help them make connections to prior knowledge in order to make the learning relevant and interesting. Teachers can learn from their students by listening to them, observing them, interviewing them, and engaging with them and their family and community. Specific strategies for doing these things are described in Chapter 2. Teachers can also learn about students' personal goals for learning and the ways in which certain teaching practices help or hinder their learning.

Phase 2. Identify Goals and Standards

Educational goals and standards are statements describing the competencies, skills, and attributes that students should possess at the completion of a class, grade, or educational level. A broad goal of PreK–12 education may be to facilitate all students in graduating from high school with the academic, sociomotional, and lifelong learning skills to be responsible and caring citizens, leaders in their community, and agents of their own success. Educational learning standards, such as the Common Core State Standards (National Governors Association Center for Best Practices & Council of Chief State School Officers, 2010; *www.corestandards.org*) and the Next Generation Science Standards, are written descriptions of what students are expected to know and be able to do at a specific stage in their education.

In addition to national learning standards, there may be state and district goals for what students should be able to know and do by the end of each grade.

Phase 3. Determine What, How, and When to Assess

Teachers select assessments that are useful to support students' learning, and assess what students are expected to know and do. Knowledge about a student's literacy and content proficiency can be obtained through individual or group assessments, as well as information from the student, the family, classroom teachers, classroom assistants, and other professionals. Evidence of content and literacy development can be obtained through multiple diagnostic, formative, and summative assessments. Students' performances, processes, and products can all be evaluated.

Evidence of a student's learning should be collected throughout the year and should be organized in a student's literacy learning portfolio. These data could include diagnostic assessment, performance-based checklists, and rubrics; self-evaluation interviews; and observation notes. At the end of each grading period or semester, specific literacy assessments can be readministered in order to evaluate and identify new literacy strengths, other improvements, and ongoing needs.

The choice of a specific assessment should be based on its relation to the stated goals and objectives. When possible, assessments should use authentic oral language, reading, and writing tasks. The assessment should provide evidence of specific literacy strengths and needs, and not just general levels and scores. Discretion is needed in selecting assessments or literacy experiences, so that the most information is gained from the fewest tasks. This allows more time for learning and less time assessing. In addition, these tasks should be within or close to a student's zone of proximal development. That is, the student is expected to complete at least part of the task correctly, but the student may not have the prior knowledge necessary to complete the task with 100% accuracy. If the student becomes too frustrated or can complete the task too easily, the literacy task may need to be stopped, and another one can be given that will be more appropriate.

The assessments included in this book are organized by specific literacy processes. The *Purposes for Assessments* chart in the Appendix (p. 357–358) provides a list of the assessments, along with their purposes and which students should benefit from them. Within each chapter, there are directions for how to administer each assessment. Some assessments include cut scores that indicate where to stop, as well as directions for continuing to higher levels.

Phase 4. Administer Diagnostic or Formative Assessments and Analyze Data

The following general assessment procedures are used for administering the literacy assessments described in Chapters 3–7 and included in the Appendix (language, word analysis, reading fluency, comprehension, and writing/visual assessments). For specific instructions, see the directions for the individual assessments.

First, as the teacher, obtain background information about each student's language and literacy development from family members, classroom teachers, and all other involved professionals to help guide the selection of assessments. You also need to determine if your students with visual, auditory, or other physical differences need any accommodations. Next, select those assessments that will provide the information needed to guide your instruction. Obviously, not all assessments need to be administered to every student; the decisions are based on developmental benchmarks, prior knowledge of each student's literacy development, and an analysis of each assessment after it is administered.

Prepare the environment for assessment. If possible, the assessments should be administered individually in a quiet, separate room in order to reduce distractions. You should usually sit next to and slightly behind the student being assessed, and hold a clipboard containing all record sheets. In this arrangement, your interactions are more conversational, you can more easily observe the student's behaviors, and the student remains focused on the task rather than what you are writing. The student should be able to sit comfortably at the table with feet on the floor; if the table is too tall, a block may be used on which to rest the feet.

To obtain more accurate documentation, equip the room with discreet audiovisual equipment. At a minimum, you should have equipment for audio-recording the student's oral responses. Record with a pencil the student's responses and behaviors during assessment, and then review the recording for additions or corrections. Only the materials needed for the assessments should be placed on the table, including at least two sharpened pencils. If necessary, you can administer some of the silent reading or writing assessments in groups; however, more useful information is obtained if each student is observed individually. In a group situation, it is sometimes beneficial to provide personal workspace dividers, to help the students stay focused on their own papers.

You should not attempt to administer all of the assessments during a single session. It is important to watch for and keep anecdotal notes of the student's behavior and to notice signs of inattentiveness, restlessness, or stress in particular. Allow students to take water, restroom, or stretch breaks as needed. The length of the assessment periods will vary, depending on the particular assessment tool(s) being used and each student's attention span. For elementary students, it is usually best to keep the assessment time to no more than 30–60 minutes per day, including breaks. Older students may be able to attend for up to 2 hours per day, with breaks. Use each student's behavior to guide your decision.

Although there is no specific order in which the assessments must be given, starting with one of the interest or literacy inventories is recommended if you do not know the student well. In doing so, you can establish rapport and help the student feel more relaxed in the assessment process. It is beneficial to administer the reading word lists prior to text reading, as the results can help determine at which level to begin the text reading. If the assessment session is longer than 30 minutes, you might consider providing a break and interspersing reading and writing assessments to help keep the student more engaged.

After administering each assessment, quickly review the student's responses to determine which assessment to give next. At the end of each assessment session, analyze and evaluate the student's literacy development according to the assessment protocol. For assessments with multiple levels, continue to the next level until the highest instructional level has been reached. Identify the student's strengths and needs for each assessed area of literacy by integrating information within or between assessments. These diagnostic data will be used to make instructional decisions. When analyzing data, always provide a qualitative analysis, not just quantitative scores. Identify the student's strengths before areas for growth, and give specific examples. See the *Guidelines for Literacy Assessment Analysis* in the Appendix (pp. 359–361).

Phase 5. Identify and Write Objectives for Literacy and Content

Education is likely to be more effective if what students need to learn and the criteria for how well the students learn it are clearly stated to students. This clarity can be achieved by first writing observable and measurable **learning objectives.** Based on assessment data, determine the specific objectives that are appropriate for the next step in the student's development. These objectives should be the ongoing focus of your lesson. You can refer to the revised Bloom's taxonomy (Anderson & Krathwohl, 2001) to identify the level of knowledge you want to assess and observable verbs related to that level. To write a comprehensive learning objective, include the following components: learner, behavior, content, assessment criteria, condition, and rationale (see Table 1.2). The objectives should be aligned to standards such as the Common Core State Standards or Next Generation Science Standards. For literacy and disciplinary lessons, objectives that integrate multiple literacy processes and modalities are recommended.

Phase 6. Plan Instruction

Planning for instruction needs to include decisions about assessment, strategies, materials, learning experiences, and sequence of instruction. The first step is thinking about the **context** of instruction: Which students are you teaching? What are their funds of knowledge? Where and in what format(s) will the instruction will take place? What part of the

TABLE 1.2. Guide to Writing a Comprehensive Learning Objective

Learner	Behavior: observable/ cognitive	Content	Assessment criteria	Condition	Rationale
The student will . . .	Say/write/visually represent a thinking process (May be Bloom's taxonomy verb)	Something	Use this assessment/ strategy and do it this well	In this situation	For the purpose of
Who? (Student or students)	Do what? (Observable action/cognitive process)	About what? (Topic)	How? (Task and how accurately, frequently)	What conditions? (Setting or with what provided)	Why? (Improving [name of strategy or skill])
Example: The student will orally and in writing compare and contrast whales and fish in a Venn diagram with at least three similarities and three differences individually, after orally reading the text *Whales and Fish* to improve comprehension of animal classification.					

instruction is individual, paired, small-group, or whole-group? Providing individual instruction or flexible grouping according to the instructional objectives for each student is suggested.

Next, using the **objectives**, plan the formative and summative **assessments.** Decide how to assess each student's learning for each of the objectives. Select or create the assessment tools. Identify the criteria for assessing the students' learning, and create scoring guides, checklists, or rubrics containing the criteria. Remember to assess not only individual skills, but the ability to apply them in context. For example, when you are assessing writing, do not forget to assess the content and purpose for the writing, not just the mechanics. Plan how you are going to record details on each student's performance and document the evaluation of each area. In addition, plan opportunities for you and the student to discuss and reflect on specific strengths and needs.

Then carefully select appropriate strategies, tasks, and materials that focus on the whole act of literacy (oral, written, and visual), are within a student's zone of proximal development, and focus on authentic literacy experiences. You should be able to explain why you have made these decisions and why you teach as you do. When teaching a **skill** or **strategy**, start with introducing it in context (e.g., select a text that contains the element to be taught), read the text or portions of the text, teach the skill or strategy, and then return to the text to use it in context. Finally, provide opportunities to apply the skill or strategy in new contexts.

In addition, the choice of appropriate reading, writing, and viewing **materials** needs to be based on the student's instructional level and interest, so that with scaffolded instruction, the student can be successful. Although students should be allowed to give some input into text selection, they should read and write texts from a variety of genres and formats to extend learning. You should consider incorporating technology, such as websites and videos, to better equip the student in gaining knowledge from other media. The texts used in language arts can also be correlated with content area learning standards. You should analyze text characteristics, features, and structures prior to assigning reading. You should plan how you are going to introduce the text, provide background knowledge, and connect the text to your students' prior knowledge. See Chapter 6 for strategies for selecting and analyzing texts.

Furthermore, plan for how you are going to teach and have your students apply general academic and content-specific language. **General academic language** is language that is used at school orally and in instructional texts; it may not be used in informal social settings. **Content-specific** or **discipline-specific vocabulary** is vocabulary that is typically only used within a particular discipline, such as math, science, social studies, or the arts.

Plan how you are going to **differentiate** the content, process, product, and environment to meet the needs of each student. Determining the appropriate sequence of instruction involves keeping in mind the whole–part–whole philosophy, the gradual-release-of-responsibility model, and the integration of all six literacy modalities.

The *Literacy Lesson Plan Format* (see Appendix, pp. 362–363) provides a guide for planning specific lessons and documenting student learning. This lesson plan format can be used for either individual or group instruction. The elements in the lesson plan include the context for learning; objectives with standards; differentiation; academic language; materials; procedure; assessment with criteria; homework and family communication; attached student work and assessment documents with analysis and feedback; and reflection (see Table 1.3). The procedure section includes an introduction, instruction with guided collaborative, and independent practice and application, and student closure.

The introduction provides interest and motivation to the students, and helps them to make connections to their background knowledge. It also focuses their attention on the lesson by communicating clear objectives, authentic purpose, connection to prior learning, and benefit for learning concepts. To help students engage in the topic, you could ask questions, show pictures or videos, tell a relevant story, or bring in realia. Although not every element may be present in every lesson, you need to make informed decisions about what you are going to teach and why you are going to teach it. This comprehensive lesson plan is detailed, to guide you in the process of making informed instructional decisions. Initially, it is very important to write everything down; eventually, you will make decisions about what essential elements are needed, and what needs to be written down. However, the objectives and the evaluation of students' learning should always be documented.

Phase 7. Implement Instruction

When implementing instruction, you should reflect on your teaching before, during, and after the literacy event. At the beginning of your lesson, clearly state and teach objectives, and connect them to the students' prior knowledge. Throughout the lesson, be sure to define, use, and provide opportunities for students to use general academic and discipline-specific vocabulary terms.

One effective general instructional strategy is the **think-aloud** strategy. Model thinking aloud for your students as you read, write, or participate in literacy activities. Talk about what you are thinking about, thereby providing them with the opportunity to become aware of the many strategies and monitoring behaviors that effective readers and writers use. Have the students keep a list of the different types of things you do to help you understand or compose the text. Then discuss and post the strategies in the students' own words. Once you model the think-aloud process, guide them in their own think-aloud process. Whichever strategy and instructional model you choose, you should anticipate your students' responses and plan adaptations for different learning styles and interests.

TABLE 1.3. Lesson Plan Elements

Element	Guidelines
Context	Describe setting, groupings, and relationship of lesson to unit or prior learning.
Objectives with Common Core State Standards or other standards	• Include objectives for **literacy processes** (language/vocabulary, word analysis, reading fluency, comprehension, and composition). • Include objectives for **content area/discipline** (language arts, math, science, social studies, and/or arts). • Incorporate multiple **literacy modalities** (speaking, listening, reading, writing, viewing, and visually representing) in the objectives.
Differentiation	Include how you will/did adapt the **content, process, product,** and **environment** for class and specific students. Describe potential **misconceptions.**
Academic language	List the **general academic vocabulary** and the **discipline-specific vocabulary** that you plan to teach and expect students to know and use.
Materials	List all teacher and student materials and resources needed for the lesson.
Procedure	Sequence what the teacher and students will say and do, along with the formative and summative assessments.
Introduction	Include engagement activities, clear objectives, authentic purpose for learning, connection to background knowledge, connection to prior learning, introduction of content, preassessment of what students know or want to learn.
Instruction	• Present and model strategies and learning activities in context. • Define and use academic and content-specific vocabulary.
Guided and collaborative practice	• Encourage application of learning with scaffolded support and specific feedback. • Reinforce use of academic and content-specific vocabulary. • Demonstrate integration of skills, strategies, or tasks into real-world applications.
Assessment with criteria and planned feedback	Describe how you will assess or check for understanding and evaluate student learning before, during, and after instruction. Include criteria for acceptability and planned feedback.
Student closure	Describe how students will or did reflect on their learning of objectives (student review or summary of learning).
Homework and family communication	Describe the homework or extensions related to this lesson. Describe how this information was or will be shared with the families.
Attached student work/ assessment documents	List and then attach students' work and other assessment and observational documents, with analysis and positive and constructive feedback provided to the student.
Teacher's reflection	Reflect on your teaching, student learning, and future plans for how to enhance the retention and transfer of the processes and content. Include how individual students met each of the objectives. Provide specific examples of student's correct and incorrect responses as well as a summary of strengths and areas for improvement.

However, you also need to adapt your lessons during teaching to meet the needs of individuals. These modifications should be recorded for future use. Monitor your instruction to see that it is meaningful and emphasizes success.

During guided practice, provide specific feedback on strengths and areas for growth. You need to focus first on what a student can do, rather than just pointing out mistakes. Mistakes are just windows into students' thinking. Mediate your students' learning by scaffolding the type and amount of your prompts and support. **Scaffolding**, provided within each student's zone of proximal development, is "a process that enables a student or novice to solve a problem, carry out a task, or achieve a goal which would be beyond his (or her) unassisted efforts" (Wood, Bruner, & Ross, 1976, p. 90). Encourage active learning and problem solving. Assess during instruction because assessment needs to be continuous as the student is learning. Adjust instruction while teaching to ensure successful learning, and do not wait until the lesson is over. Base your instructional decisions on a student's ability to construct meaning or compose writing by using information from texts and information that the student already knows. According to Clay (1993), such scaffolded instruction enables students to develop a self-extending system, whereby they utilize multiple techniques and strategies while solving problems.

You build independence by providing your students with the feedback and resources to understand themselves as effective speakers, readers, writers, presenters, and problem solvers. Elicit metacognition by first verbalizing your own thinking during the literacy process, and then guiding your students in doing the same. Select strategies that will facilitate learning in the most efficient way for the students. When you are an effective observer, listener, and responder, you are better able to meet the needs of individual students.

Phase 8. Assess, Analyze, and Give Feedback on Student Learning

Assess before, during, and after instruction in order to identify specific strengths and areas for growth. To enhance students' learning, it is important to provide them with clear explanations of what to do, how to do it, and what the criteria for judging their behavior are. Without such explanations, students may be confused and use time inefficiently in trying to figure out what they are supposed to learn. Both during and at the end of the lesson, it is essential to bring closure to a student's learning by using your own and/or the student's assessments of learning. Oral, written, or observation assessments can be used, such as oral reading records, retellings, or written reflections. Again, be sure to document each student's responses and behaviors.

Once the assessments have been administered, both the quantitative and qualitative data can be analyzed to provide specific information about each student's strengths and needs in language, reading, and writing processing. Many of the assessments in this book can help identify the independent, instructional, and frustration levels of a student's reading and writing. Since many factors (including background knowledge) have an impact on a student's functioning level, grade levels can only be approximate. In addition, an analysis can identify strategies that a student uses or neglects in problem solving. This information is often even more important when you are planning which strategies or concepts to teach. Other assessments, such as observations, work samples, checklists, or rubrics, provide additional information about how students perform during authentic oral language, reading, and writing tasks. Narrative comments and quantitative scores based on the objectives of literacy can be documented and evaluated.

Assessment is primarily used to provide specific feedback to students to support their learning. Point out to students specific examples, areas of strength on the assessment, and help them make connections between these strengths and areas for improvement. Using the assessment responses, select one to three areas for improvement, and scaffold their learning by providing specific problem-solving strategies to correct the information on the assessment and apply it to new learning. The following are examples of literacy questions adapted from Gunning (2004, p. 26) that you can ask to help you plan, revise, and improve your literacy programs and your instruction.

- Where is the student in language, reading, and writing development?
- At what grade level is the student reading and writing?
- Is the reading or writing at the independent, instructional, or frustration level?
- How adequate are the student's listening, reading, and writing vocabularies?
- What comprehension and word analysis strategies does the student use?
- Does the student know how to study?
- What are the student's interests in and attitudes toward reading or writing?
- Does the student enjoy reading or writing in a variety of genres?
- Does the student read and write on one's own?
- What kinds of writing tasks has the student attempted?
- Is the student's reading and writing improving?
- What strengths and needs does the student have in language, reading, and writing?

Phase 9. Reflect on Student Learning and Instructional Decisions

During reflection, begin by measuring each student's learning outcomes against goals, objectives, and developmental benchmarks. You and the student need to reflect on the student's learning, the student's affect, and your teaching. You could ask the student questions such as these: "What did you learn? What did I do that helped you learn? What did you like about the lesson? What was difficult for you? What might help you learn better?" If the student omits any of the objectives, talk about them and ask the student to explain what was learned. Reflecting on their own learning helps students solidify their learning. To increase active engagement during group lessons, have each student share responses with a partner before selecting a few students to respond to the class. When your students go home after school and a family member asks questions such as "What did you learn in school today?", they will (ideally) have something specific to tell them. Remind family members periodically that this is an important dialogue to have with their children.

For your own reflection on the lesson, you should answer the following questions: "What went well and why? What didn't go well and why? What did I learn about my teaching? How can instruction be adapted to meet each student's needs in the future? Finally, what does each student need instruction on next to move literacy development along?" For additional ideas or sharing concerns, talk with your colleagues and other professionals.

Finally, return to Phase 1 to measure student outcomes against goals, objectives, and developmental benchmarks. The data of student responses are interpreted and used to show individual growth over time. This approach can also be used to compare data for groups of students, the whole classroom, or the whole program. In order for this information to be useful to you, Paris and colleagues (1992) suggest giving careful consideration to the selection of methods for recording, organizing, and accessing assessment data for each student. These methods include a process portfolio, where ongoing assessment documents and data are kept; an archival portfolio, where a summary of previous assessment data are kept and passed to the next teacher; aggregated records, which are collections of assessment data from different sources; and electronic storage/retrieval, where student data are recorded in an electronic file.

These nine integrated phases in the cycle of literacy assessment and instruction support you in using assessment to inform instruction. The assessment results should then be used to improve opportunities for student learning by connecting assessment data to new instructional goals and objectives, to inform families of the students' growth, and to help students monitor and evaluate their own work. Cycling back to Phase 1 allows you to focus back on each student and plan for new or continuing goals and learning objectives.

UNDERSTANDING DIVERSE LEARNERS

Diverse learners include students from racially, ethnically, culturally, linguistically, and socioeconomically diverse families and communities. Students as individuals also have diverse cognitive, socioemotional, and physical abilities. Teachers have a responsibility to celebrate diversity and to make every student feel accepted and respected by the classroom community. Diversity is discussed further in Chapter 2.

Some students have an identified disability, some have learning or socioemotional challenges, but all students have strengths. These strengths can be used as building blocks to foster new learning. The following provides some foundational information about learning disabilities and information processing.

Learning Differences and Disabilities

Students who have learning differences, or who have been formally identified as having learning disabilities, have increased difficulties in processing information. **Learning disabilities** are neurologically based conditions that interfere with the acquisition, storage, organization, and use of skills and knowledge. They are identified by deficits in academic functioning and in processing memory, auditory, visual, and linguistic information. Students with learning disabilities have normal to above-normal intelligence, and the disabilities are not caused by emotional disturbance; social or cultural conditions; or a primary visual, hearing, or motor disability. Students should receive comprehensive vision, hearing, and overall physical exams to rule out or make adaptations for physical disabilities.

Information Processing

There are four stages of information processing used in learning, according to the National Dissemination Center for Children with Disabilities (2004): input, integration, memory, and output.

- **Input** is the process of recording in the brain information that comes from the senses; for literacy, these are predominantly visual and auditory processes.
- **Integration** is the process of interpreting the input information, such as sequencing, abstraction, and organization. Sequencing disabilities might include retelling

a story in an incorrect order, reversing words, or having to start from the beginning of a sequence (such as the days of the week or the alphabet) to determine what comes next. Students who have a disability involving abstraction have difficulty in inferring meaning. They may read a story, yet may not be able to generalize from it. They find it difficult to understand homophones, jokes, puns, or idioms. Students with organization disabilities find it difficult to make bits of information cohere into concepts and relate it to what has previously been learned. They may learn a series of facts without being able to answer general questions that require the application of these facts.

- **Memory** is the brain's storage for later retrieval. Short-term memory retains information briefly while a person attends to it or concentrates on it, such as remembering a phone number long enough to dial it. When information is repeated often enough, it enters long-term memory, where it is stored and can be retrieved later. Students with these disabilities need many more repetitions than usual to retain information.
- **Output** of information is achieved through language or motor (muscular) activity. Language disabilities almost always involve what is called demand or responsive language, rather than spontaneous or assertive language. Motor disabilities can be poor coordination of large muscle groups, called gross motor disabilities, or poor coordination of small muscles, called fine motor disabilities. Students with motor disabilities often write slowly, and/or their handwriting is unreadable. They may also make frequent spelling, grammar, and punctuation errors.

Learning disabilities can be classified by their effects at one or more of these stages. It is important to remember that each child has individual strengths as well as weaknesses at each stage. A student who has difficulties in literacy may have a diagnosed or undiagnosed learning disability. Students are typically diagnosed with learning disabilities by a triangulation of observational, norm-referenced, and criterion-referenced assessment data. Once a student's disability has been identified, an individualized education program (IEP) is developed for that student. There are several classifications of learning disabilities. Some students are diagnosed with general learning disabilities and/or nonverbal learning disabilities, while others have specific disabilities. A learning disability cannot be legally identified until a student has received specific instruction in each of the processes over a prolonged period.

A **visual processing disorder** involves the inability to process visual information, such as the identification and discrimination of letters and words, spatial awareness, and visual memory. Some students have difficulty in recognizing the position and shape of what they see. Letters may be reversed or rotated. They may jump over words, read the same line twice, or skip lines. Those diagnosed with an **auditory processing disorder** may have difficulties with auditory discrimination (distinguishing between similar sounds and words), auditory figure–ground discrimination (distinguishing between relevant speech and background sounds), and/or auditory memory (recalling what words were heard).

More recently, however, the educational focus has been less on labeling students and more on documenting their specific strengths and needs during authentic literacy tasks and providing different levels of instructional intervention for students who have difficulties. As a literacy specialist or teacher, you should be an integral member of the literacy team who can provide support to all students, especially those who have literacy processing problems. Another one of your roles is to directly assess and evaluate students' strengths and needs, or to support others in this process.

UNDERSTANDING DIFFERENTIATED INSTRUCTION

Differentiated instruction consists of the efforts teachers make to respond to the different learners in the classroom. The teachers vary their instruction when working with individuals, groups or a whole class, to create the best learning experience possible for each student. Based on students' backgrounds, development, interest, or learning profiles, teachers can differentiate at least four classroom elements: the content, process, product, and learning environment (Tomlinson & Allen, 2000).

The **content** is what the student needs to learn or how the student will get access to the information. Examples of differentiating content include the following:

- Providing students with additional resources that match their different levels of understanding.
- Using reading and instructional materials at varying readability levels.
- Opportunities for students to select their own topics for reading, writing, or projects.
- Having students use technology to gain access to content, including audio- or video-recorded information.
- Providing spelling or vocabulary words at students' readiness levels.
- Presenting ideas through visual, auditory, kinesthetic, and tactile means.
- Meeting with small groups to reteach an idea or skill for some learners, or to extend the thinking or skills of other learners.
- Providing experiences at a variety of Bloom's taxonomy levels.

The **process** is differentiated by the activities in which the student engages in order to make sense of or master the content. Examples of differentiating process or activities include the following:

- Providing activities with different levels of support, challenge, or complexity.
- Providing opportunities for paired or small-group work.
- Providing different tasks for the students to complete, with similar objectives.
- Offering manipulatives or other hands-on supports for students who need them.
- Reteach or exempt students based on performance.
- Providing information early and expecting the task to be completed at the same time.
- Varying the length of time a student may take to complete a task in order to provide additional support or to pursue a topic in greater depth.

The **product** is differentiated by the evidence for learning (assessment or project). Examples of differentiating products include the following:

- Giving students options of how to demonstrate required learning (e.g., give a performance, write a letter, or create a visual or multimedia presentation).
- Using scoring guides or rubrics that match and extend students' varied skill levels.
- Allowing students to work alone or in small groups on their products.
- Encouraging students to create their own product assignments, following specified criteria.

The **learning environment** is differentiated by the way the classroom works and feels. Examples of differentiating the learning environment include these:

- Making sure there are places in the room to work quietly and without distraction, as well as places that invite student collaboration.
- Providing materials that reflect a variety of cultures and home settings.
- Setting out clear guidelines for independent work that match individual students' needs.
- Developing routines that encourage students to get support from print and electronic resources and their peers when teachers are busy.
- Providing flexible seating and opportunities for movement.
- Providing a risk-taking and supportive environment.

Differentiated instruction can be implemented within the framework of **universal design for learning** (Meyer, Rose, & Gordon, 2014), which is designed to improve and optimize teaching and learning for all people. It is organized around three major principles: the use of multiple means of representation, multiple means of action and expression, and multiple means of engagement. Every student comes from a different background, has different experiences, and has different ways of thinking. Due to the vast diversity among learners, teachers must work diligently to get to know their students and how they learn, use different engaging instructional methods and materials, provide meaningful and challenging learning experiences, and create a caring and supportive environment that enables all students to succeed.

SUMMARY

This introductory chapter has provided background information on literacy, assessment, and instruction, which will serve as a useful foundation as you use this book. It is important to remember that "literacy" is a broad term that encompasses oral, written, and visual modes. Processes of literacy include language, word analysis, reading fluency, reading, and listening comprehension; writing composition; and viewing and visually representing—all of which is included in the subsequent chapters. Assessment is not separate from instruction, but occurs before, during, and after it. When planning and implementing instruction, you need to make numerous decisions based on your knowledge of literacy development, strategies, materials, and each student's strengths and areas for growth.

Chapter 2

Building Relationships

Learning from Students, Families, and Community

UNDERSTANDING BUILDING RELATIONSHIPS

Positive relationships are based on mutual respect and trust, and are built up and developed over time through a series of interactions. Learning in a democratic classroom includes constructing knowledge that is gained from collaborative interactions among the child, peers, family, teachers, and community members who value identity, culture, and language (Msengi & McAndrews, 2016a). "It takes a village to raise a child" is a well-known African proverb, meaning that an entire community of people must interact with children for those children to experience and grow in a safe and healthy environment.

Building Relationships with Students

As educators, our goal is to value and equitably support students to develop in- and out-of-school literacies to understand and communicate ideas, as well as to develop as caring and productive citizens. Positive relationships between teachers and students are among the most commonly cited variables associated with learning and effective instruction (Marzano, 2011). When a teacher can build relationships with a student, especially one who has difficulties with academics or behavior, that child seems to work harder and become more willing to take risks and challenges that benefit learning (Marzano, 2011). Teachers need to value, appreciate, and celebrate diversity, equity, and inclusion. To build relationships with students as educators, we need to exhibit culturally and linguistically responsive pedagogy, build upon students' funds of knowledge, and support students in having a positive attitude and motivation to learn.

Culturally Responsive Pedagogy

Culturally responsive pedagogy is a mindset that respects and honors students' individuality as well as their cultures, experiences, and histories. It involves the inclusion of these factors in the curriculum and in teaching approaches, as well as a commitment to learn about these from students, their families, and their communities (Nieto, 2013). Teachers who are culturally responsive engage in critical self-reflection about their values, biases, strengths, and limitations, and consider how these can affect their effectiveness with students of diverse backgrounds (Nieto, 2013).

Culture is a blend of thoughts, feelings, attitudes, beliefs, values, and behavior patterns that are shared by racial, ethnic, or social groups of people (Muhammad & Hollie, 2012). There are many dimensions of culture, including language (which is a part of our heritage), family, community, and education, as well as our values and beliefs (Muhammad & Hollie, 2012).

Wlodkowski and Ginsberg (1995) have developed a framework of culturally responsive teaching, based on theories of intrinsic motivation; this framework is respectful of different cultures and helps to create a common classroom or school culture that all students can accept. The framework includes four motivational conditions that teachers and students continually create or enhance: *establishing inclusion*, or creating a learning atmosphere in which students and teachers feel respected by and connected to one another; *developing attitude*, or creating a favorable disposition toward the learning experience through personal relevance and choice; *enhancing meaning*, or creating challenging, thoughtful learning experiences that include students' perspectives and values; and *engendering competence*, or creating an understanding that students are effective in learning something they value. These conditions are important to develop intrinsic motivation; they are sensitive to cultural differences; and they work together to influence students and teachers in a specific moment or over time.

Gray (2012) has identified five ways in which you as the teacher can create a culturally responsive classroom:

1. Commit to knowing your students well, including academically, socially, emotionally, and culturally.
2. No matter the subject matter, build on your students' life experiences and bring them into the classroom.
3. Create a classroom learning community, and encourage students to care for one another inside and outside the classroom.
4. Hold high academic standards and expectations for all of your students.
5. Understand your own cultural identity and its consequences.

In culturally responsive teaching, teachers and students apply all six literacy modalities (listening, speaking, reading, writing, viewing, and visually representing) to interpret and communicate information (Msengi & McAndrews, 2015). Culturally responsive teaching is directly related to understanding and incorporating our students' funds of knowledge.

Funds of Knowledge

Funds of knowledge are the "historically accumulated and culturally developed bodies of knowledge and skills essential for household or individual functioning and wellbeing" (Moll, Amanti, Neff, & Gonzalez, 1992, p. 133). Students bring with them funds of knowledge from their homes and communities that can be used for concept and skill development. Some classroom practices underestimate and constrain what children are able to display intellectually. Teachers should focus on helping students find meaning in activities, rather than merely on having them learn rules and facts. Group discussions centering around race and class should promote trusts and encourage dialogue. Funds of knowledge include students' home languages, family values and traditions, caregiving, friends and family members, family outings, household chores, educational activities, TV shows and movies, family occupations, scientific knowledge, and others (Gonzáles et al., 2005), as well as their peer groups and other networks of relationships. Teachers can use these categories to identify and list their students' funds of knowledge, and can then use this information to help the students make connections to learning experiences in school. These funds of knowledge are tools that are likely to shape each individual child's learning (Moll et al., 1992).

When teachers take on a role as learners, they can come to know their students and their families in new ways, based on their needs, interests, and personal motivations (Gonzáles et al., 2005). Therefore, there is an increased need for teachers to understand learners' out-of-school lives, cultures, knowledge, and experiences, and to integrate these into classrooms, thereby creating culturally responsive and more meaningful opportunities for students' learning and literacy development (Moje et al., 2004; Nieto, 2013). As educators, we need to promote equity by understanding and providing students with what they need in order to learn and contribute to their community and wider society. "Equity" does not mean that everybody gets the same thing; it means that all students get what they need in order to be successful.

Attitude and Motivation

Students' attitudes toward and motivation for learning are key factors affecting their success in school, out of school, and beyond school. Students' **attitudes**, or ways of thinking or feeling about learning, determine their ability and willingness to learn. **Motivation** is defined as the internal and external factors that stimulate desire and energy in people to be continually interested and committed to a job, role, or subject, or to make an effort to attain a goal (Business Dictionary, 2019). Positive attitudes and motivation can compensate for relatively weak skills, whereas negative attitudes can prevent a student from applying existing knowledge or from acquiring new information (Paris, Lipson, & Wixson, 1983). We need to change the concept of motivation from reward and punishment to communication and respect (Wlodkowski & Ginsberg, 1995). We can influence students' motivation by coming to know their perspectives, by drawing on their natural and cultural selves, and by seeing them as unique and active. Sharing our resources with theirs, and working together, we can create greater energy for learning.

There is an interdependent relationship among the cognitive, behavioral, and environmental factors that influence students' attitudes and motivation to learn (Zimmerman, 2000). **Cognitive factors** have an impact on whether students have a positive attitude about their own abilities. We can teach students practical ways to think about their own thinking, control their impulses, and stay on track to complete tasks and achieve goals. Are they able to set learning goals that are more challenging than simple performance goals, which merely involve task completion? Do they have positive self-efficacy; that is, do they believe they can learn what is being asked? Are they able to use metacognition to think about the processes of their thinking? Do they have knowledge of problem-solving strategies?

Do they perceive an individual task, or learning in general, to be valuable, and do they have a positive view of the task or learning? Teachers can influence these cognitive factors through the decisions they make in terms of tasks and materials.

Dweck (2017) coined the terms **fixed mindset** and **growth mindset** to describe people's underlying beliefs about learning and intelligence. When students believe they can get smarter, they understand that effort makes them stronger. Therefore, they put in extra time and effort, and this leads to higher achievement. When teachers treat all students as competent and developing, they focus on fostering a growth mindset. In a growth mindset, people believe that their abilities can be developed through dedication and hard work, and that their brains and talent are just the starting point (Dweck, 2017).

Behavioral factors have an impact on whether students choose to monitor their own learning, make their own judgments about what and how they are learning, and react positively to the learning or task. To promote self-regulation, teachers can provide experiences that require a higher level of engagement in tasks; they can also give students strategies to set goals and evaluate their own learning throughout the process, not just in terms of the product. Students' belief about their ability to use self-regulatory learning strategies influences their confidence with which they approach academic tasks, and this confidence correlates with reading and writing success (Zimmerman, Bandura, & Martinez-Pons, 1992). Teachers can help students understand that with hard work and the use of good learning strategies they can succeed in school, regardless of how smart they think they are or how smart others think they are.

Environmental factors can also affect whether a student has a positive attitude about the learning climate. These factors include aspects of the classroom, school, home, and community environment (Zimmerman, 2000). Ways in which you, as an individual teacher, can influence the classroom and school environment include the following:

- *Provide a supportive, risk-free classroom environment.* The classroom climate is influenced by students' feeling of acceptance by teachers and peers, their physical comfort, and their feeling of a sense of order. Your decisions about the classroom environment and how you interact with students can affect students' attitudes toward and motivation for learning. Provide a supportive, risk-free environment by responding positively to students' questions, comments, or responses, and by providing wait time before calling on students. Dignify the students' responses, restate or paraphrase questions, and provide guidance such as hints or clues to help students answer questions or solve problems. Students should not be expected to read and write perfectly or quickly. Mistakes or miscues are windows into the students' learning processes that can be used to understand these processes and help the students' select appropriate problem-solving strategies. Finally, students should have numerous opportunities to apply their learning for authentic purposes.

- *Support students' beliefs that they are accepted by adults and their peers.* Encourage them to respect each other, work together, and support each other in the learning process. Encourage especially younger students to treat each other with respect by referring to everyone in the class as friends. You can make statements such as "Can you help your friend by showing her in which paragraph you might find the answer?" or "Our friend Katherine is home sick today; can you help me write a get-well card to her?" For students in all grades, it is important that you take time to point out when students or adults help others or treat them kindly. You also must stop and address any and all statements and behaviors that can be hurtful. Students' feelings of self-worth are often related to what people say to them and how they react to them. As they leave your class, wish them a good day and let them know you are looking forward to seeing them tomorrow.

- *Remember that physical comfort influences students' attitudes and behaviors.* Carefully arrange furniture for ease of movement, with space for both group and individual work. Be sure that the students' chairs and desks or tables are at the appropriate height for students to sit comfortably. Provide an organized space for the classroom library, computers, and materials for writing and publishing. Proudly display new student work throughout the classroom. Carefully select what is put on the walls so that it is meaningful and interesting to the students, but not too overwhelming. Organize classroom materials so that students have easy access to them. Provide opportunities for students to take breaks, go to the restroom, or get a drink of water as needed.

- *Provide clear expectations for routines, tasks, and behavior, to fulfill students' sense of order.* These should be taught initially and then reinforced throughout the year. Teachers create a positive learning environment by promoting respect in all situations and encouraging open dialogue.

Another approach to identifying factors that affect students' motivation and will to succeed is to use the acronym REACH, for Relationships, Effort, Aspirations, Cognition, and Heart (Search Institute, 2016):

1. *Relationships:* Connecting young people to caring adults and to other young people who push them, support them, empower them, and expand their views of what is possible in life.
2. *Effort:* Helping students understand that with hard work and the use of good learning strategies, they can succeed in school, regardless of how smart they think they are or how smart others think they are.
3. *Aspirations:* Grounding young people in the reality that the actions they take—or do not take—each day will influence their ability to realize their dreams for the future.
4. *Cognition:* Teaching students practical ways to think about their own thinking, control impulses, and stay on track to complete tasks and achieve goals.
5. *Heart:* Giving students the opportunity to discover and develop what they love to do—or what the Search Institute calls their "sparks"—and articulate a set of core values that they want to guide their lives.

Although students should have intrinsic motivation to be successful, we as teachers need to be aware of how our own behaviors, teaching styles, curriculum designs, classroom environments, assignments, and informal interactions affect our students' motivation. When we provide each child with they need in order to optimize performance in academics as well as socioemotional realms, they become strong self-advocates and lifelong learners. To accomplish this, we need to obtain a deep understanding of the whole child's strengths, areas for growth, and interests, by actively listening, asking, and observing. We need to use this information to make decisions about assessment, plan instruction, select materials, give specific feedback, and help students set their own goals. Through providing culturally and linguistically relevant pedagogy, viewing students' funds of knowledge as assets, supporting their positive attitudes, and enhancing their motivation, we build strong student–teacher relationships and encourage students' learning.

Building Relationships with Families

Family–school collaboration involves families and educators working together to educate youth. (Note that the inclusive term "family" is used rather than "parents." There are many different configurations of families, and not all children live with or are cared for by their biological parents.) Teachers can gain a significant understanding about their students from family members. They need to see families as resources not only for their own children, but for the learning of other children. They need to learn about the assets of the families' languages, cultures, and interests. Family members should be encouraged to share these assets with the class by being guest speakers or volunteering in and out of the classroom. Family cultures need to be celebrated and included in school procedures and practices (Owens, Watabe, & Michael, 2013).

A teacher needs to find out what a family member's goals are for a child, often during family- or child-led conferences. The teacher should also ascertain the family's academic, adult literacy, linguistic, socioemotional, medical, and financial needs, and help the family members to connect to community resources. Family engagement needs to be supported in ways that are consistent with the family's goals and expectations and are culturally responsive.

Recent research by Garbacz and Weist (2019) has defined and clarified how to develop these types of family–school relationships within multi-tiered systems of support (MTSS), such as **Positive Behavioral Interventions and Supports (PBIS).** PBIS (*www.pbis.org*) is a program funded by the U.S. Department of Education to improve social, emotional, and academic outcomes for all students, including students with disabilities and students from underrepresented groups. In PBIS, family–school collaboration focuses on strengthening support for schoolwide and individual practices, such as co-creating behavior expectations and support plans across home and school settings, encouraging participation in group-based skills training, and promoting family collaboration. Family members should be viewed as equal collaborators, who have more knowledge about their children than educators or clinicians do (Weist, Garbacz, Lane, & Kincaid, 2017). Five strategies in PBIS can help create a school approach that is anchored in family–school collaboration: (1) creating a clear role for such collaboration, (2) reaching out to families proactively, (3) enhancing the school atmosphere, (4) emphasizing two-way communication, and (5) providing guidance and support for collaboration (Garbacz & Weist, 2019). Teachers need to maintain close contact with families regarding their children's academic and socioemotional progress, as well as ways in which family members can contribute to the school community. This can be done via emails, text messages, conversations, newsletters, and web-based communications.

Building Relationships with the Community

Schools alone cannot prepare our youth for adulthood. Schools can provide more support for students, families, and school personnel when they are part of the community. School–community partnerships can bring together many resources and strategies to enhance communities that support youth and their families. They can improve schools, strengthen neighborhoods and lead to a reduction in young people's problems (Mitrofanova, 2004). Community resources such as agencies, service clubs, youth organizations, sports/health/fitness groups, and other community-based organizations, as well as faith-based organizations, ethnic associations, artistic and cultural instititutions, businesses/corporations, and the mass media, can all partner with schools to support families and youth. There are many activities that can build school–community relationships, such as encouraging community use of school facilities, holding senior citizen banquets and inviting community members to school events, holding career-themed days (e.g., construction, health care, visual and performing arts, community aid, etc.), sending news releases to the media, publishing newsletters, giving business discounts for academic and behavioral achievements, and promoting "Do the Right Thing" student awards. Community members can volunteer in the schools, mentor students, offer field trips, provide learning opportunities, participate on advisory boards, and invite students and staff to community and cultural events. Students and staff can also contribute by volunteering for business, organization, and community projects.

Building Relationships with School Personnel

When teachers build relationships with other school personnel, this helps to create a positive and caring school culture. There are many people who work together at a school, both classified and certified staff, because they want to support students and their families. It is essential that each person feels valued, as these responsibilities are often very challenging. When people feel valued, they are likely to work harder, be successful, and enjoy their work. To build relationships among school personnel, it is important to have clear and open communication, show respect, praise and celebrate everyone's accomplishments in and out of school, be kind, and provide support (Younghans, 2018). It is important for all of us as school staff members to be role models for how to problem-solve and interact with others, as students notice and learn from staffers' behaviors (Younghans, 2018). We can show students how to be kind, caring, and accepting of all the people at school. When we develop trusting and caring relationships, we will be able to learn from and support each other. Other school personnel can not only provide teachers with background information about students and their families; they can share their own cultures, interests, and skills to enhance teaching and student learning.

BUILDING RELATIONSHIPS: GOALS

Building Relationships with Students

Teachers will:

- Actively listen to, show respect for, and take interest in their students.
- Seek out information about each student's background (cultural, linguistic, academic, socioemotional, and physical/health) and interests.
- Use this background information to assess, plan instruction, select materials, and provide feedback.

Students will:

- Make statements to indicate that they believe they can learn what is being asked.
- Set challenging, yet attainable, learning goals.
- Monitor and assess their own learning.
- Demonstrate problem-solving behaviors.
- Develop a growth mindset and make decisions that promote learning.

- Engage in meaningful self-selected and teacher-selected reading, writing, speaking, and listening experiences in and out of school.
- Develop or maintain a caring and respectful disposition toward all people.

Building Relationships with Families

Teachers will:

- Actively listen to, show respect for, and take interest in their students' families.
- Seek out information about each family's background (cultural, linguistic, academic, socioemotional, and physical/health) and interests.
- Use this background information to assess, plan instruction, select materials, and provide feedback.
- Suggest resources for families.
- Communicate regularly with families.
- Encourage families to contribute to the learning of the class.

Building Relationships with Community Members

Teachers will:

- Actively listen to, show respect for, and take interest in community members.
- Seek out information about their cultures, interests, and expertise.
- Connect community resources to families.
- Communicate regularly with community members.
- Invite community members to contribute to the learning of the class or school.
- Invite community members to school events or use school resources.
- Support community events and projects.

Building Relationships with School Personnel

Teachers will:

- Actively listen to, show respect for, and take interest in all school personnel.
- Demonstrate clear and open communication.
- Praise and celebrate others' accomplishments in and out of school.
- Provide support.
- Model how to problem-solve and interact with others.
- Model how to be kind, caring, and accepting of all the people at school.

BUILDING RELATIONSHIPS: ASSESSMENTS

Building Relationships with Students

There are four assessments that can be given to students to learn about their interests, attitudes, and literacy strategies: the *Getting to Know You—Student Survey*; the *Reading, Writing, and Learning Interest Inventory (Elementary Level or Middle and Secondary Level)*; the *Elementary Reading and Writing Attitude Surveys (Garfield Assessments)*; and the *Literacy Process Interview*. (All of these assessments except the Garfield surveys are included in the

Appendix to this book.) These assessments are generally designed to be given individually and orally, with a teacher or family member taking dictation. Students who are proficient writers can write the responses themselves; however, sometimes the students may not read or respond to the prompts thoughtfully and thoroughly when being asked to complete them on their own.

There are general ways in which all of these assessments can be analyzed. First, they should be analyzed according to the content of the responses: What were this student's responses, and how can this information be used to inform instruction, including selection of materials and topics of discussion? Second, if the assessments were administered orally, the student's speech and language can be evaluated to see if further assessments are needed in this area. For example, did the student comprehend the questions or statements? Was the student able to answer the questions easily, without significant delays or nonresponses? Did the student use a variety of vocabulary words and sentence structures? Was the speech clear and at an appropriate volume? By learning about each student's interests and abilities, the teacher can personalize the instruction for the student by selecting or suggesting interesting books or writing topics.

Getting to Know You—Student Survey

PURPOSE: To gain background information about a student's interests in and out of school, so that the teacher can engage the student in conversation and make connections during classroom instruction.

PROCEDURE: See the general description of administration procedures above. It is suggested that this inventory be administered before any other assessment, especially if the teacher is not familiar with the student. Students tend to be more relaxed about assessment if it begins with questions about themselves with no right or wrong answers. Typically, this assessment would only be given once and placed in a file for those who work with the student to refer to. At the very beginning of the school year, this survey can be given either as an at-home activity that can be completed with the support of family members or an in-class activity. If a student is not proficient at writing or provides limited responses, a family member or teacher can take dictation. Again, however, students may not read or respond to each item thoughtfully and thoroughly when being asked to complete them on their own. It is beneficial for family members to engage their children in conversations about their interests, and they can provide additional prompting based on their family experiences. (See Appendix, *Getting to Know You—Student Survey*, pp. 364–366.)

ANALYSIS: Upon completion, the teacher reads each of the student's responses and identifies any unique experiences or any that are similar to experiences other students have. The teacher may follow up with students and/or family members to learn more about the students and their families. Based on the information gained, the teacher can engage in individual conversations demonstrating that the teacher cares about the students' interests and can help children make connections between their experiences and learning. The teacher may also be able to help students make connections to others with similar interests. In addition, the names of family members and pets can be used as resources for understanding who is in each student's family and for helping students to spell their names correctly during writing activities. The teacher should make it a point to make at least one connection to each student via this survey within the first few weeks of school.

Reading, Writing, and Learning Interest Inventory: Elementary Level

Reading, Writing, and Learning Interest Inventory: Middle and Secondary Level

PURPOSE: To gain background information about students' reading, writing, and learning interests based on literature genres, in order to help select engaging topics and materials.

PROCEDURE: The teacher selects either the Elementary Level or the Middle and Secondary Level of this inventory, as appropriate. This inventory can be completed by a whole class or independently. If it is given to the whole class, the teacher says to the students, "I want to know what you are interested in reading, writing, or learning about. Follow along as I read aloud each category. Make a checkmark in the 'Yes' column under the happy face, if you like it; make a checkmark in the 'Maybe' column under the neutral face, if you are unsure if you like it; make a checkmark in the 'No' column under the sad face, if you do not like it. If you are unsure about any of the categories, please ask, and I will provide examples for you. When you are finished, put an asterisk or star [the teacher draws an asterisk on the board] in front of your top three choices. Then name three of your favorite books or authors." (See Appendix, *Reading, Writing, and Learning Interest Inventory: Elementary Level* and *Reading, Writing, and Learning Interest Inventory: Middle and Secondary Level*, pp. 367 and 368, respectively.)

ANALYSIS: Upon completion, the teacher reads each student's responses and identifies the categories that the student likes to read, write, or learn about. The teacher can then select or suggest reading materials or writing projects that the student might be interested in. Students can also be organized into literature or inquiry groups based on similarities in interests.

Literacy Process Interview

PURPOSE: This 12-question interview is used to determine a student's perceived strategies, strengths, and needs in reading, writing, listening, and speaking. The original concept for this interview came from Carol Burke's *Reading Interview* (Goodman, Watson, & Burke, 1987). This interview is appropriate to give to students who read and write at or above first-grade level.

PROCEDURE: The teacher says to the student, "I am going to ask you some questions about what you do when you read, write, and talk with others. I am going to write down what you say." The teacher then asks the questions and writes down the student's responses. Some questions require multiple responses, so the teacher should pause after each part and wait for a response. (See Appendix, *Literacy Process Interview*, pp. 369–370.)

ANALYSIS: This assessment provides insight into the perceived strategies a student uses during the reading, writing, listening, and speaking processes. The strategies are analyzed to determine whether they are oriented toward phonics, grammar, meaning, communication, or a combination. A teacher should ask the following questions: Does the student focus on grapho-phonemics or sounding out words? Does the student focus on semantics or trying to figure out the meaning? Does the student mention a combination of strategies? If so, the student has a more integrated view of the reading process. Does the student focus on being able to spell words? Does the student focus on communicating ideas in writing? Does the student emphasize handwriting or being able to form the letters correctly? And, what are the student's perceived strengths and needs that the teacher can build upon during instruction? Does the student realize that listening and speaking are active processes that require both the listener and the speaker to monitor comprehension?

During reading, the teacher determines whether the student's strategies are oriented toward grapho-phonemics, grammar, meaning, or a combination. During writing, the teacher determines whether the student's strategies are oriented toward content, mechanics, or handwriting. During listening and speaking, is the student oriented toward active communication, or just passive responses? The teacher should also compare what the student states to the strategies observed during the other assessments. During teaching, the teacher reinforces the student for strategies used and prompts for neglected strategies. Figure 2.1 shows a completed example of the *Literacy Process Interview,* with identifying information and directions omitted.

• Elementary Reading and Writing Attitude Surveys (Garfield Assessments)

PURPOSE: In addition to the assessments included in the Appendix to this book, the *Elementary Reading Attitude Survey* (McKenna & Kear, 1990) and the *Elementary Writing Attitude Survey* (Kear, Coffman, McKenna, & Ambrosia, 2000) can be administered to assess students' reading and writing attitudes in grades K–6.

PROCEDURE: These 20-question assessments have students respond by circling the Garfield the Cat cartoon picture that best represents their feelings about each item, from very happy to very upset. The scores are then analyzed for the students' attitudes toward academic and recreational reading and writing.

Building Relationships with Families

• Family Asset and Child Development Survey

PURPOSE: To learn about a child's family members, the languages spoken in the home, family members' interests, and possible volunteer opportunities, as well as their views of their child's academic, socioemotional, and physical/health development, in order to work together with the family members to support the student's learning and the family's well-being.

PROCEDURE: The teacher sends this survey home within the first week of school, possibly during open house. The survey introduction states, "As your child's teacher, I want to get to know your child and your family better to see how we can support your child's learning together. In addition, I want all our students to learn about the cultures, languages, and assets available in our community. Would you please complete and return this survey to me?" If the teacher knows in advance that some family members are not native English speakers, they can have the survey translated or can invite the family members to school and complete it together with the help of a translator. This survey is lengthy, so family members may need support in completing it. Questions on this survey can be omitted if the school already has records of some of the information. The teacher should also be aware that some people may find some of the questions intrusive. If so, the teacher should give them reasons why the information would be helpful, but give them permission not to answer selected questions. (See Appendix, *Family Asset and Child Development Survey,* pp. 371–376.)

FIGURE 2.1. *Literacy Process Interview,* example and analyses.

Reading Questions
1. When you are reading and you come to a word you do not know, what do you do? Do you do anything else? Look at the picture.
2. When you are reading and you do not understand something, what do you do? Do you do anything else? Sound it out. Cover up the last part of the word.
3. How would you help someone who is having trouble reading? Tell them the word they are stuck on, if I knew it.
4. During reading, what do you think you do well? Why? I can read bigger words because I can sound them out.
5. What would you like to change about your reading? Why? I would want to read faster. I want to be like Molly.
Writing Questions
1. When you are writing and you come to a difficult part, what do you do? Do you do anything else? I try to find the word on a poster or in my dictionary.
2. If you are given a writing assignment, what would you do first? Next? Then what? Last? I put my name on it. Then I think of what to write and I write it.
3. How would you help someone who is having trouble writing? I'd give them a dictionary like mine.
4. During writing, what do you think you do well? Why? I write my letters good. People tell me I write good.
5. What do you like to change about your writing? Why? That I could always spell stuff right because I am not good at spelling.
Listening and Speaking Questions
1. When you are listening to someone and you do not understand the person, what do you do? Do you do anything else? Nothing, uh, I don't know.
2. When you are speaking to someone and the person does not seem to understand you, what do you do? Do you do anything else? Say it again.
Reading Analysis: He stated three different strategies he used for figuring out unknown words: Look at the picture, sound it out, and cover up the ending. He emphasized that a good reader is one who knows the words and can read fast. He described a dominant focus on phonics rather than meaning.
Instructional Implications for Reading: Reinforce known strategies and suggest new ones, such as read on, go back, and think about what makes sense. Absent from these comments is the idea that reading is to learn something or for fun. This needs to be made explicit in teaching; reading fast should not be the main, or even primary, goal.
Writing Analysis: He explained that he used resources to figure out how to spell words he wants to write. He stated that he is a good writer because he has good handwriting. He also thinks that spelling is important.
Instructional Implications for Writing: He needs to be reinforced for using resources for spelling and having neat handwriting. However, while it is beneficial to have neat handwriting, it is more important that he understands that the real purpose is to write interesting ideas. He needs opportunities to write to communicate his ideas. He also needs to be shown how to use inventive spelling and circle words that he is unsure of the correct spelling.
Listening and Speaking Analysis: He did not list any strategies for listening. For speaking, he had named one successful strategy, "Say it again."
Instructional Implications for Listening and Speaking: Teach active listening strategies, and explain that it is the responsibility of both the speaker and the listener to make sure they are understood. Other strategies include paying attention to the speaker, getting clarification, asking questions (thereby showing the speaker you are interested in listening to what they have to say), and restating to make sure you understood it.

ANALYSIS: Upon completion, the teacher reads each family member's responses and identifies any unique experiences or ones that are similar to the experiences of other students' family members. The teacher may follow up with the student or family members to learn more about their family. Based on the information gained, the teacher can engage in individual conversations demonstrating that the teacher cares about the family's and student's culture, language, and interests, and can help the child make connections between their experiences and learning. The teacher may also be able to help families make connections to other families with similar interests.

• Child Interest Survey

PURPOSE: To gain background information about a student's interests in categories and specific topics, in order for the teacher to engage the student and make connections during classroom instruction.

PROCEDURE: This survey is given as an at-home activity that is typically completed by an adult family member with input from a child. If the student is proficient in writing, it can be completed by the student, but an adult family member should provide support. It is beneficial for family members to engage their children in conversations about their interests, and they can provide additional prompting based on their family experiences. Depending on the child's level of interests, the adult or child marks A = Strongly enjoys, B = Enjoys, C = Not sure, or D = Does not enjoy for each category. If A or B is marked, the respondent writes specific examples of the kinds of activities the child enjoys. If the respondent is unsure about any of the categories, the teacher can provide examples. (See Appendix, *Child Interest Survey*, p. 377.)

ANALYSIS: Upon completion, the teacher reads each of the responses and identifies any unique experiences or ones similar to experiences that other students have. The teacher may follow up with the student or family members to learn more about the student and family. Based on the information gained, the teacher can engage in individual conversations demonstrating that they care about the student's interests and can help the child make connections between their experiences and learning. The teacher may also be able to help students make connections to others with similar interests.

Building Relationships with Community Members

• Community Member Survey

PURPOSE: To identify community members who can support students' learning, and to identify ways students and schools can support the community.

PROCEDURE: A teacher can walk around the neighborhood or go to businesses or organizations. Or the teacher can get recommendations from family members or school personnel. The teacher begins by introducing themselves to a community member as a teacher in the school and asking when a good time would be to talk. The teacher then shares the survey and asks if the community member would be willing to answer the questions orally or would prefer to complete the survey on their own. The teacher should be sure to leave contact information and remind the community member to call with any questions. Once the teacher learns background information, follow-up questions can be asked as needed.

Finally, the teacher should be sure to send a thank-you note to everyone who responds. (See Appendix, *Community Member Survey*, pp. 378–379.)

ANALYSIS: The teacher can use the information on the survey to plan opportunities to collaborate with the community members.

Building Relationships with School Personnel

• School Personnel Class Support Survey

PURPOSE: To identify other school personnel who can support students' learning, and to identify ways a teacher and students can support the school community.

PROCEDURE: The teacher talks to various school personnel (custodians, cafeteria workers, secretaries, maintenance workers, and teacher aides, as well as certified personnel). The teacher begins by explaining the wish to have the personnel share their interests, hobbies, and expertise with students and help students support their work in the school. The teacher then asks when a good time would be to talk. The teacher shares the survey and asks if they would be willing to answer the questions orally or would prefer to complete the survey on their own. The teacher makes sure to leave contact information and reminds personnel that they can call with any questions. Once the teacher obtains background information, you might have follow-up questions that can be asked as needed. Finally, the teacher should be sure to send a thank-you note to everyone who responds. (See Appendix, *School Personnel Class Support Survey*, pp. 380–381.)

ANALYSIS: The teacher can use the information on the survey to plan opportunities to collaborate with the other school personnel.

• School Personnel Student Connection Survey

PURPOSE: To identify school personnel who can provide background information about students and their families.

PROCEDURE: The teacher identifies school personnel who have had significant contact with individual students in class (past teachers and other professionals, teacher aides, secretaries, etc.). The teacher explains the interest in having them share their knowledge about specific students, as well as in their willingness to share their expertise with students. The procedure from this point on is the same as for the *School Personnel Class Support Survey*. (See Appendix, *School Personnel Student Connection Survey*, p. 382–383.)

ANALYSIS: The teacher uses the information on the survey to plan opportunities to collaborate with other school community members.

BUILDING RELATIONSHIPS: STRATEGIES

Building Relationships with Students

• Greeting Students at the Door and Saying Goodbye

SOURCE: Coombs (2016).

PURPOSE: To give each and every student a sense of belonging, set a positive tone, and increase student engagement by greeting students at the door at the start of the day and saying goodbye at the end.

PROCEDURE: Each morning, the teacher greets students individually at the classroom door. The students have eight options for how they would like to be greeted: waving hello; giving a high five, pinky shake, hug, elbow hello, handshake, or fist bump; or doing a "shake shake" dance. (The teacher may decide to select just four of these options.) These options are placed on a poster, and each child either touches an option on the poster or orally chooses the option (see Figure 2.2). The teacher then looks the child in the eye and greets them in the preferred way, frequently also making a compliment, noticing something, or comforting the student. Here are some examples of comments: "I'm glad you are back today; we missed you yesterday," "I heard you won your baseball game," "I like your hair [or outfit]," "When is your performance? I would like to go," "Wow, you lost a tooth!", "What happened to your arm?", "How exciting! You are going to be a big brother!", "Happy Ramadan Kareem!" Or the teacher can greet students in their native language, if this is other than English. The teacher can also take this time to assess students' mood, emotion, or well-being. The teacher may make a quick comment or come talk to them privately if they seem sad, upset, unhealthy, or tired. It is also beneficial to say goodbye to each student as they leave, making a comment on their day or wishing them a good evening.

FIGURE 2.2. Morning greeting poster. Photo by the author.

Student Letters and Surveys

SOURCE: Connell (2016).

PURPOSE: To learn more about students, in order to start building relationships with them and to generate topic or discussion ideas.

PROCEDURE: At the beginning of the year, each student writes an "everything you wanted to know about me" letter to the teacher, telling about the student's family, hobbies, interests, and interests in school. The teacher typically does not include dislikes in the instructions, in order to focus on the positive, but students are welcome to add these as well. The letter is more open-ended than the interest assessments described earlier in this chapter. The teacher then makes at least one connection to each student based on the letter within the first few weeks of school.

Selecting Classroom Library Books: Windows, Mirrors, and Sliding Glass Doors

SOURCE: Sims Bishop (1990).

PURPOSE: To provide readers with diverse books, to ensure that students see themselves and others in literature

PROCEDURE: Rudine Sims Bishop (1990) coined the phrase "windows, mirrors, and sliding glass doors" to explain how children can both see themselves in books and learn about others through literature.

1. Select books to provide "windows" into other people's lives, so that students can learn about points of view, perspectives, and issues they may not have faced.
2. Select books that "mirror" or reflect students' own lives, so that they can see that their culture and interests are valued in society.
3. Select books that represent "sliding glass doors." These are books that allow readers to "walk through" in their imaginations to become part of whatever world has been created or re-created by the author.

The classroom library should include books featuring multicultural characters and settings, as well as books about socioeconomic struggles, LGBTQ issues, and characters with physical disabilities and mental health issues. To encourage reading of these diverse books, the teacher or students can give book talks, use the literature for classroom read-alouds, or conduct book studies based on topics or authors.

"Who Am I?" Riddle Book

PURPOSE: To have the teacher and students share information about themselves, to help all classroom members get to know each other better.

PROCEDURE: Students write clues about who they are and what they like. At the end of each set of clues, they state the question "Who am I?" The teacher puts a sticky note over each student's name. The students then randomly exchange "Who Am I?" riddle books, and students predict who each student is, based on the clues (see Figure 2.3 for an example).

FIGURE 2.3. "Who Am I?" riddle book sample page, by Rio Gomez Khmara. Photo of Rio and his sister Maya by the author.

Who Am I?
I enjoy rock climbing.
I play piano and guitar.
I also took capoeira lessons (Brazilian fight dancing).
I have two African aquatic frogs.
I used to collect fossils, rocks, and shells.
I like reading Manga, Japanese graphic novels, and the Lord of the Rings books.
I like reading Spanish and English books to my little sister Maya.
I was born in Tulum, Quintana Roo, Mexico.
I have brown hair and brown eyes.
Who am I?
Rio Age 13

• "All about Me" Poster

PURPOSE: To have students share information about themselves with the class.

PROCEDURE: Students are given a graphic organizer or criteria for completing an "All about Me" poster. Possible categories include "Facts about Me," "My Family and Pets," "A Few of My Favorite Things," "Activities," "Favorite Books," "My Hero," "Did You Know?", and "Pictures of Me." Students then give oral presentations about themselves, based on these posters.

• Showing Interest in Students, Advocating for Students, and Not Giving Up on Students

SOURCE: Marzano (2011).

PURPOSE: To support students as fully as possible by showing interest in and advocating for students.

PROCEDURE: As the teacher, do the following:

1. Learn the names (and their pronunciations) of all your students. On the first day, have the students create their own name tags, and photograph them holding their name tags.

Create a grid with about 12 pictures per page, and print these pages out. Use this photographic reference as you call on each student until you learn each of their names. Ask them questions about topics they have shown interest in. Suggest books and activities based on their interests.

2. Set up times or methods for students to talk to you individually. Walk around and monitor students' work, giving them constructive feedback along the way. Ask questions to support their metacognition, such as "What is the tricky part? What could you do to figure that out? Are you right? How do you know? What have you tried? What might you try next?"
3. Even if students get behind in their work or appear frustrated, do not give up on them. Continue to offer suggestions and support. Give them words of encouragement, or relate personal stories when you faced challenges in learning something new.

• Creating Student-Defined Rules of Respect

SOURCE: Coombs (2016).

PURPOSE: To create classroom rules grounded in building relationships.

PROCEDURE: At the beginning of the year, students define respect and disrespect. From the discussions, students collaborate to develop approximately five "Rules of Respect," while the teacher takes dictation. During the year when students show or do not show signs of respect, the teacher refers to the established rules. Respect should include respecting self, others, and the world.

• Choosing Civility

SOURCE: Forni (2002).

PURPOSE: To help students (middle and high school) and educators be respectful and civil toward others as well as connecting effectively and happily with others.

PROCEDURE: The teacher begins by defining civility and discussing its impacts on the classroom, school, and greater society. Civility rules from Forni's (2002) book *Choosing Civility: The Twenty-Five Rules of Considerate Conduct* are then introduced. These civility rules are listed on a chart, and each week, students discuss a different rule and examples of it. In addition, throughout the year, when a student's or other person's behavior represents or does not represent that behavior, the class takes time to discuss it and refer to the rule chart. Possible topics include pay attention, listen, acknowledge others' contributions and accomplishments, think good thoughts, be inclusive, speak kindly of others, accept and give praise, respect "no" (even subtle no), respect others' opinions, respect your body, be agreeable, assert yourself, relish silence, respect other people's time, respect other people's space, apologize earnestly, avoid personal questions, think before speaking or asking favors, refrain from idle complaints, accept and give constructive criticism, don't shift responsibility and blame, and respect environment and animals. Newspaper articles or books can also be used as a basis for civility discussions, to determine which rules of civility were followed or violated and by whom. Possible discussion questions include the following:

- Our contentment and happiness are matters of personal attitude. Does your attitude affect those around you?
- Think of things you have done that make you feel good immediately. Then think of things that made you feel good later. What do they have in common? How do they differ?
- Some say, "What's in it for me?" Can you think of a time when your life has been improved by a personal relationship?
- What do personal attitude, kindness, restraint, the Golden Rule, and relationships have to do with civility?

Making Cards for Peers, Family Members, School Personnel, or Community Members

PURPOSE: To demonstrate caring by writing birthday, get-well, thinking of you, or thank-you cards.

PROCEDURE: The teacher encourages students to write cards to other people, and suggests that they include descriptions of each person's character. Figure 2.4 shows an example of a student's birthday card.

Using "I-Statements" or "Action Statements"

SOURCE: Centervention (2019).

PURPOSE: To help students take responsibility for their own feelings while addressing a concern or problem, using an "I-statement" or "action statement."

FIGURE 2.4. Example of a student birthday card, by Rio Gomez Khmara. Photo by the author.

PROCEDURE: The class begins by discussing different emotions and noting that sometimes it is difficult to talk about emotions. The teacher says, "Think about a recent time when you felt a strong emotion. It could be positive, such as joy, excitement, or hope, or it could be something difficult, like frustration, anger, or hurt. Now think about what happened that led up to your emotion and what you were thinking." The teacher then uses and models an I-statement (and should do this on a regular basis). An I-statement names the feeling first, then names the behavior, then explains why or how that behavior is appropriate or inappropriate: "I feel [emotion word] when [event or behavior happens] because [description or explanation of thought about event]." The students then practice changing blaming statements to I-statements. For example, "You are mean. I am never going to talk to you again," can be changed to "It made me upset when you said that I am not smart because I can do many things well, and I would like to get along with you better." Students are encouraged to use I-statements with family members, peers, and others. Another simple sentence frame to teach is: I feel ___________, when you ___________ and I want ___________.

Action statements can be similarly practiced and encouraged. An action statement makes a suggestion to another person, rather than blaming the other: "If you [do a certain action], I can do [a corresponding action]." For example, "If you use nicer words with me, I can enjoy being with you."

Growth Mindset Strategies

SOURCE: Neal (2017).

PURPOSE: To help students develop perseverance, especially when something is difficult.

PROCEDURE: As the teacher, do the following:

1. Introduce students to the idea of developing a growth mindset through their dedication, hard work, and use of multiple strategies or attempts. Give personal examples of mistakes you made and how you persevered.
2. Share books such as *Wolf!* by Becky Bloom (1999), the story of a wolf who learned to read even when it was hard, or *Your Fantastic Elastic Brain: Stretch It, Shape It* by JoAnn Deak (1998), a nonfiction text about how people can stretch and grow their brains and how making mistakes is one of the best ways the brain learns. And, share videos that demonstrate a growth mindset, such as "You Can Learn Anything" (*www.youtube.com/watch?v=JC82Il2cjqA&feature=youtu.be*) or "How to Grow Your Brain" (*www.youtube.com/watch?v=GWSZ1DKjNzY*), both from Khan Academy. Ask students to think–pair–share ways the books and videos show a growth mindset.
3. Introduce the word *yet* to the students. When a student says, "I can't [do a certain thing]," suggest that they change the phrase to, "I am not able to [do this thing] yet, but I can get there by [doing these other things]."
4. Sort phrases according to whether they reflect a fixed mindset or a growth mindset, to help students see the difference. Example of a fixed mindset: "This is too hard. They are smarter than me. I'll never be able to do it." Example of a growth mindset: "I can't do it yet. I will try it a different way. I will keep practicing."
5. Help students to set and write short-term, attainable goals, and to pair each one with an action they will take to attain the goal. Examples: "Don't give up if I don't know words;

try rereading the sentences or breaking words up into parts to figure out unknown words. Don't give up if I don't understand the whole text; retell the author's message after each paragraph. Don't give up if I don't know how to spell a word I want to write; just write the letters for each sound I hear in the word, circle it, and come back later. Don't give up on writing a story; start by writing three complete sentences about my drawing."

• Questions and Feedback Comments for a Growth Mindset

SOURCE: Simpson (2019).

PURPOSE: To assist students further in developing a growth mindset.

PROCEDURE: Questions to develop a growth mindset: "What did you learn from your activities today? What steps did you take to make you successful today? What are some different strategies you could have used? How did you keep going when things got tough?" Feedback comments to develop a growth mindset: "This will be challenging, but I believe you can do it. You haven't got it yet, but you will if you keep working on it and thinking about it. I really appreciate your effort today. It is OK to take risks; that is how we learn. Getting better takes time, and I see that you are improving."

• "Find Someone Who . . ." Bingo and Discussion of Experiences

PURPOSE: To help students share and identify interests that are similar to and distinct from those of other students and teachers, and to develop a sense of community.

PROCEDURE: The teacher administers the *Getting to Know You—Student Survey* to the child, and the *Child Interest Survey* to the family members. The teacher then creates Bingo cards with a 5 × 5 grid that include experiences children may have had. Examples include the following:

- Speaks a language other than English.
- Family members speak a language other than English.
- Lived in another country.
- Traveled to another country.
- Family members from another country.
- Family celebrations or traditions
- Helps do family chores.
- Helps with family businesses.
- Is an only child.
- Lives with more than five people.
- Plays an instrument.
- Plays a sport.
- Enjoys: Art or graphic design, music, nature, reading, writing, board or card games, video games, cooking, gardening, building/making things, collecting things, bike riding, traveling, photography, drama.
- Participates in a club.

Or, the teacher can create other categories of experiences that match those of the class.

Next, the teacher and each student take a Bingo card and go around the room to find people who have one of the experiences; then each person signs their name to the card. No one can have more than two signatures from the same person on a card. Afterward, each person finds two other people who have had the same experiences and talks about them; then each person finds two other people who have had different experiences and talks to them. Finally, the students write in their journals, describing the experiences they learned about from the four different people they talked to.

Additional Student Motivation Strategies

PURPOSE: To continue developing motivation in students.

PROCEDURE: As the teacher, do the following:

1. Know your students' names, and use them frequently when addressing them or providing positive examples.
2. Plan every lesson carefully, based on students' cultures, languages, interests, strengths, and areas for growth.
3. Help students to understand how the learning is relevant to them and the world around them.
4. Encourage peer-to-peer classroom discussions.
5. Use a variety of instructional strategies that incorporate listening, speaking, reading, writing, viewing, and visually representing.
6. Explain the learning objectives. Make sure the students know what they are expected to learn, why they are learning it, how they are to demonstrate their learning, and what criteria they will be evaluated on.
7. Provide specific feedback on strengths and areas for growth during and after instruction.
8. Teach with enthusiasm and the expectation that all students can learn.

Providing Effective Feedback

PURPOSE: To encourage students to internalize feedback and use the suggested strategies on future work.

PROCEDURE: Students should always know the criteria for success in advance. The teacher should provide oral and/or written feedback as soon as possible to make the most impact; the feedback should be focused on the specific criteria; and positive feedback should always be given first. The teacher differentiates the directions for improvement on the basis of students' needs, and models examples as necessary. Finally, the teacher checks with each student that the feedback is understood, and gives students an opportunity to apply the feedback right away.

Level-of-Effort Evaluation

PURPOSE: To evaluate the levels of effort students are giving.

PROCEDURE: The teacher creates an anchor chart with the different levels, and titles this chart "How Much Effort Am I Giving?" Here are suggestions for the levels:

Level 4: I gave my best effort even when it was a challenge. I learned from the challenge.

Level 3: I gave my best effort until there was a challenge. Then I gave some effort.

Level 2: I gave some effort, but I gave up when it became challenging.

Level 1: I gave little or no effort.

Students should always try to give Level 4 effort!

Building Relationships with Families

• General Strategies

PURPOSE: To build and develop positive relationships with families.

PROCEDURE: As the teacher, follow these general strategies for building relationships with families:

1. Call every family the first week of school, and tell the family members something you enjoyed about their child.
2. Learn about families' cultures, interests, and expertise by having them complete the *Child Interest Survey*.
3. Use the background information you obtain to make connections during teaching and discussions.
4. Send positive notes home.
5. Have each student call home to tell something "awesome" they did that day.
6. Begin every interaction with a positive comment first.
7. Be an active listener when talking with families.
8. Plan family-led and child-led conferences.
9. Create a brochure with community resources for families (medical, food, clothing, counseling, GED programs, English language learning, adult literacy, community events and organizations).
10. Create a "Giving Tree" for ways families can contribute talents, time, and materials to the classroom.
11. Create a classroom newspaper (print or online) containing student written articles and stories, past and upcoming events, and celebrations.

• School–Home Learning Plan

SOURCE: Muhammad and Hollie (2012).

PURPOSE: To collaboratively develop academic or behavioral goals for students.

PROCEDURE: Together, the teacher and family members complete a school–home learning plan (a sample plan is provided in Figure 2.5).

FIGURE 2.5. A sample school–home learning plan.

Family–Student–Teacher Goal for ______________________________ (name of student)

We will work together this school year to: ______________________________

Desired results for this goal: ______________________________

Activity: What needs to be done?	When?	Student will:	Family will:	Teacher will:	Check-ins: When and how?

I can keep informed by visiting this website: ______________________________

Teacher can be reached during these times: ______________________________

Teacher phone: ______________________ Teacher email: ______________________

• Action Plan for Engaging Families in School Conferences

SOURCE: Muhammad and Hollie (2012).

PURPOSE: To create a plan to welcome, honor, and connect with families.

PROCEDURE: The teaching team identifies how the school or district will welcome, honor, and connect families during school conferences to reach school goals. A sample action plan for engaging families in school conferences is provided in Figure 2.6.

Building Relationships with Community Members

• General Strategies

PURPOSE: To build and develop positive relationships with community members.

PROCEDURE: As the teacher, follow these general strategies for building relationships with community members:

1. Invite community members to school events through emails, fliers, door hangers, or social media.
2. Invite them to share their cultures, hobbies, interests, or skills with students.
3. Invite them to volunteer, mentor, provide job shadowing, or answer student interview questions.
4. Plan topic-related career day events (construction and trade, health care, community assistance, etc.).
5. Send thank-you cards to community members.
6. Collaboratively plan ways the school can help the community by volunteering (adopting nearby parks, creating a neighborhood garden, picking up trash or recycling, participating in community events).

FIGURE 2.6. A sample action plan for engaging families in school conferences.

School: ____________________ School Year: ____________________

What result(s) do we want this plan to help achieve? ____________________

____

Action we will take to . . .	Date to be completed:	Grade level(s):	Steps to complete activity:	Who will do or help with each activity?	Funds, supplies, or resources needed:
Welcome families:			1. 2. 3.		
Honor families:			1. 2. 3.		
Connect families:			1. 2. 3.		

Building Relationships with School Personnel

• General Strategies

PURPOSE: To build and develop positive relationships with other school personnel.

PROCEDURE: As the teacher, follow these general strategies for building relationships with school personnel:

1. Make sure that school personnel receive praise and notes from students and other staff members, thanking them or congratulating them on an in- or out-of-school accomplishment.
2. Have school personnel give students "Good job!" notes for meeting academic or behavioral goals or for being kind to others.
3. Invite school personnel to share their cultures, hobbies, interests, or skills with students.
4. Model for students how to be kind and treat all staff members with respect.
5. Model for students how to problem-solve and interact with others.

Chapter 3

Language Development

UNDERSTANDING LANGUAGE

Language is a complex and dynamic system of conventional sounds and symbols for thinking and communicating in spoken, written, and/or visual modes by people of a particular community (American Speech–Language–Hearing Association, 1993). Not only is language learning a social function; Halliday (1975) notes that we humans use it to help discover meaning from the world around us. It is through language that we express and understand thoughts and feelings; think critically and solve problems; and store, transfer, and transform knowledge and experiences from one person to another. Language links present, past, and future generations together and is a means of nourishing and developing culture and relationships in a society.

Communication is a process by which information is exchanged between individuals through a common system of symbols, signs, or behavior. There are four types of communication: verbal, nonverbal, written, and visual communication. **Verbal communication** includes the use of words, phrases, and sentences in delivering an intended message, either face to face or through phone, voice chat, video conferencing, audio or video recording, or any other auditory medium. The effectiveness of oral conversations depends on the clarity of speech, voice modulation, pitch, volume, speed, and even (when the parties can see each other) nonverbal communications. **Nonverbal communication** includes facial expressions, gestures, body language, posture, movement, and other physical cues. These messages usually reinforce verbal communication, but they can also convey thoughts and feelings on their own. **Written communication** refers to the process of conveying a message through written symbols, such as handwritten, printed, or digital messages using words. **Visual communication** is the conveyance of ideas and information in forms that can be seen, such as signs, typography, drawing, graphic design, illustration, advertising, animation, color, video and other electronic resources, and other wordless messages. The written and visual types of communication are addressed in detail in Chapter 7.

Communication involves both receptive and expressive language. **Receptive language** is the ability to understand what is being communicated through listening, reading, and viewing, while **expressive language** is the ability to produce language to communicate needs, thoughts, and ideas to others through speaking, writing, or visually representing. A communication has three parts: the sender, the message, and the recipient. The sender expresses or encodes the message, usually with a mixture of words and nonverbal communication. The message is transmitted through speech, writing, and/or visual means, and the recipient receives and decodes it. In other words, **encoding** is the creation of a message, while **decoding** is the interpretation of the meaning of a message.

Languages and Orthography

Over 7,000 languages are currently spoken in the world, and these languages belong to 142 different language families that share the same origin (Eberhard, Simons, & Fennig, 2019). Indo-European languages are the most widely spoken, followed by Sino-Tibetan (including Chinese), Niger-Congo, and Afro-Asiatic. The Indo-European languages include most of the modern languages in Europe and in central and western Asia; they are also dominant in the Americas and in much of Oceania and Africa. The greatest numbers of Indo-European native speakers are those who speak Spanish, English, Hindi, Portuguese, Bengali, Russian, and Punjabi, in descending order. Spanish is an example of the Romance language subgroup, and English is an example of the Germanic subgroup.

A writing system, also called a script or orthography, is a convention for representing the units of a spoken language. There are three general categories of writing systems: alphabetic, syllabic, and logographic. In an alphabetic system, letters or graphemes represent consonant and vowel speech sounds. Latin, Greek, Russian, Tai, Arabic, and Hebrew are all alphabetic languages. The Latin alphabet is used to write many modern-day languages, such as English and Spanish. The original Latin alphabet has all of the letters of English except *J, U, W,* and *Y.* In a syllabic language system, such as Japanese or Cherokee, each symbol correlates to a syllable or stress. In logography, each character represents a word, morpheme, or meaning, such as Egyptian hieroglyphs. Chinese characters and the Mayan script are mostly syllabic but are based on logograms. Many writing systems also include symbols for punctuation, to aid in the structure and organization of ideas.

UNDERSTANDING LANGUAGE SYSTEMS

Language is a system that consists of the development, acquisition, maintenance, and use of complex systems of communication, and a language is any specific example of such a system. The study of language is called linguistics. Language is characterized by five integrated rule-governed processes or systems—phonological, morphological, syntactic, semantic, and pragmatic (American Speech–Language–Hearing Association, n.d.)—which are summarized in Table 3.1. The five language systems allow people to communicate an unlimited combination of ideas through using highly structured streams of sounds, written signs, and manual or facial gestures. People use these systems to process, understand, and produce language. Although each system is distinct, they are integrated during communication. Understanding the integration of these five systems helps educators to be better observers of language development; it also helps them to adapt instruction to meet

TABLE 3.1. Five Language Systems

Language system	Description	Related terms	Related learning goals
Phonological	Organization of sounds in a language.	• **Phoneme:** Smallest unit of sound. • **Grapheme:** Smallest unit of a writing system.	• Pronounce and distinguish sounds in words. • Speak clearly and fluently. • Read by decoding words. • Spell by encoding words.
Morphological	Word structure or word-building rules.	• **Morpheme:** Smallest grammatical unit in a language. • **Derivational morpheme:** When combined with a root, can change the semantic meaning or part of speech. • **Inflectional morpheme:** Can modify a verb's tense, aspect, mood, person, or number, or a noun's, pronoun's, or adjective's number, gender, or case, without affecting the word's meaning or part of speech.	• Identify the meaning and function of roots and affixes, in order to comprehend and appropriately use words that contain derivational and inflectional morphemes.
Syntactic	Sentence structure or grammatical rules used in word order, combining, and functional use of words in phrases, clauses, and sentences.	• **Sentence structure:** Whether sentences are simple, compound, or complex. • **Parts of speech:** Categories of words with similar grammatical properties. • **Phrases:** Groups of words that act as units. Types include noun, verb, and prepositional. • **Subject–verb agreement:** Subjects and verbs must agree in number. • **Verb tense:** Quality of a verb indicating when something happened. Types include present, past, and future. • **Pronoun use:** Correct reference.	• Communicate effectively in Standard English. • Understand how sentence structure contributes to the coherence of paragraphs and texts. • Use complete simple, compound, and complex sentences. • Understand how word order, subject–verb agreement, pronoun use, and parallel structure affect meaning.
Semantic	Meaning system of words, word combinations, and word relations.	• **Lexical semantics:** Meanings of individual words. • **Relational semantics:** Relationships between words/phrases and their literal meanings (denotation) or their associated meanings (connotation). • **Academic vocabulary:** Words generally used in academic dialogue and texts. Can be either general or content-/discipline-specific. • **Meaning construction:** Depends on interaction of knowledge of language, text structure, subjects, and broad-based world knowledge.	• Understand and use general, general academic, and content-specific academic words. • Understand the meaning of oral, written, and visual messages. • Clearly communicate meaning through selecting interesting and precise words and organizing ideas.

(continued)

TABLE 3.1. *(continued)*

Language system	Description	Related terms	Related learning goals
Pragmatic	Use of a language in social contexts, such as rules of conversation or discourse based on audience and setting.	• **Communication functions:** Declaring, greeting, requesting information, answering questions, and following rules of conversation. • **Register:** The variety of language used for a particular purpose or in a particular social setting. Choice of register depends on social skills and rules of conversation.	• Analyze and use content, vocabulary, and grammar appropriate for the audience and setting. • Vary language register to fit specific purposes. • Understand and appreciate the natural variation that occurs in language across time, social situation, and social groups, and understand language-based prejudices that may exist.

the linguistic needs of students who have difficulties with receptive and/or expressive language. When young speakers are supported in their understanding and use of these systems in English and their other languages, they will be able to communicate better with more audiences, which may lead to future academic and career success.

Phonological System

Phonology is the study of the organization and patterns of sounds or phonemes used in a language. A **phoneme** is the smallest unit of sound that can change meaning in a word, such as changing /p/ in *pat* to /b/ in *bat*. Phonemes can be combined to build larger units, such as syllables and words. This system is responsible for recognizing the distinct speech sounds heard in language. For example, a person who hears the word *cat* is actually hearing the blending of three separate sounds or phonemes: /k/ /ă/ /t/. **Phonological awareness** is the awareness that language is composed of sounds, together with the understanding of the relationships of these sounds (in sentences, phrases, words, syllables, rhymes, and phonemes). This awareness marks the ability to identify, think about, and manipulate sounds in words. **Phonemic awareness**, the last stage in phonological awareness, is the understanding that spoken words are made up of a sequence of discrete sounds or phonemes. Children begin to understand the concept of individual words. Words can have similar beginning, middle, and/or ending sounds. Sounds can be manipulated to make new words.

The study of phonology encompasses the articulation, pronunciation, and intonation of sounds in words. **Articulation** is the process of producing speech sounds in the mouth and throat, and is classified by manner, place, and voice. These are combined to produce 44 distinct speech sounds in English.

There are seven places of articulation for English consonants: bilabial (made with both lips in contact); labio-dental (made with contact between the lower lip and upper teeth); lingua-dental (tongue and teeth); lingua-alveolar (made with tongue against the ridge behind the upper teeth); lingua-palatal (made with tongue against the palate or hard roof of the mouth); velar (made with the base of the tongue and the soft back of the mouth); and glottal (made via unrestricted airflow through the larynx or vocal cords). These places of articulation are cross-referenced with the manner in which the sounds are produced.

The manner of articulation describes how the tongue, lips, vocal cords, and other speech organs are involved in making sounds, primarily consonant sounds. Voicing in articulation refers to whether the sound produced in the vocal cords vibrates or not: /TH/ in *then* is voiced, while /th/ in *thin* is voiceless. In English, there are eight manners of articulation, ranging from the greatest amount of constricted airflow to the least. There are **stop consonants,** in which the airflow is stopped abruptly: /p/, /t/, /k/ (voiceless) and /b/, /d/, /g/ (voiced). **Fricative consonants** are partially blocked with turbulent airflow: /f/, /th/ in *thin*, /s/, /sh/, and /h/ (voiceless) and /v/, /th/, /z/, and /zh/ (voiced). **Affricate consonants** start like stops and end like fricatives: /ch/ (voiceless) and /j/ (voiced). Manners that involve very little obstruction and are voiced include **nasals** (/m/, /n/, and /ng/, where air flows through the nose, not the mouth), **liquid lateral** (/l/, where the tongue touches the teeth and air flows from the side of the tongue), and **liquid rhotic** (/r/, where sound is made with the blade of the tongue and air flows from the sides in a vowel-like consonant). In addition, there are **glides:** /w/ and /y/ (voiced), and /hw/ (voiceless), which are also vowel-like consonants with the tongue closer to the roof of the mouth with slight turbulence. The last parts of diphthongs such as /ow/ and /oi/ are also glides. **Vowels**, on the other hand, have unrestricted airflow, and the lips are retracted. They are categorized by tongue height, tongue advancement, and tongue tension or relaxation. Vowels also differ in how much the mouth is open: /ĭ/ (closed), /ĕ/ (half-closed), /ŭ/ (half-open), /aw/ (half open), /ŏ/ (mostly open), and /ă/ (open). This information is useful in helping speakers correctly articulate sounds in words. Young children often make speech errors, such as *wabbit* for *rabbit*, or may leave sounds out of words, such as *nana* for *banana*. A child may have an articulation disorder if these errors continue past about age 8. A student who has difficulties with articulation may omit, substitute, or distort one or more sounds, as in /poon/ for *spoon*, /tăt/ for *cat*, or /ssip/ with a noisy /s/ for *sip*. Not all sound substitutions and omissions are speech errors; instead, they may be related to a feature of a dialect or accent. For example, speakers of African American Vernacular English (AAVE) may substitute /d/ for /th/, saying *dis* for *this*. This is not a speech sound disorder, but one of the phonological features of AAVE.

The International Phonetic Alphabet (IPA) is a standardized set of graphic symbols, including Latin and Greek symbols, for transcribing speech sounds in any language. Speech–language therapists use the IPA to transcribe and then classify students' articulation of phonemes. Table 3.2 is a consonant chart that modifies the IPA's (2005) approach to include speech sounds written with the English phonetic spelling, so that it is more understandable to professionals other than speech–language pathologists. This table shows the manner, voice, and place of articulation for English consonants. Understanding these elements of articulation is important in interpreting a student's speech or spelling and in planning subsequent instruction. Some developmental spelling assessments give credit for substituting letters that have the same place and manner but differ in voice. For example, students may write *budado* for *potato*. This spelling is not random; rather, it represents substituting /b/ for /p/ and /d/ for /t/, which are similar-sounding phonemes but should be voiceless, not voiced. Educators can help students say the correct sound, and feel the vibration difference, by putting their hands to their throats as they say these two words and then write the correct letter. Table 3.3 is a vowel sound chart that categorizes the English vowel sounds by tongue height, tongue advancement, and tongue tension or relaxation

TABLE 3.2. Consonant Sounds of English

Manner	Voicing	Place						
		Bilabial	Labio-dental	Lingua-dental	Lingua-alveolar	Lingua-palatal	Velar	Glottal
Obstruents								
Stop	Voiceless	p			t		k	
	Voiced	b			d		g	
Fricative	Voiceless		f	th (*thin*)	s	sh		h
	Voiced		v	TH (*the*)	z	zh		
Affricate	Voiceless					ch		
	Voiced					j		
Sonorants								
Nasal	Voiced	m			n		ng	
Liquid lateral	Voiced				l			
Liquid rhotic	Voiced					r		
Glide	Voiced	w				y		
	Voiceless						hw	

TABLE 3.3. Vowel Sounds of English

Vowel phoneme	Key word	Tongue height	Tongue advancement	Tongue tense or lax	Lip rounding
/ē/	*key*	High	Front	Tense	Retracted
/ĭ/	*win*	High–mid	Front	Lax	Retracted
/ā/	*rebate*	Mid	Front	Tense	Retracted
/ĕ/	*red*	Low–mid	Front	Lax	Retracted
/ă/	*had*	Low	Front	Lax	Retracted
/ōō/	*moon*	High	Back	Tense	Retracted
/ŏŏ/	*wood*	High–mid	Back	Lax	Retracted
/ō/	*open*	Mid	Back	Tense	Retracted
/aw/	*law*	Low–mid	Back	Tense	Retracted
/ŏ/	*cod*	Low	Back	Tense	Retracted
/ə/	*about*	Mid	Central	Lax	Retracted
/ŭ/	*bud*	Low–mid	Central	Lax	Retracted
/er/	*butter* (end)	Mid	Central	Lax	Retracted
/ir/	*bird*	Mid	Central	Lax	Retracted

Note. Some consonant and vowel phonemes have been adapted from the Latin symbols in the International Phonetic Alphabet (IPA), to help relate sounds to known English graphemes.

(IPA, 2005). Key words are provided for each of the vowel phonemes. This table is important to understand how different vowel sounds are produced.

The English Pronunciation and Transcription Keys in Tables 3.4 (p. 60) and 3.5 (p. 61) show the American Heritage Dictionary and IPA representations of General American English pronunciations for vowels and for consonants, respectively. It also includes sample words and spelling patterns for each sound. When transcribing speech, teachers should use the American Heritage Dictionary pronunciation key, while speech–language pathologists will use the IPA. When teachers transcribe students' speech or reading, they should use the conventional spelling of the word if a real word is pronounced correctly. If a word is pronounced incorrectly, they should use the phonetic spelling as shown in the American Heritage Dictionary pronunciation symbols. To indicate the pronunciation, they should use slashes as the beginning and the end. If a student pauses between phonemes, a teacher should put slashes around each phoneme pronounced (/k/ă/t/ for *cat*); if the student blends parts of words together, the teacher should put slashes around each group of phonemes (/tōō/ /gĕt/ /her/ for *together*).

Phonology also includes the pronunciation of words and intonation. **Pronunciation** is the way in which a word or language is spoken; it involves a generally agreed-upon sequence of sounds used in speaking a word in a specific language dialect. Some speakers may be able to articulate all of the English speech sounds, yet may mispronounce words by omitting, substituting, or inserting one or more sounds (as in /pŭskĕtē/ for *spaghetti*, /crowns/ for *crayons*, or /drawring/ for *drawing*). It should be noted that people do not always agree on the "correct" pronunciation of a word, but a dictionary pronunciation is a good reference. If a speaker pronounces a word differently than expected, it may be an individual difference, a dialect difference, a regional difference, or a non-native English speaker difference. It is only an articulation disorder when a person says the sound with the tongue, teeth, and/or lips in the wrong place. The most important aspect of language is communication of ideas. If a listener is unclear as to what word was spoken, or a mispronunciation causes a distraction from the meaning of the message, pronunciation differences need to be addressed.

Intonation refers to the patterns of pitch, stress, and juncture that affect the meaning of words, phrases, and sentences. For example, if someone says *personal* when *personnel* is meant, this will have an impact on meaning. **Pitch** is the rise and fall of the voice, such as the difference in the voice for a statement, command, or question. **Stress** involves putting more emphasis on a syllable (such as in the words *dessert* and *desert*) or on a word (such as "*I* wouldn't say that" vs. "I wouldn't say *that*"). **Juncture** refers to the flow and pauses between the sounds within and between words. This includes appropriately blending sounds or pausing within a word, such as *a note* or *an oat*. Juncture also includes taking appropriate pauses between words (e.g., "My dad coaches soccer" vs. "Peter, my dad, coaches soccer").

People from different states, regions, and countries have different accents and use different dialects. **Accents** are the ways people pronounce specific sounds within a certain group or region of people. For example, "I hiked up the moun-tain" may be pronounced "I hiked up the mou-n" in the U.S. West, or the word *bath* may be pronounced /băth/ in an American English accent or /bawth/ in a British English accent. A **dialect** is a variety of language differing in vocabulary and grammar as well as pronunciation. Dialects are usually spoken by people in a certain group or region. For example, in different U.S. regions, people call carbonated drinks "soda" or "pop," or use the generic term "Coke." Some people

TABLE 3.4. English Pronunciation and Transcription Key for Vowels

American Heritage Dictionary (alternative)	IPA general American	Example words	Spelling patterns
ă	æ	at, ran	a
ăr	æɹ	carry	ar
ā	eɪ	rain, play, same, great, eight, reign, they, gauge	ai, ay, a_e, ea, eigh, ei, ey, au
ä (ŏ)	ɑ	father	a
är	ɑɹ	arm, car	ar
âr (ār)	ɛɹ	hair, pear, there, scary, their, they're	air, ear, ere, ar, eir, ey're
ĕ	ɛ	bed, end, friend, bread	e, ie, ea
ĕr	ɛɹ	merry	er
ē	ɩ	be, eat, ease, see, piece, movie, receive, ski, theme, machine, people, key, very	e, ea, ee, ie, ei, i, i_e, e_e, eo, ey, y
ĭ	I	it, him, crystal	i, y
ĭr (ēr)	ɪɹ	syrup, Sirius, souvenir	yr, ir
ī	aɪ	I, my, bite, pie, night, height, eye, bye, buy, aisle, choir	i, y, i_e, ie, igh, eigh, eye, ye, uy, ai_e, i
ēr	ɪɹ	here, near, peer, serious	ere, ear, eer, er
ŏ	ɑ	on, not	o
ō	oʊ	go, hope, boat, low, though, oh, woe, owe, sew, plateau	o, o_e, oa, ow, ough, oh, oe, owe, ew, eau
ô (aw)	ɔ	saw, caught, bought, cough /ôf/	aw, au, ough
ōr	oɹ, ɔɹ	glory, four, hoarse, horse, more, laureate	or, our, oar, or_e, ore, aur
oi	ɔɪ	boy, noise	oy, oi
o͝o (ŏŏ)	ʊ	book, put, wolf	oo, u
o͝or (ŏŏr)	ʊɹ	poor, tour	oor, our
o͞o (ōō)	u	soon, lose, true, new, fruit, through, lute	oo, o_e, ue, ew, ui, ough, u_e
yo͞o (yōō)	ju	you, cute	you, u_e
ou (ow)	aʊ	out, house, now, bough	ou, ou_e, ow, ough
ŭ	ʌ	up, run, enough, some, onion	u, ou, o_e, o
ə (ŭ)	ə	about, sofa, item, easily, common, circus (unstressed syllable)	a, e, i, o, u
ûr (er)	ɝ	her, first, nurse, works, early	er, ir, ur, (w)or, ear
ər (er)	ɚ	enter, grammar (unstressed syllable)	er, ar

Note. The part of the word that represents the phoneme is underlined. The final *e* is also underlined if it represents a long vowel. Based on Wiktionary (2012).

TABLE 3.5. English Pronunciation and Transcription Key for Consonants

American Heritage Dictionary	IPA general American	Example words	Spelling patterns
b	b	but, able, cab, wobble, ebb	b, bb
ch	Tʃ	chat, teacher, inch, catch, nature	ch, tch, t
d	d	dot, idea, nod, paddle, odd	d, dd
f	f	fan, left, leaf, enough, phone	f, gh, ph
g	ɡ	get, magnet, bag, ghost	g, gh
h	h	ham	h
hw	ʍ (hw)	which	wh
j	dʒ	joy, ajar, gin, agile, age, edge	j, g, ge, dge
k	K	cat, kit, queen, pique, choir, ache, tack	c, k, q, que, ch, che, ck
kʜ (k)	X	loch (Scottish), ach (German)	ch
l	L	left, hello, elevator (before or between vowel sounds)	l, ll
l	l̩ (əl)	little (following vowel sounds)	le
m	M	man, animal, him, hammer, climb	m, mm, mb
m	m̩ (əm)	spasm, prism, column	(s)m, mn
n	N	note, ant, pan, winner, know, pneumonia, gnat	n, nn, kn, pn, gn
n	n̩ (ən)	hidden, button	en, on
ng	ŋ	sing, sang, playing	ng
p	P	pen, spin, top, apple	p, pp
r	ɹ(4)	run, very	r
s	s	set, list, pass, city, ice, science	s, ss, c, sc
sh	ʃ	she, ash, sure, nation, session, special, chef, ocean	sh, s, ti, si, ci, ch, c
t	T	ten, stop, mat, attend, butt, two, talked	t, tt, tw, ed
th	θ	thin, nothing, moth	th
TH	ð	this, father, clothe	th, the
v	V	voice, naval, save, love, of	v, ve, f
w	W	wet, twins	w
y	J	yes, onion	y
z	Z	zoo, quiz, fuzz, is, easy, rose, xylem	z, zz, s, x
zh	ʒ	vision, treasure, beige	si, s, ge
ks	Ks	box	x

Note. Based on Wiktionary (2012).

might say, "I'm fixin' to" for "I'm going to," or "y'all, "youse," or "you guys" for "everyone." Accents and dialects are differences, not articulation disorders.

Morphological System

Morphology is the study of how words are formed by analyzing the structure of words and word parts such as roots, prefixes, and suffixes. An English language root, also called a **base word**, is the basic form of a word that can stand by itself with meaning, such as *cycle*. Affixes can be added to the base word to make new words, such as *bicycle* or *cycling*. In addition, some English words are made up of roots from other languages, such as Greek and Latin. These **roots** are parts of words that have meaning but cannot stand alone as English words, such as the Greek root *chron* (meaning *time*) in the words *chronic* or *chronological*. In Greek, *morph* means *form* and *-ology* means *study of*; therefore, in linguistics, morphology means the study of word forms. Understanding common Greek and Latin roots can help unlock the meanings of English words. Knowing Spanish, a Latin-based language, may also help in understanding some English words. Table 3.6 includes common Latin roots, related Spanish words, their meanings, and example English words. Table 3.7

TABLE 3.6. Common Latin Roots with Related Spanish Words

Latin root	Related Spanish word	Definition	English examples
aqua	*agua*	water	*aquarium, aquamarine*
mal	*mal*	bad	*malevolent, malodor*
bene	*bueno*	good	*benefactor, benevolent*
cent	*cien*	hundred	*century, centimeter*
dict	*decir*	to say	*dictation, dictator*
fort	*fuerte*	strength	*fortitude, fortress*
scrib/scribe	*escribir*	to write	*inscription, prescribe*
struct	*construir*	to build	*construct, constructive*

TABLE 3.7. Common Greek Roots

Greek root	Definition	English examples
auto	self	*autobiography, automobile*
bio	life	*biology, biography*
graph	writing	*graphic, phonograph*
hypo	below	*hypothermia, hypodermic*
lat	side	*bilateral, quadrilateral*
logy	study of	*biology, paleontology*
photo	light	*photograph, photosynthesis*
scope	viewing	*telescope, microscopic*

includes common Greek roots. Learning the meaning of these roots will be especially helpful in learning scientific and mathematical vocabulary.

A **morpheme** is the smallest grammatical unit of meaning in a language. For example, the word *dogs* has two morphemes, *dog* + plural *s*, and the word *unforgettable* contains three morphemes, *un* + *forget* + *able*. The identification of these morphemes helps to unlock the meaning of each word. **Free morphemes** can function independently as words (e.g., *town, run, blue*) and can appear with other words (e.g., *town hall, doghouse*). **Bound morphemes,** such as prefixes and suffixes, must be attached to a word or free morpheme. There are two types of bound morphemes: inflectional and derivational. **Inflectional morphemes** are suffixes added to a word to modify a noun, verb, or comparative adjective without changing the meaning of the root or part of speech. These additions can produce changes in verb tense (*look* → *looked*) or person (*walk* → *walks*), can show changes in plurality (*fox* → *foxes*), can indicate possession (*Katherine's book*), or can help make comparisons (*small* → *smaller* → *smallest*) in English. The eight English inflectional morphemes are shown in Table 3.8. In Spanish, suffixes can also be added to change a verb's tense, aspect, mood, or person, as well as a noun's, pronoun's, or adjective's number (*gato blanco* → *gatos blancos*) or gender (*mesa blanca*). In Spanish, possession is expressed with the word *de* (meaning *of*), not by adding *-'s* (*el libro de Katherine* vs. *Katherine's book*).

Derivational morphemes are prefixes or suffixes that, when combined with a root, can change the semantic meaning to form a new word (*happy* → ***un**happy*) or change the part of speech to produce a new form of the word (*teach* → *teach**er***). Table 3.9 shows the English derivational morphemes with suffixes that change the part of speech; Table 3.10 shows the English derivational morphemes with prefixes that create words with new meaning. There are only eight types of inflectional suffixes in English, while the number of derivational prefixes and suffixes is potentially infinite. A child with a problem using inflectional morphemes may omit morphemes, such as "Yesterday, I *look* at the pig," or may use morphemes incorrectly (e.g., *untrust* for *distrust*). Instruction on linking base words and affixes to their meanings helps students analyze unfamiliar words that contain familiar morphemes, and therefore expands their vocabularies.

Brown (1973) identified the first 14 grammatical morphemes in order of acquisition, as shown in Table 3.11 on page 65. Although Brown reported that these morphemes are mastered between 19 and 50 months, I have found that some school-age children receiving language

TABLE 3.8. English Inflectional Morphemes

Inflectional morpheme	Category	Examples
-s, -es	Noun, plural	*cat**s**, dog**s**, fox**es**, pupp**ies***
-'s	Noun, possessive	*Katherine**'s** car*
-s	Verb, present tense, third-person singular	*He play**s** guitar.*
-ing	Verb, present participle/gerund	*They are play**ing**.*
-ed	Verb, simple past tense	*He play**ed** yesterday.*
-en	Verb, present perfect or past perfect participle	*She has eat**en**.*
-er	Adjective, comparative	*She is tall**er** than her mom.*
-est	Adjective, superlative	*Dad is the tall**est** in the family.*

TABLE 3.9. English Derivational Morphemes—Suffixes That Change the Part of Speech

Suffix	Root → root + suffix	Part-of-speech change	Meaning
-ful	*beauty* → beautiful	Noun to adjective	Full of beauty
-y	*health* → healthy	Noun to adjective	Full of health
-ly	*father* → fatherly	Noun to adjective	Similar to a father
-less	*care* → careless	Noun to adjective	Without care
-er	*bake* → baker	Verb to noun	One who bakes
-or	*act* → actor	Verb to noun	One who acts
-ist	*bicycle* → bicyclist	Verb to noun	One who bicycles
-ly	*quick* → quickly	Adjective to adverb	Manner of being quick
-ness	*happy* → happiness	Adjective to noun	Quality of being happy

and literacy support, as well as some English language learners, need specific instruction in using these morphemes correctly. The list of morphemes in Table 3.11 can be used as a checklist to identify the presence or absence of these morphemes in a student's speech, and then can be used to plan instruction to support the student's use of these morphemes.

Syntactic System

The **syntactic system**, or syntax, of a language refers to rules governing word order, sentence structure, grammar usage, and the relationships among the elements within a sentence. This system controls the way in which words and phrases are combined to form grammatically correct sentences, in order to communicate in a clear, formal manner. A complete sentence, or independent clause, has a subject and a verb that express a complete thought when they are put together. Syntax includes understanding the sequence of parts of speech (nouns, verbs, adjectives, adverbs, etc.), sentence patterns (simple, compound, complex, and compound–complex), sentence transformations (questions, negatives, passive vs. active voice) and embeddings (adding modifiers, compounding, conjoined, or embedded clauses). In Table 3.12 on page 66, the nine different word classes or parts of speech are defined by their functions, with example words and sentences provided. People with syntactical problems often produce sentences lacking syntactic complexity or length; make errors in verb tenses or agreement; and incorrectly or uncharacteristically

TABLE 3.10. English Derivational Morphemes—Prefixes That Create Words with a New Meaning

Prefix	Meaning	Root → prefix + root	Meaning
un-	not	*happy* → unhappy	Not happy
im-	not	*mature* → immature	Not mature
dis-	not	*agree* → disagree	Not agree
re-	again	*write* → rewrite	Write again
pre-	before	*test* → pretest	Test before
mis-	wrong	*place* → misplace	Wrong place
sub-	under	*sub* → submarine	Under sea

TABLE 3.11. Grammatical Morphemes in Order of Acquisition

Morpheme	Example
Present progressive *-ing* (no auxiliary verb)	*Mommy driv**ing**.*
Preposition *in*	*Ball **in** cup.*
Preposition *on*	*Doggie **on** sofa.*
Regular plural *-s*	*Kitt**ies** eat my ice cream.* (Forms: /s/, /z/, /ez/)
Irregular past	*came, fell, broke, sat, went*
Possessives	*Mommy**'s** balloon broke.*
Uncontractible copula (verb *to be*)	*He **is**.* (Response to "Who's sick?")
Articles	*I see **a** kitty. I throw **the** ball.*
Regular past *-ed*	*Daddy pull**ed** the wagon.* (All three sounds: /ed/, /d/, /t/)
Regular third person *-s*	*Kathy hit**s**.* /s/, /z/, /ez/
Irregular third person	*He does* or *He has.*
Uncontractible auxiliary	*He **is**.* (Response to "Who's going home?")
Contractible copula	*The man**'s** big* for *The man is big.*
Contractible auxiliary	*Daddy**'s** drinking juice* for *Daddy is drinking juice.*

use articles, prepositions, and pronouns. A person with a different dialect or nonstandard syntax might say, "He *eat* ice cream" (verb tense) or "They *is* happy" (subject–verb agreement). A native Spanish speaker learning English might say, "The book is in the table of the kitchen," for "The book is on the kitchen table." In Spanish, this sentence would be "*El libro está en la mesa de la cocina.*" The speaker uses their knowledge of the Spanish grammatical word order and confuses similar-sounding prepositions.

The nine parts of speech are commonly divided into open classes (nouns, verbs, adjectives, and adverbs) and closed classes (pronouns, prepositions, conjunctions, articles/determiners, and interjections). Although we can add to the open classes of words as language develops, those in the closed classes are pretty much finite sets of words. Table 3.12 includes the nine word classes or parts of speech, their function, and example words and sentences.

Semantic System

Semantics is the study of meaning in single words, phrases, sentences, and even longer discourse units, and the relationships between and among them. This system includes both lexical and relational semantics. **Lexical semantics** focuses on the meaning of individual words within a language's vocabulary. **Relational semantics** examines the relationship between words and phrases and their literal meaning (**denotation**) or their associated meaning (**connotation**). Denotation is the actual meaning—what the word directly refers to, or its dictionary definition. Connotation is the implied meaning, along with the negative and positive associations of that word.

In lexical semantics, vocabulary can be classified into three tiers (Beck, McKeown, & Kucan, 2013). Tier 1 vocabulary includes the common, everyday words that most children enter school knowing already, unless they are English language learners. Because these

TABLE 3.12. Word Class or Part of Speech

Word class or part of speech	Function or job	Example words	Example sentences
		Noun	
Common noun	Names a general person, place, thing, or idea.	*teacher, city, building, shoes, document*	*He plays* ***guitar*** *in a* ***band****.*
Proper noun	Names a particular person, place, thing, or idea.	*Mr. Reyes, Tucson, Adidas, Declaration of Independence*	***Kate*** *lives in* ***Denver****.*
Pronoun	Stands in for nouns in a sentence.	*I, you, he, she, it, we, them, who, which, some, anybody, ourselves*	*Katherine is athletic.* ***She*** *plays soccer and field hockey.*
		Verb	
Action verb	Tells what action someone or something does.	*read, write, sing, draw, dance, create, evaluate*	*Maya* ***danced*** *to the music.*
Linking verb, state-of-being verb, or copula	Links the subject to a noun or adjective and does not express an action. *Copula* means link or tie in Latin.	*be (am, is, are, was, were, being, and been), look, feel, taste, smell, sound, seem, appear, get, become, grow, stay, keep, turn, prove, go, remain, resemble, run, lie*	*Stephanie* ***is*** *an author.* *The pie* ***smells*** *delicious.* Contractible copula: ***I'm*** *here.* Uncontractible copula: *Here* ***I am.***
Auxiliary verb or helping verb	Is used to form the tense or time of action, voice, and mood of the following verb.	Primary auxiliaries: *be: am, is, are, was, were, being, been* *do: does, did; have: has, had* Modal auxiliaries (indicate necessity, possibility, permission, obligation, ability or habit): *can, could, may, might, shall, should, will, would, must, ought to, used to, need, dare*	*Laura* ***is*** *playing soccer.* *She* ***has*** *been playing soccer. She* ***has*** *played soccer.* *He* ***will*** *not play soccer.*
Adjective	Tells us more about or describes a noun or noun phrase. It can be used before a noun or after certain verbs.	Determining adjectives: Possessive adjectives: *my, their* Numerals: *two, twenty* Qualifiers: *every, many* Demonstrative: *this or that* Interrogative: *which* Descriptive adjectives: *big, wonderful, red, smooth, round*	*I like* ***cheesy, bean*** *burritos.* *I have* ***two*** *dogs.* ***My*** *dogs are* ***intelligent.*** *They can do* ***many*** *tricks.*

(continued)

TABLE 3.12. *(continued)*

Word class or part of speech	Function or job	Example words	Example sentences
Adverb	Describes everything except nouns. It has many different uses and can appear virtually anywhere in a sentence.	Adverbs of manner: *slowly, happily, carefully* Adverbs of degree: *very, extremely, somewhat* Adverbs of time: *now, today* Adverbs of frequency: *often, daily, annually* Adverbs of place: *here, there,* Interrogative adverbs: *where, when, how, why* Indefinite adverbs: *anywhere, sometime, somehow* Relative adverbs: *where, when, why*	*Rio climbed* ***rapidly*** *up the rock cliff.*
Preposition	Shows a relationship between a noun (or a pronoun) and the other words in a sentence	*above, across, after, at, around, before, behind, below, beside, between, by, down, during, for, from, in, inside, onto, of, off, on, out, through, to under, up, with*	*Peter cycled* ***through*** *the mountains.*
Conjunction	Joins words, phrases, and clauses in a sentence.	*for, and, nor, but, or, yet, so* (mnemonic device for these: FANBOYS)	*I'd like to go,* ***but*** *I can't.*
Article/ determiner	Functions like an adjective by modifying nouns, but is different in that it is necessary for a sentence to have proper syntax.	Articles: *a, an, the* Determiners: *these, that, those, enough, much, few, which, what*	***The*** *eagle was in* ***that*** *nest.*
Interjection	An expression that can stand on its own as a complete sentence and often expresses a spontaneous feeling or emotion.	Exclamations: *Wow! Whoops! Ouch! Oh! Hooray! Bravo!* Greetings: *Hi! Welcome! Bye!* Agreement: *Sure! OK! Yeah! No!* Sounds: *Yikes! Aww! Fhew! Hmm!*	***Wow!*** *You did great!*

words are heard frequently, they rarely require explicit instruction. Examples of Tier 1 words are *baby, walk,* and *happy*. Tier 2 and Tier 3 words are academic vocabulary words and are used in academic dialogue and texts. Tier 2 vocabulary consists of important general academic words and related word forms that are used across several content areas. These include words essential for completing tasks at school or in the workplace, such as process words (*predict, categorize, analyze, differentiate, verify*), related words (*respond, respondent, unresponsive*), shades-of-meaning words (*said, screamed, whispered*), homophones (*idle–idol*), different meanings of the same word (*table* meaning a piece of furniture, or a chart, or to delay), confusing words (*accept–except, complement–compliment*), transition words (*in addition, in contrast, of course*), and sophisticated words (*obvious, establish, complex*). Tier 3 vocabulary consists of content- or discipline-specific words—ones that are generally only used for communicating within a certain discipline or career. These words are important for building knowledge and conceptual understanding within disciplines, such as medical (*phlebotomist*), legal (*acquit*), geological (*igneous*), mathematical (*variables*), historical (*archive*), technological (*bandwidth*), or even pedagogical (*lexical semantics*) terms. In school, content-specific words are those that are often defined in textbooks or glossaries. It is important to remember that words are not all clear-cut in their tier classification, as this classification depends on a person's linguistic and background knowledge. Vocabulary instruction should focus on important Tier 2 and Tier 3 words in the contexts of authentic communication experiences.

According to Blachowicz and Fisher (2006), depth and breadth are two dimensions of vocabulary knowledge. **Vocabulary depth** involves knowing the many facets of a word, such as understanding and applying the phonology (pronunciation), morphology (word parts), syntax (grammar and part of speech), semantics (meaning), and pragmatics (use) of the word in context. **Vocabulary breadth** refers to the full span of knowledge of a word, including the number of words people know that are related to it. In other words, depth indicates how much a person knows about a word, and breadth indicates how the person connects the word to the numerous other words on that topic. When people hear or read a word, they need to have both a broad and deep knowledge of the word to understand it fully.

Students' concept knowledge needs to be developed, in addition to vocabulary knowledge. A **concept** is a category or class into which events, ideas, and objects are grouped. It may be further clarified by examples and characteristics common to members that belong to the same class (Crank & Bulgren, 1993). Word meanings are linked to schema development. A **schema** is a cognitive framework or concept that helps organize information, determine relationships between or among pieces of information, and interpret information. For example, in early language development, a child may initially categorize all four-legged animals as dogs because the child has a dog. Eventually, with more experience, the child learns to discern the differences among dogs, goats, and other four-legged animals. Unless they have particular knowledge, some adults may not be able to discern the difference between a wild goat and a wild sheep, until they develop the schema to do so. Identifying examples and nonexamples enhance student's understanding and remembering of concepts (Bos & Anders, 1990). Meaning construction depends on interactions among knowledge of language, knowledge of context, knowledge of subject and broad-based world knowledge. Learning vocabulary is a generative process going from the known to the unknown, from the simple to the complex, and from the literal to the metaphorical.

In addition to understanding word-level semantics, we need to examine semantics at the sentence and discourse levels to communicate. To be an effective communicator, speakers need to determine what to include and how to organize the information so it can be easily understood. Language content refers to the ideas that language codes, and it has to do with what people know about objects and events in the world and with the feelings and attitudes they have about what they know. Language content is often analyzed by content categories (Bloom & Lahey, 1989). Table 3.13 identifies, defines, and gives an example of each of these content categories. Bloom and Lahey (1989) reported that children become able to communicate these content categories between 10 and 40 months of age, although I have found that many school-age children still have difficulties with them. Since all of the

TABLE 3.13. Language Content Categories

Content category	Age in months	Briefly defined	Example
Existence	10–18	Object in environment.	"Doggie."
Nonexistence	14–30	Object no longer present.	"All gone."
Recurrence	20–40	Reference to reappearance.	"More milk."
Rejection	24–48	Opposing action or refusing.	"No!" "I don't want that."
Denial	24–48	Negates identity, state, or event.	"Not a kitty."
Attribution	34–38	Often includes the use of an adjective.	"Big man."
Possession	34–38	Object associated with a person.	"Mommy's car."
Action	34–38	Movement, but no change of location.	"Eat cookie."
Locative action	38–40	Movement with change of location.	"Come here."
Locative state	38–40	Spatial relationships.	"Doggie outside."
State	38–40	Refers to state of affairs: Internal state External state Attributive state Possessive state	 "He's tired." "It's cold." "It's broken." "That's mine."
Quantity	38–40	Number or plural.	"Two baby," "Birdies."
Notice	40 and above	Attention to person, object, or event.	"I see Mommy."
Dative	40 and above	Use of indirect object.	"Give cookie to me."
Additive	40 and above	Joining objects, events, or states often by *and*.	"I got a truck and a bear."
Temporal	40 and above	Reference to time.	"It broke yesterday." "I'm gonna get it."
Causal	40 and above	Cause and effect.	"I go cuz I got shoes on."
Adversative	40 and above	Two events/states in contrast.	"I want to go, but I can't."
Epistemic	40 and above	Mental states of affairs (with verbs such as *know, think, remember, wonder*).	"What does this mean?' "I don't know."
Specification	40 and above	Distinguishing one from another. Later involves joining two dependent clauses.	"I want that one." "It looks like a fishing thing and you fish with it."
Communication	40 and above	Contains communication verbs.	"Tell Mommy I want this." "Mommy said not to do this."

age ranges in Table 3.13 are before school age, any student who is unable to demonstrate the use of these categories will need support in developing it. This chart can be used to identify the content categories that students use or do not use in their speech within sentences.

Discourse in longer units of language can be ways of speaking, listening, reading, and writing, integrated with ways of acting, interacting, valuing, feeling, dressing, thinking, and believing. Engaging students in discourse, including talking on topic in an academic environment, is central to language development, engaged learning, and ultimately student achievement. Student discourse can happen with partners, groups, or the whole class, or at the student-to-teacher level. Student discourse routines need to be explicitly taught and reinforced. When there is a classroom culture where students' thoughts are encouraged and where students are expected to speak, listen, and respond to one another, in-depth discussions occur. Student "talk moves" are strategies that they engage in, such as repeating, adding on, and changing thinking, that help build a collaborative learning culture in the classroom. To increase language development and learning, it is imperative that teachers provide more opportunities for students to talk to each other, rather than just listening and responding to the teachers. Semantic skills are necessary for understanding the world around us and developing the ability to express ourselves in a concise and meaningful way.

Pragmatic System

Pragmatics examines how people use language to communicate with others. It includes understanding the function of the language used, the language choices made within specific contexts, and discourse analysis of communication. Language use categories are function categories that have been developed to describe the basic intentions a user has for making an utterance. For example, people may want to make a request, make a statement, comment on information being discussed, regulate their environment, or just maintain communication (Fey, 1986; Halliday, 1975; Lahey & Bloom, 1988). Language use categories can be divided into assertive functions, in which a person expresses a request or an assertion, and responsive functions, in which a person responds to a request or assertion (Fey, 1986). Spontaneous language occurs when we initiate speaking, such as when we select the subject, organize our thoughts, and find the correct words before opening our mouths. Demand language occurs when someone else creates the circumstances in which communication is required. A question is asked, and we must simultaneously organize our thoughts, find the right words, and answer the question. A child with a language disability may speak normally when initiating conversation, but may respond hesitantly in demand situations—pause, ask for the question to be repeated, give a confused answer, or fail to find the right words.

Pragmatics also involves examining the language choices people make in social interactions, as well as the effects of these choices on others (Crystal, 1987). This variety in the use of language for a particular purpose or in a particular context is called a **register** and is determined by the social circumstances. Most people use several registers. For example, the way in which students communicate with their teachers or principal should be a more formal register than the way they talk to their friends. It might include pronouncing *-ing* as in *walking*, rather than *walkin'*; choosing more formal words, such as *child* rather than *kid*; and refraining from using less standard words, such as *ain't*. Formal register also includes considering the types of topics that are shared, such as not sharing as much personal information. This formal register should be taught and reinforced in school, so that students will be comfortable using it when communicating with employers, business people, and professionals. The language people choose to use can positively or negatively affect the way they are perceived by others. There tends to be a spectrum of registers rather than a distinct variety.

A similar and somewhat overlapping type of language variation is a regional or age **dialect** that is characteristic of a particular group of the language's speakers. Dialect has been discussed above in connection with some of the other language systems, but it is also worth considering as an aspect of pragmatics. It is usually related to regional speech patterns but may also be related to other factors, such as socioeconomic status or ethnicity. Dialects influence pronunciation, syntax, and even word choice. For example, people in the U.S. Southeast may say /may/ for *my* or /git/ for *get*; in Boston, you may hear *dock* for *dark*, and the words *caught* and *cot* may sound alike. There are some grammatical suffixes that appear to be absent in AAVE but are present in Standard U.S. English, such as possessive *-s* (*Kim'**s** car*), the third-person singular *-s* in the present tense (*He play**s***), past tense *-ed* (*He play**ed***), and copula apostrophes (*She'**s** coming*). It is important to distinguish mistakes in speech and reading that affect comprehension from those that do not. A teacher who is unsure of a student's intended meaning should ask follow-up questions and intervene if the grammatical or pronunciation differences affect comprehension. Despite differences in dialect, the language is usually mutually intelligible; however, sometimes it may interfere with communication and affect students' academic achievement. There also may be social and psychological differences among students who speak certain dialects, which may influence the students' confidence and attitudes toward reading and schooling, their performance on assessments, teachers' perceptions of the students' abilities and behavior, and miscommunication between teachers and students. These factors may lead to lower achievement and occupational achievement (Labov & Hudley, 2009).

Variation and change are characteristics of all languages. Alterations are made in phonological, morphological, syntactic, semantic, and lexical features over time or in specific contexts. Speakers may vary pronunciation, word choice, morphology, or syntax. Pronunciations evolve; new words are borrowed from other languages or invented; the meanings of old words drift; and affixes develop or are omitted. Using the categories in the language change chart provided in Table 3.14, students can identify words or phrases from speech or texts that are examples of how language has changed over time.

UNDERSTANDING LANGUAGE ACQUISITION AND ENGLISH LANGUAGE LEARNING

Language is a system that consists of the development, acquisition, maintenance, and use of complex systems of communication. This includes the language of native English speakers, as well as of those learning English or an additional language. Most people acquire language through a subconscious, naturalistic process during which they learn to communicate according to the linguistic rules of the language. People acquire and learn language through meaningful social interaction. **Language acquisition** is the process by which humans acquire the capacity to perceive and comprehend language, as well as to produce and use words and sentences to communicate. **Language development** is the expansion of intricate sounds and symbols that individuals interpret and integrate as they evolve and grow throughout their lifespans.

TABLE 3.14. Language Change Chart

Type of language change	Examples
Phonological—changes in the sound of words	short ĕ for short ă (kĕtch/*catch*), or short ĕ for short ĭ (mĕlk/*milk*)
Morphological—changes in phonetic representation or usage rules of morphemes	• *goed:* not past tense of *go* (this is *went,* from word *wend*) • plurals: *wife/wives, radius/radii*
Syntactic—changes in the part of speech or word order	• *dress* (noun to verb in *dress up,* or change to turkey *dressing*) • *If I gave not* (Shakespeare) to *If I didn't give*
Semantic—changes in the meaning of existing words	• *awful* used to mean "full of awe" or "inspiring wonder," but now has a negative meaning; *wicked,* which was formerly negative, is now sometimes positive • *wireless* used to mean radio, but now refers to an internet connection without cables • generalizations: *silverware* to mean utensils that can be made of stainless or plastic, not just silver
Lexical—creation of new words: • Borrowing words from other languages • Based on names of people or places • Name based on association • Part standing for whole • Compounding • Clipping • Blending • Adding prefix or suffix • Abbreviations/acronyms	• *school* comes from *schule* in German • *Franklin stove* from inventor Ben Franklin, or *denim* from *serge de Nim,* a cloth from Nimes, France • *suits*: (named for business executives) • 100 *head* of cattle, not just their heads • *blackboard; crowd + funding = crowdfunding* • *flu* for influenza, *ad* for advertisement • *web + seminar = webinar* • *texting* from the word *text* • BFF ("best friend forever"); 24/7 ("all the time")

The term **English language learners** (hereafter abbreviated as **ELLs**) describes persons who are learning English in addition to their native language or any other languages they may speak. Instruction, assessment, cultural background, and the attitudes of teachers and peers are all factors in ELLs' achievement in school. We are all language learners, whether we are adding to our knowledge of our native language(s) or are learning a new language. Historically, U.S. schools were designed for native speakers of English, but now students come from diverse cultural and linguistic backgrounds, and as teachers we need to use this background to support their learning.

Both first- and second-language learners pass through a similar initial stage, the silent period, that builds competence in the learners via listening (Krashen, 1981). Second-language learners are urged to limit this silent period. The second stage is formulaic speech—expressions that are learned as a whole and used during particular occasions, such as greetings or "Can I have a . . . ?" In the third stage, first- and second-language learners apply structural and semantic simplifications to their language. Structural simplifications include omitting grammatical functions (e.g., articles or auxiliary verbs), while semantic simplifications include omitting content words (e.g., nouns and verbs). Learners show a pattern in the developmental sequences and the order in which they acquire certain grammatical morphemes (Brown, 1973); however, McLaughlin (1987) found that the pattern may depend on the amount and type of comprehensible language input a learner receives. **Comprehensible input** (Krashen, 1981) means that students should be able to understand the essence of what is being said or presented to them. Students learn a new language best when they receive input that is within their zone of proximal development (i.e., just a bit more difficult than they can easily understand on their own; see Chapter 1). Making teacher talk comprehensible involves attention not just to the choice of vocabulary, but to the presentation of background and context; the explanation and wording of unclear content; and the use of such strategies as graphic organizers, visuals, and building context through relatable experiences.

ELLs need to learn grade-level academic content, even though they are still in the process of learning English. Teachers can challenge these students with content knowledge activities and help them apply critical thinking skills, such as knowledge, comprehension, application, analysis, synthesis, and evaluation. Content knowledge can be assessed separately from their level of English proficiency. Teachers can also differentiate the process of their instruction, the products students are to produce, and the environments for responding (e.g., working in collaborative groups).

As educators, we need to value and preserve ELLs' home and additional languages, while providing these students with the tools to learn and use academic English. According to Young and Hadaway (2006), several factors have an impact on English language acquisition: the age at which children enter the school system; their level of first-language literacy; the similarities of the first language to English in terms of phonology, morphology, syntax, semantics, and type of script; and, as noted above, the amount and type of comprehensible input they receive. To support students, educators need to identify systemic patterns of home languages and dialects in their students; distinguish between speech disorders and nonstandard dialects; and make the educational system more accessible by teaching conventions while acknowledging the legitimacy of home languages and dialects. Once teachers have a better understanding of their students' familial, cultural, and language backgrounds, they can focus their attention on selecting and implementing the most effective instructional strategies (Young & Hadaway, 2006). They can give students the tools and strategies they need to organize and express their thinking, as well as to develop a vocabulary and style suited to each academic context.

The following strategies to enhance English language acquisition are a compilation of suggestions from various sources, including Collier (1995) and Young and Hadaway (2006). These strategies are beneficial not only for ELLs, but for most learners. As educators, we need to do the following:

- Emphasize activation of students' prior knowledge, show respect for their native languages and cultures, and engage in ongoing assessment with multiple measures.
- Encourage and model strategic thinking, problem solving, and comprehension strategies that emphasize the connections between language and content concepts.
- Incorporate multiple modalities (visual, auditory, and kinesthetic) during instruction and student learning experiences.
- Build content through relatable experiences, using context and visual cues, and providing enough relevant background information.
- Choose language, academic vocabulary, gestures, and visuals carefully.
- Encourage interactivity through the use of native languages.
- Use cooperative learning, peer-assisted activities, and student–student dialogue journals with feedback.
- Finally, provide more opportunities for ELLs to talk and engage in cognitively

challenging tasks. It is most important to stress the accuracy of content, rather than the precise pronunciation and syntax. The focus should be on progress, not perfection.

LANGUAGE DEVELOPMENT: GOALS

The language goals listed below include competencies, skills, and attributes students should possess in order to be effective speakers and communicators. They are organized around the topics of receptive language for vocabulary, following directions, and answering questions; articulation; phonology; and expressive language for morphology, syntax, semantics, vocabulary and pragmatics. In the Common Core State Standards (National Governors Association for Best Practices & Council of Chief State School Officers, 2010), the language standards focus on Conventions of Standard English, Knowledge of Language, and Vocabulary Acquisition and Use. In addition, there are standards for Speaking and Listening, including Comprehension and Collaboration during discussions, and Presentation of Knowledge and Ideas. Some of the goals below are based on a list given on *bilinguistics.com* under the Resources Speech Therapy Goal Bank tab and are available there in both English and Spanish. These goals have been combined in a series for space reasons; however, a teacher would select only one part of each listed goal to work on at a time.

To develop receptive language for vocabulary, students will:

- Point to pictures or objects that represent developmentally appropriate nouns, action verbs, and adjectives (size, shape, color, texture, etc.), to increase receptive vocabulary knowledge.
- Identify word relationships by pointing to or grouping pictures and objects to identify part–whole relationships or category memberships.
- Use context and sentence structure to figure out the meaning of words.
- Figure out meanings of words by their morphemes, such as prefixes, suffixes, and root words.
- Use Latin roots and affixes to expand their knowledge of new vocabulary words.
- Identify how English is enriched by words from other languages.
- Ask for clarification of any unknown words, phrases, or concepts that are heard.

To develop receptive language for following directions, students will:

- Follow one-step, two-step, and then three-step directions.
- Follow directions with modifiers such as location (spatial), quantity (number, more–less), quality (size, color, shape), and pronouns.

To develop receptive language for answering questions, students will:

- Respond to yes–no questions related to a variety of contexts (personal experiences, classroom experiences, discussions, and narrative and expository texts).
- Respond to "who, what, where, when, why, and how" questions related to a variety of content.

To develop articulation, students will:

- Articulate speech sounds in a conventional manner.
- Use a given sound or blend in isolation, and then at the beginning, middle, and/or end of a word.
- Use a given sound or blend at the sentence, phrase, paragraph, and conversation levels.

To develop phonology, students will:

- Pronounce words in a conventional manner.
- Reduce deletion of weak syllables by producing all of the syllables of two- and three-syllable words at the word, phrase, and sentence levels.
- Reduce deletion of weak consonants by producing all of the consonants at the word, phrase, and sentence levels.
- Reduce substitution of sounds by producing all of the sounds at the word, phrase, and sentence levels.

To develop expressive language for morphology, students will:

- Use article and gender agreement in activities and conversation.
- Use present progressive, present, future, and regular–irregular past-tense verbs at the phrase, sentence, and conversation levels.
- Use regular and irregular plural markers.
- Use article and number agreement.

To develop expressive language for syntax when describing or responding to questions regarding activities or thinking, students will:

- Form grammatically correct simple sentences.
- Use correct subject–verb agreement in sentences.
- Use the preterit (past) tense accurately.
- Include the necessary prepositions in a sentence.
- Use compound subjects and objects in sentences.
- Use compound sentences (with conjunctions—*and, but, or,* etc.).
- Use a variety of long, complex, and compound sentences.

To develop expressive language vocabulary, students will:

- Describe objects and pictures by identifying critical features (names, attributes, functions).
- Use vocabulary to clearly describe ideas, feelings, and experiences.
- Name items in a given category (e.g., school items, animals, clothing, transportation, food).
- Name and classify objects and words by category and function; explain their relationships.
- State whole–part relationships between words.
- Expand knowledge of word meanings by identifying antonyms, synonyms, and related words.
- Identify words with multiple meanings, and use them appropriately.

- Use context and sentence structure to figure out the meanings of words.
- Use prefixes, suffixes, and roots to figure out word meanings.
- Compare and contrast related words from other languages to words in English.
- Use precise and interesting words.
- Use a variety of general academic vocabulary words in the correct contexts.
- Use a variety of content- or discipline-specific academic vocabulary words in the correct contexts.
- Identify characteristics, examples, and nonexamples of words and concepts.
- Group and organize vocabulary words to learn their meanings.
- Provide examples of how the meanings of words move from literal to figurative.
- Interpret figurative language.
- Identify characteristics, examples, and nonexamples of concepts.

To develop expressive language for utterance expansion during an activity, students will:

- Use four- to five-word utterances to ask questions, comment, and describe.
- Include all the necessary words in a sentence.
- Use rote phrases with cues.
- Use descriptive words in utterances.
- Use complete grammatical sentences to express wants/needs and share information.
- Use complete sentences for a variety of communicative functions during daily activities.
- Use complete grammatical sentences to relate past events, and explain word relationships.
- Use complete grammatical sentences to ask and answer "wh-" questions.
- Produce statements and questions that are clearly understood.
- Respond to requests for information, action, and clarification.

To develop expressive language for discourse, students will:

- Share meaningful information on a variety of topics.
- Explain or describe objects, ideas, experiences, or processes in detail.
- Use visual cues to retell stories or events.
- Tell stories or events in sequential detail.
- Use sequence words to verbally order an event (e.g., *first, next, then*).
- Include critical and detailed features of a story, problem, or interaction (characters, setting, problem, plan or attempt, consequence, resolution, moral, theme, and main idea).
- Use descriptive language to tell stories or report an event.
- Describe opinions or convince others of their point of view.
- Describe feelings and emotions.
- Distinguish between fact and fantasy.
- Interpret figurative language.

To develop expressive language with gestures, signs, and visuals, students will:

- Pair oral language with gestures and signs to communicate meaning and maintain interest.
- Maintain eye contact and use eye gaze to direct attention or to gauge interest or confusion of the listener.

- Use facial expressions such as smiles, expressive eyes, and looks of empathy to communicate feelings and emotions.
- Stand naturally during speaking, with hands at sides and at a comfortable distance from the listener.
- Use visuals and realia to support oral language.

To develop expressive language pragmatics, students will:

- Initiate conversations.
- Initiate requests for information or help.
- Take turns during conversations.
- Demonstrate attention to speakers with eyes and body language.
- Respond to others' requests, questions, or comments.
- Make predictions after observing or listening to others.
- Modify language based on feedback.
- Communicate appropriately in a variety of settings and situations.

To develop expressive language fluency and voice, students will:

- Alter the rate of speech to maintain attention and interest, but not too fast or slow.
- Speak in an appropriate volume for varied situations.
- Alter voice pitch (high or low) to prevent sounding monotone.
- Use optimum stress patterns in syllables, words, phrases, and sentences.
- Stress certain words to add emphasis.
- Use optimal pauses and breathing while speaking (e.g., pauses after important ideas).
- Speak fluently without repetitions, revisions, unusual pauses, or fillers.

LANGUAGE DEVELOPMENT: ASSESSMENTS

Since language development is so complex, it is challenging to assess the full extent of a person's language, especially in a short period of time. Profiles of language strengths and areas for improvement can be determined by using the following assessments included in the Appendix: the *Language Observation Scale, Semantic Generative Vocabulary Assessment, Oral Presentation Assessment, Synonym Vocabulary Assessment, Antonym Vocabulary Assessment, Morphology Assessment—Inflectional Morphemes,* and *Morphology Assessment—Derivational Morphemes.* The speech–language pathologist can use this information to determine if additional assessments are needed. Transcribed language samples and standardized language assessments may be needed to analyze specific elements in students' expressive or receptive language, in order to plan intervention that develops their language proficiency. The *Peabody Picture Vocabulary Test—Fifth Edition* (PPVT-5) is a test of receptive vocabulary for Standard English and a screening test of verbal ability for ages 2½ to 90+ (Dunn, 2018).

ELLs also need to be assessed for their proficiency and progress in English. The WIDA Consortium, based at the University of Wisconsin, provides a suite of English language proficiency assessments known as the ACCESS tests; these tests measure students' academic English in the domains of listening, speaking, reading, and writing (*https://wida.wisc.edu*). The content of the assessments aligns with the five WIDA English Language Development

Standards: Social and Instructional Language, Language of Language Arts, Language of Mathematics, Language of Science, and Language of Social Studies. The scores reflect proficiency levels ranging from Level 1 (Entering) to Level 6 (Reaching). The ACCESS suite is taken annually by ELLs in grades K–12 in WIDA Consortium member states to identify initial English language proficiency and assess growth over time.

Teachers can support all students' language learning if they have a better understanding of the students' phonological, morphological, syntactic, semantic, and pragmatic processing. The literacy specialist, the speech–language pathologist, and the classroom teacher work together to assess each student's language development and to identify appropriate goals, objectives, and strategies.

Language Observation Scale

PURPOSE: To assess students' expressive language development, especially for those students who exhibit a language difference, language delay, or language processing disorder, or who are ELLs. In developing this scale, I used some of the ideas from the *Language Development Checklists* for 3- to 5-year-olds (Allen & Marotz, 1994) and the *Loban Oral Language Scale* (Loban, 1961) for elementary-grade children, as well as my own ideas.

PROCEDURE: The teacher records the student's language over time using the *Language Observation Transcription Form* (see Appendix, p. 384). Then, on the *Language Observation Scale* (see Appendix, pp. 385–387), the teacher circles the number for each of the items that best describes the student's communicative behavior, using a scale of 1–4 (1 indicates almost no evidence of this behavior, and communication is significantly interrupted; 4 indicates the student predominantly exhibits the correct behavior, with almost no interference with communication). In the Analysis section for each category, the teacher writes down specific examples for areas of need.

ANALYSIS: The teacher identifies the student's strengths and needs in the following language areas: phonemics (articulation, pronunciation, fluency), syntax and morphemics (sentence complexity and grammar), semantics (vocabulary and discourse meaning), and pragmatics (language use). If the student's score is a 1 or 2 in any language area, or a 3 in several areas, then they should be referred to a speech–language pathologist for further language or speech evaluation. Strengths need to be reinforced, and explicit or implicit instruction and modeling should be provided for the areas needing improvement. See the partial example in Figure 3.1.

Semantic Generative Vocabulary Assessment

PURPOSE: To identify a student's ability to name multiple items in a category, describe whole–part relationships, describe objects, and describe feelings and events.

PROCEDURE: The teacher reads each prompt to the student and writes down and audio-records the responses. For each question, the teacher says, "I am going to ask you some questions. I want you to answer with as many words as possible." The student is given up to 2 minutes to respond to each question. If the student stops, the teacher asks, "Can you tell me more?" After 10 seconds of no response, the teacher goes to the next question. (See Appendix, *Semantic Generative Vocabulary Assessment*, p. 388.)

FIGURE 3.1. *Language Observation Scale,* partial example for a grade 2 student.

Phonemics (Articulation, Pronunciation, and Oral Fluency)				
1. Articulation: Correctly produced speech sounds.	1	(2)	3	4
2. Pronunciation: Correctly pronounced words and did not add or delete sounds.	1	2	(3)	4
3. Linguistic fluency: Speech was fluent and not disrupted by repetitions, revisions, unusual pauses, and fillers such as *um* or *like*.	1	(2)	3	4
Comments: For phonemics, the student correctly articulated most sounds, except she said the /d/ sound for /th/, (*dis* for *this*), and omitted /s/ in blends (*tar* for *star*). She did not pronounce /-ed/ at the end of past-tense verbs. It should be noted that she also did not spell words correctly with the past tense *-ed*. She is generally fluent, but sometimes paused and said *um* when she was figuring out what to say. This was not only in pressure-induced situations, such as talking in front of the class, but also in casual conversations.				
Analysis: The student is strong in correctly articulating most sounds. She needs to improve in pronouncing and writing past-tense verbs and in pausing less when speaking.				
Instructional Implications: Refer for speech-language evaluation for the /th/ and /s/ sounds since the student is now in grade 2. Work on pronouncing the /th/ sound in front of a mirror by sticking her tongue out between her teeth and the /s/ sound by closing teeth and rapidly putting her tongue to the front of her teeth. Then practice saying words with /s/ blends (/st/, /sp/ etc.). Use kinesthetic strategies; for example, start at the wrist and slide finger up the arm and say /s-s-t/, stopping at the shoulder for *t*. Read and write words and sentences with /th/ and /s/ blends. Teach the purpose for the *-ed* suffix, and encourage speaking, reading, and writing of words with past tense *-ed*. Discuss with her about language fluency hesitations and the filler "um" and provide opportunities for the student to plan out what to say prior to being asked to speak out in class. Continue classroom support in these areas.				

DIFFERENTIATION: ELLs should be asked to respond to each question first in their native language and then in English. It may be beneficial to translate the questions into their native language to determine if they have correct responses, even if they do not have the English words for them.

SCORING AND ANALYSIS: For each prompt, the teacher marks a plus sign (+) for 10 or more correct items or the correct concept, a checkmark (✓) for 5–9 correct items or the mostly correct concept, and a minus sign (–) for 0–4 correct items or the incorrect concept. Categories of strength and areas for improvement should be identified. The teacher should give specific examples of interesting or specific terms, inclusion of words from multiple categories, words from different parts of speech, and any incorrect responses. Semantic generative vocabulary levels are as follows: Advanced = 6 or more plus signs; Adequate = 5 or more plus signs or checkmarks; Limited = 4 or fewer plus signs or checkmarks. Figure 3.2 shows a partial example and analysis.

• Oral Presentation Assessment

PURPOSE: To evaluate oral presentations in terms of language, organization, content, visual media, manner, and audience participation (for students in grade 3 and above).

PROCEDURE: The teacher should provide this assessment to students before they plan a presentation, and should model both positive and negative examples of each element. During the presentation, the teacher writes down specific observations under each heading

FIGURE 3.2. *Semantic Generative Vocabulary Assessment,* partial example and analysis for a grade 2 student.

Score +, ✓, –	Prompt and Responses
✓	1. Name as many kinds of food as you can. Pizza, cereal, PBJ, burgers. I like ice cream and cookies. (Can you tell me more?) Uh, waffles and pancakes.
–	2. Choose one food and describe it in detail. Pizza's good. It's got stuff on it, like cheese. (Anything else?) Nope!
✓	3. Name as many kinds of clothing as you can. Shirt, pants, dresses, shorts. (Can you tell me more?) I don't know, socks.

Analysis: Sarah was able to generate vocabulary at an adequate level. She was identified as a native English speaker. In this partial example, she identified eight different foods with prompting. She provided two specific details about pizza, which indicates a need for improvement in semantic generation for description. She was prompted to add more, yet did not add anything. Her words were common nouns, and the foods were examples of three categories: grains, meats, and desserts. Her description of pizza included nonspecific vocabulary such as *stuff.* She used a simple sentence structure and included one adjective, good, and no adverbs. She identified five types of clothing with prompting. She used general terms with no adjectives or descriptors.
Instructional Implications: Sarah could use some support for generating more and specific vocabulary. You might have her think about all of the food that is in her refrigerator and in the cupboards at home. You could help her to classify the food in food groups, and then add a new group of foods that would be in multiple food groups. Create a graphic organizer with the senses, to help her describe one of these multiple-food-group foods.

and scores it. After the presentation, the student completes a self-evaluation, and then the teacher gives the student specific feedback on the effective elements of the presentation and suggestions for improvement. After the initial assessment, the teacher provides constructive feedback with a group discussion. This measure can also be used by peers or for self-assessment. (See Appendix, *Oral Presentation Assessment,* p. 389–391.)

ANALYSIS: During the presentation, the teacher evaluates each element with a plus sign (+) if all of the descriptors were clearly observed, a checkmark (✓) if most of them were, and a minus sign (–) if they were rarely or never observed. See the example in Figure 3.3.

• Synonym and Antonym Vocabulary Assessments

PURPOSE: These two tests are screening instruments (Laster & McAndrews, 2004), and are used to identify reading and listening vocabulary levels for students in all grades.

PROCEDURE: Either of these assessments can be administered to groups or individuals as a reading or listening assessment, depending on the teacher's purpose and the students' reading levels. The synonym and the antonym tests should be administered separately. If students are able to read at a second-grade level, the teacher begins by administering each test as a reading assessment; otherwise, it is begun as a listening assessment. The teacher may want two copies of the assessment, if it is completed as a reading assessment, as the student and teacher will each need one to mark. An index card may be provided to help the student keep their place.

FIGURE 3.3. *Oral Presentation Assessment,* partial example and analysis for a grade 6 student.

Topic: Country Reports–Cuba

Score	The presenter:
	Language:
+	Conveyed the information clearly to the audience.
+	Pronounced words correctly and clearly.
+	Used grammatically correct sentences.
–	Used a variety of complex and compound sentence structures.
–	Included adjectives, adverbs, prepositions, and conjunctions.
✓	Used general academic vocabulary.
✓	Used content- or discipline-specific vocabulary.
✓	Used appropriate language for the audience.
	Observations: During the oral presentation, examples of her sentences include Cuba is an island. Cuba is near Florida. Cuba has a tropical climate. This indicates use of simple sentence structures with limited parts of speech and description.

Analysis: During the oral presentation, the student's language was generally appropriate, grammatically correct, and communicated clearly. However, she referred to the people as Spanish, not Cuban. She started many of her sentences with the word *Cuba* and used a limited number of different sentence structures.

Instructional Implications: Provide instruction on varying sentence structures. Have her watch and listen to her video-recorded presentation. The student or teacher can write each sentence on a separate line and examine the first word and the sentence structures. The student can then rewrite to vary the structure of the sentences and add details. Discuss the difference in vocabulary between language, ethnicity, and national origin.

The reading assessment should begin at Level 1, which equates to first grade, for all students reading at or below fourth-grade level; otherwise, it should begin at least three levels below a student's grade level. Students will continue with each level until they score 60% or below. Then that level is readministered as a listening assessment, with a different-colored pen, and again continues with each subsequent level until students score 60% or below. The teacher begins by explaining the synonym or antonym directions to the student for either reading or listening; then the teacher and student complete the practice items together. If the student does not understand the practice items, the teacher explains the reason for the correct response.

Throughout each assessment, in front of each line number, the teacher writes a plus sign (+) if correct and a minus sign (–) if incorrect. For each level, the teacher writes the total correct and calculates the percentage to determine the student's functioning level: independent (90–100%), instructional (70–80%), or frustration (60% and below). (See Appendix, *Synonym Vocabulary Assessment* and *Antonym Vocabulary Assessment*, pp. 392–396 and 397–401, respectively.)

ANALYSIS: The highest grade level at which the student scores 70% is the student's reading or listening vocabulary level. The teacher identifies whether the student's reading vocabulary is below, at, or above the current grade level. If the student's reading vocabulary is below the current grade level, the student's listening level should be assessed. Students who score below their grade level may require more attention to vocabulary development. See the example in Figure 3.4.

• Morphology Assessment—Inflectional Morphemes

PURPOSE: To assess the ability to create words by adding inflectional morphemes to root words to pluralize nouns, to show possession, to change a verb's tense, or show a comparison, without affecting the root's meaning or part of speech (for students in grades 2–12).

PROCEDURE: This assessment can be read to a student, who responds orally, or the student can read it and write the correct word. The teacher says, "I will read a key word and a sentence with a blank. Fill in the blank by adding suffixes or word parts to the key word to make the sentence complete and sound right." The teacher then provides the practice item: "*dog*—I have a dog. I used to have two ________ (dogs)." If the student doesn't get it right, the teacher provides the correct answer. (See Appendix, *Morphology Assessment—Inflectional Morphemes*, p. 402.)

SCORING AND ANALYSIS: The teacher writes the total correct out of 16, then describes the type of morphemes the student correctly said or did not say and gives examples of incorrect responses. See the example and analysis in Figure 3.5.

FIGURE 3.4. *Synonym Vocabulary Assessment*, partial example and analysis for a grade 2 student.

LEVEL 2 Functioning Level: Frustration **Score:** 5/**10** = 50%					
+, –		A	B	C	D
–	**1. go**	anything	leave	(rest)	summer
+	**2. pair**	read	should	(two)	middle
–	**3. cut**	(last)	round	slow	slice
+	**4. thin**	shout	(skinny)	live	under
+	**5. hear**	kind	magic	help	(listen)
+	**6. car**	secret	chew	(automobile)	juice
+	**7. fear**	(afraid)	lunch	yellow	welcome
–	**8. stir**	hospital	(stood)	mix	know
–	**9. below**	(live)	place	under	took
–	**10. all**	this	every	(find)	lunch

Analysis: This second-grade student was at the instructional level at the first-grade level (not shown) and at the frustration level at the second-grade level for identifying synonyms while reading. There was no particular pattern to the incorrect responses. The grade Level 2 assessment should be readministered as a listening assessment to see if he knows the synonyms orally.

Instructional Implications: Provide word card pairs to match synonyms, create cloze sentences that can be completed with several synonyms, and have the student use a thesaurus to find other words that are synonyms during speaking and writing.

FIGURE 3.5. *Morphology Assessment—Inflectional Morphemes,* example and analysis for a grade 3 student.

Score +, –	Key Word	Prompt
Inflectional bound morphemes (plurals)		
+	**1. cat**	Sam has one **cat.** Ann has two more cats______.
+	**2. ball**	Maya had one **ball.** Her friend gave her another. Now she has two balls______.
+	**3. fox**	A **fox** was playing in the field. Out of the bushes came another. Now there are two foxes______.
+	**4. dish**	I ate one **dish** of ice cream. My dad was hungry and ate two dishes______ of ice cream.
–	**5. leaf**	I picked up one **leaf** from the ground. Then I picked up a pile of leafs. (leaves)______
Inflectional bound morphemes (possessives)		
+	**6. sister**	My **sister** has a fish. My sister's______ fish is a goldfish.
+	**7. dog**	My **dog** has a collar. My dog's______ collar is red.
–	**8. Garcia**	Mr. and Mrs. **Garcia** invited me to their house. I am going to the Garcia______ house for dinner. (Garcias'______)
Inflectional bound morphemes (verb tenses)		
+	**9. play**	Yesterday, Max played______ with his truck.
+	**10. play**	Right now, he is playing______ with his robot.
+	**11. play**	Tomorrow he wants to play______ with his drums.
+	**12. play**	Sometimes he plays______ the piano.
–	**13. eat**	Yesterday, she eat______ beans. (ate)
+	**14. eat**	Right now, she is eating______ carrots.
–	**15. eat**	She always eat______ salad every day. (eats)
–	**16. eat**	She has never eat______ beets before. (eaten)
Inflectional bound morphemes (comparative and superlative)		
+	**17. small**	When we are comparing size, a softball is small. A baseball is smaller______.
+	**18. small**	A golf ball is the smallest______.
Score: 13/18		

Analysis: On the morphology assessment, she correctly added inflectional morphemes for 13/18 prompts. She correctly added inflectional morphemes for all of the plurals except *leafs/leaves* and all of the possessives except Garcia/Garcias'. She correctly added inflectional morphemes for all of the verb tenses for *play* and only the present progressive for *eat.* She correctly added the morphemes *-er* and *-est* for the comparative and superlative of *small.*

Instructional Implications: She would benefit from cloze activities that have her select the correct verb tense, especially for irregular verbs. She could sort verb tenses and restate the same ideas in the past, present, and future. She could then examine books and her own writing for verb tense usage.

Morphology Assessment—Derivational Morphemes

PURPOSE: To assess the ability to create words by adding derivational morphemes to root words to change the roots' meaning or the words' parts of speech (for students in grades 3–12).

DIRECTIONS: This assessment can be read to a student, who responds orally, or the student can read it and write the correct word. The teacher says, "I will read a key word and a sentence with a blank. Fill in the blank by adding to or changing the root word to make the sentence complete and sound right." The teacher then gives the practice item: "*test*—Before our test on Friday we will have a _______ (pretest)." If the student does not give the correct answer, the teacher provides it. (See Appendix, *Morphology Assessment—Derivational Morphemes*, p. 403.)

SCORING AND ANALYSIS: The teacher writes the total correct out of 20, then describes the type of morphemes the student correctly said or did not say and gives examples of incorrect responses. See the example and analysis in Figure 3.6.

LANGUAGE DEVELOPMENT: STRATEGIES

Language is best developed through interactions during meaningful, authentic conversations and experiences. However, focused mini-lessons can also support students' receptive and expressive language development through specific phonological, morphological, syntactic, semantic, and pragmatic language strategies. Since language is used to communicate ideas, work on those goals and objectives that significantly interfere with communication should come first. Teachers should not wait until language development objectives are met before working on other literacy and content objectives, and vice versa. These processes are interrelated and may be enhanced when students use them in the context of other processes. Students' language is often a reflection of the language(s) they hear in their home and their community; however, school can play an essential role in the development of a more formal language register.

The following are general oral language strategies that teachers can use to support language development. Teachers should provide many opportunities for children to engage in talking. The classroom context and environment are central to oral language use and development in the classroom. Oral language is not only a means to gain understanding, but also a way to display competence. General language development strategies begin with teachers' being good listeners during conversations with students. They should do the following: respond and show interest in what a student is saying; ask the student questions to learn more information or to clarify information; encourage the student to speak in complete sentences; encourage the student to use language to express feelings and needs; frequently use words the student is not familiar with and explain what these words mean, in order to expand their vocabulary; and, finally, encourage the student to participate in appropriate adult and formal English conversations.

Education must be viewed as a social activity in which students are engaged in sharing ideas and learning from others, not an individual activity where teachers attempt to transmit knowledge and students simply regurgitate that knowledge. Talking and reading

FIGURE 3.6. *Morphology Assessment—Derivational Morphemes,* example and analysis for a grade 3 student.

Score +, –	Key Word	Prompt
Derivational bound morphemes (meaning changed)		
+	**1. happy**	A person who is not **happy** is unhappy.
+	**2. do**	If you are asked to **do** your assignment again, the teacher would ask you to redo it.
+	**3. obey**	Someone who does **not obey** the rules would disobey them.
–	**4. complete**	His paper was **not complete**; therefore, it is imcomplete. (incomplete)
Derivational bound morphemes (changed to nouns)		
+	**5. teach**	A person who **teaches** is a teacher.
+	**6. biology**	A person who practices **biology** is a biologist.
+	**7. kind**	A person who was **kind** showed much kindness when she picked up the books he dropped.
–	**8. store**	A place to store something is in a big container. (storage)
+	**9. help**	A person who likes to **help** others is a helper.
+	**10. create**	He will **create** a model. When he is done, it will be his own creation.
Derivational bound morphemes (changed to adjectives)		
+	**11. nature**	A person who enjoys **nature** wants to be in the natural environment.
+	**12. care**	He took great **care** with his houseplants. He was very careful.
+	**13. week**	I go to soccer practice every **week.** We have weekly soccer practice.
+	**14. five**	There are **five** people in line. I am the fifth person.
+	**15. rain**	Today it will **rain.** Today will be a rainy day.
Derivational bound morphemes (changed to adverbs)		
+	**16. slow**	The turtle is **slow.** He walks very slowly.
+	**17. happy**	He was **happy** to help. He happily helped his teacher.
+	**18. clock**	He turned around in the direction of a **clock.** He turned clockwise.
Derivational bound morphemes (changed to verbs)		
+	**19. quiz**	Tomorrow is a **quiz.** Today we will be quizzing each other to prepare.
–	**20. accessory**	Her necklace is an **accessory.** She will need at least three things to accessory her outfit. (accessorize)
Total: 17/20		

(continued)

FIGURE 3.6. *(continued)*

Analysis: Mario correctly added prefixes and suffixes to 17/20 derivational morpheme prompts. He correctly added prefixes to the morphemes, except that he said *imcomplete* for *incomplete*. He correctly added suffixes to change the words into nouns in all the prompts except *big/storage*. The word made sense in the sentence, but he did not use the root word. He correctly added suffixes to change all the words into adjectives and adverbs. He correctly added suffixes to change the word *quiz* to a verb, but did not correctly change *accessory* into the verb *accessorize*.
Instructional Implications: Reinforce the correct addition of prefixes and suffixes to the root word to change the meaning or part of speech of the affected word. For incorrect responses on this assessment or during the student's language use, model how adding or changing bound morphemes changes the word's meaning or part of speech. Provide opportunities for the student to create new words by adding different morphemes to the root or base word and then ask them to use the new word in the context of a meaningful sentence. Have them find and explain the meaning of derivational morphemes in their reading or writing.

with students are two of the most important things teachers can do to enhance students' language development. Since talking requires no materials, it can be done not only in the classroom, but anywhere—including in the hall, at lunch, or during activities off school grounds. Students who have many conversations with adults and peers learn the words and ideas they will need to understand when they are reading and writing. Reading to students of all ages builds the desire to read, gives an educational advantage, and develops vocabulary and reading strategies. This can be an enjoyable experience for both listeners and readers; indeed, reading aloud to students develops lifelong readers and learners. For specific strategies for reading to students, refer to Chapter 6. Language can be promoted through conversations in a variety of situations; structured question–answer periods; and the use of aesthetic talk (giving emotional responses), efferent talk (informing and persuading), and dramatic talk (telling stories).

The following are more specific strategies for developing phonological, morphological, syntactic, semantic and pragmatic skills during oral language. Additional strategies for using text to enhance language and comprehension are described in Chapter 6.

Phonological Language Strategies

• Articulating Sounds

PURPOSE: To improve the articulation of specific sounds (for students in all grades).

PROCEDURE: As the teacher or other educator, do the following:

1. Identify an incorrect speech sound.
2. Use the consonant and vowel articulation charts in Tables 3.2 and 3.3, respectively, to determine the manner, place, and voice of articulation.
3. Provide pictures or objects that preferably begin with or contain that sound, name the objects, and ask the student, "What is the beginning sound in all of these words?"
4. Tell the student the sound, and demonstrate and verbalize how to articulate the sound or phoneme by manner, place, and voice.
5. Give the student a mirror to examine the manner, place, and articulation while they make the sound; correct the student as needed.

6. Introduce the sound in minimal pairs (two words that vary by only a single sound), and describe the similarities and differences between the manner, place, and voice for each word.
7. Use an audio recording for the student to practice and compare growth in the change in articulation.
8. Provide additional examples of the phoneme in the initial placement in a word, and then in the final and medial placements, for the student to practice saying.
9. Have the student read or repeat sentences from a text containing multiple examples of the phoneme. *Note:* It is not necessary for a student to be able to articulate a sound correctly before they are able to differentiate it, so continue instruction in context.

EXAMPLE: If the student says /tat/ for *cat,* the student is making the sound at the front of the mouth (alveolar ridge) instead of the back of the mouth (velar). Show the student pictures for words such as *cat, can,* and *car,* and say each word while emphasizing the /k/ sound. Model the /k/ sound, and tell the student to raise the back of the tongue and touch the roof of the mouth to make the sound. Have the student practice saying the sound in front of a mirror, and then have them practice with the picture words. Now introduce the minimal pair of *can* and *tan,* and describe the similarities and differences in manner, place, and articulation of each. Have the student practice saying the minimal pair. Introduce and practice the /k/ sound in different places in a word (*call, talk, backs*). Then have the student read or repeat sentences from the song "Jimmy crack corn and I don't care . . . "

• Pronouncing Tricky Words

PURPOSE: To improve the pronunciation of words, including word endings (for students in all grades).

PROCEDURE: As the teacher or other educator, do the following:

1. Identify a word the student has difficulty pronouncing.
2. Ask the student to use the word in a sentence to be sure they understand the meaning of the word, if not provide a sentence.
3. For the mispronounced sound, use the consonant and vowel articulation charts in Tables 3.2 and 3.3, respectively, to model the manner, place, and voice of articulation.
4. Say, "Listen for how the word is pronounced. How is it different from the way you pronounced it?"
5. Say, "Repeat the word as I say it."
6. If the student does not correctly repeat your pronunciation, you can break the word into syllables or phonemes.
7. Write the student's phonetic pronunciation directly above the correct pronunciation, and ask, "How are these the same and different?"
8. Provide other examples of words with the same sound combinations.
9. Ask the student to repeat the words in isolation and then in context of a sentence.
10. Have the student read or repeat sentences from a text containing multiple examples of the word.

Note: When students mispronounce a word in class, simply say the word correctly in a new or rephrased sentence, using a friendly tone. Remember, do not expect perfection! Some pronunciation differences are due to dialects or to students' being ELLs; therefore, you must first determine whether the mispronunciation affects communication or whether you can work on the pronunciation individually at a later time.

EXAMPLE: If the student says /l ī bărē/ for *library*, ask them to use it in a sentence. "I went to the /lībărē/ to get some books." Then say, "You said 'libary' for 'library.' How are they different? 'Library' has an /r/ after the /b/. Break it up into syllables: /l ī / /brăr/ /ē/." Another example is the word *February*, where there is also an /r/ after the /b/. Have the student read or repeat sentences from the book *Library Mouse*, by Daniel Kirk (2007), in order to practice saying the word *library*.

Morphological Language Strategies

• Making New Words by Adding Prefixes and Suffixes

PURPOSE: For students to use inflectional and derivational morphemes (prefixes and suffixes) correctly when speaking (at end of first grade and above).

PROCEDURE: As the teacher, do the following:

1. Listen to students' speech to find patterns of incorrect use of prefixes or suffixes (e.g., "He walked slow/slowly to school").
2. Identify one to three inflectional or derivational morphemes to teach from the same category; see the charts of inflectional and derivational morphemes in Tables 3.8–3.10. (In the case of *slow/slowly*, the derivational morpheme *-ly* changes an adjective to an adverb.)
3. Introduce the prefix or suffix, and elicit multiple examples of words that contain it. Write them on the board, and have students circle the affix (*-ly*: *slowly, quickly, sadly*).
4. Explain the meaning of an affix, prefix, and suffix. ("A suffix is a word part added to the end of a root that changes the meaning of the word.")
5. Ask students what they think the affix means. Define the meaning of the affix, as well as words containing the affix (*-ly* = a characteristic of; e.g., *slowly*, a way in which something moves that is not fast). You might use resources to help you find common prefixes and suffixes with their meanings (see, e.g., Scholastic, 2019).
6. Describe the category of the affix you are teaching. ("When you change *slow* to *slowly*, *-ly* changes the adjective to an adverb describing how something is done.")
7. Connect the words to the students' prior experiences by posing questions. ("How can you tell our pet turtle is walking slowly? Who at your table at lunch cleaned up quickly?")
8. Ask students how they could you use this word correctly in a sentence. ("The turtle was walking slowly toward the pond.")
9. Repeat steps 5–8 with other words in the same category or the same affix.
10. Point out examples of this affix during conversations or in texts throughout the week.

DIFFERENTIATION: For more challenge, encourage students to create sentences with additional words with the same morpheme or category. Have them explain how the meaning or part of speech changes when the affix is added. For more support, present the words as a math problem (*slow* + *ly*= *slowly*). Model the strategy first with easier or known morphemes (e.g., adding plural *-s* to nouns). For ELLs, point out similar affixes in their native language (e.g., *slow* → slowly/lento → lentamente), or identify how the idea is conveyed in their native language.

EXTENSION/APPLICATION: Have students create a page in their personal dictionaries for common definitions of affixes and Latin roots. Have them practice covering up parts of words in text as they read, to learn and understand the meaning of unknown multisyllabic words.

Separating Morphemes

PURPOSE: For students to understand word meanings by understanding the individual morphemes or word parts (in grades 4–12).

PROCEDURE: As the teacher, ask students to do the following:

1. "Separate the following words into morphemes or meaningful word parts by drawing a line between each part, such as prefix, root word and suffix."
2. "Write the meaning of each word part."
3. "Write the word in a sentence showing that you understand the meaning of the word."

EXAMPLE: *untruthful,* un/truth/ful, *un* = not truth = real facts, *ful* = full of. "She was untruthful when she said her dog ate her homework." Other words: *disobeyed, telephone, zoologist, preview, homeless.*

Adding Morphemes

PURPOSE: For students to develop new words based on the same root word and identify how the morphemes change the meaning or tense of the word.

PROCEDURE: The teacher says, "Create as many real words as possible using the root word *act* by adding the following prefixes and/or suffixes. Here's a hint: You can add more than one suffix. Select three of your new words and write a sentence for each one, showing that you understand the meaning of the word." Prefixes: *re-, de-, in-*. Suffixes: *-ly, -ary, -ive, -or, -able, -ate, -ion, -ary, -ed.*

EXAMPLES: *active, actively, action, actor, react, reactive, reactivate, reaction, reactionary, reactor, activate, actionable, reactionary, acted, reacted, activated, deactivated, inactive*

Illustrating Compare and Contrast Affixes

SOURCE: Nilsen and Nilsen (2004).

PURPOSE: For students to learn the differences between affix meanings (in grade 6 and above).

PROCEDURE: The teacher or the students select prefixes that are opposite. Each student then folds an 11″ × 17″ page of paper in half, and identifies and illustrates example words that have one prefix on one half of the paper and the opposite prefix on the other side.

EXAMPLES: On the top half of the paper, students write and illustrate *super-* with the following words: *Superman, superscript, supercilious,* and *superior.* On the bottom half of the paper, students write and illustrate *sub-* with the following words: *submit, subdivision, subservient, subliminal,* and *submerge.* Other examples of comparing only two words are *antebellum* (before war) and *anti-war* (against war), *maximum* and *minimum, inductive* and *deductive,* and *accelerate* and *decelerate.*

Morpheme Match-Up

PURPOSE: For students to define words according to the Greek or Latin meaning of morphemes.

PROCEDURE: The teacher gives students about 20 cards containing Greek or Latin morphemes that can be combined to make words, as well as a chart containing each morpheme and its meaning. Students then match the morpheme cards to make real words. The spellings may need to be altered slightly. They read the word, state the meaning of each morpheme, then create a definition for the word, and finally use or write the word in a sentence to demonstrate the meaning. As an extension, they can see how many other words they can create by using one of the listed morphemes and an additional morpheme.

EXAMPLES: Potential morphemes with definitions: *photo* (light), *auto* (self), *sub* (under), *graph* (write), *micro* (small), *tele* (distant), *marine* (in the sea), *logy* (study of), *phone* (sound), *port* (carry), *scope* (look at), *ist* (one who), *mobile* (move), *geo* (earth), *way* (move), *vision* (see), *re* (again), *scribe* (write), *de* (from), and *bio* (life)

Latin and Greek Root Family Sentence Completion

SOURCE: Nilsen and Nilsen (2004).

PURPOSE: For students to learn new words with the same or similar Latin or Greek roots (in grade 3 and above).

PROCEDURE: Students make sentences for words that contain similar roots. The teacher omits the specific word and provides a word box for students to choose from to complete the sentences. See the example in Figure 3.7.

Latin and Greek Root Seek-and-Find Lessons

PURPOSE: For students to identify meanings of words with similar Latin and Greek roots (in grade 3 and above).

PROCEDURE: The teacher selects words in a text with Latin or Greek roots that are used in multiple words, and asks students to find these words. Students say or write the roots, meanings, definitions, and a sentence to show the meaning of each word. They then write other words containing the same roots. See the example in Figure 3.8.

FIGURE 3.7. Latin root family sentence completion, example.

Sonus: Latin word referring to sound.

Word box: | *resonates resounding sonata sonnets sonorous* |

1. A __________ is a musical composition.
2. If an idea __________ with you, "it sounds right."
3. A person who speaks in __________ tones has an imposing and effective voice.
4. __________ are poems that sound almost like music because of their rhythm.
5. All speakers long for their ideas to be met with __________ applause.

FIGURE 3.8. Latin root lesson, example.

Root: fin	**Meaning:** end
Word	**Definition**
definite	Clear or exact; not vague, having settled limits.
confine	Keep within limits; restrict, keep in; shut in, boundary; border; limit.
finale	The concluding part of a piece of music or a play, the last part; end.
Sentence	The tiger was confined to a cage at the zoo.

• Morphology of Words in a Unit of Study

SOURCE: Ogle and Correa (2007).

PURPOSE: To use as a pretest and a posttest to assess and for students to learn vocabulary, by chunking words into parts that sometimes can be used to figure out word meanings.

PROCEDURE: The teacher selects vocabulary words from a text or from concepts in an instructional unit, and provides the student with a box for each word part. As a pretest, the teacher asks the student to divide the word into word parts and to write what each part probably means and what the word probably means. Afterward, the student can revise the first part if needed, write the definition, write a quote from the text, and write related words. See the example in Figure 3.9.

Syntactic Language Strategies

• Sentence Structure Activity

PURPOSE: For students to improve sentence structure, such as missing parts of speech; incorrect word order; or incorrect inflection such as verb tenses, plurality, possession, or suffixes added to adjectives and adverbs (for students in all grades).

FIGURE 3.9. Morphology example for the word *entomologist*, from the book *Buzz* (Bingham, Morgan, & Robertson, 2007).

Entomologist

Word parts	*entom*	*olog*	*ist*
Part meaning	insect	study	person

Probably means: A person who studies insects.

Dictionary definition: A scientist who studies insects, including their relationships with other animals, their environments, and human beings. Some study the classification, life cycle, distribution, physiology, behavior, ecology, or interaction of insects (EnvironmentalScience.org, 2020).

Quote from the text: "Forensic entomologists may be called to the scene of a crime to gather evidence or may be sent samples by a police forensic scientist" (Bingham, Morgan, & Robertson, 2007, p. 131).

Related words: *entomology*, the study of insects; *biologist*, a person who studies life.

PROCEDURE: As the teacher, do the following:

1. When listening to a student speak, identify syntactic elements in which the student is having difficulties such as those listed above.
2. Restate the content of what the student said by using standard sentence grammar. Evaluate the student's syntax to determine whether this is a repeated pattern and whether it is important to correct.
3. Help the student by writing down what they said in context and rewriting it in standard formal English.
4. Have the student identify the similarities and differences in the sentence structure.
5. Explain why this change is needed, based on grammar rules.
6. Have the student restate the sentence, using the correct sentence structure.
7. Have the student create a new sentence either orally or in writing, using the same formal syntactic structure.
8. In the future, point out examples of this structure in oral communication or text.

EXAMPLE: The student stated, "On Tuesdays, he *play* basketball after school." The teacher said, "Oh, so on Tuesdays, he *plays* basketball after school." The teacher then asked, "What is different in the way I added to the root word *play*? Most of the time there is no suffix on the word *play* in present tense, except in the third-person singular, when you refer to *he, she,* or *it*. This is called subject–verb agreement." The student then repeated the sentence correctly and created a new sentence: "He also *plays* soccer."

• Act Out and Say Preposition Sentences

PURPOSE: For students to orally use prepositions correctly in sentences.

PROCEDURE: Examples are from *Bears in the Night* by Berenstain and Berenstain (1971). As the teacher, do the following:

1. Say, "Today we are going to talk about a special kind of a word called a preposition. A preposition is a word or group of words that is used with a noun, pronoun, or noun phrase to show direction, location, or time, or to introduce an object." Connect this to prior learning: "Remember that a noun is a word that names a person, place, or thing. Tell your partner examples of nouns."
2. "We are going to read a story called *Bears in the Night* by Stan and Jan Berenstain. In this story, the bears leave their bed at night, and the authors use different words, called prepositions, to explain the direction or location of where the bears went. Let's look at the pictures and see where the bears went. The bears went *out* of their beds, *to* the window, *out* the window, *down* the tree. . . . When I read, I want you to put your thumb up each time you hear a preposition. What is the preposition the authors used?"
3. With the students, chorally say a complete sentence of where the bears went. (Example: "The bears went *over* the wall.")
4. Explain to the students, "I brought a teddy bear to school today. We are going to talk about where the bear is in relation to other objects like the chair." Move the bear as you say the following sentences: "The bear is *on* the chair. The bear is *over* the chair." Ask, "How is *over* the chair different from *on* the chair? The bear is *under* the chair. The bear is *next to* the chair. The bear is *between* the two chairs. The bear is *behind* the chair. The bear is *in front of* the chair."

5. Ask, "What are the prepositions I used to explain the bear's location?" (*on, under, over,* etc.).
6. With the students, chorally say a complete sentence of where the bear went. (Example: "The bear went *over* the wall.")
7. For assessment, pass out small stuffed animals such as Beanie Babies. Ask the students to state or repeat the noun or the name of the stuffed animal (i.e., *duck, dog, pony, lizard*).
8. "Now, with a partner, I want you to act out the prepositions and say in a complete sentence where you put your stuffed animal. For example, 'The duck is *over* the chair.' Do this for each of the prepositions."
9. "I am going to walk around and tell you a preposition, and I want you to act it out with your stuffed animal and say a complete sentence using the preposition."
10. "I will mark on my preposition checklist if you are able to act the preposition out and if you could tell me a complete sentence."

DIFFERENTIATION: For a challenge, the teacher can have the students take pictures of the stuffed animal and write captions using the prepositions. For support, students place the animal in a location; the teacher states two sentences; and the students answer which one is correct and then repeat the correct sentence. ELLs can be allowed to use the prepositions in their native language first.

Semantic Language Strategies for Vocabulary

Verbal interaction and vocabulary instruction result in an increase in word knowledge, concept knowledge, and listening–reading comprehension. According to Nagy (1988), the most effective methods of vocabulary instruction include providing information about word meanings and etymology (the history of the words), showing vocabulary in a variety of contexts, and creating multiple exposures to the new words. Learning words in the contexts of reading, experiences, and discussion have been found to be most effective, whereas memorizing long lists of isolated words has been found to be relatively ineffective (Nagy, 1988). Since language is a social activity, it is important that students work together to negotiate multiple meanings, rather than copy, recite, and be tested on dictionary definitions.

The teacher can help students make predictions about word meanings, based on comparing known to new words on phonological (sound) similarities, orthographical (spelling) similarities, semantic (meaning) similarities, and pragmatics (common sense and knowledge about historical connections between both words). Important Tier 2 general academic words and Tier 3 discipline-specific academic words can be chosen. Words can also be selected from the following categories: Bloom's cognitive processing verbs (*analyze, infer, summarize, evaluate, apply*); words that are often included in teacher directions and academic discussions; multiple-meaning words; words for specificity; sophisticated words; connectors and transition words; phrasal clusters; information-processing words; cognates and false cognates; sentence and question starters and frames; and figurative language (idioms, metaphors, similes, and puns).

Vocabulary needs to be taught in the context of discussions during meaningful tasks and text reading. Students need to develop both depth and breadth in vocabulary knowledge. In general, it is beneficial to use visual, auditory, and kinesthetic methods of instruction for introducing students to new vocabulary words. The teacher can specifically point out individual word parts such as affixes and roots. Students can read or use the word in context, practice pronouncing it, and then provide their own definition and/or examples. To differentiate these strategies for more challenge, students can create their own graphic organizers or apply the strategy to their own set of words. For more support, the teacher can provide more modeling or fill in portions of graphic organizers. For ELLs, images or videos for word or concept development, or oral sentence frames for expected responses, can be provided.

Six Steps to Effective Vocabulary Instruction

SOURCE: Marzano and Pickering (2005).

PURPOSE: To explicitly teach academic vocabulary.

PROCEDURE: As the teacher, do the following:

1. Give students a friendly, informal description, explanation, or example of the new word.
2. Have students give an informal description, explanation, or example of the new word in their own words.
3. Ask students to create a nonlinguistic representation of the word (e.g., by creating a visual aid or acting it out).
4. Engage in activities to deepen knowledge of the word.
5. Have students discuss the word with others.
6. Have them play games and review new vocabulary.

Depth and Breadth Vocabulary

PURPOSE: For students to learn a word deeply by identifying its pronunciation, part of speech, multiple definitions, and properties, and learn the word broadly by writing synonyms, antonyms, the category it belongs to, other words in that category, related words, and other forms of the word.

PROCEDURE: As the teacher, have students do the following:

1. Select a word from a unit of study or text with multiple meanings. Each person can become an expert on a word.
2. Write the pronunciation and part of speech.
3. Write each of the definitions with a corresponding sentence.
4. Write synonyms and/or antonyms.
5. Write the hypernym, or category the word belongs to.
6. Write the hyponyms, words that are subtypes or examples of it.
7. Write coordinate terms from the same category.
8. Write other forms of the word, including those with added prefixes, suffixes, or roots.
9. Write any other related terms.
10. Write the etymology or word origin.
11. Write root-related terms or other forms of the words from similar roots.

EXAMPLE: *table*, ta·ble, /t ā bəl/, noun and verb

Definition 1. *Noun:* A piece of furniture with a flat top and one or more legs, providing a level surface on which objects may be placed, and that can be used for such purposes as eating, writing, working, or playing games. Sentence: "We ate dinner at the kitchen table."

Definition 2. *Noun:* A set of facts or figures systematically displayed, especially in columns. Sentence: "The population has grown, as shown in Table 1."

Definition 3. *Verb:* To postpone considering. Sentence: "I'd like to table the issue for the next few months."

Synonyms: (def. 2. computing): *grid, vector.*

Hypernyms (overarching or general term): (def. 1. furniture) *furniture,* (def. 2. computing): *array.*

Coordinate terms: (def. 1. furniture): *chair, couch.*

Hyponyms (subtypes or specific types): (def. 1. furniture): *dinner table, poker table, end table, coffee table*; (def. 2. computing): *hash table.*

Idioms: 1. *on the table*—parliamentary procedure. (a) United States, postponed. (b) United Kingdom, submitted for consideration. 2. *turn the tables*—to cause a reversal of an existing situation, especially with regard to gaining the upper hand over a competitor, rival, antagonist, etc. "Fortune turned the tables and we won." 3. *under the table*—(a) drunk. (b) as a bribe; secretly: "She gave money under the table to get the apartment." 4. *wait (on) tables*—to work as a waiter or waitress: "He worked his way through college by waiting tables."

Etymology: From Latin *tabula,* meaning a board, plank, writing table, or schedule.

Root-related terms: 1. *tablet* (noun), a flat surface, often for writing. Sentence: "I used my tablet for taking notes." 2. *tabulate* (verb). Sentence: "In order to create a table, the professor must tabulate relevant data, perhaps while seated at the dinner table."

Personal Dictionaries

PURPOSE: For students to place newly learned words in a dictionary to be used for future reference (in grade 1 and above).

PROCEDURE: After learning new vocabulary words, the students can write the word, definition, and an example and/or picture clue under each letter of the alphabet. These can be general personal dictionaries, or they can be content- or discipline-specific. The teacher and students can create a class vocabulary chart with the same information.

EXAMPLE: On the "A" page: *antonym*—a word that means the opposite of another word (e.g., *up* ↑ and *down* ↓).

Act Out, Visualize, or Draw

PURPOSE: To demonstrate the meaning of vocabulary words (for students in all grades).

PROCEDURE: The teacher and students make up rules similar to those of games such as charades or Milton Bradley's *Pictionary,* where others have to guess the word that one person draws or acts out. On a card, one student writes the sentence(s) that the vocabulary word came from and underlines the word. Then the student acts out that word, and the other students try to guess what it is.

EXAMPLE: From *Holes* by Louis Sachar (1998): "The warden got a pitchfork out of the back of the pick-up. She poked it through X-Ray's dirt pile, to see if anything else might have been buried in there as well" (p. 69). The student who chose that word acts out poking a pile with a pitchfork. The other students then try to guess the word.

• Modified Cloze Procedure

SOURCE: Taylor (1953); see also Walker (2004).

PURPOSE: Originally developed to measure readability and comprehension of a passage, this strategy can be used to develop vocabulary.

PROCEDURE: Words are omitted or covered in the text, and a student needs to supply the missing words. This modified cloze technique uses semantic and syntactic clues to determine the covered vocabulary word. Grapho-phonemic cues can be provided, such as the beginning letter or letters, to enhance the student's prediction of the word.

EXAMPLE: From *The Mitten* by Jan Brett (1989). The underlined words are the ones to be covered up:

1. He wanted mittens made from wool as white as snow.
2. "If you drop one in the snow," she warned, "you'll never find it."
3. The bear gave an enormous sneeze.

• Compare and Contrast Vocabulary Words

PURPOSE: For students to identify the similarities and differences between two words (in grade 2 and above).

PROCEDURE: Students write two words, write how they are different, write how they are similar, and then write a summary statement comparing the two words. See the example in Figure 3.10.

FIGURE 3.10. Compare and contrast vocabulary words, example.

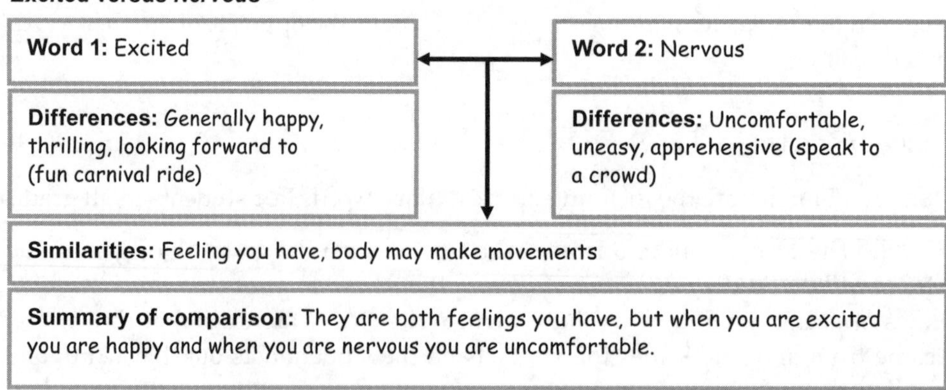

Contextual Processing

SOURCE: Walker (2004).

PURPOSE: For students to learn how to identify word meanings by the context (in grade 1 and above).

PROCEDURE: The teacher selects sentences or paragraphs from the text where the meaning of new vocabulary is apparent from the surrounding context, and writes or posts these on the board. The teacher then asks students what the paragraph tells them. The students tell or write down their predictions of what they think the word means. After the students reply, the teacher asks, "Why did you think that?" Then the students think of how the word can be used in another sentence and identify words with similar meanings. Finally, they check a dictionary to verify their predictions.

EXAMPLE: From *The Great Kapok Tree* by Lynn Cherry (1990): "They set fires to clear the underbrush, and soon the forest disappears. Where once there was life and beauty only black and *smoldering ruins* remain." The teacher asks, "What does 'smoldering ruins' mean? What does this paragraph tell us that might help us understand it?" Students respond, "They set fires to the land," and "It's what's left after a fire." Sentence: "The wood in our campfire was burning and all that was left was the smoldering ruins." Similar word: "It's like charcoal." Dictionary definitions: "The definition of *smoldering* is slow, low-temperature burning. The definition of *ruin* is the physical destruction of something." The teacher asks, "Were your predictions right? How do you know?"

Homonym/Homophone/Homograph/Heteronym Vocabulary

PURPOSE: For students to distinguish the meaning of words that are homonyms, homophones, homographs, and heteronyms (in grade 1 and above). **Homonyms** are words that have the same pronunciation and different meanings, and sometimes different spellings. **Homophones** are types of homonyms that sound alike, have different meanings, but also have different spellings (*to, two, too*). **Homographs** are words with the same spellings and different meanings, and sometimes different pronunciations. **Heteronyms** are types of homographs in which two words are spelled the same but sound different (*wind,* pronounced /wĭnd/ and /wīnd/). Note that *bank* for money and *bank* of a river can be considered both a homonym and a homograph.

PROCEDURE: Students write one or two words that are homonyms, homophones, homographs, or heteronyms; write their definitions; draw them; and then use them in sentences. See the example in Figure 3.11.

Vocabulary Building

PURPOSE: For students to define and use vocabulary words (in grade 1 and above).

PROCEDURE: Students write a vocabulary word, predict the definition, write down the dictionary definition, and then draw it. They then predict synonyms and antonyms, and then use a thesaurus to write the actual synonyms and antonyms. Finally, they write three sentences for the word, and then replace the vocabulary with the synonyms to see if it still makes sense. See the example in Figure 3.12.

FIGURE 3.11. Homonym/homophone/homograph/heteronym vocabulary, example.

Homonym vocabulary: *there* and *their*

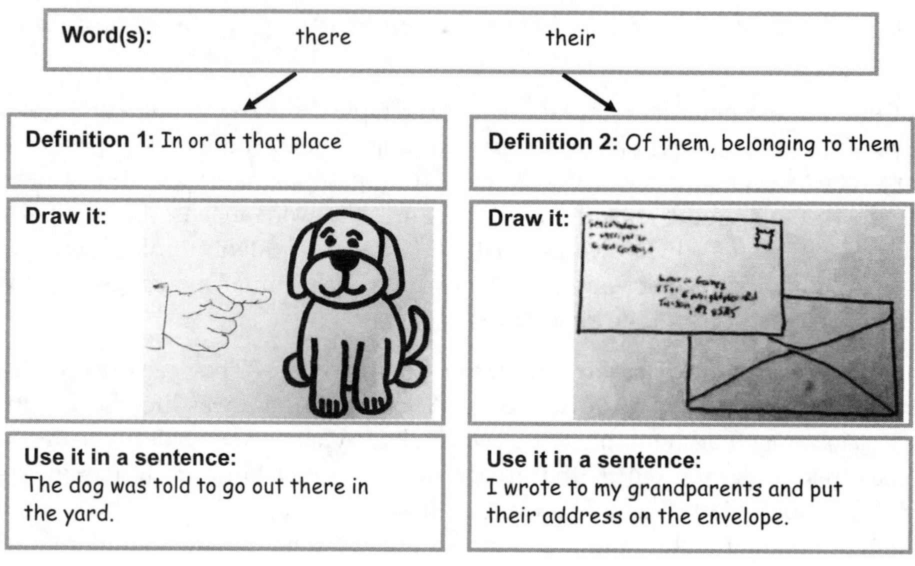

Word(s): there their

Definition 1: In or at that place

Draw it:

Use it in a sentence:
The dog was told to go out there in the yard.

Definition 2: Of them, belonging to them

Draw it:

Use it in a sentence:
I wrote to my grandparents and put their address on the envelope.

FIGURE 3.12. Vocabulary building, example.

Word: reveal **Guess the definition:** To show something
Use it in a sentence: Her smile revealed her white teeth.

Dictionary Definition:
To make known; to display or to show

Draw it:

Predict Synonym: To show
Actual Synonym: To show, display

Predict Antonym: To hide
Actual Antonyms: To hide, to cover up

Use the word in three different sentences to show the meaning.

1. The magician revealed the rabbit to the crowd.
2. She took off her hat and revealed her new haircut.
3. He asked his friend to never reveal his secret to anyone.

Write one of the sentences with a synonym, and another with an antonym.

1. The magician showed the rabbit to the crowd.
2. The magician hid the rabbit from the crowd.

Did it change the meaning of any of the sentences? Yes

• Frayer Model

SOURCE: Frayer, Frederick, and Klausmeier (1969).

PURPOSE: For students to develop word meanings by analyzing a term (definition and characteristics), and to have them synthesize/apply this information by thinking of examples and nonexamples.

PROCEDURE: As the teacher, do the following

1. Explain the Frayer model graphic organizer to the class. Students define a concept, word, or term; describe its essential characteristics; provide examples of the idea; and suggest non-examples from a related category. Use a common word to demonstrate the various components of the form. Model the type and quality of desired answers when giving this example.
2. Select a list of key concepts from a text or topic of study. Write or display the list of words, and review it with the class.
3. Assign each pair of students one of the key concepts, and have them read and use resources to define this concept. Have these groups complete the four-square organizer for this concept.
4. Ask the student pairs to share their conclusions with the entire class. Use these presentations to review the entire list of key concepts. See the example in Figure 3.13.

• Vocabulary Grid or Four-Block Vocabulary (Modified Frayer Model)

PURPOSE: For students to expand and deepen word meanings (in grade 1 and above).

PROCEDURE: For an individual word, a student divides a sheet of paper into four quadrants and writes the vocabulary word in a circle in the center with the part of speech underneath. This is similar to the Frayer model graphic organizer, but the student selects four different ways that would help them understand the word the best from the following list: the

FIGURE 3.13. Frayer model, example.

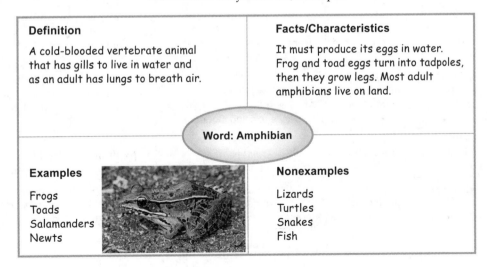

Definition	**Facts/Characteristics**
A cold-blooded vertebrate animal that has gills to live in water and as an adult has lungs to breath air.	It must produce its eggs in water. Frog and toad eggs turn into tadpoles, then they grow legs. Most adult amphibians live on land.
Word: Amphibian	
Examples	**Nonexamples**
Frogs Toads Salamanders Newts	Lizards Turtles Snakes Fish

student's own definition; the sentence where it was found; a new sentence demonstrating understanding of the word; a visual representation (the student draws or inserts a picture or a memory clue); antonyms, synonyms, examples, or nonexamples (homonyms, or words easily confused with the word); characteristics; words with the same base word or root word; word origin; *It is a type of . . .* or *It is part of . . .* ; and pronunciation and syllable. The student labels each quadrant with one of the methods they have chosen. Then the student writes responses based on the heading in each quadrant. Underneath the diagram, the student writes the word in a sentence to show the understanding of the word's meaning.

• Vocabulary Jeopardy

PURPOSE: For students to identify the parts of speech, spelling, or meaning of vocabulary words (in grade 3 and up).

PROCEDURE: This group participation game is similar to the television game show *Jeopardy!*. The following categories are used: Part of Speech (identify what part of speech a word is after hearing it used in a sentence), Spelling (spell the word correctly), Use It (use the word in an original sentence), Synonyms (name the vocabulary word after hearing synonyms for it), and Antonyms (name the vocabulary word after hearing antonyms for it). The teacher places answers in each of the boxes and has the students ask the correct questions. See the example in Figure 3.14.

FIGURE 3.14. Vocabulary Jeopardy, example.

Title: *Hitler's Daughter* — **Author:** Jackie French (2003)

Directions: The teacher identifies vocabulary words from a text or unit of study and sets up the game board from easier to harder with prompts and potential answers. Students play individually or in groups. They first pick a category and a point value (e.g., "Synonyms for $300"). The teacher reads the prompt in parentheses and the student responds with an answer based on the category, not with a question as in the game show *Jeopardy!*. The individual or team with the most money at the end of the game wins.

Part of Speech	Spelling	Use It	Synonyms	Antonyms
$100 *(scrunched)* verb	$100 *(squelched)* s-q-u-e-l-c-h-e-d	$100 *(animated)* Her face was animated when she talked.	$100 *(persisted)* *continued*	$100 *(opinion)* *fact*
$200 *(parka)* noun	$200 *(permitted)* p-e-r-m-i-t-t-e-d	$200 *(enthusiastic)* Anna is enthusiastic when she tells exciting stories.	$200 *(mournfully)* *sad*	$200 *(maximum)* *minimum*
$300 *(obligingly)* adverb	$300 *(gesturing)* g-e-s-t-u-r-i-n-g	$300 *(ointment)* She put ointment on the wound.	$300 *(dismally)* *gloomily*	$300 *(objected)* *agreed*
$400 *(mournful)* adjective	$400 *(negotiated)* n-e-g-o-t-i-a-t-e-d	$400 *(defensively)* Mark acted defensively when he thought that Hitler really had a daughter.	$400 *(paddock)* *pasture*	$400 *(offhandedly)* *purposefully*

• Vocabulary Knowledge Rating

SOURCE: Blachowicz and Fisher (2006).

PURPOSE: For students to rate their own understanding of a word (in grade 3 and above).

PROCEDURE: The teacher lists each vocabulary word from the reading on a chart. The students rate their knowledge for each of the words by placing a checkmark (✓) under the correct category: "Can define it," "Think I know it," "Have heard or seen it," or "Have no clue." They read the text and then discuss the word meanings. Finally, the students write each word in a sentence demonstrating the correct word meaning. See the example in Figure 3.15.

• Vocabulary Self-Collection Strategy

PURPOSE: For students to identify unknown words in text and then define them (in grade 1 and above).

PROCEDURE: While reading, students write down words they cannot pronounce, understand, or are particularly interesting, along with the page number where they can be found. This can be done on sticky notes. The class or group then discusses each word in the context of the story until its meaning is understood.

EXAMPLE: The words *terns* and *noddies* in *The Tale of Rabbit Island* by P. Ching (2002). The students read these sentences and put sticky notes on these two words, and the teacher explains (if necessary) that terns and noddies are birds: "Every chance he got Hapa would spend time with the birds and help them with their chores. He gathered twigs for the sooty terns and noddies to build their nests" (p. 3).

• Vocabulary Wheel

PURPOSE: To expand word meanings (for students in all grades).

PROCEDURE: A student writes a vocabulary word and its part of speech in the center. In circles around it, the student writes synonyms, antonyms, examples, and other forms of the word. The student also writes the word in a sentence and draws a picture. See the example in Figure 3.16.

FIGURE 3.15. Vocabulary knowledge rating, example.

Title: *Wanted . . . Mud Blossom*			**Author:** Betsy Byars	
Word	**Can define it**	**Think I know it**	**Have heard/seen it**	**No clue**
accusation				✓
excavation			✓	
Sentences:				
1. They made an accusation that the girl took the cookie because there were crumbs on her face.				
2. After they dug the hole to the gold, the excavation was done.				

FIGURE 3.16. Vocabulary wheel, example.

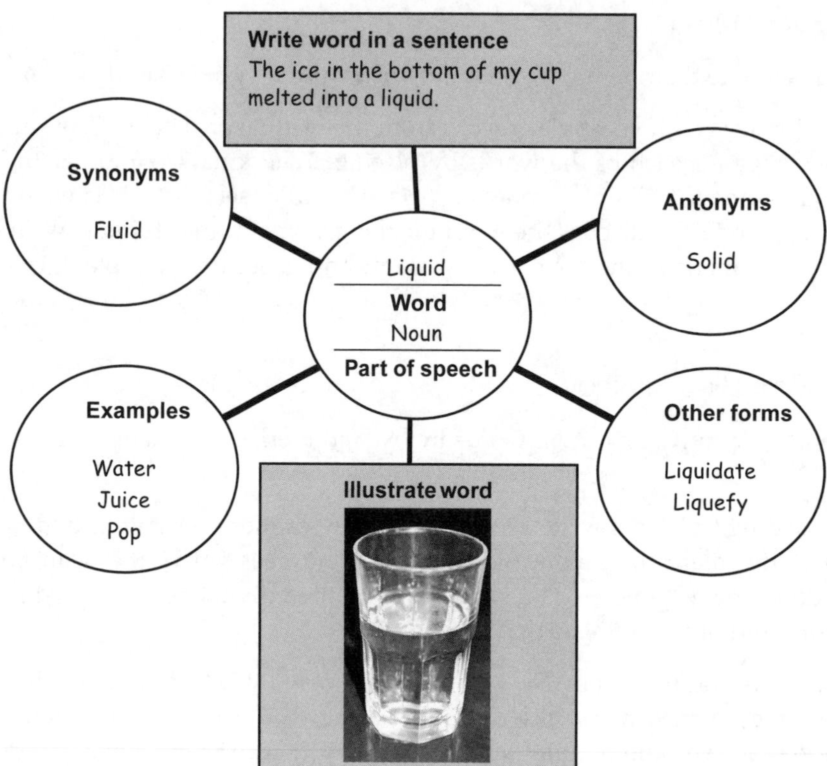

• Word Hunt

PURPOSE: For students to find and define vocabulary words in context (in grade 2 and above).

PROCEDURE: On index cards, students write the following headings for each word: vocabulary word, where I found it, the sentence the word was used, dictionary definition, my definition. Students could also identify words with affixes or Latin or Greek roots in the text.

EXAMPLE: The word *palfrey,* in *Crispin: The Cross of Lead* by Avi (2002, p. 184). Sentence: "It was there I saw a woman riding sidesaddle astride a great black palfrey whose saddle and harness were trimmed with gleaming silver." Predicted definition and reason: "A horse, because they talk about having a saddle and harness." Dictionary definition: A small saddle horse, especially for a lady.

• Word Sort for Word Meaning

SOURCE: Walker (2004).

PURPOSE: For students to categorize words based on meanings or grammatical functions (in all grades).

PROCEDURE: A student or the teacher identifies key words from a text. The students write them on index cards and then group the terms by meanings or grammatical functions. For higher-order development, the students provide the reasons why the terms are grouped together.

EXAMPLE: Word cards: *run, dog, cat, walk, hop, jump, girl, boy.* Sort: *dog, cat, girl, boy* = nouns; *run, walk, hop, jump* = verbs or things they can do.

On Your Own Vocabulary Strategies

PURPOSE: For students to figure out the meanings of unknown words when they are listening or reading and no one is around to help.

PROCEDURE: Students use some or all of the following strategies to predict the word meaning:

1. Read or reread the sentence or paragraph, to see if the meaning of the word can be figured out by the context.
2. Make a prediction about the word's part of speech.
3. Break the word up into word parts: prefix, root, and suffix. Ask yourself, "Do I know the meaning of the word parts, or do I know the meaning of words with the same or similar word parts?"
4. Determine if the word is important to your understanding of the communication or text.
5. If you think it is important, look the word up in the glossary or dictionary.
6. After reading the definition or definitions, reread the sentence to see if it makes sense.
7. Write the word down, along with the definition and a sentence or a drawing to help you remember it.
8. If you determine that the word is not important to the meaning of the text, make a prediction and read on. You might write the word down to learn its meaning later.

Figurative Language Illustrations

PURPOSE: For students to identify and describe the meaning of figurative language as it is used in conversation and text (in grade 3 and above).

PROCEDURE: Students discuss the meaning of the language, and draw first a picture of the literal meaning and then a picture of the implied meaning.

EXAMPLE: The *Amelia Bedelia* books by Peggy Parish are helpful in illustrating how the character takes everything literally. When Amelia is playing baseball and trying to steal a base, for instance, she literally steals or takes all of the bases and then literally runs home to her house. Other examples: *bank*—bank building, piggy bank, river bank.

Semantic Language Strategies for Concepts

A concept is a mental representation, image, or idea of a tangible and concrete object or an intangible idea or feeling. Visual and auditory information facilitates the development of concepts. The following strategies help students not only develop a broader sense of concepts, but develop important mental processes: identifying associated objects or ideas, analyzing and discriminating between ideas, grouping and regrouping them based on their similarities and relationships, and synthesizing information through summarizing and forming generalizations.

Concept of Definition

SOURCE: Schwartz and Raphael (1985).

PURPOSE: For students to define concepts based on categories, properties, and illustrations.

PROCEDURE: Using context and a dictionary, students complete the three parts of a concept definition map, as shown in the example in Figure 3.17.

Concept Ladder

SOURCE: Gillet and Temple (1994).

PURPOSE: For students to identify hierarchical concept relationships.

PROCEDURE: Using context, background knowledge, the dictionary, and the internet, students complete each step of the concept ladder by answering the questions about the concept. This strategy will expand the students' understanding of this concept. See the example in Figure 3.18.

Labeling Diagrams

PURPOSE: For students to use diagrams to identify word meanings.

PROCEDURE: Students add vocabulary labels to drawings.

EXAMPLES: The skeletal system of the human body, the water cycle, or the life cycle of a butterfly.

FIGURE 3.17. Concept definition map, example.

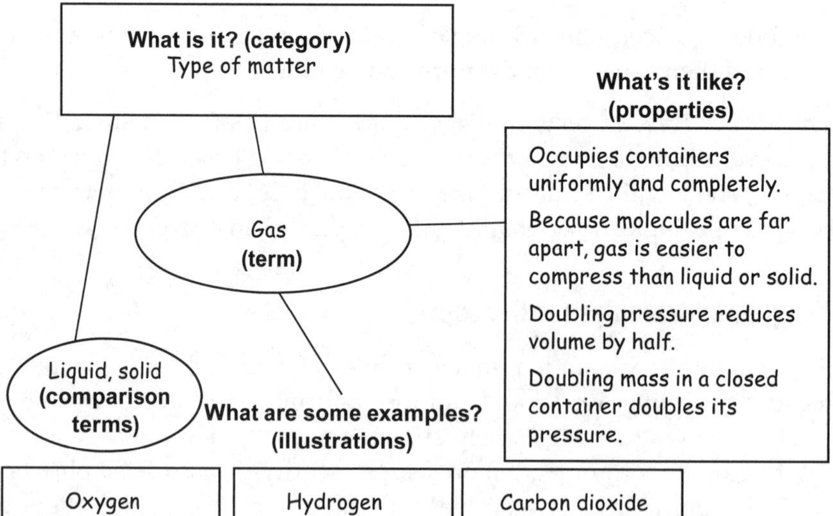

FIGURE 3.18. Concept ladder, example.

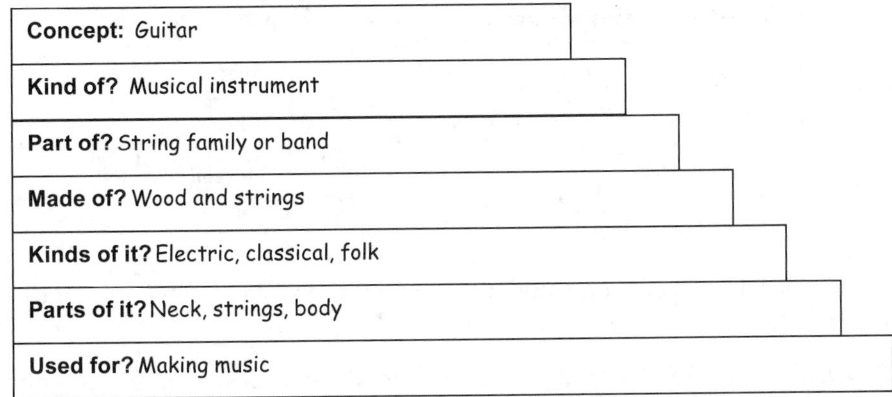

Concept: Guitar
Kind of? Musical instrument
Part of? String family or band
Made of? Wood and strings
Kinds of it? Electric, classical, folk
Parts of it? Neck, strings, body
Used for? Making music

• Linear Array

SOURCE: Nagy (1988).

PURPOSE: For students to show linear relationships of degrees of variation in words.

PROCEDURE: A student draws an array in a line with points marked with words in sequence. See the example in Figure 3.19.

• List–Group–Label

SOURCE: Taba (1967, cited in Tierney & Readence, 2005).

PURPOSE: For students to organize words based on their relationships to each other and label the relationships.

PROCEDURE: A student or the teacher identifies key words from a text and writes them on index cards. The students then group the terms by their relationships to each other. For higher-order development, the students provide the labels. See the example in Figure 3.20.

• Mnemonic Devices

PURPOSE: To assist students (in grade 3 and above) in remembering concepts or the order of concepts by learning a mnemonic device.

PROCEDURE: The teacher identifies a topic with several subtopics that the students need to

FIGURE 3.19. Linear array, example.

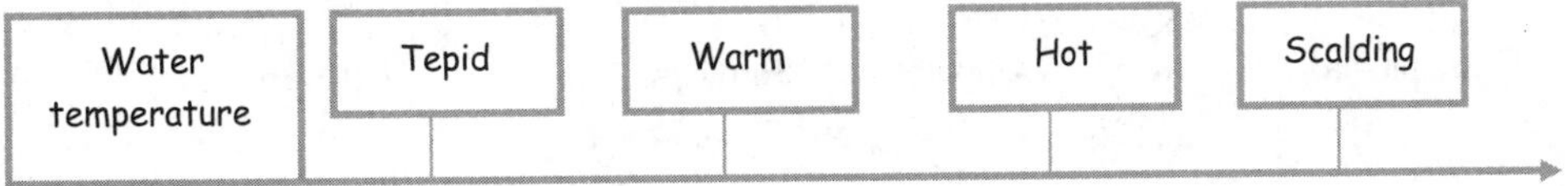

FIGURE 3.20. List–group–label responses, examples.

Digestive System	Circulatory System	Respiratory System
esophagus	heart	trachea
stomach	blood vessels	lungs
intestines	arteries	alveoli

remember in order. The teacher and students then use the first letter of each word to create a sentence or a phrase.

EXAMPLE: Scientists use the following categories to classify living things: kingdom, phylum, class, order, family, genus, and species. In order to remember the order, students can use the following sentence as a mnemonic device: "Kids Prefer Cheese Over Fried Green Spinach."

• Schematic Word Map

SOURCE: Tierney and Readence (2005).

PURPOSE: For students to identify key concepts, using lines to show how words are hierarchically related.

PROCEDURE: The teacher defines the target concept, presents the concept, and begins constructing the hierarchy. The teacher guides students to relevant and irrelevant attributes, and students then complete the map with additional examples and nonexamples.

EXAMPLE: In Figure 3.21, based on the concept of *reptiles,* the supraordinate concepts would be *cold-blooded, vertebrate,* and *animal* at the top of the hierarchy. A coordinate concept at the same level would be *amphibians,* while subordinate concepts would be examples such as *alligators, snakes,* and *lizards.*

FIGURE 3.21. Schematic word map, example.

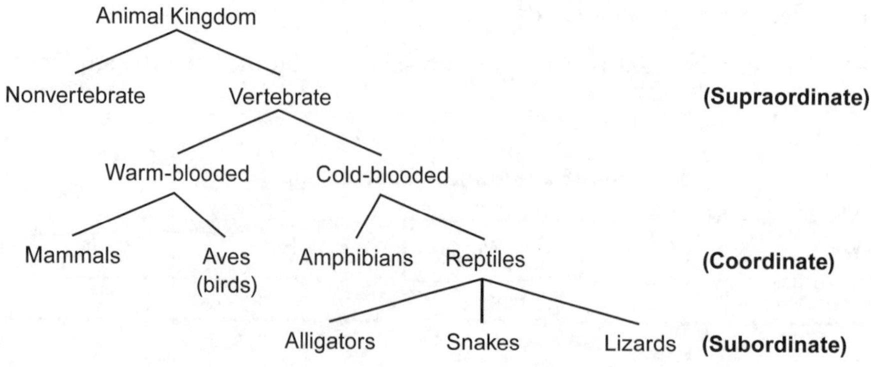

Semantic Feature Analysis Matrix

SOURCE: Johnson and Pearson (1984).

PURPOSE: For students to sort out the similarities and differences among a group of events, people, objects, or ideas.

PROCEDURE: The teacher places items to be classified on the left side of the matrix, and attributes that make them similar and different at the top. The students classify each item by its attributes, by putting a plus sign (+) or a minus sign (–) in each cell of the matrix to indicate the presence or absence of each feature. See the example in Figure 3.22.

Semantic Mapping

SOURCE: Johnson and Pearson (1984).

PURPOSE: For students to expand and develop a definition of a word by using a graphic organizer in which ovals represent concepts and the arrows and word boxes represent the relationships or properties of the word.

PROCEDURE: The teacher writes the concept in the center oval; then students supply descriptors, examples, and what it is used for, with arrows connecting them. See the example in Figure 3.23.

FIGURE 3.22. Semantic feature analysis matrix, example.

Categorizing Animals				
	Live In Water	Breathe Air	Lay Eggs	Have Fur
Whales	+	+	-	-
Seals	+ (sometimes)	+	-	+
Sharks	+	-	+	-
Fish	+	-	+	-
Bears	-	+	-	+
Snakes	- (rarely)	+	+	-
Toads	+ (young) - (adults)	- (young) + (adults)	+	-

FIGURE 3.23. Semantic mapping, example.

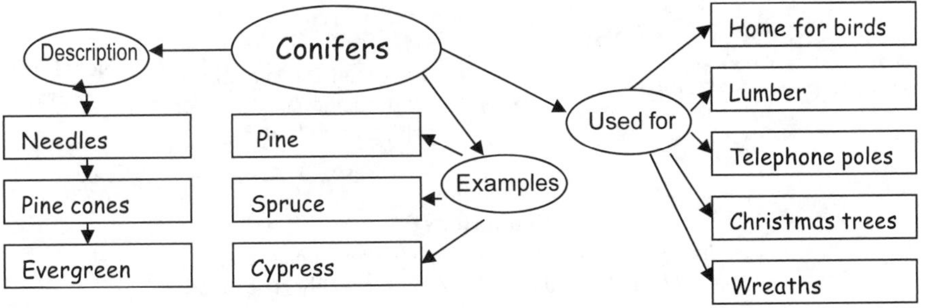

• Venn Diagram

PURPOSE: To help studevnts (in all grades) compare and contrast two or three concepts.

PROCEDURE: The teacher draws two or three interlocking circles and labels these circles with the concepts. In the center, where the circles intersect, students write the attributes that the concepts have in common. See the example in Figure 3.24.

ADAPTATION: A diagram shaped like the letter *H* is used for two concepts. Attributes of one concept are written on the left side of the *H*, and those of the other concept are written on the right side. Similarities are written on the crossbar of the *H*.

DIFFERENTIATION: For a challenge, the teacher asks students to create their own graphic organizers. For support, the teacher can prefill in portions of a graphic organizer.

• Idea Web Assessment

SOURCE: Ogle and Correa (2007).

PURPOSE: To gauge students' prior knowledge when used as a pretest, or to determine knowledge learned when used as a posttest (for students in grade 3 and above).

PROCEDURE: Students choose words from a list and put them under the appropriate category or concept. They can use as many of the words as they know, and they can only use each word once. Some categories may have blank spaces, even though all of the words have been used. See the example in Figure 3.25.

DIFFERENTIATION: For a challenge, the teacher does not provide any headings and the students can create their own headings. Students can work in groups for support. For ELLs, images can be added to the words.

Pragmatic Language Strategies

• Think–Pair–Share Language Strategy

PURPOSE: To differentiate instruction by providing all students time and structure for thinking on a given topic, enabling them to formulate individual ideas and orally share these ideas with peers. It helps students develop conceptual understandings of a topic, the ability to filter information and draw conclusions, and the ability to consider other points of view.

FIGURE 3.24. Venn diagram, example.

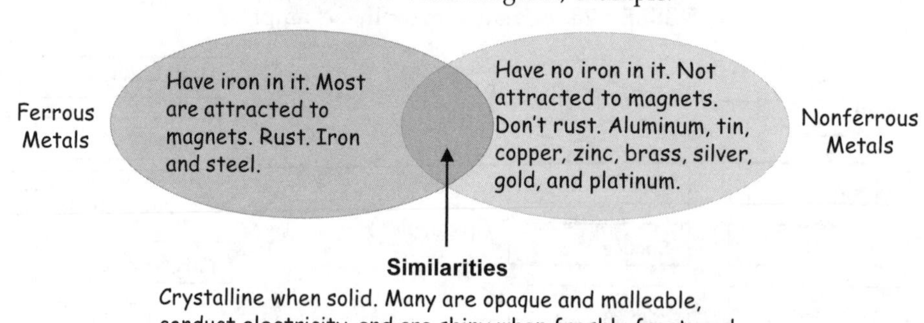

FIGURE 3.25. Idea web assessment, example (arthropod vocabulary).

antennae	exoskeleton	mantises	entomologist	arachnid	molting
thorax	cephalothorax	crayfish	abdomen	wasps	myriapod
invertebrate	scorpion	crustacean	migration	compound eye	
beetles	insecta	pollination	centipedes	metamorphosis	

Arthropods

Classification
- myriapod
- invertebrate
- arachnid
- insecta
- crustacean

Body Parts
- exoskeleton
- thorax
- abdomen
- cephalothorax
- antennae
- compound eye

Examples
- beetles
- centipedes
- scorpions
- crayfish
- wasps
- mantises

Study and Behaviors
- migration
- pollination
- metamorphosis
- molting
- entomologist

PROCEDURE: As the teacher, do the following:

1. Explain that the *think–pair–share* strategy is intended to give everyone an opportunity to talk and share their ideas and listen to the ideas of others. It has three steps: Each student (a) thinks individually about a topic or answer to a question; (b) pairs with a partner and discuss the topic or question; and (c) shares ideas with the rest of the class, sometimes sharing what the partner said.
2. Model the procedure with a student, using something familiar and closed-ended, such as "Who are the members of your family?" Model thinking, pairing with the student/partner, and sharing with the class. Then ask for a volunteer to pair with the first student and repeat the procedure.
3. Now pose a specific higher-level question or make a statement related to the topic your class is studying.
4. Say, "*Think* about what you know or have learned about ____________ [topic], and answer the question I asked. You will have ____ minutes" (usually 1–2 minutes).
5. "*Pair* with a partner, and share your thinking, compare ideas, and ask questions of your partner about their thoughts on the topic for ____ minutes" (usually 2–5 minutes). You may choose whether to assign pairs or let students pick their own partners. Remember to be sensitive to learners' needs (language skills, reading skills, attention skills) when creating pairs. Walk around, monitor, and support students as they share. You may also ask students to write their responses while doing the think–pair–share activity.

6. Say, "It's group *share* time; please share the ideas of your partner and also your own ideas." You can choose students to share based on listening to the paired conversations, or you can ask, "Who would like to share their partner's and their ideas?"
7. Then expand the sharing into a whole-class discussion about the different responses. After the class members share, you may choose to have pairs reconvene to talk about how their thinking might have changed as a result of the share element.

EXAMPLE: *Think:* "What is a tree? I want each of you to think about trees and what you know about them." *Pair:* "Now turn to the person next to you, and talk about your responses and the similarities and differences in ideas." Partner 1 says, "A tree is something you can climb," and Partner 2 says, "A tree has branches and a trunk." The partners agree that both of them have described a tree. *Share:* "Who would like to share their ideas with the class?" Partner 1 says, "We think a tree has branches, leaves, and a trunk, and is good for climbing." You then ask, "How has our understanding of a tree become better as a result of the think–pair–share strategy?"

• Discourse Moves for Student Talk

SOURCE: Blanke (2018).

PURPOSE: For students to engage in deeper conversations/discussions and ask questions of each other.

PROCEDURE: The following are seven different discourse moves, with a brief explanation of each.

1. *Revoicing.* The teacher or student revoices another student's contribution and then asks if their interpretation was accurate. Prompts can include "So you are saying that . . . ?" or "So let me clarify . . . " or "Is this what you were saying?"
2. *Repeating.* The teacher or the student restates what was said in their own words and reflects on what was said. Prompts can include "Can you repeat what ____________ [name] said in your own words?" or "Is what ____________ said what you meant? Does it need clarification?"
3. *Reasoning.* The teacher asks students to apply their own reasoning about someone else's ideas. This helps students build connections between differing ideas. Prompts can include "Were you thinking the same thing, or do you have a different idea? Why?"
4. *Adding on.* The teacher prompts students to add on to another student's idea. Prompts can include "Who can say something more about this?" or "Who can explain why this is a good idea?"
5. *Wait time.* The teacher and students need to provide students with extra time to process information, formulate ideas, develop arguments, and ask questions. Prompts can include "Take your time to think," or "Hands down, and think silently about this."
6. *Pass it on.* The teacher asks students to refrain from raising their hands, and asks them instead to share ideas in pairs or a group and then share with the class ideas from their peers. Prompts can include "When your peers share, remember to ask the clarifying questions," or "Does anyone have anything to share about my idea?"
7. *Think-alouds.* The teacher models how to think and talk about ideas and problems. Prompts include: "When I read or heard about this ____________, I thought about ____________," "This is similar to ____________ that we learned about before," or "One strategy I might try is ____________."

Sentence and Paragraph Starters

PURPOSE: To scaffold responses for students (in all grades, and especially for ELLs), in order to help them answer questions or provide information while lowering the linguistic demands. These strategies allow students to focus on the content words and phrases that demonstrate their knowledge and understanding, without having to focus on how to put words together in coherent sentences.

PROCEDURE: As the teacher, do the following:

1. Identify the content and critical vocabulary necessary for social or topical communication.
2. Identify the level of support needed for individuals or groups of students.
3. Create sentence starters, which are the initial phrases of declarative or interrogative sentences that the speakers are to complete. These sentence starters are usually open-ended, but they scaffold how to start the sentence.
4. Model how to complete a sentence starter orally, using phrases in common use by the group.
5. Have the speaker restate the sentence starter and then orally complete it to communicate information.
6. Adapt the complexity of the starter to the learners' content and language skills. As the students' language usage improves, use more complex starters. A paragraph starter is based on the same idea, except that a whole sentence is provided to begin an entire paragraph.

EXAMPLES: Sentence starters include "May I please . . . "; "I would like to . . . because . . . "; "This reminds me of . . . "; "The main idea is . . . "; "This is interesting because . . . "

DIFFERENTIATION: For more support or for ELLs, after you ask a question such as "What are the three primary colors?", give the sentence starter "The three primary colors are . . . "

Sentence and Paragraph Frames

PURPOSE: To scaffold responses for students (in all grades, and especially for ELLs), in order to help them communicate and comprehend information while lowering the linguistic demand. Again, these strategies allow students to focus on the content words and phrases that demonstrate their knowledge and understanding, without having to focus on how to put words together in coherent sentences.

PROCEDURE: As the teacher, do the following

1. Identify the content and critical vocabulary necessary for comprehension of a topic.
2. Identify the level of support needed for individuals or groups of students.
3. Create a sentence frame, which is a sentence with blanks that a speaker or writer needs to fill in with single words or short phrases, based on instructional content or background knowledge. Adapt the complexity of the frame to the learners' content and language skills. You can provide a word bank for exact answers, or these frames can be open-ended.
4. Model how to complete a sentence frame, using common background knowledge for the group. As the students' language usage improves, use more complex frames. A paragraph frame is based on the same idea, except that an entire paragraph is used. For

the paragraph, you can use different linguistic or text structures with words signaling description (characteristics), sequencing (*first, next, then*), comparison–contrast (*similar, different*), problem–solution, and cause–effect (*if . . . then*).

EXAMPLES:

Sentence frame example: "Animals need ___________ to eat, ___________ to drink, ___________ for protection, and space to ___________." (*food, water, shelter, survive*)

Open-ended sentence frame example: "My opinion is ___________ because ___________. I think that ___________ will happen because ___________."

• Making Connections

PURPOSE: To provide opportunities for students to have meaningful communication with others by connecting ideas to themselves, their environment, the world, and text.

PROCEDURE: As the teacher, do the following:

1. To help students connect ideas to *themselves,* ask them to talk about various aspects of themselves (such as their family, friends, feelings, likes, and dislikes) during sharing or show-and-tell time. Provide opportunities for make-believe or role play, including pretending about home living, jobs, and travel. Providing puppets, stuffed animals, action figures, and dolls to talk with often encourages reluctant speakers.
2. To help students connect ideas to their *environment,* ask them to talk about their experiences inside and outside the school environment. Take students on field trips (such as to a grocery store, post office, bank, zoo, park, museum, library, or hospital), and have them discuss what they learned. While there, ask for or give explanations of what is happening and what might happen next. Play games such as "I spy with my little eye something ___________" (describe it and see if they can find it), or an alphabet game where the students need to come up with adjectives or adverbs for each letter. Ask students questions about the world around them. "How," "why," and "tell me" questions encourage the students to think more deeply and answer with more than one word. Plan science, art, music, and food preparation activities that encourage discussion and vocabulary development.
3. To help students connect ideas to *literature and media,* have them share and discuss ideas and themes from a variety of fiction and nonfiction literature and media. Plan thematic units, and provide numerous opportunities for discussion and language development. Gradually increase the complexity of ideas and vocabulary in the texts. Talk about the content, graphics, and connection to other texts. Ask a variety of "wh-" questions. Ask, "What was the most important message?" Have the students retell the story or text by looking at the pictures or from memory using the language from the text. Students can even make up stories together based on common story structures, such as "Once upon a time, I met . . ." Older students can write limericks such as "There once was an old man from . . ." Provide opportunities for students to express themselves orally through story retellings, puppetry, drama, songs, finger plays, nursery rhymes, jokes, riddles, and poetry readings. It is also beneficial for students to share a summary of what they learned each day or after each lesson. For more specific suggestions for using puppets and giving oral presentations, see the next few strategies.

Puppets: Connecting Oral Language and Reading

SOURCE: Kathleen Weber (personal communication, 2001).

PURPOSE: To enhance students' oral language development; to help them connect oral language to texts; to develop creative expression of characterization, voice inflection, and storyline; to improve comprehension skills (main idea, details, sequence, setting, plot); to promote cooperative learning strategies; to develop the performance or audience connection; to integrate discipline content with language arts; to involve families with the learning process through project-based lessons; and to have students apply art concepts and skills in the creation of puppets and props.

PROCEDURE: As the teacher, do the following:

1. Create or purchase a stage.
2. Create puppets that go with specific characters in books, or more generic puppets that can be used for multiple purposes.
3. Create either dialogue based on the text or original dialogue. Be sure to identify and include important vocabulary and clear story structure.
4. Create different voices for each of the characters.
5. Act out the story or dialogue with expression in front of the students.
6. Have the students take turns acting out the same story, using specified vocabulary and structure.
7. Have students select a story or part of a story from literature, adapt a story, or create one themselves. Remind them to determine which important words and text structures they want to include.
8. Have them create their own puppets.
9. Have them create different voices for each of the puppets.
10. Have the students tell the story with expression, using their puppets in front of the class, school, and/or family members.

The puppets can be of various sizes and can be made from a variety of materials. Possibilities include stick puppets, finger and hand puppets, puppets in a cup, "big mouth" puppets, sock puppets, and glove puppets. Stuffed animals can even be made into puppets by removing stuffing from their back ends/bottoms and sewing in gloves or mittens. Stages can also be created from a variety of materials. A stage can be made with a fabric sheet pinned across a doorway. A television stage can be made from a cardboard box. A stage can even be made with a piece of long paper as the foreground, or a "roll play" can be made with a large roll of paper.

What's in the Bag?

PURPOSE: For students to develop descriptive oral language skills when talking in front of the class.

PROCEDURE: The teacher models the strategy by placing an object in a bag and preplanning clues to describe its characteristics, such as shape, size, texture, material, purpose, and where it may be found. The teacher then holds the closed bag and describes the object without stating what it is. The first clues should be general and then become more specific. The students then have to predict what the object is, based on the clues provided. The students then go home and select an object to put in a bag. With the help of family members, each student rereads the example and writes clues on an index card. The student then brings the object in the bag and the clues to class. Each student stands in front of the class and provides clues for their peers to guess what's in the bag. The teacher can help prompt students to use the written clues.

EXAMPLE: The teacher says, "I am made of smooth metal and plastic. I can be opened to put small pieces of metal inside. You push down on me. I am used to keep papers together. What am I?" (Answer: A stapler.)

Oral Presentations for Language Development

PURPOSE: For students to develop an effective oral presentation with the six major elements of language, organization, content, visual media, manner, and audience participation, in order to share information with their peers.

PROCEDURE: The teacher provides opportunities for students to express themselves orally through oral presentations of a topic they are familiar with or have researched. Familiar topics include sharing family stories, their favorite book, or favorite activity. Students can also research science, social studies, math, literature, arts, or sports topics. The teacher and students discuss each of the following elements: language, organization, content, manner, visual media, and audience participation; the *Oral Presentation Assessment* (see Appendix, pp. 389–391) can be used as a basis for this discussion. The teacher provides both appropriate and inappropriate examples of each heading, such as the following:

- For *language,* a student presenter should use appropriate language for the audience, convey information clearly to the audience, and use formal grammar structures. Questions to consider: "Who is my target audience? What do they already know about the subject?"
- For *organization,* it is important to have a clear structure so that the audience can understand the information easily. The presentation should include an introduction that captures the interest of the audience and tells why the audience would want to know about this. The presenter should tell the audience exactly what they want to say, say it, summarize the main ideas of what was said, and leave enough time for questions.
- For *content* in a 10-minute presentation, the student should keep to about three main ideas. Examples for a presentation about family events: background about the family and the historical period; the key events; and the effects, memories, and reflections of the events.
- For *manner,* the student should practice the presentation in front of a mirror until they are comfortable with the material and can speak clearly, audibly, and at an understandable pace. The student should practice correctly pronouncing difficult words. They can use notes with major headings, key words, and a few choice sentences, but should try to maintain eye contact with the audience (looking throughout the room, not just at one or two people). Also, the student should be aware of and avoid nervous gestures.
- For *visual media,* it is useful for the presentation to include visual material that is relevant and enhances the content, such as computer presentations, web links, transparencies, video, photographs, slides, charts, or objects (such as clothing or family treasures). The student should be sure to present the visuals at the appropriate points during the presentation.

- For *audience participation*, the student provides an opportunity for the audience to interact. This can be done through asking or answering questions during or after the presentation. It is important to allow time at the end for the audience to ask the presenter questions.

Finally, feedback is important to enhancing oral presentation skills. The teacher and the other students should use the six major elements to give feedback on strengths and areas for improvement.

Switching Registers

PURPOSE: For students to improve the choices of language that they make during social interactions, as well as the effects of these choices on others.

PROCEDURE: The teacher demonstrates a formal register and helps students to identify when they are not using a formal register. The teacher explains to the students that there are many different registers in the English language. How students speak at home may be different from how they speak to their grandparents, or how they speak with their friends. In school, students should be taught to use a formal register, also referred to as Standard English, so that they can be clearly understood by people from a variety of communities. For older students, the teacher can explain that a television report showed that people who use Standard English are more likely to get hired for higher-paying jobs than those who do not. Since students may not be aware of the differences in syntax between their natural speech and standard speech, it is important to teach these differences explicitly. Since writing is usually a formal form of communication, it is beneficial to use writing to point out differences between Standard English and a student's natural English. Students can write down common statements that they use, and then the teacher or class can help the students rewrite these in Standard English.

Detecting Changing Language

PURPOSE: For students to identify and demonstrate understanding of words based on language change categories.

PROCEDURE: Using the categories in Table 3.14 (see p. 72), such as borrowing words from other languages, students identify words or phrases from language and texts as examples of these change categories.

EXAMPLE: "IM me tonight and let me know what's up." *IM* is an abbreviation for *instant messaging* and is an example of using an abbreviation or acronym as a new term. There are many new terms of this type, due to advances in technology.

Chapter 4

Word Analysis

UNDERSTANDING WORD ANALYSIS

When students engage in **word analysis**, they start with the concept of the whole word, then examine the grapho-phonemic and morphemic parts that make up that word, and finally apply this knowledge when reading and writing the word to understand and communicate meaning. Reading and writing build on the wealth of oral language skills that children begin developing long before they enter school. Oral and written language share many features, such as similar vocabulary (semantics), grammar (morphology and syntax), and purposes (pragmatics). In addition to the oral language features, to construct meaning from the printed language during reading or communicate meaning during writing, students must apply **grapho-phonemic** knowledge: the recognition of symbols or letters, and the understanding that letters or symbols represent sounds of speech in written words. This knowledge is also often referred to as phonics or the alphabetic principle. A **grapheme** is a written symbol of a phoneme or speech sound that is the smallest unit of writing in a language, such as alphabetic letters, numerical digits, Chinese characters, or other individual symbols. The 26 letters in the English alphabet make up 70 graphemes, also called **phonograms**, that represent approximately 44 English phonemes or sounds (depending on dialect). Graphemes or sequences of them are placed between angle brackets to represent written letters (e.g., the word *chair* is made up of three graphemes: <ch>, <ai>, and <r>). A **phoneme** is the smallest unit of sound that distinguishes one word from another in a particular language. Phonemes include sounds represented by a single letter, as well as sounds represented by letter combinations such as consonant and vowel digraphs or diphthongs. Phonemes are written between slashes to represent individual sounds (e.g., /b/ /ă/ /th/ to indicate the three phonemes in *bath*). If you are writing a phonetic transcription of what a student says, there is only one slash between each phoneme (e.g., /b/ă/th/).

Spanish is a more phonetic language than English because there is almost a one-to-one correspondence between the 27 letters and the 24 sounds or phonemes. Spanish has only five vowel sounds and 19 consonant sounds, using 27 letters (the English letters and the addition of *ñ*). In Spanish, <ch>, <ll>, and <rr> are no longer considered separate letters, but consonant digraph phonemes. Like English, Spanish has both a hard and a soft sound for *c* and *g*. In Spanish, the consonant phonemes of /s/, /b/, and /y/ have more than one spelling, and <h> is silent.

Reading and writing are reciprocal processes referred to as decoding and encoding. **Decoding** is the process of reading words in text—for example, "My dog likes bones." The decoding process requires several steps: A person must (1) recognize each letter, (2) associate the sound represented by the letters, (3) understand how the letter sounds work together to make words, and (4) blend the letter sounds together to form words in speech or in the mind. **Encoding** is the process of using sound and letter knowledge to write words. For example, in order to write the same sentence, it is necessary to (1) identify the word to be written, (2) segment the sounds of the word, (3) recall the letter or letters represented by that sound, and then (4) write the letters in order. Initially, decoding and encoding are controlled cognitive processes; that is, significant amounts of attention and effort are required. Eventually, with more literacy experiences, decoding and encoding become more automatic processes, where less attention and effort are needed to read and write individual words.

Word analysis in this text is organized around the following concepts: phonological awareness, the alphabetic principle, emergent text concepts, word identification, and orthography. While these processes are interrelated, their descriptions, goals, assessments, and strategies are addressed separately, so that they can be more clearly understood. In teaching these processes, it is important to think about a whole–part–whole model. As the teacher, start with written or oral text that includes the concepts you want students to learn; teach a specific word analysis skill or strategy; then apply the skills and strategies to reading or writing a new text.

Phonological Awareness

Terms such as phonological awareness, phonemic awareness, and even phonics are frequently confused. **Phonological awareness** is the ability to recognize that speech is made up of sentences or phrases that can be divided into words, and that words can be further divided into smaller units of sound, such as syllables, onsets, and rimes, and finally into individual sounds or phonemes (Johnson & Roseman, 2003). A **syllable** is a unit of pronunciation having one vowel sound, with or without surrounding consonants, and forming a word or a part of a word. For example, the words *I* and *cat* have one syllable, *baby* (/bā/ /bē/) has two syllables, and *animal* (/ă/ /nĭ/ /məl/) has three. The term **onset** corresponds to the consonant or consonant cluster (also called a consonant blend) before the initial vowel sound, such as /st/ in the word *stop*. The term **rime** corresponds to the vowel–consonant cluster at the end of a one-syllable word, such as /op/ in *stop*. Rimes can also consist of just vowels, as in the word *see*, where /s/ is the onset and /ee/ is the rime. Some words such as the word *at* have a rime, but no onset.

Phonemic awareness, the final stage in phonological awareness, is the ability to recognize that a spoken word consists of a sequence of individual sounds or phonemes, to distinguish between different phonemes, and to manipulate phonemes in words to change their meaning (Yopp & Yopp, 2000b). Phonemes are combined to form syllables and words. For example, the word *cat* is made up of three distinct English phonemes: /k/, /ă/, and /t/. If the initial phoneme is changed from /k/ to /s/, the result is the word *sat*, which is a new word with a different meaning. Some phonemes sound very similar and are sometimes difficult to distinguish, such as the final phoneme in the words *half* and *have,* where /f/ is a voiceless consonant and /v/ is the corresponding voiced consonant. Acquiring phonemic awareness is important because it is the foundation for spelling and word recognition skills. ELLs may have difficulties distinguishing between English phonemes that are not in their native language. For example, /sh/ does not exist in Spanish, and therefore ELLs whose first language is Spanish may confuse the words *ship* and *chip.* Also, in Spanish, when *g* is followed by *e* or *i,* it sounds like *h* in English.

As noted earlier, some phonemic sounds correspond to individual letters, such as /ă/ in *apple;* other phonemes are made up of combinations of letters, such as the consonant digraph /th/ in *that* or the diphthong /oy/ in *boy.* According to a meta-analysis of evidence from the National Reading Panel (Ehri et al., 2001), phonemic awareness instruction helps students learn to read and write. However, learning phonemes in the context of words within stories makes them more meaningful and easier to learn. There are two major processes involved in phonemic awareness: segmenting and blending. **Segmenting** is the process of hearing a spoken word and distinguishing each of the phonemes (e.g., *fish* → /f/ /ĭ/ /sh/). Segmenting phonemes is beneficial for isolating individual phonemes in words in order to spell words. **Blending** is the process of hearing the phonemes and putting them together to form a word (e.g., /f/ /ĭ/ /sh/ → *fish*). This skill is beneficial for putting sounds together in order to read words. Phonological awareness and phonemic awareness are only auditory processes, whereas phonics, a term that is often confused with them, is both an auditory and a visual process. **Phonics** is one method of teaching people to read by correlating sounds with letters or groups of letters in an alphabetic writing system. However, phonics is only one aspect of learning to read, as students must also use morphemic, syntactic, semantic, and pragmatic cues.

Alphabetic Principle

The **alphabetic principle** is the understanding that letters represent sounds, which form words; it is the knowledge of the predictable relationships between written letters and spoken sounds. **Phonics** is a way of teaching the relationships between the sounds of a language and the letters used to represent those sounds. Phonics begins with letter and sound identification. Phonics is then used during the decoding process to read words, as well as during the encoding process to write or spell words. Although phonics is essential for learning to read, it must be coupled with other word identification and comprehension strategies (which include using morphemics, syntax, semantics, and pragmatics) in order to make reading meaningful. The English language is a semiphonetic language, in that letters or combinations of letters can represent more than one sound—for example, *-ough* makes six sounds (*bought, though, through, drought, rough,* and *cough*). The same sound can be represented by one or more different combinations of letters (e.g., *ate, eight, pale, pail,* and *lay*). Therefore, phonics alone cannot be used to identify all words, and context must be used.

There are several types of phonemes or sounds in the English language. The following definitions are based on those in *The Literacy Dictionary* (Harris & Hodges, 1995). A **consonant** is a speech sound made by partially or completely closing part of the vocal tract, while a **vowel** is a voiced speech sound, made without stoppage or restriction of the air flow as it passes through the vocal tract. The **long vowel** sounds have a relatively long duration of time in which the sound is stressed and the vocal cords are tense. In English, they are also the names of the alphabet letters that are phonetically represented with a **macron** or bar over them: ā, ē, ī, ō, and ū. The **short vowel** sounds have a relatively short duration, or a weak stress of the vowel sound, and the vocal cords are relaxed or lax. They are phonetically represented with a **breve** (similar to a *u*) over them: ă, ĕ, ĭ, ŏ, and ŭ, as heard in *bat, bet, bit, blot,* and *but.* The **schwa** is a midcentral vowel in an unaccented or unstressed syllable, such as the initial vowel in the word *alone* (əlōn) or the final vowel in the word *table* (tābəl). It is represented with an upside-down *e*, written ə. A **diphthong** is a vowel sound produced when the tongue moves or glides from one vowel sound to another vowel or semivowel sound in the same syllable, such as in the words *boy* and *coin* (/ōē/) or *cow* and *bough* (/ŏŏ/). Technically, the long *a* (/āē/) and long *i* (/īē/) are also diphthongs. A diphthong is written as a digraph, trigraph, or tetragraph; that is, it is written with multiple letters. **Vowel digraphs** and **trigraphs** are two, three, or four letters that represent a single vowel sound. Examples include *ai, ea, ee, ei, eigh, ey, ie, igh, oa, oo, ou* (/ŭ/), and *ow* (/ō/). **Controlled vowels** are those vowels that change their sound because they are followed by an /r/, /l/, or /w/ sound. The vocalic *-r* or /er/ sound can be written with *er, ir, ur, wor, ear,* and *ar.* A mnemonic device to remember them is the following sentence: "H*er* f*ir*st n*ur*se *wor*ks *ear*ly on gramm*ar*." The underline means that the *w* needs to be in front of *or* to make the /er/ sound. Vowel digraphs, trigraphs, and tetragraphs, or diphthongs collectively, are often referred to as vowel teams; English has 25 standard vowel teams. There are 18 different vowel sounds, but these are written with only five vowel letters. The letters *y, w, gh,* and *r* are also used in representations of vowel sounds. Vowel teams are probably the most common sources of reading and spelling mistakes.

A **consonant digraph** consists of two consonants that represent one sound. This combination of letters can create a brand-new sound, as in these examples:

<th>: /th/, *this*, or voiceless /th/, *thin*

<ch>: /ch/, *chair*, /k/, *chorus*, or /sh/, *chef*

<wh>: /hw/, *what*

/sh/: <ti>, *nation*, <ci>*facial*, or <si>*session*

<ph>: /f/, *phone*

One of the letters can be silent, as in these examples:

<gh>: /g/, *ghost*

<ng>: nasal n /ng/, *sing*

<ck>: /k/, *truck*

<dge>: /j/, *edge*

<gn>: /n/, *gnat*

<wr>: /r/, *write*

<kn>: /k/, *know*

<pn>: /n/, *pneumonia*

<rh>: /r/, *rhyme*

<mb>: /m/, *thumb*

A **consonant blend** or cluster is a sequence of two or more distinguishable consonant sounds before or after a vowel sound, such as *str* in *street* within a single syllable. The final terms are **hard and soft *c* and *g*** sounds—for example, the hard *c-* (/k/) in *cat* and the soft *c-* (/s/) in *city*, or the hard *g-* (/g/) in *goat* and the soft *g-* (/j/) in *giant*. The *Individual Phonics Summary* provides a chart with these phonetic elements (see Appendix, p. 414).

Emergent Text Concepts

One aspect of emergent reading is having a basic understanding of how the English written language works and of the concepts in emergent texts. Emergent text concepts are learned gradually as a student is exposed to reading and writing. Clay (1993) coined the term **concepts about print** to assess and teach emergent readers the following basic concepts: the fact that print contains a message; directionality; one-to-one matching; return sweep; letter and word identification; identification of punctuation; and concepts of a letter and a word.

Word Identification

The terms word identification and word recognition, while similar, differ slightly in their definitions. **Word recognition** is determined by those words that students can read automatically, while **word identification** is demonstrated by the process students use in their attempt to read or self-correct an unknown word. Word identification involves a complex process of integrating five cueing systems: grapho-phonemic, morphemic, semantic, syntactic, and pragmatic (McAndrews & Msengi, 2017). This revised model was based on Goodman's grapho-phonic, syntax, and semantic cueing system. Although Goodman appears to have embedded morphemic into syntactic and pragmatic into semantic cueing, research indicated a need to expand this model to explicitly include the two other language systems (McAndrews & Msengi, 2017).

Readers use **grapho-phonemic (phonic and visual) cues** by applying their knowledge of letter–sound relationships to visual information in the print (configuration and length of words). **Morphemic or word structure cues** are used when readers examine word parts (affixes and roots) to monitor if the word structure sounds right. The affixes may indicate plurality, verb tense, possession, or part of speech, or may change the meaning of the word. Readers use **syntactic or language structure cues**, such as word order and subject–verb agreement, to monitor if a sentence sounds right. Readers use **semantic or meaning cues**, such as background knowledge, context clues, and picture clues, to monitor if a word makes sense. **Pragmatic cues** (which are discussed more fully in other chapters) tend to be used by more advanced readers, as these cues are used to examine the implied meaning of language used within a specific context. In the linguistic cueing system depicted in Figure 4.1, pragmatic cues are shown in an outer ring.

Orthography

Orthography is a set of conventions for the written form of a language. It comes from Greek roots meaning "correct writing." In English and other alphabetic languages, orthography includes letter forms; handwriting conventions; the ways letters are combined to represent sounds and form words; norms of spelling, hyphenization, and capitalization; word breaks; emphasis; and punctuation. There are different physical forms of letters, including different fonts, uppercase (capital) or lowercase, bold, italics, size, text effects, and typography.

FIGURE 4.1. Linguistic cueing system.

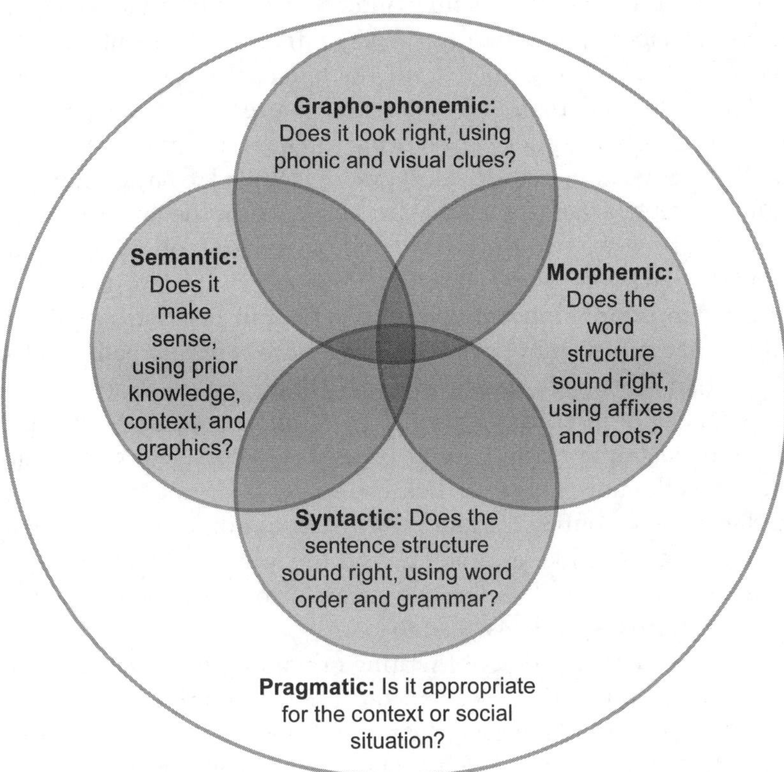
Grapho-phonemic: Does it look right, using phonic and visual clues?
Semantic: Does it make sense, using prior knowledge, context, and graphics?
Morphemic: Does the word structure sound right, using affixes and roots?
Syntactic: Does the sentence structure sound right, using word order and grammar?
Pragmatic: Is it appropriate for the context or social situation?

Emergent writing includes the preconventional forms of writing, such as scribbling, drawing, nonphonetic lettering, and phonetic or inventive spelling, that occur prior to conventional writing (Sulzby & Teale, 1991). Children need early experiences with writing materials and observing others writing to communicate information. Early writing development begins with children making marks on a paper just for fun. This progresses into communicating visual messages on paper to create texts (Morrow, 2005). Sulzby and Teale (1991) describe the development of children's writing as follows. Once they learn letter forms, children create strings of letters for their written messages without regard for the sounds represented by the letters. Children then learn that letters equate to sounds, which can be strung together to write words and ideas. They begin to use invented or phonetic spelling, which typically includes the most dominant sounds in a word, such as the beginning and ending sounds. However, it takes some time before they use phonetic clues to read what they write, and often they try to recall what was written or use pictures to remind them. Finally, the students can write the majority of the sounds in the words needed to communicate a message, and they can read it back. It is important to model for students that what they say can be written down, and that what is written down can be read by others to share information. Through emergent writing, children refine their understanding of the written language system (Jensen, 1984); this not only helps them communicate their ideas, but enhances their reading and spelling of words.

Handwriting is an additional skill that is often taught in correlation with learning letter formation, letter sounds, and writing words. However, the goal of writing is to communicate ideas, so legibility should be emphasized over the exact formation of each letter. There are three purposes for teaching and encouraging legible handwriting (Spear-Swerling, 2006). First, labored handwriting creates a drain on the mental resources needed for higher-level aspects of writing, such as attention to content, elaboration of details, and organization of ideas. Second, because handwriting is used as a tool for taking notes, taking tests, and doing classwork, poor handwriting can have a negative effect on school performance. Finally, handwriting in the earliest grades is linked to basic reading and spelling achievement; for example, when students learn how to form the letter *m*, they can also be learning its sound. There are two basic handwriting styles: Zaner–Bloser and D'Nealian. **Zaner–Bloser** is written straight up and down in manuscript printing and slanted in cursive. The vertical manuscript alphabet is written with four basic strokes and is similar to the letter forms most often seen in print. The strokes are typically balls, sticks, and slants in a specific direction. This is the easiest style for children to read and write. **D'Nealian** is written at a slight slant in both manuscript printing and cursive. Most D'Nealian letters have tails in manuscript printing, so the transition to cursive may be simpler because students just connect the tails. However, because students do not often see words printed in D'Nealian, they may be confused when trying to recognize different letters—especially the lowercase *k*, which looks like a capital *R*, and the lowercase *i* and *j*, which look very similar because they each have a tail. The D'Nealian form is also more complex to write, as it has many different strokes students need to learn.

Spelling is the process or activity of writing or naming the letters of a word. English spelling is difficult for both native speakers and ELLs, as there is more than one way to spell most sounds in English. However, there are some predictable patterns for spelling many words. Students can use knowledge of phonetic elements, word families, inflections, syllable types, roots/affixes and word origins to spell a word. Tables 3.4 and 3.5 in Chapter 3 provide spelling patterns for each of the phonetic sounds in English. Instruction should begin with the single-syllable spelling patterns. These are listed in approximate order of complexity in Table 4.1.

There are six types of syllables: closed, open, vowel–consonant–*e*, vowel teams, vowel–*r* syllables, and consonant–*le*, as described by Moats and Tolman (2009). In a **closed syllable**, the vowel is followed by a consonant, as in *cat*. Notice that the vowel is short. In an

TABLE 4.1. Single-Syllable Spelling Patterns

Spelling pattern	Example words
Vowel–consonant (V-C), short vowel	*in, at, is, on*
Consonant–vowel–consonant (C-V-C), short vowel	*cat, pet, pin, hot, nut*
Consonant–vowel–consonant (C-V-C) with initial consonant digraphs	*this, chip, when, ship*
Consonant–vowel–consonant (C-V-C) with final consonant digraphs	*with, duck, fish*
Consonant–vowel–consonant–*e* (C-V-C-*e*)	*made, like, hope, use*
Consonant–vowel–consonant (C-V-C) with long vowel digraphs	*paid, meat, night, soap*
Consonant–consonant–vowel–consonant (C-C-V-C), initial blends	*stop, spot, drip, frog, glad, crab*
Consonant–vowel–consonant–consonant (C-V-C-C), final blends	*fast, desk, band, bank, camp, gold*

open syllable, nothing comes after the vowel, as in *baby* (/bā/ /bē/). Notice that the vowel is long or says its name. **Vowel–consonant–*e*** (VC*e*) syllables typically contain long vowels spelled with a single letter, followed by a single consonant and a silent *e* (e.g., *make, like, joke, use*). Words with long *e* are rarely spelled with this pattern. Note that some high-frequency words with this spelling pattern are pronounced with a short vowel sound (e.g., *have, give, come*). A **vowel team**, as explained earlier in this chapter, may consist of two, three, or four letters that represent a long, short, or diphthong vowel sound. Sometimes letters that are typically considered consonants are also used in vowel teams (e.g., the letter *y* in *ey, ay, oy,* and *uy*; the letter *w* in *ew, aw,* and *ow*). Other vowel teams that use consonant letters are *-augh, -ough, -igh,* and the silent *-al* spelling for /aw/, as in *walk*. **Vowel–*r* syllables** ending in the vocalic *-r* sound are pronounced /er/ and can have multiple spelling, as demonstrated in the mnemonic sentence mentioned earlier: "H*er* f*ir*st n*ur*se <u>w</u>*or*ks *ear*ly on gramm*ar*." The *-or* says /er/ only when preceded by a *w* and, therefore, the underline is placed under the *w* as a reminder. **Consonant–*le*** (C-*le*) syllables are found at the ends of words. If a consonant-*le* syllable follows an open syllable (long vowel), then the consonant is not doubled (e.g., *able, cycle*). If such a syllable follows a closed syllable (short vowel), then the consonant is doubled (e.g., *apple, little*).

Any type of syllable can be simple or complex. A **complex syllable** is a syllable that contains a consonant cluster, also called a blend (e.g., ***pl**ate, **str**eet*). A **simple syllable** does not contain any consonant clusters (e.g., *late, meet*). Knowing the syllable types may help a student become a better speller. The student can say the first syllable, then write it; and can then say the next syllable and write it.

There are two different models for stages in spelling development. The first model, developed by Gentry (1982) and based on examining students' inventive spelling, includes the precommunicative, semiphonetic, phonetic, transitional, and correct (conventional) stages.

- *Precommunicative stage.* Children imitate writing by making scribbles, letter-like forms, and random strings of letters, numbers, or shapes.
- *Semiphonetic stage.* Children recognize that sounds in words are represented by letters, and they begin to write one or two letters to represent a whole word.
- *Phonetic stage.* Children represent all the major sounds by letters, generally in the correct sequence. Some of the sounds may not be represented or may be represented with incorrect letters.
- *Transitional stage.* Children write most of the common English words correctly, and the incorrectly spelled words contain letters representing all of the sounds in the words but using alternative spelling patterns.
- *Conventional or correct spelling stage.* Children spell almost every word correctly, and they have developed checking and self-correcting strategies. They know and apply the basic rules of the English orthographic system, including prefixes, suffixes, silent letters, and irregular spellings.

The second model, developed by Bear, Invernizzi, Templeton, and Johnson (2012), also has five sequential stages that describe students' spelling behavior. The stages correlate to Gentry's (1982) first four stages, but the fifth stage, instead of being correct spelling, is the stage where students are still learning derivations of words.

- *Stage 1: Emergent stage.* Children are not yet reading or communicating in writing and are typically up to 5 years old. In the early emergent stage, students may produce large scribbles with no letter-like forms. They then begin to use mock writing to "tell" about their pictures. In the middle of the emergent stage, the pretend writing becomes separate from the picture. Then children begin to write letters, particularly the letters of their own names, and begin to pay attention to the sounds in words.
- *Stage 2: Letter name/alphabetic spelling.* Children in this stage are formally taught to read (typically in kindergarten through second grade). Students use the names of letters as cues to the sounds they want to represent. For example, the word *when* might be written with a *y* instead of *wh* because of the sound it makes. Early in this stage, students spell the first sound and then the last sound of a single-syllable word, with the middle syllables or vowels usually left out. In the middle of this stage, students are learning to segment both sounds in a consonant blend and begin to represent the blends correctly. By the end of this stage, they represent most regular short-vowel sounds, digraphs, and consonant blends.
- *Stage 3: Within-word-pattern spelling.* This level typically begins as students make the transition to independent reading (toward the end of the first grade through second, third, or fourth grade, or even later if they have learning difficulties). This stage begins when students can correctly spell most single-syllable, short-vowel words correctly, as well as consonant blends, consonant digraphs, and preconsonantal nasals (such as *-ng*, *-mp*, *-nt*, *-nd*, and *-nk*). These spellers take a closer look at vowel patterns within single-syllable words. During this stage, students first study the common long-vowel patterns.
- *Stage 4: Syllables and affixes spelling.* This stage is typically achieved in the upper elementary and middle school grades, when students are expected to spell many words of more than one syllable. Students consider spelling patterns where syllables meet, and meaning units such as affixes. At the end of this stage, students begin spelling words with affixes that change the meanings of the words. They may misspell affixes, but begin studying the meaning of base words and affixes.
- *Stage 5: Derivational relations spelling.* Most spellers at this stage are found from the beginning of middle school through adulthood. It is known as *derivational relations* because this is the stage when students examine the common derivations of words, as well as related base words and words' roots. In the early part of this stage, spellers spell most words correctly, but they are still learning to use knowledge of roots and affixes to spell. For example, students writing *faverite* for *favorite* or *difrent* for *different* have not used the root word *favor* or *differ* to help spell the word. In this stage, students also build vocabulary based on Latin or Greek origins. Student may still have difficulty spelling words with a reduced vowel or schwa sound; for example they may spell *competition* as *computition,* without making the connection to the word *compete.*

WORD ANALYSIS: GOALS

Goals that are included in the Common Core State Standards are indicated with (CCSS).

Phonological Awareness Goals

Students will:

- Identify and demonstrate that spoken language is divided into words.
- Identify and demonstrate that spoken words are divided into smaller units of sound, such as syllables, onsets, and rimes.
- Identify and demonstrate that spoken words can be divided or segmented into individual sounds or phonemes.
- Aurally differentiate between different English speech sounds.
- Identify and demonstrate that spoken sounds can be blended to make words.
- Aurally differentiate between different English words.
- Identify and demonstrate that orally substituting phonemes results in creating new words.
- Identify and produce the initial, final, and then medial phonemes within words they hear.
- Identify and produce words that have the same initial, final, or medial phoneme.
- Identify or sort words based on their initial, medial, or final sounds.
- Identify and make oral rhymes. (CCSS)
- Segment and blend phonemes in words. (CCSS)
- Blend and segment onsets and rimes of single-syllable words. (CCSS)
- Count, pronounce, blend, and segment syllables in words. (CCSS)
- Add or substitute individual sounds (phonemes) in one-syllable words to make new words. (CCSS)
- Identify and demonstrate that oral words can be put together to make sentences.
- Identify and demonstrate that sentences can be put together to communicate with other people.

Alphabetic Principle Goals

Students will:

- Identify the names of the consonant letters and produce the sounds that they represent, including the soft and hard *c* and *g*. (CCSS)
- Identify the names of the vowels and produce the long and short sounds that they represent. (CCSS)
- Produce the sounds of consonant digraphs and the letters that represent them.
- Produce the sounds of vowel digraphs and identify the letters that represent them.
- Produce the sounds of diphthongs and identify letters that represent them.
- Demonstrate emergent text concepts, such as print contains a message; directionality; one-to-one matching; letter and word identification; use of capitalization; identification of punctuation; and concepts of letters and words within a sentence.
- Blend sounds to read phonetically regular words. (CCSS)
- Use knowledge of all letter-sound correspondences, syllabication patterns, and morphology to read unfamiliar or phonetically irregular words in and out of context. (CCSS)
- Recognize and know the meanings of high-frequency words automatically.
- Identify and know the meanings of words by cross-checking the grapho-phonemic, morphemic, syntactic, semantic, and pragmatic cues in the context of reading texts.

- Segment words into phonemes, syllables, and morphemes to represent the words using inventive spelling.
- Write high-frequency words using conventional spelling.
- Segment words into phonemes, syllables, and morphemes to write the words using conventional spelling.
- Identify words that are spelled incorrectly.
- Use spelling patterns to write multisyllabic words, including those with inflectional and derivational morphemes.

Emergent Text Concepts Goals

Students will:

- Demonstrate that print contains a message by pointing to the text, rather than a picture, when asked where to begin reading.
- Demonstrate directionality and return sweep by following words from left to right, top to bottom, and page to page. (CCSS)
- Recognize that spoken words are represented in writing by specific sequences of letters. (CCSS)
- Demonstrate one-to-one matching by pointing to each word written in a sentence as the teacher reads it.
- Demonstrate letter and word identification by pointing to a given uppercase and lowercase letter and identifying a specific word after a sentence is read.
- Demonstrate knowledge of punctuation marks by pointing to each type (. ? ! , " ") and telling its purpose.
- Demonstrate the concept of a letter by identifying only one letter, two letters, first letter, and last letter. This is often done by pushing together two index cards to isolate individual letters.
- Demonstrate the concept of a word by identifying that words are separated by spaces and identifying the first word and last word.
- Identify alphabetic principle goals.

Word Identification Goals

Students will:

- Decode regularly spelled words with one, then two, then three or more syllables.
- Read common, high-frequency words by sight.
- Read words by using common phonetic patterns.
- Read words by trying different consonant sounds.
- Read words by trying different vowel sounds.
- Read words by breaking words into syllables.
- Read words by separating, then blending, roots and affixes.
- Read words by using the syntax of a sentence.
- Read words by using the semantics of a sentence.
- Read words by using picture or graphic clues.
- Read words by using the pragmatics of the context of the text.
- Monitor reading by making sure that words look right, sound right, and make sense.

- Use strategies to self-correct words.
- Read words and phrases by integrating grapho-phonemic, morphemic, syntactic, and pragmatic cues.

Orthography Goals

Students at the emergent writing stage will:

- Draw pictures to communicate information.
- Dictate stories for others to write.
- Write letters to represent sounds or words.
- Write strings of letters to represent ideas.
- Write uppercase and lowercase letters with the correct formation.
- Write letters and words from left to right.
- Return to the left for the next line, using the return sweep.
- Use proper spacing between letters and words.
- Use inventive or phonetic spelling of words.
- Use resources to spell words.
- Write phrases to communicate ideas.
- Write using sentence frames or patterned sentences.
- Write using phonetic spelling, with letters representing almost all sounds.
- Write high-frequency words correctly.
- Write sentences with initial capitalization and end punctuation.
- Write more complete sentences.
- Begin to recognize mistakes in content, punctuation, capitalization, spelling, and grammar.

Students will:

- Write letters that are easily recognizable, within the lines on lined paper, and spaced properly.
- Correctly spell all high-frequency words.
- Write using transitional spelling, with letters representing all the sounds.
- Use knowledge of spelling patterns, roots, and affixes to spell words.
- Monitor their spelling and use resources to correct it.
- Write for a variety of purposes.
- Write compound and complex sentences.
- Write complete paragraphs.
- Monitor mistakes in content, punctuation, capitalization, spelling, and grammar.

WORD ANALYSIS: ASSESSMENTS

Phonological Awareness Assessments

Phonological awareness assessments are administered to determine if a student can blend, segment, and differentiate English speech sounds. While all students should be given a hearing test, if a student does not score at least 70% on these assessments, further assessment by a speech–language pathologist or an audiologist may be needed to determine if the student has an auditory processing disorder or other hearing impairment. These assessments are most appropriate for students at the emergent reading and writing level, unless there is an indication of difficulties in discriminating, blending, or segmenting sounds.

• Auditory Discrimination Assessments

PURPOSE: The Appendix to this book includes three auditory discrimination tests: one for consonants, one for short and long vowels, and one for diphthongs and controlled vowels. Each of these assessments is designed to determine the ability of students, to recognize the fine differences between English phonemes in words. These tests are generally administered to primary students unless a discrimination issue is observed. Each test consists of word pairs that differ by a single phoneme or are the same; the examiner says the word pair, and the student has to say whether the words are the same or different. These tests use a format similar to that of the original Wepman *Auditory Discrimination Test* (Wepman, 1958). The *Auditory Discrimination Assessment—Consonants* (see Appendix, p. 404) compares words that differ by auditorily similar initial or final consonant sounds. The *Auditory Discrimination Assessment—Short and Long Vowels* (see Appendix, p. 405) compares the five short vowel sounds with each other, compares the five long vowel sounds with each other, and compares the short and long sound of each vowel. The *Auditory Discrimination Assessment—Diphthongs and Controlled Vowels* (see Appendix, p. 406) compares diphthongs (/ay/, /uy/, /oy/, /ow/) and controlled vowels (/er/, /ar/, /or/, /al/, /aw/, and /ew/) to long and short vowels.

PROCEDURE: For all three of these tests, the teacher and student sit shoulder to shoulder, facing away from each other, so the student cannot see the words pronounced. The teacher says toward the student's ear, "I am going to say two words, and I want you to tell me if they are the same or different."

SCORING AND ANALYSIS: The student's responses are recorded as S for same and D for different. They are scored with a plus sign (+) for correct and a minus sign (–) for incorrect. Functioning levels are scored as independent (90–100%), instructional (70–89%), or frustration (69% or below). The teacher identifies individual or patterns of phonemes that the student did and did not distinguish between, and correlates these phonemes with those in other assessments. See Figure 4.2 for a partial example of the *Auditory Discrimination Assessment—Short and Long Vowels.*

INSTRUCTIONAL IMPLICATIONS: If students are at the frustration level on this assessment, they should be evaluated for a hearing loss and for an auditory processing disorder. They should be given a mirror and be given oral prompts for how the sounds in words should be made with the lips, mouth, tongue, and voice.

• Phoneme Blending Assessment

PURPOSE: To determine a student's phonemic knowledge of blending sounds into words (see Appendix, p. 407). I developed it (McAndrews, 2008) by using the general format of the *Yopp–Singer Test of Phoneme Segmentation* (Yopp, 1995). Blending and synthesizing sounds to form words are strategies used when decoding unfamiliar words (Walker, 2004). This assessment is generally given if a student scores at or below 70% on a first-grade reading word list, or if there is evidence that a student has difficulties blending sounds into words.

FIGURE 4.2. *Auditory Discrimination Assessment—Short and Long Vowels,* partial example and analysis for a grade 2 student.

Functioning Level: Instructional		**Score:** 35/**40** = 88%	
	Response/Score		**Response/Score**
1. get–get	S +	21. cake–cake	S +
2. hat–hot	D +	22. jean–June	D +
3. pet–pat	S –	23. high–hay	D +
4. had–had	S +	24. bite–beat	D +
5. nut–not	S –	25. home–home	S +

Analysis: This second-grade student identified all of the words that sounded the same and distinguished between each of the words with long vowel sounds. The short vowel sounds that she did not distinguish between were /ĕ/ and /ă/; /ŭ/ and /ŏ/; /ĭ/ and /ĕ/; /ĕ/ and /ĭ/; and /ă/ and /ĕ/.

Instructional Implications: Provide instruction on short vowel sounds. Try strategies such as a picture word sort with a picture of a pan and a pen, and pictures of other short /ă/ and short /ĕ/ words.

PROCEDURE: The teacher tells the student, "I am going to say separate sounds, and I want you to say the word when the sounds are blended together. For example, if I say /l/ /ī/ /k/, you should say *like*." (Note that the words are not written phonetically, but the way they are spelled.) Practice items: /m/ /ă/ /p/, /ŏ/ /n/, /b/ /ĭ/ /g/. For assessment items, the teacher puts a plus sign (+) next to items the student has correctly blended and a minus sign (–) for incorrect blendings, and records incorrect responses in the blank space.

SCORING AND ANALYSIS: The teacher identifies those phonetic elements that the student did and did not correctly blend; makes a note if the student did not say a real word; and identifies patterns of correct and incorrect responses and writes specific examples. Functioning levels are scored as independent (23–25 = 90–100%), instructional (20–22 = 70–89%), or frustration (19 or below = 69% or below). See Figure 4.3 for a partial example.

INSTRUCTIONAL IMPLICATIONS: Students who are at the frustration level on this assessment should be given scaffolded opportunities to blend words orally while reading in context and during word identification strategies such as making words with magnetic letters or alphabet blocks.

• Phoneme Segmentation Assessment

PURPOSE: To determine a student's phonemic knowledge of segmenting words into individual phonemes that is used for writing words. (For my own version of this assessment, see Appendix, p. 408.) This version of the assessment is based on the *Yopp–Singer Test of Phoneme Segmentation* (Yopp, 1995). Segmenting words into their single letter sounds, or analytic phonics, is a strategy used in spelling words. This assessment is generally given if a student scores at or below 70% on a first-grade writing word list, or if there is evidence that a student has difficulties segmenting sounds in words to write them.

FIGURE 4.3. *Phoneme Blending Assessment*, partial example and analysis for a grade 2 student.

Functioning Level: Frustration		**Score:** 14/25 = 56%	
Prompt	**Response and + or –**	**Prompt**	**Response and + or –**
1. /c/ /ă/ /t/	+	14. /d/ /āy/	+
2. /s/ /ē/ /d/	– see	15. /p/ /l/ /ā/ /ce/	– play
3. /m/ /ī/ /ne/	– my	16. /t/ /o/	+
4. /g/ /ō/	+	17. /th/ /r/ /ew/	– THē
5. /h/ /ē/	+	18. /j/ /ŏ/ /b/	– /j/ /ŏ/, jŏg

Analysis: This second-grade student blended 13/25 words correctly, including all of the words with only two sounds. Her phonemes blending is at the frustration level. The incorrect blended responses were real words except for two. The remaining were real words, yet the final sound of the target word was generally deleted or was replaced with another sound. For example, she omitted the /d/ in seed and substituted /g/ for /b/ in jog for job.

Instructional Implications: Since the final sound was deleted or changed, one strategy could be to have her listen to a segmented word and identify the picture cards that represent it and say the complete word. Based on her needs, these words should have different word endings. She could also sort pictures based on the final *b* and *g* sounds, such as *bag, crab, pig, bib, big.* To extend this into reading and writing words, she could use magnetic letters or letter cubes to make and blend words with three to four phonemes. She should also make new words by adding phonemes such as changing the word *can* to *candy.*

PROCEDURE: The teacher tells the student, "I am going to say a word. I want you to break the word apart and say each sound of the word in order. For example, if I say *sun,* you should say /s/ /ŭ/ /n/." The student's responses are recorded. Practice items: *bike, on, and.* Assessment items: The teacher puts a plus sign (+) next to items the student has correctly segmented and a minus sign (–) for incorrect segmentations, and records incorrect responses on the blank line.

SCORING AND ANALYSIS: The teacher identifies those phonetic elements that the student did and did not segment correctly, and makes a special note of whether the student separated or did not separate blends and consonant digraphs. Functioning levels are scored as independent (23–25 = 90–100%), instructional (20–22 = 70–89%), or frustration (19 or below = 69% or below).

INSTRUCTIONAL IMPLICATIONS: If the student did not correctly segment words, the teacher could use the pushing pennies strategy (described later in this chapter) for separating words into discrete phonemes.

Alphabetic Principle and Emergent Text Concepts Assessments

• Letter and Sound Identification Assessment

PURPOSE: This individual assessment provides information about a student's ability to identify the 26 uppercase and 28 lowercase letters and produce the sounds they represent out of sequence; it is used for all K–2 students and those who are unsure of letter names and sounds (see Appendix, pp. 409–410). The letters *a* and *g* are presented in two different, but commonly used, fonts. I developed this assessment, using Marie Clay's *Letter Identification Test* (1993) as a starting point.

PROCEDURE: The teacher gives the student a copy of the letter chart and places an index card under the first row of letters. The teacher says, "I want you to tell me the names of each letter and the sound or sounds it makes." Pointing to the first letter, the teacher then says, "What letter is this?" and writes the student's response on the record sheet. "Do you know what sound it makes?" If the letter is marked with an asterisk (*), there are multiple sounds, so the teacher asks, "Do you know what other sound that makes?" If the student does not know the sound, the teacher asks, "Do you know a word that starts with that letter?" All responses are recorded. If a student says, "I don't know," the teacher writes the abbreviation IDK and pauses to see if the student can try something. Although students are not scored on knowing a word, it provides a connection between known words and initial sounds during instruction.

ANALYSIS: The teacher identifies the known and unknown uppercase letters, lowercase letters, and sounds and separates the consonants and the vowels. The teacher also identifies any known words for unknown sounds; these would be the first sounds to teach, using these words as key words. Finally, the teacher identifies substitutions of visually similar letters or substitutions of similar-sounding phonemes. Functioning levels are scored as independent (90–100%), instructional (70–89%), or frustration (69% or below). See Figure 4.4 for an example with a grade 1 student.

• Phonics Skills for Grades K–3

PURPOSE: This is a checklist of the phonetic elements to be introduced and mastered for reading and writing at each primary grade level (see Appendix, pp. 411–413).

PROCEDURE: This checklist can be used as an ongoing record sheet to document a teacher's instruction or a student's learning of reading and writing specific phonemes, based on grade level. The teacher simply checks each phonetic element as it is taught or learned.

SCORING AND ANALYSIS: The teacher marks each phonetic element with a plus sign (+) or a minus sign (–), identifies patterns of correct and incorrect responses, and writes specific examples. Functioning levels are scored as independent (90–100%), instructional (70–89%), or frustration (69% or below).

INSTRUCTIONAL IMPLICATIONS: Students can be grouped according to the type of phonetic element they most need to work on: consonants, long vowels with a silent *e*, short vowels, consonant digraphs, vowel digraphs, inflectional endings, and so forth.

• Individual Phonics Summary

PURPOSE: This can be used to document all the missed phonetic elements when a student's reading and writing assessments have been completed or after classroom literacy tasks (see Appendix, p. 414). It is important to note, however, that these phonemes should be taught in the context of reading and writing, rather than in isolation.

PROCEDURE: After assessments have been completed, the teacher highlights in yellow the phonemes the student missed while reading, and highlights in blue the graphemes the

FIGURE 4.4. *Letter and Sound Identification Assessment,* example and analysis for a grade 1 student.

	Letter	Sound	Word		Letter	Sound	Word
B	+	+		b	d, s-c +	+	
O*	+	/ŭ/, IDK –	IDK	o*	+	/ŭ/, /ō/ –	OK +
S*	+	+, -/z/		s	+,-/z/	+,-/z/	
A*	+	/ă/, IDK –	apple +	a*	IDK,s-c +	/ă/,/ā/ +	
W	+	/dŭ/ –	IDK	w	+	/dŭ/ –	done –
Z	+	/zē/ –	zebra +	z	t, s-c +	/t/, s-c +	zebra +
F	+	/ĕ/ –	fish +	f	+	/ĕf/ –	fish +
H	+	/ā/ –	IDK	h	+	/āch/ –	IDK
K	+	/kŭ/ +	Katelyn	k	+	/kŭ/ +	
J	G	/jŭ/ +	IDK	j	G	/gŭ/ –	go –
U*	+	/yŭ/ –	you –	u*	+	/yŭ/ –	you –
				a*	+	/ă/, /ā/ +	
C*	+	/k/, IDK –	cat +	c*	+	/k/, IDK –	me, Cindy +
Y*	IDK	/wŭ/ IDK –	"no"	y*	+	/wŭ/, IDK –	IDK
L	+	/lŭ/ –	Laura +	l	1 –	/wŭ/, IDK –	IDK
Q	+	/kŭ/ –	IDK	q	p	/p/	IDK
M	+	+		m	+	+	
D	+	/dŭ/ +		d	B	/b/	Bear
N	+	+		n	+	+	
X	+	/ĕ/ –	x-ray	x	+	/ĕ/ –	x-ray
I*	+	/ă/, /ĕ/ –	"No"	i*	+	ĕ	IDK
P	+	+	Peter	p	+	+	
E*	+	/ĭ/, IDK –	Elizabeth	e*	+	/ĭ/, IDK –	IDK
G*	+	/g/ +, –	go	g*	+	/g/ +, –	go
R	+ speech?	/w/speech?	wabbit	r	+ speech?	/w/speech?	wabbit
V	w, s-c +	IDK –	IDK	v	+	IDK –	IDK
T	+	+		t	F	/f/	fish
				g*	IDK, 8 –	ā –	IDK
Total	24/26	Score with lowercase	No score	Total	22/28	Both 6/26	No score

Analysis: On this assessment, the student identified 24/26 capital letters, 22/28 lowercase letters, and 6/26 sounds.

Letters: She identified most of the capital letters, except J and Y. She substituted numbers for lowercase *l* and *g*. She substituted *g* for *j*, *p/q*, *b/d*, and *f/t*. She self-corrected *b*, *a*, and *z*. She identified both fonts of *a*.

Sounds: She correctly identified the capital and lowercase sounds for six letters.

Unknown consonant sounds: *c* and *g* (soft sounds), *w*, *z*, *f*, *h*, *j*, *y*, and *l*. She often began with the sound of the letter name. Sometimes she added a /ŭ/ at the end of the letter sound. I only marked it incorrect for /l/, since it clearly does not end in a /ŭ/ sound.

Unknown vowels: *e*, *i*, *o*, *u*, and *y*. She identified two sounds of "a" for the lowercase, but not the uppercase.

Known words for unknown letters: *a*, *z*, *f*, *c*, *l*, and *e*. The word *x-ray* uses the letter, but not the sound.

Instructional Implications: Begin by teaching the sounds with picture icons for *a*, *z*, *f*, *c*, and *l* since she has known words representing them. Then explain that letter names, except for the long vowel sounds, do not always start with the sound of the letter names. Teach that letter sounds do not end with an /ŭ/ sound. Be sure to teach the sounds in context of words, and help her create key words and pictures for each sound.

student missed while writing. The missed elements in both reading and writing are highlighted in green. The teacher circles elements once the student can read and write them correctly.

ANALYSIS: The teacher classifies the phonetic elements the student correctly and incorrectly read and/or wrote. For miscues, the teacher identifies any visual or auditory similarities. Finally, the teacher identifies any similarities between missed elements in reading and writing.

INSTRUCTIONAL IMPLICATIONS: The teacher selects phonic strategies to support the learning of these elements and help the student make connections to reading and writing texts.

• Emergent Text Concepts Assessment

PURPOSE: This 25-question assessment provides information about emergent text concepts, such as directionality, one-to-one matching of words to print, and concepts of letters, words, and punctuation, in the context of a storybook (see Appendix, pp. 415–416). This assessment was based on Clay's (1993) *Concepts About Print Observation Task*. Unlike Clay's assessment, this one does not require a specific published text. This assessment is appropriate for students who read at or below the first-grade reading level.

PROCEDURE: The teacher selects a picture book that has a picture and two to three lines of print on each page, and that contains most or all of the punctuation marks. For questions 1–7, the teacher first asks the questions and then reads the page. For questions 8–25, the teacher reads each page and then ask the questions. The teacher fills in the blanks on questions 15–17. The teacher writes down the student's responses and records a plus sign (+) for each correct one and a minus sign (–) for each incorrect one. For any absent concepts, the teacher writes N/A and changes the denominator of the fraction for the total number of questions.

SCORING AND ANALYSIS: Functioning levels are scored as independent (90–100%), instructional (70–89%), or frustration (69% or below). The teacher identifies patterns of correct and incorrect responses and writes specific examples. The teacher also answers the following questions, to analyze and evaluate the student's understanding of each of the emergent text concepts. Does the student understand directionality, including one-to-one matching and the return sweep (going to the next line) (questions 1–10)? Does the student know the purposes for the punctuation marks (questions 11–14)? Can the student identify and know the difference between words and letters in context (questions 15–24)? Does the student understand that reading is a comprehension process (questions 1, 25)? For instruction, the teacher identifies known text concepts to reinforce and unknown concepts to teach.

ANALYSIS EXAMPLE: The student responded correctly to 17 of 25 emergent text concepts. He did not demonstrate the return sweep and was not accurate with his one-to-one matching. He pointed to the last word in the line, not the page. He did not know what the comma and quotation marks were for. He did not discriminate between *out* and *one*, but he selected a word with the same first letter.

INSTRUCTIONAL IMPLICATIONS: The teacher reinforces the known concepts and directly teaches the specific unknown concepts while reading and writing texts with the student.

Word Identification Assessments

Since high-frequency words make up the majority of reading and writing words, these are the primary words used for assessment. Some informal reading inventories also include word lists from their included passages to help determine a student's approximate grade level based on word accuracy.

• Fry's Instant Words, Graded Reading Words Assessment, Graded Reading Words Lists, and Coding and Scoring Oral Reading Behaviors Guide

PURPOSE: *Fry's Instant Words* are 10 lists of 100 words each that are the most common words in the English language, ranked in frequency order (Fry, Kress, & Fountoukidis, 1993). These word lists can be retrieved from multiple sources, such as *www.sightwords.com*. The first 100 words make up half of all written material. The *Graded Reading Words Assessment* includes selected representative words from *Fry's Instant Words* and other lists of high-frequency, phonetically regular and irregular words. It contains nine leveled lists of words based on frequency of use and difficulty of decoding, beginning with a preprimer list and ending with a list for grades 9–12 (see Appendix, pp. 417–419). The *Graded Reading Words Lists* form presents these nine lists for students' use during the assessment (see Appendix, pp. 420–421). The *Coding and Scoring Oral Reading Behaviors Guide* is a guide to completing the *Graded Reading Words Assessment* (see Appendix, p. 422).

The *Graded Reading Words Assessment/Lists* and *Fry's Instant Words* are used to identify students' known sight words, strategies used during decoding, and patterns of miscues, as well as their knowledge of phoneme–grapheme relationships. The *Fry's Instant Words* lists are predominantly administered to students who are reading at or below the third-grade level, to determine the students' knowledge of the high-frequency words. These lists can also be used as instructional check sheets for known and unknown words identified during authentic reading. The *Graded Reading Words Assessment/Lists* contain only a representative sample of *Fry's Instant Words,* and therefore constitute a quicker screening instrument and provide an approximate grade level for students' reading of words.

PROCEDURE: For the *Graded Reading Words Assessment,* the teacher selects the list that is at least two grade levels below a student's current grade, unless there is evidence to show that the student would be reading at a lower level. It is often beneficial to provide a bookmark or index card for the student to keep their place on the appropriate list in the *Graded Reading Words Lists.* For an emergent reader, the teacher can write the words on index cards and present them one at a time. The teacher says, "Read each word, and then move the card down to the next word in the column. I cannot help you; if you don't know a word, try to figure it out. I am going to write down everything you say." The teacher then records all of the student's responses on the *Graded Reading Words Assessment,* following the directions in the *Coding and Scoring Oral Reading Behaviors Guide.* If the word is correct, the teacher writes a plus sign (+) above the word on the *Graded Reading Words Assessment.* If the student substitutes a real word, the teacher writes it above; if not, the teacher phonetically writes down each attempt, marking the vowels. A minus sign (–) is used for an incorrect word, and a checkmark (✓) for a self-corrected word. The teacher marks a slash for every 2 seconds the student pauses, in order to differentiate between an automatic word (sight word) and a decoded word or self-corrected word. If the student scores at or above 70% on a given list, the teacher goes to the next list; if the student scores below 70%, the teacher goes to the previous list unless it was already assessed. For the *Fry's Instant Words* lists, the teacher begins with the very first word. The teacher will need two copies of the words—one for the student to read from, and the other to document the student's responses. The lists are administered in the same way as the *Graded Reading Words Assessment/Lists.*

SCORING AND ANALYSIS: There are three scores for reading words: the automatic score, the identified score, and the total score. The automatic score is the percentage of words the student reads immediately within 1 second; these are often called the student's sight words. The identified score is the percentage of the words the student correctly reads after 1 second. These include the correct reading of the word after hesitations, decoded sounds, or incorrect words. The total score is the total percentage of correctly read words. Functioning levels are scored as independent (18–20, 90–100%), instructional (14–17, 70–89%), or frustration (13 or below, 69% or below). The teacher identifies the high-frequency words the student can read automatically (sight words), as well as those the student can identify through using phonics and knowledge of words. Patterns of the student's knowledge of phoneme–grapheme relationships can also be documented on the *Individual Phonics Summary* (see Appendix, p. 414). In addition, strategies used during decoding or self-correcting can be identified. An analysis would include known words, the strategies the student used when problem solving, and known grapheme–phoneme relationships. In addition, the patterns between phonetic elements in known and unknown words are identified. See Figure 4.5 for a partial example of the *Graded Reading Words Assessment* with a grade 6 student.

INSTRUCTIONAL IMPLICATIONS: Students can be grouped according to patterns of correctly and incorrectly read words and phonetic elements. These elements are taught in the context of the students' reading and writing of authentic texts, and then strategies using these elements are taught. Finally, the students apply these strategies in their reading.

Orthography Assessments

• Graded Writing Words Assessment and Fry's Instant Words

PURPOSE: These two orthography assessments are used to identify high-frequency words students can spell, the strategies used during writing, the patterns of their miscues, and their knowledge of phoneme–grapheme relationships, as well as to evaluate the students' handwriting. All the findings are used to plan word study instruction.

The words used in these assessments are the same as those in the *Graded Reading Words Assessment* and *Fry's Instant Words. Fry's Instant Words* lists are predominantly administered to students who spell at or below the third-grade level, to determine the students' knowledge of how to write all of the high-frequency words. They can also be used as instructional check sheets for known and unknown words identified during authentic writing. The *Graded Writing Words Assessment* contains only a representative sample of *Fry's Instant Words,* and therefore it is a quicker screening instrument and provides an approximate grade level for student's writing of words (see Appendix, pp. 423–425).

PROCEDURE: The teacher copies the *Graded Writing Words Lists* or downloads the *Fry's Instant Words* lists (e.g., at *www.sightwords.com* or *www.k12.reader.com*). The teacher then selects appropriate paper (lined or unlined, depending on the student's ability) for the student to write on. Kindergarteners and first graders with poor fine motor coordination can

FIGURE 4.5. *Graded Reading Words Assessment,* partial example and analysis for a grade 6 student.

Grade 4 Reading Words		Functioning Level: Instructional		
Automatic Score 14/20 words = 70%		Total Score 15/20 words = 75%		
+ been	+ different	they've they're	+ beautiful	+ piece
+ pretty	know, s-c ✓ knew	+ sign	+ brought	+ finally
+ trouble	+ learned	unusual usually	exit excited	When whether
+ half	eight weight	+ whole	+ through	+ tomorrow

Grade 5 Reading Words		Functioning Level: Frustration		
Automatic Score 10/20 words = 50%		Total Score 11/20 words = 55%		
+ heard	Could s-c ✓ couldn't	confused conclusion	+ library	+ environment
+ watched	+ sure	+ laughed	+ terrible	/ĕxkĭt/ excellent
/nōĕdj/ knowledge	+ experience	+ certain	/ăkfūzd/ athletic	different difference
spread separate	high height	problem probably	onion opinion	+ picture

Analysis: The student read word lists for grades 3, 4, and 5 on the Graded Reading Word Assessment. He read the grade 3 reading word list at an independent level. On the grade 4 list, he was at the instructional level. He attempted each word he was shown, and when he did not know the word, he substituted a different word with the same beginning sounds as the word that he was shown. He self-corrected know for knew. There were only two instances in which he did not correctly identify the beginning sounds, but correctly read the ending word sounds (*his/this* and *weight/eight*). There were two instances in which he went back to try a word again, and in both instances he successfully self-corrected the word (*know/knew* and *another/around* from the grade 3 list). As the word lists grew more difficult, he began substituting more words. In two words, he substituted the end of the contraction (*we've/we're, they've/they're*). On the grade 5 list, he was at the frustration level. He attempted all of the words and self-corrected one word. He responded with several nonwords (/ăkfūzd/, *athletic*; /ĕxkĭt/, *excellent*; /nōĕdj/, *knowledge*). Occasionally, he left out or substituted medial sounds (*onion/ opinion*). He usually attended to the beginning word sounds, although he did not consistently attend to medial and ending word sounds.

Instructional Implications: The focus should be on breaking words into parts, trying different sounds, and predicting real words. If his initial attempts are not real words, he should attempt the word again.

be given unlined paper. Other students in these grades or above can be given paper with top, middle, and bottom lines that are the appropriate distance apart for their fine motor coordination. Generally, students in third grade and up can use a sheet of regular single-lined paper; they can fold the paper in half to make two columns. For the *Fry's Instant Words* lists, the teacher begins with the very first word. For the *Graded Writing Words Assessment*, the teacher selects the list that is at least two grade levels below the student's current grade, unless there is evidence to show that the student would be performing at a lower level. For an emergent writer, the teacher first asks the student to write their first and last names and any words the student knows and then begins with the preprimer list. The teacher reads each word one at a time, provides a sentence using the word, and then reads the word again. It is especially important to provide sentences for words that are homophones, as indicated by an asterisk, so that the student can understand the words in context. The student should be reminded to write letters for the sounds in each word, even if the student is not sure how to spell the word. After dictating each word, the teacher writes a plus sign (+) above each correctly spelled word. For all incorrect responses, the teacher writes what the student wrote above each word, being sure to indicate reversals and capital letters. The teacher writes a comma between each attempt, and s/c if the student self-corrects the spelling. If the student scores at or above 70% on a given list or column, the teacher goes to the next list; if not, the teacher goes to the previous list if it was not already assessed.

SCORING AND ANALYSIS: Functioning levels are scored as independent (18–20, 90–100%), instructional (14–17, 70–89%), or frustration (13 or below, 69% or below). The teacher identifies the words the student can write automatically, as well as those the student can write through using phonics and knowledge of words. (For a student in the developmental spelling stage, Table 4.2 can be used to evaluate each word.) In addition, patterns in the student's knowledge of phoneme–grapheme relationships can be documented on the *Individual Phonics Summary* (see Appendix, p. 414). The *Handwriting Rubric Assessment* (see Appendix, p. 428, and description below) can be used to compare the student to the expected standard and to identify areas of strength and need, such as letter formation, spacing, directionality, reversals, and capitalization. Data can also be correlated with reading words, dictation, and the writing sample. See Figure 4.6 for an example of the use of the *Graded Writing Words Assessment* with a grade 3 student.

INSTRUCTIONAL IMPLICATIONS: During instruction, the teacher can help students make connections between known and unknown words in the context of authentic reading and writing. Students can be grouped according to patterns of correct and incorrectly written words and phonetic elements. These elements are taught in the context of students' reading

TABLE 4.2. Developmental Spelling Stage Rubric

Prephonetic	Semiphonetic	Phonetic	Transitional	Conventional
Scribbles, letter-like forms, or letters that do not represent the sounds that are produced.	Some sound–symbol relationships are present; one or two letters may represent a whole word.	Most of the sounds are represented graphically, and vowels are used even if incorrect.	Most words are correct. Incorrectly spelled words contain letters representing all the sounds in the word.	The word is spelled correctly, or in writing composition at least 96% of words are spelled correctly.

FIGURE 4.6. *Graded Writing Words Assessment,* partial example and analysis.

Grade 2 Writing Words **Functioning Level:** Instructional **Score:** 15/20 words = 75%

Developmental Stage: Transitional

+ Very	+ before	+ right	+ goes	+ always
around Around	wercs works	+ great	there their	+ don't
+ Where	yous use	wood would	+ who	+ your
+ wanted	+ first	+ please	+ talked	+ long

Analysis: This student wrote words from the grades 1, 2, and 3 lists from the Graded Writing Words Assessment. She was at the independent level for writing the grade 1 words, the instructional level for the grade 2 words, correctly spelling 15/20 words, and frustration for the grade 3 words. She was at the transitional spelling stage for grade 2 because her incorrect spelling words could be sounded out, and she generally included letters representing all of the sounds in the words. Some of the words were homophones, so I gave her a sentence, yet she did not spell the correct one in either case (*wood/would, there/their*). One misspelling sounded similar to the word (*yous/use*), and for the other two words she wrote the correct beginning and ending sounds, but the middle sounds were wrong: She wrote *wercs/works, arond/around.*

Instructional Implications: Praise her for including letters for almost all of the sounds. Focus writing instruction on vowels, the hard and soft *c* and *g*, and homophones. Provide opportunities in her writing to circle words that do not look right to her. Have her practice the read, cover, write, and check strategy with misspelled common words or words she writes frequently.

and writing of authentic texts; then strategies using these elements are taught; and then students apply the strategies in their writing.

• Sentence Dictation Assessment

PURPOSE: This is used to identify students' known writing words, as well as their abilities to divide words they hear into their sounds (phonemic segmentation), to write the letter or letters that represent these sounds, and to use analogies for known words to help them spell new words (see Appendix, pp. 426–427). These sentences were created to incorporate as many graphemes as possible in the fewest words in the context of a short story.

PROCEDURE: There are three different dictation stories. Preprimer- and primer-level writers are assessed on 41 graphemes; first- and second-grade-level writers are assessed on 50 graphemes; and those at or above third-grade writing level are assessed on 153 phonemes, graphemes, and controlled vowels. It can be administered to an older student if the student scores below fifth-grade level on the *Graded Writing Words Assessment*. Paper with line widths appropriate for the student's age should be used. The teacher says, "I am going to read you a story, and then I will go back and read one word at a time. Write down each word I say. If you do not know how to write a word, say the word to yourself, and write down the letters for the sounds you hear." The student is to write these words in sentence format, not in a list.

SCORING AND ANALYSIS: Above each word, the teacher writes a plus sign (+) for the correct spelling or a minus sign (–) for a deleted/omitted word, and records all incorrect spellings. The teacher then counts each correct underlined grapheme and records the total. The functioning level is determined by the percentage of correct graphemes written: independent (90–100%), instructional (70–89%), or frustration (69% or below). If the student scores at or above the instructional level on a given dictation test, the teacher goes to the story at the next highest level. The process continues until the frustration level is reached. To analyze the sentence dictation, the teacher identifies the correct and incorrect graphemes or patterns of spelling in order to plan instruction. In the story for third grade and above, those spelling patterns that are not individual graphemes such as consonant blends and controlled vowels are indicated by a double underline. The *Individual Phonics Summary* (see Appendix, p. 414) can be used to indicate the phonetic elements that the student wrote correctly and is a place to record examples of incorrect elements. In the analysis section, the headings in the *Individual Phonics Summary* are used to record patterns of correct and incorrect graphemes with specific examples. The teacher can provide additional information about use of punctuation and capitalization, as well as handwriting and spacing. See Figure 4.7 for a preprimer-/primer-level sentence dictation example and Figure 4.8 for a first-/second-grade level example.

FIGURE 4.7. *Sentence Dictation Assessment* (preprimer and primer level), example and analysis for a grade 1 student.

Preprimer and Primer Functioning Level: Frustration **Score:** 21/41 **graphemes** = 51%

\+ lik 2 f fn wf mi +DOG h+ kn dm anb gt
I like to have fun with my dog. He can jump and get
bl
balls.

Analysis: The student correctly spelled three words and attempted to write the other words with many of the correct consonant letters. She often wrote the correct graphemes for many of the initial and final consonants, but she omitted most of the vowels. She substituted the number 2 for the word *to*. She omitted the *h* in *have* and substituted the letter *f* for *v*. She also substituted *d* for *j* and omitted the *p* blend in *jump*. In *balls*, she correctly wrote two of the letters, *b* and *l*. She transposed *b* for *d*, which is typical in first-grade writing. For vowels, she substituted *i* for *y*, *i* for *e*, and *o* for *l*-controlled *a*. She also omitted the final *e*'s. She generally formed the letters correctly, except that she wrote the *o*, *a*, and *g* starting in the wrong direction. She correctly capitalized the pronoun *I*, but used capitals for *D-O-G*. She wrote a lowercase letter for *H* at the beginning of a sentence, and she omitted the two end punctuation marks.

Instructional Implications: She demonstrated that she used some phonics to write the words. She first needs explicit instruction in writing words with vowels. Strategies such as using sound boxes would be helpful. She could use a mirror and her hand to her throat to distinguish among *f*, *v*, and *th* sounds. She should be encouraged to write in her journal daily, writing a letter or letters for each sound she hears in the words.

FIGURE 4.8. *Sentence Dictation Assessment* (first- and second-grade level), example and analysis for a grade 3 student.

First and Second Grade Functioning Level: Instructional **Score:** 44 **/50 graphemes =** 88%
+ + + + + + + + + + + + wather Th e f ar m er s aw the b l a ck a n d wh i t e t oy b oa t ou t o n the w a t er. + flotid + + shine stile birgh + + + + I t f l oa t ed u n d er the sh i n y s t ee l b r i dge to a s m a ll b ea ch.

Analysis: The student correctly wrote 44/50 graphemes (letters for sounds) and 19/24 words. She represented almost all of the sounds with the correct letters for each word. She wrote the correct letters for the beginning sounds of the five words that she missed; however, she did not correctly write the middle or ending letters. She wrote all of the consonants, consonant digraphs, and consonant blends correctly, except that she wrote /th/ for the consonant *t*, bir for the *br* blend, and *gh* for the -*dge* consonant digraph. She wrote all of the vowels and vowel digraphs correctly, except that she wrote *o* for the *oa* vowel digraph in *floated* (but wrote *boat* correctly). She wrote *e* for *y* and *i* for *ee*. She wrote *id* for the past-tense -*ed*. She used capital letters correctly and remembered all the punctuation marks. She also appropriately spaced her words and letters, so her writing was was easy to read.
Instructional Implications: Begin with the making words strategy with *oa* and *ee* vowel digraphs, using word tiles. Then, during separate lessons, have her make words with the following: words ending in *y*, with /t/ and /th/, *br* blend, past-tense -*ed* with all three sounds (/ed/, /d/, /t/), and a brief lesson on *dge* words.

• Words Their Way Spelling Inventory

SOURCE: Bear, Invernizzi, Templeton, and Johnson (2012).

PURPOSE: To identify a student's developmental spelling stage to plan word study instruction.

PROCEDURE: The *Words Their Way Spelling Inventory Word List and Feature Guide* can be found in the Bear and colleagues (2012) book. The teacher selects the appropriate level: primary, elementary, or upper level. The student is asked to read each word the teacher says from the list.

SCORING AND ANALYSIS: The teacher uses the feature guide to mark each phonetic element written correctly. The number of words spelled correctly, the number of phonetic feature points, and the total are recorded. The teacher identifies the highest-level column in which the student wrote at least 80% of the features correctly; this indicates the student's spelling stage, which is used to select instructional strategies.

INSTRUCTIONAL IMPLICATIONS: Students can be grouped according to their spelling stage. The teacher provides strategies for reading and writing words at this stage, and then has the students apply these strategies to their reading and writing. When they are successful at that stage, instruction moves to the next stage.

• Handwriting Rubric Assessment

PURPOSE: To determine a student's strengths and areas for improvement in handwriting.

PROCEDURE, SCORING, AND ANALYSIS: The *Handwriting Rubric Assessment* can be used with any writing assessment or writing sample to assess the student's specific development in handwriting (see Appendix, p. 428). Using the criteria listed in the rubric under the columns labeled Exceeded, Met, and Did Not Meet, the teacher marks a plus sign (+), checkmark (✓), or minus sign (–) for each of the standards. Using the school-adopted style of manuscript or cursive, the teacher compares the student's handwriting with the expected standard and identifies areas of strength and areas for improvement, such as letter formation, spacing, directionality, reversals, and capitalization.

INSTRUCTIONAL IMPLICATIONS: Because the goal of writing is communication, the focus should be on legibility rather than exact handwriting style.

WORD ANALYSIS: STRATEGIES

Phonological Awareness Strategies

Sequence of Phonological Awareness Strategies

There are six general types of activities for teaching phonological awareness, presented here in order of complexity:

1. *Preparatory and ongoing activities.* Listen to stories, songs, and rhymes → Echo stories, songs, and rhymes → Recite stories, songs, and rhymes.
2. *Rhyme awareness activities.* Identify words that rhyme → Produce words that rhyme.
3. *Phoneme awareness activities.* Identify the beginning sound of a word → Identify the ending sound of a word → Identify the middle sound(s) of a word.
4. *Segmenting activities.* Segment sentences into words → Segment words into syllables → Segment words into sounds.
5. *Blending activities.* Blend syllables into words → Blend sounds into words.
6. *Manipulation activities.* Delete syllables from words → Substitute syllables in words → Delete sounds from words → Substitute sounds in words.

Although the following strategies are auditory, they can be extended by having the students read or write the letters or words. Since words represent meaning, and not just a sequence of sounds, it is important to incorporate and discuss the meaning of each unknown word, and never use nonsense words.

• Oral Rhyming Words

PURPOSE: For students to identify and generate rhymes (in grades K–4).

PROCEDURE: Rhymes are taught in context by first reading a rhyming couplet, then leaving off the last word and having the students complete the rhyme.

EXAMPLE: From *The Cat and the Hat* by Dr. Seuss (1957): "Would you, could you in a boat? Would you, could you with a ___________ [goat]?" Students can also say as many words as they can that rhyme with *cat* or other rhyming words in the book.

Phoneme Identification

PURPOSE: For students to identify initial, final, and then medial phonemes (in grades K–2).

PROCEDURE: The teacher asks students to identify the initial, final, and then medial phonemes within words they hear in conversations or in books (e.g., to listen for initial /s/, and then later to identify the initial sound in *sat, sit, sip,* and *sad;* to listen for final long /e/, and then to identify the final sound in *me, see,* and *bee*). The strategies used should make phonemes prominent in students' attention and perception.

EXAMPLE: The teacher models specific sounds, such as /s/ in the word *sat,* and asks students to produce each sound in isolation and in many different words until they are comfortable with the sound and understand its nature.

Blending Phonemes

PURPOSE: For students to blend individual phonemes into words (in grades K–2).

PROCEDURE: The teacher selects a familiar word and tells the students, "I am going to say the sound of each phoneme, and you need to figure out what word it is." The teacher pronounces each phoneme separately, and then asks the student to orally blend the phonemes into the word. This strategy helps students eventually decode or sound out words.

EXAMPLE: "/s/ /ā/ /t/ blended together makes what word? /m/ /ĭ/ /l/ /k/ blended together makes what word?"

ADAPTATION: The teacher can say to students: "Put your left hand on your right shoulder and say the initial sound; put your hand on the inside of your right elbow for the middle sound; then put your hand on your right palm and say the final sound. Now run your hand from shoulder to palm to blend the sounds."

Pushing Pennies for Phoneme Segmentation

PURPOSE: For students to segment words into individual phonemes so that they can eventually write each word one grapheme at a time (grades K–2).

PROCEDURE: As the teacher, do the following:

1. Prepare your phoneme mats and picture cards. Along the short side of a piece of paper folded in half, make three 1″ × 1″ boxes for words with three phonemes. On the long side of the other side of the paper, make four 1″ × 1″ boxes for words with four phonemes. Make picture cards for words with three and four phonemes. Select a picture card to put on each student's piece of paper, and give the students a penny to put under each phoneme box.
2. Model the activity by pronouncing the word slowly and pushing one penny up into each box on a card as each sound is pronounced.
3. Select a new picture card. Ask the students first to name the picture, then to say each sound of the word as they push a penny into the box. Make sure that there is a one-to-one match between the pronunciation of each phoneme and the pushing of each penny. Start with phonemes that are represented by only one letter. See Figure 4.9 for an example.

FIGURE 4.9. Pushing pennies for phoneme segmentation, example.

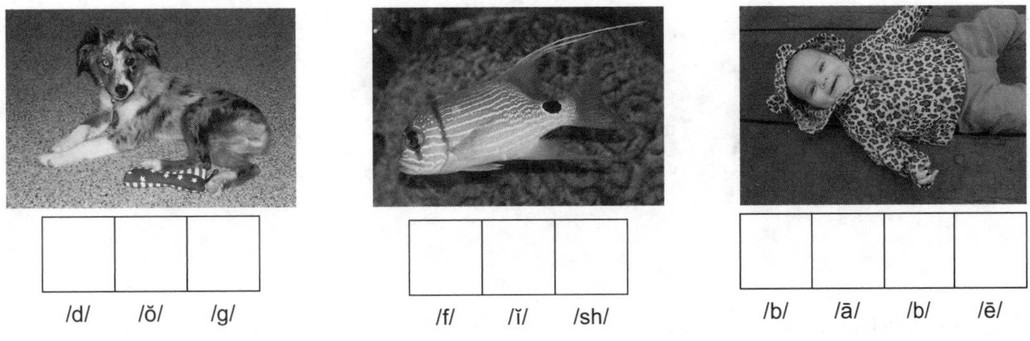

ADAPTATION: These words could come from a story or theme. For example, after reading the book *Cat on the Mat* by Brian Wildsmith (1982), tell the students, "We are going to listen to some of the words in the book and see if we can identify each sound, so that later we can write these words." Say the word *cat* slowly and separate each sound. Then ask, "How many sounds do we hear?" The answer should be "Three." If not, model by saying the word *cat* while pushing one penny for each phoneme: /k/ /ă/ /t/. Tell the students, "Now you say the word *cat*. Push one penny in each box as you say each sound." If the students are correct, try the next word; if not, model again and have the students push pennies for each sound in *cat* again. Example words from *Cat on the Mat*: *cat, sat, mat, dog,* and *goat*.

ASSESSMENT: A plus sign (+) is given for each word a student segmented correctly and a minus sign (–) for each word segmented incorrectly. For instructional feedback, point out correct responses and then for incorrect responses model how to push pennies and segment each word, then have the student do it.

● Take Apart, Put Together (Phoneme Segmentation and Blending)

SOURCE: Fitzpatrick (1997).

PURPOSE: For students to segment words into individual phonemes and blend phonemes into words so that they can eventually write and read the words (grades K–2 or as needed).

PROCEDURE: As the teacher, do the following:

1. Distribute several linking cubes to each student.
2. Say a word with three phonemes, such as *duck*. Show them a picture of the word to link the word with meaning, especially for ELLs.
3. Have students repeat the word slowly, taking one cube for each sound they hear (segmenting phonemes) and linking the cubes together.
4. Ask them to touch each linked cube from left to right, saying the corresponding sounds with each movement. Have them sweep a hand across the cubes as they blend the sounds to form the word (blending phonemes).
5. Then have students take the linking cubes apart, "breaking" the word as they say the corresponding phonemes for the last time (segmenting phonemes).
6. Repeat with other words. Once students are successful with words with three phonemes, do the same strategy with a mixture of words with three, four, or even five phonemes. See Figure 4.10 for an example.

FIGURE 4.10. Take apart, put together (phoneme segmentation and blending), example.

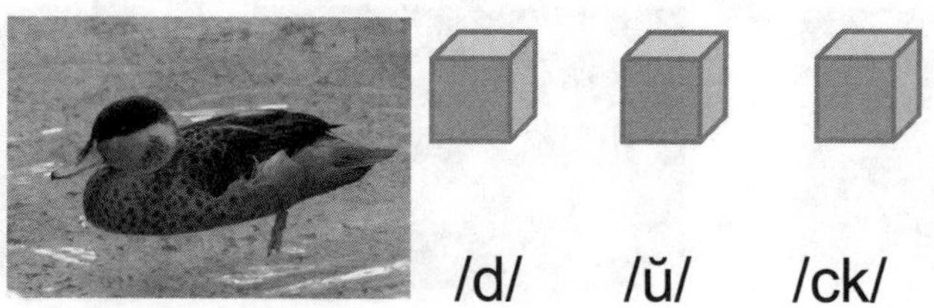

• Picture Sorts

PURPOSE: For students to hear the differences in the sounds of phonemes by sorting pictures by their initial, final, or medial sound(s) (grade level K–2 or as needed).

PROCEDURE: The teacher selects one or two initial, final, or medial sounds for the students to identify or differentiate, based on the assessment data. For closed picture sorts, students are asked to find and name all of the pictures that have that phoneme—for example, "Find all the pictures that begin with the /p/ sound" (*pig, pencil, paper, pan, purse, penguin*). For an open sort, the teacher asks, "Tell me what all the picture names have in common." For example, they may all have the *-ar* sound in them (*car, star, arm, card, jar*). The students can also sort the pictures by two different sounds.

• Seven-Step Activity

PURPOSE: For students to rhyme, blend, segment, isolate sounds, and substitute phonemes (grades K–2 or as needed).

PROCEDURE: As the teacher, say the following:

1. "I have a secret word. Can you guess what I'm saying? /s/ /a/ /t/ (*sat*). Say each sound separately, not the letters."
2. "Let's think of words that rhyme with *sat*."
3. "Which of these words doesn't rhyme with *sat*? *sat, man, rat*." (Make up several sets of words to use with the secret word of the day.)
4. "What is the *first* sound you hear in *sat*? . . . And we spell that sound with what letter? What is the *last* sound you hear in *sat*? . . . And we spell that sound with what letter?"
5. Let's say all the sounds apart, like I did: /s/ /a/ /t/. Now let's use two fingers to clap the sounds in *sat*." (Do the same with some of the rhyming words the students came up with earlier.)
6. "If we say *sat* without the /s/, what is left?" (*at*) Or substitute new beginning sounds: "If I put a /b/ in front, what is my new word?" (*bat*)
7. "If I put /th/ in front, what is the word?" (*that*)

ADAPTATION: If time allows, use wipe-off boards and write words that rhyme with the word of the day, or use magnetic letters on a cookie tray. Words can be sorted by common spelling patterns or word families. If some words rhyme, but are spelled differently, put them in a separate column. As students' skills improve, emphasize substituting beginning sounds and segmenting each word into individual sounds.

Alphabetic Principle and Emergent Text Concepts Strategies

• General Letter and Sound Identification

PURPOSE: For students to identify the names of the letters and the sound or sounds that each letter represents (grades K–1 or as needed).

PROCEDURE: The teacher selects a letter–sound correlation to teach, based on student assessment or observation and the *Phonics Skills for Grades K–3* chart (see Appendix, pp. 411–413), which will indicate the approximate grade level at which to teach the phonetic elements. Generally, instruction begins with frequently occurring consonants, followed by the other consonants, vowels, consonant digraphs, vowel digraphs, word endings, *r*-controlled vowels, and others. At first, the teacher should work with only a few letter–sound correspondences that have high utility in many words (e.g., /m/ in *man, mad, him,* and *ham*). The teaching of less frequently occurring letters and consonant digraphs should be postponed until the students have a firm understanding of how left-to-right spellings represent first-to-last sounds (alphabetic understanding). If the *Letter and Sound Identification Assessment* has been administered, teaching can begin with the unknown sounds for which the students knew a word that began with that sound. When introducing each letter, the teacher points to it and says the letter name followed by the sound or sounds, and then says a common word beginning with that sound (often illustrated by a picture). The students then say it chorally with the teacher, then echo the teacher, and then say it by themselves.

• Alphabet Books

PROCEDURE: The teacher reads aloud alphabet books to build vocabulary and teaches students the names of words that represent each letter. Then students reread the books and consult them to think of key words when making their own books about a letter.

• Key Word Alphabet Chart

PROCEDURE: The teacher creates or uses an alphabet chart with a picture and word of a familiar object for each letter. Students must be familiar with the objects, or they won't remember the key words. The key words chosen should be ones, that represent the primary sound each letter makes. Words beginning with consonant digraphs should be avoided unless such digraphs are being taught. The teacher and students recite the alphabet by pointing to each letter and saying the letter, the sound, and the name of the picture (e.g., *A, /ă/, apple*). The alphabet chart can also be used as a resource to read or spell words. If a student wants to write the word *pet,* for instance, the teacher says, "The word *pet* starts with the same sound and letter as at the beginning of *penguin.* Can you find the letter that starts with the word *penguin*? How will you write the letter *p*?" See Figure 4.11 for an example.

• Seek and Find Pictures and Objects

PROCEDURE: As the teacher, do the following:

1. Seek and find pictures in books or magazines, stickers, images from the internet, or photos depicting objects in the environment that start with certain letters. Create one book or poster for each letter.
2. Cut out the pictures or make drawings of objects to put in the book or poster.

FIGURE 4.11. Key word alphabet chart, example.

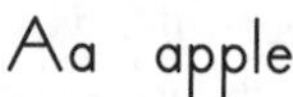

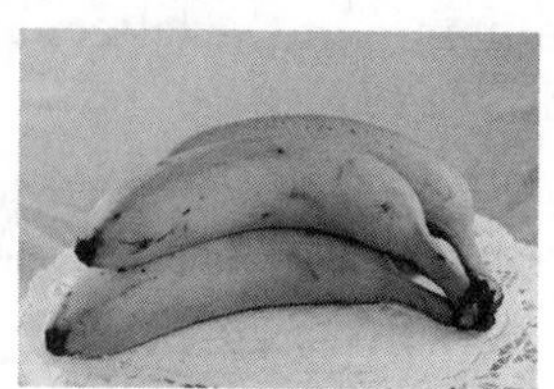

B b banana

C c cactus

D d dog

3. If a picture does not have a word, write the word, and underline the selected letter.
4. If the initial letter has multiple sounds or is a consonant digraph, sort the pictures by sound and label each with the sound.

• Letter Books and Posters

PROCEDURE: As the teacher, do the following:

1. Choose a letter (grapheme) and sound (phoneme) to study.
2. Show students an object that begins with that letter. Ask, "What sound do you hear at the beginning of that word? How do we write that word? What letter does it start with?"
3. Brainstorm: "What other words start with or contain that letter and sound?"
4. Say to students: "Using the computer, newspapers, or books, find words and/or pictures that start with that letter and sound."
5. Make a book with that letter/sound (e.g., "My *E* Book"). Each page should include the letter, the word, a picture, and a sentence. If that letter represents more than one sound, sort the words and put all the words with the predominant sound first, followed by words with the subsequent sound(s).

• Letter and Word Search Highlighting

PROCEDURE: While reading books, students look for a particular letter or phoneme represented by two or more letters at the beginning of a word or anywhere within the word. The teacher can cover the letter or phoneme with highlighting tape, or make circle-shaped letter frames from tag board, plastic bracelets, pipe cleaners, or wax-covered sticks for students to highlight particular letters on charts or in big books. Each time, the students say the letter, the sound, and the word represented by that letter. Students should be reminded that some letters represent multiple sounds.

• Environmental Print

PROCEDURE: The teacher and students collect food labels, newspaper advertisements, toy traffic signs, and other environmental print for students to sort and use in identifying letters and words. Examples for the letter *p* and sound /p/: *Peter Piper Pizza, Pepsi,* *popsicle, popcorn, peanut, pumpkin, peaches.* Or students' names can be used: *Penelope, Pedro, Paul.*

• Letter Containers

PROCEDURE: The teacher and students collect coffee cans or shoeboxes, one for each letter of the alphabet. The teacher writes uppercase and lowercase letters on the outside, and places several familiar objects that represent the letter in each container. The teacher uses these containers to introduce the letters, and the students use them at a center for sorting and matching activities.

• Letter Stamps

PROCEDURE: Students use letter stamps and ink pads to stamp letters on paper or in booklets. They also use letter-shaped sponges to paint letters, and letter-shaped cookie cutters to make cookies or to cut out Play-Doh letters.

• Magnetic Letters/Letter Tiles

PROCEDURE: Given a variety of letters, students pick all examples of a letter or match uppercase and lowercase letter forms. They also arrange the letters in alphabetical order and then use the letters to spell their names or other familiar words.

• Making Letters

PROCEDURE: Students practice making letters while saying the sound(s) that each one represents. They can use pipe cleaners, Play-Doh, shaving cream, or colored hair gel in a bag to make letters, or they can write on sidewalks, in the air, or on whiteboards.

• Show-and-Tell Bag

PROCEDURE: At home, students place items and pictures in a bag that represent a given letter or sound. They can share these items with other students, or each one can give clues as to what is in their bag for the others to guess.

• Songs, Rhymes, and Alliteration Texts

PROCEDURE: The teacher selects songs, rhymes, and alliteration texts that teach a selected letter sound. For example, if the students are studying the letter *B*, the teacher can read aloud *Brown Bear, Brown Bear, What Do You See?*; *Big Red Barn*; *Blueberries for Sal*; or *Stellaluna* (about bats and birds).

• Directionality and One-to-One Matching

PURPOSE: For students to read from left to right, differentiate between the amount of space between letters and words, correlate one written word with every spoken word, and use the return sweep.

PROCEDURE: When reading a big book to the class, the teacher uses a pointer to demonstrate reading from left to right and continuing to the next line by pointing under each word as they read. Students then take turns demonstrating these concepts, first with the big book and then with individual copies of the same book. For one-to-one matching, a student must clearly point under each word as it is read. If the spoken and written words do not match up, such as if words have multiple syllables, the teacher reminds the student to point only once for the entire word, and then has the student reread it until one-to-one matching is achieved. One motivational technique is to give the student a plastic fingertip with a long nail (found at a novelty store) to use when pointing one to one. These same concepts can be reinforced during writing instruction, especially finger spacing, the return sweep, capitalization, and punctuation.

• Segmenting Sentence Strategy

PURPOSE: For students to segment sentences into separate words.

PROCEDURE: The teacher models and demonstrates how to break short sentences into individual words. Chips, cards, or other manipulatives can be used to show how a sentence is made up of separate words and how the order of the words matters.

EXAMPLE: The sentence "Frogs eat bugs" has three words, so one chip is pushed up for each word.

• End Punctuation Reading and Writing Strategy

PURPOSE: For students to read with intonation and correct pausing marked by end punctuation, and to write with the correct end punctuation marks.

PROCEDURE: As the teacher, do the following:

1. Find an emergent text containing periods, question marks, and exclamation marks. Explain that authors write their ideas in sentences, and that each sentence ends with a period, question mark, or exclamation point.
2. State that a declarative or telling sentence is marked with a period at the end. Ask the students to point to each period on the page. Then read the sentences, taking a long breath after each period. Have students chorally read the sentences, reminding them not to stop at the end of a line if it is midsentence. Act out making a point in the air with a finger each time they come to a period. Then have them put a card with a period on it where it should go between declarative sentences, then write a declarative sentence with a period.
3. State that an interrogative sentence or question is marked with a question mark at the end. Ask students to point to each question mark on the page where the author or character asks a question. Then read the sentence, pointing out that your voice often goes up at the end of questions and you take a breath at the end of each sentence. Act out making a question mark in the air with a finger each time they come to a question mark. Have the students chorally read the sentences, reminding them to pause between sentences. Then have them put question marks in sentences and write interrogative sentences with question marks.
4. State that an exclamatory or strong emotion sentence is marked with an exclamation

point at the end. Exclamation points are used to show strong feelings such as excitement, anger, or joy. Follow this same technique for reading and writing exclamatory sentences. Point out that your voice rises with excitement and then falls.

Teaching commas and other punctuation marks is discussed in Chapters 5 and 7.

Song Chart Activities for Emergent Text Concepts, Word Identification, and Fluency

PURPOSE: For students to improve emergent text concepts, word identification, and fluent text reading using visual, auditory, kinesthetic, and tactile experiences

OBJECTIVES:

- Students will echo and then recite songs and finger plays, and use actions to demonstrate meaning.
- Students will demonstrate one-to-one matching by pointing to each word on a song chart.
- Students will identify initial sounds and letters for high-frequency words in a song.
- Students will sequence the phrases and sentences by words and related pictures.
- Students will sequence the words into phrases and sentences, and put punctuation in the correct places.
- Students will orally (or in writing) compose new words for songs, substituting nouns, verbs, and adjectives.

PROCEDURE: As the teacher, do the following:

1. Select a song/story that students know, or teach students a new song that has many common words.
2. Write the song lyrics on large chart paper or sentence strips, one phrase per line. It is best to use the Zaner–Bloser (ball-and-stick) writing style, a large font, and clear spaces between words. It is beneficial to write each line or stanza in an alternating color to help with tracking.
3. Add pictographs to selected words or phrases, especially nouns, to support one-to-one matching and word recognition.
4. Add hand or body movements to the song to help students remember the lyrics, focus on the meaning, and provide opportunities to move. You can use American Sign Language or your own made-up signs.
5. Start by singing the entire song to the students while pointing to each word.
6. Then, one line at a time, point to each word as you sing it and have students echo each line of the song.
7. Then have the whole class sing the entire song as you point to each word.
8. Each day, choose an objective or skill for the students to learn:

- *One-to-one matching.* Select a sentence or phrase of the song. Say the sentence or phrase aloud to the students. Have the students orally count how many words are in the sentence or phrase. Tell them that when words are written, they are divided by spaces. Have them put up one finger for each word in the sentence as you point to it.
- *Letter and sound identification.* Select a letter that is repeated frequently in the song. Point to the letter, and ask students what sound it makes. If they do not know, refer them to

the picture alphabet chart. Have students come up and point to each word that starts with that letter. Have the students repeat the letter, the sound, and the word that starts with that letter. Once students can find words that start with several different letters, ask students to find words that have particular letters at the end of words. Once they are successful, have them find words that have that letter in the middle of words. Start with common consonants, then vowels, then uncommon consonants. You can also have them find both lowercase and uppercase forms of selected letters.

- *Sentence sequencing.* Write each of the sentences or phrases on a sentence strip. As a class, put the sentences in order. Point out how the sentences differ, depending on differences in beginning letters of words. Then read the sentences to put them in order. In small groups, have the students put the sentence strips in order.
- *Word sequencing.* Select a sentence from the song that has several common words. Write the sentence on a sentence strip. Read the sentence aloud to the students. Cut between each word as you read it. Be sure to cut off the punctuation marks. As a class, then in small groups, and finally individually, have the students sequence the words correctly in the sentence and put the punctuation marks in the correct place.
- *Word identification.* Initially select common repetitive words in the song (three to five per day). Select the sentence or phrase with the word or words in it. Cover up the word you want to teach. Read the sentence as you point to each word, and ask the students to try to figure out what word is missing. Uncover the letter (or letters) making the first sound in the word. Ask the students what sound the letter (or letters) makes. Uncover the next letter and ask what sound it makes. Keep going until all letters in the word are uncovered. Read the word, then reread the whole sentence. Do this for several common words in the song.
- You can also create configuration boxes and sound boxes for words in the song. These are explained below under "Orthographic Strategies."
- As a class, write new words for the song/story. Using the same pattern, change some of the nouns, adjective, verbs, and adverbs. Cover up the nouns and ask the students, "What other words could we write that would make sense in this sentence?" Make sound boxes for those words. Slowly say each word, and ask the students, "What sounds do you hear, and how do you write each sound?" Have the students change the song in small groups, in pairs, and then by themselves. Have them practice reading/singing the new songs. Advanced students can write a whole new song and draw a picture for it. See Figure 4.12 for an example of a song chart for the "Five Little Ducks" song. The new version of the song begins with the line "Five brown bats went out one night."

Word Identification Strategies

General Guidelines

The teaching of a word should integrate as many cueing systems as possible (graphophonemic, morphemic, syntactic, semantic, and pragmatic). For example, if the students are learning to read and write the word *playing*, the teacher begins by finding the word in the text and reading the sentence: "The dog was *playing* in the park." The teacher can then ask:

> "What was the dog doing in the park? [Semantic and syntactic] Look at the picture. How can you tell the dog was playing? [Semantic] This word contains two meaningful parts: *play*, the verb or action the dog is doing, and *-ing*, the suffix to mean that it is happening now. [Morphemic and syntactic] How many sounds do you hear in *playing*?

FIGURE 4.12. Song chart activity, example.

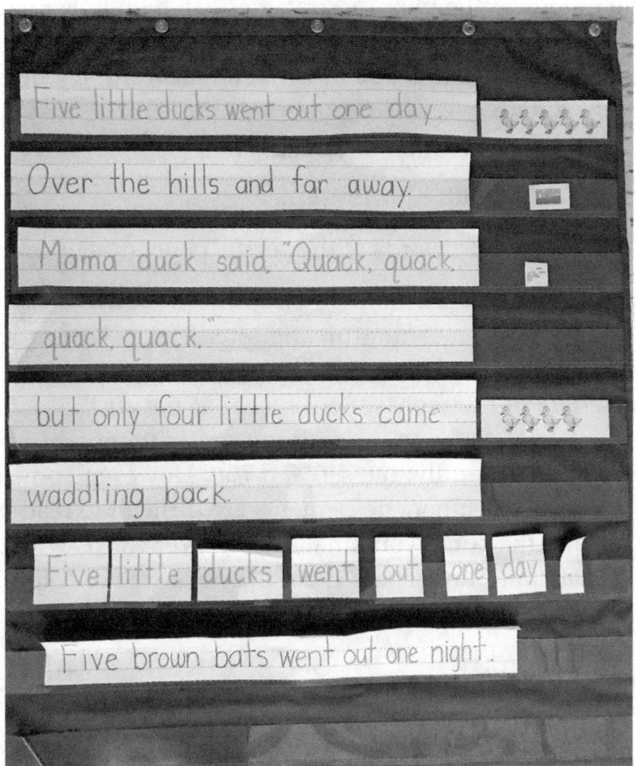

Let's make five boxes. What sound do you hear at the beginning of the word? /p/. How do we write it? What's the next sound? /l/. How do we write it? What two letters make the /ā/ sound? <ay>. What sound does /ing/ start with? /ĭ/, <i>. What two letters make /ng/? <ng>. [Grapho-phonemic] Can you use the word *playing* in a new sentence? Can you write that sentence? [Grapho-phonemic, morphemic, syntactic, semantic] There is another meaning of *playing*. If I were to say 'Quit playing around,' what would that mean? Who could give me another word for it? *Fooling around*." [Pragmatic]

Grapho-Phonemic Strategies

The general purpose of grapho-phonemic strategies is to help students identify and write words by analyzing word parts. For emergent readers, it is best to focus on high-frequency words and words the students will see regularly in their reading materials. These strategies are frequently taught in grades K–3; however, they can be used for older students when they come to words they do not know and cannot figure out through the context of the sentence.

• Grapho-Phonemic Strategies from the Good Readers Bookmarks

PURPOSE: For students to figure out unknown words, using the phonics strategies from the grade-appropriate *Good Readers Bookmark* (see Appendix, p. 438). These bookmarks are described more fully in Chapter 5.

PROCEDURE: The teacher gives a student the appropriate *Good Readers Bookmark,* and prompts the student to look at the phonics strategies listed on it. For example, the teacher can suggest, "Say the first three sounds and think about what makes sense, sounds right, and looks right. If it does not make sense or is not a real word, try breaking the word in parts, or try a different sound."

• Books with Specific Phonetic Elements

PURPOSE: For students to identify words with specific phonemes in context (grades K–3 or as needed).

PROCEDURE: As students read meaningful and predictable stories containing several examples of words that reflect the letter–sound pattern being taught, the teacher asks students to find those letters in the words. Books such at *Cat on the Mat* (Wildsmith, 1982) encourage students to read through an interesting story with repetitive sentence structure that emphasizes the *-at* word family: *cat, sat,* and *mat.* However, some books written for the purpose of teaching specific phonetic elements are difficult to read because the stories have no real meaning and the books contain just a series of words with the same phonetic pattern, such as "Nan can fan Dan." These types of books are not helpful for instruction.

• Model Decoding of Words

PURPOSE: For students to use a model to decode words on their own (in grades K–3).

PROCEDURE: Beginning with small, familiar words, the teacher models sounding out the letters left to right, blending the sounds together, searching for the word in memory, saying the words, then using them in the context of a sentence.

• Make and Break Words

PURPOSE: For students to read and make new words (grades K–3 or as needed).

PROCEDURE: With magnetic letters, letter cubes, or tiles, students make words. It is beneficial to have the vowels and the consonants in different colors, so that the students know that every word has a vowel sound. The teacher scrambles the letters needed to make a

FIGURE 4.13. Make and break words, example.

word and has the students reconstruct it. This process begins with two- and three-letter words that have one letter per sound and builds to more complex words. Once they know some words, the students can change the onset or rime to make new words. The students can also find and read the words in a story. See Figure 4.13 for an example.

• Missing Vowel Cards

PURPOSE: For students to identify and produce the correct vowel in words (grades K–3 or as needed).

PROCEDURE: The teacher makes index cards with each of the vowels *a, e, i, o, u,* and then makes cards with pictures of a variety of consonant–short vowel–consonant words (*cat, pen, pig, fox, cup*). The teacher writes each word under its picture, but draws an underline where the vowel should be. The students sort the picture cards under the correct vowels. The same activity can be done with long vowels or controlled vowel sounds.

• Missing Vowel Mix-and-Match Chart

PURPOSE: For students to read and make new words by changing the short vowel sound (grades K–3 or as needed).

PROCEDURE: The teacher creates a chart like the one depicted in Figure 4.14 on heavy paper, and cuts out the vowel tiles at the bottom. The teacher then gives the students these directions: "Put different vowels in each space to make new words. Start with the first box: h_t. Put one vowel at a time in the box. Start with the letter *a*. Now blend the sounds together. Does it make a real word? If it makes a real word, write the real word in a column on your paper. Then try each of the other vowels (*e, i, o,* and *u*) to see if they make real words. When you are finished making a word with all of the boxes, read each word you wrote on your paper. Use the word in a sentence to demonstrate understanding of the word." Example sentences include "I have a Cardinals baseball *hat*," "He *hit* the ball," "It is *hot* outside," "They lived in a *hut*." Students can also choose three words that they wrote down and draw a picture for each of them.

• Word Family Letter Slide

PURPOSE: For students to read and make new words that rhyme and are spelled with different onsets but the same rime.

FIGURE 4.14. Missing vowel mix-and-match chart, example.

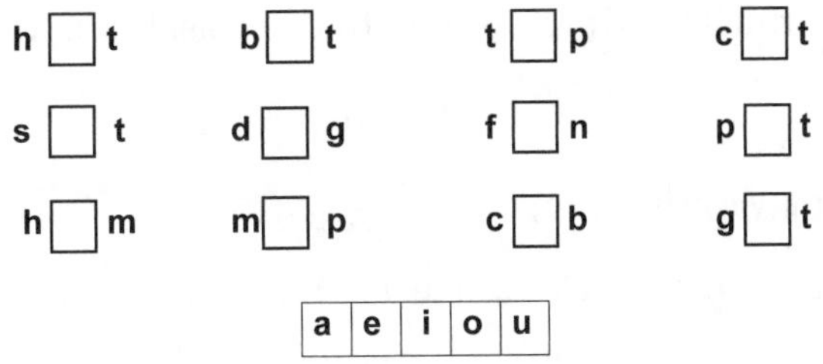

h☐t	b☐t	t☐p	c☐t
s☐t	d☐g	f☐n	p☐t
h☐m	m☐p	c☐b	g☐t

a	e	i	o	u

PROCEDURE: As the teacher, do the following:

1. Select a word family to study.
2. Give the students an outline picture of one object that contains the word family (e.g., a picture of a chick for the *-ick* word family). Write the word family on the right side of the picture. Cut two parallel 1″ vertical slots just to the left of the word family in the picture. Write possible onsets on a ⅞″ strip of paper.
3. Tell the students: "Write your name, date, and 'Word Family Letter Slide' on the top of your paper. Read the end part of the word on the picture [*-ick* → chick]. Slide the strip through the slot, so that you can see one letter or two letters that are written together at a time. Blend the beginning sound or sounds with the ending sounds, and read the word. Move the strip to read more words [examples: *chick, kick, pick, lick, stick*]. Write and read each word on your paper. Draw a picture for three of the words."

Sorting Words by Sounds

PURPOSE: For students to identify multiple sounds of letters and digraphs (grades K–3 or as needed).

PROCEDURE: As the teacher, do the following:

1. Find a story that contains numerous examples of graphemes with multiple phonemes or sounds: *c* (/k/, /s/); *g* (/g/, /j/); *ch* (/ch/, /k/, /sh/); *-ea* (ē, ĕ, ā,); *-ed* (/ēd/, /d/, /t/).
2. Make word cards that represent the phonograms in the story, and then ask students to sort word cards under the correct sound cards.
3. Have students create new word cards as they find them in print. Instead of teaching many phonic rules, teach the students to try alternate sounds, starting with the most common sound.

EXAMPLE: To help students sort and read words based on the sound of past-tense *-ed*, read a story such as "The Little Red Hen." Find the words ending in past-tense *-ed*. Put the /ed/, /d/, and /t/ on colored heading cards in three columns. Have the students read each of the words on the word sort cards (*planted, played, worked*, etc.). Underneath each column, the students sort the cards by their ending sounds. They then select one word from each column, write the sentence from the story where that word was found, and underline the word.

Seek and Find Words

PURPOSE: For students to identify and read words with different phonemes.

PROCEDURE: The teacher selects one to four categories of phonemes (blends, consonant digraphs, vowel digraphs, etc.) For more examples, see the *Individual Phonics Summary* in the Appendix (p. 414). Students skim a text and find at least three words that belong in that category.

Personal Word Wall Words

PURPOSE: For students to create a resource for reading new words (grades K–3 or as needed).

PROCEDURE: The teacher introduces a few high-frequency words as they are encountered in text. As words are introduced, students write them under the correct initial letter in a personal word chart or dictionary for ongoing reference. Students can draw or cut out picture clues to match each word.

• Printed or Electronic Dictionary and Glossary

PURPOSE: For students to look up words to identify their meanings and pronunciations (grades K–2 or as needed).

PROCEDURE: The teacher provides instruction and practice in using a printed dictionary or glossary, including how to use guide words and how to use the dictionary pronunciation key. Only after sufficient practice with printed dictionaries can students use them as effective resources. In addition, students can learn to use an electronic dictionary by typing the word or using a voice command.

• Connecting Known to Unknown Words

PURPOSE: For students to make connections between words that they know and the words written to read the new word.

PROCEDURE: When a student is reading and comes to an unknown word that has the same phonetic element(s) as a word they know, the teacher writes the new word down, says it with the known word, or points to the phonetic elements in the known word and says, "What is this word? The new word has the same sound(s). What is the new word?"

• Flip Books

PURPOSE: For students to use analogy to read words that have the same word parts (onsets, rimes, prefixes, roots, suffixes, consonant digraphs, vowel digraphs, or blends).

PROCEDURE: As the teacher, do the following:

1. Preview a book to be read by students.
2. Find a pattern of word parts, phonemes, or graphemes found in the book that the students might have difficulty reading.
3. Make at least one flip book of words with the same word parts, using strips of 1″ tag board stapled together.

EXAMPLE 1: For words with the rime of *-and*, write *and* on the right side of each strip, and then stack short strips on the left side with different onsets: *s, b, h, l, bl, br, st.*

s	and

Staple the onsets onto the left side, so that students can flip them to read each new word.

EXAMPLE 2: For words with the same consonant digraph, such as *wh-*, write *wh-* on the left side of each strip, and then stack short strips on the right side with different vowels and consonants to make words starting with *wh-: at, ere, en, y, ith.* Staple these strips onto the right side, so that students can flip them to read each new word.

EXAMPLE 3: For words with different suffixes, such as present, past, and progressive verb endings *-s, -ed,* and *-ing,* write the root word on the left side of each strip, and then stack three strips on the right side with *-s, -ed,* and *-ing* on each. Staple these strips on the right side, so students can flip through and read each new word.

STUDENT DIRECTIONS:

1. "Write your name and date on the top of your paper."
2. "Flip and read each word."
3. "Choose one word and write a sentence with that word."
4. "Underline the part of the flip word that stayed the same in the sentence."
5. "Draw a picture related to that word."

• Flap Books

PURPOSE: For students to read words by analogy that change in pronunciation, such as contractions and silent *-e* words.

PROCEDURE: As the teacher, do the following:

1. Preview a book to be read by students.
2. Find contractions or silent *-e* words found in the book that students might have difficulty reading.
3. Make at least two flap books of words with the same patterns, using long strips of 1" tag board.

EXAMPLE 1: For words ending in silent *-e* that make a long vowel sound, write the consonant–vowel–consonant combination on the left side of the strip, and then fold the right side of the strip over to the edge of the word. With the flap closed, write *-e* next to the word that was already written. You can do this with all different words that are real words with and without a silent *-e*: *can/cane, Pet/Pete, fin/fine, not/note, tub/tube.*

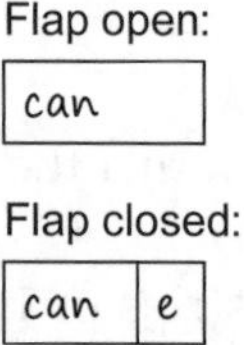

EXAMPLE 2: For the contraction *don't,* write *do not* on the left side of the strip, and then fold the right side of the strip over to cover the space and the word *not.* With the flap closed, write *-n't* next to the *do* that was already written. You can do this with all different contractions that appear in the book and those that do not.

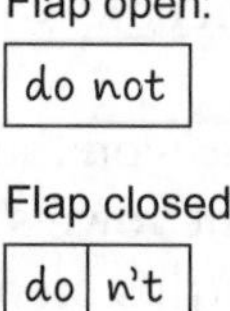

STUDENT DIRECTIONS:

1. "Write your name and date on the top of your paper."
2. "Read each word with the flap open and closed."
3. "Choose one flap book."
4. "Write a sentence using the word with the flap open."
5. "Write a sentence using the word with the flap closed."
6. "Underline the flap book word in each sentence."

Over and Under Words

PURPOSE: For students to correct a substitution of a visually similar word when reading.

PROCEDURE: On a paper or dry erase board, the teacher writes the word the student said directly above the word as it is written in the text. The teacher discusses the similarities and differences between the two words, and then has the student reread the correct word in the sentence.

EXAMPLE:

thought	very	happy
through	every	happily

H Brothers Poster

PURPOSE: For students to identify the sound of consonant digraphs (grades K–3 or as needed).

PROCEDURE: Using pictures of the four "H brothers" (see example in Figure 4.15), the teacher points to each brother and tells this story: "This brother plays with trains and says /ch/. This brother blows his whistle and says /wh/. This brother doesn't want to play and sticks his tongue out and says /th/. This last brother says, 'Mom is coming, /sh/.' " Students refer to the poster for reading or writing consonant digraphs. For example, the word *when* has the beginning sound of the brother who blows his whistle.

General Suggestions for Using Analogy and Structural Clues

PURPOSE: The general purpose of the following analogy and structural clue strategies is to have students identify and compare phonetic elements in known words to learn to read new words. These strategies are used to teach initial, medial, and final phonemes, as well as morphemes such as prefixes and suffixes. As readers begin to recognize sight words, they can use analogies to learn new words. For example, students who have seen the word *day* many times, and who know the sound for the letter *m*, will probably recognize the word *may*. Building phonemic awareness for onsets and rimes helps students to identify simple words and syllables by analogy.

Activities that engage students in word family (*cat, sat, hat*) and initial consonant substitution ("What word would I have if I changed the *c* in *cat* to an *s*?") can assist emergent readers in using analogies to read new words. Beginning with small, familiar words, students learn to sound out the letters and blend them together, searching for the word in

FIGURE 4.15. H brothers poster, example.

memory. The teacher models sounding out the word, blending the sounds together, and then saying the word. The ability to sound out new words allows students to identify and learn new words on their own. Select one or two elements at a time on which to focus. See Figure 4.16 for an example. To write words with the *-un* word family, students make an outline of a sun and add initial letters to make new words.

PROCEDURE: Readers also employ analogy cues by using the words they know to help them recognize unfamiliar words. Students can learn to manipulate onsets and rimes. For example, a student who can read *cat* can change the onset to *s-* when reading the new word *sat*. Associating sounds with a cluster of letters, such as the rime *-at*, leads to more rapid, efficient word identification. According to Cunningham (1995), beginning readers recognize very few words instantly; however, through repeated exposure to the same words, the number of sight words grows. It is particularly important that developing readers learn to

FIGURE 4.16. Analogy word family, example.

recognize those words that occur very frequently in print, since only 100 words make up 50% of the words read by adults and students alike. The *Fry's Instant Words* lists include both phonetically regular high-frequency words (*the, and, you, he, it*) and phonetically irregular high-frequency words (*of, they, have*). The English language is derived from many different languages, and therefore words are not consistently spelled phonetically. For example, words that look as if they should rhyme do not, such as the words *to* and *go*. Homophones are spelled differently yet sound the same, such as *there, their,* and *they're*. The teacher can help students identify these words by pointing them out in context and comparing them to other words with the same spelling and sound patterns.

The following are specific strategies that can be used to assist students in using analogy and structural clues to problem-solve unknown words.

Phonetic Visual Anchor Chart or Bulletin Board

PURPOSE: For students to use a chart as a resource for students who are learning to read and write words with the same phonetic element by analogy.

PROCEDURE: The teacher creates a visual anchor chart or bulletin board with pictures and key words for the most frequent phonemes represented by two or more graphemes (vowel digraphs, consonant digraphs, *r*-controlled, and vocalic *-r*). The words on the chart can have the graphemes underlined or put in a different color. The chart can also be theme-related. For example, it can depict a farm scene, and each item can be labeled with key words. Vowel digraphs: *hay, pail, rake, sheep, wheat, field, bike, light, silo, goat, post, backhoe, cow, cloud, boy, soil, boots*. Consonant digraphs: *sheep, chickens, wheel, thumb, feather*. *r*-controlled: *barn, horse*. Vocalic *r*: *farmer, bird, fur, earthworm, tractor*. When students want to spell a word, such as *stay*, the teacher can point to the chart or board and say that it is written like the /ā/ in *hay*.

Cut-Up Sentences

SOURCE: Clay (1993).

PURPOSE: For a student to read a sentence with one-to-one matching by sequencing words, graphemes, and punctuation, and to help the student develop sight word recognition. This strategy is beneficial for students who can identify initial sounds of words based on initial letters, yet are still learning how to decode many one- and two-syllable words.

PROCEDURE: A student reads, writes, and/or dictates a text. The student or teacher selects a sentence according to degree of interest or amount of challenge. The student rereads the sentence. The teacher uses the guided writing procedure to write the sentence on a sentence strip, making sure to say the entire sentence, to sound out each word as it is written, and to note when and why capitalization, spacing, and punctuation are needed. The teacher then rereads the sentence, pointing to each word. As the teacher cuts off each word and punctuation mark from the strip, the teacher and/or the student reads each word and punctuation mark. The teacher scrambles the words and punctuation marks, making sure they end up right side up. The student restates the sentence, looks for each word and punctuation mark, and places each one in order, reading the words as they go along. The student then self-assesses by pointing to each word and punctuation mark as it is read, to check that it looks like the word the student is reading. If the student does not self-correct, the teacher asks the student to say the word they are looking for. The teacher asks, "What sound starts that word, comes next, or ends that word? What letter or letters represent that sound? Can you find a word with those letters at the beginning, middle, or end?" The cut-up sentence pieces are placed in an envelope with the sentence written on the front, to be practiced later at home or at school. Students should be encouraged to point out these words when reading or writing new texts. They can also use these words as key words to read, or can write other words with the same spelling pattern. On a subsequent day, the words can be used for flash cards to assess word identification, and can be placed in the "Words I Know" and "Words I Am Learning" envelopes described below. See Figure 4.17 for an example.

DIFFERENTIATION: If the procedure is too challenging, a teacher can try selecting one of the following: a sentence that is shorter, a sentence that the student can easily remember, a sentence that the student has previously dictated or written, a sentence containing words with different initial letters that are easily decodable, or a sentence with only one end punctuation mark. The teacher models the sequencing of the words and sentences, using a think-aloud of the thought processes. Or the student can use a picture alphabet chart to identify the letter associated with the sounds. To provide more challenge, the teacher can cut up individual words by onset/rime, by syllable, or by phonemes, or can select longer sentences or ones with multiple punctuation marks.

• "Words I Know" and "Words I Am Learning" Envelopes (or Boxes)

PURPOSE: For students to identify known and new words (grades K–3 or as needed).

PROCEDURE: The teacher makes two labeled envelopes (or boxes) for each student, and

FIGURE 4.17. Cut-up sentence, example.

From *Cat on the Mat* by Brian Wildsmith (1982). The student selected the sentence "The cat sat on the mat." The teacher wrote the sentence on a sentence strip, and cut between each word or punctuation mark. The teacher then scrambled the words and the punctuation mark.

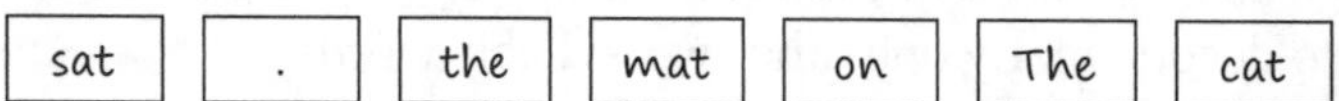

The student sequenced the words and punctuation mark as she read each word, then checked that it looked right and made sense.

gathers word cards created from word wall words, cut-up sentences, or other sight words the student is learning. These are placed (no more than five to seven words at a time) in the "Words I Am Learning" envelope. The student reads each card, if needed the teacher helps the student to break up the words into parts and try different sounds to read them. Once the student can read and/or write the word in isolation three different times, it is placed in the "Words I Know" envelope. The teacher or student can mark the card with a tally mark each time it is read correctly.

EXAMPLE: After a student successfully completes the cut-up sentence "The cat sat on the mat," the teacher assesses the student's word identification and places the words *the, cat,* and *on* into the "Words I Know" envelope, and the words *sat* and *mat* into the "Words I Am Learning" envelope. Any word that is not a high-utility word can be eliminated from the "Words I Am Learning" envelope.

Morphemic Strategies

Morphemic analysis cues for word identification involve structural analysis. This includes the identification of roots, affixes, compounds, hyphenated forms, inflected and derived endings, contractions, and in some case syllabification. See additional vocabulary strategies in Chapter 3.

• Meaningful Word Parts

PURPOSE: For students that are more advanced readers to use structural cues to figure out how to decode and learn the meaning of new words. To help students to identify and learn meanings of prefixes and suffixes from the text.

PROCEDURE: During reading, students can break words in parts (prefixes, roots, suffixes, compounds) by covering each affix. They can also add different suffixes to words (*play, plays, played, playing*) with magnetic letters or word cards. When learning contractions, they can substitute the apostrophe and subsequent letters for the word these replace.

• Morphemic Analysis Flip Books

PURPOSE: For students to identify an unknown word with multiple morphemes from the students' reading or writing, and to connect it to words with similar roots, prefixes, and suffixes.

PROCEDURE: The teacher selects words with either the same root, the same prefix, or the same suffix, and uses quartered index cards to create mini-books. Four to six mini-pages are stapled together on the left side; the known or key word is written on the top page; and the part that is the same in each word is underlined. Examples for flip books: prefix (*un-*: *unfair, unhappy, unsure*); suffix (*-ly*: *quickly, slowly, quietly*); verb tense (*played, plays, playing*); and root (*bio-*: *biology, biography, biodegradable, amphibious, symbiotic, biosphere, biopsy*). The teacher and students discuss what each prefix, suffix, or root means, and how to read and figure out the meanings of words that include these elements. The students then use each word in a sentence to make sure they understand the meaning.

Syntactic and Semantic Strategies

GENERAL GUIDELINES FOR SYNTACTIC AND SEMANTIC STRATEGIES

Context cues for word identification involve using information from the surrounding words, phrases, or sentences, such as semantic or syntactic cues, or using picture cues. The semantic or meaning cues help the reader by associating words with the topic of the text or sentences. For example, when a student is reading a story about dogs, the expectation is that the text may also contain words such as *bark, woof,* and *wagging.* The syntactic cues help the reader to predict what part of speech the unknown word is, based on the word order. The picture cues or illustrations can often help with the identification of a word if there is strong picture support for the unknown word. Typography is also a context cue that students can use to identify words that may be particularly important. Noticing typography such as boldface, capitalization, or italics draws attention to words that may be important. (Typography is addressed further in Chapter 6 with nonfiction text concepts.) Using context cues allows readers to cross-check their identification of words to be sure that each word makes sense in terms of syntactic and semantic cues.

These strategies are intended to support students in using context cues such as their knowledge of background information, sentence structure, vocabulary, and meaning from the text, as well as graphic information, to read and comprehend text. Although phonics cues are important in learning to read, students also benefit greatly from using context cues. While reading, students can be prompted to use context cues by asking them to read on or reread to collect cues to figure out unknown words. They can also ask themselves, "Does it make sense? Does it sound right?" These questions encourage the students to be self-reflective. Pictures and graphics can also support a student's reading, so when selecting books, a teacher should consider the support that the pictures and other graphics provide. Before reading, the teacher can ask the student to look at the pictures and graphics, discuss them, and predict what the text will be about. If applicable, the student could be directed to look at the pictures or graphics and think about the story to figure out a word. Some emergent books have rebus pictures above the word or in place of the word to help beginning readers.

• Cloze Procedure/Guess the Covered Word

SOURCES: Cunningham, Hall, & Sigmon (1999); Taylor (1953)

PURPOSE: For students to use context clues to predict words.

PROCEDURE: During reading, the student predicts the unknown word or part of the word, which is deleted or covered with correction tape or self-stick notes.

EXAMPLE: From *Where the Wild Things Are* by Maurice Sendak (1963): "They gnashed their terrible ___________ (teeth) and rolled their terrible ___________ (eyes)."

• Predictable Language Approach

PURPOSE: For students to use context to read texts that contains predictable or patterned language (grades K–3 or as needed).

PROCEDURE: Students read or chime in during the predictable or patterned part.

EXAMPLE: From Martin (1967): "Brown Bear, Brown Bear, what do you see? I see a ___________ looking at me."

• Creating Sentences

PURPOSE: For students to sequence words from different parts of speech to create a meaningful sentence.

PROCEDURE: The teacher creates manipulatives, such as different-colored word cards or cubes with high-frequency words. The colors correspond to each part of speech (nouns, verbs, articles, adjectives, adverbs, prepositions, conjunctions, etc.). Students use these to create meaningful sentences. Every sentence must contain at least one noun and one verb. Each student can then read their sentence and draw a picture related to it.

Orthography Strategies

General Guidelines for Handwriting Strategies

The general purpose of handwriting strategies is to help students communicate ideas in such a manner that readers can easily read what they have written. These strategies include selecting a handwriting style and teaching letter formation, word spacing, and margins. They also include choosing writing utensils and paper that are appropriate for the students' developmental level.

• Handwriting Style

PROCEDURE: The teacher can use a manual for the selected handwriting style to explain orally to students how to form each letter and write within the lines and the margins. The Zaner–Bloser handwriting style chart is depicted in Figure 4.18. While D'Nealian handwriting is often popular in schools, I have found that the Zaner–Bloser (or ball-and-stick) style is easier for many students to write and differentiate because it doesn't have the added stroke of a tail on the letters. Older students tend to develop their own handwriting styles. I contend that handwriting in the upper grades should only be addressed if it prevents other people from reading the writing easily without having to predict what is written.

• Letter Formation

PROCEDURE: Students can begin learning letter formation by forming large letters in the air, then on the sidewalk with chalk or a paint brush drenched in water, and finally on paper. As the students are making each letter, they can say the letter name and the sound(s) represented by the letter. The teacher can model letter formation with dots that show students where the initial stroke begins, and arrows that show the stroke sequence. Sometimes teaching letters together that use the same motions can be helpful. For example, the "2 o'clock" letters, *c*, *o*, *a*, *d*, *g*, and *s*, can be taught together because they all start at the 2 on a clock and then go counterclockwise up to 12 and around. Students can evaluate their own handwriting by putting a smiley face above the letter or word they wrote the best. The students should maintain a good posture when writing, with their feet on the floor and their chairs pushed in.

FIGURE 4.18. Zaner–Bloser handwriting style chart. Used with permission from Zaner–Bloser, Inc.

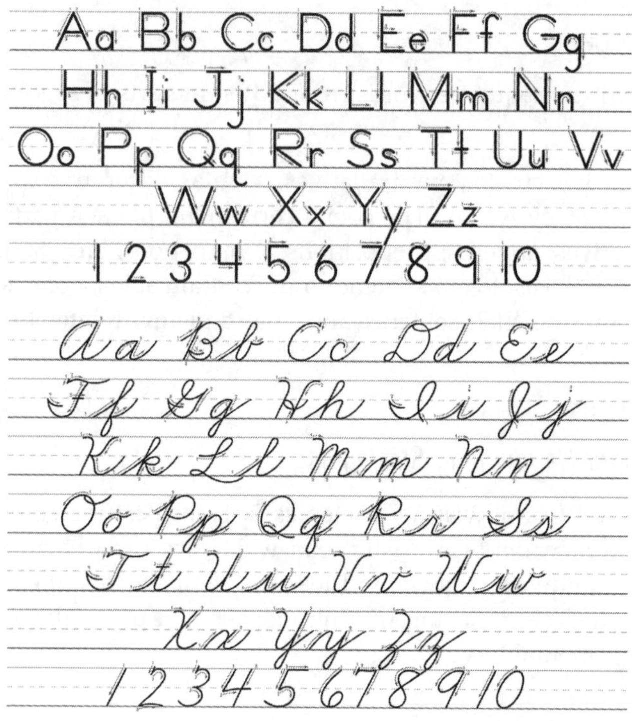

One technique for tracing letters is for the teacher to write letters, words, or sentences with thick strokes, using a color-changing marker. A student can use another marker on top that will change the original color. This will only work if the student traces directly over the original writing. The teacher can also add texture to the letters for students to follow with their fingertips by writing on a textured fluorescent light cover with a crayon or writing on sandpaper. With either of these techniques, students can trace letters of their names and high-frequency words. The sooner students can write their own compositions, the better. Having students share their writing with others is a motivating factor in writing legibly.

• Word Spacing

PROCEDURE: To develop or improve spacing between words, students can place a finger after each written word, or they can lay down a "space person" (a narrow, decorated craft stick) to leave a space before they write the next word.

• Margins

PROCEDURE: Students make a fold along the left and right margins of their paper, and are instructed to write only within the folds (i.e., the margins). Instead of encouraging hyphenating words, the teacher can suggest that the entire word be written on the next line.

• Writing Utensils

PROCEDURE: For emergent writers or those with fine motor coordination difficulties, large-diameter pencils, pens, markers, or crayons are the best choices. For motivation, the type of utensil can be changed. A student who has difficulties holding a utensil properly, or holds it too tightly, can use a pencil grip. Some varieties even have an indentation for each finger when the pencil is properly held.

• Paper

PROCEDURE: Emergent writers should use unlined paper until their letters become small enough for lines. Once they reach this point, the widest ruled paper available (which is in landscape format) should be used; eventually, older students can use regular ruled notebook paper. Some primary paper has textured and colored lines, such as green at the bottom, yellow in the middle, and blue at the top. These lines can be beneficial when students are learning letter formation.

General Guidelines for Spelling Strategies

The general purpose of spelling strategies is to assist students in using conventional and inventive spelling to communicate ideas. While spelling is important in order to accurately convey a written message accurately, it is only one aspect of the writing process. Spelling ability is dependent on writers' having a strong foundation in sound–symbol correlations as well as on their being readers, so that they are familiar with how words look. Students should be taught to spell high-frequency words in the context of reading and writing sentences, and to be inventive in using their spelling knowledge to spell unknown words. Students' writing will be stifled if they are limited to writing only the words they can spell. Spelling skills are not necessarily sequential, so instruction should not be delayed until a student has mastered one spelling pattern before moving on. For emergent readers and writers, high-frequency, phonetically regular words are introduced first, followed by high-frequency, phonetically irregular words. Students are taught to spell words by sounding them out into separate phonemes and writing the corresponding letters one by one. The teacher models the sounding and spelling process for students as they spell. Instruction begins with short words students can sound out, because these words follow regular spelling conventions (e.g., *at, can,* and *go,* instead of *see, was,* or *have*). It continues with teaching "word family" words and demonstrating how they are similar.

• Chanting and Acting Out Spelling Words

PURPOSE: For students to spell words kinesthetically, based on letter configuration (grades K–3 or as needed).

PROCEDURE: The students chant the letters or sounds as they act them out. Actions or arm movements are added as each word is spelled, based on the configuration of the letter. Arms are raised to the "attic," and students can go up on their tiptoes, for tall letters that go above the center line (*b, d, f, h, k, l,* and *t*). Arms are out front for "main floor" letters that remain between the center and bottom lines (*a, c, e, i, m,* etc.). Arms go down as students squat down and touch the ground to the "basement" for letters below the bottom line (*g, j, p, q,* and *y*). Students stand up and spell each word as they move, and then write the word.

EXAMPLE: To spell ducklings: *d*—arms up, *u*—arms out front, *c*—arms out front, *k*—arms up, *l*—arms up, *i*—arms out front, *n*—arms out front, *g*—squat down, *s*—arms out front. Chanting and acting out each letter help the students to remember how to spell words, including their weekly spelling words.

• Configuration Boxes

SOURCE: Cunningham (1999).

PURPOSE: For students to spell and recognize words, based on their configuration.

PROCEDURE: First, the teacher identifies a word or words that a student has difficulty reading and/or writing and makes a boxed outline around the shape of each letter to indicate the configuration the letters make above the center line, below the bottom line, and between the center and bottom lines, to assist memory. The teacher makes square boxes on the line for letters that are written between the center line and the bottom line (*a, c, e, i, m, n, o, r, s, u, v, w, x, z*), tall rectangular boxes that go from the bottom line to above the center line for tall letters (*b, d, f, h, k, l, t*), and rectangular boxes for letters that go from the middle line and hang down below the bottom line (*g, j, p, q, y*). These boxes are connected to show the configuration of the whole word. As the teacher tells the students each new word, the students say each sound and say what letter makes that sound and writes each letter of the word in the corresponding configuration box to assist them in spelling the word correctly.

See Figure 4.19 for examples. While this strategy supports word identification, it cannot be used alone, as there can be numerous words with the same configuration.

ADAPTATION: The teacher provides the configuration boxes and asks the students to select the correct spelling words to match.

• Sound Boxes

SOURCE: Elkonin (1973).

PURPOSE: For students to spell and recognize words, based on the number of phonemes in a word.

FIGURE 4.19. Configuration boxes, examples.

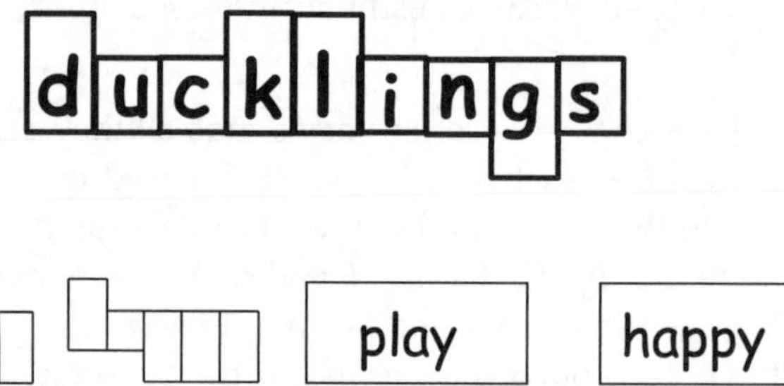

PROCEDURE: As the teacher, do the following:

1. Draw one box for every phoneme in a word. If more than one letter represents that phoneme, then divide that box vertically with dotted lines between each letter. For a silent *-e* at the end of a word, draw a line underneath where the *e* would be written, since a box would indicate it has a sound.
2. Have the students predict what the letter or letters in each box should be.
3. Ask the students, "What sound do you hear at the beginning of the word? What letter represents that sound? [Refer to an alphabet chart as needed.] How do we write that letter? [Refer to a handwriting chart as needed.] What sound [or sounds] do you hear in the middle of the word? How do we write this sound? What sound do you hear at the end of the word? How do we write it?"
4. Have the students write the letter or letters that represent the sound in each box as they say the sound. See Figure 4.20 for examples.

• Key Word Spelling

SOURCE: J. Bradley (personal communication, 1996).

PURPOSE: For students to use a key word chart for identifying English spelling patterns associated with the long and the short vowel sounds.

PROCEDURE: The teacher puts a key word chart on the wall (see Table 4.3 for an example), and also places copies of the chart in the students' writing folders for them to use as a reference for spelling. If students want to spell a word, they sound it out to determine the vowel sound. They then use the chart to identify the possible spellings for that sound. The spelling patterns are in order from most common to least common. They select and write the spelling pattern that they believe to be correct for a given word.

• Magnetic Letters

PURPOSE: For students to read and spell new words, based on the connection to known words or spelling patterns (grades K–3 or as needed).

PROCEDURE: The teacher shows the students how to make new words by changing the onset or the rime.

EXAMPLE: c **a** n (change the initial consonant to *f, m, pl*)—f **a** n, m **a** n, p l **a** n, p l **a** n t (add a *t*).

FIGURE 4.20. Sound boxes, examples.

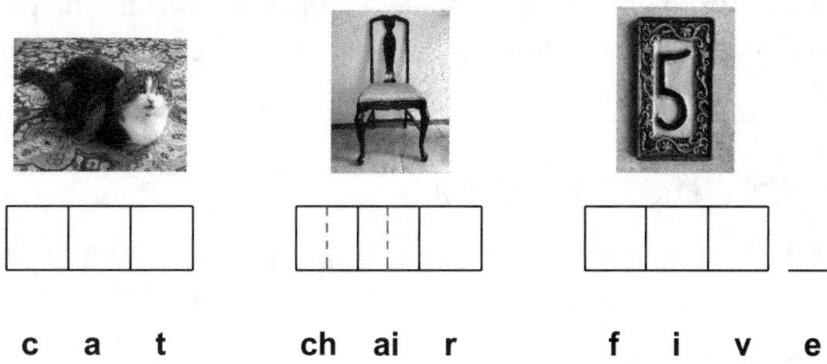

TABLE 4.3. Key Word Spelling Chart

Vowel sound	No. of spellings	Different spellings
Long a /ā/	9	day, made, bait, straight, gauge, break, sleigh, obey, veil
Short a /ă/	4	pat, laugh, have, plaid
Long e /ē/	7	scheme, each, bleed, police, key, neither, niece
Short e /ĕ/	5	net, health, friend, heifer, said
Long i /ī/	11	die, mine, aye, aisle, geyser, stein, coyote, kind, light, height, my
Short i /ĭ/	6	pin, give, been, sieve, build, myth
Long o /ō/	9	cone, sew, mauve, soul, boast, dough, brooch, glow, toll
Short o /ŏ/	2	not, wasp
Long u /ū/	3	future, pewter, beauty
Short u /ŭ/	2	nut, some
Long oo /ö/	8	do, blue, broom, brute, bruise, move, through, group
Short oo /ŏŏ/	3	put, book, could
Diphthong /oi/	2	boy, join
Diphthong /ow/	3	how, mountain, sauerkraut
Schwa /ə/	7	basal, nickel, table, civil, Mongol, cherub, porpoise
Vocalic *r* /er/	6	her, first, nurse, works, early, grammar
r-controlled /ar/	1	arm
r-controlled /or/	1	for
l-, *w*-, and *u*-controlled	3	all, awful, auto
/aw/	8	claw, cause, broad, cough, gone, bought, boss, caught

• Personal Spelling Dictionary

PURPOSE: For students to use a personal dictionary as a resource to spell words the students frequently use in their writing.

PROCEDURE: Each student creates a spelling dictionary with words the students can read and are learning to write. There should be one page for every letter of the alphabet. As the students desire to write new frequently used words, the teacher helps them to add the words to their dictionary. The students can even add drawings to help them remember the word.

• Read, Cover, Write, and Check Words

PURPOSE: For students to read and write words from short-term memory rather than copying.

PROCEDURE: As the teacher, do the following:

1. Select two to five high-frequency words that students have had difficulties with during reading and/or writing. These could be words that are visually similar. For advanced readers, these could also be important content words.
2. Fold a sheet of paper into four columns. The first column contains two to five new words to learn.
3. The student reads the first word, covers it up, writes the same word in the second column, then opens it up and checks the spelling. This process is repeated for the third and fourth columns.
4. If a word is written incorrectly, the student draws one line through it, rereads the correct word, covers it, and writes it again. See Figure 4.21 for an example.

ADAPTATION: Cut one side of a file folder into four equal flaps. The student puts the paper inside the folder and can lift the first flap, read the word, cover the word with the flap, write the word under the second flap, open the first flap to check the word, read it again, cover it, and write it under the third flap. The process is repeated for the fourth flap.

• Word Sorts for Phonemes and Word Families

SOURCE: Bear et al. (2012).

PURPOSE: For students to identify the differences and similarities of words by sight and by sound (grades K–5 or as needed).

PROCEDURE: The teacher selects words that can be sorted by sight and/or by sound, and asks students to sort the words by how the vowels sound. Students can also sort the words by similar spellings. Some exceptions to the spelling rules can be included, once students learn the common spelling patterns.

EXAMPLE: Students sort words spelled with *–ea* into three sounds, such as /ē/, *eat*; /ĕ/, *bread*; and /ā/, *great*.

• Word Study Notebook

SOURCE: Bear et al. (2012).

PURPOSE: The notebook serves as a record, an assessment, and a resource for the word study activities taught (in grades 1–12).

PROCEDURE: A student writes the spelling or sound pattern learned in each lesson, with examples on each page.

EXAMPLE: The letter *o* that says its name: *boat, stone, so, grow.*

FIGURE 4.21. Read, cover, write, and check words, example.

Read, cover, write, and check three times each			
they	~~thay~~ they	~~thay~~ they	they
there	~~ther~~ there	there	there
their	their	their	their
they're	~~they'er~~ they're	they're	they're

• Word Wall Words

SOURCE: Allington and Cunningham (2002).

PURPOSE: For students to use a word wall as a resource to spell and read explicitly taught common words.

PROCEDURE: As the teacher, do the following:

1. Introduce high-frequency words from stories a few at a time.
2. Model sounding out each word, and provide a kinesthetic method for remembering how to spell and write it.
3. Place each word on the word wall underneath its initial letter.
4. Have the students refer to the word wall when they find words in books or want to write words that are on the wall.
5. The word wall words can be written with an outline of the letter configurations as a clue.

EXAMPLE: The words *said, saw, school, sometimes,* and *stop* could be written under the letter *s*.

Chapter 5

Reading Fluency

UNDERSTANDING READING FLUENCY

Oral reading is "the process of reading aloud to communicate to one another or to an audience," according to Harris and Hodges (1995, p. 173). During this social process, people read aloud or discuss the reading to share information, to enhance their understanding of the text, and purely to enjoy the text. Teachers can also use oral reading for assessment and instruction when these are done properly, although they are not its primary purposes. When students read materials in small groups or individually at their instructional level, oral reading provides a window into the readers' processing and provides an opportunity to scaffold the instruction to enhance their problem-solving strategies.

Reading fluency is the accurate reading of connected text with appropriate prosody at a conversational pace or rate (Hudson, Lane, & Pullen, 2005). Oral reading fluency is highly correlated with reading comprehension; however, even students who sound as if they are reading fluently may not be comprehending what they read, and students who comprehend may not exhibit all of the criteria for fluent reading (Rasinski, Rikli, & Johnson, 2009). The three primary components of reading fluency are accuracy, prosody, and pace, while comprehension is related.

Word Accuracy

Word accuracy is the ability to read the words in a text as the author has written them. Since most readers (even fluent readers) make some mistakes or miscues while reading, due to making predictions of the author's words, the expected word accuracy is 90% or above. The word accuracy score is determined by dividing the total number of words correctly read by the total word count of the passage that a student read.

To attain word accuracy, readers need to use grapho-phonemic, syntactic, and semantic cues to monitor their reading and to self-correct when necessary. Goodman's (1965) seminal work examined the sources of information students use while reading. These integrated sources are called the linguistic cueing system (Goodman, 1996), which is divided into three sources: semantic (meaning), syntactic (structure or grammar), and grapho-phonemic (symbol and sound). During the reading process, effective readers integrate semantic, syntactic, and grapho-phonemic cues that interact with the reader's knowledge to support ongoing word identification and comprehension (Adams, 1990; Clay, 1991; Goodman, 1996; Rumelhart, 1994). The linguistic cueing system incorporates these three cueing sources, along with the integration of morphemic (meaningful word parts) and pragmatic (language use in context) cues. Figure 4.1 (p. 121) depicts the linguistic cueing system model of cue integration. To monitor their reading, students can reflect on the following questions correlated to each of the linguistic cues:

- *Grapho-phonemic:* Does it look right, using phonetic and visual cues?
- *Morphemic:* Does the word structure sound right, using affixes and roots?
- *Syntactic:* Does the sentence structure sound right, using word order and grammar?
- *Semantic:* Does it make sense, using prior knowledge, context, and graphics?
- *Pragmatic:* Is it appropriate for the context or social situation?

Familiarity with both syntax and semantics, through listening and reading a variety of texts, enables even very young readers to anticipate the format and predict the content of sentences in print (Singer & Ruddell, 1985). Oral reading strategies are the ways the reader makes sense of cues during reading, in making miscues, during cross-checking, and in making self-corrections. A significant difference between efficient readers and developing readers is their ability to use a variety of strategies that integrate the cues in order to comprehend a passage (Clay, 1991; Goodman, 1996; Walker, 2004).

Prosody

Prosody refers to the expressiveness with which a person reads; it includes intonation, stress placement, pauses at phrase boundaries, and the rhythm of the sound of words (Rasinski et al., 2009). Readers place vocal stress or emphasis on appropriate words; voice tone rises and falls at appropriate points; inflection reflects the punctuation (such as rising with yes–no questions); in dialogue, vocal tone reflects a character's emotional state; and pausing occurs at appropriate phrase boundaries (Hudson et al., 2005).

Intonation refers to the tone of how readers say or read phrases, rather than what they say. It is the way they use vocal pitch to express particular meanings and attitudes. Listeners can tell whether the meaning conveys being bored, surprised, angered, happy, or grateful, based on the rising or falling tone. There are also some grammatical intonation patterns, such as usually asking "wh-" questions with a falling intonation, but asking yes/no questions with a rising intonation.

Stress is part of the rhythm of the language; it includes syllable, word, and sentence stress. There are stressed and unstressed syllables. Stressed syllables are louder and longer, and tend to occur in content words such as nouns and verbs, whereas structure words such as articles and prepositions are usually unstressed. Syllable stress can change the meaning of a word, such as *dessert* versus *desert*. Word stress can change the meaning of a sentence. Reading the sentence "I love my sister" multiple times, stressing a different word each time, will show how it changes the meaning. Sentence stress focuses on saying important words a bit louder and longer. For example, in "I just got a *new bike*!", the stress is put on the words *new* and *bike*.

Pausing or **phrasing** is reading in meaningful phrases by pausing after punctuation or phrases to enhance meaning. Students should always pause at the ends of sentences as indicated by end punctuation marks, but also after most middle-of-sentence punctuation, such as commas, semicolons, and colons. In addition, readers pause within sentences after extended noun phrases, verb phrases, and prepositional phrases, as in this example: "Stella,/my Australian shepherd,/ has been whining/because she wants/to go for a walk/ in the park." Slight fluctuations in pitch, timing, and emphasis can all have an impact on meaning. For example, a lack of pausing for commas can change "Let's eat, Grandma" into the cannibalistic statement "Let's eat Grandma," or a difference in emphasis can change a question such as "What did you do?" into an expression of disapproval ("What did you *do*?"). The goal of phrasing and other aspects of prosody is for readers to take the words on the page and bring them to life through their interpretation and delivery. Readers use the author's words to guide the conversational delivery, so that they sound as if they are talking to and with people.

Lastly, **rhythm**, as related to prosody, is the intensity, duration, or melody of syllables, words, or phrases, which influences the aesthetics and the use of effective and persuasive language. It includes the rate, frequency, and pitch of sound.

Pace

Conversational pace is the ability to read words efficiently at a rate similar to that of conversational speech, in order to understand the message the author is trying to convey or to communicate a message to an audience. Shanahan (2016) has explained that if a reader reads too slowly, such as one word at a time with pauses in between, it may be difficult to keep all the information in short-term memory and may negatively affect the comprehension of the text. Those readers who have difficulty reading words easily have to devote most of their cognitive attention to decoding rather than reading comprehension. The problem may be the divided attention, not the slow speed.

Shanahan (2016) goes on to explain that speed-reading is also not the goal, as it often lowers comprehension as well. Instead of trying to teach students to read faster, it is essential to make sure that they can decode easily and maintain their concentration. Someone listening to oral reading should be able to understand the message because the reader is grouping the words appropriately into smooth-sounding phrases and clauses. Students who are reading aloud should try to read the text as well as they can, not as fast as they can. They should focus on understanding the text because they will be expected to retell and/or answer questions when they finish. Finally, they should read so that the reading sounds like a conversation—not too slow or too fast.

Reading speeds are also going to vary by content, purpose, and background knowledge. More demanding texts will require readers to slow down to maintain comprehension, while easier texts with familiar topics should allow for faster reading of a text. Students should not attempt to read in a completely steady pace, measuring out each word evenly, as this could sound monotonous or boring. The pace of reading should emphasize the meaning of the text. The pace should increase when they want to indicate urgency, excitement, or strong emotion, while the pace should slow to indicate importance, sadness, confusion, or the seriousness of a point the author is making.

There has been some confusion between reading fluently and reading quickly. The goal of reading is comprehension, not reading quickly. Because reading rate and accuracy are more easily quantifiable than conversational pace and reading prosody, they are often what are measured for fluency. Because fluent readers do not have to concentrate on decoding the words, they can focus their attention on what the text means. When students are first learning to read, they often read slowly and have very few strategies for problem-solving unknown words. As students gain experience in reading and can efficiently integrate all aspects of the linguistic cueing system, their pace of reading will improve.

Unfortunately, the act of timing children's reading causes children to focus on reading fast, and not on self-correcting their reading or on reading with phrasing, expression, and intonation, which are characteristics more closely linked with comprehension. Timing children can lead to anxiety or lack of confidence in their reading or achievement. As readers learn strategies for figuring out unknown words, and for reading with both prosody and comprehension, their reading pace will improve. The act of timing children does not improve their reading. It is not recommended to time children's reading for assessment or instruction. If a school requires this information, possibilities may include timing without the readers' knowledge, or at the very least not focusing on increasing students' words per minute. Students can just be encouraged to increase their word identification and prosody skills, so that they can read at a conversational pace and with comprehension.

Comprehension

While accuracy, prosody, and pace are beneficial, readers should most importantly be able to comprehend what they are reading. Comprehension should always be a part of oral reading assessment and instruction; it is discussed separately in Chapter 6.

Silent Reading and Reading Stamina

Silent reading gives students an opportunity to read at their own pace, practice problem-solving and fluency strategies they have learned, focus on comprehension, spend more time actually reading, and develop their interests in reading self-selected texts. During instructional time, teachers can give students a purpose for reading silently and then discuss each section in order to monitor comprehension. Students then may reread sections orally in order to support answers or verify information found in the text. Students also need opportunities for self-selected independent reading and reading for their own purposes.

In addition to reading fluently, students need to build reading endurance or stamina. **Reading stamina** is being able to stay focused on reading for a long period of time without getting too tired or giving up, as well as being able to read increasing longer and more complex texts. Students should set reading goals for themselves by slowly increasing the amount of daily independent reading based on the number of minutes, pages, or books read. Students should be able to read a complete picture book or a chapter or two in a single sitting without getting distracted or giving up. Children cannot become better readers and develop a love of reading if they only read independently for a short period of time each day.

Guided Reading versus Round-Robin Reading

Guided reading at students' instructional level gives the students the chance to apply the strategies they have learned to a new text in a supportive small-group setting. Although oral reading can be very beneficial during guided reading instruction, **round-robin reading**—a technique in which teachers call on students with different reading levels to read orally one after another in front of the whole class—concerns many researchers and educators (Opitz & Rasinski, 1998). Students may come to the inaccurate conclusion that perfect word reading and following along in the text are the goals, rather than comprehending the text. During round-robin reading, students have fewer opportunities to problem-solve on their own (as others often correct them), and orally reading in front of more able readers may cause students to feel anxious or embarrassed about their reading. In addition, because oral reading one by one is more time-consuming than silent reading, less class time is spent reading, discussing, and comprehending the text (Opitz & Rasinski, 1998). Some students have difficulty comprehending for a variety of reasons when other students read. Some students do not read loud enough; some do not read fluently enough, or model ineffective strategies; and some read too fast for others to keep up. Not all students read at the same level or can use strategies to self-correct their miscues efficiently. It is very difficult to keep all students engaged during round-robin oral reading, and therefore very few students benefit from this practice. In addition, it is inappropriate for the teacher and peers to critique a student's reading in front of the entire class, as some students would feel embarrassed or self-conscious about their reading. Therefore, round-robin reading is not an effective oral reading practice.

It is important to note that having children take turns reading at their instructional level in a small guided reading group is not called round-robin reading, as they are reading texts in which they are likely to have high word accuracy, and the teacher is scaffolding their strategy use during the reading process. In a large-group setting, either students should either hear the text read by a fluent reader (such as the teacher or a student who reads fluently), or the text should be read silently. The focus in a large- or whole-group setting should be on discussions related to comprehending the text. Students can also be given opportunities to read the text at home or at school in advance of the discussion.

READING FLUENCY: GOALS

To improve reading fluency, students will:

- Read with purpose and understanding.
  - Listen to and read a variety of genres for enjoyment, information, and vocabulary development.
  - Read to entertain or share information with others.
- Read with sufficient accuracy to support comprehension.
  - Use grapho-phonemic cues and word analysis skills to identify words in context.
  - Use syntactic cues (grammar) and morphemic cues (meaningful word parts) to identify words in context.
  - Use semantic cues (word meanings) and pragmatic cues (language use) to identify words in context.
  - Use context and the integration of cues to confirm or self-correct word identification and understanding, rereading as necessary.
- Read with sufficient prosody to support comprehension.
  - Use intonation (falling and rising tones) to show meaning and expression.
  - Use syllable, word, and sentence stress to show meaning and expression.

   - Use pausing after punctuation and grammatical phrases to show meaning and expression.
   - Use rhythm to show intensity, duration, or melody of syllables, words, or phrases to show aesthetics and use of effective language.
- Read at a sufficient pace to support comprehension.
   - Read at a conversational pace that is not too slow or too fast.
   - Read smoothly and with appropriate phrasing.
   - Modify pace according to content, purpose, and background knowledge.
   - Increase pace to indicate urgency, excitement, or strong emotion.
   - Slow pace to indicate importance, sadness, confusion, or the seriousness of a point the author is making.

READING FLUENCY: ASSESSMENTS

Teachers should assess and analyze students' oral reading to identify the students' strengths and areas for improvement. Oral reading can be evaluated with an oral reading record to analyze word identification, miscues, and reading behaviors; an oral reading strategy checklist to identify oral reading strategies used; and a fluency assessment to evaluate accuracy, prosody, pace. A comprehension assessment, addressed in Chapter 6, can also accompany the running record. Once analyzed, all assessments can be used as a teaching tool to provide immediate feedback to the students about their strengths and areas of need, and to plan instruction.

The primary way to assess oral reading is by listening to a student read and taking running records with comprehension checks. The texts can be trade books, articles, or passages in an informal reading inventory. A **running record** is a method of assessing a child's reading level by examining both accuracy and the types of miscues made. A running record gives the teacher an indication of whether material currently being read is too easy or too difficult for the child, and it serves as an indicator of the child's areas of strength and areas for improvement. For example, if a child frequently makes word substitutions that begin with the same letter as the printed word, the teacher will know to focus on getting the child to look beyond the first letter of a word, and to cross-check with syntactic and semantic cues. An **informal reading inventory** is a collection of leveled fictional and informational passages that teachers use to take a running record of students' reading, and then to have the students retell or answer comprehension questions. Such inventories may also include graded reading word lists, concept questions, prediction questions, and retelling checklists.

Published Informal Reading Inventories and Emergent Literacy Assessments

Many informal reading inventories are available. The following four published literacy assessments are probably the most influential in understanding the reading process of students: the *Observation Survey of Early Literacy Achievement* (Clay, 1993); the *Illinois Snapshot of Early Literacy* (ISEL; Barr et al., 2004); the *Benchmark Assessment System, 3rd Edition* (Fountas & Pinnell, 2016); and the *Qualitative Reading Inventory–6* (QRI-6; Leslie & Caldwell, 2017).

Observation Survey of Early Literacy

For assessing emergent literacy, Clay (1993) developed the *Observation Survey of Early Literacy Achievement*, which is used in her Reading Recovery program. This assessment includes letter identification, concepts about print, word tests, writing vocabulary, writing dictation, and text reading. Running records are taken from 30 leveled books between preprimer and third grade. For each book, an introduction is provided, and a running record of text is taken. A word accuracy score is obtained, along with an analysis of errors.

Illinois Snapshot of Early Literacy

Barr and colleagues (2004) developed the ISEL, which is based on Clay's work but is designed as a screening instrument for classroom teachers to help evaluate all of the emergent literacy areas identified in the National Reading Panel (2000) report. There are two separate tests. The kindergarten and first-grade test contains subtests in alphabet recognition; story listening; phonemic awareness; one-to-one matching and word naming; letter sounds; developmental spelling; vocabulary; passage accuracy and comprehension; and fluency. The second-grade test evaluates spelling; word recognition; fluency; extended written response; passage accuracy and comprehension; and vocabulary. Through extensive research, cut scores were obtained for the beginning and end of each grade level. I contributed to the piloting and adaptation of this assessment. The ISEL is a free assessment and can be obtained online (*https://nlb.nl.edu/media/nlu/downloadable/readingcenter/iseldocumentation%20-%20new.pdf*).

Benchmark Assessment System, 3rd Edition

The *Benchmark Assessment System, 3rd Edition* (Fountas & Pinnell, 2016) includes two leveled kits containing leveled fiction and nonfiction books for grades K–3 and grades 3–8, which correlate to Guided Reading Levels A–Z. Each grade level is subdivided into incremental levels; for example, grade 1 includes Guided Reading Levels C–I. This assessment uses running records, comprehension conversations, and an optional writing component to determine students' independent and instructional reading levels. These data can be used to make instructional decisions and to document students' progress through one-on-one formative and summative assessments.

Qualitative Reading Inventory–6

The QRI-6 (Leslie & Caldwell, 2017) is an informal reading inventory that identifies students' levels of oral reading, silent reading, and listening comprehension levels, using preprimer through 12th-grade word lists and expository and narrative passages. Although there are passages as low as preprimer in the QRI-6, the *Benchmark Assessment System* has more incremental levels for emergent readers, which are correlated to guided reading book levels. There are five to six passages per grade level in the QRI-6. At the lower levels, there are stories with pictures; at the middle and high school levels, there are longer passages based on the different content areas. To analyze a student's reading behaviors, oral reading records are taken during reading and then the miscues are analyzed. The teacher assesses the student's comprehension by analyzing the student's responses on concept questions, retelling checklists, and explicit and implicit comprehension questions after the student has read a passage orally or silently. In addition, the listening comprehension level is useful in determining if a student can comprehend a passage, even if it is at their frustration level for word accuracy. In one study, an earlier version of the QRI-6 (the QRI-3) was found to have the highest percentage of higher-level questions when it was compared with seven other informal reading inventories (Applegate, Quinn, & Applegate, 2003).

Strategies for Using Running Records and Informal Reading Inventories

Literacy experts recommend informal reading inventories for determining students' reading levels and identifying their reading behaviors to plan instruction. In the Appendix to this book, the *Analysis of Miscues Worksheet*, the *Oral Reading Analysis of Miscues Summary*, the *Oral Reading Strategies Assessment*, the *Fluency Assessment by Teachers and Peers*, and the *Comprehension Analysis Summary* can all be used to analyze the student's reading of passages in the informal reading inventories described previously, as well as any other text a student reads. There are many leveling systems for assessments and materials. Refer to the *Reading Level Correlation Chart* in the Appendix (p. 434) to compare grade levels, Reading Recovery levels, Fountas–Pinnell Guided Reading Levels, Developmental Reading Assessment levels, basal equivalent levels, and lexile levels.

• Developing Running Records with Comprehension

PURPOSE: For students to identify students' word accuracy and reading behaviors during reading of any text.

PROCEDURE: As the teacher, do the following:

1. Select a complete or coherent 100- to 400-word narrative or expository text you would like your students to be able to read.
2. Create a running record form. In the heading, write the name of the text, the genre, the reading level, and the word count. Also, add a place for a student's name and the date.
3. Type the text double-spaced, using the same words per line and text layout as in the original text. Readers may lose their place and read text directly above or below the line of text they are currently reading. In the space above, you will write the student's reading behaviors and miscues.
4. On a separate page, write two prior knowledge questions based on the main idea. Ask these questions before the student reads.
5. Create a retelling checklist containing headings and phrases for either the story elements for a fictional text, or the main ideas, details, and text structures of an informational text. Be sure to include the most important ideas and vocabulary words, but not every detail.
6. Create at least eight literal, inferential, and evaluative questions that require more than single-word responses. Be sure to include questions that address the text structure and important vocabulary words. Write potential answers to the questions.
7. To administer the running record, follow the procedures for the oral reading record and analysis of miscues, described next.

• Oral Reading Record and Analysis of Miscues

PURPOSE: For students to accurately represent oral reading behaviors while reading connected text; to identify word accuracy and functioning levels; and to analyze miscues and oral reading behaviors. The data from this assessment can be used to scaffold instruction and select appropriate leveled texts in order to improve student's oral reading.

PROCEDURE: There are five parts to this assessment: the Oral Reading Record, the *Analysis of Miscues Worksheet*, the *Oral Reading Analysis of Miscues Summary*, the *Comprehension Analysis Summary* (addressed in Chapter 6), and the analysis statement. As the teacher, do the following:

1. **Text selection.** To determine whether a text is at a student's instructional or independent functioning level, select a text that the student is interested in reading or has just begun reading. To determine the student's reading grade level or Fountas–Pinnell Guided Reading Level, select texts from an informal reading inventory or benchmark texts that have been evaluated by the publisher, leveling system, or literacy specialist to be at a certain level. Reading familiar text reveals whether the difficulty level of the material the student is using is suitable, as well as how the student is making use of the strategies they have been taught. Reading unfamiliar texts reveals the student's willingness to take risks and indicates the ability to use and integrate strategies independently (Walker, 2004). There are many factors to consider that influence a student's ability to read a given passage. Consider the student's interest, prior knowledge of the content and vocabulary, and ability to use strategies for self-monitoring. The genre, text structure, text complexity, and amount of textual and graphic support all have an impact on readability. Refer to the "Reading Fluency: General Strategies" section on page 187 for more details on readability and leveling of texts. Which text you select depends on what information you want to gather. Sometimes reading a narrative text is easier than reading an expository text because of the reader's experience with that structure. However, selecting an expository text will provide more information about a student's problem-solving strategies while reading content- or discipline-specific material. When selecting passages in an informal reading inventory, you might first find the student's instructional level on the word lists and then select a passage one grade level below. This may reduce the number of passages a student needs to read in order to find the highest instructional level. If the text has fewer than approximately 300 words, you might have the student read the entire text. For longer texts, select a chapter or coherent passage, using the following word count guidelines: preprimer–primer, 40–60 words; first grade, 100–150 words; second grade, 100–200 words; third grade, 200–300 words; fourth grade and above, 300–400 words.

2. **Materials and set-up.** You need the text for the student to read, a clipboard, at least one pencil, and an audio- or video-recording device (optional, but strongly encouraged). You will also need a form or paper to document oral reading behaviors, using one of four formats: the running record with a comprehension check (described previously), a photocopy of the text, a premade form from an informal reading inventory, or a blank sheet of paper. If you use a blank sheet of paper, one line of text should correspond to one line of coding marks; you will write a checkmark (✓) for each correct word and write each miscue on top of a line, with the word from the text below the line. Use the coding system that follows to mark all miscues. Sit next to and slightly behind the student, holding the clipboard

with the running record forms attached. This way you can see the student reading, but can document the reading behaviors without the student's seeing what is written. Place the text the student is to read in front of them. Be sure to start the audio/video recording prior to the student reading and continue until you have completed the comprehension check.

3. **Directions to the reader.** Say, "Today I am going to listen to you read. I am going to mark down exactly what you say. Read the [text, book, or passage] the best that you can, so that you can understand it. Try to read like you are talking—not too fast or too slow. I cannot help you while you are reading, so if you come to a tricky part, try your best. When you are done, I want you to retell what you read, and then I will ask you questions. This story or text is called . . ." You may choose to provide a brief introduction to the text, ask the student to do a picture walk, or ask questions to determine the student's prior knowledge about the content. While the student is reading, code all reading behaviors. If the student reads too fast, or if you have difficulty keeping up with the coding, ask the student to slow down. Audio-recording the reading is beneficial to verify that the coding was done accurately.

4. **Coding oral reading behaviors.** Take a running record by writing all of the student's reading behaviors, miscues, and comments in such a way that the passage could be reread in exactly the way the student read it. To code the student's text reading and miscues, use the *Coding and Scoring Oral Reading Behaviors Guide* (see Appendix, p. 422). The coding and analysis of oral reading was developed by integrating the procedures for running records (Clay, 1993), miscue analysis (Goodman & Marek, 1996), and the *Qualitative Reading Inventory* (the current version of which is the QRI-6; Leslie & Caldwell, 2017). This assessment can be used as a pre- and posttest or as an ongoing assessment to show growth over time. It helps determine a student's reading level, problem-solving abilities, and ability to orally read the current classroom texts or self-selected reading. The oral reading record and analysis is only the first part of the overall reading assessment; the second part is an analysis of comprehension, which is described in Chapter 6.

Miscues are any deviations from the text, including substitutions (real words and decoded sounds), omissions, insertions, hesitations, repetitions, and self-corrections. Do not count hesitations, repetitions, and self-corrections as word accuracy errors because the word is ultimately correct. To keep track of accurate reading, write a checkmark (✓) above each word read correctly. Record checkmarks for all texts below second grade, and for any text where the student typically has more than one miscue per line of text. Write the student's response above the word in the text. If the miscue is not a real word, write the phonetic spelling, and mark all the vowel sounds. Put commas between multiple attempts. For every 2 seconds of a hesitation, put a slash mark between words or letters. If a reader does not pause at a punctuation mark, it can be documented with a hyphen as an omission, but do not count it as a word accuracy error. For a repetition, mark an R with a circle around it, and draw an arrow underneath back to where the repetition began. In this assessment, never tell students a word, as it may inflate their comprehension of the passage; this also sends a message to students that if they wait long enough, an adult will tell them the word, and they will not have to use problem-solving strategies. In a non–assessment setting, however, you may provide strategy prompts to help students problem-solve. In a teaching event, mark a prompt by a P with a circle around it, and consider it a miscue. The following example of coding miscues is from the story *Annie and the Wild Animals* (Brett, 1985):

The student read: Ann fund ✓ cat cuddled ✓ ✓ /// ↑s/t/r/ă/n/g/, strong plāks s-c
The actual text: Annie found her ^ curled up in strange places.

Notice that this example shows several types of miscues. If a student actually reads like this, they are at the frustration level, and a lower-level text should be used.

5. **Comprehension check.** After every text reading, conduct a comprehension check by directing the student to retell what they read and/or asking comprehension questions. More details are provided in Chapter 6.

6. **Determining the need for additional passage reading.** If you want more information and time allows for additional text reading, quickly count the number of miscues to see if the student's word accuracy is at the instructional level. For example, if there are 181 words in the passage, the student is at least at the instructional functioning level for word accuracy if they make fewer than 18 miscues (or 10%). To check the instructional level for comprehension, determine whether the student can retell and answer most of the questions. If the student meets the criteria for both word accuracy and comprehension, continue to the next higher reading level passage; if not, select a lower-level passage for the student to read. If the student can read the passage at an instructional level, you might also have them read a different genre at the same reading level; reading fiction is different from reading nonfiction.

7. **Using the *Analysis of Miscues Worksheet*.** Analyzing miscues provides information about how the reader constructs meaning with the text. This analysis is based on several theoretical assumptions suggested by Goodman and Marek (1996) and summarized by Walker (2004): Readers read to construct meaning; reading is not an exact process; some miscues or errors are more significant than others; miscues should be evaluated for the degree to which they change meaning; and readers use a consistent pattern of correction strategies that indicate their text processing. Using the *Analysis of Miscues Worksheet* (see Appendix, p. 429), record all miscues, except repetitions and hesitations. For each miscue, mark the student's response, a slash, and then the word from the text. For insertions, write the word, a slash, and then a caret. For omissions, mark a hyphen, a slash, and the word. Although self-corrections are miscues and affect prosody and pace, they are not incorrect responses, so they are not counted against word accuracy. Hesitations and omissions of punctuation are also issues of prosody, not word accuracy, so they are also not included in the analysis of miscues. For each miscue, put a checkmark (✓) indicating the type of miscue it is (self-correction, omission, insertion, decoded, or substitution). Mark *decoded* if a student sounds out a word or says a nonword, or mark *substitution* if a student substitutes a real word. An analysis of the semantic (meaning), syntactic (structure or grammar), and grapho-phonemic (visual and sound) cues used while making miscues provides an opportunity to examine the student's processing while reading. For each miscue, check the cue used during the initial attempt at the word (grapho-phonemic, syntactic, or semantic). For grapho-phonemic cues, indicate whether the reader has used the correct initial (I), medial (M), or final (F) sounds. Grapho-phonemic cues are used when a reader predicts a word based on visual or sound similarities, such as the word *very* for *every* (marked with M and F) or when a reader attempts to sound out a word, such as /ŏ/ /t/ /h/ for *other*. Syntactic cues are predictions of a word made on the basis of the sentence structure or of what makes grammatical sense, such as the substitution of *run* for *swim* because they are both verbs. A student shows evidence of using semantic cues if the miscue has a similar meaning, such as the substitution of *little* for *small*. Generally, a student relies on the context and experience when making semantic miscues. In the last column, write *Yes* if the meaning of the text is retained. If it is self-corrected, just write the word *Yes*, as all self-corrections result in the

retention of the meaning. If it is not self-corrected but maintains the meaning of the text, write *Yes* and an asterisk (*), as it counts toward the text meaning or acceptability score. Some miscues do not have a significant impact on the meaning of the text. For example:

The student read:	Toad put the covers over his head.
The actual text:	Toad pulled the covers over his head.

Put and *pulled* generally do not have the same meaning, but in this sentence the meaning of the text is retained, and therefore the miscue is considered acceptable. Mispronunciations are another example of how the reading of the text maintains meaning—for example, saying /pŭskĕtē/ for *spaghetti*. Also, a student who says *gonna* for *going to* still maintains meaning.

Once all of the types of miscues, types of cues used, and meaning-retained miscues are recorded, tally them and write the totals of each at the bottom of the *Analysis of Miscues Worksheet*.

8. **Using the *Oral Reading Analysis of Miscues Summary*.** From the data from the *Analysis of Miscues Worksheet* (see Appendix, p. 429), you can obtain scores for word accuracy; acceptability; self-correction; and use of the grapho-phonemic, syntactic, and semantic cues. Using this information, complete the *Oral Reading Analysis of Miscues Summary* form (see Appendix, p. 430). First, calculate the word accuracy by writing the word count minus the uncorrected miscues, divided by the word count. Uncorrected miscues are omissions, insertions, decoded sounds, or substitutions that have not been self-corrected. Write the word accuracy as a fraction and a percentage, and then determine the functioning level by using the criteria at the bottom of the summary form. Next, calculate the text meaning or acceptability score by writing the words correct (the numerator in the word accuracy score), added to the total number of uncorrected meaning-retained miscues with asterisks in the last column of the *Analysis of Miscues Worksheet*; then divide this by the word count. Although word accuracy is important, the goal is comprehension. Even fluent readers make miscues. Because this assessment is also used to place students in appropriately leveled text, the acceptability of the miscues needs to be considered. By comparing the accuracy and the acceptability score, you can see if the student's miscues still retain the meaning of the text. If a student has a higher acceptability score, then the student may be able to read more challenging text than the accuracy score would reflect. Complete the rest of the form for type of miscues and type of cues. These scores are calculated by inserting the totals as the numerators and the number of miscues (or lines filled out under student response on the worksheet) as the denominator for each of them. The functioning levels for the types of miscues and types of cues are determined using the criteria on the *Oral Reading Analysis of Miscues Summary*.

Once you obtain the student's accuracy, acceptability, and comprehension scores, you can determine their functional reading levels. Betts (1946) was the first to set up three levels of reading on the basis of the word accuracy score and the comprehension score: the independent level, the instructional level, and the frustration level. Table 5.1 provides a guide for determining the functioning levels. The purpose for identifying these levels is to determine the student's reading level and to select appropriate instructional materials that will challenge yet support the student. The independent level, also called the recreational reading level, is the level at which the student should be able to read the text on their own. Select materials at this level for supplementary and independent reading. The instructional

TABLE 5.1. Functioning Levels Chart

	Independent level	Instructional level	Frustration level
Oral accuracy	95–100%	90–94%	89% or below
Oral acceptability	98–100%	95–97%	94% or below
Comprehension	90–100%	70–89%	69% or below

level, also called the guided reading level, is the level within the reader's zone of proximal development (Vygotsky, 1978; see Chapter 1). Materials used for small-group instruction such as guided reading should be at the instructional level. The frustration level is the level at which a student did not correctly read many of the words or did not demonstrate comprehension of the text. Although this level should be discouraged for individual reading, it is excellent for a teacher to read aloud and facilitate group discussions, or for students to browse through if it is a topic of interest. Reading levels are only guidelines; the amount of familiarity with content, genre, and structure can cause great variability in a student's ability to read a text with understanding.

9. **Analysis statement.** Write an analysis statement summarizing the quantitative and qualitative information obtained from the analysis of miscues and comprehension of the text. The analysis statement will include the patterns in miscues, the use of cues, and additional strategies used while reading. Use the *Guidelines for Literacy Assessment Analysis* to write the analysis statement (see Appendix, pp. 359–361).

Figure 5.1 on the next page shows an example of an *Analysis of Miscues Worksheet,* which includes the miscues and reading behaviors that a child made while reading the book *The Mitten* by Jan Brett (1989). Figure 5.2 on page 185 shows an *Oral Reading Analysis of Miscues Summary* example for the same book.

Additional Fluency Assessments

• Oral Reading Strategies Assessment

PURPOSE: This is used to identify strategies a student used during reading (see Appendix, p. 431). This is to be used for any oral reading that is at the instructional or frustration level for word accuracy, as strategies are not often oral in independent reading.

PROCEDURE AND ANALYSIS: While the student is orally reading, the teacher identifies the strategies that were used in their attempts to figure out words. The teacher records a plus sign (+) if this strategy was used frequently, a checkmark (✓) if the strategy was used occasionally, or a minus sign (–) if the strategy is used rarely or not at all. For the analysis, summarize the strategies that were used frequently, occasionally, and rarely. The analysis statement should summarize the scores and give specific examples of evidence for the scores. See Figure 5.3 on page 186 for an example.

• Fluency Assessment by Teachers and Peers

PURPOSE: This is based on Zutell and Rasinski's (1991) three dimensions of fluency—phrasing, smoothness, and pace—as well as a compilation of other fluency elements (see Appendix, p. 432). The teacher can use the data obtained with this form to plan instruction

FIGURE 5.1. *Analysis of Miscues Worksheet*, example for a grade 3 student.

Name: ______________________ **Grade:** 3 **Date:** __________

Title: The Mitten by Jan Brett **Word Count:** 198/310 **Text Level:** M

	Miscue Type					Cues Used			Meaning Retained	
Student Response /Text	Self-correction	Uncorrected miscue	Omission of word	Insertion of word	Decoded/ nonword	Substitution of word	Grapho-phonemic I = Initial, M = Medial, F = Final	Syntactic–grammar	Semantic–meaning	Yes, sentence meaning, * if not s-c
1. Nicholas /Nicki		✓				✓	I, M	✓	✓	Yes*
2. /k/nĭt /knit	✓				✓		M, F			Yes
3. like /look		✓				✓	I, F	✓		
4. turning /tunneling		✓				✓	I, F	✓		
5. decided /discovered		✓				✓	I, F	✓		
6. he /a	✓					✓				Yes
7. something /things	✓					✓	M, F	✓		Yes
8. with /the	✓					✓				Yes
9. /arg /argue		✓			✓		I, M			
10. picture, prediction, pickles /prickles		✓				✓	I, M			
11. there /through		✓				✓	I			
12. /ĕverd /eyed		✓			✓		I, F			
13. ^ /and		✓		✓						Yes*
14. then /when		✓				✓	M, F	✓		
15. deer /diggers		✓				✓	I	✓		
16. The /A		✓				✓		✓	✓	Yes*
17. spĭd /spied		✓			✓		I, F			
18. pulled /plumped		✓				✓	I, F	✓		
19. tight /tightly		✓				✓	I, M	✓	✓	Yes*
20. /arg /argue		✓			✓		I, M			
21. a /an		✓				✓	I	✓		Yes*
22. corn /acorn	✓					✓	M, F	✓		Yes
23. snap /shape		✓				✓	F			
24. dĭs /distance	✓				✓		I			Yes
25. – /silhouetted		✓	✓							
26.										
27.										
28.										
29.										
30.										
Totals:	6	19	1	1	6	17	20	12	3	5

FIGURE 5.2. *Oral Reading Analysis of Miscues Summary,* example and analysis for the same grade 3 student as in Figure 5.1.

Name: ______________ **Grade:** 3 **Date:** ______________

Title: The Mitten by Jan Brett **Word Count:** 198/310 **Text Level:** M (end of grade 2)

Genre: Fiction, narrative

ORAL READING SUMMARY				
Type of Score	**Calculation**	**Fraction**	**%**	**Functioning Level***
Word Accuracy	Words Correct = Word Count – Uncorrected Miscues (19) / Word Count	179/198	90%	Instructional
Text Meaning/ Acceptability	Words Correct + Uncorrected Meaning Retained Miscues / Word Count	184/198	93%	Frustration
Miscue Scores				
Self-Correction	Self-Corrections/Number of Miscues	6/25	24%	Sometimes used
Omissions	Omissions/Number of Miscues	1/25	4%	Rarely used
Insertions	Insertions/Number of Miscues	1/25	4%	Rarely used
Decoded Sounds or Nonwords	Decoded Sounds/Number of Miscues	6/25	24%	Sometimes used
Substitutions of Real Words	Substitutions/Number of Miscues	17/25	68%	Often used
Cueing System Scores				
Grapho-Phonemic	Number of Grapho-Phonemic Cues Used / Number of Miscues	20/25	80%	Predominantly used
Syntactic	Number of Syntactic Cues Used / Number of Miscues	12/25	48%	Sometimes used
Semantic	Number of Semantic Cues Used / Number of Miscues	3/25	12%	Rarely used

Functioning Level*	Independent	Instructional	Frustration
Oral Accuracy	95–100%	90–94%	89% or below
Oral Acceptability	98–100%	95–97%	94% or below
Comprehension	90–100%	70–89%	69% or below

***To obtain a true functioning level, comprehension must also be assessed.**

Functioning Levels for Miscue and Cueing System Scores			
75–100%	Predominantly Used Cue	20–49%	Sometimes Used Cue
50–74%	Often Used Cue	19% or below	Rarely Used Cue

(continued)

FIGURE 5.2. *(continued)*

Analysis: The student's oral reading was at an instructional level for the end-of-grade-2 text. His text meaning was at the frustration level, due to the large numbers of miscues that did not make sense. His comprehension (as evaluated and analyzed separately) was also at the instructional level. When he came to an unknown word, he sometimes self-corrected his miscues, such as *corn/acorn*. He made only one omission and one insertion. He often substituted real words, such as *snap/shape*, but sometimes said decoded sounds or nonwords, as in */spĭd/spied*. When making miscues, he predominantly used grapho-phonemics, such as *turning/tunneling*, and most of the time used the correct initial sound. Sometimes he substituted words using syntax or the same part of speech, such as *decided/discovered*. He rarely used semantics, such as *pulled/plumped*, meaning that the miscue did not mean the same.
Instructional Implications: Praise the student for making self-corrections. He should be encouraged to use the strategies on the appropriate *Good Readers Bookmark*. He needs prompting to reread when he does not come up with a real word or when the word does not make sense. Guessing the covered word might be an effective strategy to get him to predict real words that make sense.

FIGURE 5.3. *Oral Reading Strategies Assessment,* example and analysis.

When the reader came to unknown words, he/she . . .	
Score +, ✓, –	**Strategy**
✓	Looked at the pictures and graphics and thought about the text.
✓	Said beginning three sounds.
✓	Read on to collect clues and went back.
–	Went back and read again.
–	Broke words into parts.
–	Tried different sounds.
✓	Attempted to self-correct words that did not look right.
–	Attempted to self-correct words that did not sound right.
–	Attempted to self-correct words that did not make sense.
✓	Self-corrected words.

Analysis: This student used several strategies while orally reading. She generally attempted to sound out the words when she came to words she didn't know. Usually only the first sound or two were correct. Sometimes she read on and figured out the word; however, she rarely reread, broke words into parts, or tried different sounds. She self-corrected 6 out of the 25 miscues. All of these self-corrections were for words that did not initially look like the word in the text.
Instructional Implications: Use the *Oral Reading Strategy Checklist for Teachers* and the *Oral Reading Strategy Checklist for Peers and Self* to teach and reinforce word identification strategies (described later in this chapter; see also Appendix, especially focus on rereading if the text does not make sense).

that reinforces and teaches appropriate fluency behaviors. The student can use data from the teacher or peers to reflect on and improve their fluency.

PROCEDURE AND ANALYSIS: While the student orally reads a passage, a teacher or peer observes the student's fluency and compares it with the indicators for each of the fluency elements: read in phrases, paused at punctuation marks, read with expression, read smoothly, resolved word problems quickly, read at an independent level, read at a conversational pace, and could comprehend or retell what was read. Each indicator is marked with a plus sign (+) for generally fluent, a checkmark (✓) for sometimes fluent, or a minus sign (–) for rarely fluent. This assessment can be administered throughout the school year to plan appropriate fluency instruction and show growth over time. The analysis statement should summarize the scores and give specific examples of evidence for the scores. Figure 5.4 provides an example of how to complete this assessment.

- Fluency Self-Assessment

PURPOSE: This is a rubric, similar to the *Fluency Assessment by Teachers and Peers,* to help students evaluate their own reading fluency and to provide them with a guide that includes the indicators of fluent reading (see Appendix, p. 433).

PROCEDURE AND ANALYSIS: After students audio-record their reading, they replay the recording and evaluate their reading with a plus sign (+) for generally fluent, a checkmark (✓) for sometimes fluent, or a minus sign (–) for rarely fluent for each of the indicators. Students can also practice rereading the same text and reevaluate their reading to identify any areas of improvement. Again, the analysis statement should summarize the scores and give specific examples of evidence for the scores.

READING FLUENCY: GENERAL STRATEGIES

Creating a Diverse Classroom Library

To encourage children to read, they need access to diverse literature in a variety of genres, formats, and levels in both printed and digital texts. Creating a classroom library that includes a variety of genres, award-winning and diverse books, and formats and levels of printed and digital texts will provide students with such access. The "windows, mirrors, and sliding glass doors" strategy (Sims Bishop, 1990; see Chapter 2) provides guidance in choosing diverse books, to ensure that students see themselves and others in literature.

Variety of Genres

Providing access to a variety of genres is important. The primary genres in children's and young adult literature include the following categories: *picture books* (concept books, pattern books, wordless books, or those that emphasize the illustrations); *traditional literature* (myths, fables, legends, and fairy tales); *fiction* (fantasy, mystery, realistic fiction, historical fiction, science fiction); *nonfiction* (history, science, technology, arts, culture, sports, etc.); *biography and autobiography*; *poetry and verse*; and the newest genre, *media* (digital, video, audio, and visual). (Fiction and nonfiction are discussed in more detail below.) It is beneficial to have several books by the same authors or on the same topics because it may

FIGURE 5.4. *Fluency Assessment by Teachers and Peers*, example and analysis.

Title/Author: Crickwing by Janell Cannon (2000) **Level:** Guided Reading O **Genre:** Narrative

The student . . .	Generally Fluent (+)	Sometimes Fluent (✓)	Rarely Fluent (–)
Read in phrases. Score: ✓	Read sentences in meaningful phrases or clauses.	Read in a mixture of appropriate phrasing and word by word.	Read only one to two words at a time.
Paused at punctuation marks. Score: ✓	Paused after end punctuation (period, question mark, exclamation point) and middle punctuation (comma, semicolon, colon).	Usually paused at end punctuation, but not always middle punctuation.	Rarely paused at punctuation marks.
Read with expression Score: –	Read with appropriate stress and intonation; changed voice for expression as needed; read with emphasis for dramatization or read with different voices.	Read with some appropriate expression, and some changes in stress and intonation.	Read with little expression or change in stress and intonation.
Read smoothly. Score: ✓	Reading sounded smooth, with only a few short pauses for problem solving when needed.	Reading was generally smooth, with some hesitations and repetitions.	Reading sounded choppy, with several skipped words, hesitations, or repetitions.
Used problem-solving strategies efficiently. Score: –	Most meaning miscues were self-corrected after initial attempt.	Most meaning miscues were self-corrected after multiple attempts.	Most miscues were not self-corrected, and few strategies were attempted.
Read at a conversational pace. Score: ✓	The reading pace was like that of a conversation, not too fast or too slow for others to understand.	The reading pace was either a little too fast or a little too slow.	The reading was very slow and labored.
Read at an independent word accuracy level. Score: ✓	Read at an independent level (95% or higher word accuracy).	Read at an instructional level (90–94% word accuracy).	Read at a frustration level (89% or below word accuracy).
Comprehended or retold what was read. Score: –	Retold all of the important elements of the story or the main idea and major details.	Retold most of the important elements of the story or the main idea and major details.	Did not retell the important elements of the story or the main idea and major details.

Analysis: During this narrative passage, the student sometimes read in phrases, attended to punctuation, read smoothly, read at a conversational pace, and read at an instructional level, which indicated some fluency skills. However, the student did not attend to expression even when Crickwing was yelling, "Oh, noooo!" or "Wait!" The student generally skipped unknown words and rarely used strategies to attempt to self-correct. He did not retell any of Crickwing's problems or how he saved the colony from army ants.

Instructional Implications: The student needs more opportunities to hear stories read and modeled with rich expression. He needs practice on how and when to change one's voice to show expression when reading. The student would benefit from using the appropriate *Good Readers Bookmark* (see Chapter 4 and Appendix, pp. 151–152 and 438, respectively) when he comes to words he does not know. Finally, think-aloud strategies or story maps could be used to identify each of the major events in the story and the resolution.

encourage students to read additional books, and the students can conduct author or topic studies. Having multiple texts related to the topics taught in class provides opportunities for students to compare and contrast or verify information from multiple sources.

Award-Winning Literature and Media

Providing access to high-quality literature, such as award-winning books and media, is also important. The American Library Association gives annual awards to authors and illustrators (at this writing, the most recent link for the list of these awards is *www.ala.org/awardsgrants/awards/browse/bpma/all/cyad?showfilter=no*). The awards include, but are not limited to, the John Newbery Medal—awarded to the author of the most distinguished contribution to American literature for children; the Randolph Caldecott Medal—awarded to the artist of the most distinguished American picture book for children; the Coretta Scott King Book Award—given to African American authors and illustrator for outstanding inspirational and educational contributions; the Pura Belpré Award—presented to a Latino/Latina writer and illustrator whose work best portrays, affirms, and celebrates the Latin cultural experience in an outstanding work of literature for children and youth; the Robert F. Sibert Informational Book Award—awarded to the author(s) and illustrator(s) of the most distinguished informational book published in English; the Theodor Seuss Geisel Award—given to the author(s) and illustrator(s) of the most distinguished American book for beginning readers published in English; the Children's Notable Award—which identifies the best of the best in children's books, recordings, videos, and computer software; and the Excellence in Early Learning Digital Media Award—given to a producer that has created distinguished digital media for early learners. Book awards presented by other organizations include the International Literacy Association's Children's and Young Adults' Book Awards (*www.literacyworldwide.org/about-us/awards-grants-ila-children's-and-young-adults'-book-awards*); the Children's Book Council's book lists and awards (go to *www.cbcbooks.org*, click on Readers, then click on Reading Lists); and the National Science Teaching Association's awards for Outstanding Science Trade Books for Students K–12 (*www.nsta.org/publications/ostb*).

More about Fiction and Nonfiction

Why include fictional texts in a classroom library? For many students, these texts are quite entertaining and provide opportunities for the students to expand their imaginations. Fairy tales and Mother Goose rhymes are often passed down from generation to generation. Many of these stories have a predictable story structure and often include repetitive lines, which make these texts easier to read. Bookshelves for young students continue to be filled with Dr. Seuss books, Norman Bridwell's *Clifford the Big Red Dog* books, and fairy tale books rewritten by Disney with the standard "happily ever after" endings. For more contemporary books, young readers might enjoy reading the series *Diary of a Wimpy Kid* by Jeff Kinney (2007–present). Older students enjoy classics such as Swift's *Gulliver's Travels*, Twain's *Tom Sawyer*, London's *The Call of the Wild*, and Verne's *Twenty Thousand Leagues Under the Sea*. They may enjoy older series, such as the *Hatchet* series by Gary Paulsen (starting in 1987) and the *Harry Potter* books by J. K. Rowling (starting in 1998), or more contemporary series, such as the *Divergent* series (starting in 2011) by Veronica Roth or the fantasy novel series *A Song of Fire and Ice* by George R. R. Martin (starting in 1996; the best-known of these is the first one, *A Game of Thrones*). Most children's books in school are works of fiction.

Why include nonfiction texts in a classroom library? Most of what children read outside of school is nonfiction, and most of the reading we do as adults is nonfiction (Harvey, 2002). Yet, elementary school reading programs have traditionally been dominated by fictional texts; as a result, when children reach the upper grades and encounter disciplinary/content area texts and research materials, many students struggle to comprehend nonfiction texts (Caswell & Duke, 1998; Rog, 2003). Students' difficulty with nonfiction texts in the upper grades may be caused by lack of experience in primary grades (Caswell & Duke, 1998; Donovan & Smolkin, 2001). If children are to survive in this age of information and technology, they will need greater familiarity with nonfiction texts, according to Moss, Leone, and Dipillo (1997).

Not only are young children capable of interacting with nonfiction texts, but when they are provided with multiple opportunities to engage in them, their ability to comprehend them dramatically increases (Duke & Kayes, 1998; Kamil & Lane, 1997; Yopp & Yopp, 2000a). Not only are nonfiction texts essential for gaining disciplinary/content area knowledge, children are also motivated by them. Doiron (1994) suggests that the use of nonfiction books be increased at all levels for affective reasons. He argues that nonfiction books need to be included in read-alouds, guided reading, and independent reading because children are curious about and interested in learning about the world around them. Yopp and Yopp (2000a) have explained that nonfiction texts can capitalize on children's interests and lead them to be more purposeful and active readers.

With the emphasis in the United States on state standards and national legislation, it is important for teachers to provide students with experiences and texts that motivate them to read in order not only to enhance their reading development, but to provide them with valuable disciplinary/content area knowledge. Since nonfiction texts make up a larger proportion of state and district tests, it is also beneficial to devote more instructional time to them. In addition, pairing fiction and nonfiction books on the same topic, along with interactive strategies, can boost students' understanding and enjoyment (Camp, 2000; Taberski, 2000; Camp, 2000).

Criteria for Evaluating Nonfiction Texts

Again, it is important to select high-quality texts for a classroom library, both nonfiction and fiction. While award-winning books have been discussed earlier, other criteria for nonfiction texts include inviting design, engaging linguistic style, accurate content, and clear organization. As a classroom teacher evaluating nonfiction texts for a classroom library, consider these factors.

Inviting Design

Does the text include high-quality, eye-catching illustrations, photographs, maps, drawings, charts, and/or figures? Do the illustrations support and enhance the text? Are they clearly labeled and/or appropriately integrated within the text? Is the font easy to read? Is the placement of the text easy for the reader to follow? For excellent examples of design, look at any books in the Eyewitness Series—for example, *Hurricane and Tornado* (Challoner,

2004). This text contains photographs, models, illustrations, and experiments related to hurricanes and tornadoes.

Engaging Linguistic Style

The linguistic style should be engaging and appropriate for the students' interests and/or reading levels. Does the author create excitement for the subject? Is the author's style and language appropriate for the age and development of the students? Do the texts vary in difficulty from easy-to-read picture books to challenging texts for independent and instructional reading, as well as for read-alouds and browsing? Higher-level books can be explored by looking at the pictures or by having an adult or more capable peer read selections or the whole book to the students.

Accurate Content

Answer these questions about the accuracy of the text. Is the content accurate? Is the factual information clearly distinguished from fiction? What are the credentials of the author and the references? Is the information current and up to date? Is the content appropriate for the students? Do the materials accurately represent diversity in people? Are stereotypes avoided? Do the materials appeal to a wide range of students' interests and social, cultural, ethnic, and linguistic backgrounds? Do the materials relate to curricular topics or provide other learning opportunities for the students?

Clear Organization

While the organization of nonfiction texts varies, the structure should be clear. Does the text include a table of contents, index, glossary, and references? Does it contain headings, subheadings, or bulleted information? Does the text include bold or italicized fonts to identify important concepts? All of these organization structures help guide the reader for improved comprehension. Harvey and Goudvis (2017) and Harvey (2002) describe the importance of using nonfiction in the classroom, as it is the genre most likely to spur children's passion and wonder in learning. Kobrin (1995) describes more than 800 nonfiction books in her resource book. I have discussed nonfiction literacy strategies and provided a list of quality nonfiction books in an earlier article (McAndrews, 2004). Students also enjoy magazines such as *National Geographic Kids, National Geographic World, Ranger Rick, Your Big Back Yard, Sports Illustrated for Kids, Time for Kids,* and *Zoobooks.*

Criteria for Evaluating Fiction and Nonfiction Narrative Texts

In evaluating a fictional text for a classroom library, read the text and ask these questions (based on Norton, 1995): Is the plot believable, and does it contain specific details? Does the main character overcome the problem, but not too easily? Do the characters seem real? Do the characters have both strengths and weaknesses? Is the setting accurate for the time and place? Is the theme worthwhile? Do the characters seem like real people actually talking? Does the rest of the language sound natural? When reading, could you picture yourself in the story?

Formats of Printed and Digital Texts

A 21st-century classroom library should provide access to printed and digital texts in various formats. These include magazines, newspapers, brochures, and maps. Emergent books might include cardboard books, pop-out books, and shape and texture books. Digital texts might include websites, interactive books, reading apps, dictionaries, and other electronic resources. Class-made and student-made books should also be available.

Reading Levels

A classroom library should provide access to books at various reading levels. Although the readability of a text cannot be exactly determined for a given student, publishers and educators can assign an approximate reading level. The following are a variety of ways that you, as a teacher, can determine the reading level of a book.

1. Examine the book's contents and format for readability and complexity. The readability of a text, or how easy it is to read, depends on a variety of factors. Fountas and Pinnell (2016) have identified these basic factors related to text difficulty: genre, text structure, content, themes, and ideas; language and literary features, such as sentence complexity, vocabulary, and words; illustrations; and text, graphic, and organizational features. For details on these factors, refer to the Fountas and Pinnell Literacy Continuum (Pinnell & Fountas, 2016). The passage length and the density of information, such as the amount of elaboration or use of examples, also have an impact on readability. The type of content and the way in which new vocabulary is used are factors as well. The genre (such as fiction or nonfiction) or the passage format (such as expository, narrative, or persuasive) are additional important factors. The organizational structure (including headings, diagrams, and pictures) can further enhance the readability. The style of the writing, along with the grammatical complexity (such as predictable sentence patterns and word choices, or complex structures that clearly reveal causality) can facilitate comprehension. Examine the differences in text structure among between narrative, expository, persuasive, and descriptive texts. Select a text believed to be at the student's instructional level, based on the density of vocabulary or non-high-frequency words; the complexity of sentence structure; the complexity of concepts; the amount of picture, chart, or graphic support; and the typography, such as the size of text, headings, boldfaced print, and italics. Selecting a text with one concept per page with strong picture support may enhance an emergent reader's oral reading, while choosing a longer text may overwhelm the reader. By selecting appropriate texts, you can gather the information needed to make informed instructional decisions. The readability of a text depends not only on the text, but on the reader as well. The reader's interest and/or choice in reading the text, and the the background knowledge that is required to read that text, are other significant factors. To level early reading texts, refer to Figure 5.5, based on Peterson (1988).

2. Look for the reading level on the front or back cover of the book, or within the first couple of pages.

3. Download reading level apps that help you determine the reading level. Most of them work when you scan the ISBN of the book and cross-reference it with different databases.

FIGURE 5.5. Reading Recovery levels and Fountas–Pinnell Guided Reading Levels for characteristics of early reading texts. Based on Peterson (1988).

Reading Recovery Levels 1–4; Guided Reading Levels A, B, and C; Preprimer 1
Consistent placement of print; repetition of one or two sentence patterns (one- or two-word changes); oral language structures; familiar objects and actions; illustrations provide high support.
Reading Recovery Levels 5–8; Guided Reading Levels D and E; Preprimer 2–3
Repetition of two or three sentence patterns (phrases may change), opening/closing sentences vary, or varied simple sentence patterns; predominantly oral language structures; many familiar objects and actions; illustrations provide moderate to high support.
Reading Recovery Levels 9–12; Guided Reading Levels F and G; Primer
Repetition of three or more sentence patterns, or varied sentence patterns (repeated phrases or refrains); blend of oral and written language structures, or fantastic happenings in framework of familiar experiences; illustrations provide moderate support.
Reading Recovery Levels 13–15; Guided Reading Levels H and I; Grade 1
Varied sentence patterns (may have repeated phrases or refrains), or repeated patterns in cumulative form; written language structures (oral structures appear in dialogue); conventional story and literary language; specialized vocabulary for some topics; illustrations provide low to moderate support.
Reading Recovery Levels 16–20; Guided Reading Levels J, K, L, and M; Grade 2
Elaborated episodes and events, extended descriptions, links to familiar stories; literary language; unusual, challenging vocabulary; illustrations provide low support.

4. Consult book lists for the student's age or grade, such as the Scholastic Book Wizard lists (*www.scholastic.com/teachers/bookwizard*), the Great Schools grade-level lists (*www.greatschools.org/gk/book-lists*), or the New York Public Library's book lists (*www.nypl.org/books-music-movies*). For books leveled by Fountas and Pinnell, go to a frequently updated, subscription-based, online list (*www.fandpleveledbooks.com*) that contains more than 64,000 books submitted by over 300 publishers.

5. Use readability formulas. While numerous text-leveling formulas exist, they can only be used as general guidelines, as they often do not take into account the content, vocabulary, or text structure.

6. Use the *Reading Level Correlation Chart* (see Appendix, p. 434) to compare grade level, Reading Recovery level, Fountas–Pinnell Guided Reading Level, Developmental Reading Assessment level, basal equivalent level, and lexile level.

• Organizing Books

PURPOSE: To help students with their book selections.

PROCEDURE: As the classroom teacher, arrange your classroom library by genre, author, topic, and/or book level. Books can be placed in labeled baskets, or colored labels could be placed on the books indicating their topic or level. In the classroom, you might have three areas of books. In one area, the books might be grouped by genre, author, and topic. Another area might have books grouped by reading level. This arrangement is useful for selecting books for guided reading groups. The third area could be a rotating book study area for highlighting a particular author or topic.

• Wide Reading Strategies

PURPOSE: To increase the type and amount of reading. Through wide reading, students acquire knowledge about the world, as well as about the specific content, vocabulary, language, and form of written text.

PROCEDURE: As the teacher, provide opportunities for a variety of literacy experiences in the classroom:

1. Encourage students to read a variety of topics, genres, or authors in print and electronic formats.
2. Pair students with books by getting to know students' interests and recommending books to them.
3. Have students conduct author studies or topic studies and then share these with the class.
4. Enthusiastically read portions or entire texts from different genres and formats to students, including newspaper and magazine articles.
5. Model book talks, and have students give book talks on self-selected texts.
6. Prominently display new additions to your classroom library.
7. Have students share information they learned from the internet that is related to classroom experiences and topics.
8. Have students select poems, jokes, and riddles to read to the class.
9. Give students regular opportunities to discuss texts and connect them to their lives, other texts, and the world.
10. Provide opportunities for individual, paired, and small-group reading experiences, including scheduling regular self-selected reading time in class.
11. Lastly, create a positive reading environment by providing comfortable, quiet places to read.

READING FLUENCY: STRATEGIES FOR WORD ACCURACY

• Self-Selection of Reading Materials and the Five-Finger Rule

PURPOSE: To support students in selecting appropriate texts.

PROCEDURE: Here are five guiding questions students can ask themselves when selecting reading materials.

1. Does the book or text look interesting?
2. Does it look about as hard as other texts I have read?
3. Can I understand what the text is saying?
4. Can I explain what I just read?
5. Am I choosing reading materials from different genres and authors?

To figure out if the book or text is about right or too challenging, students can use the "five-finger rule." The teacher can say to them: "Read about 50 words. Put up one finger for every word you cannot read or understand. If you make five mistakes or fewer, and can retell what the text is about, it is at about the right level for you to read. If you make more than five mistakes or you cannot retell what the text is about, it is probably too hard."

Students should have opportunities to select materials even if they are not always on their instructional level. Easier or independent-level books provide recreational reading and fluency practice, while more difficult books may pique their interest and encourage experience with more complex text and more diverse vocabulary.

• Text Selection Bookmarks

PURPOSE: To let family members know the type of reading support their child needs, based on the text selected; to provide suggestions for interaction; and to encourage children to take home different levels of books based on their interests.

PROCEDURE: The *Text Selection Bookmarks* in the Appendix (p. 435) correlate to the expected levels of support students would need to read a text. The teacher should color-code each bookmark for ease of identification. The "Read to me!" bookmark is for books that the students cannot read on their own, but would enjoy having someone read to them as they look at the pictures. The "Read with me!" bookmark is for books that the students might have difficulty reading, but could read along with someone else. The "I can read this on my own!" bookmark is for books that the students could probably read on their own, by using strategies for figuring out unknown words and for comprehending the text. This may be a text they have read earlier or a text that is at their independent reading level. After students select the books they want to take home, the teacher and each individual child select which bookmark to put in the book. The teacher might ask the student to read a short section and follow the five-finger rule strategy to quickly assess the level of support needed to read it. When the children get home with their books, they can use the before, during, and after strategies on each bookmark to support their understanding of the book. They can also use the strategies listed on the *Good Readers Bookmarks* (discussed on the next page; see Appendix, p. 438) for figuring out unknown words.

• Reading Log

PURPOSE: To document each student's reading outside of class, in order to build reading interest and stamina.

PROCEDURE: Each day on the *Reading Log* (see Appendix, p. 436), the student or an adult records the date, the title and author of the book, the amount of time spent reading, and the number of pages read. The adult signs the log to verify that the reading occurred, and then evaluates the student's reading. The adult marks a plus sign (+) if the reading included only minimal mistakes and the student could retell the important ideas; a checkmark (✓) if the reading included some mistakes and the student could retell some of the important ideas; and a minus sign (–) if the reading included many mistakes and/or the student could not retell important ideas. At the end of the month, the adult totals the number of pages and amount of time the student read.

ADAPTATION: An older reader, instead of having an adult evaluate their reading, they can conduct a self-evaluation. The reader can also keep track of the different genres that they read. If a book is particularly interesting, the reader can put an asterisk (*) at the end of the line.

Good Readers Strategy Poster and Good Readers Bookmarks

PURPOSE: To provide strategies that can be used when a reader cannot figure out a word or realizes that the reading does not make sense, sound right, or look right. The icons on the *Good Readers Strategy Poster* correspond to those for each strategy on the *Good Readers Bookmarks,* to help students identify the strategies on the bookmarks quickly (see Appendix, pp. 437 and 438).

PROCEDURE: The teacher displays the *Good Readers Strategy Poster* in the classroom, and provides each student with a personal *Good Readers Bookmark.* The teacher explains to students that the title *Good Readers* was selected because good readers, not poor readers, use strategies to figure out unknown words or to make sense of their reading. The teacher then reads the strategies aloud according to the students' grade level, and provides examples for using each of the strategies while the students read. While students are reading, they should be reminded to use their *Good Readers Bookmarks* strategies if they come to words they do not know or if what they are reading does not make sense. These *Good Readers Bookmarks* can be used in conjunction with the *Oral Reading Strategy Checklists,* discussed next.

Oral Reading Strategy Checklist for Teachers

PURPOSE: To help students efficiently identify words and correct their miscues by using oral strategies when the students come to words they do not immediately recognize, and to self-correct their reading when it does not make sense, look right, or sound right (grade 1 and above).

PROCEDURE: The two-column *Oral Reading Strategy Checklist for Teachers* (see Appendix, p. 439) can be used while students are reading to identify and analyze the strategies students use while problem-solving unknown words (see the left column) and to identify and analyze the prompts given to students to encourage the use of new strategies for word identification (see the right column). Because it identifies and models the cues and strategies used by good readers, this checklist can be used to provide "critical-moment teaching" (Goodman & Marek, 1996) and to prompt for strategies that students can select when problem-solving on their own. As the teacher, do the following:

1. Select a passage that is approximately at the student's instructional level. The first time the student is evaluated, do not preteach the strategies from the appropriate *Good Readers Bookmark.* Tell the student, "I am going to mark all the good things you do while reading." Then for subsequent evaluations, provide a copy of the *Good Readers Bookmark* for the student to use as a resource and say, "I am going to mark all the strategies you use during reading." Ask, "What do you think this story or text is about from the title, the pictures, or from what you have read so far?"
2. While the student is reading, make a tally mark corresponding to each of the strategies the student uses in the left column of the checklist. Also tally the number of self-corrections. For each uncorrected miscue, note whether the miscue has a similar meaning, has similar syntax, or is visually similar. After the student has read the passage or section, ask the student to retell the important events or ideas in the text.
3. After evaluating the student's strategy use, use the right column to tally each of the prompts you provided to support the student in correctly identifying the words. The words "wait time," the first item in this column, reminds you to provide the student

with at least 3 seconds of thinking time after making a miscue, or to wait until the student has finished reading the sentence or paragraph with a significant miscue prior to prompting them. This also gives you time to think about and plan what the most efficient prompt would be to help the student problem-solve. Mark each time you provide wait time.

4. If the student needs support, ask, "What strategy from the bookmark could you try?" If the student is unsuccessful in self-correcting, suggest one of the strategies and mark it in the right column. Do not tell the student any words, as it prevents them from problem solving, but continue to offer prompts until the student figures out the word.
5. Table 5.2 lists the oral strategy prompts and indicates when you should provide them. The strategy prompts are not presented in a particular order, but should be selected first by you and then by the student, based on which strategies would result in the

TABLE 5.2. Oral Reading Strategy Prompts

Strategy prompt	When to provide prompt
(Wait time.)	Provide wait time before any prompting. Allow the student the opportunity to read to the end of the sentence before prompting.
"Look at the pictures and visuals; think about the text."	Use if the picture, diagrams, other visuals, or previous content can be used to figure out the unknown words.
"Say the first three sounds."	Use if the student pauses for an extended time or makes a guess only on the basis of the initial sound. Three sounds were selected, because using these as a basis for predicting is more effective than using only the initial sound, and using three is often more efficient than sounding out the entire word.
"Read on to collect clues."	Use if the context of the rest of the sentence would help. Then prompt the student to go back.
"Go back and read again."	Use if the beginning of the sentence or the previous sentence will help.
"Break words into parts."	Use if the student knows parts of the word, such as syllables in multisyllabic words or roots, prefixes, and suffixes.
"Try different sounds."	Use when the student is mispronouncing phonemes. If necessary, the correct sound can be provided.
"Does that make sense?"	Use when the student keeps reading and the miscue doesn't make sense.
"Does that look right?"	Use when the miscue doesn't look like the correct word.
"Does that sound right?"	Use when the miscue is the wrong part of speech.
"Where is the tricky part?"	Use when the student keeps reading well after the miscue.
"Try that again."	Use to indicate that there is one or more miscues and the student needs to figure it out, or if the student loses his/her place and skips a line or phrase.
"Are you right? How do you know?"	Highest metacognitive level: Use initially when the student is correct, to get the student to evaluate his/her own reading. Then use for both correct and incorrect reading.
"What else can you do?"	Use when the student was unsuccessful with the first strategy.
"Summarize what you've read."	Use to check comprehension of reading.

most efficient student correction of reading. Some prompts are very specific, while others allow for more metacognition on the part of the reader to analyze their own reading.

6. Multiple prompts may be necessary to help a student problem-solve. Initially, it may be necessary to provide specific prompts, such as "Look at the picture; what animal is that?" or "Try the long ā sound." As a student becomes more proficient at using the strategies, more general prompts can be given, such as "Try that again." Gradually, you can provide more metacognitive prompts, such as "Does that make sense?", to allow the student to do more of the processing to become an independent reader. The prompts "Are you right?" and "How do you know?" are often initially used after the student has self-corrected a word and you want him to evaluate it for himself. Later, these prompts can be used when the student is incorrect, but you do not want the student to rely on you to let them know if the reading is incorrect.
7. Using this right column helps you reflect on how you are prompting the student and begin to identify which prompts yield successful self-corrections and which do not. If the student predominantly uses grapho-phonemic cues, for instance, then semantic or syntactic prompts may need to be provided. Students need to be reminded that rereading and self-correcting are strengths. Even unsuccessful attempts to use strategies need to be praised because before students can correct their reading, they need to be aware that there is a problem.
8. As you analyze the checklist to determine instruction, first identify which strategies the student used and whether the strategies resulted in self-correction. Then identify the strategies the student might use efficiently to identify words. Also, analyze the prompts you provided, and evaluate whether the prompts resulted in correction of the miscues. Point out to the student one or two strengths demonstrated during oral reading, such as self-corrections or attempts at problem-solving strategies. If the student did not demonstrate these behaviors, then point out sentences with no miscues and ask if it those sentences made sense. Because it may not be practical or appropriate to review all of the miscues, first select those that affect meaning the most. Have the student reread each sentence to see if the miscue can be self-corrected. If the student does not self-correct, then read the sentence the way the student initially said it and ask where the tricky part is. Then proceed by prompting the student with strategies that eventually result in correcting the miscue. Afterward, have the student reread the sentence to see if it makes sense, sounds right, and looks right. When the session is over, ask the student, "What strategies did you try that helped you figure out unknown words?" Analyze the prompts that you provided for the student, and evaluate whether the prompts resulted in correction of the miscue. Determine the strategies and prompts that were most effective for different types of miscues.

• Oral Reading Strategy Checklist for Peers or Self

PURPOSE: To identify strategy use by peers during small-group reading instruction, to reinforce peers' use of strategies, and to help the recorders learn strategies they might use to facilitate their own strategy use when reading. It is easier to notice strategy use and miscues in others than in oneself; therefore, it is beneficial to provide opportunities for students to assess their peers' use of reading strategies before assessing themselves. When used by a student's peers, the *Oral Reading Strategy Checklist for Peers or Self* (see Appendix, p. 440) provides the peers with something positive to do, rather than calling out words when the reader does not know them. The focus is on encouraging strategy use, not on the miscues made (grade 1 and above).

PROCEDURE: As the teacher, do the following:

1. Select a passage that is approximately at the target student's instructional level. During small-group instruction, with students at the same or similar instructional level, select one student to focus on per day. Each time it is that student's turn to read, the other students listen for and identify the strategies the reader uses and mark them on the *Oral Reading Strategy Checklist for Peers or Self.*
2. When the students identify a strategy that the reader has used, they place a stamp or use markers to mark the strategy on the checklist. This provides positive reinforcement of a student's strategy use while providing wait time for the reader to process the text. If the reader does not correct a word after adequate wait time, ask the group members if they could suggest a strategy that would help the reader determine the word. Sometimes a combination of strategies is helpful. The group members prompt the student to correct the miscue. After each reader's turn ends, the reader needs to summarize what has been read. The peers put a checkmark on item 9 if the reader summarized the text.
3. At the bottom of the checklist is an evaluation area, where the students identify strategies that worked well and the strategies that might help the reader in the future. This activity leads to a discussion of how and when to use different strategies. When it is the next reader's turn to read, that student is more likely to try additional strategies and begin to internalize the use of strategies and problem-solve during reading.

• Oral Reading Strategy Checklist for Peers or Self

PURPOSE: To help readers identify their peers or own strategy use and evaluate when and which strategies to use. For self-assessment, use after listening to an audio recording of their reading (grade 1 and above).

PROCEDURE: This peer or self-assessment is used only after the student is familiar with the strategies and has had practice using them during the teacher and peer assessments, so that the student is better able to reflect on their own strategy use. When used as a self-assessment, the *Oral Reading Strategy Checklist for Peers or Self* (see Appendix, p. 440) is similar to retrospective miscue analysis (Goodman & Marek, 1996), in that the student reads a passage into an audio-recording device and then analyzes their reading after listening to the recording. When students use this checklist, they not only identify specific strategies they have used or neglected, but also may be able to correct some of their own miscues. Just as when peers use the checklist, the student uses a stamp or marker to document each time a strategy is used, but this time the student is listening to a recording of their own reading.

Once the checklist is completed, the student selects one strategy that they feel was beneficial and one strategy that they think should be used more. If a student cannot self-correct a word, the student uses removable highlighting tape or a highlighter to mark it. Afterward, the teacher and the student discuss the strategies used, and the teacher provides additional prompts to figure out any unknown words.

Audio recordings can be kept for each student throughout the year, and the students can listen to them again and reflect on their progress. As students become more fluent readers, they can self-correct more often and select the most efficient strategies for problem solving. Students are often quite surprised at how much their reading has improved over the year.

Self-Analysis of Miscues

PURPOSE: In another strategy based on concepts from retrospective miscue analysis (Goodman & Marek, 1996), students monitor and self-correct their own reading. The first method involves the interaction between the teacher and the student, and in the second method, the student does an analysis alone.

PROCEDURE: The teacher or students select an interesting text that is near the students' instructional level. Before beginning, the teacher conducts a reading interview to determine the students' prior knowledge. The students are then audio-recorded as they read the text. After the initial session, the teacher codes miscues on a printed version of the text and preselect miscues to discuss during retrospective miscue analysis. A video software program such as GoReact can be used to digitally mark the miscues. Sometimes the teacher may want the students to listen to the recording and stop when they hear a miscue. The teacher and students can listen to the recording, mark miscues on a printed version of the text, and then use the following questions taken from Goodman and Marek (1996, p. 45) to discuss the miscues:

1. Does the miscue make sense?
2. Does the miscue sound like English language? Was the miscue corrected? Should it have been?

If the answers are "No" to the first two questions, then these two questions follow:

3. Does the miscue look like what was on the page?
4. Does the miscue sound like what was on the page?

For all miscues, the teacher asks the following:

5. Why do you think you made the miscue?
6. Did that miscue affect your understanding of the text?
7. Why do you think that? How do you know?

Once the students have experienced several teacher–student sessions, they can conduct a self-analysis of their miscues. The students read a story or passage into an audio-recording device, and then play back the recording while following along in the text. At each place of difficulty, students stop the recording and highlight the words. The students then answer the seven questions listed above.

Searching and Self-Monitoring Strategies

PURPOSE: To support students in processing strategies such as searching and self-monitoring while they are reading. **Searching** includes gathering cues for an initial attempt to read, making multiple tries at difficult words, and self-correcting some miscues. **Self-monitoring** occurs when readers evaluate attempts and decide if further searching is needed. Lyons, Pinnell, and DeFord (1993) attribute the acceleration of students' reading progress to teacher–student interactions that promote effective literacy strategies and to the teacher's ability to make instructional decisions to the acceleration of students' reading progress.

PROCEDURE: As the teacher, do the following:

1. In order to effectively facilitate a student's reading, you must first select text that is within the student's instructional level. Review effective oral reading strategies, such as those listed on the *Good Reader Bookmarks*. Next, listen to the student read. If successful at self-correcting, let the student finish reading the sentence and then ask, "Are you right? How do you know?" This allows the student to use metacognition to determine whether they are right or not, rather than telling the student this.
2. If the student makes a miscue, provide a wait time of about 3 seconds before saying anything. Then ask probing questions within the student's zone of proximal development to help the student problem-solve while reading. If the student is incorrect, the highest-metacognitive-level questions you can ask are "Are you right? How do you know?" If this doesn't elicit self-correction, ask, "Where is the tricky part?" Which subsequent questions you ask will depend on the student's attempts. What cues does the student use, and what cues do they need to use? Does the student need support in using semantic, syntactic, or grapho-phonemic cues?
3. When students use **semantic** cues, they look at the context and meaning of the text they are reading. They also integrate knowledge of the text from illustrations and graphics. Examples of semantic cues in response to the question, "What word makes sense in the story?":

   I live in a __________. ("Horse or house?")
   I rode my bike down the __________ ("Hill or heel?")
   I __________ a dog. ("Was or saw?")

4. When students use **syntax**, they look at the sentence in which the word appears and the structure of the words around it. If they rely on their sense of word order, sentence patterns, and grammar (tenses of verbs, cases of nouns, etc.), they can work to unlock the meaning of the unknown word. Examples of syntactic cues in response to the question, "What kind of word makes this sentence sound right?":

   I want a __________ puppy. ("Adjective or descriptive word.")
   At the farm I saw __________. ("Noun or name of person, place, or thing.")
   I __________ in the water. ("Verb or action word.")

5. When students use **grapho-phonemic** cues, they sound out the letters or parts of a word, or read the word as a whole. Examples of grapho-phonemic cues in response to the question "What word looks right?":

   I __________ pizza. ("Lick or like?")
   He __________ off his bike. ("Fill or fell?")
   My mom __________ apples. ("Ate or eats?")

6. Examples of the three types of prompts:
   - **Semantic prompts:** "Does that make sense? Look at the pictures or graphics. Think about what you have been reading. What do you think the author is trying to say?"
   - **Syntactic prompts:** "Does that sound right? What kind of word is it? Is it a person, place, or thing? Is it an action? Is it a describing word? Look at the suffix or the ending of the word. How do we say it so it sounds right?"
   - **Grapho-phonemic prompts:** "Try the first three sounds. Are there different sounds that these letters can make? Break the word into parts [syllables, prefixes, roots, suffixes]. Do you know how to read any of those parts?"

7. Encourage students to monitor their reading and integrate all three types of these cues when they encounter an unfamiliar word or words in their reading. Once they correct the word(s), have them reread the entire sentence for fluency and meaning. Afterward, you need to evaluate the effectiveness of the facilitation, in order to enhance the students' ability to self-correct and therefore focus on comprehension of the text. When you and each student analyze the student's oral reading behaviors, this provides the basis for determining the student's strengths and needs as well as growth over time. Instruction can then be adapted to support the student's use of reading strategies for self-monitoring, in order to improve their comprehension.

• Guess the Covered Word

PURPOSE: To have students use the context of syntactic and semantic cues, plus the initial sounds, to figure out unknown words. This strategy helps students solve problems and self-correct independently while reading.

PROCEDURE: As the teacher, do the following:

1. Select a passage, and choose words students might have difficulties reading.
2. Cover each selected word with two small sticky notes. The first sticky note covers the onset or the initial sounds up to the vowel, and the second sticky note covers from the vowel to the end of the word.
3. Say, "Good readers use context to figure out words they do not know."
4. Read the entire sentence to the students, and clap at the point in the sentence with the covered word.
5. Say, "Think, pair, and then share. What word would make sense in this sentence?" Record the guesses on the board.
6. Remove the sticky note that covers the beginning sound or sounds.
7. Cross out any guesses that do not begin with that sound or sounds.
8. Ask for additional guesses, then reveal the word.
9. Reread the entire sentence with the correct word.
10. Talk with the students about what the word means and how that word makes sense within the context of the sentence.

EXAMPLE: "Miguel played the ____________ in the Latin band." Guesses—trumpet, drums, guitar, violin. "Miguel played the g__________ in the Latin band." Correct word: guitar.

• Over–Under Strategy

PURPOSE: To have a student use grapho-phonemic cues to figure out unknown words.

PROCEDURE: The teacher writes the word the reader said above the word the author wrote in the text. The teacher then asks the reader, "How are these words similar? How are they different? What word did the author write?" Now the student rereads the sentence.

EXAMPLE:

then	play	back
when	plays	black

• Analogy Strategy

PURPOSE: For a student to use word parts to figure out the rest of a word.

PROCEDURE: As the teacher, identify a known word/word part that is similar to the unknown word. If the unknown word is *sat*, ask the student, "What word is this [*cat*]? Now if I change the *c* to *s*, what is the new word?" Teach the student to break up the word into known parts. If the unknown word is *eating*, ask, "What word is this [*eat*]? What ending is this [-*ing*]? Now what is the word altogether?"

READING FLUENCY: STRATEGIES FOR PROSODY AND PACE

• Modeling Fluent, Expressive Reading

PURPOSE: To improve the student's word recognition in a meaningful context, and to demonstrate correct phrasing and expressive reading. Students need to hear what fluent reading sounds like and how fluent readers interpret text with their voices.

PROCEDURE: As the teacher, do the following:

1. Select stories or other texts that will interest the students and are slightly above their instructional level.
2. Read to students to show what fluent reading sounds like. Read naturally, with the right emotion or tone to match the words you're reading.
3. Have students follow along as you read.
4. Point out strategies you use when you come to words that are unfamiliar or difficult to pronounce.
5. Point out where and why you pause.
6. Point out how you change your voice to show expression or to differentiate characters.

ADAPTATION: Students can also listen to an expressively read audiobook and follow along with the matching book in print.

• Echo Reading

SOURCE: Walker (2004).

PURPOSE: To provide a model of fluent reading that students can then repeat, imitating the pronunciation of words, phrasing, intonation, and expression (grades K–2 or as needed).

PROCEDURE: The teacher reads one sentence with appropriate phrasing and intonation. The teacher then explains what they did while reading fluently, as in this example: "Notice how I grouped the words into phrases; notice how my voice went up at the end of the question; notice how I read it with expression when the person was sad." The students read the same line immediately, in order to remember how the text sounds, modeling the teacher's example. The teacher and the students echo-read the entire passage. Finally, the teacher increases the amount of text read for the students to model.

• Choral Reading

SOURCE: Opitz and Rasinski (1998).

PURPOSE: To improve students' fluency through guided practice in reading aloud with others. Choral reading involves groups of students orally reading the same text in unison. This can be done for the whole text or a portion of the text.

PROCEDURE: The teacher selects a text that is easy to read in unison, such as a poem, a nursery rhyme, or a predictable book. A copy of the text is provided for everyone, or it is displayed in large writing, such as on chart paper, in an overhead transparency, or in a computer projection. First, the teacher reads the text aloud to the students to model choral reading. Next, the teacher and students read the text chorally several times the first day, and then repeat it over several days.

• Chunking

SOURCE: Walker (2004).

PURPOSE: To encourage students to read in meaningful phrases by echoing the teacher's phrasing. Chunking facilitates comprehension and fluency by using thought units rather than word-by-word reading. This strategy is beneficial for students who are fairly proficient at word identification but need to improve their sentence comprehension.

PROCEDURE: As the teacher, do the following:

1. Audio-record students reading a 100- to 200-word passage to review later.
2. Model for the students how to read in meaningful phrases rather than word by word. Put slashes between phrases, such as between noun phrases, verb phrases, or prepositional phrases, or after punctuation marks or where you naturally pause. The students then repeat or echo the same phrasing.
3. You and the students continue echo-reading the entire passage. When possible, you can increase the number of sentences chunked before the students repeat.
4. As the students' ability to chunk meaningful phrases together increases, the students continue reading the passage without your modeling.
5. Finally, audio-record the students' reading of the passage again, and, along with the students, compare the fluency, intonation, and phrasing of the two audio-recorded readings. Once the students can echo-read successfully, then the students mark a new text for phrasing and orally read it.

EXAMPLE: From *Green Eggs and Ham* by Dr. Seuss (1960):

> Would you/could you/in a boat?/Would you/could you/with a goat?

• Paired Reading

SOURCES: Opitz and Rasinski (1998), Walker (2004).

PURPOSE: To improve students' intonation, fluency, and pace through simultaneous modeling.

PROCEDURE: A slower-paced reader and a proficient reader (either a peer or a teacher who serves as a model) read aloud simultaneously. Before reading, the two readers decide on a sign to be given when the slower-paced reader wants to begin reading on their own, and another one for when this reader needs help. The signs can be a nod and a tap, respectively.

The pair begins reading in unison. The proficient reader sets a pace that is appropriate for the text, modeling intonation and phrasing. The proficient reader can move their finger along the print if necessary. As the slower-paced student gains success, they signal the proficient reader to stop reading aloud, and then the slower reader continues to read independently until more support is requested.

• Repeated Readings

SOURCE: Walker (2004).

PURPOSE: To have students orally reread a passage repeatedly until they can read it with about 95% word accuracy and with expression. This strategy is beneficial for students who read word by word without much expression, but have some degree of word accuracy.

PROCEDURE: As the teacher, do the following:

1. Select a text in which the students are interested. Texts that include rhythm, patterns, and emotion are particularly good for this strategy such as poetry, songs, traditional literature, fiction, or emergent concept books. You might give students a purpose for improving their reading of that text, such as performing for the class, families, or students in other classes.
2. Take a running record or audio-record each student's initial reading, and mark the miscues and fluency behaviors.
3. Review the running records to help students problem-solve unknown words.
4. Have the students repeatedly read the passage until they feel they can read it smoothly, with accuracy and expression.
5. The students then reread the passage orally while you record miscues with a different-colored pen. You and the students compare the initial reading with the final reading and discuss the students' progress. This progress can be charted on the *Fluency Assessment by Teachers and Peers* or the *Fluency Self-Assessment* (see Appendix, pp. 432 and 433).
6. While some recommend timing the students' rate, I believe that timing detracts from the comprehension goal of reading. In order for students to comprehend a passage, it may be necessary for the students to use problem-solving strategies while reading, and these strategies take time to process. As students become more efficient at using strategies for figuring out unknown words, their reading pace will increase. Emphasis should be placed on improving word identification, phrasing, intonation, expression, and conversational pace—not on improving reading speed.

• Reading with Expression

PURPOSE: For students to read sentences with different types of expression.

PROCEDURE: As the teacher, do the following:

1. Write words on index cards from four categories (Emotions, People, Actions, and Scenarios) that indicate different ways to read with expression.
2. Write a sentence on the board, and have students read it aloud.
3. Next, have students take turns selecting an index card from a bag and reading the sentence while using the expression indicated by that card.

4. Examples of words for cards in each category: Emotions (*excited, angry, confused, bored, panicked, joking*); People (*an old lady, a baby, a giant, Abraham Lincoln, Junie B. Jones*); Actions (*whispering, sobbing, screaming, shuddering*); and Scenarios (*you just finished running a mile; you just received the best news in the world*).
5. Finally, have the students apply this strategy to reading a text that elicits significant expression.

• Punctuation Reading and Writing Strategy

PURPOSE: For students to read with intonation and correct pausing marked by punctuation, and to have them write with the correct punctuation marks.

PROCEDURE: As the teacher, do the following:

1. Find an appropriate grade-level text containing multiple forms of punctuation marks. Explain that punctuation marks help to communicate a message. Review the end punctuation reading and writing strategy described under "Alphabetic Principle and Emergent Text Concepts Strategies" in Chapter 4.
2. Begin with declarative sentences that are marked with a period. Ask the students to point to each period on the page. Then read the sentences, taking a long breath after each period. Have students chorally read the sentences, reminding them not to stop at the end of a line if it is in midsentence. Then have them write declarative sentences with periods.
3. Next, identify question marks, and repeat this technique with reading and writing interrogative sentences that are marked with a question mark. Point out that your voice often goes up at the end of questions.
4. Follow this same technique for exclamatory sentences that are marked with exclamation points. Point out that your voice rises with excitement and then falls.
5. Next, introduce commas. You might select a personal letter to demonstrate the multiple purposes for commas. Ask students to point to the commas. Ask and explain the different purposes for commas as they arise in text. Commas separate ideas in a series ("apples, oranges, and mangoes"); separate independent clauses ("I like soccer, but she likes basketball"); separate an introductory word, phrase, or clause ("Last summer, I went on a vacation to Italy"); separate an optional parenthetical element from the remainder of the sentence ("We have, in a manner of speaking, won despite our loss today"); separate coordinate adjectives ("the small, brown, fluffy rabbit"); separate an attribution from a direct quotation ("He said, 'I like soccer.' "); separate a participial phrase ("Having said that, I have my doubts"); separate a salutation from a letter ("Dear Peter,"); separate geopolitical entities (street, city, state, and countries); separate day and year in dates (July 23, 2015); and separate groups of three digits in numbers (100,000,000). While reading, demonstrate pausing and taking a short breath after commas. Model the difference between the long breaths for ending punctuation and the short breaths for commas. Students then write using commas and state their purposes.

ADAPTATIONS: For older students, demonstrate this technique with colons and semicolons. Quotation marks also need to be introduced in this way when they are found in students' reading. Have students point to the opening quotation mark and the closing quotation mark. Tell the students that the quotation marks are used in pairs to set off or show the words that someone says. Then read everything that is not in quotation marks, and have the students read what is in quotation marks. You then can take dictation from the students during a language experience story. For example:

> Laura said, "I like the mountain lions the best."

Remind the students that in direct quotes, the period, question mark, or exclamation mark goes inside the end quotation mark. Students then write using quotation marks correctly.

• Talking Books

SOURCE: Walker (2004).

PURPOSE: For students to increase their vocabulary, word recognition, and fluency by having them repeatedly read along with an audio recording of a story or informational text until the students can read the text fluently with comprehension.

PROCEDURE: The teacher procures or makes an audio or video recording of a story or informational text. Recordings should use natural phrases of language and should be segmented so that the students can easily finish a segment in one sitting. Cueing the page numbers so that the students can easily find the page is helpful, too. Students follow the line of print with a finger and listen to the audio recording to develop an overall understanding of the story or informational text. Next, students listen to and read along with the recording as many times as necessary until they can read the text fluently. The students rehearse the text alone and then read the text to the teacher. The teacher evaluates fluency and comprehension.

• Interactive Storybooks and Other Electronic Texts

PURPOSE: For students to support their word recognition and fluency. These texts often include animated graphics, sounds, or interactive elements (such as highlighting words as they are read or providing word pronunciations).

PROCEDURE: Each student selects an interactive storybook or other electronic text within their reading level or slightly more challenging. (The teacher must be careful that students do not just play with the graphics instead of reading their books.) Students can listen to text read to them as the words in the text are highlighted; the students can read the text themselves; or they can get support by clicking on any word, and the electronic text will read it to them or define it. Many programs come with additional phonetic, word identification, and comprehension activities related to the text. (One popular series is *Living Books*, which is easily found through an internet search.)

• Language Experience Approach

SOURCE: R. Van Allen, cited in Walker (2004).

PURPOSE: For students to enhance word identification in context and fluency through the repeated reading of students' dictated text. The story becomes the text for instruction, and a collection of the stories becomes the students' first reader.

PROCEDURE: As the teacher, engage the students in a dialogue about a topic or an experience, asking for specific details. The students dictate the story while you write it. Then ask questions such as these: "What happened next?" "Is this what you wanted to say?" "How can you make a story using this information?" You and the students read the story simultaneously to revise any statements that are unclear to them. Then you and the students read the story repeatedly because repetition of the entire story will promote prediction during independent reading. The students read the story independently. Sentences or meaningful phrases can be written on sentence strips and cut up, to be mixed and then resequenced by the students. This promotes a whole–part–whole philosophy of literacy learning. Stories can be collated into anthologies for the students to read. As the words are repeatedly read in context, you can check them off a word list, but do not assess word knowledge in isolation.

• Radio Reading Revised

SOURCES: Greene (1979) and Searfoss (1975), cited in Opitz and Rasinski (1998).

PURPOSE: For students to perform a fluent reading, as if they are on the radio (grade 3 and above).

PROCEDURE: Students are given preselected portions of a text. After the students have had an opportunity to rehearse the reading, the person reading each portion takes on the role of a radio announcer, and the others are the listeners. After each portion is read, the reader leads the group in a discussion about the text. This is preferable to round-robin reading because each student has an opportunity to practice their part, and the class discusses each section of the text to focus on comprehension.

• Story Drama

SOURCE: Walker (2004).

PURPOSE: For students to take on the roles of characters in a story, in order to enhance their fluency and comprehension (grade 2 and above).

PROCEDURE: Students think about how a story might or could end differently, and then role-play the scenes. By taking on the roles of various characters, the students use their knowledge of similar experiences as well as of information from the story to act out their interpretation.

• Display and Practice Poetry and Songs

PURPOSE: For students to learn poems and songs to enhance their fluency and enjoyment of language.

PROCEDURE: As the teacher, display poems and songs large enough for everyone in the class to see. Read each one aloud a few times to the students, and then have the whole class choral-read it together. Give students individual copies. Have them practice reading it in pairs or independently. Finally, periodically come back and read the poem or song.

Song Chart Activities for Emergent Text Concepts, Word Identification, and Fluency

PURPOSE: For students to improve their emergent text concepts, word identification, and fluent text reading, using visual, auditory, kinesthetic, and tactile experiences. See the strategy of the same name described under "Alphabetic Principle and Emergent Text Concepts Strategies" in Chapter 4.

Poetry Chair

PURPOSE: For students to have opportunities to share poetry and have a purpose for reading fluently.

PROCEDURE: A calendar is posted in the classroom, and students are invited to sign up to share a poetry selection for the day of their choice. Students should select a poem and photocopy it or write it on paper. Students practice reading their poem until it is their turn to share it from a chair in front of the class.

Readers' Theatre

SOURCES: Braun and Braun (1996); McAndrews (2004, 2008); Walker (2004).

PURPOSE: For students to dramatically interpret a play, poem, fiction, or nonfiction text through a fluent oral interpretive reading to entertain and engage the audience; to motivate reluctant readers; to provide fluent readers with the opportunity to explore different genres and characterization through intonation, inflection, and fluency of oral reading; to provide an opportunity for students to collaborate and communicate with one another; and to provide ELLs with a language model.

PROCEDURE: Scripts that are at the students' interest and instructional level (90% or above word accuracy) are preferable, so that the students can focus on intonation, inflection, and fluency rather than on word identification. Most Readers' Theatre scripts are literary adaptations, although others are original dramatic works. Initially, choose works that are already written as scripts and divided into several different speaking parts. Scripts should be short enough to be completed and discussed within one class period.

There are several websites for Readers' Theatre. Aaron Shepard explains Readers' Theatre and provides free scripts and practice sheets at his website (*www.aaronshep.com*). Another excellent source for Readers' Theatre scripts is the Scholastic website (search for Readers' Theatre at *www.scholastic.com*). The Playbooks website provides leveled books designed in a Readers' Theatre format with each character's dialogue in a different color; free samples of these books are available at *www.readerstheater.com*.

As a teacher planning a Readers' Theatre presentation, provide an introduction to the characters, setting, events, and problem for narratives or to the main idea and details of expository texts. Students select or are assigned appropriately leveled parts to read and are given separate scripts with each part highlighted. You should model and discuss appropriate elements such as those found in the *Readers' Theatre Rubric* (see Appendix, p. 441), including phrasing, punctuation, expression, volume, clarity, pacing, timing, facial and body language, interpretation, staging, and cooperation. Students read the script silently and then read their parts orally to themselves, practicing the elements listed in the rubric. Students perform the script with or without minimal sets, costumes, or props. Because the students read from the scripts, they do not need to memorize the text. Students convey the story line by their intonation and phrasing. Finally, listeners must use their imaginations to interpret the story line. Students' oral reading can then be evaluated for the elements on the *Readers' Theatre Rubric.*

ADAPTATION: You or the students can write original scripts based on stories, rewrites of stories, or nonfiction content being studied. This enhances the students' word recognition because they need to reread parts of the text several times, and it can improve their comprehension because they must decide what dialogue and narration are necessary to understand the story. Different reading levels can be included to allow readers of varying reading abilities to participate in the same activity.

• Syllable, Word, and Sentence Stress

SOURCE: Levy (2018).

PURPOSE: For students to improve their reading fluency by having them say words with appropriate stress to demonstrate expression.

PROCEDURE: As the teacher, you can combine several of the following strategies to promote reading with appropriate stress.

1. Read a sentence without stressing content or main idea words.
2. Ask the students if they think it sounds right. Then read the sentence with the correct stress patterns. Explain that stress is saying a syllable or word louder and longer than the others.
3. Have students clap out the syllables in a sentence.
4. Have them identify each syllable as being stressed or unstressed, and mark the stressed syllables with an accent mark (').
5. Talk about what type of words are stressed (nouns, verbs) or unstressed (structure words). Give students index cards with content words, and have them create sentences by adding structure words. Then have them practice reading the sentences.
6. Find different types of sentences, such as *wh-* questions, yes–no questions, and exclamation sentences. Model the stress patterns in each, and have students reread them with the correct stress.
7. Give out a dialogue, song, or poem with the content words deleted. Then have the students listen to a recording of it and fill in the content words. Then have them practice reading or singing the text with appropriate stress.
8. Teach specialized uses of stress, and demonstrate how meaning can shift based on stress patterns in sentences.
9. Tell students a joke without using stress, then retell it using stress. Ask the students to compare. Have students find and tell their own jokes.

DIFFERENTIATION: Some ELLs lack an understanding of English sentence stress and give each syllable equal length and loudness, so it may be important to teach several of these strategies explicitly.

Chapter 6

Reading, Listening, and Viewing Comprehension

UNDERSTANDING READING, LISTENING, AND VIEWING COMPREHENSION

Comprehension is a complex thinking process in which the reader, listener, or viewer interacts with text to construct meaning. The primary goal of comprehension is to construct meaning by monitoring understanding, enhancing understanding, acquiring and actively using knowledge, and developing insight, according to Harvey and Goudvis (2017). Proficient readers are better able to remember and apply what they have read, create new background knowledge for themselves, carefully analyze the text and author, and engage in conversations, and/or other analytical responses to what they have read (Keene & Zimmerman, 2007). **Listening comprehension** is understanding the meaning of spoken words, such as those in texts being read aloud to students. In contrast, **reading comprehension** is understanding the meaning of written words that students read in texts. Listening comprehension during read-alouds develops first because young children can listen on a higher level than they can read. Once students are proficient readers, they may find that they comprehend the same, if not better when they read themselves.

Viewing comprehension is the ability to interpret, recognize, appreciate, and make meaning from information presented through visible actions, objects, and symbols, natural or human-made (Finley, 2014). Viewing is the process of understanding the ways in which static and moving visual images communicate meaning; it enables people to acquire information and to appreciate ideas and experiences visually conveyed by others. Viewers need to develop an understanding of messages conveyed through a variety of media, such as both print and digital texts, as well as posters, illustrations, graphics, photographs, graphic novels, comic strips, interactive websites, videos, art, advertisements, animations, virtual reality, and video games. It also includes three-dimensional visuals such as theater, gestures, models, sculpture, and realia. **Realia** are objects and material from everyday life, especially those used as teaching aids.

Visual literacy is the ability to read, write, and create static and moving visual images; it extends the meaning of literacy beyond just written and oral information. The purpose of visual literacy is to explicitly teach a collection of competencies that will help students think through, think about, and think with pictures and images (Finley, 2014). In this age of technology, visual learning helps students integrate new knowledge, as they can better remember information when it is represented and learned visually, aurally, and kinesthetically. Students construct meaning by interpreting the parts (images, symbols, context) of a visual message. Learners not only observe and interpret visual information within a print or digital text, but also through visual and performance arts, realia, and gestures. In digital texts, learners need to navigate by using search engines, menus, hyperlinks, videos, and interactive graphics. These multilayered texts can enhance understanding, but can be complicated if the use of these devices is not explicitly taught.

Visual language is used for comprehending and composing visual meaning. A shared metalanguage of visual design enables students and teachers to understand and talk about how meaning can be made in both still and moving-image texts (Victoria State Government Education and Training, 2018). Understanding visual design language supports viewing and creating visual meaning (Callow, 2013; Kress & van Leeuwen, 2006). There are three visual meaning functions, as described by the Victoria State Government Education and Training (2018): (1) expressing and developing ideas in visual texts—for example, how meaning about who, what, where, when, and why can be designed through choices of lines, symbols, vectors (showing action and direction in still images), comparative size, and color; (2) interacting and relating with others through visual texts—for example, how meaning about how we interact and relate with subjects and characters, and how we feel, can be designed through choices of perspective, social distance, subject gaze, and color; and (3) composition and structure of the image—for example, how a visual text can be organized to create a cohesive, coherent whole through the choice of focus (what the viewer's attention is drawn to first), color, and viewing path.

Although most of the subsequent discussion references reading comprehension, many of the concepts can be applied to comprehending visual information as well. The term **text** is used broadly to refer to any written or visual text.

Metacognition

Reading and viewing involve high levels of metacognition. **Metacognition** is being aware of your thinking as you perform specific tasks and then using this awareness to control what you are doing (Marzano et al., 1988). According to Baker and Brown (1984), there are four major aspects of metacognition in reading (these could apply to viewing as well):

1. *Knowing oneself as a learner*—being aware of what you know and do not know, your likes and dislikes, and your ability to activate background knowledge.
2. *Regulating*—knowing what to read, how to read it, being aware of text structure, and knowing how to use this information.
3. *Checking comprehension*—evaluating your own performance, being aware when comprehension is lacking or confused, knowing what information is important, and engaging in self-questioning to determine if your reading goals have been met.
4. *Repairing*—taking steps to correct your comprehension. Comprehension problems

may be caused by unknown words or concepts, misreading punctuation or phrasing, confusing relationships between ideas, misinterpreting main or important ideas, or having inadequate or conflicting prior knowledge.

Metacognitive awareness involves self-questioning and has to be built into all literacy instruction. Gunning (2004) explains that instruction in metacognitive strategies must include teachers modeling how they recall prior knowledge, set purposes for reading, decide on a reading strategy, carry out a strategy, monitor for meaning, take corrective action, organize information, and apply the knowledge gained from reading. Again, this can also apply to viewing.

Schema Theory and Comprehension

According to Anderson (2004), **schema theory** involves an interaction between the reader's own knowledge and the text, which results in comprehension. There are two types of schemata: **content schemata**, which refers to background knowledge of the world, and **formal schemata**, which refers to knowledge of rhetorical structure (Carrell, 1983). The reading process involves the identification of genre, formal structure, and topic, all of which activate schemata and allow readers to comprehend the text (Carrell, 1983).

Readers can activate and build schemata through direct and indirect experiences. Direct experiences include experiments, field trips, video recordings, demonstrations, computer programs, web quests, and guest speakers. An effective indirect experience is reading to and with students from a wide variety of genres and having discussions to build content and formal schemata. Students need guidance in using their existing knowledge and experience, as well as visualization, to make sense of texts. Often this guidance involves providing motivational anticipatory sets; activating background knowledge; building text-specific knowledge; relating the reading to the students, other texts, and the world; providing a book introduction; previewing the text, graphics, and organizational features; preteaching vocabulary and concepts; questioning and predicting; direction setting; and suggesting comprehension strategies for during or after reading. Students also need to think about what they already know about a topic, author, vocabulary words, and text structure. To enhance comprehension, readers need to make connections between the text and themselves, the text and other texts, and the text and the world (Farris, Fuller, & Walther, 2004). According to Carrell (1983), activating background knowledge is especially useful for ELLs to develop comprehension. Activating prior knowledge and building connections before, during, and after reading enhances comprehension because it helps the readers or listeners make connections between the text and their previous experiences and understandings; all this is directly related to schema theory.

Classifications of Written and Visual Texts

Written and visual texts can be classified as fiction, nonfiction, narrative, or expository. Visual texts can also be classified as two- or three-dimensional and can be static or moving. Kissner (2011) clarifies the distinctions and relationships among these four related but different terms (see Figure 6.1). The content, or what is in the text, can be fiction or nonfiction. **Fiction** describes imaginary events and/or people, but is often inspired by the real world.

FIGURE 6.1. Relationships among fiction, nonfiction, narrative, and expository text. Adapted from Kissner (2011), by permission of Emily Kissner.

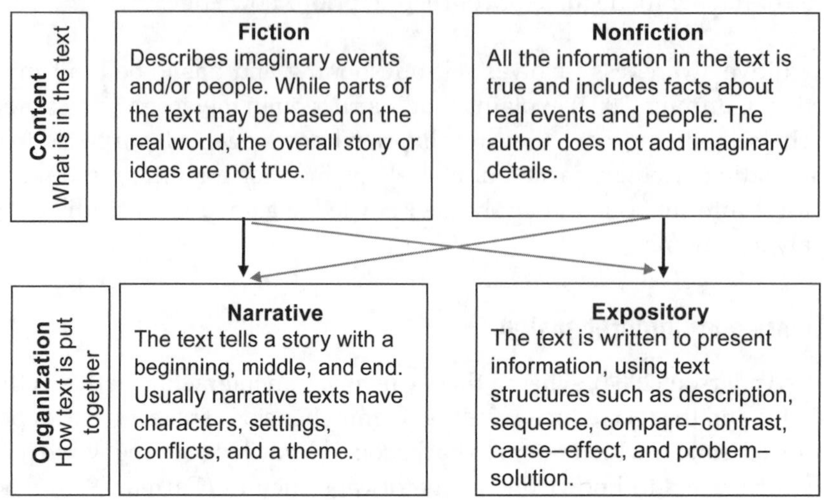

Genres of fiction include traditional literature, fantasy, mystery, adventure, humor, realistic fiction, science fiction, and historical fiction. **Nonfiction** is an account or representation of a subject, which is presented as fact. The purpose of the text is to provide facts through reliable sources. The information in the text is entirely true and includes facts about actual events and people, and the author does not add imaginary details. Examples of nonfiction include content textbooks, scientific reports, disciplinary journal articles, how-to guides, recipes, informational texts, concept texts, and reference books and resources.

The organization, or how the text is put together, can be a narrative or expository structure. A **narrative** text tells a story with a beginning, middle, and end. Usually narrative texts have characters, settings, conflicts, and a theme. They generally use a lot of emotion. Narratives can be short stories, novels, poetry, or drama. An **expository** text is written to present information, using text structures such as description, sequence, compare–contrast, cause–effect, and problem–solution. It is written to explain, inform, or describe information in a way that is educational and purposeful.

Fiction texts predominantly use narrative techniques, and nonfiction texts predominantly use expository structures. However, these terms are not synonymous. Biographies, autobiographies, memoirs, travel logs, and newspaper articles are nonfiction (or, at least, they are supposed to tell only facts), but they use a narrative style of writing. Fictional texts can also be written with expository text structures, such as cause–effect or problem–solution, in order to explain or inform us about real or realistic events, even if all the details are not completely accurate. Examples include contemporary or historical fiction that demonstrates how people solve problems. To add to the confusion of classifying texts, the Common Core State Standards use different terms and divide texts into "literature" and "informational text." The term "literature" equates to the term "fiction," and "informational text" equates to the term "nonfiction." Finally, it is important that teachers teach the general term "text" to refer to any written material—fiction or nonfiction, print or digital. The term "story" only refers to a narrative and should not be used for nonfiction expository texts.

Author's Purpose

To understand a text, it is important to determine the **author's purpose**, or reason for writing or creating a visual about a specific topic (such as to inform, persuade, entertain, or explain ideas to learners). The reason for composing changes the content and message. When authors compose to **inform**, they teach or give factual information. When they write to **persuade**, they try to convince readers of a certain point of view. When they write to **entertain**, they try to hold the attention of their readers through enjoyment. When they write to **explain**, they describe a procedure or sequence for a topic.

Narrative Text Structures

Knowing the text structure or organizational structure helps students organize the ideas in the text to enhance comprehension. Narrative texts have a sequence including a beginning, middle, and end. The basic **story grammar** is the description of the parts or elements of a story such as characters, setting, problem, events, and solution (Beck & McKeown, 1981). More advanced story grammars include the elements in a **plot diagram**, which is a tool that can be used to organize a story into segments (International Literacy Association & National Council of Teachers of English, 2019). The beginning **exposition** introduces the characters, describes the setting, sets the mood, and establishes the conflict or problem in the story. The **rising action** is where the suspense builds; it includes character development and the attempts to solve the problem. The **climax** is the turning point in the story and is usually the most exciting part. The **falling action** consists of the events that happen after the climax and lead to the resolution to the problem. The end **resolution** is the outcome of the story, or the description of how things turn out for the characters in the end. The events can be plotted in a three-section storyboard with the beginning, middle, and end to show the organization in the story. While generally sequential, plots can also include foreshadowing and flashback.

Other narrative elements identified by Buss and Karnowski (2000) include characterization, stereotypes, and theme or point of the story. The author's style and use of language are generally more informal in narratives. These texts are written from a particular point of view and often include imagery; figurative language, including similes, metaphors, and irony; humor; allusion; mood; tone; motivation; suspense; inference; and exaggeration. The story map or plot diagram strategy is often used for organizing and assessing narrative texts.

Organizational Text Structures

Text structures refer to how the text is organized. Predominantly expository texts, along with some narrative and persuasive texts, contain one or more of the following seven organizational text structures (Kletzien & Dreher, 2004). **Generalization–example** or **categorization** gives a general statement and provides examples or categories. **Question–answer** presents questions and gives answers. **Description** gives characteristics or features of people, places, living or nonliving objects, and ideas. **Sequence** or **process** explains events or steps to follow in chronological or time order. **Problem–solution** presents a problem and suggests one or more solutions. **Compare–contrast** tells how two or more things are alike and different. **Cause–effect** describes the cause of something, or why something happened, and the effect, or what happened. Teaching students to recognize these text structures help them monitor their comprehension. The writing in expository text is more formal and often includes a dense amount of information with discipline-specific vocabulary. Students may need to adjust the pace and style of their reading to their own purposes for reading and the text structures.

Persuasive texts, designed to convince others of the author's ideas, have four basic elements: the assertion, supporting evidence, the opposing view, and arguments against the opposing view. An **assertion** is a positive statement of fact or declaration of the author's beliefs. The **supporting evidence** is found in the details in the text and visual image that provide reasons for that point of view. The **opposing view** is stating what others may believe. The author then provides **arguments against** or reasons why they disagree with the opposing view. Persuasive texts generally use the **pro–con** structure, where the writer discusses the positive and negative aspects of a topic. This structure is similar to the cause–effect and compare–contrast structures. They may also include the problem–solution structure. Or the writer may try to emphasize a point by first discussing a topic and then either restating it through rephrasing or explaning it by using symbolism. Finally, the writer may integrate a narrative story within an expository or persuasive text in order to elaborate upon, personalize, or clarify a statement made. The language used is dependent on the audience for the persuasive text or advertisement and may include one or more propaganda techniques to convince the readers or viewers.

Text, Graphic, and Organizational Features

Most written texts contain a front cover with the title, author, and/or illustrator; a title page with the same information plus the publisher's name; a copyright page with publication and copyright information; pages with text and/or images; and a back cover. However, there are additional text, graphic, and organizational features that guide the readers in determining what the text is about and what is important. If they know how to use these features, they will support their understanding of the text. **Text features** include elements existing independently of the body of the main text, including the title, headings/subheadings, caption text, pronunciation guides, bullets, sidebars, and hyperlinks. It also includes elements of typography, such as boldface, italics, font style, size, capitalization, and text effects. **Graphic features** are pictures and other images that accompany a text to enhance its meaning, such as photographs, illustrations, insets, cross sections, cutaways, diagrams, labeled diagrams, maps, graphs, tables, charts, and timelines. **Organizational features** are intended to direct readers to specific locations in the text, such as the table of contents, glossary, index, references/bibliography, and appendix.

Elements of Graphic Design

There are seven basic elements of graphic design to examine while comprehending static and moving visual images: line, color, texture, size, shape, space, and value (Una Healy Graphic Design, 2019). When these elements are used together, they help convey a message. Kress and van Leeuwen (2006) have created a taxonomy of the grammar and structures of visual design. There are three structures, or components, of visual grammar that are essential for comprehending visual images and multimodal texts: composition, perspective, and visual symbols.

Six Types of Reading and Viewing Comprehension

There are multiple types of reading comprehension, depending on the sources one consults. The following are six types of comprehension that are combined from numerous sources: literal, inferential, applied, critical, affective, and lexical. The assessment or teaching of comprehension needs to address multiple types ofv comprehension. **Literal (explicit) comprehension** involves the factual information that an author directly states. This could include recognizing and recalling facts, and identifying stated main ideas, supporting details, categorizing, sequencing, and summarizing. This information can be determined by answering "who," "what," "when," and "where" questions that are stated or viewed directly in the text. Responses to these types of questions can be found in one place, referred to as "right there" (or, in multiple sources, referred to as "think and search"). **Inferential (interpretive, implicit) comprehension** deals with what the author means by what is written or viewed, but is not directly stated. The readers need to read between the lines and infer the meaning, which may not be initially apparent. This may include information that is not directly stated, such as main idea, compare–contrast, cause–effect, and theme. It may involve interpreting figurative language, drawing conclusions, predicting outcomes, determining the mood, and judging the author's point of view. Inferential comprehension is used to answer "what if," "why," and "how" questions, and is referred to as "author and you" comprehension questions. It can also include visual information, such as cartoons or images that infer what is happening or might happen.

Applied comprehension is taking what is said (literal) and what is meant by what was said (inferential) and extending the concepts or ideas beyond the text. The readers make connections from the text to their own background knowledge, to their knowledge of other texts, and to their knowledge about the world and universal truths. Information comes from both the author and the readers, which is why this type of comprehension is also often referred to as "author and you" comprehension. **Critical comprehension** involves readers' making judgments about the quality and accuracy of what they are reading and why the author wrote what they did. The readers will need to use their own experience to evaluate the quality and value of the author's reasoning. They will determine if they believe that the writing is fact or fiction and that the author is a credible authority. The readers will react both emotionally and intellectually with the writing. **Affective comprehension** involves understanding the social and emotional aspects of a text. It examines attitudes, values, thoughts, and feelings a person may have about the reading. This type of comprehension is referred to as "on your own" comprehension. **Lexical comprehension** is understanding the vocabulary used in the text. Readers need to learn to attend to the meaning of general academic vocabulary words and the discipline-specific vocabulary while reading, in order to comprehend the text.

Comprehension Levels and Dimensions of Thinking

The revised Bloom's taxonomy (Anderson & Krathwohl, 2001) includes six levels of comprehension: remembering, understanding, applying, analyzing, evaluating, and creating (see Chapter 1, Table 1.1). Marzano and colleagues (1988) have identified eight dimensions of thinking that incorporate additional ideas: focusing, information gathering, remembering, organizing, analyzing, generating, integrating, and evaluating. My literacy model organizes the comprehension process into the following categories: planning/monitoring, remembering, inferring, applying, analyzing, evaluating, and creating. Each of these categories involves metacognition and self-questioning in order for students to engage actively in the comprehension process.

Planning and monitoring comprehension refers to what students do prior to and throughout reading and viewing. Students set purposes for their reading or viewing, such as to learning about a topic, solving a problem, figuring out how to do or make something, or simple enjoyment. They decide which of the four reading styles matches their purpose for reading: (1) *skimming*—reading quickly to obtain a general idea; (2) *scanning*—reading quickly to find specific information; (3) *intensive or study reading*—careful reading for precise understanding of complex and detailed information; and (4) *extensive or pleasure reading*—reading fairly quickly for overall understanding and enjoyment. Viewing is similar, in that students can skim or scan through websites to find something they are interested in; they could carefully view a YouTube video to figure out how to fix or make something; or they could watch shows and movies on Netflix or view social media sites just for fun.

The ultimate goal is for students to monitor their own comprehension by generating and answering their own questions about their reading and viewing. In **question generation**, learners ask themselves questions about various aspects of the text, the author, and themselves, and also set a purpose for reading. In **question answering**, students answer questions posed by the teacher or themselves. Question generation and answering serves to guide students' thinking and help them develop comprehension, and also enables them or the teacher to assess comprehension. Too often, the questions that teachers ask are designed to check comprehension, rather than develop comprehension. Using questions to develop comprehension requires greater attention in the reading process. Questions can be used for students to monitor their comprehension.

During planning and monitoring comprehension, students gather information from the text by previewing the text, graphics, and organizational features. Students ask metacognitive questions to activate their prior knowledge of the topic or genre, to predict or anticipate what the text will be about, to determine what they want to learn from the text, and to identify strategies for monitoring and comprehending the text.

Remembering is recalling and storing information that is directly stated, such as literal or explicit information. This involves identifying the story elements in narratives, or the main ideas and details in expository and persuasive text. It also includes sequencing events or processes, as well as retelling and summarizing the text.

Inferring is the ability to draw conclusions, make predictions, pose hypotheses, make generalizations, and visualize. Students use their prior knowledge of the content and text structure to infer information that is not directly stated in the text. Students can read between the lines to infer story elements such as characters' motivation, cause–effect relationships, or the meaning of figurative language. They can make connections between the conclusions they draw and others' beliefs and knowledge.

Applying is the ability to use information in new situations, such as interpreting information, solving problems, and demonstrating learning. It also includes using the information from the text to make text-to-self, text-to-text, and text-to-world connections (Keene & Zimmerman, 2007).

Analyzing is the ability to draw connections among ideas by classifying, making comparisons, identifying cause–effect relationships, and identifying and separating ideas in the text into their component parts or organizational structures. Understanding the organizational structures helps students determine the importance of the information being read and decide which parts of a text deserve the most attention. Not all information is of equal importance. Some details are secondary or just provide additional background information, while others are essential for understanding.

Critical comprehension, or **evaluating**, refers to making judgments. Readers can infer the author's purpose, detect biases, and then evaluate accuracy in comparison to other sources or experiences. Readers can discriminate between reality or fantasy, and fact or opinion. Readers can examine the author's style and use of language, including identifying various propaganda techniques. Finally, readers can make judgments about whether or not the text or ideas are valuable, appropriate, acceptable, interesting, and entertaining; such judgments often help them decide what to believe or do. Students need instruction in viewing a text from different perspectives and need opportunities and instruction in locating, evaluating, and using reference sources. During evaluating, readers ask questions about who the author is and whether the author is an authority on the topic. They question the copyright date and the relevance of the text to information now. In evaluating persuasive texts, the reader needs to determine whether the author has appealed to their sense of fairness, goodness, or right and wrong.

Creating refers to applying the concepts or ideas acquired through reading, listening, or viewing to produce something new. Examples of this level of comprehension often include written composition, oral presentation, demonstration, multimedia presentations, visual representations, dramatic or artistic interpretation.

Instructional Frameworks to Support Comprehension

Several flexible instructional frameworks have been developed to support comprehension: the comprehension strategy framework (Dowhower, 1999), the scaffolded reading experience (Graves & Graves, 1994), and guided reading (Fountas & Pinnell, 1996). These frameworks are similar, in that each includes a planning or prereading phase to elicit and develop background knowledge and make connections, including the topic, text, and strategy introduction; an implementation or active reading phase with scaffolded questions and prompts; and a postreading phase with experiences to revisit, respond to, and expand upon the text. In addition, guided reading, as defined by Fountas and Pinnell (1996), includes the important stage of analysis and evaluation of student learning to plan future instruction. Fountas and Pinnell developed an instructional framework, now called a "continuum of literacy learning" (Pinnell & Fountas, 2010), which includes guided reading and has been described in Chapter 1. When constructing meaning, effective readers generate and answer questions before, during, and after reading in order to analyze, synthesize, infer, and evaluate information, and to apply this knowledge to create something new.

READING, LISTENING, AND VIEWING COMPREHENSION: GOALS

The following goals are divided into the comprehension categories of planning/monitoring, literal/inferential, analysis, critical/evaluative, and applied/creative. Some goals are specific to reading narrative, expository, or persuasive text; while others are more specific to comprehending visual information. Goals that are based on the Common Core State Standards (National Governors Association Center for Best Practices & Council of Chief State School Officers, 2010) are in the following lists.

Planning and Monitoring Comprehension

Prior to reading, listening, or viewing, students will do the following:

- Identify their own purposes for reading, listening, or viewing.
- Preview and predict what a written text will be about, based on text features (headings, captions, bullets, boldfaced/italicized words), graphic features (illustrations, photographs, charts, graphs, and maps), and organizational features (title page, table of contents, glossary, index).
- Identify the genre by both content and organization (fiction, nonfiction, narrative, expository, or persuasive).
- Identify the author's purpose for writing or creating visuals (to inform, persuade, entertain, and explain).
- Identify what they already know about this topic and what they want to learn about the topic.

During reading, listening, or viewing, students will do the following:

- Monitor and clarify what they understand and what they do not understand.
- Apply strategies to resolve problems in comprehension at the sentence, paragraph, and passage levels.
- Make and confirm predictions throughout reading, listening, or viewing.
- Generate questions about the text (literal, inferential, and critical).
- Form mental pictures to aid in understanding the text.

Literal and Inferential Levels of Comprehension

To enhance comprehension of narrative, expository, and persuasive texts at both the literal and inferential levels, students will do the following:

- Ask and answer questions to demonstrate understanding of a text, referring explicitly and implicitly to the text as the basis for the answers. (CCSS)
- Recount stories, including fables, folk tales, and myths from diverse cultures; determine the central message, lesson, or moral; and explain how it is conveyed through key details in the text. (CCSS)
- Describe characters' qualities in a story (e.g., their traits, motivations, feelings, actions, dialogue, appearance, and relationships), and explain how their actions contribute to the sequence of events. (CCSS)
- Describe setting (places, time of day, season, and year) and how it contributes to events.
- Visualize the setting, events, process, or ideas.
- Determine the meaning of general academic and domain-specific words and phrases in a text relevant to a grade-level topic or subject area. (CCSS)
- Use text features and search tools (e.g., key words, sidebars, hyperlinks) to locate information relevant to a given topic efficiently. (CCSS)
- Explain how graphic features contribute to what is conveyed by the words in a text (e.g., create mood, emphasize aspects of a character or setting in narratives) or clarify or extend information (e.g., where, when, why, and how key events occur in expository texts). (based on CCSS)
- Describe how graphic design features (line, color, texture, size, shape, space, and value) affect meaning.

- Describe the logical connection between particular sentences and paragraphs in a text (e.g., comparison, cause–effect, first–second–third in a sequence).
- Compare and contrast the most important points and key details presented in different texts.
- Describe facts and details about living things, objects, places, events, concepts, and ideas.
- Explain the sequence of events, processes, or ideas, either stated or inferred.
- Identify problems, attempts to solve problems, solutions, or potential solutions.
- Explain the stated or implied main ideas, and describe how key details support it. (CCSS)
- Explain the theme, plot, and resolution (stated or inferred).
- Summarize or paraphrase information directly or inferentially stated in the text or section of the text.
- Draw logical inferences, conclusions, and generalizations.
- Distinguish their own point of view from that of the narrator or those of the characters for literature, and from the author in informational text. (CCSS)
- Interpret figurative language such as similes, metaphors, hyperbole, oxymorons, and personification (in narrative and persuasive text).
- Explain the author's use of irony, humor, allusion, flashback, mood, tone, point of view, motivation, suspense, inference, and exaggeration (in narrative and persuasive text).
- Infer connections and relationships.
- Make connections between conclusions they draw and others' beliefs and knowledge.
- Generalize or form general concepts by inferring common properties of people, places, objects, and events.
- Predict or draw conclusions about what might happen to the characters, setting, or plot (in narrative text).
- Predict or draw conclusions about what the next part of the text will be about.
- Hypothesize, predict outcomes, or draw conclusions about ideas, problems, and solutions.
- Predict or draw conclusions about what may happen to living things, objects, places, events, concepts, and ideas in the future (in expository or persuasive text).
- Summarize or paraphrase inferred and explicit information from the text or a section of the text.
- Provide textual evidence to support responses to the text.

Analysis Level of Comprehension

To enhance comprehension at the analysis level, students will do the following:

- Analyze or classify characters, setting, plot, and resolution (in narrative text).
- Identify and analyze text structures (description, sequence, problem–solution, cause–effect, compare–contrast) within and between texts.
- Analyze or classify main ideas and details about living things, objects, places, events, concepts, and ideas.
- Compare and contrast the themes, settings, and plots of stories within or between narrative texts (CCSS), or with their own or others' experiences.
- Compare and contrast main ideas and details about living things, objects, places, events, concepts, and ideas within and between expository or persuasive texts, or with their own or others' experiences.

- Compare and contrast words or concepts within or between texts, with their own knowledge, or with that of others.
- Identify cause–effect relationships between/among characters, living things, objects, places, events, concepts, and ideas.
- Locate and compare and contrast information from a variety of sources.
- Describe the relationships between/among a series of historical events, scientific ideas, concepts, or steps in technical procedures in a text, using language that pertains to time, sequence, and cause–effect. (CCSS)
- Integrate visual information (e.g., in charts, graphs, photographs, videos, or maps) with other information in print and digital texts. (CCSS)
- Understand the purpose and analyze the elements of visuals (photographs, charts, graphs, illustrations, art, videos, theater, websites, and other visual media).

Critical or Evaluative Level of Comprehension

To enhance comprehension at the critical/evaluative level, students will do the following:

- Evaluate new information to determine if they need to change their existing knowledge to incorporate the new information.
- Discriminate between significant and irrelevant details in a paragraph or section.
- Determine importance of information.
- Evaluate the importance of words or concepts.
- Determine usefulness of information.
- Determine interest in the story or topic.
- Evaluate texts to select those that appeal to the emotions or affective domain.
- Rank information in terms of importance or interest.
- Evaluate their interest in the author's style of writing.
- Determine if events are based in reality or fantasy.
- Evaluate the accuracy and truthfulness of the material.
- Distinguish between facts and opinions.
- Recognize valid arguments.
- Compare material from several sources to verify or confirm information.
- Judge appropriateness, worth, desirability, and acceptability of the text for a specific purpose.
- Assess how an author's point of view, bias, or purpose shapes the content and style of a text. (CCSS)
- Recognize the various propaganda techniques, such as bandwagon, testimonials, glittering generalities, transfer, card stacking, "plain folks," name calling, stereotyping, and fear.
- Integrate and evaluate content presented in diverse media and formats, including visually and quantitatively, as well as in words. (CCSS)

Applied or Creative Level of Comprehension

To enhance comprehension at the applied or creative level, students will do the following:

- Combine prior knowledge with the knowledge, attitudes, or insights gained from reading to create something new.
- Apply reading to their own lives for problem solving or gaining understanding.

- Express a personal response to the text or subject.
- Apply knowledge about the characters, setting, plot, and resolution to create something new (e.g., dramatize the story, illustrate the story, create a model of the story, or produce another artistic representation).
- Apply knowledge about the characters, setting, plot, and resolution to rewrite the story in another genre or compose a new story.
- Apply knowledge about the topic to represent information in a new form, such as a chart, graph, outline, illustration, or model.
- Apply knowledge of the text to add information or go beyond the text.
- Apply knowledge from the text to solve a problem, conduct research, demonstrate a concept, or give a persuasive speech.
- Use the text or combination of texts as a guide to compose their own narrative, expository or persuasive writing, oral communication, or artistic interpretation.

READING, LISTENING, AND VIEWING COMPREHENSION: ASSESSMENTS

Reading, listening and viewing comprehension is strategic, interactive, engaging, and constructive. Assessment must also reflect the idea that comprehension is a complex process, which requires a more in-depth analysis of an individual student's literacy growth. Comprehension is dependent upon several factors, including adequate background knowledge; understanding of important concepts, vocabulary, and text, graphic, and organizational features; effective use of monitoring strategies; basic decoding skills and fluency; motivation and the ability to concentrate; and well-developed thinking skills and language development (Gunning, 2008). Comprehension should be evaluated through diagnostic assessment, followed by formative and summative assessment.

Comprehension assessment helps not only to identify a student's comprehension grade levels, but (more importantly) to identify the depth of comprehension, the story grammar elements, the main ideas and details, the text structures, the concepts, vocabulary, and visual information the student can comprehend, and areas for instructional support. Listening and reading comprehension assessment should use texts from different genres and include prior knowledge and prediction questions; a retelling checklist; and four types of comprehension questions: literal, inferential, applied, and critical. Questions should also be asked about the text structure and important vocabulary. An informal reading inventory such as the *Qualitative Reading Inventory–6* (QRI-6; Leslie & Caldwell, 2017; see Chapter 5) can be used for this purpose, as it contains these essential elements.

As a teacher who wishes to evaluate a student's reading or listening comprehension on a given text, you can develop your own evaluation by using the *Comprehension Retelling and Questioning Assessment: Guide* (described next). For formative or summative assessment, you can use your observations and notes or student writing on discussions and responses to texts, checklists for retelling or comprehension elements, graphic organizers, teacher-created or published tests, or evaluations based on the use of additional comprehension strategies. Standardized tests provide overall measures of comprehension, but they contain generally low-level, multiple-choice questions, and do not provide students with opportunities to construct their own responses (Gunning, 2008). Effective comprehension assessments should provide opportunities for multiple levels of comprehension. Every assessment tool described in this part of this chapter is provided in the Appendix.

• Comprehension Retelling and Questioning Assessment: Guide, with Comprehension Analysis Summary

PURPOSE: To analyze a student's prior knowledge before oral or silent reading, as well as the student's comprehension after reading by retelling and responding to comprehension questions, without and with looking back in the text. Listening comprehension can be also assessed after the student has heard a fluent reading of the text in person or through any form of audio media. The listening comprehension assessment is used to determine a student's ability to comprehend when the task of reading is removed. Listening comprehension is always assessed for a student who reads at or below the primer level. It can also be given to any student to determine their listening comprehension level. This assessment should be administered regularly to identify appropriate texts and instructional strategies based on the students' comprehension strengths and areas for growth. See the Appendix (p. 442) for the *Comprehension Retelling and Questioning Assessment: Guide.* It should be noted that unlike most other forms in the Appendix, this form is not to be filled in directly: The retelling checklist in the left half of the form is used to construct an assessment for a specific narrative text, and the retelling checklist in the right half to construct an assessment for a specific expository text. An *Oral Reading and Comprehension Analysis Summary,* and a *Comprehension Analysis Summary* that does not cover oral reading, are also presented in the Appendix (pp. 443 and 444).

PROCEDURE: As the teacher, choose a narrative, expository, or persuasive text, depending on which type of comprehension you want to evaluate. This could be text from a trade book, reading series, reference material, or electronic text. To determine a grade level for comprehension, use an informal reading inventory, such as the QRI-6 (Leslie & Caldwell, 2017; see Chapter 5), or leveled text. The QRI-6 is particularly valuable because it contains multiple narrative and expository passages at each level. It also contains background knowledge questions, retelling checklists, and explicit and implicit questions. The text selected should be a complete passage or complete meaningful section of a passage. If the text is less than approximately 300 words, use the entire text. The following is a general word count guide for text length by grade level: Preprimer–primer ≅ 40–60 words, grade 1 ≅ 100–150 words, grade 2 ≅ 100–200 words, and grade 3 and above ≅ 200–300 words.

Develop background knowledge questions and ask for a prediction about the story. Develop a retelling checklist with the important narrative or expository elements. Develop approximately 6–10 literal, inferential, lexical, and critical questions that address important concepts and vocabulary in the text. Include a final question that would address a connection between the text and the student, the world, or other text. Mark each question with L for literal, I for inferential, or C for critical. Add TS for text structure and V for vocabulary to literal or inferential questions that address these areas. To help develop questions, use the *Active Reading Self-Evaluation* (pp. 455–456), the *Narrative Comprehension Guide* (p. 457), and the *Expository Comprehension Guide* (p. 458) in the Appendix, and the questions at a variety of levels in Bloom's revised taxonomy as described in Chapter 1.

If the student is to read the story orally, follow the directions for recording and analyzing their miscues as described in the section "Oral Reading Record and Analysis of Miscues" in Chapter 5. Ask the student background knowledge questions about what they already know about the topic. Hand the student the text, and read the title. Ask the student to scan through the text and predict what it will be about. Write down the student's background knowledge and prediction responses, and score each response with a plus sign (+), a checkmark (✓), or a minus sign (–), depending on the accuracy and detail of the response. If oral reading is not to be analyzed, the student can listen to the story being read or can read silently. It is beneficial to audio-record the student's responses to review for accuracy, but always write the student's responses during the assessment procedure. Tell the student, "After you read, I will ask you to tell me everything you remember about the text, and then I will ask you questions about what you read." Use a retelling checklist to evaluate the student's recall of essential elements of the text by putting a plus or a minus sign next to each element, depending on whether the information is correct or not. Ask questions about the text, write the student's responses, and score with a plus or a minus sign, based on whether the question was answered correctly or not. No partial credit is given. If the student gives an incomplete response, write T.P. for teacher prompt and then write the clarifying question, such as "Anything else?" Then have the student look back into the text to find the evidence for their responses. Document the student's ability to verify their accurate responses and correct any answers after looking back at the text. Put a checkmark next to any response that the student corrects after looking back.

SCORING AND ANALYSIS: First, analyze the accuracy and depth of the student's background knowledge and then prediction by marking the total response with a plus sign (+) for accurate and complete responses, a checkmark (✓) for some knowledge, and a minus sign (–) for no knowledge or incorrect responses. Then analyze the student's ability to retell and answer different types of comprehension questions (literal, inferential, and critical). Provide specific examples of correct and incorrect responses. Comprehension is analyzed to determine independent, instructional, and frustration levels, as well as specific reading strengths and areas for growth. Although the retelling and comprehension questions are separate, both types can be used to determine a student's comprehension functioning level. If a student has correctly retold and/or answered 90–100% of the questions, the student is at an independent functioning level for comprehension; if the comprehension score is between 70% and 89%, they are at the instructional level; and if the score is 69% or below, the student is at the frustration level for that text.

A passage that the student read orally or silently at the frustration comprehension level may be read to the student to see if it is within their listening capacity level. This level is also called the potential level if the student comprehended the passage that was read to them, even though the student could not read it. In order to determine the student's functioning level when the word accuracy score and comprehension score are different, the functioning level is the lower of the two.

A student's comprehension can be affected by a variety of factors. To plan future instruction, reflect on the following questions: Did the student have background knowledge of the topic? Did the student use text features such as title, headings, typography, and graphics to predict what the text would be about? If the text was read orally, did the student read it at least at the instructional level for word accuracy? Did the student retell essential elements? If not, what elements were neglected? Did the student correctly answer literal questions, inferential questions, and/or critical questions? Did they look back into the text to verify or correct responses? Did the student comprehend narrative or expository passages better? How do the factors above affect each other? During instruction, select texts that are at the student's instructional level and select strategies that will enhance the student's comprehension in the areas for growth above.

The example of a *Comprehension Retelling and Questioning Assessment* in Figure 6.2 is a continuation of the *Oral Reading Analysis of Miscues Summary* example for *The Mitten* by Jan Brett (1989) in Chapter 5 (see Figure 5.2). See Figure 6.3 on page 229 for an example of the *Oral Reading and Comprehension Analysis and Summary*, using this same narrative text. Figure 6.4 on pages 230–231 shows an expository text example of the *Comprehension Retelling and Questioning Assessment* for the text *What on Earth Is a Chuckwalla?* by E. R. Ricciuti (1994). Figure 6.5 on page 232 provides an example of the *Comprehension Analysis Summary* for the same expository text.

• Text, Graphic, and Organizational Features Assessment

PURPOSE: To determine if the student can identify and use text features such as headings, captions, and typographical information; graphic features such as illustrations, tables, and charts; and organizational features such as title page, table of contents, glossary, and index to enhance text comprehension. See the Appendix (pp. 445–446) for this assessment.

PROCEDURE: This assessment may be administered either individually or in a group with everyone having the same text. As the teacher, select a text (usually an expository text) that contains as many of the features in the assessment as possible. Make a key for the blanks and expected responses. You or a student can read each question, and the student answers them. This assessment may be read to the student, especially if they read or write at or below third-grade level, or it can be completed independently by the student. Either the teacher or the student can write the responses. Evaluate by writing a plus sign (+) if correct, a minus sign (–) if incorrect, or N/A if the feature is absent in the selected text. If any of the features are absent, change the denominator of the fraction for the total number of questions. See Figure 6.6 on pages 233–234 for an example.

ANALYSIS: Answer the following questions to analyze the student's understanding of the layout and text features. Can the student locate and give the purpose for information on the title and copyright pages, such as the title, author, illustrator, copyright date, and publisher (questions 1–7)? Can the student locate and demonstrate the purpose for each of the organizational features, such as table of contents, glossary, and index (questions 8–16)? Can the student locate and give the purpose of text features, such as headings, captions, bolded words, and italicized words (questions 17–22)? Can the student locate and describe the graphic information that is found in illustrations, tables, and charts (questions 23–28)? Can the student identify other resources where information can be found (question 29)? Does the student understand that reading is a comprehension process and information can be obtained from these text concepts (question 30)?

INSTRUCTIONAL IMPLICATIONS: Identify the concepts the student does know and plan to reinforce them during instruction. Then go back to the text, point to all of the text, graphic, and organizational features that the student did not locate, and ask them to describe the information found there. For example, point out to the student the specific text, graphic, and organizational features and their purpose. Ask these same questions during the introduction of any disciplinary textbook or other texts students are reading that contain these features.

FIGURE 6.2. *Comprehension Retelling and Questioning Assessment,* narrative text example.

Title/Author: *The Mitten* by Jan Brett (1989)	**Grade Level:** 3 **Reading Level:** M, DRA 2 (end of grade 2)
Genre: Fiction, narrative	
Prior knowledge questions: Have you read this book before? No. ✓ What is a mitten? Things for your hands. – What is knitting? I don't know. + What happens if you lose something? My mom gets mad.	**Prediction:** What do you think this story is going to be about? Animals in the snow.

Student Retelling: There is a little boy. Grandma made mittens. He was climbing a tree and dropped a mitten. A mole came through. The rabbit and porcupine. Then the owl, badger, fox, bear, and the mouse.

Anything else? Then what happened? He went home.

Retelling Checklist:

Characters:	Setting:
✓ Boy, *Nicki*	____ In the house
✓ Grandmother, *Baba*	____ In the snow in the woods
____ Animals	____ Back to house

Plot:

Events:

✓ Grandmother knits a pair of white mittens.

____ Grandmother warns Nicki to be careful not to lose the mittens . . .

____ . . . because they are hard to find in the snow.

____ Nicki plays in the snow.

✓ Nicki climbs a tree.

Problem:

✓ Nicki drops a mitten ~~in the snow.~~

Events:

✓ A mole finds the mitten ~~in the snow~~ and crawls inside.

✓ A snowshoe rabbit finds the mitten.

____ The mole complains there is not enough room . . .

____ . . . but the rabbit climbs in.

____ The grandmother's knitting holds as the mitten stretches.

____ A hedgehog finds the mitten.

____ Each time the others complain there is not enough room . . .

____ . . . each time they crawl in.

____ The grandmother's knitting holds as the mitten stretches.

✓ An owl, ____ A badger, ✓ A fox, ✓ A bear finds the mitten.

✓ Finally, a mouse finds the mitten.

____ There is no more room in the mitten.

____ Nicki searches for the mitten.

____ Uses verbs to describe how the animals moved, such as *swoop, lumber, trot, snuffle, bump,* and *jostle.*

(continued)

FIGURE 6.2. *(continued)*

Resolution:
____ The mouse causes the bear to sneeze.
____ The mitten and all its animals go flying.
____ Nicki sees the mitten it the air and gets it.
____ Nicki goes back to grandmother with the mittens.
____ The grandmother notices how stretched out the mitten is.

Comprehension Questions: *The Mitten* (Brett, 1989)		
Score	**Question**	**Answer**
+	What is the grandma doing at the beginning of the story? L	She's making mittens.
–	What did the grandmother warn Nicki about? I	I don't know. She made him mittens.
+	How did Nicki lose his mitten? L	He was climbing a tree. He dropped it.
+	Which animals found the mitten? (At least five.) L	Mole, rabbit, owl, fox, bear, mouse.
+	What did the animals do when they found the mitten? L, TS	They went inside.
+	Why do you think the animals went into the mitten? I	They were cold.
–	According to the story, what does it mean to lumber over to the mitten? I, V	Wood.
–	Why do you think that the mitten didn't break? I	It was a big mitten.
–	How did Nicki find his mitten? I	It was on the ground.
+	How do you think the grandmother would have felt if Nicki lost the mitten? Why? I	She would have been mad, because she made the mitten. (*Stronger response:* because she warned him not to lose it.)
Critical Questions (Note: These are not used for assessing the comprehension of text, but to evaluate the text and make connections.)		
+	What do you think Nicki could do to keep from losing his mittens again? C	Put those clip things to hold them on the coat.
–	In real life, when do you think that the mitten would break? C	When the mouse climbed in.
–	Why do you think that Jan Brett made illustrations on the outside of the picture in the middle?	To make it look pretty. (It tells two different stories, one of grandma knitting and the other the animals climbing in the mitten.)
+	What is your favorite part of the story? Why? C	I like the part when all of the animals were in the mitten, because it got really big.

Note. L = Literal, I = Inferential, C = Critical, V = Vocabulary, TS = Text Structure.

FIGURE 6.3. *Oral Reading and Comprehension Analysis Summary,* narrative text example and analysis.

Name:	**Grade:** 3	**Date:**
Title: *The Mitten* by Jan Brett	**Word Count:** 198	**Level:** M (end of grade 2)
Genre: Fiction, narrative		

ORAL READING SUMMARY				
Type of Score	**Calculation**	**Fraction**	**%**	**Functioning Level***
Word Accuracy	Words Correct = Word Count – Uncorrected Miscues / Word Count	181/198	91%	Instructional
Text Meaning/ Acceptability	Words Correct + Uncorrected Meaning Retained Miscues / Word Count	185/198	93%	Instructional

COMPREHENSION ANALYSIS SUMMARY		
Criteria	**Scores with Examples**	
Prior Knowledge (+, ✓, –)	✓ Knew what a mitten was and what happens if you lose something.	
Prediction (+, ✓, –)	✓ Thought it would be about animals in the snow.	
Retelling (+, ✓, –) **Narrative** / **Expository** Characters / Main Idea Setting / Details Problem / Main Idea Plot / Details Resolution / Text Structure	C = ✓ S = – P = – (didn't identify problem) P = – (animals in the mitten, but not much else) R = –	
Comprehension Score	**Without Look-Backs**	**With Look-Backs***
Literal Questions:	4/4 = 100%	__/__ = __%
Inferential Questions:	2/6 = 33%	__/__ = __%
Application Questions	NA/NA = NA%	__/__ = __%
Critical Questions:	2/4 = 50%	__/__ = __%
Total Correct:	6/10 = 60%	__/__ = __%
Comprehension Functioning Level Frustration		*** Not used for determining level**

Functioning Levels for Text Reading			
	Independent	Instructional	Frustration
Oral Reading Accuracy	**95–100%**	**90–94%**	**89% or below**
Oral Acceptability	**98–100%**	**95–97%**	**94% or below**
Comprehension	**90–100%**	**70–89%**	**69% or below**

Analysis: This end-of-second-grade text is at the student's instructional level for oral accuracy, yet at the frustration level for comprehension. She correctly answered all of the literal questions that were directly stated in the text, as well as 2/6 inferential questions and 2/4 critical questions. During the retelling, she named the characters of the animals that went into the hat, but not the setting, problem, or solution.

Instructional Implications: Since the text was at the frustration level for comprehension, reading instruction should be at a lower text level. I would reinforce the identification of literal information and model using the think-aloud method on how to use information from different parts of the text and prior knowledge to answer the inferential questions in this and other texts.

FIGURE 6.4. *Comprehension Retelling and Questioning Assessment,* expository text example.

Title/Author: *What on Earth Is a Chuckwalla?* by E. R. Ricciuti (1994)	**Grade Level:** Grade 5 **Reading Level:** T (middle of grade 5)
Genre: Nonfiction, expository	
Prior knowledge questions: Have you read this book before? No. ___ What is a chuckwalla? I don't know. ✓ Describe the desert. It is hot. ✓ How do animals adapt to their environment? They change.	**Prediction:** What do you think this story is going to be about? A lizard. (Looked at the front cover.)
Retelling Checklist:	
✓ Main Idea: What does it look like? Details: ___ Large head ✓ Big flat belly ___ Long, thick tail ___ Folds of skin hang from throat, neck, and shoulders ___ Skin is rough and scaly ✓ Dark skin with spots of yellow or grey ___ Is about 18 inches long ✓ Main Idea: How is it classified? Details: ✓ Chuckwalla is a lizard ___ Related to iguanas in the family Iguanids ___ Scientific name: *Sauromalus obesus* ___ *Sauros* means lizard, and *omalus* means flat ✓ Main Idea: Habitat: Details: ___ Lives in the Southwest United States (California, Nevada, Utah, Arizona, and Baja California) ✓ in rocky places in the desert	✓ Main Idea: Food Details: ✓ It eats only plants ___ Eats leaves, fruits, and flowers ___ Likes yellow flowers on the prickly pear cactus and the creosote bush ___ Food for hawks and big birds – Main Idea: Reproduction Details: ___ Mate between 4 and 7 years ___ Male attracts mate by bobbing its head and selecting a place with plenty of food and rocks ___ Lays 6–30 eggs in a burrow and fills it up ___ In 3 months, young dig out ✓ Main Idea: Survival ___ Burrows to get out of the heat ___ Eats in the morning and evening when it is not hot ✓ Wedges itself between cracks in rocks ✓ Puffs up its lungs so it can't be pulled out

(continued)

FIGURE 6.4. *(continued)*

Comprehension Questions: *What on Earth Is a Chuckwalla?*		
Score + –	**Question**	**Answer**
+	**1. What does a chuckwalla look like? Describe at least three physical characteristics. (L)** Large lizard with a large head, a fat body, and a thick tail; about 18 inches long (46 cm) and weighs more than 3 pounds (I kilogram). Folds of skin droop from its throat, neck, and shoulders. It usually has dark scaly skin with yellow or grey dots sprinkled on its back.	A big lizard with a big belly and loose skin. T.P. Anything else? It has spots all over.
+	**2. Describe its habitat. (L)** It lives in the desert, especially in rocky places.	It lives in the rocks in the desert.
+	**3. On the map, where does it live? (L)** It is found in southern California, southern Nevada and Utah, western Arizona, northern Mexico, and an island in Mexico's Gulf of California.	In the United States. T.P. Specifically where? Like California, Arizona, and Mexico.
+	**4. How does it adapt to living in the desert? (I)** When it is hot, it crawls into holes. It eats in the morning and evening, because it is not too hot or too cold.	It goes into holes when it is too hot.
+	**5. What kind of defense does it have against its enemies? (L)** It goes into a crevice, inflates its lungs with air, and swells up its body so it cannot be pulled out.	It goes between rocks and gets fat and nothing can pull it out.
+	**6. What does it eat? (L)** It eats only plants: leaves, fruits, and flowers. They are attracted to yellow flowers.	They eat yellow flowers. Anything else? Just plants.
– LB +	**7. How do male chuckwallas attract mates? (L)** They bob their heads and stake out a territory with plant and boulders.	They call them.
– LB –	**8. How do changes in the environment affect mating? (I)** If it is too cold or there is not enough food, they do not mate.	I don't know.
+	**9. What dangers do chuckwallas face? (I)** Hunted by hawks and large birds, their habitats are being destroyed and people are taking them as pets?	Birds can eat them T.P. Anything else? People take them.
– LB –	**10. Why do you think chuckwallas lay so many eggs? (I)** Because the desert is hot and dangerous, and many won't survive. They have to dig themselves out after they are hatched. They have to be at least 4 years old to mate.	Because there are a lot of them.
+	**11. Would a chuckwalla be comfortable living where you live? Why or why not? (C)**	No, because it is too cold here and they couldn't eat.
+	**12. How might you protect chuckwallas? (C)**	Don't let people tear up the land and not take them home.

Note. L = Literal, I = Inferential, C = Critical, V = Vocabulary, TS = Text Structure, LB = Look-Backs.

FIGURE 6.5. *Comprehension Analysis Summary,* expository text example and analysis.

Name:		**Grade:** 6	**Date:**
Title: *What on Earth Is a Chuckwalla?* by E. R. Ricciuti (1994)		**Word Count:**	**Level:** T (middle of grade 5)
Genre: Nonfiction, expository			
COMPREHENSION SUMMARY			
Criteria	**Scores with Examples**		
Prior Knowledge (+, ✓, –)	✓ Did not know what a chuckwalla was, but could minimally describe the desert and adaptation.		
Prediction (+, ✓, –)	+ Said the book would be about a lizard in the desert.		
Retelling (+, ✓, –) **Narrative** / **Expository** Characters / Main Idea Setting / Details Problem / Main Idea Plot / Details Resolution / Text Structure	MI = Looks ✓ D = ✓ MI: Food ✓ D = – MI = Classified – D = – MI: Reproduction – D = – MI = Habitat ✓ D = ✓ MI: Survival ✓ D = ✓ TS = ✓ Retold events in order		
Comprehension Score	**Without Look-Backs**	**With Look-Backs***	
Literal Questions:	4/6 = 83%	6/6 = 100%	
Inferential Questions:	2/4 = 50%	2/4 = 50%	
Application Questions	__/__ = N/A%	__/__ = N/A%	
Critical Questions:	2/2 = 100%	__/__ = N/A%	
Total Correct:	7/10 = 70%	8/10 = 80%	
Comprehension Functioning Level Instructional		*** Not used for determining level**	

Functioning Levels for Comprehension			
	Independent	Instructional	Frustration
Comprehension	**90–100%**	**70–89%**	**69% or below**

Analysis: She was at the instructional level for comprehension when reading this middle-of-grade-5 book silently. She answered 4/6 literal questions, 2/4 inferential questions, and both critical questions correctly. She did not have any background knowledge on chuckwallas, and her response was limited to how animals adapt to their environment. During her retelling, she mentioned how it looks, the habitat, food, and survival. She did not mention how it was classified or anything about reproduction. She did not provide many of the important ideas or details in the text. However, for the comprehension questions, she answered all but one literal question and 2 out of the 4 inferential questions. After the assessment, when she looked back into the text, she correctly answered the remaining literal questions, but not the inferential ones.

Instructional Implications: After the assessment, I had her orally read sections that would contain clues to the inferential questions. I explained that the answers were not directly in the text, but had to be inferred from the information in the text and her own knowledge. I will continue teaching using this level of materials, and will focus on answering inferential questions and providing more details during retelling.

FIGURE 6.6. *Text, Graphic, and Organizational Features Assessment,* example.

Title/Author: Habitats: Tropical Rain Forests, by Libby Romero (2005) **Level:** Beginning of grade 3

Questions	Responses	Score
1. What is the title of the text?	Tropical Rain Forests.	+
2. Who is the author of the text?	Libby Romero.	+
3. Who is the illustrator of the text?	It doesn't say.	N/A
4. Is there any information about the author or illustrator? If yes, state one fact.	No. (*There is author info. on the back cover.*)	–
5. What is the copyright date?	2005.	+
6. Why is it important?	It's a new book.	+
7. Who is the publisher?	I don't know. (*T.P. Try to find it.*)	–
8. Where is the table of contents?	Right here. (*Student pointed.*)	+
9. What information do you find there?	What's in the book and page number.	+
10. What page can you find What Lives in Tropical Rain Forests? on?	Page 10.	+
11. Where is the glossary?	I don't know.	–
12. What information do you find there?	Words. (*Anything else?*) No.	–
13. What is the definition of habitat?	Where stuff lives. (*Not from book*)	–
14. Where is the index?	Right here. (*Student pointed.*)	+
15. What information do you find there?	Words (*Anything else?*) No.	–
16. What page is *deciduous* on?	Page 9.	+
17. Where is a heading?	Page 4.	+
18. What information does it tell you?	What Are Tropical Rain Forests?	+
19. Where are bolded or italicized words?	Tropics.	+
20. Why are they bolded or italicized in the text?	They're important.	+
21. Where is a caption?	I don't know.	–
22. What information does it tell you?		–
23. Where is a photograph or illustration?	(*Student pointed.*)	+
24. What information does it tell you?	It's a howler monkey.	+
25. Where is a diagram or map?	(*Student pointed to page 4.*)	+
26. What information does it tell you?	It's the world. (*Anything else?*) It's where the rainforests are.	+
27. Where is a table or chart?	*Student pointed to page 9.*	+
28. What information does it tell you?	Stuff about rain forests?	–
29. Where can you go to get additional information on this topic?	On the Internet.	+
30. As you look through the text, what do you think it is going to be about?	It's about rain forests. (*Anything else?*) Where they are and what's in them.	+
Total Correct:		20/29

(continued)

FIGURE 6.6. *(continued)*

Analysis: The student correctly identified 20/29 text, graphic, and organizational features in the text Habitats: Tropical Rain Forests. She did not find or identify the author information on the back cover, the publisher information, or the glossary. She could not describe the information found in the index or captions. She was not specific about what information the chart provided.
Instructional Implication: Select a nonfiction text that includes all of the text, graphic, and organizational features she missed on this assessment. Quickly point out several features she identified correctly, then define the features she missed and guide her to find and explain the information found in the features.

• Text Structure Assessment

PURPOSE: To assess a student's ability to identify text structures and related signal words. In addition, to assess the student's ability to select an appropriate graphic organizer and write important details related to that structure. See the Appendix (pp. 447–448) for this assessment.

PROCEDURE: As the teacher, say, "Common text structures include descriptive, compare–contrast, sequence, problem–solution, and cause–effect. Read each paragraph, write the overall text structure, and identify the signal words. Next, create a graphic organizer related to the text structure, and write at least five important details in the graphic organizer."

ANALYSIS: Calculate the student's score out of 35 total points. Students get 1 point for each correct text structure identified, 1 point for identifying two or more signal words, and 5 points for selecting an appropriate graphic organizer and writing at least five details from each paragraph related to the text structure. In the analysis, provide examples of correct and incorrect responses for text structure, signal words, and graphic organizer.

INSTRUCTIONAL IMPLICATIONS: If students are unable to identify the text structure in the assessment paragraphs, refer them to the text structure chart with the related signal words. Then show them graphic organizers appropriate for each text structure, and ask which one would be helpful to document the important information the author wrote. Next, have them identify text structures authors used in other texts. Finally, support students in using a particular text structure and graphic organizer to write their own paragraphs.

• Guided Reading Checklist

PURPOSE: To evaluate students during guided reading. The *Guided Reading Checklist* is divided into an evaluation of reading silently, reading orally, and comprehension. This assessment was developed from multiple sources, including my own assessments (McAndrews, 2008), as well as those of Fountas and Pinnell (2001) and Robb (2001). See the Appendix (pp. 449–450) for this assessment.

PROCEDURE: During guided reading, evaluate each student in a reading group. It is often easiest to focus on one or two students in the group per day.

SCORING AND ANALYSIS: Mark each element with a plus sign (+) if a student usually exhibits the behavior, a checkmark (✓) if the student sometimes exhibits the behavior, or a minus sign (–) if the student rarely or never exhibits the behavior. Summarize strengths, and provide specific examples of areas for growth. See Figure 6.7 for an example.

FIGURE 6.7. *Guided Reading Checklist,* example and analysis.

	Score +, ✓, –
Reading Silently	
Stayed on task.	✓
Chose to read.	+
Used organizational features (table of contents, glossary, and index) to clarify information.	–
Referred back to parts already read to clarify or extend new information.	–
Read for detail rather than just skimming.	✓
Actively participated in discussion about the text.	+
Contributed to discussion and questioning that indicated an appropriate level of comprehension.	✓
Connected text to self, to other texts, or to the world.	✓
Reading Orally	
Accuracy	
Used a variety of strategies to problem-solve unknown words.	–
Reread if the reading did not make sense, look right, or sound right.	✓
Self-corrected miscues that affected the meaning of the text.	–
Made fewer than 5 miscues in 50 words.	–
Used resources to gain meaning of unknown words.	–
Fluency	
Read in phrases.	✓
Paused at punctuation.	✓
Changed expression and intonation according to the author's style.	–
Generally, read smoothly and resolved any problems quickly.	–
Adjusted pace according to material and purpose.	✓
Read at a conversational pace.	✓
Comprehension	
Predicted content based on cover page, table of contents, graphic information, headings, and/or reading the first paragraph.	✓
Identified the genre and text structure.	+
Made inferences and evaluated them during reading.	–
Reread to clarify meaning.	–
Used resources or asked questions to clarify meaning.	–
Identified and explained the narrative story elements in his/her own words.	✓

(continued)

FIGURE 6.7. *(continued)*

	Score +, ✓, –
Identified and explained the main ideas and details of an expository text.	–
Identified and explained the expository text structures in his/her own words.	–
Summarized the text in his/her own words.	✓
Made connections within the text, to other texts, to self, and to the world.	✓
Evaluated the text for author bias, content, and interest.	✓

Analysis: He generally participated in the group discussion about the text. He is beginning to understand the texts more with group discussion. He did not use resources such as the glossary when he didn't know the meaning of a word. He did not use a variety of strategies to figure out unknown words, especially strategies that might result in self-correcting miscues that affected the meaning of the text. With support, he used organizational and graphic features to make predictions about the text. He identified the genre, but did not identify any text structures. He has improved in summarizing, making connections to the text, and evaluating the content, and has increased his interest in text reading.

Instructional Implications: The first lesson should include learning how to use organizational features such as table of contents, glossary, index, and headings. Next, I would use this information to help the student predict what the text will be about. I would then teach the student that the main purpose for reading is to understand what the author is saying and how it is similar or different from what we already know. I would use the appropriate *Good Readers Bookmark* to teach the student multiple strategies to use when identifying unknown words or concepts. Later lessons would include identifying text structures and strategies for comprehending texts with those structures.

• Oral or Written Story Retelling Analysis

PURPOSE: For students to improve their oral language complexity, story comprehension, and understanding of story structure. I developed this assessment, using Mariotti and Homan (1997) as a basis. See the Appendix (p. 451) for this assessment.

PROCEDURE: As the teacher, give the student a copy of this retelling analysis as a reference. Say, "Tell me [or write] everything you remember about the story in order as if you were telling a friend about it." After the student is finished, ask, "Can you tell me anything else?" Mark each element (characters, setting, events, resolution, and sequence) with a plus sign (+) if the student provides a complete correct response, a checkmark (✓) if it is a partial or partially correct response, or a minus sign (–) if the response is incorrect or not given. Add comments to clarify behaviors.

ANALYSIS: Identify which elements the student retold or did not retell, such as theme, main idea, description and sequence of events, use of text vocabulary, and use of story grammar elements with details. Provide examples of correct and incorrect responses.

INSTRUCTIONAL IMPLICATIONS: Point out the student's strengths, and identify one or two elements to improve. Have the student return to the text and reread to help them enhance the retelling.

READING, LISTENING, AND VIEWING COMPREHENSION: STRATEGIES

Instruction that actively engages students in asking questions, summarizing, and synthesizing text, and identifying important ideas improves comprehension (Keene & Zimmerman, 2007). Strategies are included for enhancing comprehension before, during, and after reading and viewing. Some of these strategies are helpful when used alone, but many are more effective when used as part of a multiple-strategy method, and/or through collaborative experiences where students comprehend text with the support of their peers. Additional strategies that support comprehension can be found in the other chapters. Chapter 2 also includes strategies for selecting appropriate texts from different genres that engage and facilitate students' interests, abilities, and culturally responsive understanding.

General Listening Comprehension Strategies

Almost all of the reading comprehension strategies can be used as listening strategies; however, here are some guidelines for using read-alouds and think-alouds during listening.

• Read-Alouds and Think-Alouds

PURPOSE: For students to build comprehension and interest in books during read-alouds and think-alouds.

PROCEDURE: As the teacher, do the following:

1. Select a wide range of high-quality, diverse books that children can relate to and that will help them learn about others. They need to see themselves as well as other people, cultures, and communities. Themes can include family traditions, friendship, immigration, and so forth, or they can relate to content areas. These read-aloud books are typically above the reading level of most students, in order to develop language and comprehension skills.
2. Start with an introduction to the topic of the book, with a "hook" to get students interested in it.
3. Conduct a text and picture walk, discussing some of the organizational, text, and graphic features that may help them predict what the text will be about. Talk about the author's purpose and the genre of the text.
4. Ask questions that help students to connect the book to their own experiences, to other texts, and to the world around them.
5. Model fluent reading of text by reading with appropriate expression, intonation, and pace. Use different voices or dialects for stories with dialogue.
6. Use think-alouds to model your process for comprehending the text. Model how to make connections between the text and students' experiences, the text and other texts, and the text and the world or universal truths. Talk about connections to similar text structures, topics, and authors.
7. While reading books, point out and discuss the graphic, text, and organizational features.
8. Point out vocabulary, concepts, or text structures that the students may not be familiar with.
9. Show your students that you enjoy reading books, magazines, newspapers, and digital resources.

Emergent Listening Comprehension Strategies

Many students (especially those at lower reading levels) can comprehend a text better when it is read orally to them because they can concentrate on the meaning rather than on decoding the text. It is important for students to hear, discuss, and comprehend text above their reading level to develop reading comprehension and a love of literature. According to Harris and Hodges (1995), a student's **listening comprehension level** is "the highest grade level of material that can be comprehended well when it is read aloud to the student" (p. 140).

• Guidelines for before and during Reading

As the teacher, you could do the following:

1. Reread familiar texts, talk about students' favorite books, and introduce new texts.
2. Reading instruction should begin with a topic and/or book introduction and discussion to develop and make connections to background knowledge and language. It should not begin with phonics skills.
3. For emergent readers, begin with a picture walk, where you preview and talk about the pictures to familiarize the students with the content of the text and key vocabulary words the author used.
4. Read the story with expression and use different voices for different characters to get your students more involved in the story.
5. Help students make predictions based on the context, picture clues, and background knowledge by pausing and asking prediction questions.
6. Point to details in the pictures that show what you read or to reinforce vocabulary words—for example, "Look, there are the two scared cats," or "That's where the mouse escaped to."
7. Use a modified oral cloze procedure, in which you as the reader omit words for the listeners to provide. Encourage the students to chime in on repeated phrases or patterns, by stopping to see if your students can supply the repeating phrase or the last word of the rhyme. An example from "The Three Little Pigs": "He huffed and he puffed and ________________" (he blew the house down).
8. In both stories and expository texts, encourage wondering—for example, "I wonder what Pooh will do now?", "How do you think the father feels?", or "I wonder what frogs do in the winter. Do you think that's a problem? Why?", or "What do you think is going to happen next?"
9. Make brief comments during the story, and answer students' questions as well.

• Guidelines for after Reading

Have a conversation with the students about the story after you read it. Ask questions such as "What was your favorite part?" or "How is the story or text similar or different from your life?" Make connections to their lives with questions such as "Where does *your* cat sleep?" or "How is this character like you?" After reading the story on several different days, encourage your students to pretend read by retelling from the pictures, or actually read by saying, "Now how about you read to me? Remember to look at the pictures to help you." Suggest that students draw pictures related to the story or their lives. Have them tell you about the pictures, and write down what they say above or below the pictures. Help the students to write their names and/or their ideas on the pictures. Connect their writing and art activities to the reading, and make puppets based on the books to help the students expand their vocabulary.

General Reading Comprehension Strategies

• Guidelines for Teaching Comprehension Strategies

PURPOSE: For students to use strategies on their own to enhance their comprehension.

PROCEDURE: The following are general directions for planning, modeling, and teaching strategies.

1. Select a text from the same genre as what the students will be reading.
2. Read the text on your own.
3. Select a strategy that would be helpful in understanding that text.
4. Practice using the strategy on your own. Write out your thinking and how you incorporate listening, speaking, reading, writing, viewing, and/or visually representing during the strategy.
5. In class, explain the purpose for reading the text and the purpose for the strategy you selected.
6. Read the text or a coherent section of the text aloud.
7. Model the strategy, explaining your thinking along the way.
8. Try not to break up the text too much; otherwise, comprehension could be impeded.
9. You or the students select a text that is judged to be at their independent or instructional comprehension level.
10. Provide guided practice with this strategy, asking specific questions to guide the students.
11. Provide paired and/or independent practice in using this strategy.
12. Explain when, why, and how the students can use this strategy on their own.
13. Have students keep a list or a notebook of strategies they have learned as a reference.

• Creating Anchor Charts

SOURCE: Linder (2014).

PURPOSE: For students to use charts created by teachers and students that are displayed in the classroom as references to recognize instructional goals; review concepts; set expectations; and apply specific strategies, concepts, or procedures.

PROCEDURE: The teacher and students create anchor charts at the onset of new learning and revisit them throughout the lesson and into independent practice. The teacher begins by identifying the focus and purpose of an anchor chart (strategy, procedure, concept), and then engages all students in shared creation. The chart should include only the essential information (it is not a narrative). It should organize information so that it is neat and easy to follow and reinforces the purpose. Simple icons and graphics will enhance the chart's usefulness, and different colors can be used to code related information. The completed anchor chart should be placed in a strategic location where students can visually access it easily. They should refer to the anchor chart frequently as part of a literacy-rich, collaborative environment.

EXAMPLES: Topics for anchor charts can include using context clues, making connections, identifying text structures, steps for retelling story elements, literature circle roles, independent reading response options, and many others.

• Eight Types of Comprehension Strategies

SOURCE: Harvey and Goudvis (2000).

PURPOSE: For students to use an integration of comprehension strategies while reading.

PROCEDURE: As the teacher, help students to do the following:

1. *Make predictions.* Think what will the text be about and what will happen next.
2. *Make connections.* Connect the topic or information to what they already know about themselves, about other texts, and about the world.
3. *Ask questions.* Ask themselves questions about the text, their reactions to it, and the author's purpose for writing it.
4. *Visualize.* Make the printed word real and concrete by creating a "movie" of the text in their minds.
5. *Determine text importance* by (a) distinguishing between what's essential and what's interesting; (b) distinguishing between fact and opinion; (c) determining cause–effect relationships; (d) comparing and contrasting ideas or information; (e) discerning themes, opinions, or perspectives; (f) pinpointing problems and solutions; (g) naming steps in a process; and (h) locating information that answers specific questions.
6. *Make inferences.* Merge text clues with their prior knowledge, and determine answers to questions that lead to conclusions about underlying themes or ideas.
7. *Summarize.* Make a brief statement of the main points of the text.
8. *Synthesize.* Combine new information with existing knowledge to form original ideas, new lines of thinking, or new creations.

• Questions for Types of Reading Comprehension

PURPOSE: For students to ask and answer questions based on the different types of comprehension (literal, inferential, applied, critical, affective, lexical). See the descriptions of each type in the "Understanding Reading, Listening, and Viewing Comprehension" section earlier in this chapter.

PROCEDURE: When assessing and teaching comprehension, teachers need to address multiple types of comprehension. The following are general strategies to teach to students along with examples of questions that could be asked after reading the story of Cinderella.

- **Literal (explicit) comprehension.** *Strategies:* "During reading, ask/answer your own questions from the beginning, middle, and end of the story; after reading, look in the text to find the answers." *Examples:* "Where did Cinderella live at the end of the story [right there]? What did the animals do to help Cinderella get ready for the ball [think and search]?"
- **Inferential (interpretive, implicit) comprehension.** *Strategies:* "Use textual and graphic context to know information that is not stated directly in the text." *Examples:* "How did

the pumpkin turn into a carriage? What would have happened to Cinderella if she hadn't lost her slipper?"

- **Applied comprehension.** *Strategies:* "Use your background knowledge and make text-to-self, text-to-text, and text-to-world connections. Support your answers with logic and reason, but there are no right or wrong answers." *Example:* "Do you think Cinderella was wrong for going to the ball after her stepmother told her she couldn't go [author and you]?"
- **Critical comprehension.** *Strategies:* "Make judgments about the quality, accuracy, and value of the text, and the author's reasoning for the text." *Examples:* "Describe the author's style of writing. Do you enjoy this style? Why or why not? Why do you think the author wrote the Cinderella story?"
- **Affective comprehension.** *Strategies:* "Connect motive to plot and to the characters' social and emotional development." *Examples:* "What do you do when you are disappointed because you can't do something you want to do? What did you like or dislike about Cinderella's character?"
- **Lexical comprehension.** *Strategies:* "Use context or other resources to figure out the meaning of unknown words during reading." *Examples:* "What does *enchanted* mean? What word is more like *enchanted—magical* or *funny*? Can you use *enchanted* in a sentence to show you understand its meaning?"

Predicting Comprehension Strategies

• Author's Purpose and Perspective Strategy

SOURCE: Dearborn Schools (2011).

PURPOSE: For students to analyze the author's purpose and perspective in a variety of texts, and understand how these affect meaning; to help them recognize bias; and to help them understand why authors write the way they do.

PROCEDURE: Explain and model examples of author's purpose, such as to persuade readers to think about an issue in a certain way and to take action; to provide readers with information or to describe a person, event, or issue (inform); or to entertain the reader. Explain the Persuade, Inform, Entertain (PIE) diagram in Figure 6.8. Explain and model examples of the author's perspective/point of view, or of how the author feels about the topic, based on the content of the text and the language used. Ask the following questions:

1. **Author's purpose questions:** (a) "Why do you think the author wrote this selection?" (b) "Which words do you think best describe the main reason the author wrote this selection?" (c) "Why did the author write the article from a particular perspective?" (d) "How did the author influence your response to the selection?" (e) "Do you think that the author achieved the intended purpose?" (f) "What examples from the text support your conclusions about the author's purpose?"
2. **Author's perspective questions:** (a) "What opinions or belief statements are evident in the selection?" (b) "Why do you think the author has this particular opinion or point of view?" (c) "What background information about the author do you have that may help understand the author's perspective? Would another author have a different perspective, depending on their background experiences?" (d) "What evidence did the author include to support their opinions?" (e) "What facts were missing?" (f) "What words and

FIGURE 6.8. What's the author's purpose? It's as easy as PIE.

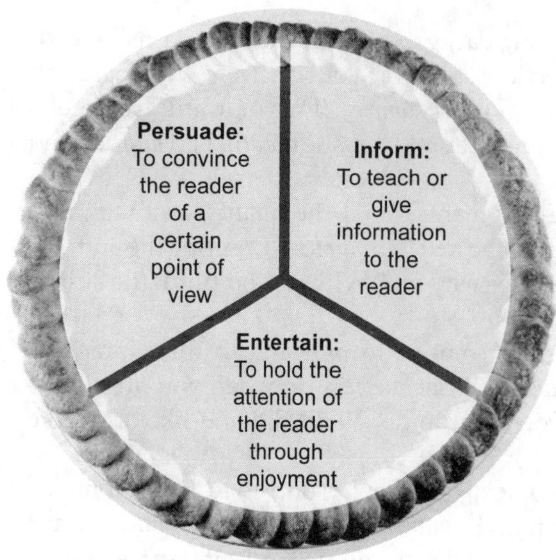

Purpose	Examples
Persuade	Opinions, commercials, advertisements, political campaigns
Inform	Nonfiction, news articles, science articles, recipes, biographies, documentaries
Entertain	Fiction, fantasy, mystery, comics, jokes, adventure, movies

phrases did the author use to present the information?" (g) "Did the words the author chose have strong connotations?" (h) "Why did the author write this selection? Identifying the author's purpose helps you recognize possible perspectives, especially in persuasive writing."

• Visual or Guided Imagery

SOURCE: Walker (2004).

PURPOSE: For students to increase their active comprehension and activate their background knowledge about situations and characters in fiction or key concepts in expository text.

PROCEDURE: As the teacher, use sensory images related to the story line to introduce the text. For example, to introduce the book *On the Far Side of the Mountain* (George, 1990), you might begin by saying to students, "Close your eyes and picture yourself in the mountains. What can you hear, what can you see? You are all alone. How are you going to eat? Where are you going to sleep?"

• Prediction Maps or Logs

SOURCE: Walker (2004).

PURPOSE: For students to predict and revise predictions during reading to enhance comprehension.

PROCEDURE: As the teacher, ask the students to predict what the text will be about before and during reading, based on cover, introduction, and/or the beginning sentences. Make a visual map of predictions and revisions or verifications.

EXAMPLE: From *Holes* by L. Sachar (1998):

Predictions	Revisions or Verifications
The boys dig holes to plant trees.	They have to dig holes to please the rancher in search of buried treasure.
He runs away and gets help.	He runs away and gets caught.

• THIEVES Strategy

SOURCE: Manz (2002).

PURPOSE: For students to activate and provide background knowledge and organizational structure for expository texts by surveying parts of a textbook or nonfiction text.

PROCEDURE: Before reading an expository text, the students preview each element in the THIEVES acronym: Title, Headings, Introduction, Every first sentence in a paragraph, Visuals and Vocabulary, End-of-chapter questions, and Summary. They then write or think about each of the questions (see Figure 6.9).

• Text, Graphic, and Organizational Features Chart

PURPOSE: For students to identify and apply text, graphic, and organizational features to enhance their comprehension of texts.

PROCEDURE: As the teacher, select a text containing numerous text features (headings, captions, boldfaced and italicized words), organizational features (title page, table of contents,

FIGURE 6.9. THIEVES questions. Based on Manz (2002).

T	**Title:** What is the title? What do I already know about this topic? What does it have to do with the preceding chapter? Does the title express a point of view? What do I think I will be reading about?
H	**Headings:** What does this heading tell me I will be reading about? What is the topic of the paragraph beneath it? How can I turn this heading into a question that is likely to be answered in the text?
I	**Introduction:** Is there an opening paragraph? Does the first paragraph introduce the chapter? What does the introduction tell me I will be reading about? Do I know anything about this topic already?
E	**Every first sentence in a paragraph:** What do I think this chapter is going to be about, based on the first sentence in each paragraph?
V	**Visuals and vocabulary:** Does the chapter include photographs, drawings, maps, charts, or graphs? What can I learn from the visuals? How do the captions help me better understand the meaning? Is there a list of key vocabulary terms and definitions? Are there important words in boldface type? Do I know what the boldfaced words mean? Can I tell the meaning of the boldfaced words from the sentences around them?
E	**End-of-chapter questions:** What do the questions ask? What information do they identify as important? What information do I learn from the questions? (Keep in mind the questions while reading, and note where the important information is located.)
S	**Summary:** What do I understand and recall about the topics covered in the summary?

glossary, index), and graphic features (pictures, charts, graphs). Model and provide students with practice in identifying the features, understanding their purposes, and applying the features to support comprehension. Use the *Text, Graphic, and Organizational Features Chart* in the Appendix (pp. 452–454) to define the features, explain their purposes, and view examples. You could even have the students create their own anchor chart with these features.

These concepts should be taught when you are introducing a new science or social studies textbook, or using a text with many of these features. Take turns with students asking and answering questions to demonstrate their understanding of each of these parts or features. Example pages can be shown with a computer projector. For independent practice, give each student a copy of the text and have them demonstrate their understanding of the text concepts by finding and explaining the purpose for each of the text concepts, while you walk around. Discuss why these parts and features are important, and how they can help them in reading and in writing their own texts.

• Story Impressions

SOURCE: McGinley and Denner (1987).

PURPOSE: For students to predict what is going to happen in a story before they see the text.

PROCEDURE: The teacher creates a list of words or of two- to three-word phrases from the story that show key aspects of the story, including setting, character names or descriptions, plot, and resolution for fiction or nonfiction narratives. Students write short stories, using these words and phrases in the order they were given. The stories are then shared with the class. The students then read the original text and compare and contrast their stories to the one they read. (These words should be written in a single column; for space reasons, the words in the example below are given in a row.)

EXAMPLE: List of words and phrases from *Goin' Someplace Special* by Patricia C. McKissack and Jerry Pinkney (2001):

> Tricia Ann, someplace special, bus, colored section, stand, empty seats, Peace Fountain, bench, Whites only, Bloomin' Mary, Grandmother's voice, Grand Music Palace, go 'round back, doorway to freedom, Public Library

Example story:

> Tricia Ann went someplace special on a bus. The colored section was full. She had to stand even though there were empty seats in the white section. She went to Peace Fountain and there was a bench that said, "Whites Only." Bloomin' Mary' called out, in a grandmother's voice, "Let's go to the Grand Music Palace." They told her she had to go 'round back. She went to another building, on the door was a sign that read, "doorway to freedom." It was a Public Library, so she went in. The library was a special place where everyone could go.

• Anticipation Guide

SOURCE: Vacca et al. (2006).

PURPOSE: For students to evaluate statements prior to reading in order to assess their current knowledge or beliefs. This strategy uses a series of oral or written statements, including key concepts and vocabulary words, that individual students respond to before reading the text.

PROCEDURE: As the teacher, prepare a document for the students to read or listen to that includes statements about key concepts and vocabulary words. The types of responses can include agree–disagree, true-false, fact–opinion, or a Likert scale of 1–5 rating how strongly students believe a statement. Discuss the students' predictions and anticipations before reading. After reading, discuss and reevaluate the statements to see if their ideas remained the same or changed.

EXAMPLE: From *The River Road* by Meish Goldish (2000): True or false?

1. The Mississippi River is the longest river in the U.S. (T)
2. In this book, cars drive on the river road. (F; the river road is for the barges.)
3. Barges carry many people down the river. (F; the barges carry materials and goods.)
4. People live along the river in farms, towns, and cities. (T)
5. The river is useful to carry people and goods. (T)

Monitoring Comprehension Strategies

As they are reading, students need to be aware of what they do not understand, identify what they do not understand, and use strategies to resolve problems in comprehension. At the sentence level, students can use the oral reading strategies on the *Good Reader Bookmarks* (see Appendix, p. 438) to problem-solve words, such as rereading sentences and pausing at the periods to see if the text makes sense. At the paragraph level, students also need to stop and think if what they are reading makes sense. The students may need to look back or skim through the previous sections of text to remember important information. In addition, looking at the pictures, graphs, maps, diagrams, charts, or illustrations may help to clarify the text. Using the context, glossary, or dictionary can provide the meaning for unknown words. Students can also use an encyclopedia, reference book, or the internet to clarify confusing concepts. If the text is difficult, the students may need to slow down their rate of reading.

• Self-Questioning

PURPOSE: For students to monitor their reading comprehension through explicit self-questioning of their thinking processes.

PROCEDURE: As the teacher, have students ask themselves the following questions: "Did I understand what I was reading? How do I know that I understand what I am reading? Did I have any problems reading any word or understanding ideas? What did I do to solve those problems? Was it successful? What else might I try?"

• Everyone Reads to . . .

SOURCE: Cunningham et al. (1999).

PURPOSE: For students to read sections of a text for a purpose.

PROCEDURE: Students read silently (or orally to themselves) an identified page, paragraph, or section, or read until they find the answer to a question posed by the teacher or another student. Then they discuss what was read. See Figure 6.10 for an example.

FIGURE 6.10. Everyone Reads to . . . , example.

"Jackie Joyner-Kersee" in *And Not Afraid to Dare: The Stories of Ten African-American Women*, by T. Bolden (1998)	
Question:	**I found out:**
Read to the end of page 189 to find out how Pop Miles decided to mentor Jackie Joyner to be an Olympian.	Pop ran the community center where Jackie participated in sports activities. He noticed that she had high athletic aptitude. She had the talent and character to be a champion.

• Think–Pair-Share

SOURCE: Lyman (1981).

PURPOSE: For students to increase their engagement in comprehension by having them share ideas with peers.

PROCEDURE: The teacher poses a topic to discuss or a question. Students think about the topic, get with a partner, and discuss the topic. The teacher monitors the conversations and selects a few students to share with the class. To enhance listening and to learn differing ideas, students are asked to share what their partners said.

Connecting and Visualizing Comprehension Strategies

• Text Connections

SOURCE: Harvey and Goudvis (2000).

PURPOSE: For students to make connections and analyze ideas while reading texts.

PROCEDURE: As the teacher, explain to students that readers make three main types of connections while reading texts: *text-to-self* (T-S) connections ("This reminds me of when I . . ."); *text-to-text* (T-T) connections ("This reminds me of something else that I read about . . ."); and *text-to-world* (T-W) or *universal understandings* connections ("This makes me think about . . ."). While reading a text to the students, stop at least three times (one for each type of connection), and tell the students your connection and which type it is. After students have had sufficient practice making each type of connection, assess their learning by having them read a text and make the three types of connections, using the abbreviations T-S, T-T, and T-W.

• Structured Overviews

SOURCE: Baron (1969), cited in Gunning (2004).

PURPOSE: For students to use vocabulary words to relate new ideas in the text to old ideas in the text.

PROCEDURE: As the teacher, select two to four important concepts and the related vocabulary. Then arrange the words into a diagram to show their interrelationships, with lines connecting the words. Add known words to show how they relate to new words, and evaluate whether the major relationships are clearly shown. Then introduce the overview to the students and explain why the words were arranged that way.

ADAPTATION: The students can learn to make their own structured overview after it has been modeled.

Photographs of the Mind

SOURCE: Keene and Zimmerman (2007).

PURPOSE: For students to visualize while reading the text and make connections to the ideas.

PROCEDURE: The students preview the text to be read. They read the text. Then at predetermined or self-selected points in the text, they stop and sketch a visualization related to the reading. After reading, the students share the sketches in small groups.

Graphic Prediction

PURPOSE: For students to predict the content of the text and activate background knowledge.

PROCEDURE: Students page through the text and look at each of the pictures, graphs, charts, maps, or other sources of visual information. Students then predict the main idea of the text and share what they learned with a partner before reading.

Text Introduction and Picture Walk

PURPOSE: For students to use visual clues, hear text language, and set a purpose for reading to improve comprehension.

PROCEDURE: As the teacher, sit comfortably where you and the students can see the pictures. Read the title, author, and illustrator and explain the role of each. Give students a "hook" or a purpose for reading the book. Conduct a picture walk that focuses on the graphic and organizational features, and ask the students to predict what the text might be about. Using the pictures, discuss the meaning of important vocabulary words. For important complex or phonetically irregular words, have students predict what the initial letters would be and locate these in the text. Add more information or relate information in books to something that is familiar to them.

Prereading Plan (PREP)

SOURCE: Langer (1981).

PURPOSE: For students to develop background knowledge about the topic to improve their comprehension of the text.

PROCEDURE: First, the teacher engages students in group discussion of key concepts. This starts with choosing a word, phrase, or picture to start the conversation. Students then brainstorm what comes to mind when they hear this word or phrase. Students make associations between the concept and prior knowledge. The teacher writes the responses on the board. Students then orally reflect on these associations. Then the students refine and expand their knowledge of concepts.

Say Something

SOURCE: Walker (2004).

PURPOSE: For students to create personal responses to a text.

PROCEDURE: Students take turns saying something at intervals during the reading of the story. They can make comments about what they have learned, what is surprising, what it reminds them of, how it is different from something else, or any questions they have about it.

ADAPTATION: Students can use sticky notes to mark their comments in the text.

Response Journal

PURPOSE: For students to express personal reactions in writing and wonder about events, themes, and ideas in a book.

PROCEDURE: Students read a book or section of a book and then write reflections on it. These reflections could be open-ended or teachers could provide sentence starters such as "An interesting quote from the text was ________. I chose it because ________." "I agree or disagree with the author or character because ______." "The part of the text about __________ made me feel _______ because _________." These may be shared with peers or the teacher.

K-W-L and K-W-L Plus for Expository Text

SOURCES: Carr and Ogle (1987); Ogle (1986).

PURPOSE: For students to monitor their reading by identifying their prior Knowledge, questioning what they Want to learn, and documenting what they Learned.

PROCEDURE: For a K-W-L chart, the teacher makes three columns and elicits students' responses to complete each column. The K-W-L Plus strategy involves creating a map or web of what was learned and then summarizing the text. See Figure 6.11 for an example of a K-W-L chart, and Figure 6.12 for an example of a K-W-L Plus map.

Guided Writing Procedure Outline

SOURCE: Smith and Bean (1980).

PURPOSE: For students to activate and synthesize their prior knowledge and set a purpose for reading (grade 4 and above).

PROCEDURE: As the teacher, identify the key concept in the selection to be read (e.g., pollution). Ask students to brainstorm any associations they have with the word. Record the

FIGURE 6.11. K-W-L chart, example.

Time for Kids: Mammals, by D. Housel (2005)		
What I **K**now	What I **W**ant to Know	What I **L**earned
Mammals are animals. Dogs and cats are mammals. Bears are mammals. Mammals have fur. Lions and tigers are animals.* They live on the ground.*	What is a mammal?	D: Mammals are warm-blooded because their body temperature stays the same. D: They are vertebrates because they have backbones. G: There are 4,550 kinds of mammals.
	What are other kinds of mammals? Where do mammals live?	E: Rabbits and seals are mammals. L: Some mammals, like whales, live in the sea. D: All mammals breathe with their lungs. D: Most mammals grow inside their mothers and are born alive. D: They are born helpless, so they need their parents' care. D: They drink their mothers' milk. T: This was not answered in the text, so we will need to use other resources to find out how many families of mammals there are. G: Primates. E: Humans, apes, and monkeys. E: Wolves, lions, and otters are carnivores. G: Rodents. E: Chipmunks. G: Hoofed mammals are herbivores. E: Deer, giraffes, and cows.
	What are some unusual types of mammals?	E. Bats are the only mammals that can fly. G: Marsupials have pouches. Kangaroos are marsupials. Most marsupials live in Australia. G: Monotremes (like the platypus) lay eggs, but drink milk.
D = description, G = groups of mammals, E = examples of mammals, L = live where?, *Partially correct response		

FIGURE 6.12. K-W-L Plus map, example.

Mammals

Description	Group and example	Where they live
• Vertebrate • Warm-blooded • Breathe air • Born alive and helpless • Drink milk • Fur (most)	• Primates: Humans, apes, and monkeys • Carnivores: Cats, dogs, lions, and tigers • Herbivores: Deer, giraffes, and cows • Marsupials: Kangaroos • Rodents: Chipmunks	• Most mammals live on land. • Some mammals, like whales, live in the sea. • Monkeys live in rainforests. • Most marsupials live in Australia.

different responses on the board (e.g., smoke, ponds, cars, noise, garbage, factories, oceans, death, and diseases). Through a class discussion, group the responses into categories, and label these categories. Use the categories to create an outline of information. Have each student write a passage, perhaps one or two paragraphs in length, using the information in the outline. Asking a few students to read their passages aloud will demonstrate that even though they have all used the same outline, each person's writing is unique. Have students read the selection to compare the outline and text, identify points of agreement and disagreement, and identify additional information in the text that could be used to enhance or clarify their passages. After reading, discuss the selection in terms of these purposes. See Figure 6.13 for an example of a guided writing procedure outline.

• Sticky Note Reflecting Strategy

PURPOSE: For students to reflect on their thinking while reading and to provide a focus for small-group comprehension discussions.

PROCEDURE: As the teacher, do the following:

1. Determine what kinds of responses and how many responses you want students to make during reading.
2. Create symbols for each type of response and its meaning.
3. For reference, create a poster with a key for the symbols and their meanings.
4. Explain the meaning of the symbols. Next, read a short passage, and place sticky notes to reflect your thinking. Then go back to each sticky note, explain why you put the note there, and use it to have a conversation with the group related to your understanding of the text.
5. Give students a stack of small-sized sticky notes, and tell students to prewrite at least two of each symbol. (The words are not needed, as they will be on the poster.)
6. Ask students to read a different passage on their own.

FIGURE 6.13. Guided writing procedure outline, example.

POLLUTION

I. Sources
  A. Cars
  B. Factories

II. Products
  A. Smoke
  B. Noise
  C. Garbage

III. Water Pollution
  A. Ponds
  B. Oceans

IV. Results
  A. Diseases
  B. Death

7. Tell them to put at least *six* sticky notes on parts of the passage that they are reflecting about. You might suggest that in a short passage, they can use a symbol no more than two times.
8. Tell students, "Now turn to your group and share where you put the sticky note, why you put it there, and what you were thinking about."

See Figure 6.14 for an example with symbols and discussion notes.

Strategies for Asking Questions for Comprehension

• Guidelines for Question Generation and Question Answering

SOURCE: McAndrews (2004).

PURPOSE: For students to create and answer questions to improve listening, reading, and viewing comprehension.

PROCEDURE: The following are some guidelines for asking and answering questions to help develop comprehension of narrative and expository texts. As the teacher or peer, do the following:

1. Ask good metacognitive questions before, during, and after text reading or viewing—ones that require students to think about how they are thinking.
2. Ask predictive questions about what is going to be read/viewed next. This helps students set a purpose for reading/viewing. Ask predictive questions that explore more than one possibility.
3. Ask questions that access prior knowledge and encourage students to use what they've already read/viewed.
4. Ask important questions about the story elements, including the problems and theme.

FIGURE 6.14. Sticky note reflecting strategy, example with symbols and notes.

* important	? question	! interesting	connection	agree	disagree
wonder	change	love/like	quote	~ similar	≠ not same

Discussion Notes:

"When I was reading *Tom Thumb* by Richard Jesse Watson (1989), I put [connection symbol] next to Merlin because it is a connection to Merlin in the King Arthur's books we read. I put ? because I don't know what a tunic means. I put [wonder symbol] because I wonder what will happen when others meet Tom Thumb. I put [quote symbol] next to the quote 'Good shell, Nice ocean, pretty sound' because the giant liked the shell and stopped the battle."

5. Ask questions that focus on main ideas and details, problem–solution, or cause–effect.
6. Ask questions as to what the students have learned so far and what they still want to know about.
7. Ask questions during reading/viewing that clarify the author's meaning or make the student want to learn more.
8. Ask questions that follow naturally from an initial question.
9. Avoid using too many diversionary questions in the middle of the text, such as "What would you do in this situation?" or "Have you ever had this problem?"
10. Save some of the good thought-provoking questions until after the text is completed (e.g., "Did the character make the right decision? Why or why not?").
11. After reading/viewing, reflect on and analyze the meaning of the story or text.
12. Ask questions that help the students to connect the text to themselves, the world, and other texts.

• Active Reader Self-Evaluation Questions

PURPOSE: For students to guide narrative and expository reading comprehension.

PROCEDURE: Active readers ask six types of questions before, during, and after reading: predicting, questioning, clarifying, making connections, summarizing, and evaluating. The Appendix includes examples for each of these types of *Active Reading Self-Evaluation* questions (see pp. 455–456). The students use these questions to monitor their reading comprehension.

• Self-Directed Questioning

SOURCE: Walker (2004).

PURPOSE: For students to improve comprehension through self-questioning.

PROCEDURE: Students write questions before and during reading, and then answer them after reading. They can do this on sticky notes for the class to organize and answer.

• Question–Answer Relationships (QARs)

SOURCE: Raphael (1982).

PURPOSE: For students to identify the type of response necessary to answer comprehension questions.

PROCEDURE: Students read each question and identify the response needed: "right there" (explicit comprehension—the answer is in the text and easy to find); "think and search" (implicit comprehension—the answer is in the text, but students need to put together different parts of the text to find it); "author and you" (implicit and critical comprehension—the answer is not in the text, and the students need to combine what they already know with what the author states); and "on my own" (creative comprehension—the answer is not in the text, but it can be answered by using the students' own experience). Students then read the passage to answer the questions. See Figure 6.15 for a chart with the four response types and examples of questions.

ADAPTATION: Students can use highlighting tape to identify the answers to "right there" questions.

• Question Generation Strategy

SOURCE: Walker (2004).

PURPOSE: For students to question and identify important ideas in a text.

PROCEDURE: Before, during, and after reading/viewing, the students write and answer questions about important information in the text. These questions and answers are then compared to those the teacher wrote.

• Guided Questioning Activity

PURPOSE: For students to answer questions that guide their comprehension during text reading.

PROCEDURE: As the teacher, divide the text into sections based on important stopping points. Develop questions to ask after each stopping point. See Figure 6.16 for an example.

• RACE Strategy for Writing Constructed Responses

SOURCE: Larson (2019).

PURPOSE: For students to write answers to constructed response questions with textual evidence.

PROCEDURE: As the teacher, explain that RACE is an acronym for answering constructed response question using textual evidence. Give students an example of a question and a constructed response. Teach each step of the RACE strategy to the students, and show them where that element is in the example response.

FIGURE 6.15. Question–answer relationships, example.

Title: *F Is for Freedom*	**Author:** Roni Schotter (2000)
Right There (Literal/Explicit) The answer will be found almost word for word in the story. Who got out of one of the sacks of grain?	**Author and Me (Critical/Implicit)** The author will give clues to the answer, but the students must also think about it. Why do you think Amanda says that there are probably Christmas presents behind the locked door?
Think and Search (Literal/Implicit) The answer will be found in the book, but students may have to look in several places on more than one page for the answer. Where does the father put the mysterious family when they get inside the house?	**On My Own (Inferential/Creative)** The students can answer the question without having read the story, but reading the story will help. How would you feel if your family had to be hidden?

Restate the question: Change the question into a statement by removing the question word, and restate the key words in the question.

Answer the question: After restating the question, finish the sentence, and answer the question by using your own knowledge and inferences from the text. Be sure to answer the specific question and every part of the question.

Cite text evidence: Find relevant evidence in the text to support the answer. Then write it correctly, using a sentence stem such as "According to the text . . ." or "The author stated . . ." Quote the text exactly, and write the year and page number according to an appropriate style guide (American Psychological Association, Modern Language Association, etc.).

Explain what it means: Tell how your text evidence proved your point. Sentence starters might include "This shows . . ." or "This proves . . ." or "This means . . ."

FIGURE 6.16. Guided questioning activity, example.

Title: *Ronald Morgan Goes to Bat* **Author:** Patricia Reilly Giff (1990)	
Book Introduction:	What sport are they playing? Baseball. How do you think the boy in the picture feels? Nervous, because if he strikes out, he may have to wait a long time. He may also be scared, because the ball may hit him.
Page 7	How does Ronald feel now? Why? He is excited because he gets to play baseball.
Page 10	Do you think that this boy knows how to play baseball? Why? No, because he is holding the bat wrong.
Page 13	What will Ronald Morgan do after he hears someone say he is the worst? He might punch him or do something to him.
Page 16	What will keep happening if Ronald keeps his eyes shut when he swings? He's going to keep striking out. Why does he close his eyes? He's afraid of the ball. It might hit his glasses, and then he won't be able to see.
Page 23	What is Ronald doing when he should be watching the ball? He is playing with a stick and drawing things with it.
Page 25	Why do the kids want Ronald on their team? Because he helps them feel good.
Page 29	What does Ronald's father help him do? Open his eyes.
Ending	How do you think Ronald feels at the end of the story? Why? Happy, because he is going to be a good player, and his dad practiced with him and taught him to open his eyes.

Radio Reading Procedure

SOURCE: Steward and Borgia (2004).

PURPOSE: For students to improve comprehension of a text through using literal, inference, and evaluative questions.

PROCEDURE: The teacher explains the three questioning types: literal, inference, and evaluative. The reading text is then cut into parts for each reader. All students silently read their parts, looking for unfamiliar vocabulary. They then use resources and/or discuss the word meanings. After reading silently again, each student writes a question for the audience to answer later. Once speaking and listening rules are reviewed, one student uses a microphone to read the part to the audience and ask the question. The audience answers the question, and the speaker verifies the correctness of the answer.

Narrative and Expository Structure Comprehension Strategies

Narrative Comprehension Guide

PURPOSE: For students to improve comprehension of a narrative text through self questioning.

PROCEDURE: During and after reading, students ask themselves questions about the characters, setting, plot, mood, style, theme, point of view, and author's purpose and perspective to help them understand the story better. See the Appendix (p. 457) for the *Narrative Comprehension Guide,* which supports students through this process.

Retelling of Plot Structure, Advanced Narrative Story Elements

PURPOSE: For students to identify advanced story elements and literary techniques to improve narrative text comprehension (grades 6–12).

PROCEDURE: As the teacher, select appropriate grade-level books and identify the story elements each of them exemplify. Introduce the definitions to the students and provide examples in short stories. Have students read and discuss the text. As individuals or in groups, they can explain orally or in writing how the book uses these story elements.

Provide the following definitions for the elements of the plot: **exposition**—the introduction of setting, situation, and main characters; **rising action**—the series of events leading to the climax of the story, including the conflicts or problems of the main character; **conflict**—the problem that controls or triggers the action in the story; **climax**—the point of highest interest in terms of the conflict, and a major turning point in the action; **falling action**—the sequence of events that follow the climax and end in the resolution; **resolution**—the point of the story when the conflict is resolved; **moral**—the lesson to be learned from the story. Give an example of each, and then have students identify the elements in another text.

Now provide the following definitions of literary techniques: **mood**—the feeling the reader gets from the story; **tone**—the author's attitude or feeling about a story; **point of view**—the angle from which the story is told (it depends on who is telling the story); **irony**—the use of words to indicate a meaning that is the opposite of the literal meaning; **allusion**—a reference to another work of fiction, a film, a piece of art, or even a real event;

foreshadowing—the use of clues about what will happen; **flashback**—going back to an earlier time to fill in missing information; **suspense**—tension or excitement that makes you want to read more; **surprise ending**—twist in the plot at the end of the story. Give an example of each, and then have students identify the elements in another text.

EXAMPLES: Some grade 8 short stories and the story elements: "The Dinner Party" (suspense, stereotype); "The Treasure of Lemon Brown" (characters, conflict); "The Ransom of Red Chief" (irony, conflict, tone, inference, character, allusion); "Rules of the Game" (conflict, inference, character); "Flowers for Algernon" (characterization, inference, point of view, humor, allusion, irony, suspense, and tone); "Block Party" (theme); "The Bet" (flashback, mood, and irony), "The Million-Pound Bank Note" (exaggeration, characterization); "A Mother in Mannville" (setting, motivation, conflict, irony); "The Great Rat Hunt" (point of view, conflict); "The Lady, or the Tiger?" (surprise ending, irony, and character); and "The Tell-Tale Heart" (mood and tone).

• Expository Comprehension Guide

PURPOSE: For students to comprehend an expository text through answering questions related to the text structure, content, graphics, accuracy, and author's style.

PROCEDURE: During and after reading, students ask themselves questions to help them understand the expository text better. See the Appendix (p. 458) for the *Expository Comprehension Guide*. See Figure 6.17 for signal words for each of the organizational structures.

• Identifying Common Text Structures

PURPOSE: For students to recognize and use text structures, such as cause–effect, comparison–contrast, sequence, description, problem–solution, question–answer, generalizations, and examples, to better understand and recall information in both nonfiction and fiction expository texts.

PROCEDURE: As the teacher, select short texts with clear text structures. Introduce the idea that texts have organizational patterns called text structures. Some texts may have multiple structures. Introduce the text structures in the chart in Figure 6.17, which describes common organizational text structures, definitions, signal words, and examples of graphic organizers. In a think-aloud, show examples of each text structure, and point out signal words for each of the given types. The students learn to recognize each text structure as you walk them through the text by asking questions based on text structure and the author's writing. The students then create a graphic organizer related to the text structure to organize and comprehend the ideas in the reading. Afterwards, students can create graphic organizers as a prewriting activity to write their own texts using each of the text structures.

Inference Comprehension Strategies

According to Keene and Zimmerman (2007), when proficient readers infer, they draw conclusions from the text; make, test, and revise predictions as they read, use background knowledge and explicitly stated information to answer questions they have as they read.

FIGURE 6.17. Common text structures.

Text Structure	Definition	Signal Words	Graphic Organizer
Generalization–example, or categorization	Gives a general statement and provides examples or categories.	*for example, types of, such as*	Concept → Example, Example, Example
Question–answer	Presents questions and gives answers.	*who, what, why, when, where, how*	Question → Answer
Description	Gives characteristics or features of people, places, living–nonliving objects, and ideas.	Words related to the five senses, such as color, size, shape, texture, smell, sound, and taste	Idea; Detail, Detail, Detail, Detail
Sequence or process	Explains events or steps to follow in time order.	*first, next, then, finally, last, number words, steps*	1st → 2nd → 3rd
Problem–solution	Presents a problem and suggests one or more solutions.	*problem, because, cause, solution, so, so that, in order to, since*	Problem → Solution
Compare–contrast	Tells how two or more things are alike and different.	*different from, like, alike, compared to, similar to, same as, on the other hand*	Different; Different; same
Cause–effect	Describes the cause, or why something happened, and the effect, or what happened.	*because, cause, if, so, as a result of, since, in order to, therefore*	Cause → Effect

• Think-Alouds

SOURCE: Wilhelm, Baker, and Dube (2001).

PURPOSE: For students to listen to the metacognitive thought processes of others during comprehension or composition of texts and then verbalize their own thinking.

PROCEDURE: As the teacher, read aloud to students and verbalize the thinking you are doing to make inferences that help you comprehend the text. Examples of metacognitive thought processes include making predictions, visualizing, making connections, monitoring comprehension, and using self-correction strategies. Locate evidence from the text from which you draw your inferences. As you read, think out loud, showing students how to put together prior knowledge and facts from the text. Model this inferencing procedure until students can begin to take over. Here are some examples: "Hm, what does that mean? Let me reread." "Well, I know that . . . so maybe it could be . . . Let me keep reading to see if that makes sense." "I wonder what that means?" Students then work with partners while they take turns reading and orally demonstrating their thinking processes. Students practice these strategies while reading silently. Sticky notes can be used to write down their thinking process and self-questions. Finally, the students apply think-alouds to their everyday reading, and after reading they are asked to discuss their comprehension processes.

Directed Listening/Reading Thinking Activity (DLTA, DRTA)

SOURCE: Stauffer (1969).

PURPOSE: For students to infer using prior knowledge and textual information, monitor their thinking, and justify their responses to a text.

PROCEDURE: Before reading, students predict and develop purposes for reading, based on the title, picture walk, and/or beginning paragraph. They question what the text might be about, what might happen next, and why they think that. During reading, the students read a predetermined amount of text and think about what they are reading. They confirm or revise their predictions and ask what new information verifies this. After reading, the students reexamine their purposes for reading, ask if their prediction is still possible, determine whether they want to change their prediction, and make new predictions about what will happen next.

Generative–Reciprocal Inference Procedure

SOURCE: Walker (2004).

PURPOSE: For students to read and write paragraphs that require making an inference.

PROCEDURE: As the teacher, select paragraphs with an inference as the key idea, and project these for the students to read. Short mysteries are good for this purpose. Explain that inferences are not directly stated in the text. Highlight key words that help the students identify the key idea. Pose questions to help students identify the inferred idea. On subsequent examples, the students identify the key words and the inference. In pairs, the students write their own inference paragraphs then share with others to predict what happened.

Inference and Questioning Strategy

PURPOSE: For students to pose questions, make inferences, and provide evidence to improve comprehension.

PROCEDURE: As the teacher, have students write down questions as they read. Ask them, "What can you infer from what you have read already? What evidence supports this inference?"

EXAMPLE:

Questions	Inferences	Evidence
Why did the stepmother hide Cinderella when the prince came?	The stepmother wanted one of her daughters to be selected by the prince.	The stepmother locked Cinderella in her room. She had only her daughters try on the glass slipper.

Description Comprehension Strategies

The general purpose of description comprehension strategies is for students to list characteristics, features, and examples of a specific topic. A simple description can be extended so that the characteristics, features, and examples of that specific topic are all described. Sometimes a description can be more complex, and vivid details are used. A description can also be used to clarify vocabulary words. Questions: "What are you describing? What are its qualities?" Examples of these strategies include a radial diagram, a story pyramid, a five-senses chart, and a retelling word sort.

• Radial Diagram

PURPOSE: For students to show relationships between a core idea and descriptions/examples of that idea.

PROCEDURE: Students write the topic in a circle in the center of a piece of paper, and then add descriptors and examples on circles around the topic circle. Example: "Rocks—igneous, metamorphic, sedimentary, oil sands, meteorite." See Figure 6.18 for another example.

• Story Pyramid

PURPOSE: For students to describe overall elements of a text.

PROCEDURE: Students draw a triangle and divide it with four parallel lines into five parts. Then they follow the directions for each line of the pyramid. The following is an example from *Sarah, Plain and Tall* by Patricia MacLachlan (1985): Line 1—write the name of a character (*Sarah*); write two words that describe the setting (*Kansas prairie*); write three words that describe the character (*plain, tall, friendly*); write four words in a phrase that describe one event (*responds to wife's advertisement*); and write five words in a phrase that describes another event (*cares for and teaches children*). See Figure 6.19 for an illustration of this example.

FIGURE 6.18. Radial diagram, example.

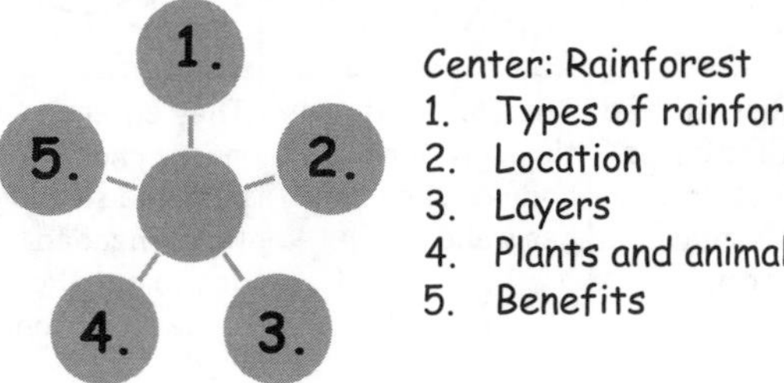

FIGURE 6.19. Story pyramid, example.

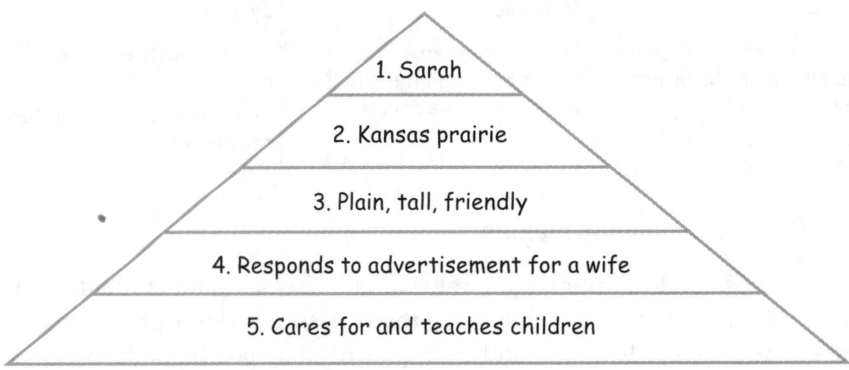

• Five-Senses Chart

PURPOSE: For students to increase their descriptions of details in a text.

PROCEDURE: Students list details from a story that are related to each of the five senses. See Figure 6.20 for an example.

• Retelling Word Sort

PURPOSE: For students to retell a text using important words from that text.

PROCEDURE: A teacher or student can write down important words from the whole text or a chapter. Students then do a word sort that organizes the words by their relationship to each other and retells the important information.

EXAMPLE: From *I Love Birds: 52 Ways to Wonder, Wander and Explore Birds with Kids*, by Jennifer Ward (2019). Words after sorting: *soaring, pecking, perching, waddling* = bird behaviors;

FIGURE 6.20. Five-senses chart, example.

Title: *Harry Potter and the Sorcerer's Stone*			**Author:** J. K. Rowling (1998)	
See	**Hear**	**Feel**	**Smell**	**Taste**
The owls delivered millions of letters to Harry through every crack in the house, inviting Harry to go to Hogwarts.	The Snitch whizzed through the air as Harry tried to get it on his Nimbus 2000 broom.	The electricity ran through Hermione's body as she used her wand.	They entered the musty chamber past the sleeping three-headed dog to get the sorcerer's stone.	They sat down to a delicious feast of meats and fruit in the great hall when Harry's team was awarded the cup.

chisel beak, forked tail, wingbars, crown stripe = field marks; *red-tailed hawk, purple martin, chipping sparrow* = species of birds; *suet, seeds, worms, nectar* = food.

Narrative Story Grammar Comprehension Strategies

The general purpose of these strategies is for students to comprehend a story through creating a graphic representation of all or part of the elements of story grammars and the relationships between and among them. While there are multiple strategies for retelling and comprehending narratives both orally and in written form, they generally contain similar elements (such as describing the characters, setting, problems, events, resolution, and theme presented in the story), but these elements are represented in different ways. Teachers model and explain graphic organizers before reading, so students know what they are looking for.

• Story Map

SOURCE: Walker (2004).

PURPOSE: For students to identify the important elements of a story to comprehend it.

PROCEDURE: As a class or individually, students write each element on the story map, including the sequential plot episodes. See Figure 6.21 for an example.

• Herringbone Map

PURPOSE: For students to identify the main idea of a story after answering "wh-" and how questions.

PROCEDURE: Students write responses to "Who?" "Where?" "When?" "What?" "How?" and "Why?" on each of the lines, resembling the bones of a fish. On the backbone, they write the main idea. Figure 6.22 provides a template for a herringbone map.

FIGURE 6.21. Story map, example.

<table>
<tr><td colspan="2">Title: How Many Days to America?: A Thanksgiving Story</td><td>Author: Eve Bunting (1988)</td></tr>
<tr><td colspan="2">Setting: Village home and fishing boat</td><td>Where: A Caribbean island to America</td></tr>
<tr><td colspan="3">When: October in about the 1970s</td></tr>
<tr><td colspan="3">Main Character(s): Brother, Mama, Papa, and little sister, who were refugees</td></tr>
<tr><td colspan="3">Other Characters: Soldiers and other refugees who arrived by boat</td></tr>
<tr><td colspan="3">Important Events in the Story:</td></tr>
<tr><td>Event 1: The family had to hide in their house from soldiers. Papa said they must leave for America.</td><td>Event 2: They traveled in a small, crowded fishing boat. The engine broke, thieves came, and soldiers came.</td><td>Event 3: They finally made it to America. They were welcomed, given food, and they celebrated a day they called Thanksgiving in the U.S.A.</td></tr>
<tr><td colspan="3">But the most important thing in this story is . . . the family was finally free and safe in America.</td></tr>
</table>

FIGURE 6.22. Herringbone map, template.

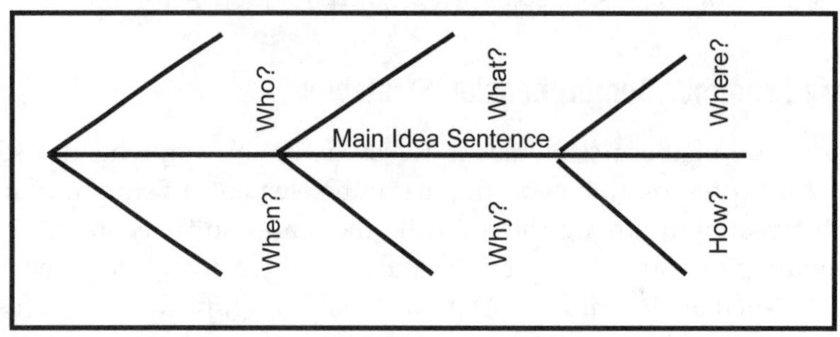

• Sequencing Map

PURPOSE: For students to identify the sequence of the story events. See Figure 6.23 for an example.

PROCEDURE: The teacher presents the sequencing map to the students prior to reading to set a purpose for reading. State, "While reading the story, identify the characters; setting; beginning, middle, and end events; and the conclusion or author's message." If needed, define and give examples from a previously read story for each of these elements. Tell students that after reading, they are to write in these elements on the sequencing map.

• Beach Ball Retelling

PURPOSE: For students to retell story elements to improve comprehension.

PROCEDURE: Using a marker, students write story element questions on each of the six sections of a beach ball, such as "Describe the characters," "Describe the setting," "What

FIGURE 6.23. Sequencing map, example.

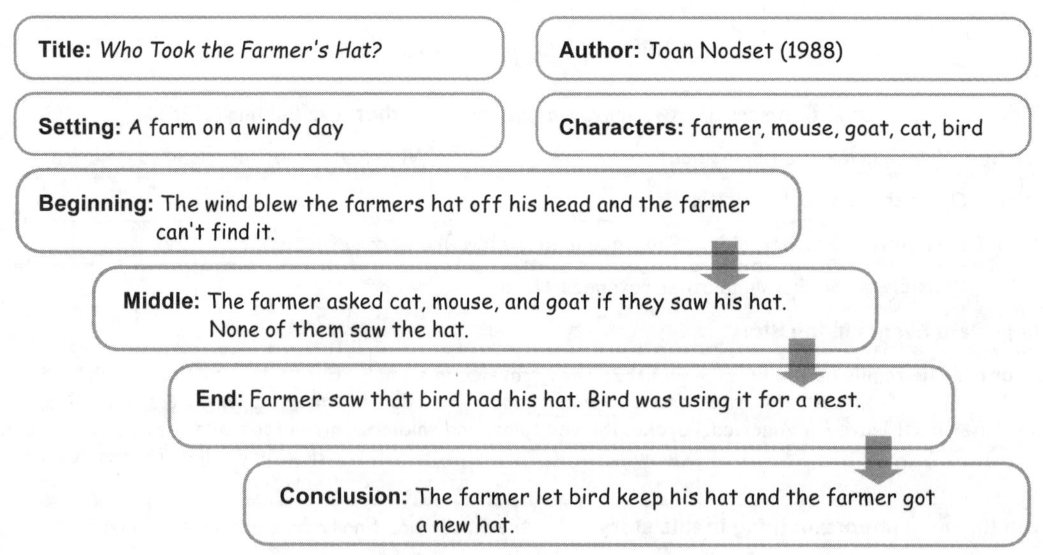

happened in the beginning?", "In the middle?", "At the end?," and "What was your favorite part?" The beach ball is then tossed, and the student who catches it must answer the question written on the color that is under their right thumb. If the student cannot recall it, the teacher or students supply a clue. The students keep playing until all questions have been answered. See Figure 6.24 for an image of a labeled beach ball to be used in this activity.

ADAPTATION: For higher-level comprehension, students can answer questions such as "Describe the relationship between characters," "How does the setting influence the story?", "What is the problem?", "Describe three important events in the plot," "What is the resolution?", and "What is the theme or lesson in the story?"

• Retelling Rope, Bookmark, and Story Map

PURPOSE: For students to retell story elements to improve comprehension.

PROCEDURE: The teacher creates a rope with the retelling pictures and objects glued on it. Students are told that when they retell a story, they need to include the *setting* (the house picture), the *characters* (two people), the *problem* (rope in a knot), the *events* (buttons with B for Beginning, M for Middle, and E for End), and the *solution* (tied up nicely with a bow). The students can hold each element on the rope as they retell the story. A bookmark and map with the same images can be created. See Figure 6.25 for an example of such a map.

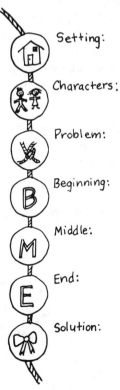

FIGURE 6.24. Beach ball retelling, image.

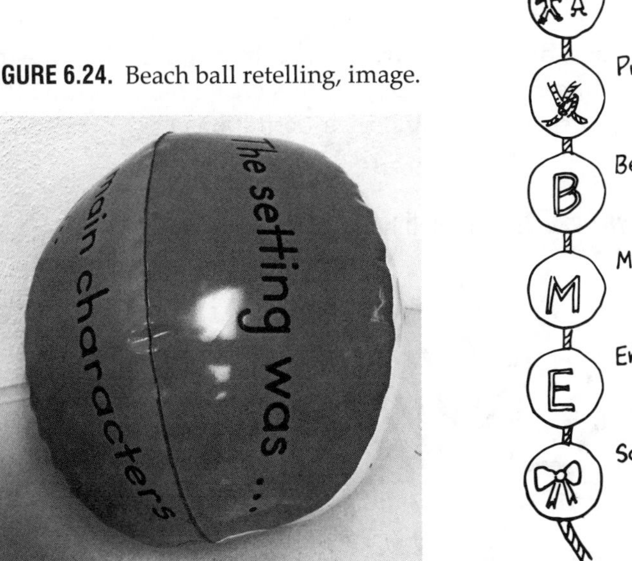

FIGURE 6.25. Retelling rope map, example.

Story Retelling Rope

Setting:

Characters:

Problem:

Beginning:

Middle:

End:

Solution:

• Five-Finger Retell

PURPOSE: For students to retell story elements to improve comprehension.

PROCEDURE: The teacher tells students that each finger in the five-finger retell (see Figure 6.26 for a template for this) represents an element: (1) Describe characters, (2) describe setting, (3) describe problem, (4) describe events, and (5) describe solution.

• Manipulative Retell

PURPOSE: For students to retell story elements to improve comprehension.

PROCEDURE: The students can use or make puppets, pictures, or felt cutouts to go with a story. They put these in order and then retell or explain the sequence of events.

• Retelling Origami Fortune Teller

PURPOSE: For students to retell story elements to improve comprehension.

PROCEDURE: Using a square piece of paper, students make an origami fortune teller (see *www.origamiway.com/origami-fortune-teller-instructions.shtml* for directions). On each of the outer four petal-shaped flaps, they put a labeled colored dot; the dots should be different colors (e.g., red, yellow, green, and blue). They number each triangle on the other side from 1 to 8. They then write the names of story elements on each of the flaps: (1) title, (2) author and illustrator, (3) setting, (4) description of main character, (5) descriptions of additional characters, (6) main problem, (7) events, and (8) solution. To play, a student begins with the thumb and index finger of each hand in the four pockets. The student asks a partner to choose a color, and the student spells it out as they alternate between pinching and pulling the fingers. Then the student shows the partner the numbers on the inside and asks the partner to choose one. The student pinches and pulls that number of times. The student then asks for another number, opens up that flap, and reads the question. Students take turns asking and answering questions based on the story elements. See Figure 6.27 for an example.

VARIATION: A student opens the flaps, draws a picture in the center square that illustrates their favorite part, and writes a sentence about it. Or students create more fortune tellers and write other ideas on the flaps, such as words and their definitions.

FIGURE 6.26. Five-finger retell hand, template.

FIGURE 6.27. Origami fortune teller retelling, example.

1. Title: Little House in the Big Woods
2. Author and Illustrator: Laura Ingalls Wilder, Garth Williams
3. Setting: Big Woods of Wisconsin
4. Description of Main Character: Laura is an adventurous tomgirl.
5. Additional Characters: She lives with her Ma, Pa, sisters Mary and Carrie, and dog Jack.
6. Main Problem: Winter was coming.
7. Events: Putting up venison, making sausages.
8. Solution: Working hard to have enough food and wood.

Center: Favorite Part: Sitting by the fire listening to Pa play his fiddle and tell stories.

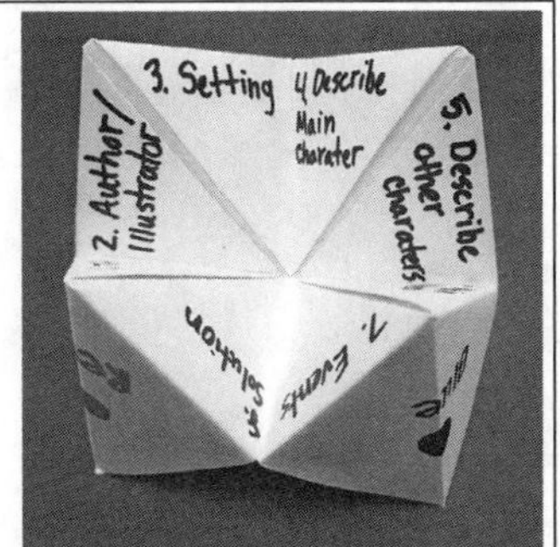

Getting to Know the Characters

PURPOSE: For students to describe each character's appearance, personality, and actions in a text.

PROCEDURE: A student draws a character in the middle of a page with a name tag, and makes five boxes around the character:

Box 1—Appearance. (What does the character look like? Give textual evidence.)
Box 2—Personality. (What are the character's thoughts and feelings? Give textual evidence.)
Box 3—Actions. (What does the character do? Give textual evidence.)
Box 4—Quotes. (Statements made by the character to show their personality. Include page numbers.)
Box 5—What do others say about the character?

VARIATION: A student draws an outline of a person. On the head, the student draws the character's face with an expression they might make; on the left arm, the student writes what the character looks like and clothing style; in the center by the heart, the student writes about the character's feelings; on the right arm, the student writes what the character does; on the left leg, the student writes how the character feels about the problem; and on the right leg, the student writes how the character feels about the solution. The class can brainstorm character traits that students might use to describe characters.

How and Why Characters Change

SOURCE: *www.readwritethink.org/classroom-resources/lesson-plans/inferring-characters-change*

PURPOSE: For students to describe the changes in characters throughout a story.

PROCEDURE: Students provide evidence from the story to show what each character was like in the beginning and at the end, how the character changed, and why they changed. See Figure 6.28 for a template.

FIGURE 6.28. Character change chart, template.

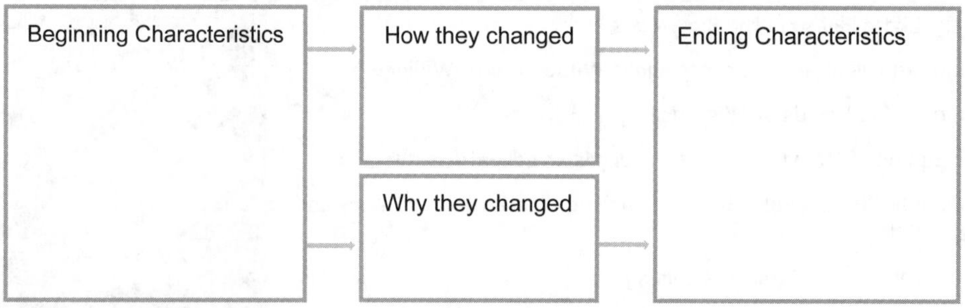

Beginning Characteristics	How they changed	Ending Characteristics
	Why they changed	

Problem–Solution Comprehension Strategies

In problem–solution comprehension strategies, the information is stated as a problem, and one or more solutions for that problem are listed. Sometimes these strategies include identifying the problem, multiple attempts to solve the problem, and then the resolution, which can be presented as in the question–answer, problem–solution map in Figure 6.29.

• Problem–Solution Story Map

PURPOSE: For students to identify a problem, examine how a main character acts and reacts to it, and then identify the solution.

PROCEDURE: Students complete each of the elements in the map, including setting, characters, problem, events, and solution. See Figure 6.30 for an example.

• Story Web

PURPOSE: For students to retell the characters, setting, problem, and solution.

PROCEDURE: Students draw a circle in the center and write the title and author. In four surrounding circles, they write the setting, characters, problem and solution for the text. See Figure 6.31 for an example.

FIGURE 6.29. Question–answer, problem–solution map, example.

Title: *Corduroy*	**Author:** Don Freeman (1968)
Questions	**Answers**
What is the problem or problems in the story?	Corduroy, a stuffed bear, was missing a button and nobody bought him.
What are the attempts made to solve the problem?	He decided to look for a button everywhere in the department store. He didn't find one.
How does the main character solve them?	Lisa came back and bought him, even though he was missing a button.
Why does resolution come about?	Lisa and her mother realized it isn't important that Corduroy is perfect. Lisa can love him anyway.

FIGURE 6.30. Problem–solution story map, example.

Title: *The Three Little Javelinas* **Author:** Susan Lowell (1992)	
Setting:	Sonoran Desert in Arizona
Characters:	First little javelina, second little javelina, third little javelina, and coyote
Problem:	The coyote wanted to eat the javelinas.
Event 1:	The first little javelina built a house of tumbleweeds.
Event 2:	The coyote blew it down, and the first little javelina ran to brother's house.
Event 3:	The second little javelina built a house of saguaro cactus ribs.
Event 4:	The coyote blew the house down, and the first and second javelina ran to their sister's house.
Event 5:	The third little javelina built her house with adobe brick.
Solution:	The coyote huffed and puffed and couldn't blow the adobe house down. He squeezed into the stove pipe, where the third little javelina lit a fire. The coyote howled and ran away. If you ever hear a coyote's voice, way out in the desert at night . . . well, you know what he's remembering!

FIGURE 6.31. Story web, example.

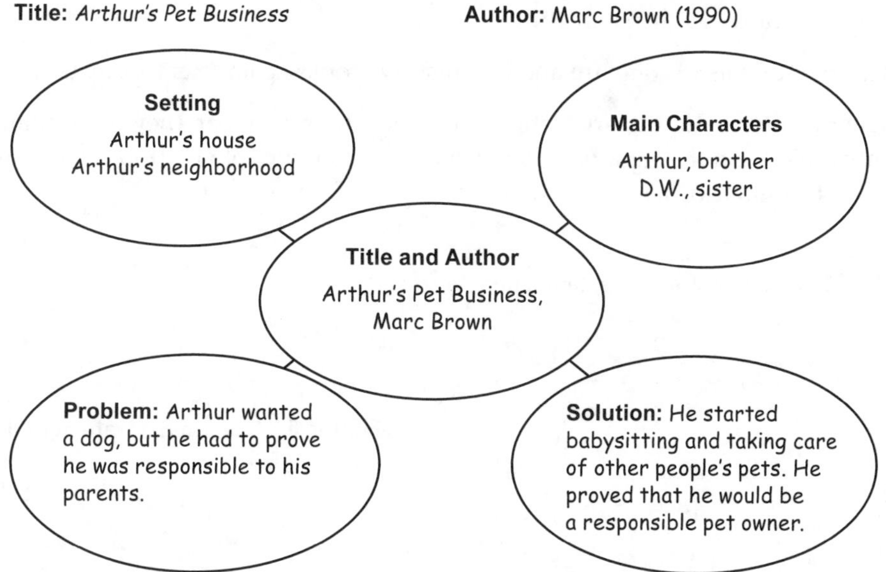

• Circular Story Map

PURPOSE: For students to retell the events of a story in sequence.

PROCEDURE: Students divide a circle into six sections and write the following information in each: (1) Characters, setting, place; (2) first event and problem; (3 and 4) attempts to solve the problem; (5) solution; and (6) resolution. Figure 6.32 provides a template for a circular story map.

Compare–Contrast Comprehension Strategies

Compare–contrast comprehension strategies involve describing how two or more events, places, characters, or other ideas are similar and different. Two or more elements within a story are explored, or the story itself is compared to another story in order to develop a listing of similarities and differences. Comparing two characters is just one use for this type of strategy. Questions can include "What are the similar and different qualities of these things? What qualities of each thing correspond to one another? In what way do they?" Examples of the strategies include a Venn diagram, an H chart, and a compare–contrast diagram.

• Venn Diagram

PURPOSE: For students to compare and contrast two or three ideas.

PROCEDURE: Students make a circle for each idea. Characteristics that are unique go in the main part of the circle; those that are shared go in the intersection(s) of the circles. If a concept is shared by all three of three ideas, it goes in the center. Figure 6.33 provides a template.

• H-Compare and Contrast Chart

PURPOSE: For students to compare and contrast two topics, characters, or texts.

PROCEDURE: Students draw a large letter *H.* On the left vertical bar, they write characteristics of only topic 1. On the right bar, they write characteristics of only topic 2. In the center bar, they write similarities.

FIGURE 6.32. Circular story map, template.

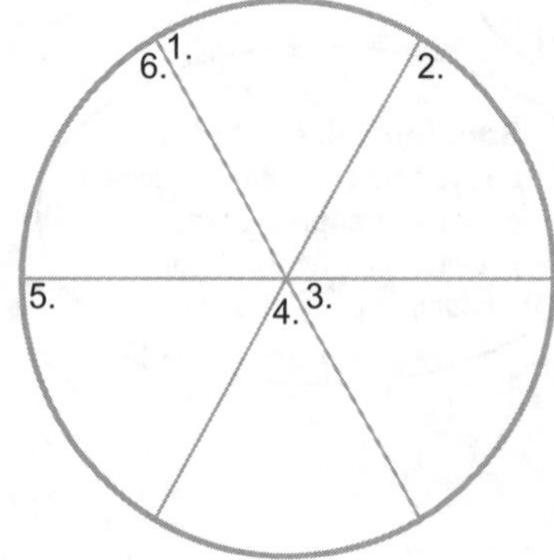

FIGURE 6.33. Venn diagram, template.

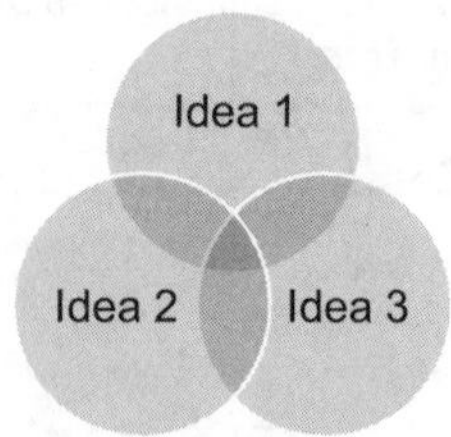

• Compare–Contrast Diagram

PURPOSE: For students to compare and contrast two topics, characters, or texts.

PROCEDURE: Students compare two characters or topics through using categories of information, and answering questions such as "How are they alike?" and "How are they different?" See Figure 6.34 for an example of a compare–contrast diagram for characters, and Figure 6.35 for an example of a compare–contrast diagram for concepts.

Sequence Comprehension Strategies

Sequence comprehension strategies involve students identifying a series of events, steps, or processes leading to a conclusion or a current happening. Sometimes signal words such as *first, then, next, during, while, soon,* and *after* are used to indicate the order of the events. Events from within a text are placed in sequential order and examined for the significance of this ordering. These strategies are used for ordering events in a narrative story or for ordering steps in a process (even a cyclical process) in an expository text for either comprehension or as a structure for student writing. Questions can include "What happened at the beginning, middle, and end? What are the steps in the process? What are the stages

FIGURE 6.34. Compare–contrast diagram for characters, example.

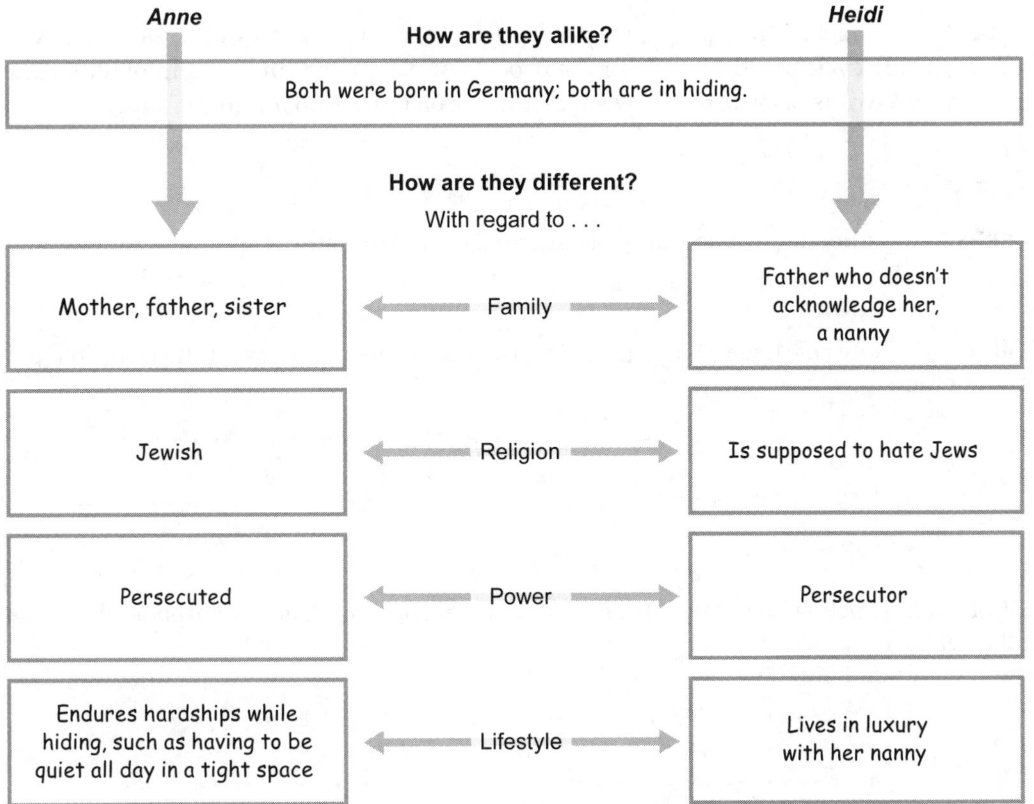

FIGURE 6.35. Compare–contrast diagram for concepts, example.

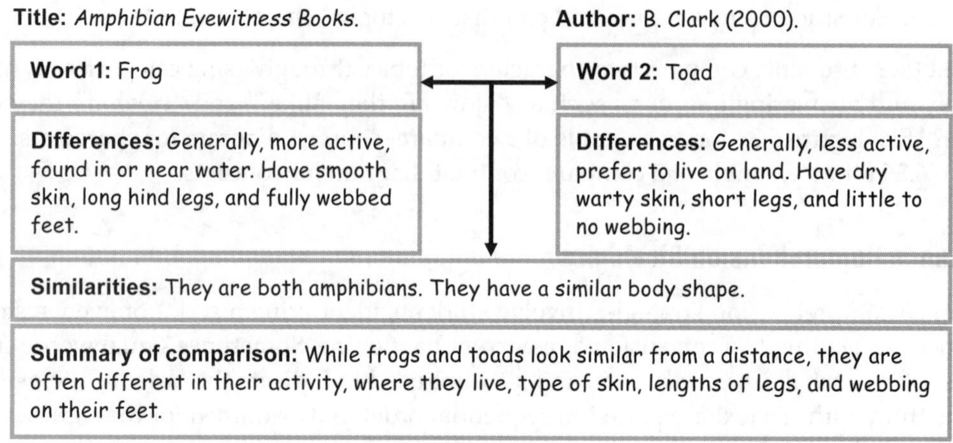

and substages?" Examples of sequence comprehension strategies include the flow chart (Figure 6.36 below), the timeline (Figure 6.37 below), the cycle diagram (Figure 6.38 on the next page), and the story board (Figure 6.39 on the next page).

Title: Amphibian Eyewitness Books.
Author: B. Clark (2000).
Word 1: Frog
Word 2: Toad
Differences: Generally, more active, found in or near water. Have smooth skin, long hind legs, and fully webbed feet.
Differences: Generally, less active, prefer to live on land. Have dry warty skin, short legs, and little to no webbing.
Similarities: They are both amphibians. They have a similar body shape.
Summary of comparison: While frogs and toads look similar from a distance, they are often different in their activity, where they live, type of skin, lengths of legs, and webbing on their feet.

• Cycle Diagram

PURPOSE: For students to show the steps in a process with a continuous cycle.

PROCEDURE: Students draw a circular progression of arrows to show each step in a cycle, such as the life cycle of a dragonfly or the process of plants' making food in photosynthesis. They add words or pictures between arrows. See Figure 6.38 for an example.

• Story Board

PURPOSE: For students to map out the sequential events in a story.

FIGURE 6.36. Flow chart, template: Students write the events in a story, or the steps in a process, in order.

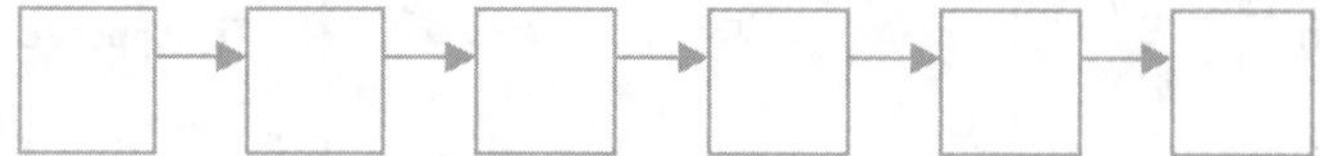

FIGURE 6.37. Timeline, template: Students put a sequence of events in chronological order and label them by date or event.

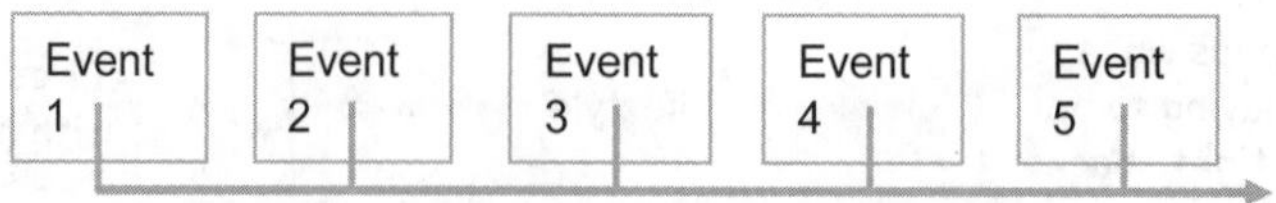

FIGURE 6.38. Cycle diagram, example.

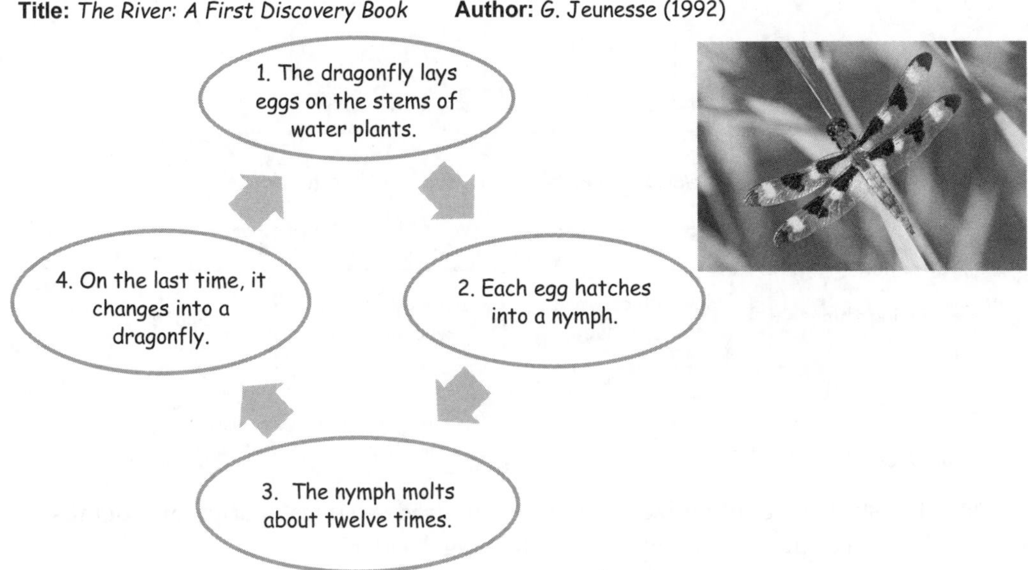

PROCEDURE: Students divide a sheet of paper into a 2 × 3 grid. They think about six major events in the text and draw or write the main events in order in each section, making sure to provide details. Figure 6.39 provides a template for a story board.

Classification Comprehension Strategies

Classifying involves organizing information from a text into classes or groups. The general connections between multiple items can be examined by using these strategies. Questions can include "What sort of idea or object is this? What are the subcategories? What other things can go into these subcategories?" Examples of these strategies include a hierarchy diagram, stacking up ideas, and a cluster web.

• Hierarchy Diagram

PURPOSE: For students to show hierarchical relationships between/among a main topic, subordinate ideas, and coordinate ideas.

PROCEDURE: Students organize the concepts by their relationships. They draw boxes and lines to show how these concepts are related. See Figure 6.40 for an example.

FIGURE 6.39. Story board, template.

Event 1	Event 2	Event 3
Event 4	Event 5	Event 6

FIGURE 6.40. Hierarchy diagram, example.

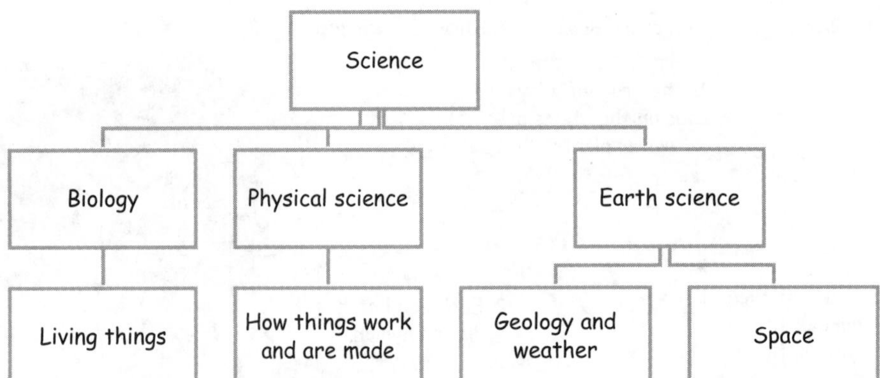

• Stacking Up Ideas

PURPOSE: For students to organize ideas into a main idea, subcategories, and details. See Figure 6.41 for an example of a diagram for stacking up ideas.

PROCEDURE: The teacher or students draw the *Stacking Up Ideas* graphic organizer. The students then write the main idea, subcategories, and details in each box.

• Cluster Web

PURPOSE: For students to identify a main concept in a story or text and add details about that concept.

PROCEDURE: Students draw an oval or circle for the main concept at the top of a page and add details about the concept in the ovals/circles connected to it below. They add supporting details in the third tier of ovals/circles and can insert additional details in a fourth tier, if needed. See Figure 6.42 for an example.

FIGURE 6.41. Stacking up ideas diagram, example.

				The three branches of the U.S. government				
Legislative branch			Executive branch			Judicial branch		
Makes laws	Senate	House of Representatives	President/Vice President	Cabinet members	15 major departmental secretaries	Supreme Court	Oversees the court systems of the U.S.	1 Chief Justice, 8 Associate Justices

FIGURE 6.42. Cluster web, example.

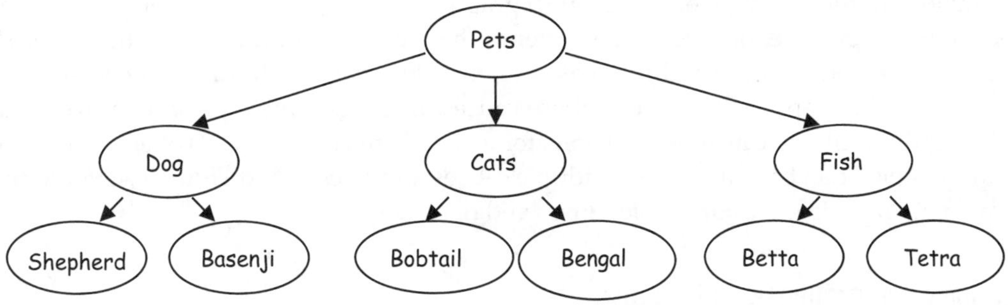

Pets

Dog Cats Fish

Shepherd Basenji Bobtail Bengal Betta Tetra

Cause–Effect Comprehension Strategies

The general purpose of cause–effect comprehension strategies is for students to identify the reason(s) why an event occurred and the end result. An event can have one or more causes and one or more resulting effects. Events from within a story or text are looked at for their connections. Questions can include "What are the causes and effects of this event? What might happen next?" This type of strategy can also be used to show how events in a story are affected by the characters' actions.

• Cause–Effect Map

PROCEDURE: Students write the cause(s) of an event on the left, and its effect(s) on the right. See Figure 6.43 for an example.

FIGURE 6.43. Cause–effect map, example.

Title: "Ida Bell Wells-Barnett" in *Rabble Rousers* **Author:** C. Harness (2003)		
Cause:		**Effect:**
People were being sold as slaves.	→	13th Amendment made it illegal in 1865.
Fever struck.	→	Parents and brother died.
Ida was asked to leave the train car because she was black.	→	Ida sued the railroad for discrimination and was awarded $500.
This decision was overturned in the state supreme court.	→	She wrote about courtrooms where blacks were unfairly tried and harshly punished.
Ida described her school, where she taught, as being shabby and poorly equipped.	→	Ida lost her teaching job at the school for black children.
Three black businessmen were jailed and hung for false charges.	→	She began gathering and publishing evidence that over 1,000 black men, women, and children had been hung.
She feared for her safety.	→	She formed anti-lynching societies in the U.S. and in Great Britain.

• Cause–Effect Graphic Organizers

PROCEDURE: In the first type of cause–effect graphic organizer, students write the topic or problem that they are exploring in the center of the organizer. At the left, in the "Causes" section, they record what they think makes the problem happen. In the "Effects" section, they record what happens because of these causes. In the second type of organizer, students identify multiple causes with details for a single effect (Moss, 2004). See Figure 6.44 for an example of an organizer with multiple causes and effects, and Figure 6.45 for a diagram for an organizer with multiple causes and one result.

Summary Comprehension Strategies

• Story Frames

PURPOSE: For students to summarize a text by completing a prompt that scaffolds appropriate responses. A story frame can be used to aid students in retelling a story, prompt them for a summary paragraph, give them a sentence starter to demonstrate comprehension; guide them to places in stories where information can be found; and help them to organize information in order to identify important ideas, analyze characters and their problems, make comparisons, and summarize passage content. These frames are helpful for students who need support in written language, especially ELLs.

PROCEDURE: The teacher selects or creates a story frame with a sequence of spaces hooked together by key language elements that would be appropriate for a given passage. Over time, a student's ability to use the same frame may demonstrate growth in specific comprehension skills. As independent assignments, frames can be used to help students deal with a variety of ideas, concepts, and information, and are excellent tools to use for quick, informal evaluations. See Figure 6.46 on page 276 for templates for several types of story frames.

FIGURE 6.44. Cause–effect organizer, type 1, example: Multiple causes, multiple effects.

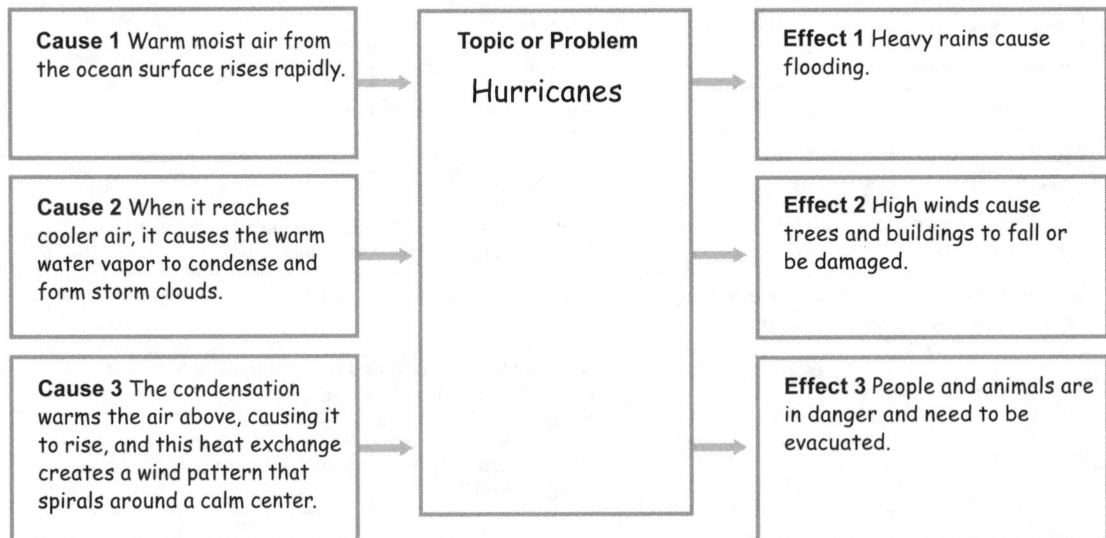

FIGURE 6.45. Cause–effect organizer, type 2, template: Multiple causes, single result.

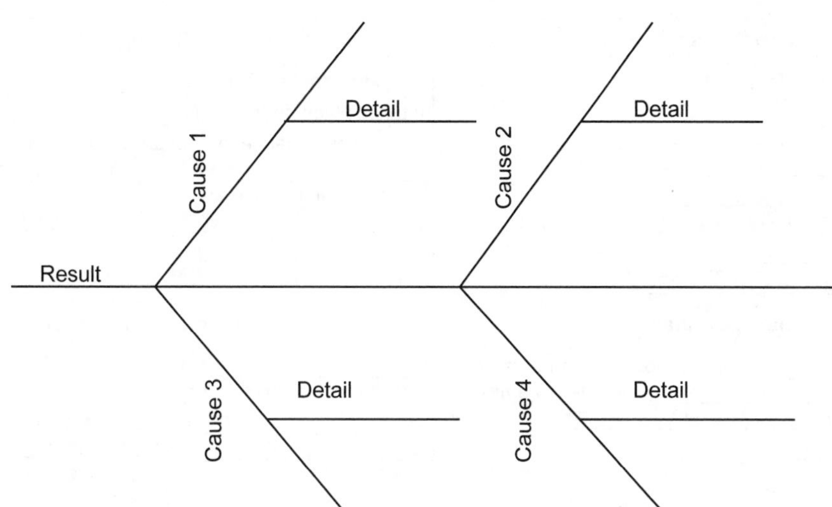

• Predict, Organize, Rehearse, Practice, and Evaluate (PORPE)

SOURCE: Simpson (1984).

PURPOSE: For students to actively plan, monitor, and evaluate their learning of content; to help them prepare for essay exams; and to use process writing to learn content (predominantly for secondary students).

PROCEDURE: Students first predict potential essay questions and clarify their purpose for reading. They then organize key information to answer the predicted questions. They summarize and synthesize the material, and outline or make concept maps of the answers. They next rehearse the key ideas, examples, and organization to put these in long-term memory. They practice writing out in detail what they rehearsed in the rehearsal step. Finally, they evaluate the quality of their own answers, based on how they think the teacher would evaluate them. The teacher should model each of these steps.

• Read, Ask, Put in Paragraph, Question (RAPQ) Strategy

SOURCE: Schumaker, Denton, and Deshler (1984).

PURPOSE: For students to identify main ideas, question reading, and summarize paragraphs (grades 3–12).

PROCEDURE: The teacher explains to students that RAPQ is an acronym for the following:

Read the paragraph.
Ask and answer questions about the main ideas and important details.
Put the paragraph in your own words.
Question—create a question about what you read, write it on a note card, and put the answer on the back. Students can use these cards as study guides.

See Figure 6.47 for an example.

FIGURE 6.46. Story frames, templates.

Important Idea or Plot

In this story, the problem starts when ____________________.
After that, ____________________.
Next, ____________________.
Then, ____________________.
The problem is finally solved when ____________________.
The story ends ____________________.

Setting

This story takes place in ____________________.
It takes place during ____________________.
I know this because the author used the words "____________________." Other clues that show when the story takes place are ____________________.

Character Analysis

____________________ is an important character in our story. ____________________ (character's name) is important because ____________________.
Once he/she ____________________.
Another time, ____________________.
I think that ____________________ (character's name) is ____________________ (character trait) because ____________________.

Character Comparison

____________________ and ____________________ are two characters in our story.
____________________ (character's name) is ____________________ (character trait), while ____________________ (other character's name) is ____________________ (character trait).
For instance, ____________________ tries to ____________________, and ____________________ tries to ____________________.
When ____________________, he/she learns a lesson of ____________________.

Story Summary with One Main Character

Our story is about ____________________ ____________________. ____________________ is an important character in our story. ____________________ (character's name) tries to ____________________.
The story ends when ____________________ ____________________.

Topic Comparison

____________________ and ____________________ are main ideas in our text.
____________________ (one main idea) is ____________________ (meaning).
____________________ (another main idea) is ____________________ (meaning).
These two ideas are similar because ____________________.
These two ideas are different because ____________________.

Subject Analysis

____________________ is an important idea/subject in our text. ____________________ is important because ____________________.
One example is ____________________.
One way it is used is ____________________.
I think that ____________________ is ____________________ because ____________________.

Text Summary with One Main Idea

The article is about ____________________.
____________________ is an important fact in our article. ____________________ (event or fact) resulted in or influenced ____________________ (another event or fact).
In summary, then ____________________ ____________________ (what happened and why).

Somebody Wanted But So (Cunningham & Allington, 2003)

Somebody, ____________________, wanted ____________________.
But ____________________. So ____________________

Story Summary

____________________ (title) takes place in ____________________ (place) during ____________________ (when).
____________________ is an important character who ____________________ (characteristics).
A problem occurred when ____________________.
After that, ____________________. The problem is solved by ____________________.
The story ends when ____________________.

FIGURE 6.47. RAPQ strategy, example.

Rand McNally (1994). *Discovery Atlas of Native Americans*	
Read a paragraph or a section of the material you are working on.	"The Hopi are thought to be descendants of the Anasazi, who lived in the area hundreds of years earlier. Like the Anasazi they built large pueblos. These buildings had many levels and were made from sun-dried bricks of mud and straw called adobe. Towns were usually placed atop high mesas—flat-topped hills or mountains with cliff-like sides."
Ask yourself what the main ideas are.	Hopi are probably descendants of the Anasazi.
Put the main ideas in your own words.	Hopi, who are probably descendants of the Anasazi, live in adobe pueblos with many levels on top of mesas.
Questions about the reading: Create and answer these.	On the front of a note card the student wrote: What do the Hopi towns called pueblos look like? On the back of the card, the student wrote: The buildings have many levels and are made of straw and brick. They are built on top of flat mountains with steep sides.

Reciprocal Teaching

SOURCE: Palinscar and Brown (1986).

PURPOSE: For students to predict, summarize, clarify, and ask questions while reading.

PROCEDURE: In pairs, the students predict what the text or the next part of the text will be about. They read a section of text and then summarize in one or two sentences what the passage was mainly about or the main idea. Students clarify what they did not understand, such as a word, phrase or statement, and then ask each other questions about what they just read.

SQ3R Strategy

SOURCE: Walker (2004).

PURPOSE: For students to study content-area texts and monitor comprehension and learning.

PROCEDURE: The teacher explains to students that the SQ3R acronym includes five steps:

Survey: skim the passage to construct a framework.
Question: develop questions that may be answered in the text.
Read: read to answer the questions, paying attention to graphics and diagrams for extra information.
Recite: construct an answer and possibly write down important information.
Review: review questions and answers, then relate the information to the framework of the text.

Writing Summaries

PURPOSE: For students to write short summaries containing the important information.

PROCEDURE: The teacher models by reading a section of text, writing a summary, and sharing how only the important information is included, while some less important information is not included. Students then work in groups, pairs, and finally individually to write their own summaries.

Triple-Read Outline

SOURCE: Walker (2004).

PURPOSE: For students to identify the main idea and supporting details of an expository text, and then write a summary of the text.

PROCEDURE: The teacher states that the purpose for the first reading is to identify the main idea of each paragraph, and they model it by writing it in the margin of a photocopy of the text. During the second reading, the purpose is to identify the supporting details. The third reading is to organize the information into an outline. The teacher then writes a summary of the passage, using the main idea as the topic sentence and adding the details to support it. The teacher also points out the irrelevant information that they left out. The students then follow the same procedure on their own, using a new passage, and compare their outline with what the teacher wrote.

GIST Procedure

SOURCE: Cunningham (1982).

PURPOSE: For students to improve their abilities to comprehend the GIST of paragraphs. GIST is an acronym for Generating Interactions between Schemata and Text.

PROCEDURE: A student selects a paragraph to summarize. The student reads the first sentence and generates a summary. Then they read the first two sentences and generate a summary for both of these sentences. The student continues with the procedure for the remainder of the paragraph. They eventually move from reading individual sentences and summarizing to reading individual paragraphs and summarizing sections of text.

Cornell Notes

SOURCE: *http://lsc.cornell.edu/notes.html.*

PURPOSE: For students to take notes and retain information during a reading or lecture.

PROCEDURE: Students are instructed to do the following:

1. *Create a template.* Divide a piece of paper into three sections. Draw a horizontal line across the bottom two inches and label it "Summary." Then divide the top section into two columns; the "Notes" column is twice the size of the "Cues" or "Questions/Keywords" column.
2. *Record.* During the reading/lecture, use the left column to take notes and record key ideas.
3. *Cues or questions/key words.* Afterward, formulate questions and key words based on the notes in the right-hand column. This helps to clarify meanings, reveal relationships, and strengthen memory, and is helpful for studying for exams later.

4. *Recite.* Cover the note-taking column with a sheet of paper. Then, looking at the questions or key words, say aloud, in your own words, the answers to the questions, facts, or ideas indicated by the key words.
5. *Reflect.* Reflect on the material by asking yourself questions—for example, "What's the significance of these facts? What principle are they based on? How can I apply them? How do they fit in with what I already know? What's beyond them?"
6. *Review.* Spend at least 10 minutes every week reviewing all your previous notes. If you do, you'll retain a great deal for current use, as well as for the exam.

See Figure 6.48 for a Cornell Notes template and a partially filled-in example.

Critical Thinking Comprehension Strategies

Critical comprehension involves reasoning to go beyond the ideas in a passage and make inferences or draw conclusions about them. Examples include recognizing the author's purpose, identifying the author's overall organizational pattern, and recognizing explicit and implicit relationships between the words, phrases, and sentences. It involves students making connections between conclusions they draw and others' beliefs and knowledge; making critical or analytical judgments about what they read; and developing perceptions of biases, assessments of truth, and values. Finally, it involves aesthetic value, such as enjoyment, enlightenment, or appreciation of something worthwhile.

FIGURE 6.48. Cornell Notes, template and partial example.

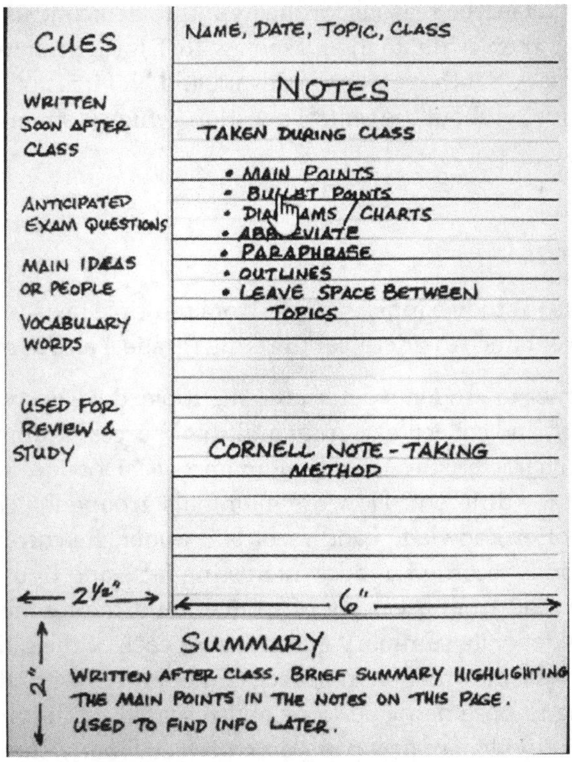

• Questioning the Author (QTA)

SOURCE: Beck, McKeown, Hamilton, and Kucan (1997).

PURPOSE: For students to question the author's writing to improve text comprehension.

PROCEDURE: The teacher identifies major understandings that the students are to construct, as well as potential problems they may face while reading. The teacher segments the text into meaningful parts. The teacher then writes a series of initiating, follow-up, and narrative questions, such as these: "What is the author trying to say here? Does the author explain it clearly? How does this connect to what the author has already told us? Does the author tell us why? Given what the author already told us about the character, what do you think will happen? How does the author let you know something has changed?" The teacher strategically guides the students' contributions and discussions to help them construct an understanding of the ideas in the text. Finally, the students create their own questions for questioning the author.

• Dialogical-Thinking Reading Lesson

SOURCE: Commeyras (1993).

PURPOSE: For students to engage in reflection and critical thinking about issues in narrative text reading.

PROCEDURE: The teacher selects a text that can be viewed from multiple viewpoints and that the students would find interesting. After the students read, they discuss a central question, such as "What should a character do?", and discuss two hypothesized conclusions. Next, students dictate the reasons for the hypothesized conclusions, which are written on the board. They then evaluate the reasons with T for true, F for false, and D for "it depends." They also mark Y if the reason is relevant and N if it is not. Finally, each student draws their own conclusion about the central question, which is shared orally or in writing.

• Inquiry Chart

SOURCE: Hoffman (1992).

PURPOSE: For students to study a topic in depth from multiple texts with possible different points of view and to enhance their critical thinking (grade 4 and above).

PROCEDURE: The teacher or students determine the topic, develop two to four questions, create an inquiry chart, and collect texts from multiple sources. Examples of guiding questions: "What are the characteristics of marine mammals? How are they similar to other mammals? How are they different? How are mammals grouped?" The teacher then asks students about their prior knowledge and records it under the correct guiding question. Additional information is recorded under "Interesting facts and figures" and "New questions." Students then read from a variety of sources, and the teacher records what they learned. The students generate summary questions for each of the guiding questions. The students then compare the information from each of the sources with their prior knowledge. The students continue to pose new questions and research to answer them. The inquiry chart can become an individual or group research project. Finally, the students report their findings to the whole class. Figure 6.49 provides a template for an inquiry chart.

FIGURE 6.49. Inquiry chart, template.

	Guiding Questions						
	Topic	1.	2.	3.	4.	Interesting Facts and Figures	New Questions
Sources	What we know						
	1.						
	2.						
	3.						
	Summary						

• Group Investigation Approach

SOURCE: Walker (2004).

PURPOSE: For students to study and present a topic in cooperative groups (grade 4 and above).

PROCEDURE: The teacher or class selects a topic and gathers resources. Then students develop a list of questions to investigate, which is then organized by key categories and subtopics. Research groups are organized around subtopics. Students select appropriate resources to read. They summarize their learning and share it during reporting sessions. Each group prepares a product (webpage, PowerPoint, poster, etc.) to share the information the members have learned about their subtopic.

EVALUATION: The teacher and students develop summary questions to ask the class. Students write a reflection about what they learned from each group.

• Critical Reflections

PURPOSE: For students to examine a text for challenges to their beliefs and values.

PROCEDURE: The teacher says to students, "As you read a text for the first time, mark an X in the margin at each point where you felt a personal challenge to your attitudes, beliefs, or status. Make a brief note in the margin about what you feel, or about what in the text created the challenge. Now look again at the places you marked in the text where you felt personally challenged. What patterns do you see?"

• Fact, Opinion, or Inference

PURPOSE: For students to distinguish among a statement of fact, an opinion, and an inference.

PROCEDURE: As the teacher, first define facts, opinions, and inferences for your students.

Fact: A piece of information that can be directly observed or can be verified or checked for accuracy.

Opinion: An evaluation based on a personal judgment or belief, which may or may not be verifiable.

Inference: A logical conclusion or a legitimate implication based on factual information.

Then, write a list of statements that contains examples of each. Have the students mark each statement with F, O, or I. Afterward, select texts that contain facts, opinions, and inferences, such as some newspaper articles and historical narratives. Have the students find examples of each.

• Persuasive Analysis Strategy Argument Chart

SOURCE: Moss (2004).

PURPOSE: For students to identify elements of a persuasive argument.

PROCEDURE:7 The students create a four-column chart, in which they write what the author is asserting, what the supporting evidence is for this assertion, what the opposing views are, and finally what the arguments against the opposing views are. Figure 6.50 provides a template for such a chart.

• Literature Circles

SOURCE: Short, Harste, and Burke (1996)

PURPOSE: For students to engage in student-led group discussions of self-selected reading (grade 2 and above).

PROCEDURE: Each member of the group is given a role sheet with required roles: discussion director, literary luminary/passage master, connector, and illustrator. Optional roles include researcher, summarizer, character captain, vocabulary enricher/word master, and travel tracer/scene setter. Each role sheet includes guiding questions and responses. The discussion director guides the group's discussions and develops a list of questions to ask the group. The literary luminary selects key sections of the text that the group would find interesting. The connector thinks of ways the story connects personally, to other group members, their community, and experiences. The illustrator draws a picture, chart, web, or cartoon and explains it to the group. The summarizer prepares a summary and the key points of the reading for the day. At the end of the literature circle, each group determines

FIGURE 6.50. Persuasive analysis strategy argument chart, template.

<table>
<tr><td colspan="3">Analysis of ______________________________ (Title)</td></tr>
<tr><th>Assertion</th><th>Supporting Evidence</th><th>Opposing View</th></tr>
<tr><td rowspan="3"></td><td rowspan="3"></td><td></td></tr>
<tr><th>Arguments against the Opposing View</th></tr>
<tr><td></td></tr>
</table>

what to share with the rest of the class. The group members' roles should be rotated so that students get an opportunity for each job.

Book Club

SOURCE: Raphael, Pardo, and Highfield (2002).

PURPOSE: For students to engage in conversations about books and to use a framework to develop reading and writing for all ages.

PROCEDURE: There are four parts to the framework: community share, book club discussions, reading, and writing. In community share, the teacher introduces and models strategies, including those for communication and introduces conventions and vocabulary. Students hear and use language of literacy and discussion and share about their discussions from their book club group. The discussions are authentic conversations between students in the group (groups are not necessarily formed according to ability). Students learn to focus more on appreciating others' ideas than on competition. During reading, the students read for at least 15 minutes per day by themselves, with peers, or with the teacher. Emphasis is given to reading strategy development. Writing is important for personal responses and involves extending thinking with analysis and synthesis of the text. This can include the use of reading logs and think sheets. The writing includes planning, revision, and publishing.

Questions and Strategies Based on Bloom's Revised Taxonomy

SOURCES: Anderson and Krathwohl (2001), based on Bloom (1956).

PURPOSE: For students to comprehend both narrative and expository texts, using multiple levels of Bloom's revised taxonomy.

PROCEDURE: The teacher uses the verbs of the cognitive domain in Bloom's revised taxonomy to develop objectives for instruction before, during, and after reading: *creating, evaluating, analyzing, applying, understanding,* and *remembering*. There are several strategies that use these six levels of thinking. The *Questioning Strategies Based on Bloom's Taxonomy of Thinking* chart (see Appendix, p. 459) includes guidelines for asking questions, starting at the lowest level of questioning (remembering) and moving to the highest level (creating). The *Bloom's Taxonomy—Narrative Comprehension Activities* chart (see Appendix, pp. 460–461) provides literacy questions and activities that can be used to assess students' understanding of a narrative at each of the revised Bloom's taxonomy levels.

Thick and Thin Questions

SOURCE: McLaughlin and Allen (2000).

PURPOSE: For students to create different depths of questions for comprehending a text.

PROCEDURE: The teacher models the difference between "thick" and "thin" questions. *Thick questions* are those that involve the big picture or main idea, important concepts, or major themes. They involve complex answers and are open-ended. Questions that start with "Why . . ." or "What if . . ." are thick questions. *Thin questions* deal with specific content or words. The answers are short and closed-ended (usually single words or phrases, or yes–no responses). Questions that start with "Who . . ." or "When . . ." are thin questions.

Creative Comprehension Strategies

Creative comprehension goes beyond the text, through oral, written, and visual communication. For the sake of brevity, the following is a list of a few strategies to enhance students' creative comprehension. As the teacher, ask students to do any of the following:

1. Share favorite, interesting, or thought-provoking parts of texts.
2. Share what it would be like to meet or be any of the characters.
3. Make connections to your own experiences.
4. Write response journals and include your feelings, what you know, what don't understand, and/or drawings of what is happening in the chapter; then orally explain your entries.
5. Share books by creating oral, written, or multimedia reports, stories, and newspaper articles.
6. Create book reviews, newspaper articles, travel brochures, letters to the author, letters to the characters, or oral reading advertisements (such as those found at the end of *Reading Rainbow* segments on TV).
7. Design and illustrate a book jacket with a biography of the author for a book.
8. Design a book poster with setting and problem. This can include captions with descriptive words.
9. Draw a comic strip about one part of the story.
10. Write a story with a different ending, a sequel, or a spinoff with different characters, setting, and/or problem, based on another story.
11. Make puppets or create a play and act out the story.
12. Write poetry or a song based on the reading.
13. Write an acrostic poem using the letters of a character or a topic, and provide descriptions that start with each letter.
14. Research the same topic by different authors, or different books by the same author.
15. Relate and apply reading to disciplinary concepts (social studies, science, math, arts).
16. Create mnemonic devices for remembering sequences of events or concepts in the text. For example, the expression "Kings Play Cards On Fairly Good Soft Velvet" can be a mnemonic for the orders of classifications of life: Kingdom, Phylum, Class, Order, Family, Genus, Species, Variety.
17. Develop art, construction, cooking, or music activities related to the reading.

Visual and Digital Text Comprehension Strategies

• Watching Videos the Way You Read a Book

SOURCE: Heick (2019).

PURPOSE: For students to develop comprehension before, during, and after viewing a video.

PROCEDURE: Like reading a text, video comprehension is a matter of decoding, but with different symbols based on the modalities. Videos can add light, sound, moving images, scene cuts, dialogue, voiceovers, video speed, music, text, shape, color, and other modalities as ways to communicate ideas. The following strategies support students' comprehension before, during, and after watching a video; they also provide extended learning about the video content. As the teacher, ask students to do the following:

Before-Viewing Strategies

- Set a viewing purpose.
- Predict (sequence of events, video creator's position on a given topic, etc.).
- Preview video (editing conventions, length, title, etc.).
- Identify media connections ("I read a book on a related topic recently," "I saw a Tweet that described this same idea but in sarcastic terms," etc.)
- Make true–false statements about general video topic.
- Begin K-W-L chart.
- Roughly summarize (e.g., what you know about topic, video creator, channel).
- Create a concept map for the video topic in a given or self-selected context.
- Complete an anticipation guide.
- Create self-produced guiding questions.

During-Viewing Strategies

- Stop (or pause) the video while viewing, either as personal preference or for monitoring of own understanding.
- Rewind to clarify understanding or uncover subtle data/events.
- Rewatch video with new purpose and perspective.
- Form relevant questions based on viewing.
- Clarify (information, bias, fact vs. opinion, "author" position, etc.).
- Monitor and repair understanding.
- Evaluate use of primary and secondary modalities.
- Make meaningful and personalized inferences (e.g., primary and secondary audiences).
- Infer underlying assumptions of video.
- Adjust viewing speed (i.e., use slow-motion) as necessary (e.g., for physics videos).

After-Viewing Strategies

- Retell what happened; paraphrase "standout" ideas.
- Summarize main idea and key supporting details.
- Recall own thinking and/or emotions during video (metacognition).
- Engage in modality analysis (i.e., identify and analyze prevailing modalities and their effect).
- Engage in metric analysis (to infer social context with respect to total views, number of viewers currently watching, social shares, etc.).
- Analyze organization of ideas in video.
- Create a word cloud (that reflects diction, tone, theme, etc.); Tweet, comment on, blog, or otherwise socialize initial impressions in a way that reflects digital citizenship.
- Socialize extended responses (in writing, on social media, etc.).
- Categorize information and perspectives.
- Separate explicit and implicit ideas.

Extended Strategies

- Reflect on "fit" of video with viewing purpose.
- Compare and contrast video with videos that have similar content.

- Create an anticipation guide (for viewers who haven't seen this video).
- Identify the "big idea" of the video.
- Critique video for which modalities supported video purpose and theme, and which seemed to distract from these.
- Roughly determine history of topic in similar and dissimilar media.
- Engage in RAFT (Role, Audience, Format, Topic/Theme) thinking and extensions of this.
- Prioritize ideas and information from least to most important.
- Distinguish between tone and mood of video.
- Design follow-up medium that extends and deepens purpose of video.

Digital Technology Tools

SOURCE: Renwick (2013).

PURPOSE: For students to comprehend and navigate digital texts using technology tools.

PROCEDURE: As the teacher, select example websites with hyperlinks, videos, and interactive graphics embedded within digital text. Then select a technology tool to help students navigate these websites. The following are five technology tools that can help students comprehend digital text.

- Instapaper can be used to save an article online, using a web clipper, and then to read it in a paper-like format. The hyperlinks and images are still available, but all advertisements and unrelated information is omitted. This information can also be exported to an eReader.
- GoodReader can be used to read PDFs, annotate and highlight text, and send revised documents to others via email. GoodReader can be used to model close reading for students, using a mobile device projected on a whiteboard. The ability to import and export files through web storage tools, such as Google Drive and Dropbox, is also available.
- Skitch can be used for understanding the message of an image. A photo of anything can be marked up with arrows, shapes, and text. It also has annotation capabilities for PDFs. If GoodReader is too complex for younger children to navigate, Skitch allows any school-age student to highlight important words and share their thinking in the margins. Afterward, the marked-up file can be saved in Evernote or shared via email and social media.
- Diigo allows readers to annotate digital texts and then save them in an online library. The highlights, comments, and tags show up under the article's link. Users can create several libraries based on topics of interest. Also, anyone can be granted access to add to these online repositories. Diigo can help create a community of readers because students can collaboratively develop these libraries, with the purpose of helping everyone understand the texts.
- Readability is a tool to use with Twitter via the app Tweetbot to remove all the advertisements just by sliding a button to the right, following the arrow.

Analyze a Photograph

SOURCE: National Archives and Records Administration (2018).

PURPOSE: For students to analyze a photograph and understand its purpose.

PROCEDURE: Students select a photo and answer the following questions:

1. *Meet the photo.* Quickly scan the photo. What do you notice first? What is the type of photo (more than one may apply): portrait, landscape, panoramic, aerial/satellite, action, architectural, event, family, posed, candid, documentary, nature, selfie, other? Is there a caption?
2. *Observe its parts.* What are the people, objects, and activities you see?
3. *Try to make sense of it.* Who took this photo? Where is it from? When is it from? What was happening at the time in history this photo was taken? Why was it taken? List evidence from the photo or your knowledge about the photographer that led you to your conclusion.
4. *Use it as historical evidence.* What did you find out from this document that you might not learn anywhere else? What other documents or historical evidence are you going to use to help you understand this event or topic?

Analyze a Map

SOURCE: National Archives and Records Administration (2018).

PURPOSE: For students to analyze a map and understand its purpose.

PROCEDURE: Students select a map and answer the following questions:

1. *Meet the map.* What is the title? Is there a scale and compass? What is in the legend? Type of map (more than one may apply): political, topographic/physical, aerial/satellite, relief (shaded or raised), exploration, survey, natural resource, planning, land use, transportation, military, population/settlement, census, other.
2. *Observe its parts.* What place or places are shown? What is labeled? If there are symbols or colors, what do they stand for?
3. *Try to make sense of it.* Who made this map? When is it from? What was happening at the time in history this map was made? Why was it created? List evidence from the map or your knowledge about the mapmaker that led you to your conclusion. Write one sentence summarizing this map. How does it compare to a current map of the same place?
4. *Use it as historical evidence.* What did you find out from this map that you might not learn anywhere else? What other documents or historical evidence are you going to use to help you understand this event or topic?

Analyze a Cartoon

SOURCE: National Archives and Records Administration (2018).

PURPOSE: For students to analyze a cartoon and understand its purpose.

PROCEDURE: Students select a cartoon and answer the following questions:

1. *Meet the cartoon.* Quickly scan the cartoon. What do you notice first? What is the title or caption?
2. *Observe its parts.* Words: Are there labels, descriptions, thoughts, or dialogue? Visuals: List the people, objects, and places in the cartoon. List the actions or activities.

3. *Try to make sense of it.* Words: Which words or phrases are the most significant? List adjectives that describe the emotions portrayed. Visuals: Which of the visuals are symbols? What do they stand for? Who drew this cartoon? When is it from? What was happening at the time in history it was created? What is the message? List evidence from the cartoon or your knowledge about the cartoonist that led you to your conclusion.
4. *Use it as historical evidence.* What did you find out from this cartoon that you might not learn anywhere else? What other documents or historical evidence are you going to use to help you understand this event or topic?

Analyze a Video

SOURCE: National Archives and Records Administration (2018).

PURPOSE: For students to analyze a video and understand its purpose.

PROCEDURE: Students select a video and answer the following questions:

1. *Meet the video.* What is the title? What do you think you will see? Type of video (more than one may apply): animation, propaganda, promotional, training film, combat film, newsreel, news report, informational, documentary, entertainment, commercial. Other elements (more than one may apply): music, live action, narration, special effects, background noise, color, black and white, animation, dramatizations. What is the mood or tone?
2. *Observe its parts.* What are the people, objects, and activities you see? Write one sentence summarizing this video.
3. *Try to make sense of it.* When is this video from? What was happening at the time in history it was created? Who made it? Who do you think is the intended audience? How do you think the creator wanted the audience to respond? List evidence from the video or your knowledge about who made it that led you to your conclusion.
4. *Use it as historical evidence.* What did you find out from this video that you might not learn anywhere else? What other documents or historical evidence are you going to use to help you understand this event or topic?

Analyze an Artifact

SOURCE: National Archives and Records Administration (2018).

PURPOSE: For students to analyze an artifact and understand its purpose.

PROCEDURE: Students select an artifact and answer the following questions:

1. *Meet the artifact.* Material (more than one may apply): bone, pottery, metal, wood, stone, leather, glass, paper, cardboard, fabric, plastic, other.
2. *Observe its parts.* Describe it as if you were explaining it to someone who can't see it. Think about shape, color, texture, size, weight, age, condition, movable parts, or anything written on it.
3. *Try to make sense of it.* Answer as best you can. Where is it from? When is it from? Who used it? List reasons you think so. What was it used for? List reasons you think so. What does this tell you about the people who made and used it? What does it tell you about technology at the time it was made? What is a similar item from today?

4. *Use it as historical evidence.* What did you find out from this artifact that you might not learn anywhere else? What other documents or historical evidence are you going to use to help you understand the event or time in which this artifact was used?

• Analyze an Artwork

SOURCE: National Archives and Records Administration (2018).

PURPOSE: For students to analyze an artwork and understand its purpose.

PROCEDURE: Students select an artwork and answer the following questions:

1. *Meet the artwork.* Quickly scan the artwork. What do you notice first? Type of artwork (more than one may apply): painting, drawing/sketch, engraving/lithograph, mural, sculpture, mixed media, scene/event, portrait, landscape, abstract, other. What is the title?
2. *Observe its parts.* What are the people, objects, and activities you see? Write one sentence summarizing this artwork.
3. *Try to make sense of it.* What do the colors, people, objects, or activities represent? Who made this? When was it created? Does it depict a different time? When? What was happening at the time in history it was created? What is the message? List evidence from the artwork or your knowledge about the artist that led you to your conclusion.
4. *Use it as historical evidence.* What did you find out from this artwork that you might not learn anywhere else? What other documents or historical evidence are you going to use to help you understand this event or topic?

• Noticings–Meanings–Implications: Comprehending Visual Images in Multimodal Texts

SOURCE: Serafini (2011).

PURPOSE: For students to expand their interpretive repertoires to comprehend visual images, graphic design, and multimodal texts through learning art theory and criticism, the grammar of visual design, and evaluating media literacies (grades 6–12).

PROCEDURE: In addition to predicting, summarizing, and asking questions for comprehending written texts, older students can learn (1) art theory and criticism, (2) the grammar of visual design, and (3) media literacies. As the teacher, select examples of multimodal texts with elaborate visual images, unusual narrative structures, complex design elements, and unique formats, as well as video games, websites, expository texts, magazines, textbooks, advertisements, picture books, and graphic novels. Create a noticings–meanings–implications chart (see Figure 6.51 for a simple example). Begin by calling students' attention to the visual and design elements presented in picture books or other multimodal texts. Have them create an inventory of what is represented, and develop a vocabulary for naming and describing the various elements (line, shape, pattern, texture, color, value). In the first column of the chart, have students describe and classify "what we notice" about the elements. In the second column, have students describe what the elements might mean. The third column asks students to consider what the visual elements might imply outside the text in sociocultural contexts.

FIGURE 6.51. Noticings–meanings–implications chart, example.

What We Notice	What It Might Mean	Implications
The use of the color blue.	The person is feeling blue.	Either the artist or the character is feeling sad or depressed.

• Question Guide for Analyzing Visual and Design Elements of a Contemporary Picture Book

SOURCE: Serafini (2011).

PURPOSE: For students to analyze visual and design elements of a picture book (grades 6–12).

PROCEDURE: As the teacher, select several picture books, and choose one of them to model the response to the questions. Then, in small groups, have the students answer the following questions about a different picture book.

- *Book format.* What can you determine about how the book's size, its format (e.g., square, horizontal, vertical), and the materials used in its construction are related to the book's content?
- *Author/artist.* What do you know about the author's and artist's previous work?
- *Cover.* What expectations does the cover (including the title and illustration) set up for you as you approach the book? What does the cover suggest? What media are used in the cover illustrations?
- *Body.* What fonts are used? Where is the text located on the page? How do the text and illustration(s) connect? What do you think of the format of the images and their placement in the picture book? Where is the text located? Within the image? Separated by borders or white space? Are the illustrations spreads, single-page images, collages, overlapping images, or portraits? Do the series of images in the book change over the course of the book? Do they get bigger or smaller? Is there a relationship between form and content? How does the design of the book enhance the content's presentation?
- *Select one illustration.* What are the dominant colors? What effect do they have on you as a reader? Are there any recurring patterns? Are there any anomalous elements (i.e., elements that stick out or seem out of place)? Are they important to consider?
- *Style.* Are the style and artistic choices appropriate? How do they add to the book's meaning? How are the illustrations framed? Are there thick borders or faded edges? How is the story's setting realized in the images? Realistically? Metaphorically?

• Question Guide for Analyzing Visual Structures

SOURCE: Serafini (2011).

PURPOSE: For students to comprehend visual images by analyzing the composition, perspective, and visual symbols.

PROCEDURE: As the teacher, do the following:

1. *Composition.* Explain that **visual composition** is how objects are organized and positioned in a visual image. The arrangement and placement of various objects determine their relative importance and how they interact with other elements in an image. Three compositional techniques that artists and graphic designers use to call attention to particular aspects of an image are (a) the relative size of the object, (b) color and contrast, and (c) foregrounding and focus. Select an image, model the responses to the following questions, and then have students work in groups to answer the questions for different images: What is foregrounded and what is included in the background? What catches your eye first? What are the dominant colors? What effect do they have on you? How is white, or negative, space used? Are the illustrations framed or full-bleed? How does this position you as a viewer? Is the image symmetrical, or does one section (top–bottom, left–right) dominate the image? How does this add to the meaning of the image? What is the artist trying to get you to look at through leading lines, colors, contrast, gestures, and lighting? How are size and scale used? What is large? Why are certain elements larger than others? How does this add to the meaning of the image?
2. *Perspective.* Explain that **visual perspective** is how close or far away a viewer is positioned relative to the objects and participants in an image, and that it affects the viewer's relationship to these visual elements. When the characters or actors in an image are positioned close to the viewer, the viewer tends to feel a strong relationship with them. In contrast, the farther away objects and participants are positioned, the less the viewer can connect to them. Additionally, an artist may depict a particular character or object from straight on (face to face), or above or below the viewers' position. When viewers are positioned to look up at a character, or a character is positioned to look up, they tend to view the character as powerful. In contrast, when viewers are positioned to look down on a character, or a character is positioned to look down, they tend to view the character as less powerful than a character who is looking up. Attending to how perspective is used gives viewers clues to the relationship among characters and objects in a story or image, and the way the viewers are being asked to consider these characters and objects. Select picture books where characters or objects are positioned in various ways. Focus the discussion on how the various perspectives emphasize a particular relationship with different characters. How are readers invited to interact with and understand these characters in different ways, based on the character's positioning? For example, in Chris Van Allsburg's (1988) *Two Bad Ants,* he portrays everything from the ants' perspective. The bad ants are terrified as they land in a huge cup of coffee, are threatened by an enormous garbage disposal, and are nearly electrocuted when they enter an electrical outlet.
3. *Visual symbols.* Explain that visual symbols represent abstract ideas that are common through their use in sociocultural contexts. For example, a rose signifies love or caring, a butterfly signifies transformation, a dove represents peace, and the color red might signify anger. Artists use visual symbols to convey meanings beyond the literal level. Explain that a **motif** is a recurring pattern of symbols or visuals—one that often refers to a theme or particular meaning. For example, color could be a motif. In the book *Miss Nelson Is Missing* (Allard & Marshall, 1997), the mean substitute teacher is wearing black clothes and the images are all in black and white, whereas when Miss Nelson is teaching, everything is bright and in color. The repeated pattern of dark color represents problems. Select picture books that have symbols or motifs. Help students to identify and interpret these symbols and motifs by analyzing their implied or connotative meaning, not just their literal meaning. For example, in J. K. Rowling's (1998) *Harry Potter and*

the Sorcerer's Stone, the use of a snake represents evil, and the symbol of the Slytherin house is a serpent.

Question Guide for Analyzing Media Literacies

SOURCE: Serafini (2011).

PURPOSE: For students to comprehend the visuals in media and advertisements that influence their thoughts, ideas, and actions.

PROCEDURE: As the teacher, do the following:

1. Explain that **media literacy** is the ability to critically understand, question, and evaluate how media work, produce meaning, and provide content (information, news, and entertainment). Individuals may interpret cultural texts differently, depending on their interests and their social and historical contexts (Messaris, 1997). The production techniques of each medium interact with content elements to create meaning (Heiligmann & Shields, 2005).
2. Explain that advertisers use persuasive or propaganda techniques to influence opinions, emotions, attitudes, and behaviors. Be careful not to villainize advertising, as people often have positive feelings about ads and products. Ads help to pay for media products and help consumers make decisions. Advertising presents images of objects that consumers are supposed to desire, people whom consumers are supposed to envy, and a lifestyle that consumers are supposed to emulate (Sturken & Cartwright, 2001). Modern societies produce more goods than are necessary for them to function; therefore, advertising is used to produce the drive and desire to consume products that members of such a society may not necessarily need or want.
3. Select several print, online, and video advertisements. Choose a few to model the response to the following questions. Then have students work in groups to answer the following questions on different advertisements:
   - Consider the *company* that created the advertisement and its possible intentions. (a) What company produced the ad? (b) What does this company primarily sell? (c) What other products does the company sell? (d) Why do you think the company has chosen to advertise its products here? (e) What materials and resources were used to create the ad?
   - Consider the *contents* of the advertisement. (a) What is your first impression? (b) What do you notice first? What seems to stand out for you? (c) What are the visual and textual contents of the ad? (d) Where is the product positioned in the advertisement? (e) What is the "catch" or "hook" for this ad? What concept of the target audience does the advertisement appeal to (e.g., fear, vanity, needs)? What propaganda techniques were used (bandwagon, testimonials, glittering generalities, transfer, card stacking, "plain folks," name calling, stereotyping, fear)?
   - Consider the *context* of the advertisement (where you receive it). (a) Who might buy (magazine), see (billboard), or care about (target audience) this advertisement? (b) Why is the advertisement located where it is? (c) Why are you looking at the images in this context? To get information? To make a purchase? (d) What background knowledge might be necessary to understand the ad? (e) How is the advertisement distributed? Target audiences or general public?

Guiding Questions for Examining Images in Context

SOURCE: Victoria State Government Education and Training (2018).

PURPOSE: For students to use as a guide in discussions about understanding images in context.

PROCEDURE: As the teacher, use the following sequence of questions to guide your discussions. Start by examining an image as a whole. For each question, ask students to expand on their responses by explaining reasons why, and encourage them to use evidence from the image to justify their responses, using visual design language. Through these discussions, different interpretations of the image may emerge which forms the basis for further discussion and exploration.

- Where does this image come from? Is it part of a sequence (e.g., page from a book or website, clip from a film), or does it stand alone (artwork, poster, advertisement)?
- What is its purpose? Who is it for? What is it about?
- What do you think about it? Why? How does it make you feel? Why? What puzzles you? What does it remind you of?
- What connections can you make to other images, texts, and experiences?
- How do you think this image is positioning the viewer? What might be missing from this image? Why has the image maker chosen to show this image this way? How else might this be shown? What difference might this make?

Literal, Inferential, and Evaluative Close Reading of an Image

SOURCE: Victoria State Government Education and Training (2018).

PURPOSE: For students to analyze how visual texts make meaning using Literal, Inferential, and Evaluative (LIE) levels of comprehension.

PROCEDURE: As the teacher, select an image to model the responses to the following questions. Then have students select another image and respond to the same questions.

Level 1. Literal: Locate, recall, and connect. What do you see? The answer is in the image. Justify answers with evidence from the text. (Students search for the information within the text.)

Level 2. Inferential: Infer and interpret. What do you think this means? Why? What evidence in the text supports your answer? (Students use the literal information and combine it with other information from the image or context, as well as their prior knowledge, to make inferences based on this information. This requires close analysis of the text and deeper thinking about this.)

Level 3. Evaluative/applied: Evaluate, generalize, hypothesize, synthesize, think critically, think creatively, and apply to other contexts. What do you think about this? (Students combine the literal and inferential information from the text with other ideas and knowledge to extend thinking beyond the text.)

Analyzing Visual Semiotic Choices

SOURCE: Victoria State Government Education and Training (2018).

PURPOSE: For students to identify how creators of visual images use a range of visual semiotic (meaning-making) choices, including symbols, lines, vectors, and size, to express actions and ideas; to represent the participants (the characters or things/objects seen); to depict the nature of the events; and to describe the circumstances.

PROCEDURE: As the teacher, select images to examine. Model how to respond to the questions, using one image. Then, in small groups, have students answer the questions about other images. For each topic, provide the background information; ask each discussion question; ask students to expand on their responses by explaining reasons why; and encourage them to use evidence from the image to justify their responses, in visual design language.

CONTEXT QUESTIONS: What type of text is this image from? What is this image about? Who and what is in this image? Who are the main participants (characters or things/objects) seen? What is happening? What are different participants/objects doing? Where, when, and why is this happening? What information is provided in the image about the circumstances surrounding these participants and actions?

SYMBOLS—BACKGROUND: Explain that symbols or signs can be used as shortcuts to represent ideas or concepts. Symbolic aspects can include choices of casting, hair design, makeup, costumes, props, and objects. They can also include icons. For example, the Eiffel Tower is a symbol often used to represent the city of Paris; heart symbols are used to represent love; and the color red is used to symbolize danger, or perhaps romance, depending on the context. Symbols can also be used to present concepts and information in diagrams, graphs, timelines, and other types of visual information texts.

SYMBOLS—DISCUSSION QUESTIONS: What things do you see in this image that you recognize from somewhere else? Why has the image maker chosen to use these symbols? What might this mean for what is happening in this image?

LINES—BACKGROUND: Explain that choices about use of line in an image include straight or curved, length, angle, intersection of vertical and horizontal lines, and direction. Lines are used in images to indicate movement and direction. Lines can be natural (formed by objects in the image) or artificial (created by the image maker through, e.g., using subject gaze or pointing).

LINES—DISCUSSION QUESTIONS: What sort of lines do you see in this image? Are these lines formed by natural objects in the image or created by the image maker? Where do the lines take your eye? What information does this use of straight/curved/intersecting lines give the audience about the circumstances of this situation? Why has the image maker chosen to use these lines like this? How would meaning change if these straight/curved/intersecting lines were replaced with a different type of line?

VECTORS—BACKGROUND: Explain that a vector shows action and direction in an image through lines. A vector can be a visible line (e.g., a line used to indicate direction). A vector can indicate movement in a still image; for instance, arrows in a diagram or sets of lines can indicate that an object or animal is moving. A vector can also be created by using the line of a shadow or an object, a subject's gaze or eyeline, or a pointing arm or finger.

VECTORS—DISCUSSION QUESTIONS: What sort of vectors do you see in this image? Are these vectors formed by natural objects in the image or created by the image maker? What information does this use of vectors give the audience about the circumstances surrounding these participants and actions?

SIZE—BACKGROUND: Explain that making choices about the sizes of objects in an image is a comparative process.

SIZE—DISCUSSION QUESTIONS: How big is something in the image in relation to something else? What information does this use of size give the audience about the circumstances of this situation? Why has the image maker chosen to use size like this? What might this mean? How would meaning in this image change if the size of the objects changed or were reversed?

Interacting and Relating with Others through Images

SOURCE: Victoria State Government Education and Training (2018).

PURPOSE: For students to learn that creators of images make visual design choices to build relationships and interactions between/among the participants in the images.

PROCEDURE: As the teacher, explain that the creator of an image makes visual design choices to build relationships and interactions between/among the participants in the image—the creator, the audience, and the subjects (the characters or main things/objects in the image). The creator also makes visual design choices to express knowledge, skills, trustworthiness, power/status, attitudes, feelings, and opinions. For example, the creator makes choices that can establish a particular attitude or point of view about the topic or subject, and tries to align the audience with this position. For each question below, ask students to expand on their responses by explaining reasons why, and encourage them to use evidence from the image to justify their responses, in visual design language.

1. As the audience, how are you positioned to see and interact with the subject(s) in this image?
   - Who are you positioned to see this image as? (focalizer)
   - How close or far away is the subject to you? (social distance)
   - Is the subject looking directly at you or away from you? (gaze)
   - Is the subject turned toward or away from you?
   - Does the subject appear to have the same level of power as you, more power, or less power in this interaction?
2. How do these design choices affect how you feel about the subject(s) and what is happening in this image?

Chapter 7

Writing Composition and Visual Representation

UNDERSTANDING WRITING COMPOSITION AND VISUAL REPRESENTATION

Writing composition is the "process or result of arranging ideas to form a clear and unified impression in order to create an effective message" (Harris & Hodges, 1995, p. 38). Writing is essential to life: It gives voice to people's inner thoughts, empowers them to interact with the world, and provides a form of communication that can transcend time. It is necessary to have a strong foundation in writing in order to be successful in school, in life, and in most careers. As Routman (2005) states, "I want students to write with passion and ease. I want them to be motivated, confident writers who see writing as an everyday, useful, even enjoyable tool" (p. 1). Writing instruction is sometimes neglected in the teaching curriculum, especially if it is not tested. In the *Standards for the Preparation of Literacy Professionals 2017*, the International Literacy Association (2018) has embraced the need for effective instruction in writing and visually representing, in addition to the other modalities.

Visually representing is the communication of ideas and information through the creation and sharing of static or moving visual images. Static forms of visual images can include two-dimensional photographs, drawings, paintings, comics, graphs, maps, and diagrams, as well as three-dimensional models, sculptures, or dioramas. Moving forms of visual representation include video presentations, multimedia presentations, interactive web designs, and performing arts. The creator needs to consider how the visual elements and principles of design are used together to communicate meaning within the visual or by integrating visuals with text.

Understanding Emergent Writing and Drawing

Emergent writing is what takes place when "children begin to understand that writing is a form of communication and their marks on the paper convey a message" (Mayer, 2007, p. 35). During emergent writing, children learn what the functions of writing are, how to write letters and words, and how to write phrases and sentences to communicate a message. Children learn that what they think and say can be written down, and that what they write can be read by others. They learn that print moves from left to right and from top to bottom, and that it carries a message. They learn that there are spaces between words, and that letters are formed in specific ways and represent sounds. Children learn that print conventions (punctuation, capital letters, size of print) help readers interpret a writer's meaning. Through emergent writing, children refine their understanding of the written language system (Jensen, 1984), which helps them communicate their ideas in written form.

Stages of Early Writing Development

There are five basic stages of early writing development. These writing stages encompass the meaning of the message and therefore should not be confused with spelling stages (see Chapter 4).

- **Stage 1: Awareness, exploration, or role-play writing, drawing, and scribbling.** Children at this stage make random marks and scribbles. Then scribbling begins to resemble writing, and letter-like forms emerge, sometimes randomly placed. They learn to hold and use writing tools as adults do. They begin to tell about their writing and drawing.

- **Stage 2: Emergent or experimental writing.** Children scribble with some legible letters, begin to form letter strings, and are developing some sound–letter relationships. They usually use capital letters. They generally have not begun spacing. Their writing is more purposeful, and they can tell others more about what they wrote.

- **Stage 3: Transitional or early writing.** Children begin to use letter–sound relationships for writing initial consonant sounds in words, and later final and medial sounds. They begin to see the differences between a letter and a word, but still may not leave space between words. They may mix uppercase and lowercase letters. They then begin to write words using letters to represent each sound that is heard, correctly spelling some sight words and spelling other words phonemically. The words make sense and may be used for writing longer texts. They also begin to use punctuation and write sentences that tell ideas. A message matches a picture.

- **Stage 4: Conventional writing.** The writing shows individuality, is focused on a topic, and makes sense. Children write complete ideas and use standard forms of writing. Their writing is readable, and they approach conventional spelling patterns. Children are becoming familiar with most aspects of the writing process and are able to select forms to suit different purposes. Their control of structure, punctuation, and spelling may vary according to the complexity of the writing task.

- **Stage 5: Proficient writing.** Writers have developed a personal style of writing and are able to manipulate forms of writing to suit their purposes. They have control over spelling and punctuation. They choose from a large vocabulary, and their writing is cohesive, coherent, and satisfying. They are able to write complete organized paragraphs, using complex sentence structures, appropriate transitions, and a variety of sentence types. They can compose a variety of essays, letters, reports, poetry, and plays for specific purposes.

Stages of Drawing Development

The four stages of children's drawing include the scribble, preschematic, schematic, and preteen stages (Steel, 1997). In the **scribble stage**, the scribbles are random, and children explore art materials in a playful way. The scribbles move from uncontrolled to progressively more controlled. A child may point to some of the scribbles and name them. In the **preschematic stage**, at about ages 3–5, the drawings become more complex, although they are usually unrealistic. Children will tend to use their favorite colors, rather than to represent objects in accurate colors. Drawings of people are very simple, with few features. Objects in drawings float in space and are not anchored. A person is often drawn with an oversized head on a small body with extended arms. In the **schematic stage**, at about ages 5–8, children's drawings of people become more proportional and more detailed. The colors become more realistic and stereotypical (e.g., grass is green, the sky is blue). The skyline and ground lines start to show. Children develop schemata about ways of drawing. For example, a house will be drawn the same way in many drawings. Children will often create stories to go along with their drawings. By the **preteen stage**, at about ages 9–11, drawings become far more detailed, and much more spatial perspective is evident. Children at this stage may become very frustrated if they are unable to create realistic pictures.

Understanding Text Composition

Composing and comprehending are interrelated processes. The more students use reading, writing, and visuals together, the more they learn, and the more effectively they are able to communicate their ideas. Understanding text and visual composition, as well as the writing and graphic design process, is necessary to create coherent texts and visuals. During writing, an author needs to make decisions about the content, purpose, text type, genre, text structure, writer's craft, format, and layout. The **content** is what the author wants to communicate; it often requires research to make sure that the information is detailed and accurately represents ideas. The **purposes** of writing are often summarized in four categories: to inform, persuade, explain, and entertain. However, Graham and Perin (2007) have identified additional purposes with examples:

1. Communicating with others (personal letters, business letters, notes, cards, email, texting).
2. Informing others (writing reports; explaining how to do something; describing an event, object, or place).
3. Persuading others (expressing an opinion about a controversial topic).
4. Learning content material (writing to summarize, analyze, and evaluate information; learning logs; journal entries).
5. Entertaining others (writing stories, plays, poems).
6. Reflecting about self (writing about personal events, autobiography, diary).
7. Responding to literature (book evaluations, analyzing authors' intentions).
8. Demonstrating knowledge (classroom tests, high-stakes tests involving writing).

Text Types

The narrative, descriptive, expository, and persuasive **text types** describe the variety, conventions, and purposes of the major kinds of writing. **Narrative writing** describes a sequence of fictional or nonfictional events in the form of a story. **Descriptive writing** provides vivid details of a person, place, object, event, and or feeling in a way that can be clearly seen in the reader's mind. This type of writing enables the reader to feel whatever is being described by using the senses of sight, smell, touch, hearing, taste, and emotion. **Expository writing** is a mode of writing in which the purpose of the author is to inform, explain, describe, or define a subject to the reader. The content is presented as fact, and the author often researches the topic to gain specific information. Examples include essays, journals, documentaries, histories, scientific papers, biographies, textbooks, technical manuals, legal and medical documents, articles, and other reference materials. **Persuasive writing** is designed to convince the reader to believe or do something; the writer argues a case from a particular point of view, often taking a position for or against an issue. There are three types of persuasive writing: appealing to reason, using facts and proof to convince the reader; appealing to emotion, using heart and the writer's sense of what is right to convince the reader; and appealing to character, using the qualities and virtues of personal character to appeal to the reader. Examples of persuasive writing include speeches, advertisements, and some business letters. These text types differ in their purpose, organizational structure, language use, and format (see Table 7.1).

As discussed to some extent in earlier chapters, **genres** are categories of literature or other forms of art or entertainment that follow agreed-upon characteristics, structures, or organization. Works may fit the criteria for a single genre or multiple genres. Genres can change or develop over time. In literature, two major genres are **fiction** (texts describing imaginary events and/or characters) and **nonfiction** (texts describing true or real things, people, events, and places). Examples of genres within fiction include folklore, fairy tales, legends, fantasy, mystery, horror, humor, science fiction, historical fiction, realistic fiction, short stories, drama, and poetry. Genres within nonfiction include biographies, essays, speeches, textbooks, works of reference, reports, instructional manuals, and other disciplinary texts. For characteristics or elements of the genres, refer to websites such as *https://literary-devices.com/literary-genres*. Learning to comprehend in a given genre supports composition in that same genre, and vice versa. It is important to make explicit the elements of each genre as they are taught during the reading process; this allows students to become successful in including these elements during writing. The ideas in a text should be organized in logical ways, based on genre and text structures.

Text Structure

Text structure refers to how the information within a text is organized. Narratives typically follow a story grammar or narrative plot structure that includes the sequential parts of a story, such as characters, setting, problem, plot, and resolution. Most narratives have **a linear or chronological structure.** It can include flashbacks, but most of the narrative is told in the order in which it occurs. There is also a **nonlinear** or **fractured structure,** in which the story is not in chronological order and jumps throughout time, sometimes switching between characters at different points of time. In a **circular structure,** the story ends where it began; often the characters go through transformations that are brought about or affected by the events. In a **parallel structure,** the story follows multiple story lines, which are tied together through an event, character, or theme. In an **interactive structure,** the reader makes choices leading to new options and alternate endings, as in "choose your own adventure" stories.

TABLE 7.1. Writing Text Types and Elements

Type	Elements
Narrative	To tell a story with a beginning, middle, and end. **Introductory paragraph:** Captures the reader's attention and introduces the characters and the setting. **Development paragraph(s):** Gives details about the characters and what's happening to them, builds the plot, and leads to the point of the story. **Concluding paragraph:** Summarizes the story, expresses a reaction to the events, offers an opinion, or reaches a conclusion.
Descriptive	To create vivid images in journaling, poetry, song lyrics. **Introductory paragraph:** Gets the reader's attention, uses vivid details to introduce the setting, creates the mood, and provides an overview. **Development paragraph(s):** Focuses on the details of one event, appealing to the reader's senses. **Concluding paragraph:** Builds to a conclusion.
Expository	To present facts, explain ideas, or give directions. **Introductory paragraph:** Defines the topic, states the thesis, and provides an overview. **Development paragraph(s):** Explains the process and gives supporting facts, details, and examples; uses key words to identify the text structure. **Concluding paragraph:** Restates or supports the topic or thesis and draws a conclusion.
Persuasive	To convince the reader to support a certain point of view. **Introductory paragraph:** States the purpose, identifies the audience, introduces the subject, includes the status of the writer, provides two reasons in support of the idea, and provides the opinion of the author. **Development paragraph(s):** Gives the topic sentence for the first reason of support, includes several sentences explaining the reason and then restating the reason; includes subsequent paragraphs for the second and third reasons. **Concluding paragraph:** Includes a sentence that restates the topic, a sentence or two that supports this reason, and a summary of the author's opinion and a conclusion.
Short report, book report, research paper, newspaper article	To share information learned. Gather resources, take notes, group notes by topic, make an outline with headings, and sequence notes to put in outline. **Introductory paragraph:** Introduces the topic, the audience, and the author's reason for writing about it; defines the topic and answers "who, what, where, when, and why"; includes a conclusion sentence that provides a transition from the introduction to the development paragraphs. **Development paragraph:** Provides details and cites the specific sources of information. **Concluding paragraph:** Restates the topic, explains the up-to-date status of the topic or what was learned so far and what the author hopes to learn in the future, provides the author's personal view and conclusion. **Bibliography:** An alphabetical list by authors of the resources used in writing the report.
Friendly letter, business letter	To communicate in a friendly letter or thank-you note. It can also be a business letter asking for information, requesting something, or making a complaint; or a cover letter for an application. Return address, date line, inside address, greeting. **Introductory paragraph:** Explains why the author is writing. **Development paragraph(s):** Develops ideas. **Concluding paragraph:** Summarizes what the author wants the reader to know or do; closing and signature block.

Expository texts include one or more text structures, such as description, sequence or process, problem–solution, cause–effect, and compare–contrast. A persuasive text structure includes an introduction with a thesis or opinion, reasons, evidence, and a conclusion. The narrative, expository, and persuasive text structures have been described in detail in Chapter 6.

Writer's Craft

Writer's craft is the art of writing by intentionally using text structure, text features, sentence structure, stylistic devices, dialogue, word choice, word placement, imagery, details, and figurative language to create an effect on the reader. Writer's craft includes style, tone, voice, audience awareness, structure/organization, and technique (Laminack, 2007; Wood Ray, 1999). There are four basic craft categories: word craft, structural craft, audible craft, and visual craft (Laminack, 2007; Wood Ray, 1999). **Word craft** is the careful deliberate choice of words, including details, imagery, interesting words, vivid verbs, and figurative language. **Structural craft** includes text structure, paragraph types, transitional devices, parallel structure, and repetition of words or phrases. **Audible craft** includes alliteration, assonance, onomatopoeia, rhythm, cadence, and hard–soft sounds. **Visual craft** includes print features (bold, italics, fonts, punctuation, and text shaped to match meaning), line breaks, white space, and graphics (pictures, illustrations, charts, maps, etc.).

In addition to the typical narrative and expository text structures, Wood Ray (1999) has described the craft of other, less typical text structures: circular texts, texts with thread-backs, seesaw texts, framing-question texts, conversation texts, texts embedded with response, "time flies" texts, texts where time is a constant but settings change, narrative poem texts, thematic poem texts, lyrical fact texts, alphabet texts, vignette texts with repeating lines or phrases, two-part texts changing situation, shifting focus or perspective, "story within a story" texts, inanimate voice texts, photo-poetry, photo-narratives, cumulative texts, multigenre texts, participation texts, geographical texts, texts that borrow a structure from nature, and repeated/wraparound paragraph structures. Teachers should start collecting examples of these structures to share as mentor texts for students' writing. Wood Ray (1999) explains that the different kinds of writing serve different purposes for different audiences and have typical features in common; the language used is crafted in particular ways; the words and illustrations hold consistent meaning over time; different publishing formats have particular features writers use to make meaning; and writers use graphics, layout, and written text to make meaning.

Text Format and Layout

Text format and layout must also be considered in creating books. Print books, especially for children, may include such formats as board books, pop-up books, flap books, peek-through books, and flip-flop books (two texts in two halves of a book, one turned 180 degrees from the other one). They can also include picture books with illustrations dominating every page; books for early readers (ages 5–8) with large font and fewer pictures; chapter books with limited illustrations; comic books; and graphic novels. Books can be a variety of shapes and sizes; they can be vertical, horizontal, square, or in a shape related to the content. The texts can be in the form of newspapers, magazines, or brochures. Decisions need to be made about the organizational features, such as table of contents, glossary, index, or menus and hyperlinks in electronic texts. The author needs to determine what visuals and graphics are needed to support the meaning of the text. The author and designer also need to consider the layout of how the type, images, graphics, color and white space come together, so that the book not only looks good but is also functional and effective at communicating ideas, information, or emotion. The layout includes deciding on the different levels of headings and subheadings, which can be distinguished from each other by size, font, style, and color to communicate a hierarchy. Words can also be emphasized with bold, italics, capitalization, or text effects. The size and location of the text body, captions, graphics, and illustrations need to be considered, along with the amount of white space between the lines, the margins, the columns, and the graphics. The graphic and text elements need to be visually aligned.

Understanding the Writing Process

The **writing process** is a series of actions required to produce a coherent written text, including prewriting activities, producing a first draft, revising, editing, conferring, revising subsequent drafts, and publishing. These actions have been described in detail by Graves (1983) and Calkins (1983). The complete writing process approach includes publishing one's writing; however, not all writing must go through all stages of the writing process. Students should select those pieces that are most meaningful to them to take all the way through the publishing stage.

During **prewriting** activities, students identify the purpose and audience for writing, identify the genre and text type, brainstorm ideas for writing, make a graphic organizer of major ideas, and/or sequence ideas in an outline. During the **first draft** stage, students may want to write their ideas on every other line to allow room for revising and editing, or to save drafts in different files. Upon completion of the draft, they may read it aloud and then research more ideas and details on the topic. During **revising**, students reread multiple times while focusing on the revision of ideas, organization, voice, word choice, and sentence fluency. They add, delete, rearrange, or substitute ideas. Once they are satisfied with the content, they enter the **editing** stage, where they edit for grammar/usage, paragraphing, punctuation, capitalization, and spelling. In the **conferring** stage, each student shares their writing with a partner and gets feedback. The partner needs to be instructed to look for the revision of ideas first and then the editing of conventions. The writer reflects on and **revises subsequent drafts** based on their own and the peer's evaluation. The writer rereads in order to refine writing and uses an editing checklist to complete a final edit of content and mechanics. The writer shares the writing with a partner again and then with the teacher to get feedback. Final revisions are made in preparation for publishing. During the **publishing** stage, students type or rewrite their compositions in their finest handwriting and then illustrate them or add graphics (maps, charts, diagrams, etc.). If their compositions are multiple pages in length, students can create a cover, title page, and any organizational features that seem needed (table of contents, glossary, index, etc.). In paper texts, they can add any publishing format features such as flaps, peek-throughs, and pop-ups, and choose from a variety of binding techniques. Finally, students share their writing orally, display it, or publish it online for an audience. This is the basic model of the writing process; however, depending on the genre and style of writing, specific criteria may need to be added to the process.

Understanding Visual Composition

Visual composition refers to how such elements of art and design as "line, shape, color, value, texture, form and space are organized . . . according to the principles of balance, contrast, emphasis, movement, pattern, rhythm, unity/variety to give the visual structure and convey the intent" of the artist or composer" (Boddy-Evans, 2019, p. 1). Taheri (2018) has described these basic elements of design:

1. A *line* is a stroke of a pen or any connected two points. Lines are useful for dividing spaces and drawing the eye to a specific location.
2. *Color* can stand alone, be used as a background, or be applied to other elements (such as lines, shapes, textures, or typography). Color creates a mood.
3. *Shapes*, geometric or organic, add interest, and they are often used to emphasize a portion of the page. Creators need to think about how the elements of their design are creating shapes, and how the shapes are interacting. The creator can also add repeated geometric or organic patterns.
4. *Space*—negative space, or the parts that are left blank—helps to create the overall image. Negative spaces can also create shapes.
5. *Texture*, even in two-dimensional websites and graphic design, can create a more three-dimensional appearance.
6. *Typography*, the fonts creators use, tell readers what's important. A variety of fonts can be used to make the text look distinctive and memorable.
7. The *scale and size* of the objects, shapes, type, and other elements add interest and emphasis.

The principles of art and design as identified and explained by Boddy-Evans (2019), Rosengren (2016), and Stribley (2019) are summarized in Table 7.2.

WRITING COMPOSITION AND VISUAL REPRESENTATION: GOALS

As in previous chapters, goals that are part of the Common Core State Standards are indicated by (CCSS) in parentheses.

Emergent Writing Goals

Students will do the following:

- Draw pictures to communicate information.
- Dictate stories for others to write.
- Write letters to represent sounds in words.
- Write letters and words from left to right.
- Return to the left for the next line, using the return sweep.
- Use proper spacing between letters and words.
- Use resources to spell words.
- Write phrases to communicate ideas.
- Write using sentence frames or patterned sentences.
- Write using transitional spelling, with letters representing every sound.

TABLE 7.2. Principles of Art and Design

Principle with guiding question	Example in photography	
Unity: Do all the parts of the composition feel as if they belong together?		 Gazelle photo by Erik Rosengren.
Focus: Does the viewer's eye rest on the most important part of the image? In the rule of thirds, the design or image should be divided into three rows and three columns. Is the focal point where the lines meet at one or more points? Does the image show impact with action, bright colors, lighting? Does it tell a story?	 Photos by Erik Rosengren.	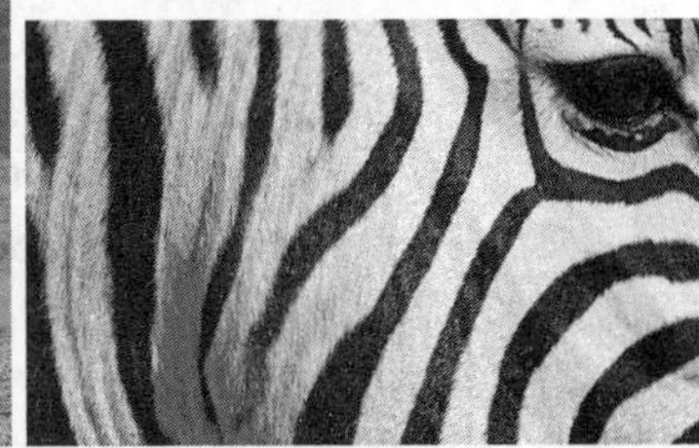
Balance: Is it symmetrical to create a calm, clean, or elegant impression, or asymmetrical to create a dynamic feeling?		
Movement: Is the viewer drawn to the subject by leading lines? Are there leading lines (actual or implied) to direct the viewer toward the subject or into the art? Is there a sense of movement in the subject, with some parts blurry?		
Rhythm: Do the viewer's eyes travel easily from one component to another, often from the use of lines or color? Think of Vincent van Gogh's sky in "The Starry Night."		

(continued)

TABLE 7.2. *(continued)*

Principle with guiding question	Example in photography 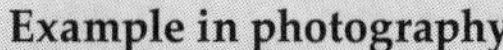
Pattern: Is there a repetition of lines, shapes, colors, or values? In typography, are typefaces, line weights, and colors repeated throughout to tie everything together?	 
Contrast: Is there a strong or slight contrast between light and dark, shape, color, size, texture, and types of lines?	 
Proportion: How do objects fit together and relate to each other in terms of size, scale, and depth of field?	 

Note. All photos by the author, except as noted by Erik Rosengren, her father.

- Write high-frequency words correctly.
- Write sentences with initial capitalization and end punctuation.
- Write for a variety of purposes.
- Write more complete sentences.
- Write stories of three sentences on one topic.
- Begin to recognize mistakes in content and conventions.

Writing Composition Goals

Students will do the following:

- Read with a writer's perspective, and apply that knowledge to their own writing.
- Write for a specific audience and with a meaningful purpose.

- Compose writing of different genres and text types (narrative, descriptive, expository, persuasive).
- Write informative/explanatory texts to examine a topic and convey ideas and information clearly. (CCSS)
- Write informational or explanatory texts by introducing, developing, and concluding a topic in a logical manner; include headings and visuals to aid comprehension; and use precise language and domain-specific vocabulary. (CCSS)
- Produce clear and coherent writing in which the development and organization are appropriate to task, purpose, and audience. (CCSS)
- Demonstrate daily functional writing, such as making lists, making notes, completing forms, and writing thank-you cards.
- Compose personal and dialogue journals, stories, poems, and songs.
- Compose writing to demonstrate comprehension of a text or concept, such as content journals, note taking, book reports, and responses to essay questions.
- Compose writing to share or request information: letters, emails, invitations, directions, reports, presentations, newsletters, speeches, persuasive essays, and webpages.
- Use story grammar elements, such as character, setting, problem, and solution.
- Use narrative plot structures of exposition, rising action, climax, falling action, and resolution.
- Use such text structures as description, sequencing, problem–solution, cause–effect, and compare–contrast.
- Use different aspects of writer's craft and different language structures, such as figurative language, dialogue, sensory descriptions, humor, and point of view.
- Use prewriting strategies such as drawing, brainstorming, diagramming or outlining, and sharing to select and narrow topic.
- Use drafting strategies such as elaborating on ideas by providing details, support, and descriptions of people, places, objects, processes, and events, and adding details in complete sentences.
- With guidance and support from peers and adults, develop and strengthen writing as needed by planning, revising, and editing. (CCSS)
- Use revising strategies such as adding, deleting, organizing and substituting words and sentences.
- Write ideas and details clearly, in an organized manner, using appropriate transitions.
- Use voice in writing to fit purpose and audience, such as tone (friendly, formal, distant), word choice (descriptive words, precise words, discipline-specific words), sentence patterns, and personal style.
- Write using varied, specific, and interesting nouns, verbs, adjectives, and adverbs.
- Write using a variety of sentence structures, such as compound, complex, declarative, interrogative, and exclamatory.
- Use editing strategies to check for appropriate grammar, punctuation, capitalization, spelling, and legible handwriting.
- Use text features (headings, captions, typography, etc.).
- Use graphic features (images, illustrations, graphs, charts, photography, etc.).
- Use organizational features (table of contents, glossary, index, etc.).
- Use different text formats and layout features.
- Share writing orally or make it available for others to read, such as by publishing for the classroom, library, family, community, newspaper, or internet.

Visual Representation Goals

Students will do the following:

- Create meaningful visuals (illustrations, photographs, charts, graphs, maps, videos, websites, models, theater sets, etc.), either to convey information on their own or to support textual information.
- Use a variety of media to create two- and three-dimensional visuals (e.g., crayons, paint, colored pencils, clay, craft materials, photographs, digitally created graphics, video).
- Integrate visuals with other information in print and digital texts.
- Use such design elements as line, color, shape, space, texture, typography, and scale to create two- and three-dimensional, static and dynamic (moving) graphics and arts.
- Use such design principles as balance, contrast, emphasis, movement, pattern, rhythm, and unity–variety to give visuals structure and convey their intent.
- Use digital and web design tools with static and dynamic content, and with navigation menus and hyperlinks.
- Use photo, video, and audio editing tools.

WRITING COMPOSITION AND VISUAL REPRESENTATION: ASSESSMENTS

Writing composition and visual representation can be assessed and evaluated in many ways. Unless an assessment is for diagnostic purposes, it is important that students be provided with the criteria for the assessment. There can be ongoing informal assessment of the sort that would occur during writing conferences or written feedback, where positive and constructive feedback can be provided. Self-evaluation can occur as students interact with their own work, as they use checklists provided by the teacher, or as they share their writing or presentations with their peers. Analytic assessment can be used by providing criteria for such elements as content, organization, and mechanics. Formative assessment can be used to improve current and ongoing compositions, whereas summative assessment can be used to identify the quality of writing in completed compositions that were independently written, revised, and edited.

• Emergent Writing Stage Assessment

PURPOSE: To document the emergent writing behaviors of a student, from exploring with writing materials to writing complete sentences; to identify the student's emergent writing stage. I developed the *Emergent Writing Stage Assessment* (see Appendix, pp. 462–465) with descriptors based on Beaty (1994) and Morrow (2005) (grades K–1 or as needed).

PROCEDURE: As the teacher, observe and collect several writing samples from the student. Read each of the descriptors in the checklist and evaluate it, using a plus sign (+) to indicate that the student exhibited this behavior frequently, a checkmark (✓) to indicate that the behavior was sometimes exhibited, or a minus sign (–) to indicate that the student rarely or never exhibited this behavior. There are five stages of emergent writing development, as described earlier in this chapter. Kindergarten includes stages 1–4, and the typical expectation for the end of first grade is stage 5. The stage with the most checkmarks or plus signs is the student's emergent writing stage. Review the student's specific areas of strength and need in writing, and plan instruction to reinforce the strengths and develop the areas of need. Add comments to record clarifying information. See the example in Figure 7.1.

FIGURE 7.1. *Emergent Writing Stage Assessment,* example and analysis for a grade 1 student in stage 4.

Score +, ✓, –	Descriptor	Date Observed and Comments
Stage 4		
CONTENT		
+	Wrote on a self-selected topic.	10/20 journal: *I GO 2 thɘ* PK W MI DG
✓	Communicated a clear message.	Somewhat clear except missing sounds
+	Illustrations matched text.	10/20 drew a picture of herself and her dog
SENTENCE STRUCTURE		
✓	Wrote one sentence with at least four words.	10/20 wrote letters for eight words
CAPITALIZATION/PUNCTUATION		
–	Used some correct capitalization.	10/20 wrote mostly capital letters
–	Used some correct end punctuation.	10/20 no punctuation
SPELLING		
✓	Wrote short sentences using inventive spelling.	10/20 wrote 2/to, PK/park, MI/my, DG/dog
✓	Wrote his/her name and some sight words correctly.	10/20 wrote name, *I*, *GO*, and *the*
✓	Wrote words with beginning and ending consonant sounds.	10/20 3/5 words had correct beginning and ending sounds
–	Wrote each word with a vowel sound.	10/20 only *I*, *GO*, *the* had vowels
✓	Used some written resources for spelling.	Wrote *the* using the word wall
HANDWRITING		
✓	All letters were recognizable.	10/20 all letters except ɘ/e
–	Mostly wrote within lines.	Did not write within the lines
✓	Wrote from left to right.	Wrote left to right, but not return sweep
–	Used some spacing between words.	Limited spacing

Analysis: This assessment evaluated several first-grade journal writing entries. Based on the descriptors, her writing is at stage 3. She wrote *IGO 2 thɘ* PK W MI DG, transcribed as "I go to the park with my dog." When evaluating her content, she communicated a message, and her picture and text matched. She communicated a complete thought, even though it wasn't a sentence and she did not use any punctuation. She wrote her ideas with letters representing many of the initial and final consonant sounds. She used the word wall to spell the word *the*. While she represented some of the sounds in words, she did not represent all of the sounds in the words *with* and *dog*. She wrote uppercase letters in the middle of words. Her handwriting was mostly recognizable with an upside-down e. She did not use consistent spacing between her words.

Instructional Implications: This student needs to be praised for writing a complete idea and having her picture match her writing. She needs daily opportunities to practice communicating her ideas using inventive spelling. During journal writing, she should be encouraged to sound out each word and write the letters for the sounds she hears. Provide sound boxes for each of the common unknown words to help her include vowel sounds. Initially select phonetically regular words, such as *to* and *zoo*, from her journal, and have her say a letter that could represent each sound. To write the words with lowercase letters, provide an alphabet strip with lower- and uppercase letters. Have her find each lowercase letter on the strip and copy it to write the words in her sentence. Use a familiar book to show her that the first letter of every sentence has an uppercase letter and that there is a period at the end of every statement. Have her select her favorite journal page to rewrite.

Writing Composition Assessment Summary

PURPOSE: To analyze a student's writing for ideas, organization, voice, sentence fluency, word choice, and conventions. It provides diagnostic and progress-monitoring data about how the student is able to communicate in writing. These data can be used to provide specific feedback on areas of strength and areas for growth, and to plan writing conferences or mini-lessons.

PROCEDURE: The *Writing Composition Assessment Summary* (see Appendix, pp. 466–467) provides a summary of the student's specific strengths and areas for growth in writing. As the teacher, select a genre and a prompt for the students to write about such as one of the following:

- For a narrative sample: "Write about an important event in your life."
- For an expository sample: "Write about a specific topic or how to make or do something."
- For a persuasive sample: "Write about what you would like to change."
- For a descriptive sample: "Write a poem or song about something you like."

For grades K–1, ask each student to draw a picture with details of what they want to write first, talk about it, and then write about it. For older students, provide the *Writing Composition Assessment Summary* form as a reference, so the students know the criteria that they will be evaluated on, including content and conventions. Give the selected prompt and then say, "I want you to think about an event or topic you know well." Ask the students to do prewriting and brainstorming, and/or to talk about their topics. Make notes of what they say and write, or changes they make throughout the writing process. Say, "Now explain it in writing with as much detail as possible. Please write on every other line. When you are done, please reread it and make any additions or changes to help the reader understand what you wrote." Although this is not a timed assessment, students should be encouraged to continue to write or revise for an allotted time, based on their grade (grades K–1, 15 minutes; grades 2–3, 30 minutes; grades 4–5, 45 minutes; and grades 6–12, 1 hour) or developmental ability. Because writing (especially emergent writing) may be difficult to read, have each student read what they have written while you transcribe what the student says on a separate paper, and note any revisions or editing the student makes. Ask students to title their pieces, if they haven't already.

ANALYSIS: In the left column for each writing element, write a plus sign (+) if it was excellent, a checkmark (✓) if it was satisfactory, or a minus sign (–) if it needed improvement or was incomplete. Use the *Writing Composition Rubric for Writer, Peer, or Teacher* (described on page 311) for criteria guidelines. In the right column, write details and examples for each element. In the analysis, indicate areas of strength or areas for improvement. Also write comments about the length of the writing and any evidence of prewriting or revisions. Additional notes can be made if the handwriting is a concern; the *Handwriting Rubric Assessment* (see Appendix, p. 428) also may be used. An evaluation of these data is used to plan lessons to develop each student's writing further. This writing composition can be used as a rough draft; then, after instruction, it can be edited and revised as a published piece of writing. In addition, this assessment can be repeated, such as at the end of every grading period, to identify areas of growth and need in the student's writing. Figure 7.2 provides a *Writing Composition Assessment Summary* example.

FIGURE 7.2. *Writing Composition Assessment Summary,* example and analysis.

Title or Topic: Unstated topic: *Going down the hill on a bike.*	
Score	**Writing Trait**
Content	
–	Ideas and Details: He had four events that he described with some detail, but he did not write a complete story.
–	Organization/Text Structure: He had the beginning of the story, a lead-up to an event but it didn't occur, and no ending.
✓	Voice: He described a personal event that happened to him with some detail, but with limited emotion.
✓	Sentence Fluency: His sentences flowed from one to another. He had one fragment: *As I wos going down the hill.*
✓	Word Choice: He used several adjectives (*both, front, motor*). He added a description of what he sounded like.
Conventions	
✓	Grammar: Correct except for *I staer did doing a front flip.*
✓	Punctuation: All correct except for the sentence fragment starting with "As . . ."
✓	Capitalization: All correct except for the sentence fragment starting with "As . . ."
–	Spelling: Most spelling mistakes were decodable but common words: *wos/was*; *bowt/both*; *tier/tire*; *mack/make*; *sawnd/sound*; *moter/moter*; *sicol/cycle*; *with owt/without*; *hamit/helmet*. One misspelling affected the meaning of the sentence: *staer/started.*

Length: Number of sentences: 4 Number of paragraphs: 1 (incomplete)

Average number of words per sentence 10 Appropriate length for topic (yes or no): No

Evidence of prewriting: He briefly talked about doing a front flip on his bike.

Evidence of revision and editing: He correctly changed *go* to *going* and *dawn* to *down*. He added new descriptive information *like a motor sicol* and changed *with a* to *with out*.

Writing Composition: One day I wos on a hill. As I was go (^ing) dawn (down) the hill. I had bowt feet on the front tier to mack it sawnd. (^ like a moter sicol) I staer did doing a front flip with a owt a hamit.

Transcription: One day I was on a hill. As I was going down the hill, I had both feet on the front tire to make it sound like a motorcycle. I started doing a front flip without a helmet.

Analysis of Content and Conventions: In his writing, this student communicated ideas about an event, using the voice of a personal narrative. His sentences flowed from one idea to the next and included some adjectives, such as *both, front,* and *motor*. The plot of the story was beginning to be developed. He did not include a strong introduction, and the story ended abruptly without a resolution. He did not explain to the reader that he was on a bicycle. He did some revision by adding information that the sound was like a motorcycle. He generally wrote with correct grammar, except for *staer/started* and one sentence fragment. He included descriptive words and some complex sentence structures with prepositional phrases. He corrected the verb tense from *go* to *going* and corrected the spelling from *dawn* to *down*. He correctly spelled a few common words, but did not correctly spell many others.

Instructional Implications: Instruction should begin with rereading the story orally to see if everything makes sense. Select a narrative story to use as a mentor text to model the story structure with a beginning, middle, and end and the development of ideas. Have the student revise this initial piece, because it is a good beginning. Phonics and spelling instruction should focus on teaching vowels, vowel diphthongs, and r-controlled vowels. He can then edit the story for conventions.

Writing Composition Rubric for Writer, Peer, or Teacher

PURPOSE: To help a writer, peer, or teacher assess the proficiency of the writer's use of writing traits and conventions in any composition. The traits include ideas/details, organization/text structure, voice, sentence fluency, word choice, and conventions (which include grammar, punctuation, capitalization, and spelling). The traits are based on the "six traits of writing" described by Spandel (2004).

PROCEDURE AND ANALYSIS: The writer, peer, or teacher reads the descriptors for each of the traits, reads the entire composition, and evaluates each trait with a plus sign (+) for excellent, a checkmark (✓) for satisfactory, or a minus sign (–) if it needs improvement. The teacher underlines any descriptive words that seem appropriate. Then the teacher writes an analysis with specific examples from the composition. This can be used to provide specific feedback and plan instruction. See the Appendix (pp. 468–469) for this assessment.

Writing Process Rubric for Writer, Peer, or Teacher

PURPOSE: To help a writer, peer, or teacher assess the writer's use of each step of the writing process during writing composition (prewriting, drafting, conferencing, revising, editing, and publishing/sharing), to provide feedback to enable the writer to improve their use of these steps.

PROCEDURE AND ANALYSIS: For each step of the writing process, the writer, peer, or teacher evaluates the student's performance. The teacher reads each of the descriptors in the rubric and evaluates each element with a plus sign (+) for excellent, a checkmark (✓) for satisfactory, or a minus sign (–) if it needs improvement. The teacher also underlines any descriptive words that seem appropriate. Then the teacher writes an analysis with specific examples from observations and anecdotal notes on the writing process. The information obtained about the writer's strengths and areas for improvement can be used during writing conferences. See the Appendix (p. 470) for this assessment.

Visual Representation Assessment for Self, Peer, or Teacher

PURPOSE: To help a student, peer, or teacher assess the student's use of visual representation elements in creating visuals to communicate ideas, and the effectiveness of these elements.

PROCEDURE AND ANALYSIS: The teacher provides students with a copy of this assessment and directions for the creation of visuals. The teacher then describes the elements and principles of art and design, along with the characteristics of the particular type of visual to be created (two- vs. three-dimensional, static vs. moving visuals). After students create the visual(s), each student self-assesses, has a peer assess, and then has the teacher assess the elements as excellent (+), satisfactory (✓), or needs improvement (–). This assessment tool is then used to provide specific feedback to improve the creation and use of visuals to communicate ideas. See the Appendix (p. 471) for this assessment.

Multimedia Presentation Assessment for Self, Peer, or Teacher

PURPOSE: To help a student, peer, or teacher assess the student's use of the elements of a multimedia presentation, and the effectiveness of these elements.

PROCEDURE AND ANALYSIS: The teacher provides students with a copy of this assessment and directions for the creation of a multimedia presentation. The teacher then discusses the content, organization, graphic design elements, principles of art and design, layout, and mechanics; they may show them a model of an effective multimedia presentation and go through the assessment to evaluate it. After students create the multimedia presentation, each student self-assesses, has a peer assess, and then has the teacher assesses the elements as excellent (+), satisfactory (✓), or needs improvement (–). This assessment tool is then used to provide specific feedback to improve the creation and use of visuals to communicate ideas. See the Appendix (pp. 472–473) for this assessment.

WRITING COMPOSITION: STRATEGIES

The writing composition strategies are organized under the following headings: emergent writing and drawing strategies, mentor text strategies, writing process strategies (including prewriting strategies, drafting strategies, revising strategies, conferring strategies, editing strategies, and sharing and publishing strategies), journal-writing strategies, narrative and descriptive strategies, expository strategies, and persuasive strategies.

Routman (2005) has identified five important things she does to ensure that students become excellent writers:

- Have them say to themselves, "I am a writer who always writes with a reader in mind," and make the writing process visible.
- Have them connect writing to reading through literature, and notice what authors do.
- Guide students to choose topics they care about (by offering them choices within structure), and give students time to talk and write about them.
- Teach students the strategies they need to draft, revise, edit, polish, and publish.
- Rely primarily on regular conferences with students to assess and evaluate; note strengths, give feedback, teach, and set mutual goals.

Although there are many strategies for writing, depending on the genre or purpose, it is important that students reread what they write to be sure that it accurately and clearly conveys the message they want to communicate. To improve in their writing development, students need to write on a daily basis and for different purposes. They should also be given models or mentor texts to read with the type of writing that is expected. The *Writing Process Rubric for Writer, Peer, or Teacher* (see Appendix, p. 470) can be used to evaluate students at every stage in the writing process. Students should write for authentic purposes. Writing can help people to discover ideas, relationships, connections, and patterns in their lives and in their world. Writing is also used to communicate by sharing ideas and information with an audience. The audience can be students themselves, peers, educators, family members, community members, businesspeople, or people with whom they may never come in contact.

Emergent Writing and Drawing Strategies

While emergent writing begins with scribbles, students quickly learn that writing and drawing communicate a message. Students need daily opportunities to see writing and journaling modeled; have their ideas written down by others; and begin seeing that their oral sentences are made up of words, the words are made up of sounds, and the sounds can be written with letters. When kindergarten students are guided to represent their ideas with drawings and written words, most of them can meet the expectation of composing one or two complete sentences by the end of the year. The following strategies support students in communicating a message by matching the sounds they hear to writing letters for words. Access to a personal alphabet chart with pictures, so that the students can use it as a model for identifying and writing letters, is essential. It is beneficial to begin with teaching students to write their names because a child's name is a very important word, and it is needed to sign written or visual work. These emergent strategies are all useful for kindergarten and first-grade children, those with writing composition difficulties, or ELLs.

• Students' Names

PURPOSE: For students to learn to correctly write their names in order to sign their work.

PROCEDURE: As the teacher, write the student's preferred first and last names on a lined sentence strip, using the school-selected handwriting style. Keep it available for the student to see. Model for students how to write their names with the initial letters uppercase and the rest of the letters lowercase, unless a name (e.g., McAndrews) requires internal capitalization. Have them write their names with a variety of media, such as markers, crayons, paints, and pencils. Be sure to remind students to put their names on their drawing and writing.

• Drawing and Dictating

PURPOSE: For students to observe what they say can be written and what is written can be read to support them in reading the words that they say

PROCEDURE: After students draw a picture, ask them to tell you (the teacher) about it. Write what they say on the paper, using the school-selected handwriting style. Then reread each student's writing, pointing to each word and asking the student to "read" it to you.

• Emergent Drawing Strategies

PURPOSE: For students to communicate their ideas through drawing.

PROCEDURE: As the teacher, ask students to describe to you what they want to draw. Start by having them describe and draw the basic shape or outline of the person, animal, or object they want to draw; then describe and draw details of the subject; and then describe/draw the setting or the location of the subject, and eventually any action of the subject. For example, if a child wants to draw a person, ask them to look at a friend and talk about the basic body parts—head, body, arms, and legs—and eventually add hands, feet, neck, and shoulders. Have the child draw those parts. Next, have them describe and draw features of the face (including eyebrows) and then ears and hair, followed by clothing, the setting (such as outdoors or in a building), and eventually the action of the subject. Once students begin drawing multiple objects, you can talk about perspective, beginning with showing bigger and smaller objects. To add interest to the drawing, students can use color. Do not expect students to include all of these details at first. Be sure to remain within each child's zone of proximal development (see Chapter 1) for drawing. After you ascertain what the child is drawing, you can ask them to describe it and add a detail or two.

Drawing and Labeling

PURPOSE: For students to correlate sounds in words with writing letters to label their drawings.

PROCEDURE: As the teacher, provide blank paper, and ask students to draw a picture and then label their drawing. Proceeding in developmental stages, start by suggesting that students write the letter for the initial sound of each word. They can use a personal alphabet chart with picture cues to help them with selecting the appropriate letter. When students are successful, ask them to write letters for other sounds they hear in the word; often these are the consonants, and eventually they begin to include letters for the medial sounds.

Message Writing

PURPOSE: For students to observe the writing process being modeled, so that they can write their own messages.

PROCEDURE: While you (the teacher) write a message to the students or a dictated message from the students, segment words into their sounds by modeling the writing process on the board. Pronounce each word slowly, and enunciate each sound as you write it. Make connections to known words or parts of words.

EXAMPLE: Say, "I am going to begin by writing *Dear Class*. What sound does the word *dear* start with? /d/. How do I write that sound?" If the students do not know, say, "Let's look on our alphabet chart. *Dear* starts like the picture of the dog. Because the *D* it is at the beginning of my greeting, I need a capital *D*. Next, I hear /ē/, and that is written with two letters *ea* like in the word *eat*. Finally, I hear the /r/, written with the letter *r*. That word is done, so I need a finger space. What is the next word? *Class*. It begins with the /k/ sound, and it is written with the letter *c*, then l/ă/s/ with two *s*'s. Now I need a comma for the end of my greeting." Continue modeling the writing of the entire message, and then chorally read the whole message.

ADAPTATION: Students can take turns dictating a message of the day while you model writing it.

Sentence Frames

PURPOSE: For students to write a complete sentence using a structure or model (grades K–3 and ELLs).

PROCEDURE: As the teacher, select a sentence that students can complete, based on a pattern in a book or based on a topic. Write the sentence frame on each student's paper or on the board, leaving underlines for words that need to be inserted. For example, after reading *Brown Bear, Brown Bear, What Do You See?* (Martin, 1967), students can write the same sentence pattern and substitute a color and a name of an animal for the underlines, such as "Red ant, red ant, what do you see?" Students can then illustrate their writing.

• Emergent Journal Writing

PURPOSE: For students to have a place and time to write their personal ideas, reflections and questions on a daily basis.

PROCEDURE: This should be a free-writing experience. Sometimes it is helpful if students draw a picture first, talk about it, and then write about it. For writing unknown words, they can be taught to say each word slowly and to write letters for each of the sounds that they hear in the word. They can also use resources such as a word wall, personal dictionary, posters, and alphabet charts for spelling words. The classroom can have charts listing color, number, and topic words. If you (the teacher) keep a personal journal, share parts of it with your students and encourage them to write about their day.

• Smiley Sentence Strategy

PURPOSE: For students to self-assess their writing of complete sentences.

PROCEDURE: After students write one or more sentences in their journal, they self-assess that they included each element of the Smiley Sentence (see Figure 7.3). If they correctly included that element, they write each part of the happy face on their journal page. If all elements are completed, they end up with a happy face wearing a hat on their paper.

• Emergent Functional Writing

PURPOSE: For students to write for authentic purposes.

PROCEDURE: Provide frequent opportunities for students to write for authentic purposes. Students can make grocery lists, things-to-do lists, or wish lists. Or students decide what to write on letters, thank-you cards, and invitations. Pretend checks, prescriptions, airline tickets, menus, or grocery lists can be provided for the students to write on while they are playing.

FIGURE 7.3. Elements of the Smiley Sentence.

I wrote complete sentences that describe ideas or pictures.

I used capital letters for the first word, the pronoun I, and all proper nouns.

I wrote end punctuation marks: . ? !

I put a space between each word and wrote each letter clearly.

I spelled sight words correctly. For other words, I sounded them out and wrote letters for each sound.

Mentor Text Strategies

Modeling and Writing Using Mentor Texts

PURPOSE: For students to use literature or informational texts as a guide to write a specific type of writing, text structure, and/or element of writer's craft.

PROCEDURE: As the teacher, do the following:

- Choose a type of writing (narrative, expository, persuasive, or descriptive writing), text structure, and/or an element of writer's craft to study. Gather books that are good examples of what you want to students apply in their own writing. Refer to the types of writer's craft (word craft, structural craft, audible craft, and visual craft) discussed at the beginning of this chapter. Refer to Table 7.1 for a description of the writing text types and elements.
- Either explicitly state what students are going to study, or, for a student inquiry approach, ask them to notice what is common in each of the texts you selected. You might put sticky notes on parts you want them to attend to.
- Have them read, share, and discuss how others have used the target elements in their writing. Teach students how to read like writers and see writer's craft everywhere. Show how writers structure texts; how they use words, sentences, and paragraphs; and how they incorporate graphics in powerful and interesting ways.
- Ask and guide students to articulate and name the characteristics the authors have used to demonstrate the type of text, structure, or craft. With the students, create an anchor chart with these characteristics, and include specific examples from the texts.
- Explain to the students that they will be composing their own texts with the same characteristics.
- During writing conferences with the students, have them articulate how they have incorporated these characteristics in their writing. Encourage each student to keep a list and examples of each form or craft of writing that is taught, or that the student notices, in a writer's notebook.
- Students should be exposed to writing drafts, using each of the types of writing or crafts that are studied. Due to different student interests, they should be allowed to select which composition draft they want to take through the writing process.
- As students learn different types, structures, and crafts, they may combine elements in a single composition.

Using Mentor Texts to Teach the Six Traits

SOURCE: Spandel (2004).

PURPOSE: For students to use literature or informational texts as a guide to write using each of the six traits of writing.

PROCEDURE: As the teacher, select one or more books to model each of the six traits of writing during mini-lessons. Then have the students write their own text using the mentor text as a guide.

- *Ideas:* Use books to discuss imagination, creativity, main ideas, and the importance and relevance of specific themes.
- *Organization:* Use books to model thoughtful sequencing and good beginnings and endings of paragraphs and plots.

- *Voice:* Select books that use a variety of imaginative perspectives and opinions.
- *Word choice:* Use books to exhibit the importance of word choice in creating metaphors, playing with onomatopoeia, achieving preciseness of meaning, and occasionally making effective use of nonsense.
- *Sentence fluency:* Model sentence fluency with books filled with lyrical phrases and rhythmically poetic lines.
- *Conventions:* Identify how authors use grammar, punctuation, capitalization, and spellling.

• Guided Writing Blocks

SOURCE: Fountas and Pinnell (2001).

PURPOSE: For students to have experience with shared writing, interactive writing, guided writing, and independent writing.

PROCEDURE: As the teacher, for shared writing, you work with students to compose messages and stories; then support the process as a scribe. For interactive writing, as in shared writing, you compose messages and stories with the students; use a "shared pen" technique that involves the students in the writing. In guided writing or writers' workshop, students engage in writing a variety of texts. You guide the process and provide instruction through mini-lessons and conferences. In independent writing, students write their own pieces, including stories, informational pieces, retellings, labeling, speech balloons, lists, and so forth.

Writing Process Strategies

• Steps to Model for the Writing Process

PURPOSE: For students to improve their writing by having them apply each of the steps in the writing process: prewriting, drafting, conferring, revising, editing, and sharing/publishing. Between each of these steps are rereading and often sharing. Although not all writing is published, those pieces that are published need to go through the writing process. The following are steps to model and go through the entire writing process:

- As the teacher, orally share a mentor text and/or their own writing, using the same genre as the writing assignment.
- Talk about the crafts, structures, and features that were used.
- Talk about and/or show drafts of revision and editing.
- Describe the writing assignment.
- Ask the students to think of several ideas to write about (brainstorming).
- Have each student choose a topic.
- Have each student create a story map for narrative writing ideas, or a concept map/text structure graphic organizer for expository writing.
- Ask each student to talk to a partner about ideas, and add further ideas to the graphic organizer.
- Have students write words or phrases related to the six senses: see, hear, smell, taste, touch and feel (emotions).
- Have each student write a first draft on every other line of sheets of lined paper.

- Ask students to reread their writing and make initial changes (if a writing checklist is provided, the students should use it for self-evaluation).
- Now ask each student to orally share the draft and discuss writing with a different partner.
- Have the students revise for content and organization.
- Identify resources to enable students to add details to their writing—other participants, photos, maps, brochures, the internet.
- Have students insert new ideas and details.
- On the second draft, have students use at least one craft.
- Ask students to reread and revise for voice and word choice.
- Then have students edit for grammar, punctuation, capitalization, and spelling.
- Have each student exchange with a new partner for positive feedback and suggestions for additional revision and editing. (Again, students should use a writing checklist if one is provided.)
- Have each student read their writings aloud to an audience.
- Publish the writings in the classroom, in the school newspaper, or online.

The following are specific sets of strategies to improve writing composition at each stage of the writing process.

Prewriting Strategies

General Guidelines and Specific Strategies

PURPOSE: For students to identify a topic with main ideas, the writer's craft, and the prewriting strategy.

PROCEDURE: Students first brainstorm topics they want to write about and think about the purpose, audience, and type of writing (narrative, descriptive, expository, persuasive, or poetic). For writing ideas, the class can brainstorm shared experiences, important events, favorite people, a special place, or something they like to do. Writers can go through family photos, magazines, books, and images on the internet to find ideas that inspire them. Ideas can be written on a class chart or in their writing ideas notebooks and can be used when they want a new idea to write about. Students read and examine the writer's craft in examples of the type of writing they want to compose. Students then select and complete one or more of the following prewriting strategies, or select one or more graphic organizers from Chapter 6.

- ***Talking and drawing.*** Especially for young children, ask them first to talk about what they want to write, and then to draw pictures with details. You (the teacher) can prompt them with "who, what, where, when, why, how" questions.
- ***List–group–label.*** Say to students, "List all the ideas or terms related to your topic, group the items into categories, label the categories. Write a sentence about each label."
- ***Idea web.*** Say, "Put the subject in the center of your paper with a circle around it. Think of ideas related to the topic, write them around the center circle, and link them with lines. Add details and draw lines to the ideas they relate to."
- ***Five-finger planner.*** Students draw an outline of one hand. In the palm, they write their topic; on each finger, they write a detail about that topic; and on the thumb, they write how they feel about that topic (Rog, 2003).
- ***Asking journalist's questions.*** Have students write down questions related to their

topics starting with "Who? What? Where? When? Why? How?" Then have them answer those questions. Note that some writing will include more information on some of the questions, and less on others.

- ***Use Your Senses chart.*** To develop description using sensory images, tell students to select an event in their lives, and then write a word or phrase in the column under each sense on a Use Your Senses chart to describe the event. See the example in Figure 7.4. Then have them write a personal narrative that uses this sense-based description.
- ***Outlining.*** For longer compositions, after students have completed one of the prewriting ideas above, say to them, "Organize your ideas into an outline, including the introduction; body with topics, details, and evidence; and conclusion. This will be used to write your first draft." See the example in Figure 7.5.

Drafting Strategies

General Guidelines

PURPOSE: For students to write initial ideas in complete sentences.

PROCEDURE: As the teacher, explain to students that the first draft can be free writing, or it can be organized writing based on a prewriting graphic organizer or outline.

- ***Free writing.*** Say to students, "Write on your topic nonstop for several minutes. Do not stop to revise or edit; just get as many ideas down as possible related to the topic. After you are finished, reread it and highlight the most important ideas. Then start all over again, and this time write by organizing your main points and details."
- ***Organized writing.*** Students use one of the prewriting graphic organizers. They look at all the ideas they wrote down, and they sequence them (possibly even numbering the ideas). Sometimes it helps to write on every other line, to allow room for revising and editing later (students might highlight the lines they do not write on). Students should focus on the content and not be concerned with grammar or mechanics at this time. If they are unsure how to spell a word, they should use inventive spelling by sounding it out and writing letters for each sound they hear, and then circle the word so they can return to it later. The ideas are the most important things at this stage. They first write an

FIGURE 7.4. Use Your Senses chart, example (bicycle accident).

See	Hear	Feel	Smell	Taste	Emotion
a deer leaping, not seeing each other	car crashing into bike, squealing tires	slamming on brakes, face colliding against metal, cuts on face and body	burning rubber, asphalt	metallic taste of blood in my mouth	pain embarrassed

FIGURE 7.5. Outline, example.

I. Title 1
  1. Subject 1
    a. Item 1: Description
    b. Item 2: Description
    c. Item 3: Description
  2. Subect 2
II. Title 2
  1. Subject 1
    a. Item 1: Description
    . . .

introductory sentence or paragraph. Then they write each main point and detail in order. Then they write a concluding sentence or paragraph. If they are unable to complete the first draft in one sitting, suggest that they draw a line under where they stopped and write brief notes about the ideas they want to write next. If time allows, they immediately reread the first draft and proceed to the revising stage.

Specific strategies for various stages of drafting follow.

• Four-Square Writing

SOURCE: Gould and Gould (1999).

PURPOSE: For students to develop prewriting and organizational skills in writing details that support a topic. This strategy can be applied to narrative, expository, persuasive, and descriptive forms of writing.

PROCEDURE: Students fold paper into four equal squares and write a topic in the middle of the paper. In the first three squares, they write details to support the topic. In the last square, they write feelings or concluding statements about the topic. Then they draw a picture in each box that describes the sentences. Finally, they use the information on the four-square writing organizer to write a complete text. This strategy can be adapted for use with words, phrases, or whole sentences in each box.

EXAMPLE:

Topic—It takes great responsibility to take care of a dog.
Box 1—First, you need to make sure the dog has food and water every day.
Box 2—Next, you need to make sure that the dog's place to live is clean and has enough room.
Box 3—Finally, the dog needs lots of exercise to stay healthy.
Box 4—Proper care is rewarded with love and attention from the dog.

• Eight-Sentence Accordion Paragraph

SOURCE: Auman (2005).

PURPOSE: For students to develop an eight-sentence paragraph with a topic sentence, two details, explanation or examples, and restatement of the topic (grade 2 and above).

PROCEDURE: As the teacher, select a writing prompt. Give students color-coded strips of paper that correlate to the colors of a traffic light in this order: green, yellow, red, yellow, red, yellow, red, green. Green means *Go,* and students write a topic sentence. Yellow means *Slow down,* and students give a reason, detail, or fact and use a transition. Red means *Stop,* and students explain or give an example. On the second yellow strip, students write another reason, detail, or fact. On the second red strip, they explain or give an example of the detail on the previous yellow strip. They then repeat with another reason and example. The final green strip means *Go back,* and students write a sentence that reminds the reader of their topic. Each student then writes a first draft of a paper, using the sentence strips. See Figure 7.6 for a template for this type of paragraph.

Revising Strategies

• General Guidelines

PURPOSE: For students to revise the content (ideas/details, organization, sentence fluency, voice, and word choice) to make sure that the message is clear, accurate, coherent, and appropriate, with the necessary supporting details.

PROCEDURE: In the revising stage, students will reread their drafts multiple times, focusing on revision of the first five traits identified in the six-trait writing model (Spandel, 2004). Students begin by clarifying the ideas and details and verifying that they are accurate and

FIGURE 7.6. Eight-sentence accordion paragraph, template.

Creative Title:
Topic Sentence:
Reason/Detail/Fact with Transition:
Explain:
Reason/Detail/Fact with Transition:
Explain:
Reason/Detail/Fact with Transition:
Explain:
Conclusion with Closing Word:

complete. They may need to research the topic more to expand on or clarify the information. They then need to organize and sequence the information. Depending on the genre and style of writing, students may need to include specific elements and types of language and structures. The writing should include descriptive and content-specific vocabulary. They should add their personal voices to the text, selecting powerful and interesting words. To improve sentence fluency, students can use a variety of sentence structures and transitions to make the sentences flow from one idea to the next. The following are specific revising strategies.

• Revising and Editing Bookmarks

PURPOSE: For students to use a resource to revise and edit their writing.

PROCEDURE: As the teacher, select the appropriate bookmark from the *Revising and Editing Bookmarks* form (see Appendix, p. 474). The first bookmark is for emergent writers, to help them revise and edit their writing. The second bookmark is a checklist to help students revise and edit narrative/descriptive writing, and the last bookmark is a checklist for revising and editing expository/persuasive writing. Prior to writing, go over each step with the students. During writing, the students refer to the checklist and then do a self-assessment after they complete their writing. Point out that the first step is for them to reread what they have written. This is an essential step in improving the students' writing composition. The students begin with revising the content; when the content is complete, they then go back and edit for conventions.

• ARMS Revision Anchor Chart

PURPOSE: For students to revise their writing by Adding, Removing, Moving, or Substituting ideas.

PROCEDURE: Students can create and use an ARMS to Revise anchor chart (see Figure 7.7 for an example) as a reference to remember how to revise by following the ARMS acronym.

• Adding Content through Research

PURPOSE: For students to improve their writing by self-assessing and revising the content for complete, clear, and accurate writing.

FIGURE 7.7. ARMS to Revise anchor chart.

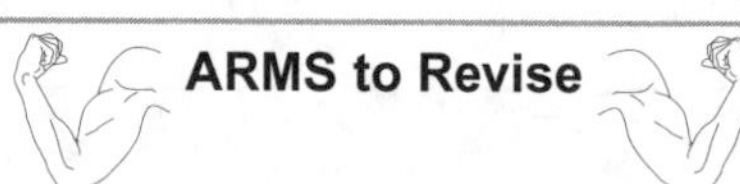

Add: Content, sentences, and words (details, descriptions, senses, vivid words).

Remove: Unneeded sentences, words, or ideas that are unclear.

Move: Change a sentence or a word placement for clarity or emphasis.

Substitute: Trade words or sentences for precise meaning; use a thesaurus if necessary.

PROCEDURE: Students reread their compositions and search for areas where more information is needed. They ask themselves, "Did my writing answer the reader's questions of 'who, what, where, when, why, and how'? Are my ideas explained thoroughly? Do I have evidence for my claims or statements? Did I include specific details? Are there any gaps in the information?" Almost all writing requires research, so students can seek out credible sources of information from reading multiple print and electronic documents, interviewing people, and/or engaging in experiences. They go through their resource materials and list all of the key terms or concepts related to the writing topic; they then then check their writing to be sure that they included and defined these key terms. They ask themselves, "How would graphics (photos, illustrations, diagrams, charts, graphs, maps) support my writing?" Finally, they add important textual content and integrate it with carefully selected or created graphics to communicate their ideas clearly.

• Removing Content

PURPOSE: For students to narrow their focus and include the most important and relevant information.

PROCEDURE: As the teacher, say to students, "Reread the composition. Remind yourself about the purpose of the writing and the message of the writing. Important ideas could get lost if there are too many extraneous details. Try to delete sentences or words that are not needed or redundant."

• Moving Information for Organization

PURPOSE: For students to monitor and self-assess their composition so that it follows a clear organization and structure.

PROCEDURE: As the teacher, say to students, "Reread the composition. Is the organization clear? Is the text structure clear and in the appropriate sequence? Does the information fit underneath the headings and subheadings? Does any information need to be moved? Would you be able to create an organized outline from what you have written?"

• Questions for Using Specific Language or Word Choice

PURPOSE: For students to monitor and self-assess their use of precise, interesting, and content-specific words.

PROCEDURE: As the teacher, have students reread their compositions and examine their word choices to see if the words are accurate, specific, and interesting. Have them ask themselves the following questions:

Did I use specific terms or proper nouns (for example, *Canon EOS 7D* vs. *camera,* or *Subway teriyaki chicken sandwich* vs. *lunch*)?

Did I use content-specific terms and explain their meaning to the reader? (A student writing about soccer might use terms such as *in the box* [penalty area], *bicycle kick, offside,* or *left wing.*)

Are my words too vague, such as *things* and *stuff*?

Did I use vivid verbs that show action (*strolled* vs. *went, whispered* vs. *said*)?

Did I use active voice, where the subject is doing the action, rather than passive voice, where the action is happening to the subject (*the bear caught the fish* vs. *the fish was caught by the bear*)? (The passive voice often uses helping verbs such as *was*.)
Did I use multiple adjectives to describe nouns (*the enormous, lumbering grizzly bear*)?
Did I use adverbs to describe the verbs (*ran quickly*)? Or, better yet, did I just use stronger verbs, such as *sprinted*?
Did I use the right word, as some words sound similar (*affect* vs. *effect*)?
Is my sentence too wordy? (For example, *regardless of the fact that* can be reduced to *although*.)
Am I being redundant by using the same words too often, or is it beneficial to repeat key terms to emphasize them?
When I use new words, am I using the words correctly?

Word Choice Mini-Lessons

PURPOSE: For students to improve their use of interesting and specific words.

PROCEDURE: The students brainstorm and make anchor charts for the following:

- Vivid verbs: Students list common words, and then list vivid verbs that could be used instead. A list of words can be retrieved from *weareawesome5.weebly.com/vivid-verbs.html*.
- "Said is dead": Students make a tombstone and write all the words they can use instead of *said* (e.g., *explained, shouted*).
- Sensory detail words: Students create five columns (sight, sound, touch, taste, and smell) and list words in each column. A list of words can be retrieved from *www.34kiwis.files.wordpress.com*.
- Emotion words (*exhausted, hopeful*): Students can go to *www.wire.wisc.edu* for an emotion word list.
- Discipline-specific vocabulary for areas of current study (e.g., for the U.S. Civil War: *abolitionist, brutality, carpetbagger*).
- Description brainstorm: Students select an object or picture to observe. They then brainstorm as many describing words they can in 2 minutes, and post these words under the object or picture.
- Word choice application: Students think about their topic and review their writing, looking for how they applied each word.

Sentence Fluency Strategies

PURPOSE: For students to write better sentences that get ideas across clearly, use different sentence patterns, and connect to the sentences before and after them.

PROCEDURE: Students reread their sentences and ask themselves the following questions:

Is the meaning of the sentence clear, or is it awkward, vague, or unclear?
Did I use transition words to link ideas from one sentence to another?
Did I use different sentence patterns (compound, complex, declarative, interrogative, and exclamatory)?
Did I have correct pronoun–noun agreement?

Was it clear who a pronoun was referring to (for example, *John, Mark, and I went to the store. I gave **him** five dollars*)?

Did I use correct subject–verb agreement (for example, *He **eats** pizza* vs. *He **eat** pizza*)?

Is my verb tense clear and consistent throughout the writing, or do I jump back and forth between past and present?

Add Transition/Linking Words

PURPOSE: For students to make their writing flow more smoothly; add transition words to link words, phrases, or sentences together; enable the reader to progress from one idea to another' and build the connections between thoughts.

PROCEDURE: As the teacher, call attention to or highlight transition words in texts. (A list of transition words can be found at *www.readingrockets.org/content/pdfs/transition%20words.pdf*.) Ask students to find places in their writing where transition words will clarify the writing or help make connections. The transition words can be grouped by purpose, such as words or phrases to help sequence ideas or transition between sentences (*first, next, also, then*); to show location (*between, in front of, around*); to show time (*while, afterward, as soon as*); to indicate more information (*besides, further, in addition*); and to conclude a piece of writing (*in conclusion, finally, to sum up*).

Sentence Expanding

PURPOSE: For students to increase the complexity and detail in their sentences.

PROCEDURE: As the teacher, model this process by writing a noun and a verb and asking students to add words to make an interesting sentence. Have them add parts of speech such as articles, adjectives, adverbs, conjunctions, prepositions, and pronouns. Students then edit their own writing by expanding their sentences.

EXAMPLE:

Dog ran.
The enormous speckled dog ran rapidly as he chased a rabbit into the raspberry bushes.

Sentence Combining

SOURCE: Walker (2004).

PURPOSE: For students to combine sentences to make compound and complex sentences that show the relationship between the ideas.

PROCEDURE: Using students' examples of short related sentences, show how to delete repeated words or phrases and combine sentences with a variety of conjunctions and prepositions. Students can then edit their own writing by combining sentences.

EXAMPLE:

I went to a party. It was for Laura's birthday. It was at the park. The park was next to the zoo.
I went to Laura's birthday party at the park near the zoo.

• Compound and Complex Sentences: Sentence Expanding

PURPOSE: For students to create interesting and varied sentences that show relationships between ideas, using coordinating and subordinating conjunctions.

PROCEDURE: As the teacher, help students identify short choppy sentences in writing, and model how to combine sentences to make compound or complex sentences. Say to students:

> "A **compound sentence** refers to a sentence made up of two independent clauses (or complete sentences) connected to one another with a **coordinating conjunction.** Coordinating conjunctions are easy to remember if you think of the words FAN BOYS: For, And, Nor, But, Or, Yet, So. For example, if you have the sentences *Maya asked to go to the park. Her Nana was coming from Mexico today,* you can connect them by using *but*: *Maya asked to go to the park,* **but** *her Nana was coming from Mexico today.*"

> "A **complex sentence** joins an independent clause with one or more dependent clauses. Dependent clauses begin with **subordinating conjunctions,** such as the following common ones: *after, although, as, because, before, even though, if, since, though, unless, until, when, whenever, whereas, wherever,* and *while.* Note that when a dependent clause comes first, a comma should be used to separate the two clauses. No comma is used when the dependent clause comes afterwards. For example, ***After*** *we pick up Nana, we can go to the park.*"

• Subordinating Conjunctions with Cut-Up Sentence Strips

SOURCE: Mims (2019).

PURPOSE: For students to identify and use subordinating conjunctions.

PROCEDURE: Grammar is best taught in context by having students identifying grammar used in published texts, by editing grammar in peers' writing, and by applying grammar to their own writing. As the teacher, do the following:

- For each of the subordinating conjunctions on the AAAWWUUBBIS list (*as, after, although, when, while, until, unless, before, because if, since*), write two sentences. One sentence should start with the subordinating conjunction; the other should be the same sentence, but flipped so the coordinating conjunction is in the middle. Example: (a) *After school today, I plan to go home and take a nap.* (b) *I plan to go home and take a nap after school today.*
- Cut each strip after the subordinating phrase. Place all sentence strips into an envelope.
- Give each student or each pair of students one envelope. Instruct students to reconstruct the sentences, paying attention to capital letters to start sentences.
- Once students have completed this task, they are primed for a lesson on the rules of subordinating conjunctions, since they have now seen 20 examples of correct sentence models.
- Explain coordinating conjunctions.
- Students should return to a piece of their own writing (or write something new) and apply the new skill.

DIFFERENTIATION: For more support, copy sentences that begin with subordinating conjunctions on one color of paper, and sentences with subordinating conjunctions in the middle on another piece of paper. For an extension, cut the commas as a third piece of each sentence strip, so that students must correctly place the commas.

• Fluency Mini-Lessons

PURPOSE: For students to develop sentence fluency in their writing.

PROCEDURE: As the teacher, present examples of current and past students' writing with fluency issues. Have students identify or highlight incomplete, unclear, awkward, vague, or disconnected sentences. Then, in small groups, have the students rewrite the sentences. Next, have students review their own writing, identify any areas for improvement, and rewrite the sentences.

Conferring Strategies

• General Guidelines

PURPOSE: For students to give and receive supportive and constructive feedback to reinforce effective writing and to provide suggestions for improvement.

PROCEDURE: In the conferring stage, which can occur at multiple times during the writing process, the students share their writing with a partner and then with the teacher to get feedback. The initial feedback needs to include identifying specific strengths in writing, followed by questions to revise the ideas and organization of the writing. Next, provide editing feedback. In the final conference, provide suggestions for publishing. Teachers and peers can use a think-aloud strategy, in which they respond to or question a student's writing as they are reading it. The teacher can model this process first by thinking aloud about their own writing, and then students can use this same process as they revise. Specific conferring strategies follow.

• Characteristics of Writing Conferences

SOURCE: Graves (1983).

PURPOSE: For students to get support during writing conferences.

PROCEDURE: As the teacher, review characteristics of successful writing conferences. Conferences should have a predictable structure, focus on a few points, demonstrate solutions to students' problems, permit role reversals, encourage use of vocabulary appropriate for writing, and stimulate pleasure in writing. Demonstrate how to use a writing rubric or checklist, and provide evidence with specific examples of strengths and areas for growth from students' writing. Support students in identifying their own strengths and writing goals. They will write "I can . . ." statements (compliments to themselves) and "My new goal . . ." statements (what the students should consciously be working on and what will be looked for in the next conference).

• Questions for Writing Conferences

SOURCE: Wood Ray (1999).

PURPOSE: For students to improve their writing by answering questions posed by the teacher or peers.

PROCEDURE: As the teacher interviewing a student writer, you need to know this: "What are you doing, and where are you in the process?" You might begin the conference by asking, "Tell me about . . . " Ask open-ended questions rather than yes–no questions. Keep the tone positive, so that the students have the emotional energy to keep writing. Be specific about what students are doing well, and show interest in what they are writing. Choose something to teach the writers that is within their zone of proximal development and that will help them beyond just writing that piece. Make connections to previously read literature, shared conversations, or other students' work to exemplify your teaching point. The following are questions to ask the writer to help support the writing process: "Where did you get the idea(s) for your text? How long have you been working on this text? What are your plans for continued work on this text? Have you made any interesting decisions about your words or illustrations? Why did you decide to write or illustrate this part this way? How does this text fit with other things you have written?"

Make a record of the conference by noting the content of the teaching and information you learned about the writer that might be helpful in the future. The *Writing Conference Record Form* in the Appendix (p. 475) can be used for this purpose. Review the notes for future mini-lessons and for writing assessment. At the end of the writing workshop time, share interesting process stories from your conferences that day. Encourage children to make connections with other writers' processes as you share.

• Writing Record

SOURCE: Solley (2000).

PURPOSE: For students to keep a record of their own writing topics, "I can . . . " statements, and goals.

PROCEDURE: Students write daily on a chart information such as the date, type of writing, topic, stage of writing, and the plans for tomorrow, "I can . . . " statement of things done well, and future goals such as things to work on and plans for learning. See the example in Figure 7.8.

• Writer-Led Peer Conference Form

PURPOSE: For students to improve their revising and editing of writing compositions. Records such as these can be part of the students' writing portfolio.

FIGURE 7.8. Writing record, example.

Date	Type, Topic, Stage of Writing	What I want to work on tomorrow
9/10	Narrative, story about our camping trip, first draft.	Reread and revise story. Include more sensory images like the mentor text.

I can . . . do these things well	Goal 1: I'm working on these things	Goal 2: I plan to learn these things
I can write the whole time and stay on topic.	Add details to setting up camp and the raccoon getting in the tent.	New words that mean *fun*, and name and location of the campground and park.

PROCEDURE: The writer shares any writing rubrics or criteria they want the peer to look for, and then reads the writing aloud. The writer next asks the questions in the *Writer-Led Peer Conference Form* (see the Appendix, pp. 476–477) and makes notes based on the responses. Notes can be written on the conference form, on sticky notes, or on a separate piece of paper, but should not be placed on the writer's composition. The writer gets the final say as to what to keep or change in the composition. These conference forms can be analyzed to demonstrate growth or need in students' writing development over time.

After conferring with the teacher and/or peers, students reflect on the ideas discussed and go back to the revising stage to add, remove, move, or substitute information or words. Once all the revisions of ideas, organization, sentence fluency, voice, and word choice are complete, the students move on to the editing stage.

Editing Strategies

• General Guidelines

PURPOSE: For students to polish their writing with correct grammar, capitalization, punctuation, and spelling so that their ideas are more clearly communicated to readers.

PROCEDURE: Students should reread their writing multiple times for different purposes. Students can use an editing checklist such as the *Primary Narrative Revising and Editing Checklist* or the *Advanced Revising and Editing Checklist* (see Appendix, pp. 478 and 479–480) to help them focus on one type of editing at a time. When you (as the teacher) are introducing one of these checklists for the first time, select a piece of writing that matches the genre and grade level. Review each element of the checklist, and evaluate that piece of writing together with the students. Then have the students work in pairs to evaluate a piece of writing, and finally have them work individually to evaluate their own writing. Specific editing strategies follow.

• CUPS Editing Anchor Chart

PURPOSE: For students to use the chart to edit their writing by checking Capitalization, Usage, Punctuation, and Spelling.

PROCEDURE: Students create and use a CUPS Editing Anchor Chart (see Figure 7.9 for an example) as a reference to remember how to edit by following the CUPS acronym.

• My Writing Seek and Find

PURPOSE: For students to identify sentence types and parts of speech in their own writing and to revise their writing by incorporating a variety of sentence structures (grade 3 and above).

PROCEDURE: As the teacher, instruct students to look in their writing portfolios to find an example of one of each of the following types of sentences and copy it: a declarative sentence, an interrogative sentence, an imperative sentence, a sentence with a compound subject, a sentence with a compound predicate, a compound sentence, a sentence with a concrete noun, a sentence with a proper noun, a sentence using a plural noun that does not end in *s*, a sentence using a collective noun, a sentence with an appositive, a sentence with

FIGURE 7.9. CUPS to Edit anchor chart.

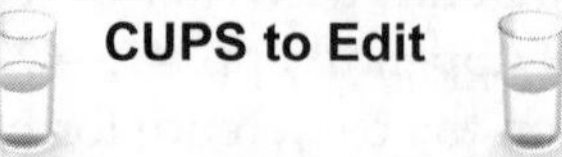

CUPS to Edit

Capitalize: Check for capitalization of proper names, places (companies, cities, states, countries), months, days of the week, holidays, religions, languages, first word in a sentence, and pronoun.

Usage: Check that subject and verb match in number, verb tenses are correct and match, pronouns refer to previous subject, words are used correctly, and sentences are complete.

Punctuation: Check for correct end punctuation. Use commas, quotation marks, semicolons, and colons appropriately.

Spelling: Check for correct spelling, including homophones and commonly misspelled words. Check for correct use of apostrophes for contractions and possession. The word *its* has no apostrophe when it means "belonging to it."

a simile, and a sentence with figurative language. Then ask students to write 10 words they have learned how to spell. Adaptations include selecting only a few of the choices above or finding examples in published texts.

• Writing Half Sentences

SOURCE: Fitzpatrick (1997).

PURPOSE: For students to write complete, grammatically correct sentences with a subject and predicate.

PROCEDURE: As the teacher, make a "Build a Sentence" poster that shows somebody doing something. Put the poster on the chalkboard. Alongside the poster, write incomplete sentences, leaving enough space for the missing words. Review the parts of a sentence. Explain that the sentences on the chalkboard are only partially complete—that either the subject (somebody or something) or the predicate (doing or being) is missing. Invite students to play a "whodunit" game by having them use their imaginations to decide which subject and which predicate is missing from each sentence. Share their answers aloud as you write the corresponding words on the chalkboard. Complete the activity by drawing separate boxes around the subject and the predicate of each sentence.

EXAMPLES:

1. The funny clown ____________.
2. ____________ was driving the new car.
3. The big black bear was ____________.
4. ____________ is swimming in the water.

• Backward Sentence Reading

PURPOSE: For students to monitor and correct their use of grammar in each of their sentences to communicate ideas clearly to readers.

PROCEDURE: As the teacher, say to students, "Reread your writing and examine the sentence structure. Read your writing backward, sentence by sentence, so you can focus on each sentence individually to identify incomplete sentences, grammatical errors, or sentences that do not make sense. Keep a list of grammar comments that your peers or I make, and focus on those (e.g., run-on sentences; subject–verb agreement; use of *that, which,* and *who*)."

Punctuation Strategies

PURPOSE: For students to monitor and correct their use of punctuation in order for the communication to be clear.

PROCEDURE: As students read literature and informational text, ask them (as the teacher) to find examples of each of the ending and medial punctuation marks. Then ask students why each punctuation mark was used that way. Punctuation needs to be taught with grammar, as the two are related. Create a punctuation anchor chart with the students, with definitions and examples (see Figure 7.10 for an example). Begin by teaching periods, question marks, and exclamation points. Next teach comma usage, but because it is complex, teach each rule as it is used in reading materials and is needed in students' writing. Teach the other punctuation marks as they are experienced in reading or writing. More punctuation rules can be found at *www.iue.edu* and *www.grammarly.com*.

Spelling Strategies

PURPOSE: For students to monitor and correct the spelling of words so that the message is clear.

PROCEDURE: As the teacher, say to students, "When you are writing a word, say the word, listen for each sound; and write a letter or letters that represent that sound. After you write the word, decide if it looks right. If it does, continue with your composition; if it doesn't, circle it and come back to it later so you can continue your thought process. Once you are ready for the editing stage, go back and review your writing for any possible spelling mistakes, or use the spell check feature in Microsoft Word. Remember, however, that spell check (and you) may not pick up on words that are homophones or words that you write that sound similar to the intended word. Keep a list of your common spelling mistakes so that you can check for those first. Most words follow spelling patterns; if the word you wrote doesn't look right, try another spelling pattern for that sound. You can also use resources for spelling words, such as books you read, word wall words, or dictionaries." Additional spelling strategies are provided in Chapter 4 of this book.

Editing Mini-Lessons

PURPOSE: For students to identify the correct use of grammar, punctuation, and capitalization and apply them when editing their own writing.

PROCEDURE: During literature or informational text reading, students pay attention to the author's grammar and use of other conventions. As the teacher, ask, "Where did the author place commas? How did they use punctuation to separate sentences, phrases, or ideas?

FIGURE 7.10. Punctuation anchor chart.

	Definitions	Examples
. period	Used at the end of a declarative statement, after complete thoughts, and after abbreviations.	I play with my dog.
? question mark	Used at the end of an interrogative sentence to indicate a question.	What kind of dog do you have?
! exclamation point	Used at the end of an exclamatory sentence to express a sudden outcry or to add emphasis.	Wow, that is a huge dog!
, comma	Used to indicate a pause; to set off a phrase; to separate items in a series; to set off quotations; and with dates, addresses, titles, and numerals.	After I finish my work, I am going to the park. March 14, 1983
" " quotation marks	Used to show what someone said.	"I love reading!" exclaimed Maya.
' apostrophe	Used to show possession or to represent missing letters in contractions.	My dog's leash is red.
( ) parentheses	Used to set aside information that is not essential. It may be a clarification or an afterthought.	Maya (3 years old) can write her name.
: colon	Used to show that something is following, like a list, example, or quotation. It is also used in time and ratios.	I saw three cities in Italy: Firenze, Roma, and Cerveteri. Never forget this point: Think before you speak.
; semicolon	Used to join two independent causes (related sentences) or separate items in a series that have commas.	Katherine scored three goals; she got a hat trick.
- hyphen	Used to divide a word, or in compound words, or to show connections between words that are working as a unit.	She played a one-on-one game of basketball.
— dash	Used to separate words into statements, with more emphasis than a colon.	She is most grateful for three things—being a wife, a mom, and a nana.

How did the author format quotations or long sentences? What structures did they use in writing sentences? How did the author conjugate the verb *to be*?" Find examples of subject–verb agreement, pronoun agreement, and compound and complex sentences.

• Text, Graphic, and Organizational Feature Strategies

PURPOSE: For students to identify and add text, graphic, and organizational features to their writing in order to engage the reader and enhance understanding of their composition.

PROCEDURE: The students read the *Text, Graphic, and Organizational Features Chart* described in Chapter 6 and provided in the Appendix (see pp. 452–454). They think about each of the features. They reread their writing to decide what features they might include. For example, if a student's narrative is about a hiking and camping trip, the student might do the following:

1. Use the format of a travel log, and change the font and color for the headings of each entry, using a font such as Comic Sans to emulate handwriting.
2. Add photographs of the mountain views and the campsite; a map of the trail the student and family took; and drawings of the plants, animals, and animal tracks they saw.
3. Add a diagram of the contents of the student's backpack.
4. Create a table of contents listing each chapter, such as "Packing for the Trip," "Climbing the Mountain," "Meeting the Bear."
5. Include a glossary with photos or drawings for the plants and animals mentioned in the journal, and put those words in boldface in the body of the text.
6. Add an "About the Author" page and a dedication page. The book then could be bound like a spiral notebook.

• Format, Covers, and Book Bindings Strategies

PURPOSE: For students to present their texts attractively and effectively.

PROCEDURE: As discussed earlier in this chapter, print books may be produced in different formats (e.g., board books, pop-up books, flap books, peek-through books, accordion books, and flip-flop books). Books can also be made in a variety of shapes and sizes. The front and back covers may be paper, tagboard, cardboard, or cloth, and may be covered with contact paper or be laminated. Students' families can be asked to cut cereal boxes a certain size and use them for covers. The bindings can be stapled, taped, sewn, or plastic, or books can be sent away to be professionally bound. Students often take pride in their writing when they illustrate and bind their books.

Sharing and Publishing Strategies

• General Guidelines

PURPOSE: For students to have an audience for their writing.

PROCEDURE: Students should share their writing orally or make it available for others to read, such as in the classroom, in the school library, in a newspaper, or online. Young Authors' or Young Writers' Conferences are held in most states, and these provide other outlets for students to share their writing.

• Author's Chair

PURPOSE: For students to share their writing with a supportive audience.

PROCEDURE: Each author sits in a special chair in front of the class and orally shares their writing. Since the writing has already gone through the revising and editing stages, this is the opportunity for students to receive positive feedback from their classmates. After listening to the author, the audience members provide specific examples for elements of the writing that they liked. The teacher should model the type of specific feedback that is helpful to the author. For example, "The language that you used to describe the opening scene was excellent! When you gave details about the crashing of the waves and the sand squishing between your toes, I felt as if I was at the beach with you." The teacher then elicits comments from about three students per writing composition shared.

Author Share

PURPOSE: For students to share their writing with a variety of audiences.

PROCEDURE: Students should be given regular times to share their writing publicly with other classes, faculty and staff members, family, and community members. Teachers can organize school or community performances, such as poetry readings or author nights. The audience asks questions of each author, and vice versa. Students often take pride in their writing when they illustrate and bind their books.

Writing Portfolios

PURPOSE: For students to organize, present, and show growth in their writing using two types of writing portfolios. A **process portfolio** is used to guide and evaluate a student's writing and provides data to inform specific writing instruction. A **showcase portfolio** is used to celebrate the student's published works. Portfolios can be used for students in all grades.

PROCEDURE: Students can create their own writing portfolios by designing covers and writing their names on these. Students' process portfolios can contain many documents, including self-made lists of topics to write about; open-ended writing prompts; drawings and graphic organizers for planning writing; lists of authors and books whose style of writing the students prefer; lists and examples of writer's craft, or lists of powerful and intriguing words that the students could use (verbs, adverbs, adjectives); lists of high-frequency words as references for spelling; revising and editing checklists and bookmarks; the students' writing records; the students' journal writing; their writing in different stages of the writing process; conference forms; and writing assessments such as those in this book's Appendix. A writing process portfolio should be used for daily writing. A student's showcase portfolio contains a table of contents and the student's published pieces of writing with "copyright" dates, so that both the teacher and student can see progress over time. Students' writing portfolios should be shared with their families during family conferences and celebrations.

Publishing Strategies

PURPOSE: For students to publish and share their writing with a wide audience.

PROCEDURE: Class or individual books can be displayed in the classroom or school library for others to read. Student writing can also be published in a class or school newspaper or on school websites.

Publishing and Contest Opportunities for Student Writing

PURPOSE: For students to publish and share their writing with a wide audience, including online.

PROCEDURE: As students go through the writing process, they can get feedback from a variety of sources. Teachers and students should search the internet, newspapers, and magazines for writing publishing and contest opportunities. Students must read the criteria for each venue carefully, to be sure that their compositions meet the criteria or can be adapted to meet the criteria.

EXAMPLES OF OPPORTUNITIES:

1. The Scholastic Art and Writing Awards (*www.artandwriting.org*).
2. PBS Kids Writers Contest (*www.pbssocal.org/education*).
3. TIME for Kids reporter contest, for ages 14 and younger (*www.timeforkids.com*).
4. National Council of Teachers of English (NCTE) Achievement Awards in Writing, for high school juniors (*https://ncte.org/awards/achievement-awards-in-writing*).
5. *Skipping Stones*, an international multicultural magazine with the Youth Honor Award that recognizes creative and artistic works by young people, and that promotes multicultural and nature awareness (*www.skippingstones.org/wp*).
6. Letters About Literature, a contest in which a student (grades 4–12) writes an essay in the form of a letter describing how a book or author has had a profound effect on their outlook on life, sponsored by the Library of Congress Center for the Book (*www.read.gov/contests*).

Journal-Writing Strategies

• Scaffolding Students' Journal Writing

SOURCE: Fahsl and McAndrews (2012)

PURPOSE: For students to record personal experiences; explore reactions and interpretations to reading and videos; or record, analyze, or enhance information about literature or other subject areas in a journal as a tool for thinking and learning.

PROCEDURE: As the teacher, develop a journaling unit that includes students' identifying journal formats and writing from different perspectives, understanding content by translating accurate information into their journals from multiple resources, reflecting on their learning, and improving individual writing skills. Use Table 7.3 to select the type of journal writing to teach. Then see the sample lesson plan for writing a simulated content journal entry in Figure 7.11 on page 337.

• Personal Journals

PURPOSE: For students to have a place and time to write for their own purposes.

PROCEDURE: As the teacher, provide paper or digital journals for students to write in daily. Explain that a journal is a safe place for writing whatever they want, and that students will not be criticized or corrected. You can suggest prompts or writing topics, or students can write on self-selected topics. Model journaling by using the think-aloud strategy. Then have students write on their own, and encourage them to reread for clarity of their message. Let them know that the meaning of the message is the most important, and that their spelling will not be graded. However, for a reader to understand their message, they need to say a problematic word slowly, write letters for the sounds heard, and then circle the word if they do not think they spelled it correctly. Periodically encourage them to reread their past entries. Remember that even kindergarteners can write in journals: They can use the resources in their environment and their knowledge of phoneme–grapheme correlations to write in their journals and draw pictures.

TABLE 7.3. Types of Journals

Form	Description	Example	
Personal	Students record events in their lives and explore issues that concern them.	"Last summer my family and I went to Disney World for vacation. I got to ride on lots of rides, and I had a good time. I want to go back again soon."	
Dialogue	Same as a personal journal, except that it is shared with the teacher or a peer, and the reader responds to the journal.	"Last summer my family and I went to Disney World for vacation. I got to ride on lots of rides, and I had a good time. I want to go back again soon." Reader Response: "What rides did you go on? What was your favorite?"	
Reading logs	Students respond to books they are reading, write and draw entries after reading, record vocabulary words, make charts, and write memorable quotes.	*Charlie and the Chocolate Factory* by Roald Dahl (1964): "What will or should happen to Violet? What is an oompaloompa?" Compare and contrast imagery in two of Dahl's works (*Charlie and the Chocolate Factory* and *James and the Giant Peach*).	
Learning logs	Students write in learning logs as part of science, social studies or math units. They write "quick writes," draw diagrams, and take notes.	Draw and label different ways to represent paying for 10-cent candy. 10 cents = one dime, two nickels, 10 pennies, or one nickel and five pennies.	
Double-entry journals	Students divide pages into two columns; write different information in each column, such as quotes on the left and reactions on the right, or predictions on left and what actually happened on right.	1. "Four score and seven years ago"	20 (4) + 7 = 87 years ago. Current year minus 87.
		2. Prediction: All coins are magnetic because they are made of metal.	U.S. coins were not magnetic, but the two pence from England and 20 colones from Costa Rica were.
Simulated journals	Students assume role of a fictional character or historical person and write entries from that person's viewpoint. Include details from the story or historical events to the entries.	*The Lion, the Witch and the Wardrobe* by C. S. Lewis (1950): Journal from the viewpoint of Lucy: "Although I was scared to enter the wardrobe, I wanted to see what was inside of it because I knew it was not an ordinary wardrobe." "The first time I saw Aslan, I was taken back by his beauty, grace, and kindness. How could such a large animal be so caring and loving? I knew immediately I could trust him no matter what."	
Graphic	Students create pictures, drawings, or charts.	Diagram of life cycle of a frog:	

• Dialogue Journals

PURPOSE: For students to regularly communicate with you as the teacher, to build student–teacher relationships, and to promote English language learning.

PROCEDURE: You and the students write back and forth on topics of their choosing, or you can provide prompts. This ongoing written interaction can take place weekly to exchange experiences, ideas, or reflections. Provide specific responses to the content of students' writing. You can assign students to turn in their dialogue journals on different days, so that you will have time to respond to each student.

FIGURE 7.11. Example of a lesson plan for writing a simulated content journal entry.

- **Prerequisites/Background Knowledge:** Identify important information from a text; restate information from text; orally compose or write complete sentences.
- **Assessment/Evidence of Student Learning:** Writing will be evaluated by using a simulated journal entry scoring guide to assess the use of the six traits.
- **Materials:** *Saguaro Moon: A Desert Journal* by Kristin Joy Pratt-Serafini (2002), paper, pencils, reference materials, science content journal.
- **Introduction:** Read book with class, and identify elements of a simulated journal entry for the desert biome. Question students throughout story about the writer's craft, background knowledge, and science content. Share how journal entries from the book relate to scoring guide.
- **Lesson Presentation:** Using teacher and student input, brainstorm a topic based on the reading selection and additional references; create a graphic organizer about the topic, event, key concepts, vocabulary, description of event, and sensory details. Using information from the graphic organizer, create a simulated journal entry to model journal format (include date and first-person narrative based on the six traits of writing). Include pictures or drawings to support content. Use the scoring guide to revise and edit work.
- **Guided Practice:** Have students brainstorm in pairs, select a different topic from the text, and create a graphic organizer from the text and additional references. Have each pair write a simulated journal entry based on the graphic organizer, including pictures or drawings to support content. Have them use the scoring guide to revise and edit work. Have pairs read aloud their journal entries to the class. The students will provide constructive feedback based on the scoring guide and ideas learned from the journal entry.
- **Independent Practice:** Individually, have students choose a new book from teacher or student selected texts. Using the new book, have them select a topic and related reference materials to create a graphic organizer. Based on the graphic organizer, have them write a simulated journal entry, including pictures or drawings to support content. Have them use the scoring guide to revise and edit work. Have individuals read aloud their journal entries to the class. The students will provide constructive feedback based on the scoring guide and ideas learned from the journal entry. Students will peer-assess independent journal entries, using scoring guide and provide constructive feedback. Students will use feedback to revise work. Students will sign up to meet with the teacher for additional feedback and then make a final copy with illustrations. Students will share their work by reading their simulated journal entries and showing their illustrations to the class.
- **Closure:** Review important components of a simulated journal entry based on the scoring guide. Briefly explain to students that the next type of journal entry they will be working on is a learning log from their upcoming science experiment.

Content-Learning Log

PURPOSE: For students to record their reflections about what they are learning and how they are going about learning it, in order to promote metacognition. These journals can reveal students' perceptions and misperceptions of the information, as well as their reactions to the way the material is being taught.

PROCEDURE: Students write about each subject area and reflect on their thinking and learning, using a guide. This guide can provide sentence starters, such as "This topic reminds me of . . ."; "I've been learning about . . ."; "The part I know the most about is . . ."; "The part that is the most confusing is . . ."; "I'd like to know more about . . ."; and "Knowing about this topic helps me . . ."

Narrative and Descriptive Writing Strategies

• Narrative Writing Guide

PURPOSE: For students to use an organizational structure for writing narratives.

PROCEDURE: Students answer the questions presented in Table 7.4 before, during, and after writing. After writing the initial draft, students reread it and revise it for meaning, edit for grammar and conventions, and share it with others.

• Alternate Endings

PURPOSE: For students to use the author's style in a text to write a different ending to a published story.

PROCEDURE: After reading a complete story or reading up to the point of the resolution, students write an original ending to the story.

• Adaptations of Stories

PURPOSE: For students to rewrite a story by changing one or more of the story elements.

PROCEDURE: First, as the teacher, model this by sharing different versions of stories such as "Cinderella" and "The Three Little Pigs." Then discuss the common elements and what was different. For example, the characters and the setting could be different, and the problem could be modified to fit the new setting.

• Writing as a Character

PURPOSE: For students to identify elements of characterization and then write in the role of a character in a text.

TABLE 7.4. Narrative Writing Guide

Parts	Questions to answer with your writing
Setting	Where and when does your story take place? Identify and provide details of the setting (place, time period, time of year, time of day).
Initiating event	What happened to the main character to cause him/her to do something?
Problem	What is the problem?
Character's feelings	What are the main character's feelings about what happened (emotions, goals, desires, intentions, thoughts)?
Events	What does each character do? Sequence the story, and add details that include the five senses.
Attempt	How does the main character attempt to solve the problem?
Additional attempts	What else does the character do?
Consequences	What happened as a result of the attempts? Are there any complications?
Resolution	How does the character feel about the consequences?

PROCEDURE: Students write a letter to the author or to another character in the role of one of the characters. Students examine the character's actions, motivations, feelings, regrets, limitations, aspirations, experiences, and appearances. They also examine the other characters' comments and actions toward this character. The students then take on that personality and write to the author or another character about how this character is feeling and what they would like to do.

Dear Diary

PURPOSE: For students to connect reading and writing instruction by writing a diary entry for a selected character.

PROCEDURE: Students first learn that a diary is a place to write down the events of the day and personal feelings. They then create a diary for a character in the book they are reading. The following are possible questions to consider in the journal writing and can be adjusted to fit a particular book or topic: "What kind of day have you had? What is one feeling you've had today? Has anything special happened to you today [describe events]? Where were you [describe setting]? Why do you think this happened? Is there anything else you'd like to tell us?" By writing in the diary, students become actively involved in the story and "become" the character.

Narrative Plot Scoring Guide

PURPOSE: For students to write beginning, rising, and ending actions in personal or other narratives.

PROCEDURE: First, as the teacher, write an example of a problem that you have had. Then show the students the *Narrative Plot Scoring Guide* (see Appendix, p. 481) and help them to identify the problem, rising action, and ending action in your writing. Then have the students write a personal narrative about a problem that they had, the events leading up to the solution, and how the problem was solved.

EXAMPLE:

> Problem—We moved to a new house, and my dog ran away.
>
> Rising Actions—We went looking for her. We called the police and put up signs with her picture. We got a phone call from a man saying he found our dog.
>
> Ending Action—We went to his house and brought her home. We got her new dog tags and made sure she didn't get out again.

Letter Writing

PURPOSE: For students to write friendly and business letters for authentic purposes in the correct format.

PROCEDURE: Students first review examples of friendly letters and business letters and learn to identify all the parts of a letter. They can then write to pen pals, authors, friends, or family members. Students' letters can be mailed or emailed.

• Literary Devices—Claim It, Name It, Frame It Strategy

SOURCE: Philbeck (n.d.).

PURPOSE: For students to identify and correctly use literary devices and figurative language.

PROCEDURE: First, as the teacher, select a piece of literature or a song with numerous examples of literary devices and figurative language. Read the story aloud or have students listen to the song. Then have them underline examples of literary devices and figurative language. They can then complete a Claim It, Name It, Frame It strategy chart (see Figure 7.12 for an example) with a quote from the work in the Claim It column, a label for the device or technique in the Name It column, and an explanation or analysis of the author's purpose in the Frame It column.

• Name That Emotion

SOURCE: Newingham (2008).

PURPOSE: For students to identify and correctly use aspects of voice such as mood or personality in their writing.

PROCEDURE: As the teacher, write each of the following emotion words on a card: *happiness, excitement, fear, confusion, anger, boredom, jealousy, envy, greed, joy, guilt, pride, compassion, arrogance, hunger, relief, satisfaction, love, regret, sadness, gratitude, panic, embarrassment, empathy, sympathy, hope, anxiety, concern, loneliness, surprise, shame, curiosity, disappointment, shock, exhaustion, confidence, disapproval, remorse.* Give each student a card. Students write a paragraph describing the emotion on their card. The students then read their paragraph to the class, and the other students try to guess the name of the emotion. Students must include at least one of their emotion words in their next piece of narrative or descriptive writing.

• Similes and Metaphors

PURPOSE: For students to interpret and write similes and metaphors.

FIGURE 7.12. Claim It, Name It, Frame It strategy, example for *Hatchet*, by Gary Paulsen (1987).

Claim It (Quote from the work)	Name It (Label the device or technique)	Frame It (Explain or analyze author's purpose)
"skip once on the water as hard as concrete"	*concrete* = simile	To show that they hit the water really hard.
"Somebody was screaming, screaming as the plane drove down into the water." "He was free. Tearing free. Ripping free."	repetition	To emphasize the strong emotion.
"tight *animal screams* of fear and pain"	metaphor	To show the intensity and primal sound of the screams.
" *raked* at the seatbelt catch," "He *clawed* up into the blue"	*raked* = vivid verbs *clawed* = vivid verbs	*To help the reader visualize how frantic he was to get out.*

PROCEDURE: As the teacher, provide poems with examples of similes and metaphors. Ask students questions such as these: "What are some ways authors write to make their details more vivid? What are some good words to describe a ______________ [give an example]? How can we write things to show comparisons?" Next, provide definitions for similes and metaphors. Use a list of sample similes and metaphors, and have the students identify each. Also have the students identify what is being compared in the examples. Ask students to change the similes to metaphors and the metaphors to similes. As a class, choose a person from television or an era in history, and write several similes and metaphors to describe the person. Afterward, students write their own similes and metaphors and share them. Assess students' similes and metaphors: Did they use *like* or *as* in similes? Did they use comparisons? Is the information accurate about the person they chose?

• Hyperbole

PURPOSE: For students to identify examples of hyperbole and use them appropriately in their writing.

PROCEDURE: First, as the teacher, define *hyperbole* as an exaggeration or overstatement that is used to make a point but is not to be taken literally. Hyperbole is appropriate to use in narratives, but not in essays or reports. Provide examples such as "I've told you a million times not to exaggerate," or "This box weighs a ton." Provide other examples within poems or short stories. Have students dictate as many instances of hyperbole as possible and discuss their meanings. Students then work in pairs to write a poem or short story with characters who use hyperbole repeatedly.

• Poems and Songs

PURPOSE: For students to write creative poems and songs.

PROCEDURE: Students read several poems or song lyrics in the style that the class is studying and discuss the characteristics of that type of poem or song. First as a class, and then individually, students write poems or songs of the same type. They then write or rewrite their own poems or songs. The following are a few examples of poem/song types:

- **Acrostic.** A type of poem consisting of words or phrases about a topic, using each of the letters in the topic's name. Examples: For the word *read, Relaxing in a chair/Escaping reality/Anticipating the climax/Delighting in my favorite book.*
- **Haiku.** A Japanese poem with three lines of five, seven, and five syllables, respectively. Example: *A pond under trees/The sound of a frog jumping/In cool, green water.*
- **Limerick.** A humorous Irish poem containing a five-line, A-A-B-B-A rhyme pattern. Example: *There once was a man from Nantucket/Who kept all his cash in a bucket,/But his daughter, named Nan,/Ran away with a man,/And as for the bucket, Nan "tuck" it.*
- **Cinquain.** A five-line poem with adjectives based on a single topic and following this pattern: Line 1—a one-word title (two syllables). Line 2—a two-word phrase that describes the title, or just two words (four syllables). Line 3—a three-word phrase that describes an action relating to the title, or just action words (six syllables). Line 4—a four-word phrase that describes a feeling relating to the topic, or just feeling words (eight syllables). Line 5—one word that refers back to the title (one syllable).

- **Autobiographical poem.** A poem about yourself, following this pattern: Line 1—Your first name. Line 2—Four adjectives that describe you. Line 3—Son/daughter of ______________, Brother/sister of ______________. Line 4—Lover of [three people or ideas]. Line 5—Who feels [three sensations or emotions]. Line 6—Who finds happiness in [three things]. Line 7— Who needs [three things]. Line 8—Who gives [three things]. Line 9—Who fears [three things]. Line 10—Who would like to see [three things]. Line 11—Who enjoys [three things]. Line 12—Who likes to wear [three things]. Line 13 —"It is the memory of [name of a person], who taught me [two abstract concepts such as honesty]." Line 14—Your last name. You may change any ideas.

• Collaborative Alternate Writing

SOURCE: Walker (2004).

PURPOSE: For students (and the teacher) to collaboratively compose a story together.

PROCEDURE: Writing for a specified time—5 minutes, for example—each person alternately continues the development of a cohesive story line. They must first read what has been written so far and then continue the story. When it is completed, one person reads the story to the class.

• Collaborative Dot-to-Dot Narrative Writing

PURPOSE: For students to collaboratively write stories about people, places, and problems, and share these with the class.

PROCEDURE: First, as the teacher, review the story elements of characters, setting, and problem, and select sticker dots in three colors (e.g., yellow, red, blue) to represent them. Put one dot on each of a pack of index cards, and distribute one card to each student. Students who receive yellow dots write the name of a person; students with red dots write the name of a place; and students with blue dots write a problem. Students then form groups of three, with one student representing each color. Students share with their group what they wrote on their cards. Instruct each group to write a story using all three elements, thus connecting the dots. After students write their stories, they share them with the class. Students will be surprised at how different their stories are, even though they have the same elements.

ADAPTATION: Form groups with more than one problem, place, or person in each group. After the group writes the first story, instruct one student from each group to rotate to a new group and write a new story with the elements.

• Partner Plot Writing

PURPOSE: For pairs of students to write a short story, using the narrative plot elements of exposition (setting character) conflict, rising action, climax, falling action, resolution, and theme.

PROCEDURE: First, as the teacher, explain a plot diagram that visually represents the important events in a story (see Figure 7.13 for an example). The climax is at the top of the triangle; the introduction is the base; the rising and falling action are the sloping sides; and

FIGURE 7.13. Plot-writing map.

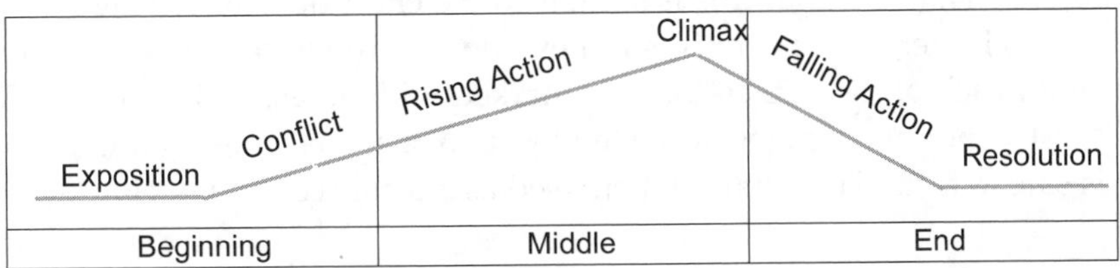

the resolution is the last base. Next, divide students into pairs, and give topics or beginning prompts on the board. The first student in each pair writes a topic or prompt and then begins to write a story. After a certain amount of time, instruct students to switch roles: Students who are writing must stop and pass their papers to their partners, even if they are in midsentence. The second student in each pair reads what is written and continues with the story. This continues until writing time is almost up. It is best to tell students when it is about "half time" and when there are 5 minutes left, to let partners know they need to start wrapping up their stories. This strategy can be used to emphasize certain areas of story writing, such as using quotations, using action words, sensory words, or transition words.

Expository Writing Strategies

• Using an Expository Text Structure for Writing

PURPOSE: For students to use an organizational structure to write expository texts.

PROCEDURE: The teacher selects short texts that are examples of these five expository text structures: description, sequence, compare–contrast, cause–effect, and problem–solution. Students identify which type of text each one is, using a text structure chart like Figure 6.17 (see Chapter 6, p. 257); this chart includes definitions, signal words, and sample graphic organizers for all of these text structures. Once students have learned about each of the text structures, they select one of them to use for their writing, depending on their purpose. They then create a graphic organizer for the selected text structure to use as a prewriting activity. They next write their own expository text, using that text structure and its signal words to guide the writing. After writing the initial draft, they reread it and see if the text structure is evident in the writing. For example, if they chose the compare–contrast text structure, did they explain how two ideas were similar and then how they were different, using the same categories? If they contrasted alligators and crocodiles, for instance, they would need to explain how they differ in the shape of their snouts (alligators have wide U-shaped snouts, while crocodile snouts are more pointed and V-shaped). They would not list all of the characteristics of an alligator and then all of the characteristics of a crocodile. Finally, students revise their writing for meaning, edit for grammar and conventions, and share it with others.

• Five Senses for Descriptive Writing

PURPOSE: For students to use their five senses to observe and describe their environment to improve descriptive writing.

PROCEDURE: Students review the descriptions in the second row of a five-senses chart like the one in Figure 7.14. (Note that this is similar to the chart depicted in Figure 7.4, for use with descriptions in personal narratives.) They add specific observations or memories in the third row for each of the senses. Taste is marked with an asterisk (*) in the Figure 7.14 chart because it is not encouraged to taste objects in nature, unless an expert says that something is safe to taste. This chart is then used as a resource for descriptive writing.

• Scientific/Nature Journal

PURPOSE: For students to document observations, questions, and learning in descriptive writing.

PROCEDURE: Each student creates and designs their own nature journal. It can be filled with blank pages or a template. Students can record observations, questions, data about their questions, measurements and quantities, and results of experiments. They can sketch their observations and label them or take pictures and insert them later. They can write reflections about their learning and their nature experiences. See the example in Figure 7.15.

• "Are, Have, Can, Eat, Live" Animal Report Planning Guide

PURPOSE: For students to write an animal report using a description of its characteristics.

PROCEDURE: Using an animal report planning guide like the one shown in Figure 7.16, students select an animal and describe what it is, what it has, what it can do, what it eats, and where it lives in phrases under each column head. Students then use this information as a planning guide to write an animal report. Figure 7.17 on page 346 gives an example for a report on a frog.

FIGURE 7.14. Five-senses observation chart for expository writing, example. (The asterisk after "Taste" indicates that tasting things in nature is not recommended unless an expert says it is safe to do so.)

A Walk in the Woods				
See	**Hear**	**Smell**	**Feel**	**Taste***
Color, size, shape, movement, pattern, physical characteristics	Loud, noisy, musical, softly	Earthy, moldy, fragrant, fresh, sweet flowery, musty, piney, minty, aromatic, smelly	Rough, smooth, soft, hard, moist, dry, hot, cold, prickly, sticky, delicate	Sweet, sour, salty, bitter, bland, crunchy
Deer tracks, animal homes, running swiftly, frog's vocal sac, antennae	Birds singing, squirrels chattering, deer crunching, frogs croaking	Honeysuckle, lavender, ponderosa pine, lemon verbena, fresh air, skunk	Toad's rough, bumpy skin; prickly pine cone	Sweet raspberries, sweet persimmons

FIGURE 7.15. Nature journal entry, example and photos.

Peter's **Nature Journal Entry** page 10

Date: April 28 **Time:** 7:00 a.m. to 8:15 a.m.

Location: Watershed Nature Center

Weather: Partially sunny with small cumulus clouds, 53°F

Describe what I . . .

See: I saw deer tracks across the path going towards the water, then all of the sudden I saw a newborn white-tailed deer wobble across the grass. I saw a muskrat coming out of his den. I saw a red-winged blackbird with bright red and yellow shoulder patches, perched on a cattail. It leaned forward and drooped his wings, spreading his tail feathers.

Hear: As the red-winged blackbird spread his tail feathers, he called out, "conk-la-ree!"

Smell: I smelled the fragrant sweet flag plant.

Feel: I felt the cool breeze blowing through my hair.

Think: I am at peace when I can be out in nature. I am in awe of the beauty around me.

Draw/photo of what I see: Muskrat, red-winged blackbird, and newborn white-tailed deer.

FIGURE 7.16. Animal report planning guide.

Are	Have	Can	Eat	Live
Animal classification and characteristics	**Physical description**	**Movement and behaviors**	**Eat or eaten by**	**Habitat**
Mammals, birds, reptiles, amphibians, fish, insects, spiders, worms	Covering (feathers, fur, scales, skin)	Run, jump, swim, fly	Herbivore: Plants Carnivore: Animals Omnivore: Both	Desert, forest, rainforest, grassland, Arctic, fresh water, ocean
Warm-blooded, cold-blooded, vertebrates (with bones)	Body parts: legs (how many?), thorax, wings, bones, antennae, horns, etc.	Lay eggs, breathe air, nurse babies	Grass, fruit, flower nectar, insects, mammals	Air, land, trees, water, underground

FIGURE 7.17. Animal report planning guide, example.

	Are	Have	Can	Eat	Live
	Amphibians Cold-blooded, backbone	Short bodies; moist, smooth skin; long legs; bulging eyes; gills as tadpoles, lungs as adults	Swim, hop, lay eggs in clusters, change from water breathing to air breathing	Meat (carnivores): Insects, worms, flies, mosquitoes, moths, and dragonflies	Moist environments, often in ponds and marshes

• "What Am I?" Riddle Book

PURPOSE: For students to use descriptive language to describe an animal, so that the reader can make a prediction about what it is.

PROCEDURE: Students write "What am I?" on the title page of a notebook. On each subsequent page, they write clues describing an animal. On the last page, they write "What am I?" at the top. Then they draw a picture or insert a picture of the answer to the riddle and cover the picture with a sticky note so the reader can't see it. Students then share their riddle books, and their peers predict what each animal is. Once several have made predictions, they uncover each picture to reveal the answer. Students can also take pictures of parts of the subject to help with the prediction. See the example in Figure 7.18.

FIGURE 7.18. "What am I?", example.

What am I?
I am very social. I enjoy swimming and walking on land. I have five digits in my hind limbs. I don't have arms or legs.

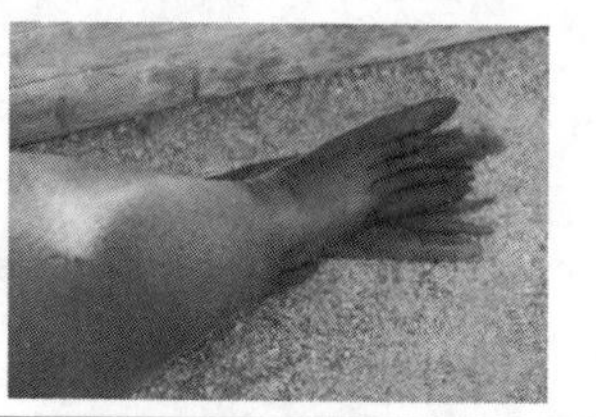

I have large front flippers. My body is covered in a chestnut brown fur coat that is water-resistant. I give birth on land in rookeries, and I nurse my young.

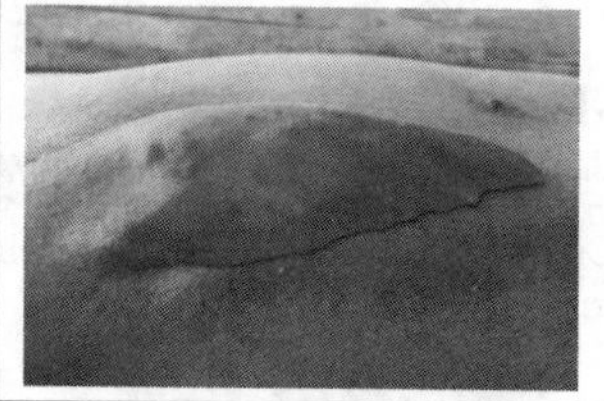

I have ear flaps and whiskers. I bark loudly. I am a carnivore and eat mostly fish. I am endangered.

What am I?

I am a Galapagos sea lion.

• List–Group–Label for Categorization, Generalization, and Examples

PURPOSE: For students to write a text that includes categorization, generalization, and examples.

PROCEDURE: The teacher uses a mentor text such as *Feathers and Hair: What Animals Wear* by Jennifer Ward (2017a) to demonstrate how the author categorizes animals by their skin coverings (feathers, hair, scales, horns, etc.). Next, the students select a topic that they would like to write about, such as classification of animals. They list all of the animals they want to include in their writing. They group them into categories by their physical characteristics, and then label the groups, such as invertebrates, fish, amphibians, reptiles, birds, and mammals. Figure 7.19 shows an example of a list–group–label animal classification chart. Students then create classification cards or posters describing each animal's characteristics. They should be sure to include characteristics that describe how they are different from similar animals (e.g., sea lions have ear flaps, and seals do not).

• Flip-Flop Books for Compare–Contrast

PURPOSE: For students to write a text that demonstrates the compare–contrast text structure.

PROCEDURE: As the teacher, read a mentor text such as *Forest Bright, Forest Night* by Jennifer Ward (2005). Have the students identify what is being compared, such as diurnal and nocturnal animal behavior. Point out that this text uses a flip-flop format. The first half of the book tells the "forest bright" diurnal part of the book; flip the book over, and the second part of the book tells the "forest night" nocturnal part of the book. Students then brainstorm sets of two things they can compare in their writing, such as bats and birds in the book *Stellaluna* by Janell Cannon (1993), or frogs and toads in *Frogs and Toads* by Bobbie Kalman (1994). Students can begin their writing by creating a Venn diagram comparing the two subjects (see Figure 7.20 for an example using *Stellaluna*). Then they can write their own text and make a flip-flop book.

FIGURE 7.19. List–group–label animal classification chart.

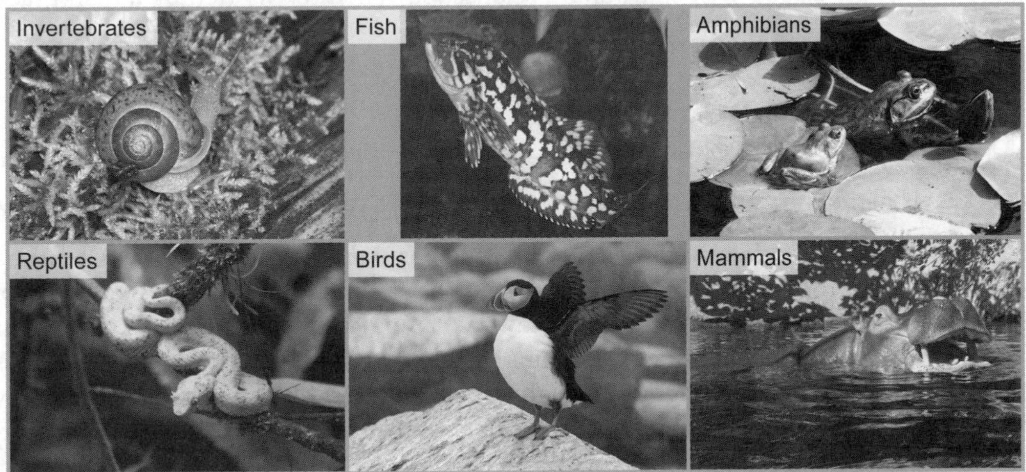

FIGURE 7.20. Venn diagram, example for *Stellaluna.*

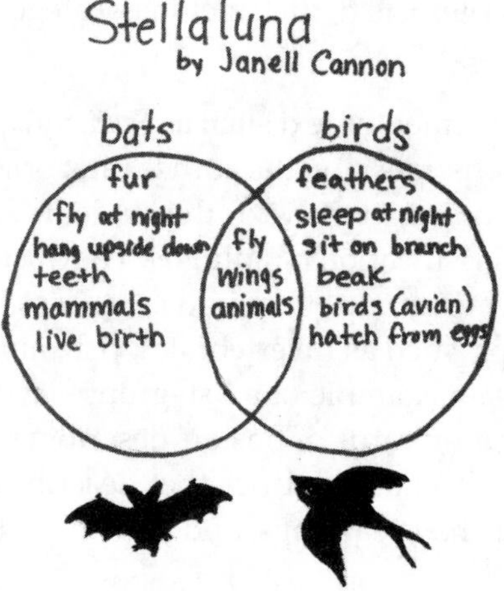

• Life Cycle/Cumulative Tale Strategy for Sequence or Process Text Structure

SOURCE: Ward and McAndrews (2019).

PURPOSE: For students to write a text that demonstrates a sequence or process text structure.

PROCEDURE: As the teacher, read a mentor text such as *The Seed and the Giant Saguaro* by Jennifer Ward (2003), which is about the life cycle of the saguaro cactus. Students identify the stages of the saguaro's life cycle. They photocopy or draw each stage and tape it to a hula hoop. Through doing this, they will see that each stage is part of a cycle that goes back to the start. Note that *The Seed and the Giant Saguaro* is also an example of a cumulative tale; as the text for each new stage is added, the previous text is repeated. For their own writing, students brainstorm other cycles that they might want to write about (e.g., the water cycle, butterfly metamorphosis, the oxygen–carbon dioxide cycle, food chains). Each student creates a graphic organizer to demonstrate the chosen cycle or process. Figure 7.21 shows a food web chart and a science journal entry written by a fifth-grade student.

• "Will We Miss Them?" Strategy for Cause–Effect Text Structure

PURPOSE: For students to write a text that demonstrates a cause–effect text structure.

PROCEDURE: As the teacher, read a mentor text such as *Will We Miss Them?* by Alexandra Wright (1992). In this book, children learn about the fascinating lives and challenges of endangered species, which is the first step toward saving them. Students then write their own text based on this book, using the frame "If ______________ disappear, will we miss them?" (Ideas for the blank might include bees, water, trees, birds, bugs, or frogs.) They then create a cause–effect map and write a text about the effect of something's disappearance on the other things that depend on it.

FIGURE 7.21. Food web figure for sequence on text structure.

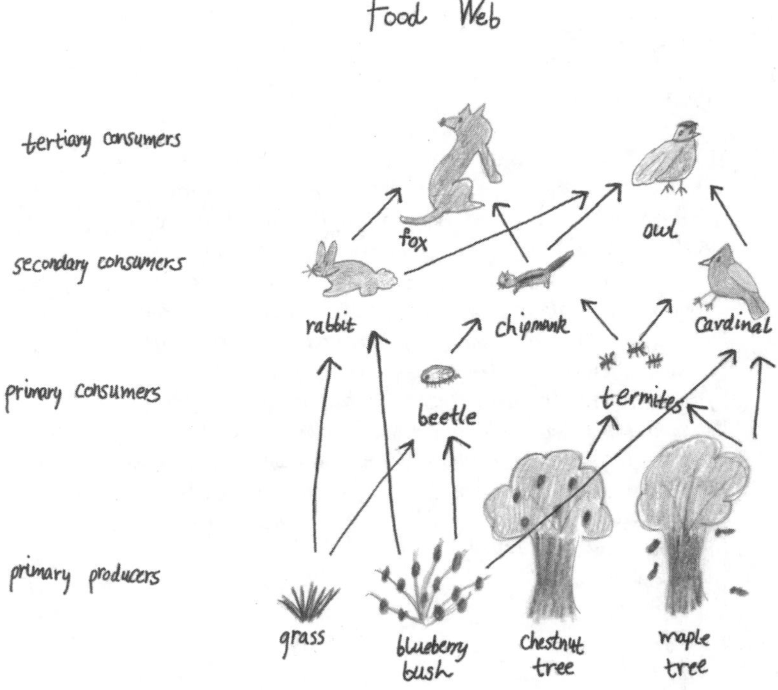

• Map Strategy for Problem–Solution Text Structure

PURPOSE: For students to write a text that demonstrates a problem and solution text structure.

PROCEDURE: As the teacher, read a mentor text such as *Mama Dug a Little Den* by Jennifer Ward (2018), which poses these problems: How will the polar bear protect her young? How will she have enough food for winter? How will she survive weather extremes? Next, have students create a problem–solution map with problems on the left, possible solutions and concerns in the middle, and a final solution on the right. Now have the students brainstorm other possible problems and solutions. See the example in Figure 7.22 for a lesson on baby rabbits.

• Strategy for Question–Answer Texts

PURPOSE: For students to write a text that demonstrates a question-and-answer text structure.

PROCEDURE: As the teacher, read a mentor text such as *What Will Grow?* (Ward, 2017b) or *What Will Hatch?* (Ward, 2013). In each of these texts, one page asks a question and the following page answers the question. Students then brainstorm their own topics and possible questions they could ask. The students will need to find resources to answer the questions. The following are questions they could ponder: How are plants and animals classified? How are plants and animals interrelated in a watershed? How are birds' beaks adapted to

FIGURE 7.22. Science journal, example for sequence on process.

March 2, 2011

Dear Journal,

In science we have been learning about food chains and webs in different biomes. A food chain is a sequence of who eats who in an ecosystem. There are different levels in a food chain. First there are the primary producers like grass and other plants that make their own food. Then are animals that eat grass such as grasshoppers, these are called primary consumers. Then there are secondary consumers that eat the primary consumers like rats. Next are the tertiary consumers that eat the secondary consumers like snakes. The quarternary consumers eat the tertiary consumers like hawks. The food chain ends with animals that have almost no natural enemies. It would be great to be a hawk because you could glide through the air without worrying about being eaten.

example
1. grass
2. grasshopper
3. rat
4. snake
5. hawk

I live near a deciduous forest, a forest that has trees with large leaves that completely fall off for part of every year. The trees around here still have no leaves and we just had another snow storm. I can't wait until spring. In our forest there are plants and animals that are connected in many ways to help them all survive. My food web on the next page shows how they are related. If something happens to even one thing the ecosystem in our forest will get all out of wack!

eat specific kinds of food? How do animals protect themselves? How can people identify animals' presence in an environment if they are not seen?

• Traveling Paragraphs

PURPOSE: For students to reread ideas and supporting details in peers writing and then add additional ideas and details to the paragraphs using complete sentences.

PROCEDURE: To prepare for this activity as the teacher, write five main idea sentences on strips of paper or sticky notes and then as a group students write supporting details. For example, "How do dogs help people" or "How to live a healthy lifestyle." Organize students into groups of five. Distribute one main idea sentence to each student, and give each student 1 minute to write a supporting detail for their main idea. When time is up, instruct students to pair up and trade paper strips with each other. Give students another minute to read this new main idea and its detail, and to add a different supporting detail. Then have students trade papers again. Continue in this manner until each student has written a supporting detail for all five ideas and traded to get their original paper strip back.

ADAPTATION: Have students share paragraphs with the class, allowing students to listen very carefully for details. Instruct them to give it a thumbs up, thumbs sideways, or thumbs down, and discuss reasons.

Newspapers and Newsletters

PURPOSE: For students to write a news article about an event by answering "who, what, where, when, why, and how" questions

PROCEDURE: Students identify events to write about and answer who, what, where, when, why, and how questions. Students create their own class newspaper and publish their own expository writing about what they are learning and upcoming events. This newspaper could also be a place to publish creative writings as feature stories.

ADAPTATION: When reading narratives, students write a newspaper article about the events in a story.

Discipline-Specific Reports

PURPOSE: For students to write reports related to academic disciplines using inquiry and academic language (grade 1 and above).

PROCEDURE: Students identify research topics, conduct literature reviews and investigations, and write reports to share their learning and findings using the *Expository and Persuasive Writing Checklist* (see Appendix, p. 482). Remind them to use multiple sources and include text features such as headings, illustrations, graphs, tables of contents, and glossaries.

Recipes and How-To Books

PURPOSE: For students to write specific directions for how to make or do something.

PROCEDURE: Students select something that they know how to make or do that they want to share with others. Read examples of recipes and how-to books. Write their own recipes or books on how to make something; be sure to include all of the materials and detailed steps. Ask someone else to follow the steps exactly as written to see that they are clear and nothing is left out.

PowerPoint and Other Media Presentations

PURPOSE: For students to use technology to present information in a visually engaging manner.

PROCEDURE: Students identify and narrow their topic; gather information, images, and audio; and then create PowerPoint or other types of media presentations to share information from group or individual projects. Be sure to revise and edit the text for accuracy and clarity and use graphic design elements to make the presentation engaging to the audience.

• Webpages or Blogs

PURPOSE: For students to create a personal or class webpage or blog to share their learning and creative writing.

PROCEDURE: After teachers share elements of example webpages or blogs, students create their own or collaborate to create one for the class. A class webpage or blog should be maintained by the teacher and can include regular entries of class or school events, commentary, assignments, teacher and student writing, messages to families, photos, and videos. A blog is actually a website, but the entries are commonly displayed in reverse chronological order. Readers can leave comments in an interactive format in a blog. Some blogs could discuss a certain topic or function as an online diary. Select and invite a wide audience for the webpages and blogs.

• Website Creation Strategies

SOURCE: *www.design-training.com/web-design/website-creation-for-children.html.*

PURPOSE: For students to create a website to share writing compositions and information with a broader audience.

PROCEDURE: For building a website, it is best to start with using a basic template with drag-and-drop features. The teacher and students can seek out free website builders and hosting sites, such as Ning, Weebly, or Homestead. Students can use the templates, choose colors and fonts, and add photos and graphics to create a page or a social network for family and friends. The following are the steps needed to create a website: choose a topic for the website; register a domain name; select a web hosting service; find or create graphics and photos; build a home page; write content; add extras (such as music, a hit counter, a photo album, or videos); and, if desired, make it a multilanguage site. Once the website is created, students can continue to add to it and redesign it.

Persuasive Writing Strategies

• Persuasive Writing Guide

PURPOSE: For students to use organizational structure to revise and edit their writing of persuasive texts.

PROCEDURE: The teacher selects short persuasive texts. Students identify the persuasive elements in these texts. Students then select a topic that is important to them, such as why they should be allowed to participate in an after-school activity. They answer the questions in a persuasive writing guide like the one in Table 7.5 before, during, and after writing. After writing their initial drafts, students reread them and revise them for content and clarity and edit them for grammar and other conventions. They then share their writing with others in an attempt to persuade them to think or do something differently.

TABLE 7.5. Persuasive Writing Guide

Parts	Questions to answer within your writing
Assertion and introduction	What do I believe? Why is it important to me?
Supporting evidence	What are the reasons I believe it?
Opposing view	What do others say they believe?
Arguments against the opposing view	Why do I disagree with them?
Summary	What do I want the reader to do?

• Power of Persuasive Writing

SOURCE: Norris and Brock (2001).

PURPOSE: For students to read and write persuasive arguments and advertisements in print and electronic formats.

PROCEDURE: This instruction could be a 3-week unit that begins with the students and teacher searching magazines and the internet for persuasive arguments and advertisements. Students use critical reading skills to deconstruct the arguments and advertisements to identify persuasive techniques; discriminate between the stated and inferred; differentiate between fact and opinion; and articulate how persuasion in media can affect and manipulate people's thinking. Students will then create a multimedia presentation, webpage, or advertisement reflecting an effective argument, with evidence and attention to differing perspectives, using at least one persuasive technique. The teacher provides questions to guide their research and projects. Students are evaluated on the basis of their responses to the following questions: "What makes your project an effective persuasive argument or advertisement?", "What persuasive techniques did you use?", "Were your opinions, reasons, and examples clearly stated?", and "What research did you conduct to understand differing perspectives?

• Letters to the Editor or Election Speeches

PURPOSE: For students to write a persuasive letter or speech to convince an audience to support their ideas and opinions.

PROCEDURE: Students write letters or speeches persuading someone to do something using persuasive techniques. Students revise and edit them based on persuasive criteria. Letters can be mailed and speeches can be presented to the class or to another audience.

• OREO Persuasive Writing Strategy

SOURCE: Tracey (2011).

PURPOSE: For students to compose a persuasive essay with opinions, reasons, and examples.

PROCEDURE: Students complete an OREO graphic organizer by giving Opinions, Reasons, and Examples, and then restating the Opinion (see Figure 7.23 for an example).

FIGURE 7.23. OREO persuasive writing graphic organizer, example.

Opinion: I want to get a new puppy.

Reason #1: Our old dog isn't fun to play with.

Examples:
1. She doesn't run.
2. She doesn't play fetch.

Reason #2: I want to teach a dog to do tricks.

Examples:
1. Our other dog doesn't do tricks.
2. I saw dogs doing fun tricks on T.V.

Reason #3: I am now more responsible.

Examples:
1. I have been feeding our other dog every day.
2. I have been helping to pick up after her.

Opinion: I am ready to get a new puppy.

VISUAL REPRESENTATION: STRATEGIES

General Guidelines

PURPOSE: For students to communicate ideas with visuals alone or by using visuals to support textual information.

PROCEDURE: As the teacher, instruct students to do the following:

- Determine the purpose for your visual(s).
- Select the type of two- or three-dimensional visuals you want to create (e.g., illustrations, photographs, charts, graphs, maps videos, websites, models, theater).
- Decide on the best media or materials to create it (e.g., crayons, paint, colored pencils, clay, craft materials, photographs, digitally created graphics, video).
- Decide how you might integrate visuals with other information in print and digital texts.
- Plan and incorporate design elements such as line, color, shape, space, texture, typography, and scale, to create two- or three-dimensional, static or dynamic (moving) graphics and arts.
- Plan and incorporate design principles of balance, contrast, emphasis, movement, pattern, rhythm, and unity–variety to give the visual structure and convey the intent.
- Identify and use digital and web design tools with static and dynamic content with navigation menus and hyperlinks.
- Identify and use photo, video, and audio editing tools.
- Evaluate your visual(s), using the same questions as those posed for viewing comprehension in Chapter 6.

Appendix

Assessments and Resources

Purposes for Assessments

Assessments	Purpose: To identify . . .	Which students? When?
Literacy Process Interview	Strategies student uses for listening, speaking, reading, writing, viewing and visually representing.	At least first-grade reading level if you want to know what literacy strategies they can identify.
Interest/Activity Inventories	Interests and activities for learning activities/connections.	PreK–12 if you want to know the student's interests.
Language Observation Scale	Speech or language problems that may require further assessment by speech–language pathologist.	PreK–12 if student is not a native English speaker or speech–language difficulties are noted.
Semantic Generative Vocabulary Assessment	Ability to name multiple items in a category, describe whole–part relationships, describe objects, and describe feelings and events.	PreK–12 if student appears to use limited vocabulary.
Oral Presentation Assessment	Important elements included in oral presentations.	3–12 for oral presentations (adapt to your criteria).
Synonym Vocabulary Assessment	Synonym vocabulary knowledge and to inform text-reading starting level.	K–12 if there are language/vocabulary concerns. Start listening level at frustration vocabulary reading level.
Antonym Vocabulary Assessment	Antonym vocabulary knowledge and to inform text-reading starting level.	K–12 if there are language/vocabulary concerns. Start listening level at frustration reading level.
Morphology Assessment—Inflectional Morphemes	Addition of inflected endings such as plurality, verb tense, and possession.	At or above first-grade reading level if student omits or adds incorrect inflectional morphemes.
Morphology Assessment—Derivational Morphemes	Addition of prefixes and suffixes that change word meaning and/or part of speech.	At or above first-grade reading level if student omits or adds incorrect derivational morphemes.
Auditory Discrimination Assessments—Consonants and Vowels (Long/Short and Others)	Ability to hear differences in phonemes in words.	At or above PreK for those with difficulties in blending, segmenting, or substituting phonemes in reading or writing words.
Phoneme Blending Assessment	Oral blending of sounds as needed for reading.	At or below first-grade level on reading word lists.
Phoneme Segmentation Assessment	Oral segmenting of sounds as needed for writing.	At or below first-grade level on writing word lists.
Letter and Sound Identification Assessment	Identification of known and unknown letters, sounds, and example words.	At or below first-grade level on reading or writing lists.
Emergent Text Concepts Assessment	Concepts of directionality, letters/words, and punctuation.	K–2, if not reading at or above first-grade level.
Graded Reading Words Assessment and Word Lists	Known sight words and ability to identify new words.	K–12; start at least two grade levels below actual grade.
Graded Writing Words Assessment	Spelling of high-frequency words (K–5) and commonly misspelled words (6–12).	All K–3 initial screening; K–12 students with spelling difficulties.

(continued)

Purposes for Assessments *(page 2 of 2)*

Assessments	Purpose: To identify . . .	Which students? When?
Sentence Dictation Assessment (PP/P, 1–2, 3+)	Phoneme–grapheme correlation and developmental spelling level.	All 1–3 initial screening; 1–12 with spelling difficulties, pre–post.
Handwriting Rubric Assessment	Formation and spacing within lines, words, and page.	K–2 and/or anyone with difficulties in handwriting.
Oral Reading Record Analysis of Miscues	Word identification and strategy use, in order to select appropriate materials and instructional strategies.	1–3 and all 12 who have difficulties with decoding and word identification in texts; should be paired with comprehension assessment.
Oral Reading Strategies Assessment	Oral reading strategy use and selection of additional strategies.	1–12 who may have difficulties with decoding and word identification.
Fluency Assessments by Teachers and Peers, Fluency Self-Assessment	Phrasing, intonation, expression, smoothness, and pace.	First-grade reading level and above for those who have difficulty.
Comprehension Retelling and Questioning Assessment: Guide	Comprehension of narrative and expository texts.	K–12 after all oral reading records and to monitor comprehension only.
Text, Graphic, and Organizational Features Assessment	Concepts such as the use of title page, parts of books, graphic information, and typographical features.	2–12, if student may not utilize nonfiction text concepts.
Text Structure Assessment	Text structures, related signal words, and ability to select and complete correlated graphic organizers.	3–12, before or after teaching text structures to improve comprehension.
Emergent Writing Stage Assessment	Ability to write letters, words, and a sentence with phonetic or standard spelling.	K–1, or any student who does not yet write conventional sentences.
Writing Composition Assessment Summary	Writing elements such as content, organization, and conventions.	Narrative and expository (K–12) and persuasive (3–12).
Writing Composition Rubric for Writer, Peer, and Teacher	Content, organization, and conventions.	K–12, for all writing throughout the year.
Writing Process Rubric for Writer, Peer, and Teacher	Concepts of prewriting, drafting, conferencing, revising, editing, publishing.	1–12, for all published writing throughout the year.
Visual Representation Assessment for Self, Peer, or Teacher	Ability to compose visuals, such as pictures, graphics, electronic texts, media, and models.	K–12, for all visual representations.
Multimedia Presentation Assessment for Self, Peer, or Teacher	Ability to create a multimedia presentation.	1–12, for all multimedia presentations.

Guidelines for Literacy Assessment Analysis

General Suggestions:

- Write in past tense.
- Put the child's name in the first statement in each section, and then use the correct pronoun thereafter.
- Begin by stating the observable task, assessment, and the grade or levels completed.
- Identify the independent functioning levels, stages, and scores, followed by specific patterns of strengths, and specific examples of incorrect responses.
- Identify the instructional functioning levels, stages, and scores, followed by specific examples of strengths and areas for improvement, with specific examples of incorrect responses.
- Identify the frustration functioning levels, stages, and scores, followed by specific examples of strengths and areas for improvement, with specific examples of incorrect responses.
- Write at least one positive comment first.
- Group related concepts together (e.g., word accuracy, use of cueing systems, word analysis, phonetic elements, fluency elements, comprehension, writing content, and writing mechanics). For miscues, write what the student said or did first, then a slash followed by the expected or correct response. In describing the correct or incorrect responses, use academic vocabulary followed by a family-friendly definition or example. If you are discussing a phonetic pattern, underline the element you are focusing on (e.g., *He incorrectly read vowel diagraphs such as* m<u>e</u>t/m<u>ee</u>t *and* r<u>a</u>n/r<u>ai</u>n).
- Write observable behaviors, not subjective comments.
- Write what the student did or did not do; do not write that the student "struggled with" something or "didn't pay attention."

Analysis of Reading Words (word lists or text reading):

- Attempted to read/did not attempt to read all words.
- Appealed/did not appeal for help.
- Attempted/did not attempt to sound out words.
- Tried/did not try alternate sounds for graphemes.
- Substituted real words/miscues that were not real words.
- Substituted words that looked similar.
- Said words with the same/different beginning, middle, and/or ending sounds.
- Blended/did not blend sounds together.
- Broke/did not break words into known parts. Did/did not read words with the correct consonant digraphs, consonant blends, vowel digraphs, diphthongs, vocalic *-r*, and *r-*, *l-*, *w-*, and *u*-controlled vowels (give specific examples).
- Read/did not read inflectional and derivational word endings.
- Self-corrected (most, some, a few, or no) miscues or mistakes.
- Read words at, above, or below grade level.

Analysis of Text Reading (in addition to the analysis of reading words):

- Used or did not use strategies to attempt to correct miscues (list which ones).
- Substituted words that looked/did not look similar (grapho-phonemics).
- Substituted words that had the same/different part of speech (syntax).
- Substituted words that made/did not make sense (semantics).
- Reread/did not reread when it did not make sense.
- Self-corrected/did not self-correct when it did not make sense.
- Read/did not read fluently.
- Stopped/did not stop at punctuation marks.
- Read/did not read in phrases.
- Read/did not read with expression.
- Read/did not read with intonation (voice going up and down).
- Read/did not read at a conversational pace.
- Read words in text at, above, or below grade level.

(continued)

Analysis of Comprehension:

- Identified/did not identify prior knowledge of concepts in the text.
- Retold/did not retell the characters, setting, problem, and/or resolution.
- Described/did not describe the main idea and/or the important details.
- Answered/did not answer questions that could be directly found in the text.
- Answered/did not answer questions that required the student to imply or connect information.
- Answered/did not answer questions about definitions of specific vocabulary words.
- Comprehended text at, above, or below grade level in narrative stories.
- Comprehended text at, above, or below grade level in (specify: narrative fiction, narrative nonfiction, expository fiction, or expository nonfiction) texts. Make a separate bullet for each type of text read.

Analysis of Writing Words:

- Attempted to write/did not attempt to write all words.
- Did not/did appeal for help.
- Attempted/did not attempt to sound out words to write them.
- Wrote/did not write words with correct beginning, middle, and/or ending letters.
- Wrote/did not write words with the correct:
  - Consonants.
  - Consonant digraphs.
  - Consonant blends.
  - Silent or double consonants.
  - Vowels.
  - Short vowels.
  - Long vowels, vowel digraphs, silent *-e*, diphthongs.
  - *r*-, *l*-, and *w*-controlled vowels, vocalic *-r*.
  - Prefixes and/or suffixes (e.g., inflectional—plurals, tenses; derivational—prefixes such as *un*-, *re*-, etc.; or suffixes such as *-ly*, *-ment*).
  - Apostrophes (contractions and possessives).
  - Homophones.
- Self-corrected (most, some, a few, or no) spelling mistakes.
- Wrote most words at the prephonetic, semiphonetic, phonetic, transitional, or conventional stage.
- Wrote words at, above, or below grade level.

Analysis of Writing Composition and Dictation Sentences (in addition to the analysis of writing words):

- Used/did not use prewriting strategies.
- Wrote/did not write the elements for narrative, expository, or persuasive writing.
- Included/did not include important ideas and details.
- Wrote with effective/ineffective organization (e.g., sequencing, opening, closing).
- Wrote with effective/ineffective sentence and/or paragraph fluency (e.g., sentence flow, variety, transition words).
- Wrote/did not write words that made sense.
- Wrote/did not write specific and descriptive words (proper nouns, vivid verbs, descriptive adjectives and adverbs).
- Used/did not use formal grammar and sentence structure (e.g., subject–verb agreement, verb tense, compound/complex sentences).
- Used/did not use correct end or middle punctuation (e.g., , ? ! , : : ( ) “ ”).
- Used/did not use correct capitalization for beginning of sentence, proper nouns, pronoun *I*, titles.
- Wrote/did not write with correct letter formation.
- Wrote/did not write with correct spacing.
- Revised/did not revise writing.
- Edited/ did not edit writing.

Analysis of Language:

- Used/did not use correct articulation of sounds or pronunciation of words.
- Speech was fluent/was not fluent as it was disrupted by repetitions, revisions, unusual pauses, or fillers.
- Spoke/did not speak in complete sentences.
- Spoke/did not speak using correct sentence structure, subject–verb agreement, verb tenses, and/or pronoun use.
- Used/did not use academic, content-, or discipline-specific words.
- Responded/did not respond appropriately to statements, questions, instructions, and/or requests for clarification.
- Maintained/did not maintain the topic while speaking.
- The listener understood/did not understand the meaning of the student's statements and questions.

(continued)

Example of Analysis:

*Laura read four graded reading word lists from preprimer through second grade. She was at the independent functioning level for the preprimer list at 100% and the primer list at 95%. She was at the instructional level for the first-grade list and at the frustration level for the second-grade list. She attempted to read all of the words and successfully self-corrected three words. On her miscues, she often substituted real words that began with the same initial sounds (*when/where*). Patterns of miscues included incorrectly reading words with vowel diagraphs (*plĕăs/please*) and leaving off word endings (*want/wanted*).*

Suggested Recommendations for Family Support (please revise for the individual student):

- Talk with your child [name] every day, and use interesting and specific words.
  - Discuss what you both did, like, learned, are concerned about, and want to do.
- Read to and with him/her every day.
- Go to the library or bookstore for your child to select new books to read.
- Have your child read something of his/her choice every day:
  - Books, newspapers, magazines, recipes, internet, computer programs, or email.
- Use the developmentally appropriate *Good Readers Bookmark* to try multiple strategies when he/she comes to unknown words.
- After reading each sentence, think, "does it make sense, sound right, and look right?"
- Have your child reread something to improve his/her fluency and understanding.
- Ask questions about what your child read.
  - Talk about how it is similar or different from his/her experiences.
  - Talk about how it is similar or different from another book or movie.
  - Ask what the child liked or learned from it.
- Write to and with your child every day.
- Have your child write something of his/her choice every day:
  - Journals, diaries, letters, email, stories, description of pictures, or grocery lists.
- Have your child reread what he/she wrote, to make sure that it makes sense, the words can be sounded out, and common words are spelled correctly.
- Encourage your child to create or add images to his/her writing.
- Talk about signs, maps, menus, brochures in the environment.
- Model your own reading and writing to your child, and talk about it.

Literacy Lesson Plan Format

Heading: Your name, name of student or group, grade, instructional level, and date of the lesson.

Objectives with Learning Standards: Based on each student's strengths and needs, what will the student(s) do in observable and measurable terms? What is the purpose of the task? How will you assess their learning? Write ABCD objectives: A = Audience, B = Behavior, C = Conditions, D = Degree of acceptable performance with criteria. Identify the state standard or Common Core State Standard that is met by each objective. Share the objectives with students.

- Language/vocabulary objective
- Reading fluency objective
- Comprehension objective
- Composition objective
- Word analysis objective

Materials: Include names and authors of books, and all curricular or prepared materials.

Procedure: Put the following headings in order of instruction.

Concept Introduction: Write a summary of what you are going to say to students to get them interested in the book/concepts. Include an introduction to the genre, text structure, concepts, characters, vocabulary words, pictures, and connections to students' prior learning or experiences. Identify possible misunderstandings. Read the title, author, and illustrator, and discuss the pictures or other graphic information to make predictions.

Reading Fluency Strategies: Describe how the text is going to be read (guided, paired, shared reading; by the paragraph or page; echo, oral, or silent). For instructional-level reading, identify and discuss specific oral reading strategies, such as those from the appropriate *Good Readers Bookmark*. For independent-level reading, identify and discuss fluency strategies such as reading in meaningful phrases, pausing for punctuation, reading with expression, reading smoothly, problem-solving efficiently, and reading at a conversational pace.

Assessment/Analysis/Feedback: How will you assess students' learning? How did they do? Examples: Write down oral reading strategies used, self-corrections, miscues, strategies prompted, and fluency behaviors. Analyze miscues for use of grapho-phonemic, syntactic, morphemic, semantic, and pragmatic cues. Analyze their ability to use strategies for unknown words. Write down areas of strength and areas for improvement. Provide examples of specific responses and specific changes made, and list specific phonetic elements of strength or improvement. Describe specific feedback you provided to support the students' learning.

Language/Vocabulary Strategies: Describe syntactic, morphemic, semantic, and/or pragmatic strategies. List unknown general academic and discipline specific vocabulary words or phrases and the strategies for teaching them. The definitions or explanations of these words may be discussed before, during, or after literacy activities.

Assessment/Analysis/Feedback: How will you assess students' learning? Evaluate by recording a +, ✓, or – after each concept or word, depending on how well the students demonstrated the meaning of the word. Analyze their ability to use vocabulary strategies and comprehend vocabulary. Describe specific feedback you provided to support the students' learning.

Reading, Listening, and Viewing Comprehension Strategies: Describe the strategies and/or questions used to assess comprehension before, during, and after listening to, reading, or viewing a text at a variety of the revised Bloom's taxonomy levels. For narratives, students may describe the characters, settings, plot, events, and resolution; for expository texts, they may describe main ideas and details.

Assessment/Analysis/Feedback: How will you assess students' learning? It is often beneficial to tell students in advance what you want them to know and do after reading. Write down and evaluate with a +, –, or ✓the students' retellings, their answers to questions, and/or their responses to activities. Write down areas of strength and areas for improvement. Provide examples of specific responses and specific changes made. Describe specific feedback you provided to support the students' learning.

(continued)

Writing Composition and Visually Representing Strategies: Emergent writers should write at least one complete sentence, and those at or above the third-grade writing level should write multiple sentences. Students may also visually represent ideas with drawings, images, diagrams, or other visuals. (1) Introduce the writing content and genre. Provide a prompt based on the text or students' experiences. Suggest precomposition strategies and resources they can use to enhance their content. (2) Introduce composition criteria. Make a scoring guide in advance, and preteach students your criteria for evaluating the content, genre, and conventions. Suggest resources for students to use to help with vocabulary and spelling. (3) Help them to revise and edit their writing and visuals. Focus on the revision of content before any editing of conventions in their writing. (4) Determine if the writing is to be published or not. **Assessment/Analysis/Feedback:** State the assessment tool or criteria for assessing the students' writing and visual compositions. Evaluate students' writing based on the predetermined elements above, using a rubric or scoring guide. How did the students do? Write down areas of strength and areas for improvement. Provide examples of specific responses and specific changes made. Describe specific feedback you provided to support the students' learning.
Word Analysis Strategies: Identify specific phonemes, graphemes, morphemes, rimes, and/or spelling patterns to work on within the context of common words. Include strategies such as making and breaking words, "read, cover, and write," sound boxes, or a personal dictionary. For spelling, focus on approximately three to five high-frequency words the students had trouble reading or spelling. **Assessment/Analysis/Feedback:** Write how you will assess students' learning of the strategy and words. Examples: Record a +, ✓, or – after each word, depending on the level of independence with which they were able to read or write. Describe specific feedback you provided to support the students' learning.
Modifications/Adaptations: How did you preplan and/or change the lesson to differentiate instruction to meet the students' specific needs?
Extensions/Technology: How are you going to extend the learning? How did you include technology?
Closure with Students' Reflection: Ask the students what they learned in the lesson. If they did not mention all of the objectives, discuss them, and ask students if they felt they learned them or had questions about them. Ask what the teacher or peers did to help them learn better.
Evidence of Student Work: Write down the names of the materials completed during the lesson. Keep examples of the actual student and teacher work for each student's portfolio.
Family Communication: Write notes to or have discussions with each student's family. Share a summary of the student's strengths and needs during the lesson, and give suggestions for support at home. Ask for family feedback and document any information that is shared with you. Write additional methods of sharing class information with families.
Your Reflection: Reflect on your teaching, feedback, students' learning, and students' affect. Provide a specific evaluation of the students' learning of each of the objectives. What went well and why? What did not go well and why? What did you learn? What will you do differently in the future? Based on your observations and documentation of students' learning, what do they need instruction on next? Discuss and write about additional ideas with colleagues. If applicable, write any concerns.

Getting to Know You—Student Survey

Full Name: ______________________________

Directions: Write the answers to these questions, so I can get to know you better. Family members can help.

Name you would like to be called by in school: ______________________________

List three words to describe yourself: ______________________________

____

What language(s) are spoken at home? ______________________________

____

List names of and your relationships to family members, in order from oldest to youngest: __________

____

List types and names of pets: ______________________________

____

What do you know a lot about? ______________________________

____

What do you want to know more about? ______________________________

____

What makes you happy? ______________________________

____

What makes you laugh? ______________________________

____

What makes you sad? ______________________________

____

What makes you scared? ______________________________

____

What accomplishments are you proud of? ______________________________

____

(continued)

Out of School:

What activities do you like to do by yourself? ______________________________

____

What activities do you like to do with others? ______________________________

____

What do you like to read? ______________________________

____

What do you like to write? ______________________________

____

What do you like to talk about? ______________________________

____

What do you like to see? ______________________________

____

What do you like to listen to? ______________________________

____

What do you like to make? ______________________________

____

What do you like to eat? ______________________________

____

Where do you like to go? ______________________________

____

What celebrations or traditions do you participate in? ______________________________

____

What is the best thing you learned about in life last year? Why is it so memorable? ______________

____

In School:

How do you feel about school? Why? ______________________________

____

What school activities do you like to do? ______________________________

____

(continued)

Getting to Know You—Student Survey *(page 3 of 3)*

What are you good at in school? ____________________

____

What is something you would like to do better in school? ____________________

____

What is your favorite subject? Why? ____________________

____

What is your least favorite subject? Why? ____________________

____

What is the best thing you learned about in school last year? Why is it so memorable? ____________________

____

Think about your favorite teacher. How did this teacher help you to be successful? ____________________

____

What are your concerns about school? ____________________

____

What are you most excited about this school year? ____________________

____

What is one goal you have for school this year? ____________________

____

What else should I know about you that I might not think to ask? ____________________

____

Reading, Writing, and Learning Interest Inventory: Elementary Level

Name: ______________________________ **Date:** ____________

For each category, mark: Yes, you like it; maybe you like it; or no, you do not like it.

	Yes	Maybe	No
I like to read, write, or learn about . . .	☺	😐	☹
Kids my age.			
Important people.			
People and places around the world.			
History of people.			
Arts, language, culture, and religion.			
Sports and athletes.			
Scientific discoveries.			
Health and the human body.			
Animals, plants, and the environment.			
Earth, weather, and space.			
How things work.			
How to make things.			
Folk tales and fairy tales.			
Animal tales.			
Funny stories or jokes.			
Adventure stories.			
Mysteries.			
Make-believe stories of things that can't happen.			
Comics.			
Poetry.			
Interest in Literacy	☺	😐	☹
I like to get new books or borrow books from the library.			
I like to read on a computer, laptop, or tablet.			
I like to write stories, journals, reports, and letters.			
I like to talk and listen to others about reading, writing, and learning.			
I like to look at art or watch videos about my reading, writing, and learning.			
I like to draw or create art about my reading, writing, and learning.			

Put an asterisk (*) in front of each of your top three choices.

Name three of your favorite books or authors: ______________________________

____

Reading, Writing, and Learning Interest Inventory: Middle and Secondary Level

Name: ____________________ **Date:** __________

For each category, mark: Yes, you like it; maybe you like it; or no, you do not like it.

	Yes	Maybe	No
I like to read, write, and learn about the following types of nonfiction:	☺	😐	☹
Biographies, autobiographies, journals			
Documentaries			
Current news			
Modern people—language, culture, religion			
Historical people—language, culture, religion			
Fine and applied arts, music, and theater			
Sports and athletes			
Political science—government and citizenship			
Psychology and sociology			
Geography and travel			
Scientific discoveries			
Health and the human body			
Biology—animals, plants			
Environmental science			
Geology and meteorology—rocks, minerals, weather, and natural disasters			
Astronomy and space science			
Prehistoric earth, plants, and animals			
Physical science/technology—how things work, what things are made of			
Mathematics—logic, statistics, algebra, geometry, probability, applied mathematics			
I like to read, write, and learn about the following types of fiction:	☺	😐	☹
Traditional literature—folk tales, fairy tales, tall tales, legends			
Modern realistic fiction			
Historical fiction			
Science fiction and space fantasy			
Fantasy			
Action/adventure			
Mysteries			
Horror and thrillers			
Comics			
Graphic novels			
Poetry			
Drama/theater			

Put an asterisk (*) in front of each of your top three choices.

Name three of your favorite books or authors: ____________________

____

____

Literacy Process Interview

Name: ______________________________ **Date:** ______________

Directions: Say to the student, "I am going to ask you some questions about what you do when you read, write, and talk with others. I am going to write down what you say."

Analysis: Write specific examples of the student's areas of strengths and areas for improvement.

Reading Questions
1. When you are reading and you come to a word you do not know, what do you do? Do you do anything else?
2. When you are reading and you do not understand something, what do you do? Do you do anything else?
3. How would you help someone who is having trouble reading?
4. During reading, what do you think you do well? Why?
5. What would you like to change about your reading? Why?
Writing Questions
1. When you are writing and you come to a difficult part, what do you do? Do you do anything else?
2. If you are given a writing assignment, what would you do first? Next? Then what? Last?
3. How would you help someone who is having trouble writing?
4. During writing, what do you think you do well? Why?
5. What would you like to change about your writing? Why?

(continued)

Listening and Speaking Questions
1. When you are listening to someone and you do not understand the person, what do you do? Do you do anything else?
2. When you are speaking to someone and the person does not seem to understand you, what do you do? Do you do anything else?
Reading Analysis:
Writing Analysis:
Listening and Speaking Analysis:

Family Asset and Child Development Survey

Child's Name: ______________________________

As your child's teacher, I want to get to know your child and your family better, to see how we can support your child's learning together. In addition, I want all our students to learn about the culture, languages, and assets available in our community. Would you please complete and return this survey to me?

Family

	Adult 1	Adult 2	Emergency contact
Name			
Relation to child			
Home phone			
Cell phone			
Workplace/occupation			
Work phone			
Email			

Other family members or people living in the home:

Name	Relationship to the child	Age/grade/occupation

Language

Languages spoken in the home: ______________________________

Preferred language for oral and written communication: ______________________________

	Levels of language proficiency and comments: Strong = 1, Adequate = 2, Basic = 3, Limited = 4
Child's level of speaking English	
Child's level of reading English	
Child's level of writing English	

(continued)

	Levels of language proficiency and comments: Strong = 1, Adequate = 2, Basic = 3, Limited = 4
Child's level of speaking other language	
Child's level of reading other language	
Child's level of writing other language	
Adult's level of speaking English	
Adult's level of reading English	
Adult's level of writing English	

Interests

Activities family members enjoy doing together in and out of your home: ______________________________

____

Celebrations and traditions your family enjoys together: ______________________________

Community events your family enjoys going to or participating in: ______________________________

Places your family enjoys going together: ______________________________

Interests or hobbies family members could share with the class: ______________________________

Your child's interests or hobbies: ______________________________

Volunteer Opportunities

Would you be willing to volunteer your time or resources to our class? If so, how? (Examples: Be a guest speaker and share about your interests, hobbies, culture, or your job; listen to students reading to you, or have students share their writing with you; help with classroom activities, field trips, binding or publishing student writing, preparing instructional materials at home, sending in supplies needed for activities; do other things that would support student learning.)

Do you know of any community or cultural events that our students would benefit from learning about or participating in?

(continued)

Academic Development

What activities does your child enjoy at school? Why? ______________________

What activities is your child concerned about? Why? ______________________

In what subjects and topics is your child most successful in? Why? ______________________

____

In what subjects and topics does he/she need the most support in? Why? ______________________

____

What kind of reading does your child do at home? ______________________

____

Can your child remember and tell you about what he/she read? ______________________

Does your child attempt to figure out unknown words or ideas on his/her own? ______________________

How much time does the child spend reading or listening to reading at home per week? ______________________

____

What kind of writing does your child do at home? ______________________

Does your child share his/her writing with family members? ______________________

How much time does the child spend writing or listening to others' writing per week? ______________________

____

What kind of conversations does your child have at home? ______________________

____

What goals do you have for your child this year? ______________________

____

What concerns or questions do you have? ______________________

____

Describe any special services your child has received at school (reading, writing, math, speech, language, special education for learning disability, special education for behavioral disability, physical therapy, occupational therapy): ______________________

When? ______________ How often? ______________, How much time per day? ______________,

Does your child have an individualized education plan (IEP)? ______________ If so, bring a copy.

Describe any tutoring your child has received: ______________________

By whom? ______________ When? ______________ For how long? ______________

As compared with other children of your child's age, do you think that your child's academic development is: ______ Above average? ______ Average? ______ Below average?

Please provide copies of previous report cards or any testing results.

(continued)

Social and Emotional Development

Describe how your child gets along with other children and adults in the family: ____________________

____

Describe how your child interacts with other children: ____________________

____

Describe how your child interacts with other adults: ____________________

____

Describe what your child does when he/she is successful: ____________________

____

Describe what your child does when he/she is faced with challenges: ____________________

____

Describe what your child does when he/she gets frustrated: ____________________

____

How does your child help and show compassion for others? ____________________

____

Write four words to describe your child outside of school from the following list, or write your own words:

______________ ______________ ______________ ______________

Write four words to describe your child at school from the following list, or write your own words:

______________ ______________ ______________ ______________

Words to describe your child: *ambitious, anxious, angry, annoyed, brave, bossy, calm, cautious, caring, cheerful, cooperative, complaining, concerned, courageous, defiant, dependable, depressed, disagreeable, discouraged, determined, excited, embarrassed, empathetic, friendly, frustrated, grumpy, happy, hardworking, helpful, honest, impulsive, irritable, joyful, nervous, optimistic, outgoing, perfectionistic, pessimistic, quiet, respectful, sad, silly, self-confident, self-conscious, shy, stressed, uninterested.*

Does your child have any tensions, fears, or insecurities? ______ If so, please describe: ____________

____

Is there anything else I should know about your child? ____________________

____

____

Is there anything I can do as your child's teacher to support him/her? ____________________

____

____

(continued)

Health and Physical Development History

Does your child have any health concerns? _______ If so, please describe: ______________________

____

Does your child need any accommodations at school? If so, what? ______________________________

Date and findings of last physical exam: ____

Does your child currently take any medications? _______ If so, please specify and explain their purpose:

____

____

Does your child have a physical disability? _______ If so, please describe: ______________________

____

List complications at birth, as well as serious illnesses, injuries, or surgeries, and the age at which each occurred: ____

____

Does your child have any difficulties with fine motor skills (writing, holding a pencil, cutting)? __________

Is your child right- or left-handed? ______________ Does he/she change use of hands? ___________

Does your child have any vision problems? _______ If so, please describe: ______________________

____

Does your child wear glasses or contacts? _______ If so, when did he/she begin to wear them? _____

____

Date and findings of last vision exam: ____

By whom? ____ (optometrist, family doctor, school personnel)

Does your child have any hearing problems? ______ If so, please describe: ______________________

____

Does your child wear hearing aids? ____________ If so, when did he/she begin to wear them? _____

____

Date and findings of last hearing test: ____

By whom? ____ (audiologist, family doctor, school personnel)

Did or does your child have any delays in language development? __________ If so, please describe: _

____

Does your child have any speech problems? ______ If so, please describe: ______________________

____

(continued)

Has your child received a psychological exam? _______ Date and findings of exam: ______________

____

__________ Examined by whom? ______________________________________ (school or private)

Is there anything else that you would like me to know about your child or family?

How can the school or community help you and your family?

Thank you for your support. Feel free to contact me at any time.

Sincerely,

____

Child Interest Survey

Child's Name: ______________________________ **Date:** ______________

Based on your child's interests, mark A = Strongly enjoys, B = Enjoys, C = Not sure, or D = Does not enjoy for each category. If A or B, write specific examples of the kinds of activities your child enjoys.

My child . . .	Select One	Examples
Enjoys creating or viewing visual arts (drawing, painting, sculpture, models, design, crafts, photography, video, and architecture).	A B C D	
Enjoys participating in or viewing performance arts (dance, music, opera, drama, magic, oratory, circus).	A B C D	
Enjoys participating in or viewing sports (individual and team).	A B C D	
Enjoys nature (observing, walking, camping, hiking).	A B C D	
Enjoys cultural or religious activities.	A B C D	
Enjoys belonging to clubs or organizations.	A B C D	
Enjoys reading stories—traditional literature, short stories, picture books, drama, realistic fiction, historical fiction, science fiction, plays, poem, comics.	A B C D	
Enjoys reading for information—articles, reports, biography, interviews, instruction, recipes, brochures, advertisements, other nonfiction.	A B C D	
Enjoys writing stories, poetry, lyrics.	A B C D	
Enjoys writing factual information, messages, and letters.	A B C D	
Enjoys mathematics—arithmetic, logics, statistics, algebra, geometry, probability, applied mathematics.	A B C D	
Enjoys science—life, health, earth, space, physical, chemical, technology environmental science, engineering.	A B C D	
Enjoys social studies—history, geography, political science, anthropology, psychology, sociology.	A B C D	

Community Member Survey

Dear Community Member,

I am a teacher at ______________________ school. I teach ______________________.
As a member of our community you are very important. I want our students to learn about the culture, languages, and assets available in our community. I was wondering if you would be willing to answer a few questions to see how you might support students' learning at our school.

1. What would you like our school to know about your organization or business?

2. Could you please describe your job or organization? What skills are necessary to be successful?

3. Would you be willing to have our students come for a field trip? If so, what could you teach them?

4. What other interests, hobbies, or skills could you share with our students?

5. Would you be willing to volunteer your time? If so, how? (Examples might include being a guest speaker by sharing your interests, hobbies, or skills; listening to students reading books or their own writing; becoming pen pals with a student; working with students on a community improvement project; or doing other things.)

6. Are there any resources you could share with me or the class (materials for projects, etc.)?

(continued)

7. Would you be willing to mentor one or more students? If so, what skills could you teach?

8. Do you know of any community or cultural events that our students would benefit from participating in?

9. What do you think are the strengths of the graduates from our school district?

10. What do you think are areas for improvement for our graduates?

11. How might students or our school help support the community?

12. Is there anything else that you would like to share with me?

13. Would you be willing to meet with me to discuss how together we can better support the learning of children at our school?

14. How can I contact you, and when is the best time?

Thank you for your time!

Sincerely,

School Personnel Class Support Survey

Dear School Personnel,

I teach ________________________. As a member of our school community, you are very important. I want our students to learn about the culture, languages, and assets available in our school community. I was wondering if you would be willing to answer a few questions to see how you might provide additional support for students' learning at our school.

1. Would you be willing to give our students a tour of what you do? Briefly describe.

2. What interests, hobbies, or skills could you share with our students?

3. Would you be willing to volunteer your time? If so, how? (Examples might include being a guest speaker by sharing your interests, hobbies, or skills; listening to students reading books or their own writing; rewarding students for their good choices; working with students on a school improvement project, such as recycling or a school garden; or doing other things.)

4. Would you be willing to mentor one or more students? If so, what skills might you be interested in teaching them?

5. Are there any resources you could share with me or the class (materials for projects, etc.)?

(continued)

School Personnel Class Support Survey *(page 2 of 2)*

6. Are you familiar with any community or cultural events that our students would benefit from participating in?

7. Is there anything else that you would like to share with me or our class?

8. Would you be willing to meet with me to discuss how together we can better support the learning of children at our school?

9. How can I contact you, and when is the best time?

Thank you for your time!

Sincerely,

School Personnel Student Connection Survey

Dear School Personnel,

I teach ___________________________. I am going to be working with ___________________________ this year. Since you have had an opportunity to know and interact with this student in the past, I was wondering if you would be willing to answer a few questions to see how you might help me support this student's learning.

1. Name and position:

2. How do you know this student? For how long have you known him/her?

3. What three words would you use to describe this student?

4. What do you know about the student's interests, language, culture, and family that would help me?

5. What can you tell me about the student's social/emotional strengths?

6. What can you tell me about the student's areas for improvement in social/emotional development?

(continued)

7. What can you tell me about the student's academic strengths?

8. What can you tell me about the student's academic areas for improvement?

9. What strategies have worked well for this student?

10. What strategies have not worked well?

11. Is there anything else I should know in order to support my teaching of this student?

Thank you for your time!
Sincerely,

Language Observation Transcription Form

Transcription: During any oral communication or assessment where the student exhibited language concerns, write exactly what the student said in context.
Analysis: Include the topics on the Language Observation Scale with student examples.

Language Observation Scale

Name: ______________________ **Grade:** __________ **Date:** ____________

Directions: After observing the student's language over time, circle the number on each of the scales below that best described the student's communicative behavior.

Scoring: Mark each behavior on a scale from 1 to 4:

1 = Almost no evidence of this behavior; communication was significantly interrupted.
2 = Rarely exhibited the correct behavior; frequent interference with communication.
3 = Sometimes exhibited the correct behavior; some interference with communication.
4 = Predominantly exhibited the correct behavior; almost no interference with communication.

Analysis: Describe areas of strengths, and provide specific examples for areas for improvement.

Phonemics (Articulation, Pronunciation, and Oral Fluency)				
1. Articulation: Correctly produced speech sounds.	1	2	3	4
2. Pronunciation: Correctly pronounced words and did not add or delete sounds.	1	2	3	4
3. Linguistic fluency: Speech was fluent and not disrupted by repetitions, revisions, unusual pauses, and fillers such as *um* or *like*.	1	2	3	4
Analysis:				
Syntax and Morphology (Sentence and Word Structure)				
4. Used a variety of long, complex, and compound sentences in the correct word order.	1	2	3	4
5. Used conjunctions (coordinating: *and*, *but*, *or*; subordinating: *because*, *when*, *unless*).	1	2	3	4
6. Used action verbs.	1	2	3	4
7. Used adverbs.	1	2	3	4
8. Used adjectives.	1	2	3	4
9. Used prepositions.	1	2	3	4
10. Used correct subject–verb agreement.	1	2	3	4
11. Used the copula (*to be*) correctly.	1	2	3	4
12. Used correct past-tense irregular verbs.	1	2	3	4

(continued)

13. Used correct past-tense *-ed* appropriately: /ed/, /d/, /t/.	1	2	3	4
14. Used present progressive *-ing* with auxiliary verb.	1	2	3	4
15. Used regular and irregular plurals correctly.	1	2	3	4
16. Used possessives correctly.	1	2	3	4
Analysis:				
Semantics (Vocabulary and Word Choice)				
17. Used words in the correct context, including question words.	1	2	3	4
18. Used a variety of words.	1	2	3	4
19. Used general academic and content- or discipline-specific vocabulary.	1	2	3	4
20. Used pronouns correctly so that the references were clear.	1	2	3	4
21. Used specific terms instead of *stuff* or *things* when the listener had no way of knowing the reference.	1	2	3	4
Analysis:				
Semantics (Meaningful Discourse)				
22. Shared meaningful information with listeners.	1	2	3	4
23. Shared information on a variety of topics.	1	2	3	4
24. Explained or described objects, ideas, experiences, or processes in detail (expository speech).	1	2	3	4
25. Told stories or events in sequential detail (narrative speech).	1	2	3	4
26. Described opinions or convinced others of his/her point of view in detail (persuasive speech).	1	2	3	4
27. Described feelings and emotions in detail.	1	2	3	4
Analysis:				

(continued)

Language Observation Scale *(page 3 of 3)*

Pragmatics (Language Use)				
28. Communication of ideas: Statements and questions were clearly understood.	1	2	3	4
29. Prompt responding: Paused less than 2 seconds before responding to a question or other verbal stimulus.	1	2	3	4
30. Appropriate responses: Utterances seemed to follow naturally what had been said or asked previously by someone else.	1	2	3	4
31. Introduced topic appropriately: Obtained listener's attention and provided listener with sufficient background information.	1	2	3	4
32. Topic maintenance: Maintained a topic appropriately while adding new and relevant information. Kept topic going.	1	2	3	4
33. Changed topic appropriately: Provided information to the listener when changing topic, to help the listener follow the conversation.	1	2	3	4
34. Asked questions for clarification: Asked for clarification when uncertain of information.	1	2	3	4
35. Repetition not needed: Did not require or request repetition for apparently clear statements or questions.	1	2	3	4
36. Responded to request for clarification: Responded to requests by others such as "Tell me more" or "I don't understand."	1	2	3	4
37. Followed three-step instructions: Repetitions and visual cues were not required in order to understand.	1	2	3	4
38. Changed language register for listener: Used appropriate register or style for adults, family, and peers.	1	2	3	4
Analysis:				

Semantic Generative Vocabulary Assessment

Name: ______________________________ **Grade:** ___________ **Date:** _____________

Directions: Read each prompt to the student. Write down and audio-record his/her responses. For each question, say, "I am going to ask you some questions. I want you to answer with as many words as possible." Give the student up to 2 minutes to respond to each question. If he/she stops, ask, "Can you tell me more?" After 10 seconds of no response, go to the next question. For ELLs, ask them to respond in either English and/or their native language. It may be beneficial to translate the questions into their native language, to determine if they have correct responses even if they do not have the English words for them.

Scoring and Analysis: Mark a plus sign (+) for 10 or more correct items or concepts (this is *appropriate*); a checkmark (✓) for 5–9 correct items (this is *adequate*); and a minus sign (–) for 0–4 correct items (this is *limited*). For each response, describe use of interesting or specific terms, as well as inclusion of words from multiple categories and from different parts of speech. For additional analysis, use the *Language Observation Scale.*

Semantic Generative Vocabulary Levels: Advanced = 6 or more pluses; Adequate = 5 or more pluses or checks; Limited = 4 or less pluses or checks.

Score +, ✓, –	Prompt and Responses
	1. Name as many kinds of food as you can.
	2. Choose one food and describe it in detail.
	3. Name as many kinds of clothing as you can.
	4. What kinds of clothing go together, and why?
	5. Name parts of a car.
	6. A car is a kind of transportation. Name other kinds of transportation.
	7. Describe a person that you know. Tell me what this person looks like, acts like, and does.
	8. Describe a day in your life. Tell me what you did and how you felt.

Analysis:

Oral Presentation Assessment

Presenter: ______________________ **Grade:** __________ **Date:** ____________

Topic: ____

Directions: Provide a copy to the student before he/she plans the presentation. During the presentation, the teacher and/or peers write down specific observations under each heading and score it. After the presentation, the student completes a self-evaluation, and then the teacher and/or class provide the student with specific feedback on the effective elements of the presentation and suggestions for improvement.

Scoring and Analysis: Evaluate each element with a plus sign (+) if all of the descriptors were clearly observed, a checkmark (✓) if most of the descriptors were observed, or a minus sign (–) if they were rarely or never observed. Write an analysis with specific examples of the student's areas of strengths and areas for improvement.

Score	The Presenter:
	Content:
______	Included accurate information.
______	Included information from a variety of sources, demonstrating deep knowledge of the topic.
______	Included details appropriate for the audience.
______	Included information the audience did not already know.
______	Described information clearly.
______	Included evidence and examples.
______	Presented content in an original and creative manner.
______	Followed the directions of the assignment.
	Observations:
	Organization:
______	Had an interesting introduction.
______	Stated objectives/goals clearly.
______	Stated main ideas and details clearly and in an appropriate order.
______	Thoughts and ideas flowed in a logical manner.

(continued)

Oral Presentation Assessment *(page 2 of 3)*

Score	The Presenter:
________	Had smooth transitions between ideas.
________	Summarized main ideas at the end.
	Observations:
	Language:
________	Conveyed the information clearly to the audience.
________	Pronounced words correctly and clearly.
________	Used grammatically correct sentences.
________	Used a variety of compound and complex sentence structures.
________	Included adjectives, adverbs, prepositions, and conjunctions.
________	Used general academic vocabulary.
________	Used content- or discipline-specific vocabulary.
________	Used appropriate language for the audience.
	Observations:
	Visual Media:
________	Included visuals directly related to the topic.
________	Visuals added information.
________	Visuals did not detract from the purpose of the presentation.
________	Visuals were creatively displayed.
________	Visuals were neatly displayed.
	Observations:

(continued)

Oral Presentation Assessment *(page 3 of 3)*

Score	The Presenter:
	Manner:
________	Maintained good eye contact.
________	Spoke clearly, at the appropriate volume, and at an understandable pace.
________	Conveyed interest in the topic enthusiastically.
________	Used gestures and body language to maintain the attention of the audience.
________	Timed the length of the presentation appropriately.
	Observations:
	Audience Participation:
________	Asked audience questions before, during, and/or after the presentation.
________	Engaged audience members in making connections to their experiences.
________	Provided adequate time for questions after the presentation.
________	Answered audience members' questions to the best of his/her knowledge.
	Observations:

Analysis:

Synonym Vocabulary Assessment

Name: ______________________ **Grade:** __________ **Date:** __________

In the left margin before each level, mark R for Reading and L for Listening, or RL for both.

Reading Directions: Say, "Read each line of words. Draw a circle around the word that means the same or almost the same as the first word in each line." Continue until the student reaches the frustration level or becomes frustrated; then repeat that grade level by having the student listen as you read the words.

Listening Directions: Say, "Follow along as I read the words in each line, and draw a circle around the word that means the same or almost the same as the first word in each line."

Scoring and Analysis: In front of each line number, write a plus sign (+) if correct and a minus sign (–) if incorrect. For each level, write the functioning level, total correct, and percentage correct. Write examples of incorrect responses.

Functioning Level: Independent, 90–100%; instructional, 70–80%; frustration, 60% or below.

Practice Item		A	B	C	D
	1. fast	run	more	look	quick
LEVEL 1 Functioning Level:			**Score: /10 =**	**%**	
Score: +, –		**A**	**B**	**C**	**D**
	1. see	run	more	look	us
	2. little	come	long	away	small
	3. say	talk	goes	like	just
	4. mom	dog	mother	many	with
	5. start	begin	last	round	slow
	6. big	door	right	fun	large
	7. hop	hard	ball	dark	jump
	8. alike	grew	pot	same	most
	9. glad	happy	sail	rope	hold
	10. street	time	thin	very	road
Analysis:					

(continued)

From *Literacy Assessment and Metacognitive Strategies: A Resource to Inform Instruction, PreK–12* by Stephanie L. McAndrews. Copyright © 2020 The Guilford Press. Permission to photocopy this material is granted to purchasers of this book for personal use or use with students (see copyright page for details). Purchasers can download additional copies of this material (see the box at the end of the table of contents).

Synonym Vocabulary Assessment *(page 2 of 5)*

LEVEL 2 Functioning Level:		Score: /10 =	%		
Score: +, –		**A**	**B**	**C**	**D**
	1. go	anything	leave	rest	summer
	2. pair	read	should	two	middle
	3. cut	last	round	slow	slice
	4. thin	shout	skinny	live	under
	5. hear	kind	magic	help	listen
	6. car	secret	chew	automobile	juice
	7. fear	afraid	lunch	yellow	welcome
	8. stir	hospital	stood	mix	know
	9. below	live	place	under	took
	10. all	this	every	find	lunch
Analysis:					

LEVEL 3 Functioning Level:		Score: /10 =	%		
Score: +, –		**A**	**B**	**C**	**D**
	1. like	cure	enjoy	tall	high
	2. beautiful	tired	asleep	seven	pretty
	3. close	shut	grow	leg	fat
	4. choose	busy	select	exactly	figure
	5. fix	busy	city	stop	repair
	6. gift	present	play	test	earth
	7. find	control	discover	listen	learn
	8. forest	job	desert	woods	book
	9. wrong	keep	kind	loose	incorrect
	10. cried	rabbit	wept	years	enough
Analysis:					

(continued)

LEVEL 4 Functioning Level:		Score: /10 = %			
Score: +, –		**A**	**B**	**C**	**D**
	1. drink	beverage	taco	salt	clover
	2. harm	meadow	misty	injure	enjoy
	3. perhaps	maybe	necklace	squeeze	strange
	4. vacant	machine	empty	hopefully	wrapper
	5. divide	frighten	separate	finally	statue
	6. quarrel	wander	grab	argue	puppet
	7. prison	meter	handle	churn	jail
	8. collect	through	young	belong	gather
	9. heal	cure	join	prepare	bring
	10. gloomy	scratch	dreary	creature	ocean
Analysis:					

LEVEL 5 Functioning Level:		Score: /10 = %			
Score: +, –		**A**	**B**	**C**	**D**
	1. slender	language	piece	thin	valley
	2. able	capable	sudden	goal	entire
	3. toil	suddenly	tongue	model	work
	4. achieve	grant	start	accomplish	youth
	5. careful	shout	cautious	agree	state
	6. motion	dangerous	cellar	movement	shriek
	7. drapes	daze	curtains	treasure	giggle
	8. thief	pebble	blanket	gallop	criminal
	9. ascend	climb	harpoon	stitch	swung
	10. continue	persevere	separate	finish	level
Analysis:					

(continued)

LEVEL 6 Functioning Level:		Score: /10 = %			
Score: +, –		**A**	**B**	**C**	**D**
	1. grateful	detest	appreciative	response	attain
	2. protect	shelter	officer	bounce	porch
	3. prohibit	engaged	possess	restrict	detest
	4. conceal	lawyer	female	hide	braids
	5. deposit	fountain	gophers	knotted	leave
	6. think	contemplate	assist	develop	discover
	7. delete	tardy	silent	repair	omit
	8. renew	restore	attend	wound	recent
	9. conclude	end	ransom	salt	fortress
	10. liquid	prejudice	fluid	radish	distemper
Analysis:					

LEVELS 7–9 Functioning Level:		Score: /10 = %			
Score: +, –		**A**	**B**	**C**	**D**
	1. surplus	design	hearth	extra	mansion
	2. revise	alter	computer	militia	museum
	3. reduce	oxygen	condense	chariot	pliers
	4. erupt	allowance	huff	incredible	explode
	5. deport	ooze	banish	turret	walrus
	6. exhibit	trophy	accountant	privacy	display
	7. solitary	gravel	starvation	tassel	alone
	8. pout	bolt	wizard	sulk	fertilizer
	9. recede	lemonade	market	bruising	ebb
	10. precious	valuable	embarrass	smolder	injection
Analysis:					

(continued)

LEVELS 10–12 Functioning Level:			Score:	/10 =	%
Score: +, –		**A**	**B**	**C**	**D**
	1. hazardous	aluminum	lavender	dangerous	famine
	2. elongate	portrait	stretch	retrieve	pigeon
	3. fierce	indelible	lariat	diplomat	savage
	4. caribou	scaffold	slalom	reindeer	awesome
	5. competition	rivalry	quench	ogre	sculpture
	6. demeanor	vanish	parallel	behavior	vertical
	7. inexhaustible	chancellor	derrick	infamy	tireless
	8. dissuade	dislocate	arouse	discourage	jovial
	9. aggregate	egret	total	obsidian	veer
	10. advisor	transistor	riveter	pageant	consultant
Analysis:					

Antonym Vocabulary Assessment

Name: ______________________ **Grade:** __________ **Date:** ____________

In the left margin before each level, mark R for Reading and L for Listening, or RL for both.

Reading Directions: Say, "Read each line of words. Draw a circle around the word that means the opposite of the first word in each line." Continue until the student reaches the frustration level or becomes frustrated; then repeat that grade level by having the student listen as you read the words.

Listening Directions: Say, "Follow along as I read the words in each line. Draw a circle around the word that means the opposite of the first word in each line."

Scoring and Analysis: In front of each line number, write a plus sign (+) if correct and a minus sign (–) if incorrect. For each level, write the functioning level, total correct, and percentage correct. Write examples of incorrect responses.

Functioning Level: Independent, 90–100%; instructional, 70–80%; frustration, 60% or below.

Practice Item		**A**	**B**	**C**	**D**
	1. stop	boy	go	her	luck
LEVEL 1 Functioning Level:			**Score: /10 =**	**%**	
Score: +, –		**A**	**B**	**C**	**D**
	1. hot	red	help	cold	up
	2. in	to	out	down	way
	3. big	fast	little	give	her
	4. wet	soon	help	dry	like
	5. easy	hard	liked	old	look
	6. tall	come	well	short	see
	7. sick	well	dark	sing	call
	8. up	made	down	love	come
	9. happy	car	pit	sad	silly
	10. kind	big	before	play	mean
Analysis:					

(continued)

LEVEL 2 Functioning Level:		Score: /10 =	%		
Score: +, –		**A**	**B**	**C**	**D**
	1. sit	play	stand	help	be
	2. true	need	able	false	part
	3. push	pull	name	fall	love
	4. front	back	lower	side	simple
	5. sweet	small	taste	sour	eat
	6. smile	near	mean	frown	pretty
	7. wrong	part	first	quiet	right
	8. over	sign	under	listen	care
	9. early	on	late	bump	moon
	10. forget	lost	hurry	school	remember
Analysis:					

LEVEL 3 Functioning Level:		Score: /10 =	%		
Score: +, –		**A**	**B**	**C**	**D**
	1. quick	tired	rough	draw	slow
	2. moist	dry	exit	taste	scent
	3. alone	perfect	together	camp	light
	4. weak	strong	sweet	guard	ring
	5. empty	long	different	moment	full
	6. poor	polite	hour	wealthy	missing
	7. neat	messy	drive	regular	cook
	8. dull	same	waste	bright	game
	9. add	follow	subtract	pay	fancy
	10. deep	shallow	never	warm	sell
Analysis:					

(continued)

LEVEL 4 Functioning Level:		**Score: /10 = %**			
Score: +, –		**A**	**B**	**C**	**D**
	1. certain	county	honest	cause	doubtful
	2. enjoy	trust	dislike	punish	attack
	3. southern	eastern	western	northern	map
	4. despair	hope	shy	clumsy	change
	5. nervous	pleased	relaxed	calm	asleep
	6. ashamed	middle	proud	curious	friendly
	7. forgive	blame	send	drive	promise
	8. expert	fitness	building	amateur	object
	9. confident	trust	insecure	forget	hungry
	10. vanish	hide	allow	jealous	appear
Analysis:					

LEVEL 5 Functioning Level:		**Score: /10 = %**			
Score: +, –		**A**	**B**	**C**	**D**
	1. poverty	support	replay	wealth	inform
	2. rejected	related	special	interested	accepted
	3. alive	deceased	ancient	predator	attention
	4. abundance	scarce	liar	increase	profit
	5. isolate	improve	disagree	reassure	include
	6. genuine	intelligent	natural	artificial	serious
	7. shrink	desire	expand	rotate	dissolve
	8. illegal	clumsy	compromise	lawful	observe
	9. reluctant	enthusiastic	increase	remain	begin
	10. avoid	honor	confront	replace	surrender
Analysis:					

(continued)

LEVEL 6 Functioning Level:		Score: /10 = %			
Score: +, –		**A**	**B**	**C**	**D**
	1. vacant	mammal	occupied	rested	irresponsible
	2. authentic	impossible	elderly	imitation	physical
	3. cease	begin	minor	respect	measure
	4. apathetic	exhausted	concerned	motivated	professional
	5. disregard	active	understand	consider	believe
	6. excess	shortage	deny	gather	expensive
	7. destruction	association	foundation	reconsider	creation
	8. oblivious	typical	aware	frustrated	cheap
	9. arrogant	humble	official	convinced	brutal
	10. fatigue	heavy	energy	careless	imply
Analysis:					

LEVELS 7–9 Functioning Level:		Score: /10 = %			
Score: +, –		**A**	**B**	**C**	**D**
	1. novice	experienced	praise	reprimand	cascade
	2. assault	resolve	expand	attempt	absorbent
	3. exhibit	concave	conductive	conceal	condescending
	4. conform	relocate	porous	revolt	distract
	5. withdrawn	outgoing	levitate	abrasion	implicit
	6. mediator	juvenile	legislator	adversary	monarch
	7. abolish	establish	apprehensive	diminish	aggressive
	8. sporadic	strict	optional	constant	restless
	9. extravagant	revived	restrained	intricate	retained
	10. harmless	tranquil	appeased	calamity	detrimental
Analysis:					

(continued)

Antonym Vocabulary Assessment *(page 5 of 5)*

LEVELS 10–12 Functioning Level:		**Score: /10 = %**			
Score: +, –		**A**	**B**	**C**	**D**
	1. harmony	reliable	discord	tentative	incline
	2. flustered	composed	hostility	slender	modest
	3. redundant	obliged	mediocre	concise	undeserving
	4. collaborate	flatter	resist	condescend	incapable
	5. discriminate	stabilized	generalize	hesitate	justifiable
	6. degrade	successful	retrospect	assessment	compliment
	7. naïve	sophisticated	pilgrim	fictitious	superficial
	8. precarious	tentative	emulate	stable	agitated
	9. substantiate	challenge	avoid	admire	incoherent
	10. expedite	irritable	impede	extensive	strict
Analysis:					

Morphology Assessment—Inflectional Morphemes

Name: ______________________________ **Grade:** ____________ **Date:** ______________

Directions: You can read this assessment to the student and have him/her respond orally, or the student can read it and write the correct word. Say, "I will read [or you will read] a key word and a sentence with a blank. Fill in the blank by adding suffixes or word parts to the key word to make the sentence complete and sound right."

Practice Item: ***dog*** *I have a dog. I used to have two* ______________. (dogs)

Scoring and Analysis: Write total correct out of 18; then describe the type of morphemes the student correctly said or did not say, and give examples of incorrect responses.

Score +, –	Key Word	Prompt
Inflectional bound morphemes (plurals)		
	1. cat	Sam has one **cat.** Ann has two more ______________.
	2. ball	Maya had one **ball.** Her friend gave her another. Now she has two _____.
	3. fox	A **fox** was playing in the field. Out of the bushes came another. Now there are two ________________.
	4. dish	I ate one **dish** of ice cream. My dad was hungry and ate two __________________ of ice cream.
	5. leaf	I picked up one **leaf** from the ground. Then I picked up a pile of ________________.
Inflectional bound morphemes (possessives)		
	6. sister	My **sister** has a fish. My ______________ fish is a goldfish.
	7. dog	My **dog** has a collar. My ______________ collar is red.
	8. Garcia	Mr. and Mrs. **Garcia** invited me to their house. I am going to the ________________ house for dinner.
Inflectional bound morphemes (verb tenses)		
	9. play **10. play** **11. play** **12. play**	Yesterday, Max _________ with his truck. Right now, he is _________ with his robot. Tomorrow he wants to ______________ with his drums. Sometimes he _________ the piano.
	13. eat **14. eat** **15. eat** **16. eat**	Yesterday, she _________ beans. Right now, she is __________________ carrots. She always ___________ salad every day. She has never __________________ beets before.
Inflectional bound morphemes (comparative and superlative)		
	17. small **18. small**	When we are comparing size, a softball is small. A baseball is ________________. A golf ball is the ________________.

Score: ____/18

Analysis:

Morphology Assessment—Derivational Morphemes

Name: ________________________________ **Grade:** __________ **Date:** ____________

Directions: You can read this assessment to the student and have him/her respond orally, or the student can read it and write the correct word. Say, "I will read [or you will read] a key word and a sentence with a blank. Fill in the blank by adding to change the root word to make the sentence complete and sound right."

Practice Item: ***test*** *Before our test on Friday, we will have a* ______________ (pretest).

Scoring and Analysis: Write total correct out of 20; then describe the type of morphemes the student correctly said or did not say, and give examples of incorrect responses.

Score +, –	Key Word	Prompt
Derivational bound morphemes (meaning changed)		
	1. happy	A person who is not **happy** is ________________.
	2. do	If you are asked to **do** your assignment again, the teacher would ask you to _____________ it.
	3. obey	Someone who does **not obey** the rules would ______________ them.
	4. complete	His paper was **not complete**; therefore, it is ________________.
Derivational bound morphemes (changed to nouns)		
	5. teach	A person who **teaches** is a __________________.
	6. biology	A person who practices **biology** is a ____________.
	7. kind	A person who was **kind** showed much __________ when she picked up his books.
	8. store	A place to **store** something is in a ______________ container.
	9. help	A person who likes to **help** others is a ___________.
	10. create	He will **create** a model. When he is done, it will be his own _____________.
Derivational bound morphemes (changed to adjectives)		
	11. nature	A person who enjoys **nature** wants to be in the ____________ environment.
	12. care	He took great **care** with his houseplants. He was very _________________.
	13. week	I go to soccer practice every **week**. We have ____________ soccer practice.
	14. five	There are **five** people in line. I am the ___________ person.
	15. rain	Today it will **rain**. Today will be a ______________ day.
Derivational bound morphemes (changed to adverbs)		
	16. slow	The turtle is **slow**. He walks very _____________.
	17. happy	He was **happy** to help. He __________________ helped his teacher.
	18. clock	He turned around in the direction of a **clock**. He turned ________________.
Derivational bound morphemes (change to verbs)		
	19. quiz	Tomorrow is a **quiz.** Today we will be _________________ each other to prepare.
	20. accessory	Her necklace is an **accessory**. She will need at least three things to ____________ her outfit.

Total: ___ **/20**

Analysis:

Auditory Discrimination Assessment—Consonants

Name: ______________________________ **Grade:** ____________ **Date:** ______________

Directions: Sit shoulder to shoulder with the student but facing away from him/her, so the student cannot see the words pronounced. Toward the student's ear, say, "I am going to say two words, and I want you to tell me if they are the same or different."

Scoring and Analysis: Record the student's response as S for same and D for different. Score with a plus sign (+) for correct and a minus sign (–) for incorrect. Write the functioning level and total score. Identify patterns of correct and incorrect responses, and write specific examples.

Functioning Level: Independent, 36–40 correct, or 90–100%; instructional, 28–35 correct, or 70–88%; frustration, 27 correct or below, or 68% or below.

Functioning Level:		**Score: /40 = %**	
Prompt	**Response and + or –**	**Prompt**	**Response and + or –**
1. let–wet		21. pet–bet	
2. pass–pass		22. van–fan	
3. nine–line		23. wake–rake	
4. much–much		24. not–not	
5. think–sink		25. what–hut	
6. jet–jet		26. time–dime	
7. hiss–his		27. head–head	
8. map–nap		28. zoo–shoe	
9. hit–wit		29. pot–tot	
10. quick–quick		30. came–game	
11. big–dig		31. been–been	
12. kite–tight		32. quit–kit	
13. fat–that		33. gate–date	
14. gave–gave		34. where-where	
15. sell–shell		35. sun–sung	
16. right–right		36. jump–chump	
17. yell–well		37. some–some	
18. jeep–sheep		38. men–when	
19. share–chair		39. this–this	
20. come–come		40. dim–gym	

Analysis:

Auditory Discrimination Assessment—Short and Long Vowels

Name: ______________________________ **Grade:** ____________ **Date:** ______________

Directions: Sit shoulder to shoulder with the student but facing away from him/her, so the student cannot see the words pronounced. Toward the student's ear, say, "I am going to say two words, and I want you to tell me if they are the same or different."

Scoring and Analysis: Record the student's response as S for same and D for different. Score with a plus sign (+) for correct and a minus sign (–) for incorrect. Write the functioning level and total score. Identify patterns of correct and incorrect responses, and write specific examples.

Functioning Level: Independent, 36–40 correct, or 90–100%; instructional, 28–35 correct, or 70–88%; frustration, 27 correct or below, or 68% or below.

Functioning Level:		**Score: /40 = %**	
	Response and + or –		**Response and + or –**
1. get–get		21. cake–cake	
2. hat–hot		22. jean–June	
3. pet–pat		23. high–hay	
4. had–had		24. bite–beat	
5. nut–not		25. home–home	
6. him–him		26. tube–tube	
7. lad–lid		27. line–loan	
8. ham–hum		28. mule–mail	
9. pin–pen		29. week–week	
10. hip–hop		30. heap–hope	
11. tub–tub		31. rude–ride	
12. rod–red		32. name–name	
13. hut–hit		33. not–note	
14. job–job		34. teen–ten	
15. bet–but		35. mop–mop	
16. heat–heat		36. cute–cut	
17. tone–tune		37. big–big	
18. we–way		38. Tim–time	
19. hike–hike		39. mad–made	
20. cope–cape		40. feet–feet	

Analysis:

Auditory Discrimination Assessment—
Diphthongs and Controlled Vowels

Name: ______________________ **Grade:** __________ **Date:** __________

Directions: Sit shoulder to shoulder with the student but facing away from him/her, so the student cannot see the words pronounced. Toward the student's ear, say, "I am going to say two words, and I want you to tell me if they are the same or different words."

Scoring and Analysis: Record the student's response as S for same and D for different. Score with a plus sign (+) for correct and a minus sign (–) for incorrect. Write the functioning level and total score. Identify patterns of correct and incorrect responses and write specific examples.

Functioning Level: Independent, 18–20 correct, or 90–100%; instructional, 14–17 correct, or 70–85%; frustration, 13 or below correct, or 65% or below.

Functioning Level:		**Score: /20 = %**	
Prompt	**Response and + or –**	**Prompt**	**Response and + or –**
1. hall–hail		11. grow–grew	
2. pool–pole		12. shook–shook	
3. few–few		13. town–tune	
4. her–here		14. talk–took	
5. bowl–boil		15. shoot–shut	
6. foot–foot		16. cloud–clawed	
7. fair–far		17. our–or	
8. mood–mud		18. fund–found	
9. care–care		19. pull–Paul	
10. stir–steer		20. fur–for	

Analysis:

Phoneme Blending Assessment

Name: ______________________ **Grade:** __________ **Date:** __________

Directions: Say to the student, "I am going to say separate sounds, and I want you to say the word when the sounds are blended together. For example, if I say /l/ /i/ /k/, you should say *like.*"

Practice Items: /m/ /a/ /p/, /o/ /n/, /b/ /i/ /g/

Scoring: Write a plus sign (+) for correct blending and a minus sign (–) for incorrect blending, and write the incorrect response.

Analysis: Write the functioning level, total score, and examples of incorrect blending and pronunciation.

Functioning Level: Independent, 23–25; instructional, 20–22; frustration, 19 or below.

Functioning Level:		**Score: /25 = %**	
Prompt	**Response and + or –**	**Prompt**	**Response and + or –**
1. /c/ /a/ /t/		14. /d/ /a/ y/	
2. /s/ /ee/ /d/		15. /p/ /l/ /a/ /ce/	
3. /m/ /i/ /ne/		16. /t/ /o/	
4. /g/ /o/		17. /th/ /r/ /ew/	
5. /h/ /e/		18. /j/ /o/ /b/	
6. /s/ /a/ /ve/		19. /th/ /i/ /s/	
7. /b/ /l/ /ue/		20. /n/ /i/ /ce/	
8. /wh/ /e/ /n/		21. /s/ /u/ /n/	
9. /b/ /e/ /d/		22. /s/ /t/ /o/ /p/	
10. /sh/ /e/		23. /m/ /y/	
11. /d/ /o/ /g/		24. /f/ /i/ /sh/	
12. /ch/ /i/ /n/		25. /b/ /oo/ /k/	
13. /k/ /ey/ /s/			

Analysis:

Phoneme Segmentation Assessment

Name: ______________________________ **Grade:** ____________ **Date:** ______________

Directions: Say to the student, "I am going to say a word. I want you to break the word apart and say each sound of the word in order. For example, if I say *sun*, you should say /s/ /u/ /n/."

Practice Items: *bike*, *on*, *and*

Scoring: Write a plus sign (+) for correct segmentation and a minus sign (–) for incorrect segmentation, and write the incorrect responses.

Analysis: Write the functioning level, total score, and examples of incorrect segmenting or pronunciation.

Functioning Level: Independent, 23–25; instructional, 20–22; frustration, 19 or below.

Functioning Level:		**Score: /25 = %**	
Prompt	**Response and + or –**	**Prompt**	**Response and + or –**
1. ran	/r/ /ă/ /n/	14. go	/g/ /ō/
2. pet	/p/ /ĕ/ /t/	15. keys	/k/ /ē/ /z/
3. chin	/ch/ /ĭ/ /n/	16. nice	/n/ /ī/ /s/
4. have	/h/ /ă/ /v/	17. clay	/k/ /l/ /ā/
5. up	/ŭ/ /p/	18. true	/t/ /r/ /ōō/
6. am	/ă/ /m/	19. call	/k/ /aw/ /l/
7. sheep	/sh/ /ē/ /p/	20. we	/w/ /ē/
8. dig	/d/ /ĭ/ /g/	21. is	/ĭ/ /z/
9. stop	/s/ /t/ /ŏ/ /p/	22. to	/t/ /ōō/
10. fun	/f/ /ŭ/ /n/	23. book	/b/ /ŏŏ/ /k/
11. my	/m/ /ī/	24. threw	/th/ /r/ /ōō/
12. this	/th/ /ĭ/ /s/	25. jog	/j/ /ŏ/ /g/
13. yes	/y/ /ĕ/ /s/		

Analysis:

Letter and Sound Identification Assessment

Name: ______________________ **Grade:** __________ **Date:** __________

Directions: Give the student a copy of the letter chart (next page), and place an index card under the first row of letters. Say, "I want you to tell me the name of each letter and the sound or sounds it makes." Point to the first letter and say, "What letter is this?" Write the student's response on this record sheet. "Do you know what sound it makes?" Letters marked with an asterisk (*) have multiple sounds, so ask, "Do you know what other sound it makes?" If the student does not know a sound, ask, "Do you know a word that starts with that letter?"

Scoring and Analysis: Write a plus sign (+) for each correct letter and correct sound, and a minus sign (–) for incorrect. Write all incorrect responses. If a student says, "I don't know," write IDK. See the "Sound" columns for correct responses. Write the scores for uppercase, lowercase, and letter sounds. Identify patterns of correct and incorrect responses, and write specific examples of each.

Uppercase Letter Names: /26 **Lowercase Letter Names:** /28 **Letter Sounds:** /26

	Letter	Sound	Word		Letter	Sound	Word
B		/b/		b		/b/	
O*		/ŏ/ /ō/ /ö/		o*		/ŏ/ /ō/ /ö/	
S*		/s/ /z/		s*		/s/ /z/	
A*		/ă/ /ā/ /ŏ/		ɑ*		/ă/ /ā/ /ŏ/	
W		/w/		w		/w/	
Z		/z/		z		/z/	
F		/f/		f		/f/	
H		/h/		h		/h/	
K		/k/		k		/k/	
J		/j/		j		/j/	
U*		/ŭ/ /ū/		u*		/ŭ/ /ū/	
				a*		/ă/ /ā/ /ŏ/	
C*		/k/ /s/		c*		/k/ /s/	
Y*		/y/ /ē/ /ī/ /ĭ/		y*		/y/ /ē/ /ī/ /ĭ/	
L		/l/		l		/l/	
Q		/kw/		q		/kw/	
M		/m/		m		/m/	
D		/d/		d		/d/	
N		/n/		n		/n/	
X		/ks/		x		/ks/	
I*		/ĭ/ /ī/		i*		/ĭ/ /ī/	
P		/p/		p		/p/	
E*		/ĕ/ /ē/		e*		/ĕ/ /ē/	
G*		/g/ /j/		g*		/g/ /j/	
R		/r/		r		/r/	
V		/v/		v		/v/	
T		/t/		t		/t/	
				g*			
Total	/26	/26		Total	/28	/26	

Analysis:

(continued)

B	O	S	A	W	Z
F	H	K	J	U	
C	Y	L	Q	M	
D	N	X	I	P	
E	G	R	V	T	

b	o	s	ɑ	w	z
f	h	k	j	u	a
c	y	l	q	m	
d	n	x	i	p	
e	g	r	v	t	g

Phonics Skills for Grades K–3

Name: ______________________________ **Grade:** ___________ **Date:** _____________

Directions: Use this as a grade-level instructional guide or assessment summary.

Scoring and Analysis: Mark with a + or –. Analyze patterns of correct and incorrect responses.

Skills Introduced and Mastered in Kindergarten	
	Identified all lowercase letters
	Identified all uppercase or capital letters
	Identified the sounds of the following consonant letters: _____ b, _____ d, _____ f, _____ h, _____ j, _____ k, _____ l, _____ m, _____ n, _____ p, _____ q, _____ r, _____ s, _____ t, _____ v, _____ w, _____ x, _____ y, _____ z
	Identified the hard sound of _____ c: *cat*, _____ g: *get*
Skills Introduced in Kindergarten	
	Identified the sounds of the short vowels: _____ a, _____ e, _____ i, _____ o, _____ u
	Identified the sounds of the long vowels: _____ a, _____ e, _____ i, _____ o, _____ u
	Identified the soft sounds _____ c: *city*, _____ g: *giant*, followed by e, i, or y
	Correctly wrote all letters
	Used inventive spelling; wrote words with several correct consonants
Skills Mastered in First Grade	
	Identified both sounds of the following consonant letters: _____ c, _____ g, _____ s
	Identified the sound of ck, when it follows a short vowel
	Identified the sounds of the vowels: _____ a: *at, ate, want*; _____ e: *end, me*;
	i: *is, I*; _____ o: *on, open, do*; _____ u: *up, use, put*; _____ y: *my, baby, gym*
	Identified the long vowel sound with a silent e at the end of a word
	Identified the sounds of the consonant digraphs _____ th: *the, think*; _____ sh: *she*; _____ ch: *chair, chorus;* _____ wh: *when*
	Identified the endings _____-ing, _____-ed: /ed/ *wanted*, /d/ *smiled*, /t/ *jumped*; _____-s: /s/ *cats*, /z/ *dogs*
	Read and wrote phonetically regular words correctly
	Used inventive spelling, wrote words with most of the correct sounds
	Read at least 100 words and wrote at least 50 words on the *Fry's Instant Words* lists

(continued)

	Skills Introduced in First Grade
	Identified the sounds of the vowel digraphs ______ ie: *pie, piece, friend*; ______ ei: *either*; ______ ea: *eat, bread, great*; ______ ee: *see*, ______ oa: *boat*, ______ ai: *sail*, ______ ay: *say*, ______ ui: *fruit*
	Identified the sound of igh: *night*
	Identified the sounds of these digraphs/diphthongs: ______ ou: *out, four, you, should*; ______ ow: *cow, grow*;
	oi: *oil*; ______ oy: *boy*; ______ ew: *new*
	Identified the sounds of ey: *they, key*
	Identified the sounds of oo: *moon, book, floor*
	Identified the sounds of the vocalic r: ______ er: *her*; ______ ir: *first*; ______ ur: *nurse*; ______ or: *works*; ______ ear: *early*; ______ ar: *grammar*
	Identified r-, l-, w-, and u-controlled vowels: ______ ar: *car*, ______ or: *for*, ______ al: *all*, ______ aw: *saw*, ______ au: *author*
	Identified the endings ______-es, ______-ly
	Identified the sound of ng: *sing, song*
	Identified the sound of the consonant digraph ph
	Identified the sounds of the vowel digraphs ______ ie: *pie, piece, friend*; ______ ei: *either*; ______ ea: *eat, bread, great*; ______ ee: *see*; ______ oa: *boat*; ______ ai: *sail*; ______ ay: *say*; ______ ui: *fruit*
	Identified the sound of igh: *night*
	Identified the sounds of these digraphs/diphthongs: ______ ou: *out, four, you, should*; ______ ow: *cow, grow*; ______ oi: *oil*; ______ oy: *boy*; ______ ew: *new*
	Identified the sounds of ey: *they, key*
	Identified the sounds of oo: *moon, book, floor*
	Identified the sounds of the vocalic r: ______ er: *her*; ______ ir: *first*; ______ ur: *nurse*; ______ or: *works*; ______ ear: *early*; ______ ar: *grammar*
	Identified r-, l-, w-, and u-controlled vowels: ______ ar; ______ or; ______ al; ______ aw; ______ au
	Identified the sound of ng: *sing, song*
	Identified the sound of the consonant digraph ph
	Read at least 200 words and wrote at least 100 words on the *Fry's Instant Words* lists

(continued)

Phonics Skills for Grades K–3 *(page 3 of 3)*

Skills Introduced in Second Grade	
	Identified the sound of kn: *knock*
	Identified silent *l* and *b*: *walk*, *climb*
	Identified the sound of dge: *edge*, used after a short vowel
	Identified the sound of gh: *ghost*, used at the beginning of a word
	Identified the sound of wr: *wrap*
	Identified words that end in a v sound and are followed by an *e*: *have*, *love*
Skills Mastered in Third Grade	
	Identified the sound of kn: *knock*
	Identified silent *l* and *b*: *walk*, *climb*
	Identified the sound of dge: *edge*, used after a short vowel
	Identified the sound of gh: *ghost*, used at the beginning of a word
	Identified the sound of wr: *wrap*
	Identified words that end in a v sound and are followed by an *e*: *have*, *love*
Skills Introduced and Mastered in Third Grade	
	Identified the sounds of ough: *though*, *through*, *rough*, *cough*, *thought*, *bough*
	Identified the sounds of eigh: *eight*, *height*
	Identified the sounds of ei: *veil*, *forfeit*
	Identified the sound of gn: *gnat*, *reign*
	Identified the sounds of /sh/ti: *nation*; si: *session*, *vision*; ci: *special*; ch: *machine*
	Identified all the previous phonics skills
	Read at least 300 words and wrote at least 200 words on the *Fry's Instant Words* lists
	Read and wrote most irregularly spelled words

Analysis:

Individual Phonics Summary

Name: ______________________ **Grade:** __________ **Date:** __________

Directions: Use after literacy assessments have been completed and then after instruction. Highlight in yellow for missed elements while reading. Highlight in blue for missed elements while writing. Highlight in green for missed elements in both reading and writing. After instruction, circle each element once the student has read and written it correctly. In the analysis, write patterns of correct and incorrect responses for phonetic elements.

Consonants	Vowels
Initial Consonants: b, c, d, f, g, h, j, k, l, m, n, p, qu, r, s, t, v, w, y, z, x, /z/	**Short Vowels:** a, e, i, o, u, y (/ĭ/) Also a in *father*, o in *to*, o in *gone*
Final Consonants: b, d, f, g, k, l, m, n, p, t, x (/ks/), s (/z/, /s/), z, v (followed by e)	**Long Vowels:** a, e, i, o, u, y (/ē/, /ī/) Spelling: Change y to i when adding suffix
Initial Blends: bl-, br-, cl-, cr-, dr-, fl-, fr-, gl-, gr-, pl-, pr-, sc-, scr-, sk-, sl-, sm-, sn-, sp-, spl-, st-, str-, squ-, sw-, tr-, thr-, tw-	**Long and Short Vowels with Silent -e:** a_e, e_e, i_e, o_e, u_e
Final Blends: -ct, -ft, -ld, -lf, -lp, -lt, -mp, -nd, -nk, -np, -nt, -pt, -rb, -rd, -rk, -rl, -rm, -sk-sp, -st	**Vowel Digraphs:** ai, ay, ea, ee, ei, eigh, ey, ie, igh, oa, oe, ooin *good*, ooin *moo*, ou /ŭ/ in *country*, ow /ō/ in *mow*, uy in *buy*
Consonant Digraphs with New Sound: th (voiced, voiceless), wh, ch (/ch/, /k/, /sh/), ph, ng, dge, dj, sh, ti, ci (/sh/), si (/sh/ or /zh/); also -ck	**Diphthongs** (written as digraphs with vowel sound shifts)**:** oi, oy, ou in *ouch*, ow in *cow*, "No highway cowboys"; long ā, ī, and ō are diphthongs if at the end of a syllable
Consonant Digraphs with Silent Consonants: gh (/g/, /f/, silent), kn, wr, pn, rh	**-ough Digraphs and/or Diphthongs:** /ō/ in *though*, /oo/ in *through*, /ŭf/ in *tough*, /awf/, in *cough*, /aw/ in *bought*, /ŏw/ in *bough*
Hard c and Soft c: /k/ /s/ **Hard g and Soft g:** /g/ /j/	**Vocalic -r:** /er/: "Her first nurse works early on grammar"
Verb Tenses: **-s, ing, -ed**(/ed/ /d/ /t/)	**r-, l-, w-, and u-Controlled Vowels:** /ar/ in *car*, /er/ in *there*, /or/ in *corn*, /al/ in *all*, /aw/ in *saw*, /au/ in *autumn*, /ew/ in *new*
Suffixes: -er, -est, -ly, -ful, -y, -able, -ible, -ate, -al, -ial, -en, -ic, -ity, -ive, -tion, -less, -ment, -ness, -ous	**Change y to i** when adding a suffix: *baby* → *babies*, *happy* → *happiness*
Plurals: -s, -es, irregular	**Drop final -e** before a suffix that begins with a vowel: *care* → *caring*
Double Consonants after short vowels and before a suffix that begins with a vowel (*stopping*)	

Analysis:

Emergent Text Concepts Assessment

Name: ______________________________ **Grade:** ____________ **Date:** ______________

Title/Author: ______________________________________ **Level:** ____________________

Directions: Select a picture book with a picture and primarily two lines of print on each page. For questions 1–7, first ask the questions, then read the page. For questions 8–25, read each page and then ask the questions. Fill in the blanks on questions 15–17.

Scoring and Analysis: Write the student's responses and a plus sign (+) if correct and a minus sign (–) if incorrect. Write N/A for absent concepts and change the total number of questions. See the response column for examples of correct responses. Identify patterns of correct and incorrect responses, and write specific examples.

What You Do	What You Say	Response
Hold book with spine to the student.	1. Where is the front of the book?	Pointed to cover.
Show the cover and read the title and author of the book. Ask the question. Read the statement.	2. What do you think this book is going to be about? I'll read this story and you can help me.	Named the topic based on the title and picture.
Find the first page with a picture and print. (Read preceding pages.)	3. Where do I begin reading? Read the page.	Pointed to words.
On the next page with at least two lines of text, ask questions, then read page.	4. Show me where to start? 5. Which way do I go? 6. Where do I go next? 7. Point to each word as I read.	Pointed to the first word. Moved finger from left to right. Pointed to first word on second line. Pointed to each word read.
On the next page, read the following prompts:	8. Point to the first word on the page. 9. Point to the last word on the page. 10. Show me the bottom of the picture.	First word. Last word. Bottom of picture.
Read along until you come to a period, question mark, comma, and quotation marks. Stop, point, and ask questions.	11. What's this for (.)? 12. What's this for (?)? 13. What's this for (,)? 14. What are these for ("")?	Period, stop, end of sentence. Question mark, ask questions. Comma or pause. Quotation or talking marks.
Find two letters that have both a capital and lowercase letter on that page. Point to the capital letter and ask:	15. Can you find a lowercase letter like this? (point to uppercase ____.) 16. Can you find a capital/uppercase letter like this? (point to lowercase ____.)	____ ____

(continued)

What You Do	What You Say	Response
Read until you find a page with two words that start with the same lowercase letter. Select the second.	17. Can you find the word __________?	__________
Find a page with one line of text, or cover all except one line of text. Read the page. Hand the student two index cards, and demonstrate how to close them like a curtain.	18. Close the cards like this until you see one letter. 19. Now show me two letters. 20. Show me just one word. 21. Now show me two words. 22. Show me the first letter of a word. 23. Show me the last letter of a word. 24. Show me a capital letter.	One letter. Two letters. One word. Two words. First letter of a word. Last letter of a word. Capital letter.
Read to the end of the book.	25. What was this story about?	Named topic.
		Score: /25

Analysis:

Graded Reading Words Assessment

Name: ______________________ **Grade:** __________ **Date:** __________

Directions: Give the student the reading word list and an index card. For an emergent reader, write the words on index cards and present them one at a time. Say, "Read each word, and then move the card down the column. I cannot help you, so if you do not know a word, try to figure it out." Continue until the frustration level is reached.

Scoring and Analysis: Above each word, write a plus sign (+) for correct words, a minus sign (–) for incorrect words, and a checkmark (✓) for a self-corrected word. Write all incorrect responses. If a response is not a real word, write it phonetically with all vowels marked. Put a slash for every 2 seconds the student pauses and between decoded parts of words. Write the functioning level, automatic score, and total score. Identify patterns of correct and incorrect responses, and write specific examples.

Functioning Level: Independent, 18–20; instructional, 14–17; frustration, 13 or below.

Preprimer Reading Words			Functioning Level:	
Automatic Score: /20 words = %			Total Score: /20 words = %	
a	to	in	is	he
I	at	have	go	see
cat	can	like	the	mom
on	dog	dad	and	we
Primer Reading Words			Functioning Level:	
Automatic Score: /20 words = %			Total Score: /20 words = %	
by	what	are	for	his
then	with	my	this	all
you	from	she	do	made
was	her	how	saw	that
Analysis:				

(continued)

Graded Reading Words Assessment *(page 2 of 3)*

Grade 1 Reading Words			Functioning Level:	
Automatic Score: /20 words = %			Total Score: /20 words = %	
of	about	many	each	when
why	which	there	play	down
little	they	new	out	one
some	good	said	going	other
Grade 2 Reading Words			Functioning Level:	
Automatic Score: /20 words = %			Total Score: /20 words = %	
very	before	right	goes	always
around	works	great	their	don't
where	use	would	who	your
wanted	first	please	talked	long
Grade 3 Reading Words			Functioning Level:	
Automatic Score: /20 words = %			Total Score: /20 words = %	
favorite	really	family	because	people
friend	again	another	everyone	sometimes
thought	walked	called	writing	carried
doesn't	early	once	we're	believe
Grade 4 Reading Words			Functioning Level:	
Automatic Score: /20 words = %			Total Score: /20 words = %	
been	different	they're	beautiful	piece
pretty	knew	sign	brought	finally
trouble	learned	usually	excited	whether
half	weight	whole	through	tomorrow
Analysis:				

(continued)

Graded Reading Words Assessment *(page 3 of 3)*

Grade 5 Reading Words			Functioning Level:	
Automatic Score: /20 words = %			Total Score: /20 words = %	
heard	couldn't	conclusion	library	environment
watched	sure	laughed	terrible	excellent
knowledge	experience	certain	athletic	difference
separate	height	probably	opinion	picture
Grades 6–8 Reading Words			Functioning Level:	
Automatic Score: /20 words = %			Total Score: /20 words = %	
absence	challenge	government	humorous	curious
business	attendance	emergency	unnecessary	exercise
secretary	similar	straight	thorough	sincerely
receipt	success	restaurant	special	familiar
Grades 9–12 Reading Words			Functioning Level:	
Automatic Score: /20 words = %			Total Score: /20 words = %	
achievement	beneficial	accidentally	extraordinary	analyze
permanent	exception	especially	independence	naturally
acceptable	efficiency	conscientious	committee	technique
tournament	vision	ridiculous	guarantee	acquaintance
Analysis:				

Graded Reading Words Lists

a
to
in
is
he
I
at
have
go
see
cat
can
like
the
mom
on
dog
dad
and
we

by
what
are
for
his
then
with
my
this
all
you
from
she
do
made
was
her
how
saw
that

of
about
many
each
when
why
which
there
play
down
little
they
new
out
one
some
good
said
going
other

very
before
right
goes
always
around
works
great
their
don't
where
use
would
who
your
wanted
first
please
talked
long

(continued)

favorite	been	heard	absence	achievement
really	different	couldn't	challenge	beneficial
family	they're	conclusion	government	accidentally
because	beautiful	library	humorous	extraordinary
people	piece	environment	curious	analyze
friend	pretty	watched	business	permanent
again	knew	sure	attendance	exception
another	sign	laughed	emergency	especially
everyone	brought	terrible	unnecessary	independence
sometimes	finally	excellent	exercise	naturally
thought	trouble	knowledge	secretary	acceptable
walked	learned	experience	similar	efficiency
called	usually	certain	straight	conscientious
writing	excited	athletic	thorough	committee
carried	whether	difference	sincerely	technique
doesn't	half	separate	receipt	tournament
early	weight	height	success	vision
once	whole	probably	restaurant	ridiculous
we're	through	opinion	special	guarantee
believe	tomorrow	picture	familiar	acquaintance

Coding and Scoring Oral Reading Behaviors Guide

Behavior	Example student response	Example word from list or text	Description: Record above the correct word
Correct pronunciation of word	+ or ✓	come	Plus sign (+) for word lists, or checkmark (✓) for text reading
Substitution with another word	house	horse	Word said
Substitution: nonword with different vowel sounds	rēb	red	Write phonetic pronunciation; mark all incorrect vowels with breve (ĕ, short) or macron (ē, long)
Substitution: with alternate consonant sounds	dēkīd	decide	Use dominant letter, such as *k* for hard c, *s* for soft c, *g* for hard g, and *j* for soft
Substitution: decoded with pauses between sounds	/m/ă/d/	mad	Put slashes for pauses, and mark all incorrect vowels with breve (short, ĕ) or macron (long, ē)
Substitution: chunked sounds	/to/get/her/	together	Put slashes between each group of sounds
Substitution: spelled letters	r-e-a-d	read	Hyphens for each letter said
Substitution: mispronunciation due to articulation	pŭskĕtē	spaghetti	Record phonetic pronunciation with vowels marked. If in doubt, ask for a sentence. Not an error.
Substitution: Mispronunciation due to reader's dialect	goin'	going	Record phonetic pronunciation. If in doubt, ask for a sentence. Not an error.
Omission of word	—	friends	Hyphen for omitted word
Insertion of word	little	^	Caret for inserted word during text reading
Multiple attempts	thr, three	there	Write each attempt with a comma between them
Self-correction*	saw, /w/ s-c	was	Word(s) said incorrect initially, then self-corrected
Hesitation*	// ✓	He // laughed	1 slash per 2 seconds. Not an error.
Repetition of word or phrase*	✓Ⓡ	✓because Ⓡ	Checkmark, underline repetition, and put a circled R each time repeated, and score as correct. During text reading, put an arrow back to where the repetition began.
Correct, then incorrect	✓ three	there, three	Put a check, then write incorrect response; score as incorrect

* Not counted against word accuracy in text reading.

Graded Writing Words Assessment

Name: ______________________ **Grade:** __________ **Date:** __________

Directions: Give the student lined paper folded into two columns. Read each word clearly, provide a sentence, then repeat the word. Homophones are indicated by an asterisk (*). Say, "Write each word I say, and then go to the next line. If you do not know a word, try to write letters for each sound you hear." For the preprimer list, ask the student to write his/her name and the words on the list; then, if the student is at frustration level, ask if he/she can write any other words. Continue until frustration level is reached.

Scoring and Analysis: Above each word, write a plus sign (**+**) for the correct word, a minus sign (–) for incorrect word, and a checkmark (✓) for a self-corrected word. Write all incorrect responses. Be sure to record reversals and capital letters. Write the functioning level, total score, and developmental stage. Identify patterns of correct and incorrect responses, and write specific examples.

Functioning Level: Independent, 18–20; instructional, 14–17; frustration, 13 or below.

Developmental Spelling Stage:

Prephonetic	Semiphonetic	Phonetic	Transitional	Conventional
Scribbles, letter like forms, or letters that do not represent the sounds.	Some sound–symbol relationships, one or two letters could represent a whole word.	Most of the sounds are represented graphically, and vowels are used even if incorrect.	Most words are correct. Incorrectly spelled words contain letters representing all the sounds in the word.	The word is spelled correctly, or in writing composition at least 96% of words are spelled correctly.

Preprimer Writing Words **Functioning Level:** ___/___ **words asked =** __________ **%**
Developmental Stage:

Ask, "Can you write your first name and last name?" ______________________

a	to	in	is	he
I	at	have	go	see
cat	can	like	the	mom
on	dog	dad	and	we

"Do you know how to write any other words?" ______________________

____

Primer Writing Words **Functioning Level:** ___**/20 words =** _____**%**
Developmental Stage:

by*	what	are	for*	his
then	with	my	this	all
you	from	she	do*	made*
was	her	how	saw	that

Analysis:

(continued)

Graded Writing Words Assessment *(page 2 of 3)*

Grade 1 Writing Words **Functioning Level:** **Developmental Stage:** **Score: _____ /20 words = ____%**

of	about	many	each	when
why	which*	there*	play	down
little	they	new*	out	one*
some*	good	said	going	other

Grade 2 Writing Words **Functioning Level:** **Developmental Stage:** **Score: _____ /20 words = ____%**

very	before	right*	goes	always
around	works	great*	their*	don't
where*	use	would*	who	your*
wanted	first	please	talked	long

Grade 3 Writing Words **Functioning Level:** **Developmental Stage:** **Score: _____ /20 words = ____%**

favorite	really	family	because	people
friend	again	another	everyone	sometimes
thought	walked	called	writing	carried
doesn't	early	once	we're	believe

Grade 4 Writing Words **Functioning Level:** **Developmental Stage:** **Score: _____ /20 words = ____%**

been	different	they're*	beautiful	piece*
pretty	knew*	sign	brought	finally
trouble	learned	usually	excited	whether*
half	weight	whole	through*	tomorrow

Analysis:

(continued)

Graded Writing Words Assessment *(page 3 of 3)*

Grade 5 Writing Words **Functioning Level:** **Developmental Stage:** **Score: ____ /20 words= ___%**

heard*	couldn't	conclusion	library	environment
watched	sure	laughed	terrible	excellent
knowledge	experience	certain	athletic	difference
separate	height	probably	opinion	picture

Grades 6–8 Writing Words **Functioning Level:** **Developmental Stage:** **Score: ____ /20 words= ___%**

absence	challenge	government	humorous	curious
business	attendance	emergency	unnecessary	exercise
secretary	similar	straight	thorough	sincerely
receipt	success	restaurant	special	familiar

Grades 9–12 Writing Words **Functioning Level:** **Developmental Stage:** **Score: ____ / 20 words = ___%**

achievement	beneficial	accidentally	extraordinary	analyze
permanent	exception	especially	independence	naturally
acceptable	efficiency	permanent	committee	technique
tournament	vision	ridiculous	guarantee	acquaintance

Analysis:

Sentence Dictation Assessment

Name: ______________________ **Grade:** __________ **Date:** __________

Directions: Give the student lined paper. Say, "I am going to read you a story, and then I will go back and read one word at a time. Write down each word I say. If you do not know how to write a word, say the word to yourself, and write down the letters for the sounds you hear." Continue to the next grade until the frustration level is reached.

Scoring and Analysis: Above each word, write a plus sign (+) for the correct spelling or a minus sign (–) for incorrect spellings or deleted words, and write all incorrect spellings. Count each correct underlined grapheme and write the total. In the analysis, use the *Individual Phonics Summary* headings to write patterns of correct and incorrect graphemes and phonetic elements, with specific examples.

Functioning Level: Independent, 90–100%; instructional, 70–89%; frustration, 69% or below

Preprimer and Primer Functioning Level: **Score: ____/41 graphemes = ____%**

I l i k e t o h a v e f u n w i th m y d o g . H e c a n j u m p a n d g e t

b a ll s .

First and Second Grade Functioning Level: **Score: ____/50 graphemes = ____%**

Th e f ar m er s aw the b l a ck a n d wh i t e t oy b oa t ou t o n the w a t er.

I t f l oa t ed u n d er the sh i n y s t ee l b r i dge to a s m a ll b ea ch.

Third Grade and Above Functioning Level:
Score: ____/153 graphemes, blends, controlled vowels = ____%

T o d ay I s aw a l i tt le g ir l w a l k i ng i n th e c oo l w a t er a l o ng the (31)

br ee z y b ea ch in Fl or i d a. Sh e a sk ed, "Ph i l , d o y ou kn ow wh er e m y (27)

tw o bl ue t oy s ai l b oa t s ar e? " I s ai d, "I th i nk th ey f l oa t ed u n d er th a t (19)

n ew br i dge a n d the h u g e w a v e s m igh t h a v e br ough t th e m u p o n (17)

th e j a gg ed sh or e o v er th e r e. Wh y d o n't y ou p u t o n y ou r sh oe s (11)

(continued)

b e c au s e y ou c ou ld g e t h ur t cl i mb i ng." We f ou nd o n l y a sm a ll (15)

p ie c e o f o n e boat i n th e s oi l. I e x cl ai m ed, "L e t 's h ea d b a ck. I t 's (17)

g e tt i ng qu i t e d ar k! N ow d o n 't w or r y; we 'll st a r t l oo k i ng a g ai n (13)

ear l y t o m o rr ow." (3)

Analysis:

Handwriting Rubric Assessment

Name: ______________________ **Grade:** __________ **Date:** __________

Directions: This rubric can be used with any writing assessment or writing sample to indicate the student's specific development in handwriting. Note: Since the goal of writing is communication, emphasize legibility over exact handwriting style.

Scoring and Analysis: Using the criteria listed, mark a plus sign (+) if the student exceeded the standard, a checkmark (✓) if the student met the standard, or a minus sign (–) if the student did not meet the standard. Identify standards that were met or exceeded; then give specific examples of standards that were not met.

Standard	Score	Exceeded (+)	Met (✓)	Did Not Meet (–)
Letters were easily recognizable.		Letters were always recognizable.	Letters were mostly recognizable.	Letters were rarely recognizable.
Letters were formed correctly.		Letters were always formed correctly.	Letters were mostly formed correctly.	Letters were rarely formed correctly.
Letters started and ended in the correct place.		Letters always started and ended correctly.	Letters mostly started and ended correctly.	Letters rarely started and/or ended correctly.
Letters were placed correctly within the lines.		Letters were always placed correctly within the lines.	Letters were mostly placed correctly within the lines.	Letters were rarely placed correctly within the lines.
Letters were usually spaced properly.		Letters were always spaced properly.	Letters were usually spaced properly.	Letters were rarely spaced properly.
Words were usually spaced properly.		Words were always spaced properly.	Words were usually spaced properly.	Words were rarely spaced properly.
Return sweep was used properly.		Return sweep was always used properly.	Return sweep was usually used properly.	Return sweep was rarely used properly.
Capital letters were used appropriately.		Always used capital letters appropriately.	Usually used capital letters appropriately.	Capital letters were rarely used appropriately.

Analysis:

Analysis of Miscues Worksheet

Name: ______________________ **Grade:** __________ **Date:** __________

Title: ______________________ **Word Count:** __________ **Text Level:** __________

Student Response /Text	**Miscue Type**						**Cues Used**			**Meaning Retained**
	Self-correction	Uncorrected miscue	Omission of word	Insertion of word	Decoded/ nonword	Substitution of word	Grapho-phonemic I = Initial, M = Medial, F = Final	Syntactic–grammar	Semantic–meaning	Yes, sentence meaning, * if not s-c
1.										
2.										
3.										
4.										
5.										
6.										
7.										
8.										
9.										
10.										
11.										
12.										
13.										
14.										
15.										
16.										
17.										
18.										
19.										
20.										
21.										
22.										
23.										
24.										
25.										
26.										
27.										
28.										
29.										
30.										
Totals:										

Oral Reading Analysis of Miscues Summary

Name: ______________________ **Grade:** _____ **Date:** __________

Title: ______________________ **Word Count:** _______ **Level:** __________

Genre: ______________________

ORAL READING SUMMARY				
Type of Score	**Calculation**	**Fraction**	**%**	**Functioning Level***
Word Accuracy	Words Correct = Word Count – Uncorrected Miscues / Word Count			
Text Meaning/ Acceptability	Words Correct + Uncorrected Meaning Retained Miscues / Word Count			
Miscue Scores				
Self-Correction	Self-Corrections/Number of Miscues			
Omissions	Omissions/Number of Miscues			
Insertions	Insertions/Number of Miscues			
Decoded Sounds or Nonwords	Decoded Sounds/Number of Miscues			
Substitutions of Real Words	Substitutions/Number of Miscues			
Cueing System Scores				
Grapho-Phonemic	Number of Grapho-Phonemic Cues Used / Number of Miscues			
Syntactic	Number of Syntactic Cues Used / Number of Miscues			
Semantic	Number of Semantic Cues Used / Number of Miscues			

Functioning Level*	Independent	Instructional	Frustration
Oral Accuracy	95–100%	90–94%	89% or below
Oral Acceptability	98–100%	95–97%	94% or below
Comprehension	90–100%	70–89%	69% or below

***To obtain a true functioning level, comprehension must also be assessed.**

Functioning Levels for Miscue and Cueing System Scores			
75–100%	Predominantly Used Cue	20–49%	Sometimes Used Cue
50–74%	Often Used Cue	19% or below	Rarely Used Cue

Analysis:

Oral Reading Strategies Assessment

Name: ______________________________ **Grade:** ___________ **Date:** _____________

Purpose: To identify strategies used during reading. This assessment is to be used for any oral reading that is at the instructional or frustration level for word accuracy.

Directions and Scoring: While the student is orally reading, identify the strategies that are used in order to attempt to figure out words. Write a plus sign (+) if this strategy was used frequently, a checkmark (✓) if the strategy was used occasionally, or a minus sign (–) if the strategy was used rarely or not at all. For the analysis, group and summarize those strategies that were used frequently, occasionally, and rarely.

When the reader came to unknown words, he/she . . .	
Score +, ✓, –	**Strategy**
	Looked at the pictures and graphics and thought about the text.
	Said beginning three sounds.
	Read on to collect clues and went back.
	Went back and read again.
	Broke words into parts.
	Tried different sounds.
	Attempted to self-correct words that did not look right.
	Attempted to self-correct words that did not sound right.
	Attempted to self-correct words that did not make sense.
	Self-corrected words.

Analysis:

Fluency Assessment by Teacher and Peers

Name: ______________________________ **Date:** ____________

Title/Author: ______________________ **Level:** ______ **Genre:** ____________

The student . . . **Score: +, ✓, –**	**Generally Fluent (+)**	**Sometimes Fluent (✓)**	**Rarely Fluent (–)**
Read in phrases. Score:	Read sentences in meaningful phrases or clauses.	Read in a mixture of appropriate phrasing and word by word.	Read only one to two words at a time.
Paused at punctuation marks. Score:	Paused after end punctuation (period, question mark, exclamation point) and middle punctuation (comma, semicolon, colon).	Usually paused at end punctuation, but not always middle punctuation.	Rarely paused at punctuation marks.
Read with expression. Score:	Read with appropriate stress and intonation; changed voice for expression as needed; read with emphasis for dramatization or read with different voices.	Read with some appropriate expression, and some changes in stress and intonation.	Read with little expression or change in stress and intonation.
Read smoothly. Score:	Reading sounded smooth, with only a few short pauses for problem solving when needed.	Reading was generally smooth, with some hesitations and repetitions.	Reading sounded choppy, with several skipped words, hesitations, or repetitions.
Used problem-solving strategies efficiently. Score:	Most meaning miscues were self-corrected after initial attempt.	Most meaning miscues were self-corrected after multiple attempts.	Most miscues were not self-corrected, and few strategies were attempted.
Read at a conversational pace. Score:	The reading pace was like that of a conversation, not too fast or too slow for others to understand.	The reading pace was either a little too fast or a little too slow.	The reading was very slow and labored.
Read at an independent word accuracy level. Score:	Read at an independent level (95% or higher word accuracy).	Read at an instructional level (90–94% word accuracy).	Read at a frustration level (89% or below word accuracy).
Comprehended or retold what was read. Score:	Retold all of the important story elements or the main idea and major details.	Retold most of the important elements of the story or the main idea and major details.	Did not retell the important elements of the story or the main idea and major details.

Analysis:

Fluency Self-Assessment

Name: ______________________ **Date:** __________

Title/Author: ______________________ **Level:** ______ **Genre:** __________

Score: +, ✓, –	Generally Fluent (+)	Sometimes Fluent (✓)	Rarely Fluent (–)
I read in phrases. Score:	I read sentences in phrases.	I read some sentences in phrases.	I often read word by word.
I paused at end punctuation (. ? !) and middle punctuation (, ; :). Score:	I paused at end and middle punctuation.	I paused at most end punctuation, but not always for middle punctuation.	I often did not pause.
My voice changed to show expression and match the meaning and emotions in the passage. Score:	I changed my voice to show expression or different characters when needed.	I sometimes changed my voice to show expression or different characters when needed.	I often did not change my voice to show expression or different characters when needed.
I read smoothly. Score:	I sounded smooth, with only a few short pauses if I needed to figure out words.	Sometimes my reading was smooth, and sometimes I needed to stop or reread more often.	My reading sounded choppy. I skipped words, stopped, or reread often.
I used strategies to correct my reading if it didn't make sense. Score:	I was able to correct my reading quickly if it didn't make sense.	It took some time, but I used several strategies to correct my reading if it didn't make sense.	I did not correct my reading if it didn't make sense.
I read at a conversational pace. Score:	I read at a conversational pace.	Sometimes I read at a conversational pace, but other times I read too fast or too slow.	I read very slowly.
I read most of the words correctly. Score:	I read almost all of the words.	I read most of the words.	I could not read many words.
I retold what I read. Score:	I retold all of the important parts of the story in fiction, or explained the main idea and major details in nonfiction.	I retold most of the important parts of the story in fiction, or explained the main idea and major details in nonfiction.	I did not retell the important parts of the story in fiction, or the main idea and major details in nonfiction.

Analysis:

Reading Level Correlation Chart

Grade Level	Reading Recovery	Fountas–Pinnell Guided Reading	Developmental Reading Assessment	Basal Equivalent	Lexile
Kindergarten	A, B	A	A	Readiness	
	1		1		
	2	B	2	Preprimer 1	
	3	C	3		
Grade 1	4		4	Preprimer 2	
	5	D	6		
	6				
	7	E	8	Preprimer 3	
	8				
	9	F	10	Primer	
	10				
	11	G	12		
	12				
	13	H	14	Grade 1	200–299
	14				
	15	I	16		
	16				
Grade 2	18	J, K	20	Grade 2	300–399
	20	L, M	28		400–499
Grade 3	22	N	30	Grade 3	500–599
			34		
	24	O, P	38		600–699
Grade 4	26	Q, R, S	40	Grade 4	700–799
Grade 5	28	T, U, V	44	Grade 5	800–899
Grade 6	30	W, X, Y		Grade 6	900–999
Grade 7	32	Z		Grade 7	1000–1100
Grade 8	34	Z		Grade 8	

Note. Reprinted with permission from Larry Madden.

Text Selection Bookmarks

Read to me!

Before Reading:

Talk about the front cover and pictures throughout the text. Predict what it will be about and talk about what you already know about that topic.

During Reading:

Listen to the text as it is read aloud. Stop briefly to talk about the author's message and the meaning of new words.

After Reading:

Talk about what you learned and liked. Make connections between the text and your experience or knowledge.

Read with me!

Before Reading:

Talk about the front cover, pictures, and graphics throughout the text. Predict what it will be about and talk about what you already know about that topic.

During Reading:

Take turns reading aloud. Use strategies to figure out unknown words. Stop briefly to talk about the author's message and the meaning of new words.

After Reading:

Talk about what you learned and liked. Make connections between the text and your experience or knowledge.

I can read this on my own!

Before Reading:

Look at the front cover, pictures, graphics, and headings throughout the text. Predict what it will be about and think about what you already know about that topic.

During Reading:

Read aloud or silently. Use strategies to figure out unknown words. Stop briefly to think about the author's message and try to figure out the meaning of new words.

After Reading:

Think about what you learned and liked. Make connections between the text and your experience or knowledge. If possible, share these ideas with someone.

Reading Log

Name: ______________________________

Directions: Record each time you read outside of class. Adults, put a plus sign (+) if it was read with minimal mistakes and the student could retell the important ideas; a checkmark (✓) if it was read with some mistakes and/or the student could retell some of the important ideas; and a minus sign (–) if it was read with many mistakes and/or the student could not retell important ideas.

Date	Title and Author	Minutes	Pages	Adult Signature	Score +, ✓, –

Reading Goal:

The more that you read, the more things you will know.
The more that you learn, the more places you'll go.—Dr. Seuss

Good Readers Strategy Poster

Good readers . . .

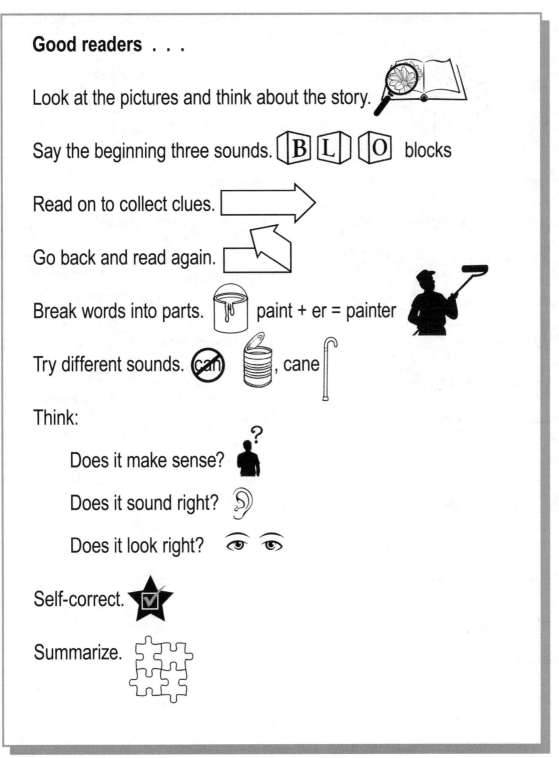

Look at the pictures and think about the story.

Say the beginning three sounds. B L O blocks

Read on to collect clues.

Go back and read again.

Break words into parts. paint + er = painter

Try different sounds. can, cane

Think:

Does it make sense?

Does it sound right?

Does it look right?

Self-correct.

Summarize.

Good Readers Bookmarks

Primary Bookmark

Good readers . . .

- Look at the pictures and think about the story. 
- Say the beginning three sounds. 
- Read on to collect clues. 
- Go back and read again. 
- Break words into parts. 
- Try different sounds.
- Think:

  Does it make sense? 

  Does it sound right?

  Does it look right? 
- Self-correct. 
- Summarize.

Intermediate and Secondary Bookmark

Good readers . . .

- Look at the graphics and headings; think about the story. 
- Say the beginning three sounds and predict the word. 
- Read on to collect clues. 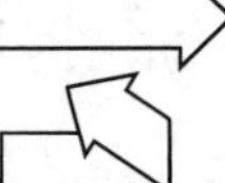
- Go back and read again. 
- Break words into parts.  (Think about prefix, suffix, and root meanings.)
- Try different sounds.
- Use a glossary or dictionary. 
- Think:

  Does it make sense? 

  Does it sound right?

  Does it look right? 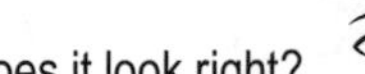 
- Self-correct. 
- Summarize. 

Oral Reading Strategy Checklist for Teachers

Name: ____ **Date:** ____________

Title/Author: __________________________ **Level:** __________ **Genre:** __________

Strategies: Put a tally mark each time a strategy is used by the student.

_____ Look at the pictures and think about the story.

_____ Say the beginning three sounds.

_____ Read on to collect clues.

_____ Go back and read again.

_____ Break words into parts.

_____ Try different sounds.

_____ Miscues have similar meanings.

_____ Miscues are visually similar.

_____ Miscues have similar syntax.

_____ Self-correct.

_____ Summarize.

Teacher Prompts: Put a tally mark for each prompt given.

_____ Provide wait time.

_____ Look at the pictures and think about the story.

_____ Say the beginning three sounds.

_____ Read on to collect clues.

_____ Go back and read again.

_____ Break words into parts.

_____ Try different sounds.

_____ Does that make sense?

_____ Does that look right?

_____ Does that sound right?

_____ Where is the tricky part?

_____ Are you right?

_____ How do you know?

_____ What else can you do?

_____ Try that again.

_____ Summarize.

Observations:

Oral Reading Strategy Checklist for Peers or Self

Name: ______________________ **Date:** ____________

Reader's Name: ______________ **Title/Author:** ______________

Directions: Put a stamp or a mark after the strategy each time the reader uses it.

1. **Look at the pictures and graphics; think about the message.**
2. **Say the beginning three sounds.** B L O **blocks**
3. **Read on to collect clues.**
4. **Go back and read again.**
5. **Break word into parts.** **paint + er = painter**
6. **Try different sounds.** can **cane**
7. **Think:** **Does it make sense?** **Does it sound right?** **Does it look right?**
8. **Self-correct.**
9. **Summarize.**

Strategy number that worked well X: ____________ Strategy number that might help ✓: ____________

Analysis:

Readers' Theatre Rubric

Name: ______________________________ **Date:** ______________

Reader's Name: ____________________ **Title/Author:** ____________________

Directions: For each element of this rubric, read the indicators and rate each student (or have the student rate him-/herself) on the basis of the student's performance. Write a plus sign (+) for excellent, a checkmark (✓) for satisfactory, and a minus sign (–) if it needs improvement.

Element and Score: +, ✓, –	**Excellent (+)**	**Satisfactory (✓)**	**Needs Improvement (–)**
Phrasing and punctuation Score:	Read sentences in meaningful phrases or clauses, and paused appropriately for punctuation.	Read with some appropriate phrasing and pausing for punctuation.	Read only one to two words at a time, rarely pausing for punctuation.
Expression Score:	Changed expression, stress, intonation, and voice as appropriate for character or narrator.	Some change in expression, stress, intonation, and voice as appropriate for character or narrator.	Rarely used or changed expression.
Volume Score:	Read at an appropriate volume and loudly enough for the audience to hear.	Usually read loudly enough for the audience to hear.	Read too loudly or too softly for the audience to hear.
Clarity Score:	All words were pronounced correctly and clearly.	Most words were pronounced correctly and clearly.	Many words were pronounced incorrectly or not clearly.
Pace Score:	Read at a conversational pace.	Often read at a conversational pace, but might be inconsistent.	The pace was either too fast or too slow.
Timing Score:	Consistently took turns in a timely fashion.	Took turns, but not always in a timely fashion.	Rarely took turns in a timely fashion; had to be prompted to read.
Facial and body language Score:	Frequently used facial expressions and body language to communicate the story.	Used some facial expressions and body language to communicate the story.	Rarely used facial expressions and body language to communicate the story.
Interpretation Score:	Correctly and imaginatively interpreted each scene.	Most scenes were interpreted correctly.	Most scenes were not correctly interpreted.

Analysis:

Comprehension Retelling and Questioning Assessment: Guide

Title: **Author:**	**Grade Level:** **Reading Level:**
Genre:	
Prior knowledge questions: **Score: +, ✓, –**	**Prediction:** What do you think this text is going to be about?
Retelling Checklist for Narrative (fiction or nonfiction): Score: +, ✓, –	**Retelling Checklist for Expository (fiction or nonfiction): Score: +, ✓, –**
Characters: _____ _____ _____ Setting: _____ Problem (conflict): _____ Events (plot—rising action, climax, falling action): _____ _____ _____ _____ _____ Solution (resolution): _____ _____	_____ Main Idea: _____ Details: _____ Details: _____ Details _____ Main Idea: _____ Details: _____ Details: _____ Details: Text Structure (select one or more): _____ Description _____ Cause–effect _____ Sequence _____ Compare–contrast _____ Problem–solution

Comprehension Questions		**Answers**
Score: **+, ✓, –**	1. _____ Literal 2. _____ Literal 3. _____ Literal 4. _____ Inferential 5. _____ Inferential 6. _____ Inferential 7. _____ Text Structure (L or I) 8. _____ Vocabulary (L or I) 9. _____ Application 10. _____ Critical	1. 2. 3. 4. 5 6 7. 8. 9. 10.

Analysis:

Oral Reading and Comprehension Analysis Summary

Name:	Grade:	Date:
Title:	Word Count:	Level:
Genre:		

ORAL READING SUMMARY				
Type of Score	**Calculation**	**Fraction**	**%**	**Functioning Level***
Word Accuracy	$\frac{\text{Words Correct = Word Count – Uncorrected Miscues}}{\text{Word Count}}$			
Text Meaning/ Acceptability	$\frac{\text{Words Correct + Uncorrected Meaning Retained Miscues}}{\text{Word Count}}$			

COMPREHENSION ANALYSIS SUMMARY		
Criteria	**Scores with Examples**	
Prior Knowledge (+, ✓, –)		
Prediction (+, ✓, –)		
Retelling (+, ✓, –) **Narrative** / **Expository** Characters / Main Idea Setting / Details Problem / Main Idea Plot / Details Resolution / Text Structure		
Comprehension Score Literal Questions: Inferential Questions: Application Questions: Critical Questions: Total Correct:	**Without Look-Backs** ___/___ = ___% ___/___ = ___% ___/___ = ___% ___/___ = ___% ___/___ = ___%	**With Look-Backs*** ___/___ = ___% ___/___ = ___% ___/___ = ___% ___/___ = ___% ___/___ = ___%
Comprehension Functioning Level		*** Not used for determining level**

Functioning Levels for Text Reading			
	Independent	Instructional	Frustration
Oral Reading Accuracy	**95–100%**	**90–94%**	**89% or below**
Oral Acceptability	**98–100%**	**95–97%**	**94% or below**
Comprehension	**90–100%**	**70–89%**	**69% or below**

Analysis:

Comprehension Analysis Summary

Name:		**Grade:**	**Date:**
Title:		**Word Count:**	**Level:**
Genre:			
COMPREHENSION SUMMARY			
Criteria	**Scores with Examples**		
Prior Knowledge (+, ✓, –)			
Prediction (+, ✓, –)			
Retelling (+, ✓, –) **Narrative** / **Expository** Characters / Main Idea Setting / Details Problem / Main Idea Plot / Details Resolution / Text Structure			
Comprehension Score Literal Questions: Inferential Questions: Application Questions:* Critical Questions:* Total Correct:	**Without Look-Backs** ____/____ = ____% ____/____ = ____% ____/____ = ____% ____/____ = ____% ____/____ = ____%	**With Look-Backs*** ____/____ = ____% ____/____ = ____% ____/____ = ____% ____/____ = ____% ____/____ = ____%	
Comprehension Functioning Level		*** Not used for determining level**	

Functioning Levels for Comprehension			
	Independent	Instructional	Frustration
Comprehension	**90–100%**	**70–89%**	**69% or below**

Analysis:

Text, Graphic, and Organizational Features Assessment

Name: ______________________ **Date:** ______________

Title/Author: ______________________ **Level:** ______________

Directions: Select a text with as many of these features as possible. Make a key for the blanks and expected responses. You or student reads each question and then answers them. Write the responses.

Score: Mark a plus sign (+) if correct, a minus sign (–) if incorrect, and N/A if the feature is not in the text.

Analysis: Describe areas of strength and areas for improvement, with specific examples.

Questions	Response	Score
1. What is the title of the text?		
2. Who is the author of the text? 3. Who is the illustrator of the text? 4. Is there any information about the author or illustrator? If yes, state one fact.		
5. What is the copyright date? 6. Why is it important? 7. Who is the publisher?		
8. Where is the table of contents? 9. What information do you find there? 10. What page can you find __________ on?		
11. Where is the glossary? 12. What information do you find there? 13. What is the definition of __________?		
14. Where is the index? 15. What information do you find there? 16. What page is __________ on?		

(continued)

Questions	Response	Score
17. Where is a heading? 18. What information does it tell you?		
19. Where are bolded or italicized words? 20. Why are they bolded or italicized in the text?		
21. Where is a caption? 22. What information does it tell you?		
23. Where is a photograph or illustration? 24. What information does it tell you?		
25. Where is a diagram or map? 26. What information does it tell you?		
27. Where is a table or chart? 28. What information does it tell you?		
29. Where can you go to get additional information on this topic?		
30. As you look through the text, what do you think it is going to be about?		
Total Correct:		

Analysis:

Text Structure Assessment

Name: ______________________________ **Date:** ______________

Directions: Tell students, "Common text structures include descriptive, compare–contrast, sequencing, problem–solution, and cause–effect. Read each paragraph, write the overall text structure, and identify the signal words. Next, create a graphic organizer related to each text structure, and write at least five important details in the graphic organizer."

Scoring and Analysis: Text structure, 1 point each; signal words, 1 point each; graphic organizer, 5 points each. Identify correct responses, and write specific examples of incorrect responses.

1. Butterflies and moths are both insects in the class of Lepidoptera. They look similar and have the same body parts, including two sets of wings. They are the only group of insects that have scales covering their wings. However, here are a few differences so you can tell them apart. Moths tend to have stout and hairy-looking bodies, while butterflies have slender and smoother abdomens. Butterflies have fine scales; however, moths have larger scales on their wings, which make them look more dense and fluffy. Butterflies have long thin antennae, with most of them having small clubs at the end. The antennae on moths vary in appearance, but are often feather-like, and most do not have the club-shaped end. Most moth caterpillars spin a cocoon made of silk within which they change during the pupa stage. Most butterflies, on the other hand, form an exposed pupa made from hardened protein called a chrysalis. Most moths are nocturnal or active during the night, while most butterflies are diurnal or active during the day. Also, most butterflies have bright colors on their wings, while nocturnal moths are usually plain brown, grey, white, or black with patterns. This helps camouflage moths from predators when they rest during the day. Moths usually rest with their wings spread out to their sides, but butterflies frequently fold their wings above their back when perched and will occasionally spread their wings. While butterflies and moths are similar insects, these are a few ways you can tell them apart.

Text Structure: ______________________ Signal Words: ______________________

2. Butterflies are insects or arthropods with three main body parts: a head, thorax, and abdomen. On the head, they have compound eyes, a pair of antennae, and a mouth called a proboscis.Their antennas are important because they detect odors, taste, wind, heat, moisture, and touch. They are also used for balance. Another characteristic of butterflies is that they have a proboscis, which is made up of two long hollow tubes that can uncoil to suck nectar out of flowers. The thorax is the middle part of their body, where three pairs of jointed legs and two pairs of wings are attached.Their feet have taste receptors to help them find plants to eat and to lay their eggs on. In addition, butterfly wings are the only ones covered in small scales, which reflect light in different colors. The abdomen contains the heart, spiracles for breathing, reproductive organs, and most of the digestive system. There are about 17,500 species of butterflies in the world, each with a unique pattern and color. One example of a common butterfly is the monarch. It has bright orange wings with black lines and white spots. Butterflies are beautiful, yet very fragile insects.

Text Structure: ______________________ Signal Words: ______________________

3. There are four stages in the life cycle or metamorphosis of a butterfly. All butterflies have "complete metamorphosis." The first stage is the egg. A butterfly starts as a very small round or oval egg. The

(continued)

eggs are laid by an adult female, often on leaves of plants. After the eggs hatch, they are in the second stage, called the larva or caterpillar stage. During this stage, the caterpillars mostly eat so they can grow quickly. Their skin molts or sheds several times as they grow. Next is the pupa stage or third stage. During this stage, butterflies form a hard shell called a chrysalis. While inside the chrysalis, the old body parts of the caterpillar begin to change. The fourth stage is when it finally becomes an adult. When the caterpillar has done changing inside the pupa, an adult butterfly will emerge or come out of the pupa. It will pump blood into its wings to get them working. Once it learns to fly, it will begin to search for a mate to reproduce. When the adult female lays eggs, the life cycle will start again.

Text Structure: ______________________________ Signal Words: ______________________________

4. There has been a 95 percent decline in the monarch butterfly population in the last 20 years. Scientists believe that this is caused by climate change and loss of habitat. In March, the eastern population of monarch butterflies begins their annual migration north from Mexico. Every year, a new generation of butterflies follows the same path as the generations before them. The only thing guiding them on the migration is temperature telling them when they need to travel. But in recent years, the monarch's fall south migration from Canada has been delayed by up to 6 weeks, due to warmer than normal temperatures. By the time the temperature in the north has cooled enough to trigger the migration south, it's been too cold in the Midwest, and many monarchs die on their trip. Climate change has also increased the frequency and intensity of extreme weather events, which can have terrible effects on migrating monarchs. In 2002, a severe and sudden storm killed most of the monarch population that wintered in Mexico. The population has yet to recover. Also, hotter and drier weather has killed monarchs in the larva stage, which reduces the reproduction ability of adult butterflies. Because of rising temperatures and extreme drought, there are fewer milkweed habitats, and this further limits where monarch butterflies can feed and reproduce. As a result, there are fewer and fewer of these beautiful butterflies.

Text Structure: ______________________________ Signal Words: ______________________________

5. Sadly, the numbers of monarch butterflies have decreased significantly from climate change and loss of habitat. We need to work together to solve this, or they will be gone forever. While governments and corporations can help reduce the amount of greenhouse gases that go into the atmosphere and warm the earth, individuals and groups can make a difference too. People can create more habitats that monarchs need by planting milkweed in backyards, gardens and community spaces along the monarch migration route from Mexico to the U.S.–Canadian border. Butterflies need milkweed and other nectar plants for eating and laying their eggs. We can stop using pesticides that destroy the milkweed and other plants. We can also help scientists track butterflies by helping with the butterfly count and reporting the numbers of butterflies seen. It is also important to educate others about the how to help increase the butterfly population. Even though butterfly populations have significantly declined, we can help bring them back.

Text Structure: ______________________________ Signal Words: ______________________________

Analysis: Score: ____/35

Text Structure:

Signal Words:

Graphic Organizer with Details:

Guided Reading Checklist

Name: ______________________________ **Date:** ______________

Directions: During guided, group, and independent reading time, evaluate each student. Write a plus sign (+) for excellent, a checkmark (✓) for satisfactory, and a minus sign (–) if the student's reading needs improvement.

	Score: +, ✓, –
Reading Silently	
Stayed on task.	
Chose to read.	
Used organizational features (table of contents, glossary, and index) to clarify information.	
Referred back to parts already read to clarify or extend new information.	
Read for detail rather than just skimming.	
Actively participated in discussion about the text.	
Contributed to discussion and questioning that indicated an appropriate level of comprehension.	
Connected text to self, to other texts, or to the world.	
Reading Orally	
Accuracy	
Used a variety of strategies to problem-solve unknown words.	
Reread if the reading did not make sense, look right, or sound right.	
Self-corrected miscues that affected the meaning of the text.	
Made fewer than 5 miscues in 50 words.	
Used resources to gain meaning of unknown words.	
Prosody	
Read in phrases.	
Paused at punctuation.	
Changed expression and intonation according to the author's style.	
Generally, read smoothly and resolved any problems quickly.	
Adjusted pace according to material and purpose.	
Read at a conversational pace.	

(continued)

Guided Reading Checklist *(page 2 of 2)*

Comprehension	Score: +, ✓, –
Predicted content based on cover page, table of contents, graphic information, headings, and/or reading the first paragraph.	
Identified the genre and text structure.	
Made inferences and evaluated them during reading.	
Reread to clarify meaning.	
Used resources or asked questions to clarify meaning.	
Identified and explained the narrative story elements in his/her own words.	
Identified and explained the main ideas and details of an expository text.	
Identified and explained the expository text structures in his/her own words.	
Summarized the text in his/her own words.	
Made connections within the text, to other texts, to self, and to the world.	
Evaluated the text for author bias, content, and interest.	

Analysis:

Oral or Written Story Retelling Analysis

Name: ______________________________ **Date:** ______________

Title/Author: ______________________________ **Genre:** ______________

Oral Retelling or **Written Retelling** (underline one)

Directions: Before and after the student reads a narrative story, say, "I want you to tell me [or write] everything you remember about the story in order."

Scoring: Record the student's responses, and mark each element with a plus (+) if the student provides a complete correct response, a checkmark (✓) if it is a partial or partially correct response, or a minus (–) if the response is incorrect or not given.

	Score +, ✓, –
Introduction of Characters and Setting	
Began story with an introduction.	
Named the main character.	
Described the main character.	
Named other characters (total number of other characters = _______).	
Described other characters.	
Included statement about the setting: Place(s) and time of day, time of year, or time period.	
Theme, Plot, and Events	
Described the important message or lesson that the author was trying to convey.	
Described the primary goal or problem to be solved.	
Number of events recalled (total number of events = _______).	
Recalled details of events and attempts to solve problem.	
Resolution	
Described the solution to the problem.	
Described the ending of the story.	
Sequence	
Retold story in structural order: characters, setting, theme, events, resolution.	

Note. Based on ideas from Mariotti and Homan (1997) and Morrow (2001).

Analysis:

Text, Graphic, and Organizational Features Chart

Type of Feature and Definition	How Feature Helps Readers	Example of Feature
	Text Features	
Title: The name of a text located on the front cover or at the beginning of a chapter.	Indicates the topic and/or main idea of the entire text.	*Reptiles*
Heading/subheading: A line of text to show what the section is about; sometimes differentiated from a title by font size or color.	Indicates the main idea of a section of text.	Scaly skin
Caption text: Words located near a graphic feature (such as a picture, map, diagram, etc.), to explain what it is or what it's about.	Explains the graphic feature near it.	Maya standing near a tall tree.
Pronunciation guide: A phonetic representation of a word, usually located in parentheses after the word has appeared in the text.	Shows the reader how to pronounce a new or unusual word.	chameleons /kŭmēlēŏnz/
Bullets: Listed text that is indented and aligned, with a bullet, dot, symbol, or dash in front of each idea.	Summarizes or lists information in a text.	Reptile characteristics: • Cold-blooded • Scaly skin • Soft eggs
Sidebar: Boxes of additional information beside, above, or below the main text.	Provides additional details, facts, or information related to the text.	A chameleon can swivel its eyes in different directions at the same time, so it can see all around.
Hyperlink: A reference to online information that the reader can follow by clicking or tapping.	Provides additional information from an online document or part of an element within a document.	*www.nationalgeographic.com/animals/reptiles*
Boldfaced words: Written in a dark and thick print within the main body of text; often, these words are also defined in the glossary.	Signals important vocabulary and/or a phrase that is integral to understanding the content of the text.	**Basking** Lying in the sun to get warm.
Italics: Font slanted to the right within the main body of text	Helps to emphasize words in a sentence, to show a title of a work, to indicate foreign words, and to set off some proper nouns.	Example from *Mama Dug a Little Den* by Jennifer Ward.
Font type, size, capitalization, or text effect: Features of the font.	Helps to emphasize words in a sentence or heading.	He was so **BIG**.

(continued)

Note. Based on ideas from Capstone Publishers (n.d.) and Wilkes-Barre Area School District (n.d.).

Text, Graphic, and Organizational Features Chart *(page 2 of 3)*

Type of Feature and Definition	How Feature Helps Readers	Example of feature
	Graphic Features	
Photograph: A picture that emphasizes key points and adds interest (with or without a caption).	Helps to visualize real events, steps, or objects described in the text.	
Drawing/painting (with or without caption): A hand-created sketch or painting; a caption explains what is in the drawing.	Helps to visualize and better understand something from the text.	
Inset: A small photo, picture, or map inside or next to a larger picture; insets magnify a part of the larger picture.	Helps to visualize something in the text in both large and small scale, in combination with the larger picture.	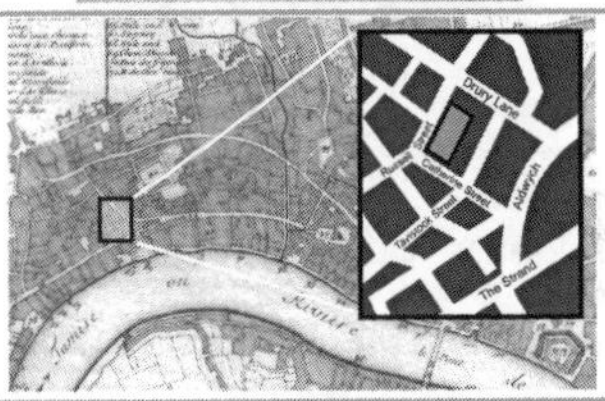
Cross-section: A picture of a person, place, or thing that has been cut completely in half, with the open half facing forward so the entire inside is revealed.	Helps to visualize all the layers of a person, place, or thing in the text.	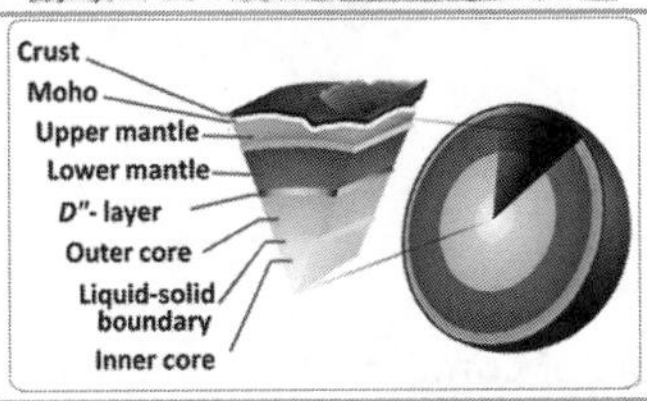 Crust Moho Upper mantle Lower mantle D"- layer Outer core Liquid-solid boundary Inner core
Cutaway: A picture of an object with part of the side dissolved, partially revealing the inside.	Helps to visualize both the interior and exterior of a person, place, or thing in the text.	
Labeled diagram: A picture with labels on lines pointing to various parts, or a series of pictures with captions showing steps, stages, or the progression of events.	Shows the different components of something in the text, or explains steps in a process or how something is made.	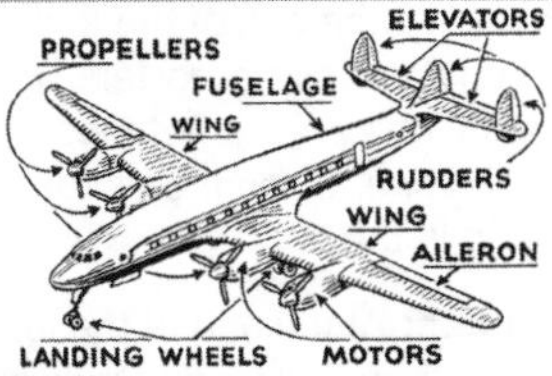 PROPELLERS ELEVATORS FUSELAGE WING RUDDERS WING AILERON LANDING WHEELS MOTORS
Map: An aerial-view picture showing the geographic location of something or someone.	Shows where something or someone is located, as well as trends for a geographic area, like population; helps to quickly understand the relative location or impact of something in the text.	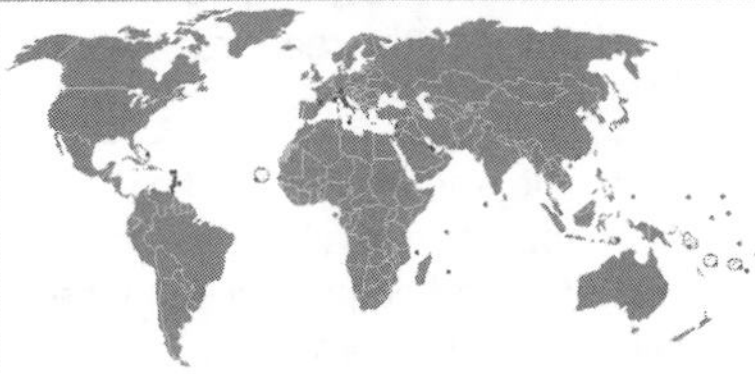

(continued)

Text, Graphic, and Organizational Features Chart *(page 3 of 3)*

Type of Feature and Definition	How Feature Helps Readers	Example of feature
Graph: Data in diagram form, such as a bar graph, line graph, or pie graph.	Condenses data and/ or displays numeric information important to the text; can be used to compare amounts or show changes over time.	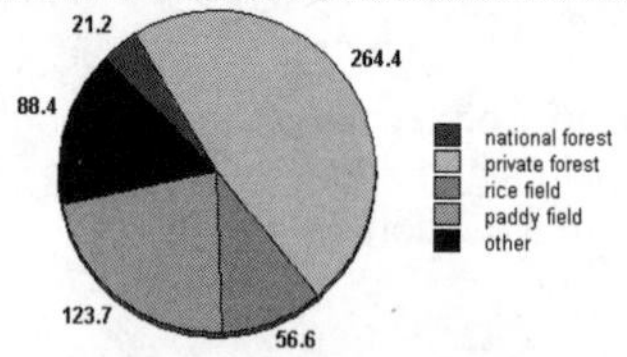
Table/chart: Data organized and condensed into columns and rows with headings, or as a visual representation.	Helps to easily read and compare data related to the text.	
Timeline: Events listed in linear format in the order that they occurred.	Helps to understand when events in the main body of text occurred, relative to other events.	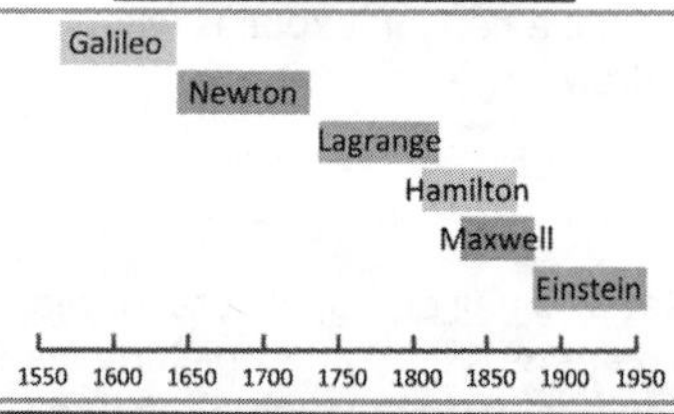
Infographic: Use of icons or images to show ideas.	Helps to capture attention with visuals and enhance comprehension.	
Organizational Features		
Table of contents: At the beginning of the text, a list of chapters or key topics in sequential order with page numbers.	Helps to quickly find a chapter or topic.	Chapter 8: Reptile Homes, pg. 111
Preface: An introduction to a book or literary work written by an author. Sometimes provides an overview of the text.	Helps to understand the author's purpose of the text.	This book tells you about reptiles: how they live, what they look like, and how they survive.
Glossary: At the end of the text, a list of alphabetically important words with definitions and sometimes pronunciations. Often the words are boldfaced in the text.	Helps to understand new or text-critical words; definitions can be easily found.	**Venom** A poisonous liquid that some snakes use to kill their prey
References: At the end of the text, it lists the authors, titles, and publishing information for all the resources referred to in the text.	Helps to find the book or resource the information came from, based on the name of the author	Bessesen, B. (2016). *Arizona highways wildlife guide.* Phoenix, AZ: Arizona Department of Transportation.
Index: At the end of the text, an alphabetical listing of all of the key topics, terms and authors cited in the text with page numbers.	Helps to find the page where a topic, term or author is mentioned.	cold-blooded, p. 5
Appendix: A section at the end of the text that gives additional information that is important, but not in the main text.	Helps to provide additional resources related to the text.	Arizona Wildlife Organizations

Active Reading Self-Evaluation

Name: ______________________________ **Date:** ______________

Title/Author: ______________________________ **Genre:** ______________

Directions: While reading or after reading, mark a plus sign (+) if you responded to the question or statement, a checkmark (✓) if you responded but are unsure of your response, and a minus sign (–) if you did not or could not respond to the question. Notice that some sections are for narrative texts and some for expository text, so mark N/A if the section does not apply.

Score +, ✓, –	Active Reader Questions by Topic
Ask Questions	
	Narrative: Who is involved? What are they doing? Why? What do they want? Why? What is the situation or problem? How might it be solved? How was it solved? Who is telling the story? Why?
	Expository: What do I want to learn? Why? What it the main idea or topic? What details support the ideas? What did I learn? What else do I want to learn?
Predict	
	Narrative: What will happen next? Why do you think so? What effect will that have on the story or the text?
	Expository: What will the next section be about? What do I already know about this topic?
Clarify	
	Identify what you do not understand. Read on and reread to help you understand. Use the illustrations and headings to help you. Use resources such as the glossary, dictionary, and technology to support your understanding. Discuss the information with other people.

(continued)

Active Reading Self-Evaluation *(page 2 of 2)*

Score +, ✓, –	Active Reader Questions by Topic
Make Connections	
	How does the information in the text relate to my experiences and understanding? How does information from one part of the book or text relate to other parts of the text? How does the information in the book or text relate to other texts? How does information in the texts relate to the world?
Summarize	
	Narrative: What happened in the beginning, middle, and end? Why did it happen?
	Expository: What was the text mostly about? What details supported this? What new information did I learn?
Evaluate	
	Narrative: What did I like about the story and characters? Would I recommend this book? Why?
	Expository: Was the information accurate? How do I know? Why is this information important?

Narrative Comprehension Guide

Directions: During and after reading, ask yourself these questions to help you understand the story better.	
Characters	Describe the characters in the story. How are they related to each other? How do the characters behave? How do the characters change their behavior in the story? How are they similar or different from each other? How are they similar or different from me or people you know? Would I want one of the characters as a friend or family member? Why or why not?
Setting	Describe where the story takes place. Does it change? How do I know when the story took place (time of day, year, history)? How is the setting similar to or different from places I am familiar with?
Plot	What are the main events that happened in the story? As I read, what do I think will happen next? Why? What is the situation or problem in the story? How might it be solved? What were the attempts to solve the problem? How was it solved? What would I do differently if I was the character?
Mood	How did this story make me feel in the beginning, middle, and end? What was the most exciting or interesting event that happened? What is the funniest, saddest, strangest, or scariest event that happened? What will I remember most about this story?
Style	What interesting words or phrases does the author use? What do I like about the way the author wrote the story? How would I have written the story differently? Would I like to write a story using this author's style?
Theme	Why do I think the author wrote the story? Is there a message in the story? What was the message? What message would I like to write about?
Author	Who is telling the story? What was the point of view of the author? What did the author have to know to write this book? Do I want to read other books by this author? Why?
Illustrator	Who is the illustrator? How did the illustrations help me to understand the story? What did I like about the illustrations? How could I use illustrations in my writing?

Expository Comprehension Guide

Directions: During and after reading, ask yourself these questions to help you understand the text better.	
Text Structure	What kind of structure is used to present the information? Does it give information in a sequence, like steps in a process or instructions for how to do or make something? Does it describe information in detail? Does it compare something or tell how things are different? Does it tell what causes something to happen and the effect of that cause? Does it tell about a problem and about a solution to a problem? Does it tell a main idea or topic and then give details to support the idea or topic?
Content	Explain the text structures that have "yes" answers above. What is the topic of the book, chapter, or text? What do the headings and captions tell me about the topic? What facts do I find most interesting? Would I like to read more books on this topic? Why? What else would I like to learn about this topic?
Graphics	What information did I get from the graphics, such as illustrations, pictures, charts, and graphs? Did the illustrations help me understand the information? How? Which illustrations or pictures are the most interesting? Why? What could the author or illustrator do to make the information easier to understand?
Accuracy	What information do I know about the author? What qualifies the author to write on this topic? What would I want to ask the author? What research did the author have to do to write this information? What is the copyright date? Does this book or text provide recent information? Where else can I find current information on this topic? Give examples of how the author lets the reader know he/she is stating facts or opinions.
Style	Do I understand what the author is saying? What did the author do to make it easier or harder to understand? Do I want to read more books by this author? Why? How is this book similar to or different from other books or texts I have read?

Questioning Strategies Based on Bloom's Taxonomy of Thinking

Bloom's Taxonomy Level	Key Words	Questions
Creating: Combines elements or parts in meaningful construction. Compiles information together in a different way.	*build create design integrate compose predict formulate imagine elaborate plan propose modify choose suppose solve construct invent hypothesize organize produce rewrite perform*	What changes would you make to solve . . . ? What would happen if . . . ? Suppose you could . . . ; what would you do? Can you elaborate on the reason?
Evaluating: Presents and defends opinion by making judgments about information.	*determine choose defend judge prove justify compare estimate appraise support decide interpret rate prioritize disprove criticize predict assess*	How would you prove . . . ? How could you determine . . . ? What information would you use to support the view that . . . ? Why was it better than . . . ? Why do you think he/she should . . . ?
Analyzing: Examines information and separates elements or parts, using meaningful categories.	*analyze compare contrast categorize classify examine simplify survey differentiate dissect test for conclude inspect classify divide deduce discover motive separate research distinguish relate outline separate diagram discriminate*	What motive is there . . . ? What conclusions can you draw . . . ? What evidence can you find . . . ? Can you make the distinction between . . . ?
Applying: Uses abstract concepts/ ideas to solve problems to new situations by applying acquired knowledge.	*apply develop interview construct organize solve plan model identify utilize select build choose experiment transfer compute produce change demonstrate draw paint show prepare dramatize make use of*	How would you use . . . ? How would you solve . . . , using what you've learned? What approach would you use to . . . ? What facts would you select to show? What would you do if . . . ?
Understanding: Demonstrate understanding of facts and ideas by working with main ideas. Use examples or paraphrasing.	*compare translate show extend infer explain summarize relate contrast interpret classify illustrate outline demonstrate tell discuss restate illustrate paraphrase review report*	How would you compare . . . ? How would you contrast . . . ? What facts or ideas show . . . ? How would you summarize . . . ? Which statements support . . . ? Explain in your own words . . .
Remembering: Exhibit memory of previously learned material by recalling, remembering, or locating facts, terms, basic concepts, and answers.	*who what where when name label choose find match recall recite write list spell count show define select describe identify sequence quote*	Who are the characters? What happened at the end of the story? When and where did the story take place? What definition is given for . . . ?

Bloom's Taxonomy—Narrative Comprehension Activities

Creating:
This level provides the student with an opportunity to put parts from the story together in a new way to form a new idea or product. Success at this level will be evidenced by the student's ability to: • Create a story from just the title before the story is read (as a pre-story exercise). • Write three new titles for the story that would give a good idea of what it was about. • Create a poster to advertise the story so people will want to read it. • Create a new product related to the story. • Restructure the roles of the main characters to create new outcomes in the story. • Compose and perform a dialogue or monologue that will communicate the thoughts of the main character(s) at a given point in the story. • Imagine that he/she is one of the main characters, and write a diary account of daily thoughts and activities. • Create an original character, and tell how the character would fit into the story. • Write the lyrics and music to a song that one of the main characters would sing if he/she/it became a rock star, and perform the song.
Evaluating:
This level provides the student with an opportunity to form and present an opinion backed up by sound reasoning. Success at this level will be evidenced by the student's ability to: • Decide which character in the selection he/she would most like to spend a day with and why. • Judge whether or not a character should have acted in a particular way and why. • Decide if the story really could have happened, and justify reasons for the decision. • Consider how this story can help the student in his/her own life. • Appraise the value of the story. • Compare the story with another one the student has read. • Write a recommendation as to why the book should be read or not.
Analyzing:
This level provides the student with an opportunity to take parts of the story and examine these parts carefully, in order to better understand the whole story. Success at this level will be evidenced by the student's ability to: • Identify general characteristics (stated and/or implied) of the main characters. • Distinguish what in the story could happen in real life from what couldn't happen in real life. • Select parts of the story that were the funniest, saddest, happiest, and most unbelievable. • Differentiate fact from opinion. • Compare and/or contrast two of the main characters. • Select an action of a main character that was exactly the same as something the student would have done.

(continued)

Applying:
This level provides the student with an opportunity to use information from the story in a new way. Success at this level will be evidenced by the student's ability to: • Classify the characters as humans, animals, or things, and list them on a chart. • Transfer a main character to a new setting, and write or tell how the story would be different. • Make finger puppets and act out a part of the story. • Select a meal that one of the main characters would enjoy eating. Plan a menu and a method of serving it. • Think of a situation that occurred to a character in the story, and write about how he/she would have handled the situation differently. • Give examples of people the student knows who have the same problems as the characters in the story.
Understanding:
This level provides the student with an opportunity to demonstrate a basic understanding of the story. Success at this level will be evidenced by the student's ability to: • Interpret pictures of scenes from the story and describe it in his/her own words. • Explain selected ideas or parts from the story in his/her own words. • Draw a picture showing what happened before and after a passage or illustration found in the book. • Write a sentence explaining what happened before and after a passage or illustration found in the book. • Predict what could happen next in the story before the reading of the entire book is completed. • Construct a pictorial timeline that summarizes what happens in the story. • Explain how the main character felt at the beginning, middle, and/or end of the story.
Remembering:
This level provides the student with an opportunity to recall fundamental facts and information about the story. Success at this level will be evidenced by the student's ability to: • Match characters' names with pictures of the characters. • Match statements with the characters who said them. • List the main characteristics of one of the main characters in a "Wanted" poster. • Arrange scrambled story pictures or sentences in sequential order. • Recall details about the setting by creating a picture of where a part of the story took place. • Write one sentence from the story that tells what the main character did first.

Emergent Writing Stage Assessment

Name: ______________________ **Grade:** __________ **Date:** ____________

Directions and Scoring: Observe and collect several writing samples from the student. Read each of the descriptors in the checklist and evaluate it, using a plus sign (+) to indicate that the student exhibited the behavior frequently, a checkmark (✓) to indicate that the behavior was sometimes exhibited, or a minus sign (–) to indicate that the student rarely or never exhibited this behavior. N/A indicates not applicable. The writing stage is the one with a majority of checkmarks and/or pluses, with no more than two minuses.

Score +,✓, –	Descriptor	Date Observed and Comments
Stage 1		
CONTENT		
	Dictated words or phrases to be written down.	
	Began to differentiate between scribbled picture and scribble writing.	
HANDWRITING		
	Scribbled on page with no message intended.	
	Scribbled, including random, circular, vertical, and/or horizontal marks.	
	Used a variety of writing utensils (crayon, pencil, markers, paintbrush).	
Stage 2		
CONTENT		
	Dictated sentences to be written.	
	"Read" story with consistent oral text.	
	Differentiated between picture and story.	
HANDWRITING		
	Symbols or scribbles represented letters, words, or strings of words.	
	Wrote mock letters or letters, but without phonetic representation.	
	Began to write alphabet letters.	

(continued)

Note. Based in part on ideas from Morrow (2001) and Solley (2000).

Emergent Writing Stage Assessment *(page 2 of 4)*

Score +,✓, –	Descriptor	Date Observed and Comments
Stage 3		
CONTENT		
	Dictated more complete stories to be written.	
	Completed sentence frames or patterned sentences.	
	Drew recognizable pictures.	
	Attempted to label pictures, and wrote letters for words.	
SPELLING		
	Wrote letters to represent a word or idea.	
	Attempted inventive spelling of words with some correct sound–symbol association.	
	Heard and wrote letters for beginning consonant sounds.	
	Heard and wrote letters for ending consonant sounds.	
HANDWRITING		
	Evidence of letter and word spacing began.	
	Evidence of left-to-right sequence of letters and words.	
	Copied some words from resources.	
	Most letters were recognizable; some might be mixed between capitals and lowercase letters.	
Stage 4		
CONTENT		
	Wrote on a self-selected topic.	
	Communicated a clear message.	
	Illustrations matched text.	
SENTENCE STRUCTURE		
	Wrote one sentence with at least four words.	
CAPITALIZATION/PUNCTUATION		
	Used some correct capitalization.	
	Used some correct end punctuation.	

(continued)

Emergent Writing Stage Assessment *(page 3 of 4)*

Score +,✓, –	Descriptor	Date Observed and Comments
SPELLING		
	Wrote short sentences using inventive spelling.	
	Wrote his/her name and some sight words correctly.	
	Wrote words with beginning and ending consonant sounds.	
	Wrote each word with a vowel sound.	
	Used some written resources for spelling.	
HANDWRITING		
	All letters were recognizable.	
	Mostly wrote within lines.	
	Wrote from left to right.	
	Used some spacing between words.	
Stage 5		
CONTENT		
	Wrote at least three sentences on one topic.	
	Sequenced ideas.	
	Wrote on different self-selected topics.	
	Wrote on different teacher-selected topics.	
	Wrote narrative texts.	
	Wrote expository texts.	
	Wrote for functional purposes (notes, lists, sharing of ideas).	
	Illustrations were detailed and matched text.	
SENTENCE STRUCTURE		
	Wrote complete sentences.	
	Wrote with correct subject–verb agreement.	
	Wrote using a variety of words.	
	Wrote using interesting and discipline-specific words.	
	Wrote with adjectives.	
	Wrote some complex and compound sentences.	

(continued)

Emergent Writing Stage Assessment *(page 4 of 4)*

Score +,✓, –	Descriptor	Date Observed and Comments
CAPITALIZATION/PUNCTUATION		
	Used capital letters at the beginning of a sentence.	
	Capitalized names of people and pronouns.	
	Some capitalization of other proper nouns.	
	Used periods at the end of statements.	
	Used question marks for interrogative sentences.	
	Experimented with other punctuation marks (! , : ; ' " ").	
SPELLING		
	Spelled many common words correctly.	
	Used mostly transitional spelling for unknown words, with letters representing the consonant sounds and vowel sounds.	
	Used written resources for spelling.	
HANDWRITING		
	Appropriate spacing between words.	
	Appropriate text wrapping.	
	Correct formation of letters (might still have some reversals).	
	Wrote the letters correctly between the lines.	
REVISING		
	Made some changes in content, such as adding, deleting, or rearranging information.	
	Made some changes in word choice.	
EDITING		
	Made some changes in grammar, capitalization, punctuation, spelling, and handwriting if needed.	

Emergent Writing Stage: ______________________________

Analysis:

Writing Composition Assessment Summary

Name: ______________________________ **Date:** ______________

Directions: Select a genre and a writing prompt. Examples of prompts are given below. Provide this form or the appropriate *Revising and Editing Bookmark* as a reference. Read the prompt, and ask the student to do prewriting brainstorming or talk about his/her topic. Take notes on the student's ideas. Ask him/her to write a draft. When the student is finished, ask him/her to reread it, and then to revise and edit their writing based on each trait. Finally, ask the student to title the piece.

Scoring and Analysis: In the left column for each writing element, write a plus sign (+) if it was excellent, a checkmark (✓) if it was satisfactory, or a minus sign (–) if it needed improvement or was incomplete. In the right column, write details and examples for each element. In the analysis, indicate specific areas of strength or areas for improvement.

Prompt: (select one)	Narrative: "Write about an important event in your life." Expository: "Write about a specific topic or how to make or do something." Persuasive: "Write about something you would like to change." Descriptive: "Write about a person, place, or thing with sensory details and/or feelings."

Title or Topic:	
Score	**Writing Trait**
Content	
	Ideas and Details:
	Organization/Text Structure:
	Voice:
	Sentence Fluency:
	Word Choice:
Conventions	
	Grammar:
	Punctuation:
	Capitalization:
	Spelling:

(continued)

Writing Composition Assessment Summary *(page 2 of 2)*

Length: Number of sentences: ______________ Number of paragraphs: ____________________

Average number of words per sentence: ________ Appropriate length for topic: (yes or no) ________

Evidence of prewriting: ____

____

____

____

Evidence of revision and editing: ____

____

____

____

Record of Writing Composition:
Translation, if needed:
Analysis of Content and Conventions:

Writing Composition Rubric for Writer, Peer, or Teacher

Writer: ______________________________ **Date:** ______________

Title: ____________________ **Genre:** __________ **Evaluator:** __________

Directions and Scoring: After reading the entire composition, read each of the descriptors in the rubric and evaluate each element with a plus sign (+) for excellent, a checkmark (✓) for satisfactory, or a minus sign (–) if it needs improvement. Underline any descriptive words that seem appropriate. Then, write an analysis with specific examples from the composition.

CONTENT			
Score	**Excellent (+)**	**Satisfactory (✓)**	**Needs Improvement (–)**
Ideas/Details	Interesting, well focused; clear purpose or theme. Accurate, specific details and description. Showed insight, originality, and careful thought. No irrelevant details.	Generally clear purpose, but had limited details. Not very specific. Some ideas were important, while others were not. Parts lacked specific details or description.	Seemed to lack purpose or focus. Limited or unclear information. Didn't seem meaningful or real. Lacked specific details or description.
Organization/ Text Structure	Inviting introduction; ideas connected and in a logical sequence; used transition words. Details fit. Strong conclusion added impact. Followed text structure for genre.	Some organization, but lacked focus and impact. The introduction and/or conclusion seemed weak. Limited transitions. Some evidence of text structure	Almost no identifiable introduction and/or conclusion. Details strung together without logical order. No transitions. Gaps in information. Text structure was unclear.
Voice	Appropriate tone and mood for purpose and audience; showed unique style, personality, interests, and feelings of writer.	Some evidence of writer's personality in writing, but parts lacked interest or personal feeling.	Almost no evidence of the writer's personality or interest in writing.
Sentence Fluency	Complete sentences with clear meaning, varied structure and length. Ideas flowed easily. Used transition words and paragraphs as needed.	Some sentences seemed awkward or did not flow. Most followed a single pattern. Sentences seemed somewhat isolated and forced.	Difficult to understand. Choppy sentences. Simplistic word patterns. Unnatural, disjointed, monotonous.
Word Choice	Used interesting, precise, general academic, and discipline-specific words. Description with strong images, vivid verbs, adjectives and proper nouns.	Words were ordinary, but conveyed message. Some words lacked precision. Some language seemed redundant.	Limited, vague, or abstract words. Repetitious, monotonous words and worn-out expressions. Few images. Weak verbs.

Analysis:

(continued)

CONVENTIONS			
Score	**Excellent (+)**	**Satisfactory (✓)**	**Needs Improvement (–)**
Grammar	Complete sentences. Correct grammar and word forms, subject–verb and noun–pronoun agreement, verb tenses.	A few grammatical errors, but meaning was maintained.	Several grammatical errors, making it hard to read.
Punctuation	Correct usage of end punctuation, commas, semicolons, colons, and quotation marks.	Ending punctuation correct, with other minor punctuation errors.	Several punctuation errors, making it hard to read.
Capitalization	Correct capitalization: first word of sentences and quotes, pronoun *I*, proper nouns (specific person, place or thing), days, months, holidays, most words in titles.	Correct capitalization at beginning of sentences, with minor mistakes on proper nouns.	Several capitalization errors.
Spelling	Correct spelling: checked for homophones, words that sound similar, use of apostrophes for possession or contractions, use of *its* for possession.	Most common words spelled correctly; others were decodable.	Spelling made the writing hard to read.

Note. Based on Spandel (2004).

Analysis of Writing Content and Conventions:

Writing Process Rubric for Writer, Peer, or Teacher

Writer: ______________________ **Date:** ____________

Title: ______________________ **Genre:** ____________

Directions and Scoring: For each step of the writing process, evaluate the student's performance. Read each of the descriptors in the rubric and evaluate each element with a plus sign (+) for excellent, a checkmark (✓) for satisfactory, or a minus sign (–) if this step needs improvement. Underline any descriptive words that seem appropriate. Analyze with specific examples from observations and anecdotal notes on the writing process.

Score	Excellent (+)	Satisfactory (✓)	Needs Improvement (–)
Prewriting	Included a prewriting plan with ideas and details.	Limited prewriting plan found.	No evidence of prewriting plan.
Drafting	One or more rough drafts each showed significant work. Final draft showed careful revising and editing.	One or more rough drafts showed minor work. Some revising/editing on final rough draft, but more needed.	One draft only. No significant changes or corrections.
Conferencing	Conference form completed. Significant evidence of revising and editing if needed. Partner's signature.	Conference form mostly completed. Some evidence of revising and editing. Partner's signature.	Conference form incomplete. Little evidence of revising and editing. No signature.
Revising	Significant evidence of adding, removing, moving, or substituting words or phrases to enhance the content, text structure elements, and craft of the writing. Final draft required almost no changes.	Some evidence of adding, deleting, arranging, or substituting words or phrases to enhance the content, text structure elements and craft of the writing. Final draft required some changes.	Limited evidence of adding, deleting, arranging, or substituting words or phrases to enhance the content and craft of the writing. Final draft required several changes.
Editing	Evidence that writer edited paper. Almost no capitalization, usage (grammar), punctuation, spelling, or format errors found on final draft.	Evidence that the author made some edits; yet some grammar, convention, or format errors were found on final draft.	Limited evidence of editing, and several grammar, convention, or format errors found on final draft.
Publishing/ Sharing	Final piece was visually pleasing, with effective graphic design to support content. It was shared or published appropriately and with pride.	Final piece was legible and included related graphics. It was shared or published appropriately.	Final piece was difficult to read, not legible, and/or not appropriately shared or published.

Analysis:

Visual Representation Assessment for Self, Peer, or Teacher

Creator: ______________________ **Date:** ______________

Title: ______________________ **Evaluator:** ______________

Directions: Once a student has created a visual to communicate ideas, assess each of the following elements as excellent (+), satisfactory (✓), or needs improvement (–). Analyze with specific examples.

Score +, ✓, –	**Visual Representation Elements and Responses**		
	Title, caption, and description:		
	Type of visual and materials used:		
	Purpose and audience:		
	Integration with text:		
Elements of art and design—effective use of:		Principles of art and design—effective use of:	
	Line		Balance
	Shape		Contrast
	Color		Emphasis
	Value		Movement
	Texture		Pattern
	Form		Rhythm
	Space		Unity–variety
	Characteristics of **photographs, drawings, paintings, illustrations, and videos:** Subject was clear, showed setting, action, and told a story or provided details.		
	Characteristics of **labeled diagrams and organizational diagrams:** Labeled diagram included a clear image, arrows or lines to parts, labels for each part. Organizational diagram showed a clear list, process, cycle, hierarchy, relationship, matrix, pyramid, or image (such as a SmartArt Graphic in Microsoft Word).		
	Characteristics of **charts/graphs/tables:** Showed meaningful data; accurate representation of graphical elements of the particular form, such as lines, bars, pie wedges; easy to read; labels for the *Y* and *X* axes on charts; legends or keys for identifying grouping of data; scale for the data; source of the data.		
	Characteristics of **maps:** Showed geographic area (with location insert, if appropriate); data were relevant and current; effective choice of symbols, color, line widths, icons, and labeling. Legends for key to decipher the symbols. Concise title; notation of scale; orientation with a north arrow. Documentation for all sources of data, date created, and author. Effective choice of orientation and placement of map elements.		
	Characteristics of **three-dimensional models and dioramas:** Created a durable model, base, and setting; objects were accurate and proportional; identified scale; labeled parts as needed.		
	Characteristics of **drama/dance/musical performances:** Designed sets and costumes; movement, expression, and music told a story or expressed a feeling.		
	Characteristics of **websites:** Accurate, current, cited and organized content; included menu and hyperlinks.		

Analysis:

Multimedia Presentation Assessment for Self, Peer, or Teacher

Creator: ________________________________ **Date:** ______________

Title: ______________________________ **Evaluator:** ______________________

Directions: Once a student has created a multimedia presentation to communicate ideas, assess each of the following elements as excellent (+), satisfactory (✓), or needs improvement (–). Analyze with specific examples.

Score +, ✓, –	Visual Representation Elements and Responses		
	Topic:		
	Purpose and audience:		
	Types of media included:		
Content:			
	Research on topic: Used three or more reputable sources.		
	Effective focus of topic (not too broad or narrow).		
	Important and interesting topic.		
	Accurate information.		
	Content was revised for clarity, specific word use, support, evidence, and examples.		
	Use of media (graphic, audio, video, music) contributed to understanding of topic.		
Organization:			
	Logical sequence of text and graphic information.		
	Clear menus, navigation, and links.		
	Users could easily navigate back and forth through pages.		
Graphic design:			
	Graphics accurately conveyed the message and would entice audience.		
	Original and creative design.		
	Consistent design and typography across pages.		
	Effective combination of multimedia and text design elements.		
Elements of art and design—effective use of:		Principles of art and design—effective use of:	
	Line		Balance
	Shape		Contrast
	Color		Emphasis
	Value		Movement
	Texture		Pattern
	Form		Rhythm
	Space		Unity–variety

(continued)

Multimedia Presentation Assessment for Self, Peer, or Teacher *(page 2 of 2)*

Layout design:	
	Pages were attractive, eye-catching, easy to read, not too busy or too dull.
	Backgrounds were subtle and appropriate.
	Spacing and alignment of text made reading easy.
	Photos, images, icons, clip art, and other graphics were appropriate.
	Graphics were of high quality and downloaded fairly quickly.
	Graphics were used creatively and might follow a theme.
Mechanics:	
	Edited for grammar, capitalization, punctuation, and spelling.

Analysis:

Revising and Editing Bookmarks

My Writing Bookmark

___ I reread.

___ It made sense.

___ Ideas were in order.

___ I added details.

___ It sounded right.

___ It looked right.

___ I checked.

___ I wrote complete and correct sentences.

___ I used capitals. T, I

___ I used punctuation . ? !

___ I used resources for spelling. cud/could

___ I added graphics to support my writing.

Narrative/Descriptive Writing

___ I reread my writing.

___ I answered "who, what, where, when, why, and how" questions.

I described the:

___ characters.

___ places.

___ time (day, season, year).

___ plot with the events in sequence.

___ end or resolution.

___ point of view of the storyteller.

I included:

___ sensory images.

___ figurative language.

___ graphics.

I checked for:

___ complete, interesting, and grammatical sentences.

___ capitalization.

___ punctuation.

___ spelling.

Expository/Persuasive Writing

___ I reread my writing.

___ I wrote an interesting opening statement or question.

___ I focused on a single topic.

___ I used text structures for my organization.

___ I supported my ideas with specific details, examples, and evidence.

___ I used multiple resources for information.

___ I used transitions for sequencing or connecting ideas.

___ I wrote a concluding sentence/paragraph that summarizes my main idea.

___ I checked for correct grammar, capitalization, punctuation, and spelling.

___ I added organization and text features.

___ I added graphic features.

___ I cited sources.

Writing Conference Record Form

Writer: ________________________________ **Date:** ______________

Title: ________________________ **Genre:** ________________________

Potential Teacher Prompts	Writer's Responses
Tell me about your writing.	
Where are you in the writing process?	
What is going well in your writing?	
What do you want support with?	
Who is your audience?	
What is your purpose for writing?	
What text structure or structures did you use?	
What is your main idea?	
How did you support that idea?	
What resources did you use? Do you need any more?	
Show me where you used good description. Is there a place that might need more description? Did you use multiple senses?	
Show me where you used interesting or content-specific words. How else might you incorporate such words?	
How did you transition between ideas? Did you use any transition words?	
Did you use a variety of sentence structures?	
Revise: Do you need to add, remove, move, or substitute any words or ideas?	
Did you review any criteria given for writing?	
Edit: Did you check for grammar, capitalization, punctuation, and spelling?	
Did you or could you add any graphics to support the text?	
What are you going to work on next?	
What could I do to support your writing?	

Teacher Notes:

Writer-Led Peer Conference Form

Writer: ______________________________ **Date:** ______________

Title: ______________________ **Peer:** ______________________

Directions: Writer shares any writing rubrics or criteria he/she wants the peer to look for, and then reads the writing aloud. Afterward, writer asks the following questions and makes notes based on the responses.

What do you like best about my writing?

What parts of the beginning were clear and interesting? What parts might need revising?

What parts of the middle were clear and interesting? What parts might need revising?

What parts of the ending were clear and interesting? What parts might need revising?

What details or descriptions might I add for clarification?

(continued)

What ideas or words might be removed, changed, or moved?

What interesting words or phrases did I use? Do I need to add or explain any words?

How did my graphics support my writing? Do you have any suggestions for improving them?

Did I use correct grammar, capitalization, punctuation, and spelling? If not, what should I change?

Any other strengths or areas for improvement?

Primary Narrative Revising and Editing Checklist

Writer: ______________________________ **Date:** ______________

Title: ____

Directions: Reread your story, and put a checkmark (✓) in front of each item you have completed.

Content	
	The story made sense and stayed on topic.
	The story had a clear beginning, describing the characters, place, and time (setting).
	The story had a clear middle, describing the problem or events (plot).
	The story had a clear ending or solution (resolution).
	I included important details so the reader could visualize my story.
	I used strong, descriptive, precise, and interesting words in each sentence.
	My ideas flowed from one to another.
	I added graphics to support my writing.
	I wrote a catchy title.
Conventions	
	Each sentence was a complete idea.
	Each sentence was grammatically correct.
	I used capitals correctly (beginning of sentences, proper nouns, and pronoun *I*).
	Each sentence ended with the correct punctuation (period, question mark, or exclamation point).
	I used commas for pauses.
	I used quotation marks when someone was talking.
	I organized my writing into paragraphs and indented each one.
	I circled the words I did not know how to spell.
	I used writing resources to correct the spelling of the words.
	My handwriting was clear and legible.

Advanced Revising and Editing Checklist

Writer: ______________________ **Date:** __________

Title: ______________________ **Genre:** __________

Ideas and Details	
	I wrote a catchy title and capitalized the appropriate words.
	My topic was focused, was appropriate, and had a clear main idea.
	My ideas and details were clearly stated, made sense, were accurate, and related to the main idea.
	All major points were supported with specific details, examples, or evidence.
	I integrated information from a variety of sources, including research and experience.
	I included information that would answer the reader's questions without gaps in information.
Organization/Text Structure	
	My lead was inviting, and the introduction clearly presented the main ideas.
	My ideas followed a sequence that made sense.
	I maintained focus and logic throughout my text.
	Each of my paragraphs had one main idea with related details and examples.
	I had an effective conclusion that summarized or restated the main idea.
	I followed the organizational structures of the genre and text types:
	For a narrative text, I had a clear beginning (characters and setting), middle (plot), and end (resolution).
	For an expository text, I used clear informational text structures and provided examples and evidence.
	For a persuasive text, I clearly stated my thesis or opinion, gave reasons, and provided evidence.
	For descriptive writing, I included sensory images and figurative language; I followed criteria for poetry and drama structure.
Sentence Fluency	
	I wrote in complete sentences with no fragments or run-on sentences.
	The meaning of each sentence was clear, and my sentences were concise (not too wordy).
	My sentences flowed well and were clearly connected to each other.
	I used linking/transition words to connect ideas, such as by time, location, comparison, and contrast, using subordinating and coordinating conjunctions.
	I used a variety of sentence structures (simple, compound, complex) that started with different words.

(continued)

Word Choice and Voice	
	My word choice and voice were appropriate for the topic, purpose, and audience.
	Every word showed the exact meaning I wanted to communicate.
	I used words specific to the content, and I defined or provided examples for them.
	I used a variety of interesting and descriptive words (vivid verbs, descriptive adjectives, precise nouns).
	My words painted pictures in the reader's mind to show ideas, not just tell them.
	I avoided vague language like *stuff* or *things* that might confuse the reader.
	My writing showed my unique style, personality, interests, and feelings.
Conventions	
	Every sentence in my paper was grammatically correct (I checked subject–verb and noun–pronoun agreement, verb tenses).
	I capitalized first word in sentences, pronoun *I*, and proper nouns (people, places, dates, and titles).
	I used end punctuation, commas, colons, semicolons, and quotation marks correctly.
	I used quotation marks around dialogue.
	I used apostrophes correctly in contractions and possessives.
	I edited my paper for spelling and checked for homophones and similar-sounding words.
	I organized my writing into paragraphs and indented each one.
	I followed the conventions for the genre.
	My handwriting or printed text was legible.
Text Features, Organizational Features, Graphic Features, and Layout	
	I used appropriate text features:
	Title, subtitles, captions, bullets.
	Boldfaced/italicized words.
	Font style, size, text effects, color.
	I used appropriate organizational features:
	Title page with author and related graphics (could include "About the Author" and dedication).
	Table of contents with all major headings and page numbers.
	Glossary with all important words defined.
	Bibliography of all in-text references and resources in appropriate format.
	I used appropriate graphic features (pictures, illustrations, graphs, charts, diagrams, icons) to clarify or enhance the meaning of the text.
	I used an interesting and unifying layout to integrate text and graphics.
	I followed the criteria for the genre or assignment.

Writing Goals:

Narrative Plot Scoring Guide

Writer: ______________________ **Date:** ____________

Title: ______________________

Directions: After the teacher writes a narrative with a conflict (problem), attempts to solve the problem and resolution (solution), the teacher shares the story and identifies the elements. Each student then writes a narrative and evaluates it with the scoring guide below, including specific examples in the analysis.

Score: Mark each element as excellent (+), satisfactory (✓), or needs improvement (–).

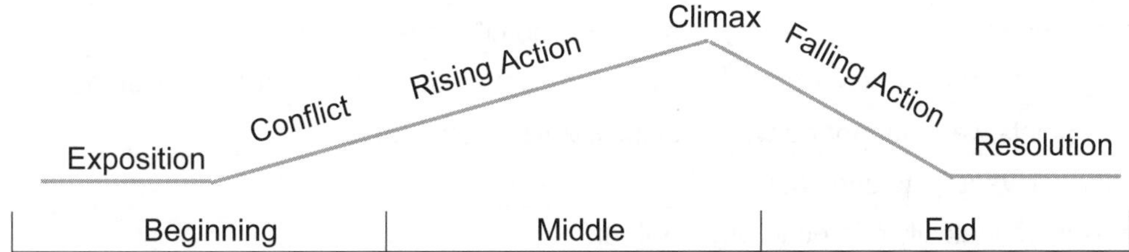

Score +, ✓, –	Narrative Plot Elements
Beginning Action (Exposition) and Conflict	
	Characters were introduced not only with physical attributes, but also with what they were thinking and doing and their relationships to others.
	Setting was established by describing the place and time (year, season, day).
	Primary conflict or problem was clearly presented.
Rising Action and Climax	
	Events created tension and excitement as the story built and began to lead up to a solution.
	Climax of the main event occurred. The main character faced the conflict and left the reader wondering what would come next.
	Events created tension and excitement as the story built and began to lead up to a solution.
Falling Action and Resolution	
	The story slowed, loose ends were tied up, and questions were answered.
	The solution to the problem was clear and followed logically from the previous events.
	Explanations were given for how the conflict was resolved, and the story was satisfactorily concluded.

Analysis:

Expository and Persuasive Writing Checklist

Writer: ______________________ **Date:** ____________

Title: ____________________ **Genre:** ____________________

√	
Ideas/Details	
	I focused on a single topic throughout my paper to explain an idea or process or to persuade.
	I used brainstorming, a concept map, or an outline to identify and organize ideas.
	I generated questions or identified problems related to my topic.
	I gathered information from a variety of sources and cited them correctly.
	Details gave the reader important information and demonstrated my knowledge of the topic.
	All major points were supported with specific details or examples.
	I included relevant facts and figures.
	My ideas were logically related to one another.
	Ideas were written in my own words.
Organization/Text Structures	
	I wrote an interesting opening statement or question.
	My ideas were sequenced in a logical order.
	Each paragraph had one main idea with related details and examples.
	My ideas flowed well and were clearly connected to one another.
	I had an effective conclusion that summarized or restated the main idea.
	I used one or more text structures: description, sequencing, problem–solution, cause–effect, compare–contrast.
Voice and Word Choice	
	Voice and word choice were formal and appropriate for my topic, purpose, and audience.
	I used words specific to the content and defined or provided examples for them.
	I used signal words to indicate the text structure.
	I used transition words to show relationships between ideas.
Presentation	
	I used text features (heading, captions, font, etc.) and organizational features (table of contents, glossary, etc.).
	I used graphic features (illustrations, photos, diagrams, graphs, and charts) to support my writing.

Writing Goals:

References

Abromeit, J. (2001). Assessment essentials: Definition of terms. Retrieved March 26, 2008, from *depts.alverno.edu/saal/terms.html.*

Adams, M. J. (1990). *Beginning to read: Thinking and learning about print.* Cambridge, MA: MIT Press.

AIMSweb overview. (2011). Retrieved from *www.mpsri.net/uploaded/documents/resources/teacherresources/aimsweb/mps_overview_spring2011.pdf.*

Allen, K. E., & Marotz, L. (1994). *Developmental profiles: Pre-birth through eight* (2nd ed.). Albany, NY: Delmar.

Allington, R. L., & Cunningham, P. M. (2002). *Schools that work: Where all children read and write.* Boston: Allyn & Bacon.

American Speech–Language–Hearing Association. (1993). Definitions of communication disorders and variations. Retrieved from *www.asha.org/policy.*

American Speech–Language–Hearing Association. (n.d.). Language in brief. Retrieved from *www.asha.org/practice-portal/clinical-topics/spoken-language-disorders/language-in-brief.*

Anderson, L. W., & Krathwohl, D. R. (Eds.). (2001). *A taxonomy for learning, teaching, and assessing: A revision of Bloom's taxonomy of educational objectives* (complete ed.). New York: Longman.

Anderson, R. C. (2004). Role of reader's schema in comprehension, learning, and memory. In R. Ruddell & N. Unrau (Eds.), *Theoretical models and processes of reading* (5th ed., pp. 594–606). Newark, DE: International Reading Association.

Applegate, M. D., Quinn, K. B., & Applegate, A. J. (2002). Levels of thinking required by comprehension questions in informal reading inventories. *The Reading Teacher, 56*(2), 174–180.

Auman, M. (2005). *Step up to writing.* Dallas, TX: Sopris West.

Baker, L., & Brown, A. L. (1984). Metacognitive skills and reading. In P. D. Pearson, R. Barr, M. L. Kamil, & P. B. Mosenthal (Eds.), *Handbook of reading research* (pp. 353–394). New York: Longman.

Barchers, S. (1993). *Readers Theatre for beginning readers.* Englewood, CO: Teacher Ideas.

Barr, R., Blachowicz, C., Buhle, R., Chaney, J., Ivy, C. A., Uchtman, A., et al. (2004). *Illinois Snapshot of Early Literacy (ISEL).* Springfield, IL: State Board of Education.

Bear, D., Invernizzi, M., Templeton, S., & Johnson, F. (2012). *Words their way: Word study for phonics, vocabulary, and spelling instruction* (5th ed.). Boston: Pearson/Allyn & Bacon.

Beaty, J. (1994). *Observing development of the young child* (3rd ed.). Englewood Cliffs, NJ: Merrill.

Beck, I. L., & McKeown, M. G. (1981). Developing questions that promote comprehension: The story map. *Language Arts, 58*(8), 913–918.

Beck, I. L., McKeown, M. G., Hamilton, R., & Kucan, L. (1997). *Questioning the author: An approach for enhancing student engagement with text.* Newark, DE: International Reading Association.

Beck, I. L., McKeown, M. G., & Kucan, L. (2013). *Bringing words to life: Robust vocabulary instruction* (2nd ed.). New York: Guilford Press.

Betts, E. A. (1946). *Foundations of reading instruction.* New York: American Book.

Blachowicz, C. L. Z., & Fisher, P. (2006). *Teaching vocabulary in all classrooms* (3rd ed.). Upper Saddle River, NJ: Pearson.

Blanke, B. (2018, November 30). 7 discourse moves that let the kids talk! Retrieved from *www.teachercreatedmaterials.com/blog/article/7-teacher-discourse-moves-that-let-the-Kids-talk.*

Bloom, B. S. (1956). *Taxonomy of educational objectives: The classification of educational goals. Book 1. Cognitive domain.* New York: David McKay.

Bloom, L., & Lahey, M. (1978). *Language development and disorders.* New York: Wiley.

Boddy-Evans, M. (2019, May 22). The 8 elements of composition in art. Retrieved from *www.liveabout.com/elements-of-composition-in-art-2577514.*

Bos, C. S., & Anders, P. L. (1990). Effects of interactive vocabulary instruction on the vocabulary learning and reading comprehension of junior-high learning disabled students. *Learning Disability Quarterly, 13*(1), 31–42.

Braun, W., & Braun, C. (1996). *A readers theatre treasury of stories.* Calgary, Alberta, Canada: Braun & Braun Education Educational Enterprises.

Brown, R. (1973). *A first language: The early stages.* Cambridge, MA: Harvard University Press.

Business Dictionary. (2019). Motivation. Retrieved at *www.businessdictionary.com/definition/motivation.html.*

Buss, K., & Karnowski, L. (2000). *Reading and writing literary genres.* Newark, DE: International Reading Association.

Calkins, L. (1983). *Lessons from a child: On the teaching and learning of writing.* Portsmouth, NH: Heinemann.

Callow, J. (2013). *The shape of text to come: How image and text work.* Newtown, New South Wales: Primary English Teaching Association Australia.

Cambourne, B. (1988). *The whole story: Natural learning and the acquisition of literacy in the classroom.* New York: Scholastic.

Camp, D. (2000). It takes two: Teaching with twin texts of fact and fiction. *The Reading Teacher, 53*(5), 400–408.

Capstone Publishers. (n.d.). Text feature definitions and examples. Retrieved from *www.capstonepub.com/classroom/sites/PDFs/teaching-text-features/Chapter_1/Table_1-2_Text_Feature_Definitions_and_Examples.pdf*

Carbo, M. (1978). Teaching reading with talking books. *The Reading Teacher, 32*(3), 267–273.

Carr, E., & Ogle, D. M. (1987). K-W-L Plus: A strategy for comprehension and summarization. *Journal of Reading, 30*(7), 626–631.

Carrell, P. L. (1983). Some issues in studying the role of schemata, or background knowledge, in second language comprehension. *Reading in a Foreign Language, 1*(2), 81–92.

Caswell, L. J., & Duke, N. (1998). Non-narrative as a catalyst for literacy development. *Language Arts, 75*(2), 108–117.

Centervention. (2019). I statement worksheet for elementary educators. Retrieved from *www.centervention.com/i-statements/.*

Clay, M. M. (1991). *Becoming literate: The construction of inner control.* Portsmouth, NH: Heinemann.

Clay, M. M. (1993). *An observation survey of early literacy achievement.* Portsmouth, NH: Heinemann.

Collier, V. P. (1995). *Promoting academic success for ESL students.* Elizabeth, NJ: NJTESOL-BE.

Commeyras, M. (1993). Promoting critical thinking through dialogical-thinking reading lessons. *The Reading Teacher, 46*(6), 486–494.

Connell, G. (2016, September 15). 10 ways to build relationships with students this year. Retrieved from *www.scholastic.com/teachers/blog-posts/genia-connell/10-ways-build-relationships-students-year-1.*

Coombs, E. (2016, May 11). Four strategies for building relationships with students. Retrieved from *www.tolerance.org/magazine/four-strategies-for-building-relationships-with-students.*

Cooper, D. (2006). *Talk about assessment: Strategies and tools to improve learning.* Toronto: Thomson Nelson.

Crank, J. N., & Bulgren, J. A. (1993). Visual depictions as information organizers for enhancing achievement of students with learning disabilities. *Learning Disabilities Research and Practice, 8*(3), 140–147.

Crystal, D. (1987). *The Cambridge encyclopedia of language.* Cambridge, UK: Cambridge University Press.

Cunningham, J. W. (1982). Generating interactions between schemata and text. In J. A. Niles & L. A. Harris (Eds.), *New inquiries in reading research and instruction: 31st yearbook of the National Reading Conference* (pp. 42–47). Chicago: National Reading Conference.

Cunningham, P. M. (1995). *Phonics they use: Words for reading and writing* (2nd ed.). New York: HarperCollins.

Cunningham, P. M., & Allington, R. L. (2003). *Classrooms that work: They can all read and write* (3rd ed.). Boston: Allyn & Bacon.

Cunningham, P. M., Hall, D., & Sigmon, C. (1999). *The teacher's guide to the four blocks: A multimethod, multilevel framework for grades 1–3.* Greensboro, NC: Carson-Dellosa.

Dearborn Schools. (2011). A study guide for author's purpose and perspective. Retrieved from *https://iblog.dearbornschools.org/deller/wpcontent/uploads/sites/232/2014/01/authors-purpose-packet.pdf.*

Doiron, R. (1994). Using nonfiction in a read-aloud program: Letting the facts speak for themselves. *The Reading Teacher, 47*(8), 616–624.

Donovan, C. A., & Smolkin, L. B. (2001). Genre and other factors influencing teachers' book selections for science instruction. *Reading Research Quarterly, 36*(4), 412–440.

Dowhower, S. L. (1999). Supporting a strategic stance in the classroom: A comprehension framework for helping teachers help students to be strategic. *The Reading Teacher, 52*(7), 672–689.

Duke, N. K., & Kays, J. (1998). "Can I say 'Once upon a time'?": Kindergarten children developing knowledge of information book language. *Early Childhood Research Quarterly, 13*(2), 295–318.

Dunn, D. M. (2018). *Peabody Picture Vocabulary Test–Fifth Edition.* Minneapolis, MN: Pearson.

Dweck, C. (2017). The journey to children's mindsets—and beyond. *Child Development Perspectives, 11*(2), 139–144.

Eberhard, D. M., Simons, G. F., & Fennig, C. D. (Eds.). (2019). *Ethnologue: Languages of the world* (22nd ed.). Dallas, TX: SIL International. Retrieved December 17, 2019, from *www.ethnologue.com.*

Ehri, L. C., Nunes, S. R., Willows, D. M., Schuster, B. V., Yaghoub-Zadeh, Z., & Shanahan, T. (2001). Phonemic awareness instruction helps children learn to read: Evidence from the National Reading Panel's meta-analysis. *Reading Research Quarterly, 36*(3), 250–287.

Elkonin, D. B. (1973). U.S.S.R. In I. Downing (Ed.), *Comparative reading* (pp. 551–580). New York: Macmillan.

Fahsl, A., & McAndrews, S. (2012). Journal writing: Support for students with learning disabilities. *Intervention in School and Clinic,* 47(4), 234–244.

Farris, P. J., Fuhler, C. J., & Walther, M. P. (2004). *Teaching reading: A balanced approach for today's classrooms.* Boston: McGraw-Hill.

Fey, M. (1986). *Language intervention with young children.* San Diego, CA: College-Hill Press.

Finley, T. (2014, February 19). Common Core in action: 10 visual literacy strategies. Retrieved from *www.edutopia.org/blog/ccia-10-visual-literacy-strategies-todd-finley.*

Fisher, D., & Frey, N. (2014). *Better learning through structured teaching: A framework for the gradual release of responsibility* (2nd ed.). Alexandria, VA: Association for Supervision and Curriculum Development.

Fitzpatrick, J. (1997). *Phonemic awareness: Playing with sounds to strengthen beginning reading skills.* Cypress, CA: Creative Teaching Press.

Forehand, M. (2005). Bloom's taxonomy: Original and revised. In M. Orey (Ed.), *Emerging perspectives on learning, teaching, and technology.* Bloomington, IN: Association for Educational Communications and Technology.

Forni, P. M. (2002). *Choosing civility: The twenty-five rules of considerate conduct.* New York: St. Martin's Press.

Fountas, I. C., & Pinnell, G. S. (1996). *Guided reading: Good first teaching for all children.* Portsmouth, NH: Heinemann.

Fountas, I. C., & Pinnell, G. S. (2001). *Guiding readers and writers (grades 3–6): Teaching comprehension, genre, and content literacy.* Portsmouth, NH: Heinemann.

Fountas, I. C., & Pinnell, G. S. (2016). *Benchmark Assessment System* (3rd ed.). Portsmouth, NH: Heinemann.

Frayer, D., Frederick, W. C., & Klausmeier, H. J. (1969). *A schema for testing the level of cognitive mastery.* Madison: Wisconsin Center for Education Research.

Freire, P. (1970). *Pedagogy of the oppressed.* New York: Continuum.

Fry, E. B., Kress, J. E., & Fountoukidis, D. L. (1993). *The reading teacher's book of lists* (3rd ed.). Upper Saddle River, NJ: Prentice Hall.

Garbacz, S. A., & Weist, M. D. (2019, February 1). PBIS Forum 8: Practice Brief. Family–school collaboration in positive behavioral interventions and supports: Creating a school atmosphere to promote collaboration. Retrieved from *www.pbis.org/resource/family-school-collaboration/in-positive-behavioral-interventions-and supports-creating-a-school-atmosphere-to-promote-collaboration.*

Gentry, J. R. (1982). An analysis of developmental spelling in GYNS AT WRK. *The Reading Teacher, 36*(2), 192–200.

Gillet, J. W., & Temple, C. (1994). *Understanding reading problems: Assessment and instruction* (4th ed.). New York: HarperCollins.

Gonzáles, N., Moll, L., & Amanti, C. (Eds.). (2005). *Funds of knowledge: Theorizing practices in households, communities and classrooms.* Mahwah, NJ: Erlbaum.

Goodman, K. (1965). A linguistic study of cues and miscues in reading. *Elementary English, 42*(6), 639–643.

Goodman, K. (1987). *Language and thinking in school.* New York: Richard C. Owen.

Goodman, K. (1996). *On reading: A common-sense look at the nature of language and the science of reading.* Portsmouth, NH: Heinemann.

Goodman, Y. M., & Marek, A. (1996). *Retrospective miscue analysis in the classroom.* Katonah, NY: Richard C. Owen.

Goodman, Y. M., Watson, D., & Burke, C. (1987). *Reading miscue inventory: Alternative procedures.* Katonah, NY: Richard C. Owen.

Gould, J. S., & Gould, E. J. (1999). *Four square writing method: A unique approach to teaching basic writing skills, grades 1–3.* Carthage, IL: Teaching & Learning.

Graham, S., & Perin, D. (2007). *Writing next: Effective strategies to improve writing of adolescents in middle and high schools. A report to Carnegie Corporation of New York.* Washington, DC: Alliance for Excellent Education.

Graves, D. H. (1983). *Writing: Teachers and children at work.* Portsmouth, NH: Heinemann.

Graves, M. F., & Graves, B. B. (1994). *Scaffolding reading experiences: Designs for student success.* Norwood, MA: Christopher-Gordon.

Gray, S. (2012, August 22). 5 ways to create a culturally responsive classroom. Retrieved from *https://blog.nationalequityproject.org/2012/08/22/5-ways-to-create-a-culturally-responsive-classroom.*

Great Schools Partnership. (2018). Elements of effective instruction. Retrieved from *www.greatschoolspartnership.org/resources/elements-of-effective-instruction.*

Gunning, T. G. (2004). *Creating literacy instruction for all students in grades 4–8.* Boston: Allyn & Bacon.

Gunning, T. G. (2008). *Creating literacy instruction for all students* (6th ed.). Boston: Pearson/Allyn & Bacon.

Halliday, M. A. K. (1975). *Learning how to mean: Explorations in the development of language.* New York: Elsevier.

Harris, T. L., & Hodges, R. E. (1995). *The literacy dictionary: The vocabulary of reading and writing.* Newark, DE: International Reading Association.

Harvey, S. (2002). Nonfiction inquiry: Using real reading and writing to explore the world. *Language Arts, 80*(1), 12–22.

Harvey, S., & Goudvis, A. (2000). *Strategies that work: Teaching comprehension to enhance understanding.* York, ME: Stenhouse.

Harvey, S., & Goudvis, A. (2017). *Strategies that work* (3rd ed.). Portsmouth, NH: Stenhouse.

Heick, T. (2019, January 3). 40 viewing comprehension strategies: Watching videos like you read a book. Retrieved from *https://teachthought.com/literacy/viewing-comprehension-strategies-watching-videos-like-you-read-a-book.*

Heiligmann, R., & Shields, V. R. (2005). Media literacy, visual syntax, and magazine advertisements: Conceptualizing the consumption of reading by media literate subjects. *Journal of Visual Literacy, 25*(1), 41–66.

Hoffman, J. (1992). Critical reading/thinking across the curriculum: Using I-charts to support learning. *Language Arts, 69*(2), 121–127.

Hudson, R. (2004). Why education needs linguistics (and vice versa). *Journal of Linguistics, 40,* 105–130.

Hudson, R. F., Lane, H. B., & Pullen, P. C. (2005). Reading fluency assessment and instruction: What, why, and how. *The Reading Teacher, 58*(8), 702–714.

International Literacy Association (ILA). (2018). *Standards for the preparation of literacy professionals 2017.* Newark, DE: Author.

International Literacy Association (ILA) & National Council of Teachers of English (NCTE). (2019). Student interactive: Plot diagram. Retrieved from *www.readwritethink.org/classroom-resources/student-interactives/plot-diagram-30040.html.*

International Phonetic Association. (2005). The International Phonetic Alphabet (rev.). Retrieved January 10, 2008, from *www.arts.gla.ac.uk/ipa/ipachart.html.*

International Reading Association (IRA) & National Council of Teachers of English (NCTE). (2005). How and why characters change. Retrieved from *www.readwritethink.org/files.resources/lesson_images/lesson858/change/pdf.*

Jensen, J. (Ed.). (1984). *Composing and comprehending.* Urbana, IL: National Conference on Research in English.

Johnson, D. D., & Pearson, D.D. (1984). *Teaching reading vocabulary* (2nd ed.). New York: Holt, Rinehart and Winston.

Johnson, K. L., & Roseman, B. A. (2003). *The source for phonological awareness.* East Moline, IL: LinguiSystems.

Kamil, M., & Lane, D. (1997, March). *A classroom study of the efficacy of using informational text for first grade reading instruction.* Paper presented at the annual meeting of the American Educational Research Association, San Diego, CA.

Kear, D. J., Coffman, G. A., McKenna, M. G., & Ambrosia, A. L. (2000). Measuring attitude toward writing: A new tool for teachers. *The Reading Teacher, 54*(1), 10–15.

Keene, E. O., & Zimmermann, S. (2007). *Mosaic of thought* (2nd ed.). Portsmouth, NH: Heinemann.

Kissner, E. (2011, July 30). Fiction, nonfiction, expository, narrative . . . Retrieved from *https://emilykissner.blogspot.com/2011/07/fiction-nonfiction-expository-narrative.html.*

Kletzien, S. B., & Dreher, M. J. (2004). *Informational text in K–3 classrooms: Helping children read and write.* Newark, DE: International Reading Association.

Knowles, M. S., Holton, E. F., III, & Swanson, R. A. (2015). *The adult learner* (8th ed.). New York: Routledge.

Kobrin, B. (1995). *Eyeopeners II: Children's books to answer children's questions about the world around them.* New York: Scholastic.

Krashen, S. D. (1981). *Second language acquisition and second language learning.* New York: Pergamon Press.

Kress, G., & van Leeuwen, T. (2006). *Reading images: The grammar of visual design* (2nd ed.). New York: Routledge.

Labov, W., & Hudley, A. C. (2009, October). *Symbolic and structural effects of dialects and immigrant minority languages in explaining achievement gaps.* Paper presented at the Workshop on the Role of Language in School Learning: Implications for Closing the Achievement Gap, Hewlett Foundation, Menlo Park, CA.

Lahey, M., & Bloom, L. (1988). *Language disorders and language development.* New York: Macmillan.

Laminack, L. (2007). *Cracking open author's craft.* New York: Scholastic.

Langer, J. A. (1981). From theory to practice: A prereading plan. *Journal of Reading, 25*(2), 152–156.

Larson, J. (2019, August 18). Using the RACE strategy for text evidence. Retrieved from *www.the-teacher-next-door.com/my-blog/reading/using-the-race-strategy-for-text-evidence.*

Laster, B., & McAndrews, S. (2004, December). *Using vocabulary assessments to guide text selection in the QRI-3.* Paper presented at the 54th National Reading Conference, San Antonio, TX.

Leslie, L., & Caldwell, J. S. (2017). *Qualitative Reading Inventory–6.* Boston: Pearson.

Levy, S. (2018). yes Yes YES!: How to teach sentence stress. Retrieved from *www.busyteacher.org/6213-how-to-teach-sentence-stress.html.*

Linder, R. (2014). *Chart sense: Common sense charts to teach 3–8 informational text and literature.* Atlanta, GA: The Literacy Initiative.

Loban, W. (1961). *Language ability in the middle grades of the elementary school.* Berkeley: University of California Press.

Lyman, F. (1981). Think–pair–share: An expanding teaching technique. *MAA-CIE Cooperative News, 41*(1), 1–2.

Lyons, C. A., Pinnell, G. S., & DeFord, D. E. (1993). *Partners in learning: Teachers and children in reading recovery.* New York: Teachers College Press.

Manz, S. L. (2002). A strategy for previewing textbooks. Teaching readers to become THIEVES. *The Reading Teacher, 55*(5), 434–435.

Mariotti, A. S., & Homan, S. P. (1997). *Linking reading assessment to instruction: An application worktext for elementary classroom teachers* (2nd ed.). Mahwah, NJ: Erlbaum.

Marzano, R. J. (2011). Art and science of teaching/relating to students: It's what you do that counts. *Educational Leadership, 68*(6), 82–83.

Marzano, R. J., Brandt, R. S., Hughes, C. S., Jones, B. F., Presseisen, B. Z., Rankin, S. C., et al. (1988). *Dimensions of thinking: A framework for curriculum and instruction.* Alexandria, VA: Association for Supervision and Curriculum Development.

Marzano, R. J., & Pickering, D. J. (2005). *Building academic vocabulary: Teacher's manual.* Alexandria, VA: Association for Supervision and Curriculum Development.

Mayer, K. (2007, January). Research in review: Emerging knowledge about emergent writing. *Young Children, 62*(1), 34–40.

McAndrews, C. (2004). Question generation and question answering [Handout for course]. Unpublished manuscript, Southern Illinois University Edwardsville.

McAndrews, S. L. (1999). *Reading discovery: The development of an early literacy program through reflective practice and analysis.* Ann Arbor, MI: UMI.

McAndrews, S. L. (2004). Linking literacy to life: Teaching concepts through informational books. *Missouri Reader, 28*(2), 55–64.

McAndrews, S. L. (2008). *Diagnostic literacy assessments and instructional strategies: A literacy specialist's resource.* Newark, DE: International Reading Association.

McAndrews, S. L., & Msengi, S. G. (2014). Keys for teaching and evaluating writing composition. In D. Coffey & E. Roberts (Eds.), *Keys for opening doors to achievement and lifelong literacy.* Dubuque, IA: Kendall/Hunt.

McAndrews, S. L., & Msengi, S. G. (2017, November). *Facilitating literacy modalities and strategies for meaningful university and k-12 instruction across disciplines.* Paper presented at the Literacy Research Association Annual Conference, Tampa, FL.

McGinley, W. J., & Denner, P. R. (1987). Story impressions: A prereading/writing activity. *Journal of Reading, 31*(3), 248–253.

McKenna, M. G., & Kear, D. J. (1990). Measuring attitude toward reading: A new tool for teachers. *The Reading Teacher, 43*(8), 626–639.

McLaughlin, B. (1987). *Theories of second language learning.* London: Edward Arnold.

McLaughlin, M., & Allen, M. B. (2000). *Guided comprehension: A teaching model for grades 3–8.* Newark, DE: International Reading Association.

Messaris, P. (1997). *Visual persuasion: The role of images in advertising.* Thousand Oaks, CA: SAGE.

Meyer, A., Rose, D. H., & Gordon, D. (2014). *Universal design for learning: Theory and practice.* Wakefield, MA: CAST.

Mims, A. (2019). Subordinating conjunctions: Cut-up sentence strips [Presentation for course]. Unpublished manuscript, Southern Illinois University.

Mitrofanova, Y. (2004). Building community–schools relations. Retrieved from *www.lancaster.unl.edu/community/articles/communityschools.shtml.*

Moats, L. C., & Tolman, C. (2009). *Spellography for teachers: How English spelling works* (LETRS Module 3). Boston: Sopris West.

Moje, E. B., Ciechanowski, K. M., Kramer, K., Ellis, L., Carrillo, R., & Collazo, T. (2004). Working toward third space in content area literacy: An examination of everyday funds of knowledge and discourse. *Reading Research Quarterly, 39,* 38–70.

Moll, L. C., Amanti, C., Neff, D., & Gonzalez, N. (1992). Funds of knowledge for teaching: Using a qualitative approach to connect homes and classrooms. *Theory into Practice, 31*(2), 132–141.

Morrow, L. M. (2001). *Literacy development in the early years: Helping children read and write* (4th ed.). Boston: Allyn & Bacon.

Morrow, L. M. (2005). *Literacy development in the early years: Helping children read and write* (5th ed.). Boston: Pearson/Allyn & Bacon.

Moss, B. (2004). Teaching expository text structures through information trade book retellings. *The Reading Teacher, 57*(8), 710–718.

Moss, B., Leone, S., & Dipillo, M. (1997). Exploring the literature of fact: Linking reading and writing through information trade books. *Language Arts, 74*(6), 418–429.

Msengi, S. G., & McAndrews, S. L. (2015, December). *Developing a shared understanding of accessible and equitable multi-modal literacy practices by cultivating a professional learning community and engaging in critical dialogue across disciplines.* Paper presented at the annual conference of the Literacy Research Association, Carlsbad, CA.

Msengi, S. G., & McAndrews, S. L. (2016a). Third space theory: Teacher, do you think I share space with only my family? What about you and others? *Learning for Democracy: An International Journal of Thought and Practice, 6*(2), 59–81.

Msengi, S. G., & McAndrews, S. L. (2016b). What does literacy mean in my content specific discipline?: Applying literacy modalities during instructional practices. *Journal of Modern Educational Review, 6*(6), 372–386.

Msengi, S. G., & McAndrews, S. L. (2017). Teachers' application and integration of multiple literacy modalities in teaching as students learn and communicate knowledge within and across disciplines: Integrating teacher content knowledge and literacy pedagogy. In R. Johnson, J. Araujo, & N. Cossa (Eds.), *Association of Literacy Educators and Researchers yearbook: Vol. 39. Literacy: The critical role of teacher knowledge* (pp. 275–297). Richmond, KY: Association of Literacy Educators and Researchers.

Muhammad, A., & Hollie, S. (2012). *The will to lead, the skill to teach: Transforming schools at every level.* Bloomington, IN: Solution Tree Press.

Nagy, W. E. (1988). *Teaching vocabulary to improve reading comprehension.* Newark, DE: International Reading Association.

National Archives and Records Administration. (2018, December 18). Document analysis worksheets. Retrieved from *www.archives.gov/education/lessons/worksheets.html.*

National Dissemination Center for Children with Disabilities. (2004). *Reading and learning disabilities.* Washington, DC: Author.

National Governors Association Center for Best Practices & Council of Chief State School Officers. (2010). *Common Core Standards for English language arts and literacy in history/social studies, science, and technical subjects.* Washington, DC: Authors.

National Reading Panel. (2000). *Report of the National Reading Panel. Teaching children to read: An evidence-based assessment of the scientific research literature on reading and its implications for reading instruction. Reports of the subgroups* (NIH Publication No. 00-4769). Washington, DC: National Institute of Child Health and Human Development.

Neal, M. (2017, August 6). Activities to jumpstart a growth mindset classroom. Retrieved from *www.teachingwithsimplicity.com/2017/09/6-activities-to-jumpstart-a-growth-mindset-classroom.html.*

Nelson Assessment. (2017). Gates–MacGinitie Reading Tests (GMRT) (4th ed.). Available from *www.nelson.com/assessment/classroom-GMRT.html.*

Newingham, B. (2008). Lots of voice: Helping students develop strong writing voices. Retrieved from *www.scholastic.com/teachers/lesson-plans/teaching-content/adding-strong-voice-your-writing.*

Nieto, S. (2013). *Finding joy in teaching students of diverse backgrounds: Culturally responsive and socially just practices in U.S. classrooms.* Portsmouth, NH: Heinemann.

Nilsen, A. P., & Nilsen, D. L. F. (2004). *Vocabulary plus high school and up: A source-based approach.* Boston: Allyn & Bacon.

Norris, B., & Brock, D. (2001). WebQuest: The power of persuasive writing. Retrieved from *volweb.utk.edu/Schools/bedford/harrisms/teahpage.htm.*

Norton, D., with Norton, S. E. (1995). *Through the eyes of a child: An introduction to children's literature* (4th ed.) Englewood Cliffs, NJ: Merrill.

Ogle, D. M. (1986). K-W-L: A teaching model that develops active reading of expository text. *The Reading Teacher, 39*(6), 564–570.

Ogle, D. M., & Correa, A. (2007, May). *Motivating and scaffolding middle school English language learners: Focus on content and collaboration.* Symposium at the annual convention of the International Reading Association, Toronto, ON, Canada.

Opitz, M. F., & Rasinski, T. V. (1998). *Good-bye round robin: 25 effective oral reading strategies.* Portsmouth, NH: Heinemann.

Owens, J. S., Watabe, Y., & Michael, K. D. (2013). Culturally responsive school mental health in rural communities. In C. S. Clauss-Ehlers, Z. N. Serpell, & M. D. Weist (Eds.), *Handbook of culturally responsive school mental health: Advancing research, training, practice, and policy* (pp. 31–42). New York: Springer.

Palincsar, A. S., & Brown, A. L. (1986). Interactive teaching to promote independent learning from text. *The Reading Teacher, 39*(8), 771–777.

Paris, S. G., Calfee, R. C., Filby, N., Hiebert, E. H., Pearson, P. D., Valencia, S. W., et al. (1992). A framework for authentic literacy assessment. *The Reading Teacher, 46*(2), 88–98.

Paris, S. G., Lipson, M. Y., & Wixson, K. K. (1983). Becoming a strategic reader. *Contemporary Educational Psychology, 8,* 293–316.

Pearson. (2010). *Stanford Achievement Test* (10th ed.). Boston: Author.

Pearson, P. D., & Gallagher, M. C. (1983). The instruction of reading comprehension. *Contemporary Educational Psychology, 8,* 317–344.

Peterson, B. (1988). *Characteristics of texts that support beginning readers.* Unpublished doctoral dissertation, Ohio State University, Columbus, OH.

Philbeck, K. (n.d.). Analyzing writer's craft [PowerPoint presentation]. Retrieved from *www.kellyphilbeck.com/writing-strategies.html.*

Pinnell, G. S., & Fountas, I. C. (2010). *The continuum of literacy learning, grades 3–8: A guide to teaching* (2nd ed.). Portsmouth, NH: Heinemann.

Pinnell, G. S., & Fountas, I. C. (2016). *The Fountas and Pinnell literacy continuum, expanded edition: A tool for assessment, planning, and teaching, PreK–8.* Portsmouth, NH: Heinemann.

Raphael, T. E. (1982). QARs: Question-answering strategies for children. *The Reading Teacher, 36*(2), 186–190.

Raphael, T. E., Pardo, L. S., & Highfield, K. (2002). *Book club: A literature-based curriculum* (2nd ed.). Lawrence, MA: Small Planet Communications.

Rasinski, T., Rikli, A., & Johnson, S. (2009). Reading fluency: More than automaticity? More than a concern for the primary grades? *Literacy Research and Instruction, 48*(4), 350–361.

Renwick, M. (2013, July 25). 5 tools for reading digital text. *EdTech Magazine*. Retrieved from *https://edtechmagazine.com/k12/article/2013/07/5-tools-reading-digital-text*.

Robb, L. (2001). *35 must-have assessment and record-keeping forms for reading*. New York: Scholastic.

Rog, L. J. (2003). *Guided reading basics: Organizing, managing, and implementing a balanced literacy program in K–3*. Portland, ME: Stenhouse.

Rosengren, E. (2016, March 22). *The art and science of critiquing nature images*. Presentation to the St. Louis Camera Club, St. Louis, MO.

Ross, S. (1998). Self-assessment in second language testing: A meta-analysis and analysis of experiential factors. *Language Testing, 15*(1), 1–20.

Routman, R. (2005). *Writing essentials: Raising expectations and results while simplifying teaching*. Portsmouth, NH: Heinemann.

Rumelhart, D. E. (1994). Toward an interactive model of reading. In R. B. Ruddell, M. R. Ruddell, & H. Singer (Eds.), *Theoretical models and processes of reading* (4th ed., pp. 864–894). Newark, DE: International Reading Association.

Scarino, A., & Liddicoat, A. J. (2009). *Teaching and learning languages: A guide*. Carlton South, Victoria, Australia: Curriculum Corporation. Retrieved from *www.tllg.unisa.edu.au/lib_guide/gllt.pdf*.

Scholastic. (2019). Most common prefixes and most common suffixes. Retrieved from *http://teacher.scholastic.com/reading/bestpractices/vocabulary/pdf/prefixes_suffixes.pdf*.

Schrank, F. A., McGrew, K. S., & Mather, N. (2014). *Woodcock–Johnson IV Tests of Cognitive Abilities*. Rolling Meadows, IL: Riverside.

Schumaker, J. B., Denton, P., & Deshler, D. D. (1984). *The paraphrasing strategy*. Lawrence: University of Kansas Press.

Schwartz, R. M., & Raphael, T. E. (1985). Concept of definition: A key to improving students' vocabulary. *The Reading Teacher, 39*(2), 198–205.

Search Institute. (2016, July 26). Five factors that impact student motivation. Retrieved from *www.search-institute.org/five-factors-impact-student-motivation*.

Serafini, F. (2011). Expanding perspectives for comprehending visual images in multimodal texts. *Journal of Adolescent and Adult Literacy, 54*(5), 342–350. Retrieved from *http://frankserafini.com/publications/serafini-jaal.pdf*.

Shanahan, T. (2016, October 27). Oral reading is more than speed. Retrieved from *www.shanahanonliteracy.com/blog/oral-reading-fluency-is-more-than-speed*.

Shanahan, T., & Shanahan, C. (2012). What is disciplinary literacy and why does it matter? *Topics in Language Disorders, 32*(1), 7–18.

Short, K., Harste, J., & Burke, C. (1996). *Creating classrooms for authors and inquirers*. Portsmouth, NH: Heinemann.

Simpson, L. (2019). Teach kids a growth mindset and watch their confidence flourish. *Huffington Post*. Retrieved from *https://www.huffingtonpost.ca/linda-simpson/growth-mindset-child-development_a_23682897/*.

Simpson, M. L. (1984). PORPE: A study strategy for learning on the content areas. Retrieved from *www.kendallhunt.com/contentarealiteracy/Articles/Simpson.pdf*.

Sims Bishop, R. (1990). Mirrors, windows, and sliding glass doors. *Perspectives: Choosing and Using Books for the Classroom, 6*(3), ix–xi.

Singer, H., & Ruddell, R. B. (1985). *Theoretical models and processes of reading* (3rd ed.). Newark, DE: International Reading Association.

Smith, C. C., & Bean, T. W. (1980). The guided writing procedure: Integrating content reading and writing improvement. *Reading World, 19*(3), 290–294.

Solley, B. A. (2000). *Writer's workshop: Reflections of elementary and middle school teachers.* Boston: Allyn & Bacon.

Spandel, V. (2004). *Creating young writers: Using the six traits to enrich writing process in primary classrooms.* Boston: Allyn & Bacon.

Spear-Swerling, L. (2006). The importance of teaching handwriting. Retrieved from *www.readingrockets.org/article/importance-teaching-handwriting.*

Stauffer, R. G. (1969). *Directing reading maturity as a cognitive process.* New York: Harper & Row.

Steel, B. (1997). *Draw me a story: An illustrated exploration of drawing-as-language.* Worcester, MA: ESCS Child Street.

Steinberg, S. (2007). *An introduction to communication studies.* Cape Town, South Africa: Juta.

Steward, F., & Borgia, L. (2004, March). *Radio reading: Broadcasting and higher order thinking questions.* Paper presented at the annual conference of the Illinois Reading Council, Springfield, IL.

Stribley, M. (2019). Design elements and principles: 10 rules of composition all designers live by. Retrieved from *www.canva.com/learn/visual-design-composition.*

Strickland, D. S. (1998, March). What's basic in beginning reading?: Finding common ground. *Educational Leadership, 55*(6), 6–10.

Sturken, M., & Cartwright, L. (2001). *Practices of looking: An introduction to visual culture.* Oxford, UK: Oxford University Press.

Sulzby, E., & Teale, W. (1991). Emergent literacy. In R. Barr, M. Kamil, P. Mosenthal, & P. D. Pearson (Eds.), *Handbook of reading research* (Vol. 2, pp. 727–758). New York: Longman.

Taberski, S. (2001). Fact and fiction: Read aloud. *Instructor, 110*(6), 24–26.

Taheri, M. (2019, September 28). 10 basic elements of design. Retrieved from *www.creativemarket.com/blog/10-basic-elements-of-design.*

Taylor, W. L. (1953). Cloze procedure: A new tool for measuring readability. *Journalism Quarterly, 30,* 415–433.

Tierney, R. J., & Readence, J. E. (2005). *Reading strategies and practices: A compendium* (6th ed.). Boston: Allyn & Bacon.

Tomlinson, C. A., & Allen, S. D. (2000). Leadership for differentiating schools and classrooms. Alexandria, VA: Association for Supervision and Curriculum Development.

Tracey. (2011, October 23). Persuasive writing: Oreo. Retrieved from *http://our-cool-school.blogspot.com/2011/10/persuasive-writing-oreo.html.*

Una Healy Graphic Design. (2019). The 7 elements of good graphic design. Retrieved from *www.unahealydesign.com/elements-of-good-graphic-design.*

University of Iowa College of Education. (2019). Iowa Assessments, Forms E and F. Retrieved from *http://itp.education.uiowa.edu/ia/default.aspx.*

Vacca, J. L., Vacca, R. T., Gove, M. K., Burkey, L. C., Lenhart, L. A., & McKeon, C. A. (2006). *Reading and learning to read* (6th ed.). Boston: Pearson/Allyn & Bacon.

Victoria State Government Education and Training. (2018, August 29). Literacy teaching toolkit: Visual literacy. Retrieved from *www.education.vic.gov.au/school/teachers/teachingresources/discipline/english/literacy/readingviewing/Pages/litfocusvisual.aspx.*

Vogt, M., & Shearer, B. A. (2007). *Reading specialists and literacy coaches in the real world* (2nd ed.). Boston: Pearson/Allyn & Bacon.

Vygotsky, L. S. (1978). *Mind in society: The development of higher psychological processes* (M. Cole, V. John-Steiner, S. Scribner, & E. Souberman, Eds.). Cambridge, MA: Harvard University Press.

Walker, B. (2004). *Diagnostic teaching of reading: Techniques for instruction and assessment* (5th ed.). Upper Saddle River, NJ: Pearson/Merrill/Prentice Hall.

Walker, B. (2011). *Diagnostic teaching of reading: Techniques for instruction and assessment* (7th ed.). Boston: Pearson.

Ward, J., & McAndrews, S. L. (2019, May). *Linking literacy and STEM.* Paper presented for the College Instructors of Literacy Professionals of the Illinois Reading Council, Edwardsville, IL.

Weist, M. D., Garbacz, S. A., Lane, K. L., & Kincaid, D. (Eds.). (2017). *Aligning and integrating family engagement in positive behavioral interventions and supports (PBIS): Concepts and strategies for families and schools in key contexts.* Eugene: Center for Positive Behavioral Interventions and Supports, University of Oregon.

Wepman, J. (1958). *Auditory Discrimination Test.* Chicago: Language Research Associates.

Wiggins, G., & McTighe, J. (2005). *Understanding by design* (2nd ed.). Alexandria, VA: Association for Supervision and Curriculum Development.

Wiktionary. (2012, July 1). English pronunciation. Retrieved from *http://en.wiktionary.org/w/index.php?title=Appendix:English_pronunciation&oldid=17032194.*

Wilhelm, J. D., Baker, T. N., & Dube, J. (2001). *Strategic reading: Guiding students to lifelong literacy, 6–12.* Portsmouth, NH: Heinemann.

Wilkes-Barre Area School District. (n.d.). Text features chart. Retrieved from *www.wbasd.k12.pa.us/Downloads/text_feature_chart_handout.pdf.*

Wlodkowski, R. J., & Ginsberg, M. B. (1995, September). Strengthening student engagement: A framework for culturally responsive teaching. *Educational Leadership, 53*(1), 17–21.

Wood, D. J., Bruner, J. S., & Ross, G. (1976). The role of tutoring in problem-solving. *Journal of Student Psychology and Psychiatry, 17*(2), 89–100.

Wood Ray, K. (1999). *Wondrous words.* Urbana, IL: National Council of Teachers of English.

Yopp, H. K. (1995). A test for assessing phonemic awareness in young children. *The Reading Teacher, 49*(1), 20–29.

Yopp, H. K., & Yopp, R. H. (2000b). Supporting phonemic awareness development in the classroom. *The Reading Teacher, 54*(2), 130–143.

Yopp, R. H., & Yopp, H. K. (2000a). Sharing informational text with young children. *The Reading Teacher, 53*(5), 410–423.

Young, T. L., & Hadaway, N. L. (Eds.). (2006). *Supporting the literacy development of English learners: Increasing success in all classrooms.* Newark, DE: International Reading Association.

Younghans, M. (2018, January 25). The steps to creating a positive school culture. Retrieved from *https://inservice.ascd.org/the-steps-to-creating-a-positive-school-culture.*

Zimmerman, B. J. (2000). Attaining self-regulation: A social cognitive perspective. In M. Boekaerts, P. R. Pintrich, & M. Zeidner (Eds.), *Handbook of self-regulation* (pp. 13–39). San Diego, CA: Academic Press.

Zimmerman, B. J., Bandura, A., & Martinez-Pons, M. (1992). Self-motivation for academic attainment: The role of self-efficacy beliefs and personal goal setting. *American Educational Research Journal, 29*(3), 663–676.

Zutell, J., & Rasinski, T. V. (1991). Training teachers to attend to their students' oral reading fluency. *Theory into Practice, 30*(3), 211–217.

Literature Cited

Allard, H., & Marshall, J. (1997). *Miss Nelson is missing.* Boston: Houghton Mifflin.

Avi. (2002). *Crispin: The cross of lead.* New York: Hyperion Books.

Berenstain, S., & Berenstain, J. (1971). *Bears in the night.* New York: Random House.

Bingham, C., Morgan, B., & Robertson, M. (2007). *Buzz: What's all the buzz about these bugs?* New York: Dorling Kindersley.

Bloom, B. (1999). *Wolf!* New York: Scholastic.

Bolden, T. (1998). *And not afraid to dare: The stories of ten African-American women.* New York: Scholastic.

Brett, J. (1985). *Annie and the wild animals.* Boston: Houghton Mifflin.

Brett, J. (1989). *The mitten.* New York: Scholastic.

Brown, M. (1990). *Arthur's pet business.* Boston: Joy Street Books.

Bunting, E. (1988). *How many days to America?: A Thanksgiving story.* New York: Clarion.

Byars, B. C. (1991). *Wanted . . . mud blossom.* New York: Delacorte Press.

Cannon, J. (1993). *Stellaluna.* San Diego, CA: Harcourt Brace Jovanovich.

Cannon, J. (2000). *Crickwing.* San Diego, CA: Harcourt.

Challoner, J. (2004). *DK eyewitness books: Hurricane and tornado.* New York: Dorling Kindersley.

Cherry, L. (1990). *The great kapok tree.* San Diego, CA: Harcourt Brace Jovanovich.

Ching, P. (2002). *The tale of Rabbit Island.* Waipahu, HI: Island Heritage.

Clark, B. (2000). *DK eyewitness books: Amphibian.* New York: Dorling Kindersley.

Dahl, R. (1964). *Charlie and the chocolate factory.* New York: Knopf.

Deak, J. (1998). *Your fantastic elastic brain: Stretch it, shape it.* New York: Scholastic.

Freeman, D. (1968). *Corduroy.* New York: Viking Press.

French, J. (2003). *Hitler's daughter.* New York: HarperCollins.

George, J. C. (1990). *On the far side of the mountain.* New York: Dutton.

Giff, P. R. (1990). *Ronald Morgan goes to bat.* New York: Puffin.

Goldish, M. (2000). *The river road.* Northborough, MA: Newbridge Educational.

Goodrich, F., & Hackett, A. (1996). *The diary of Anne Frank: And related readings.* Evanston, IL: McDougal Littell.

Harness, C. (2003). *Rabble rousers.* New York: Dutton.

Herrington, L. M. (2015). *What's the difference?: Frogs and toads.* New York: Scholastic.

Housel, D. J. (2005). *Time for kids: Mammals.* New York: HarperTrophy.

Jeunesse, G. (1992). *The river: A first discovery book.* New York: Scholastic.
Kalman, B. (1994). *Frogs and toads.* New York: Crabapples.
Kirk, D. (2007). *Library mouse.* New York: Abrams.
Lewis, C. S. (1950). *The lion, the witch and the wardrobe.* New York: Macmillan.
Lowell, S. (1992). *The three little javelinas.* Flagstaff, AZ: Rising Moon.
MacLachlan, P. (1985). *Sarah, plain and tall.* New York: Harper & Row.
Martin, B., Jr. (1967). *Brown bear, brown bear, what do you see?* New York: Henry Holt.
McKissack, P., & Pinkney, J. (2001). *Goin' someplace special.* New York: Scholastic.
Nodset, J. (1963). *Who took the farmer's hat?* New York: Harper & Row.
Paulsen, G. (1987). *Hatchet.* New York: Simon & Schuster.
Pratt-Serafini, K. (2002). *Saguaro moon: A desert journal.* Nevada City, CA: Dawn.
Rand McNally. (1994). *Discovery atlas of Native Americans.* Skokie, IL: Author.
Ricciuti, E. R. (1994). *What on earth is a chuckwalla?* Woodbridge, CT: Blackbirch Press.
Romero, L. (2005). *Habitats: Tropical rain forests.* Carlsbad, CA: Dominie.
Rowling, J. K. (1998). *Harry Potter and the sorcerer's stone.* New York: Scholastic.
Sachar, L. (1998). *Holes.* New York: Dell Yearling.
Schotter, R. (2000). *F is for freedom.* London: Dorling Kindersley Children.
Sendak, M. (1963). *Where the wild things are.* New York: Harper & Row.
Seuss, Dr. [T. S. Geisel]. (1957). *The cat in the hat.* Boston: Houghton Mifflin.
Seuss, Dr. [T. S. Geisel]. (1960). *Green eggs and ham.* New York: Random House.
Van Allsburg, C. (1988) *Two bad ants.* Boston: Houghton Mifflin.
Ward, J. (2003). *The seed and the giant saguaro.* Lanham, MD: Cooper Square.
Ward, J. (2005). *Forest bright, forest night.* Nevada City, CA: Dawn.
Ward, J. (2013). *What will hatch?* New York: Bloomsbury.
Ward, J. (2017a). *Feathers and hair: What animals wear.* New York: Beach Lane Books.
Ward, J. (2017b). *What will grow?* New York: Bloomsbury.
Ward, J. (2018). *Mama dug a little den.* New York: Beach Lane Books.
Ward, J. (2019). *I love birds! 52 ways to wonder, wander, and explore birds with kids.* New York: Penguin Random House.
Watson, R. J. (1989). *Tom Thumb.* San Diego, CA: Harcourt Brace Jovanovich.
Wilder, L. I. (1932). *Little house in the big woods.* New York: Harper & Brothers.
Wildsmith, B. (1982). *Cat on the mat.* Oxford, UK: Oxford University Press.
Wright, A. (1992). *Will we miss them?: Endangered species.* Watertown, MA: Charlesbridge.

Index

Note. Page numbers followed by *f* or *t* indicate a figure or a table.